Marketing in Australia

Marketing in Australia

Philip Kotler

Northwestern University

Robin Shaw

Monash University

Peter FitzRoy

Monash University

Peter Chandler

Chisholm Institute of Technology

PRENTICE-HALL OF AUSTRALIA PTY LTD

Prentice-Hall of Australia Pty Ltd, Sydney
Prentice-Hall International Inc, London
Prentice-Hall da Brasil Ltda., Rio de Janeiro
Prentice-Hall of Canada Ltd, Toronto
Prentice-Hall of India Private Ltd, New Delhi
Prentice-Hall of Japan Inc, Tokyo
Prentice-Hall of Southeast Asia Pte Ltd, Singapore
Whitehall Books Ltd, Wellington
Prentice-Hall Inc, Englewood Cliffs, New Jersey

Typeset by Savage & Co. Pty Ltd,
Valley, Brisbane, Qld.
Printed and bound in Australia by
Griffin Press Limited,
Marion Rd, Netley, S.A.

2 3 4 5 87 86 85 84 83

National Library of Australia
Cataloguing-in-publication data

Marketing in Australia.

American ed. published as: Principles of
marketing. Englewood Cliffs, N.J.:
Prentice-Hall, 1980.
Includes index.
ISBN 0 7248 0757 8
ISBN 0 7248 0758 6 Paperback

1. Marketing management — Australia.
I. Kotler, Philip, 1931–.

658.8'00994

Original English language edition published by
Prentice-Hall Incorporated, Englewood Cliffs, New
Jersey. Copyright © 1980 by PRENTICE-HALL
INCORPORATED.

Contents

1   Marketing's Role in the Economy

2   Marketing's Role in the Company

③ Target Market Analysis

4 **Marketing-mix Strategy**

5 Marketing's Role in Society

21 Marketing and Society 510

Social criticisms of marketing — Citizen actions to regulate marketing — Public actions to regulate marketing — Business actions toward socially responsible marketing — Principles for future public policy toward marketing — Summary

Cases

Sources

The authors and publisher have made an effort to trace the source of copyright for material used in this book; however, they would be glad to hear of any errors or omissions in the following list.

Pages 49–52, 159–160, 174, 183–4, 335–6, 395–6, 514, 535: Reproduced by permission of the *Australian Financial Review*.

Pages 77–8, 107–8, 235–7, 471–2: Courtesy Rydge Publications Pty Ltd.

Pages 137–8: Courtesy of B. J. Beilby.

Pages 161, 259–60, 412–13, 441, 518–19, 520: Reprinted from *The Age*.

Pages 212–14: Advertisement reproduced with permission of Cessna Aircraft Co.

Page 354: Table 14 – 1 courtesy of the *Columbia Journal of World Business*.

Page 356: Table 14 – 2, © MCB Publications Limited, Bradford, England. Reproduced here with permission.

Pages 364–5: Courtesy *Business Review Weekly*, who have given permission to reprint the article.

Pages 446–7: Copyright © Diane Willman and reproduced with her permission.

Pages 471–2: Courtesy Michael Batten.

Pages 473–4, 560, 574, 581, 597–9: Tables by permission of the Australian Bureau of Statistics.

Pages 490–91: Tables 20 – 1 and 20–2 courtesy of the Australian Government Publishing Service.

Pages 510–12: Courtesy of John Clemenger Pty Ltd.

Page 549: Table courtesy of the Melbourne Metropolitan Board of Works.

Page 581: Appendix IV courtesy of the Attorney-General's Department.

Preface

Marketing is an old subject and a new subject. Its roots go back to the first appearance of trade among people. Before trade or exchange, people obtained what they needed either by producing it themselves, taking it away forcefully from others, or begging for it. The emergence of trade allowed people to specialize in producing particular goods and services and exchange them in markets for other goods and services they needed.

Marketing is a new subject in the sense that the formal study of the forces and conditions that make for successful exchange became an organized academic discipline only in the twentieth century. Before this century, scattered writings could be found on selling, advertising, pricing, product design, packaging, branding, physical distribution – but they were neither treated in an integrated way nor scientifically developed. It is only in the last seventy years that various scholars and practitioners have attempted to put together a formal science of marketing.

Marketing consists of a set of principles for choosing target markets, measuring their needs, developing want-satisfying products, and delivering them at a value to the customer and a profit to the company. Many of the most successful companies in the world owe their success to practising a thoroughgoing marketing orientation. McDonald's owes its success to meeting people's needs for fast food service; Kodak to meeting their needs for inexpensive reliable cameras; and Avon to meeting their needs for personal advice on cosmetics. Practitioners of the marketing concept see consumer problems as company opportunities.

A major surprise that students experience in studying marketing is how universally applicable it is. Marketing is relevant not only to economic institutions such as manufacturing companies, wholesalers, and retailers, but to every organization 'that has something to sell'. Lawyers, accountants, and management consultants are increasingly using marketing ideas to expand their practices. Educational institutions and performing arts groups are turning to marketing in the face of low or declining demand for their services. No politician can get the required votes, and no resort area can get the needed tourists, without developing and carrying out marketing plans. And students, when they enter the job market, must do 'marketing research' to determine the best opportunities and the best way to 'market themselves' to prospective employers. Students report that their study of marketing is an 'eyeopener' and they see familiar things in an entirely new and challenging way.

MAJOR FEATURES OF THIS BOOK

More students than ever before are studying marketing. It therefore should come as no surprise that many different textbooks (brands) are available. Each textbook bears the imprint of the authors' particular mindset, style, and enthusiasm for the subject. This text is built on six principles:

Australian Context

We all learn more efficiently — and more enjoyably — if we can relate the material to be learned to a familiar frame of reference. So it makes sense to introduce and discuss marketing in the context of Australian activity, where such Australian content is relevant. But we must not be unduly egocentric or insular in our outlook, and it is grossly inefficient to attempt to 're-invent the wheel' in terms of structuring a text or summarizing the extensive marketing literature from elsewhere in the world. Therefore, this book is an Australian adaptation of Philip Kotler's *Principles of Marketing*, wherein the core of Professor Kotler's work has been retained and supplemented by the Australian authors. This Australian edition is a companion volume to *Australian Marketing Management* which provides an extended treatment of some material which may be more suitable for some graduate and advanced post-experience programmes.

Comprehensive

The student's first exposure to marketing should present the subject primarily in its breadth. This book covers the major marketing topics of interest to marketing students and practitioners. Readers will read about the *major institutions* that are involved in the marketing process — manufacturers, wholesalers, retailers, advertising agencies, marketing research firms, banks, shippers, storage warehouses, and many others. Readers will also examine the *major tools* used by modern marketers — product design, packaging, branding, ancillary services, pricing, advertising, sales promotion, publicity, and personal selling. Finally, readers will examine the *major environmental forces* affecting the marketing process — demographics, economics, ecology, technology, politics, and culture.

Systematic

Marketing can easily become overwhelming in its multitude of topics, concepts, theories, and examples. The great need is to present this abundant material in a systematic framework so that readers know where they have been, where they are, and where they are going in the subject. This text utilizes a five-part structure. Part I introduces the reader to *marketing's role in the economy*. It explains how marketing is the link between consumer needs and industrial activity, how marketing systems are organized on the national, industry, and company levels, and how marketing practices affect society and are in turn affected by society. Part II introduces *marketing's role in the company*. Marketing contributes critically to the company's growth strategy and is supported by certain planning, information, and organizational structures. Part III introduces the first major step in company marketing planning, namely *target market analysis*. This consists of analyzing the opportunities and threats in the environment, the dynamics of buying behaviour in consumer and industrial markets, the segmentation of markets, and the choice of target market segments to serve. Part IV examines the second major step in company marketing planning, namely *marketing mix strategy*. The various chapters in this Part discuss new product development, product life-cycle strategies, product design, branding, packaging, service, pricing, distribution, advertising, sales promotion, publicity, and personal selling. Finally, Part V returns to examining *broader marketing issues*, specifically the role of international marketing, the role of nonprofit marketing, and the various controversies surrounding marketing that have led to citizen action, public regulation, and constructive marketing responses by business.

Scientific

To the extent possible, this text presents concepts, generalizations, and theories of marketing that are supported by scientific research and evidence. Marketing is treated as an applied science built on the foundations of economic science, behavioural science, and modern management theory. Economic science reminds us that marketing involves the use of scarce resources to satisfy competing ends and therefore these resources must be allocated carefully. Behavioural science reminds us that marketing is about people – people who make up markets and who run organizations – and it is essential to understand their needs, motivations, attitudes, and behaviour. Finally, management theory reminds us that our approach has the practical purpose of answering how people and organizations can best achieve the marketing objectives they set for themselves.

Practical

Every marketing situation is unique. The decision maker has to know how to analyze a marketing problem and apply the relevant marketing theory to solve it. This book describes numerous situations in which well-known, as well as little-known, companies applied marketing to solve the marketing problems they were facing – whether there was too little demand for their goods or services, the wrong kind of demand, or even too much demand. The situations are illustrated in indented examples running through the text, in special exhibits appearing in boxes, and in longer case studies. They illustrate marketing problems faced by actual companies and the actions taken by these companies to solve their problems.

Lively

A book has to be lively or else it cheats the reader. It must not read like a telephone book or an encyclopaedia. Marketing is a fascinating subject and the authors must be able to communicate enthusiasm for the subject. Almost every chapter starts with a vignette about a company involved in a particular marketing problem that will be discussed in the chapter. Throughout the chapter, important points are illustrated by timely and interesting examples.

Thus the authors' intention in writing this book is to present marketing in an Australian context in a comprehensive, systematic, scientific, practical, and lively manner. Whether the intention has been achieved will be determined by the market – how satisfied the users are, and how much use they can make of its ideas.

PEDAGOGICAL AIDS

This book employs the latest pedagogical aids to facilitate its use by students and teachers. The main ones are:

1. *Opening Vignettes.* Each chapter opens with a vignette to engage the reader's interest and attention.
2. *Major Chapter Issues.* Following the vignette, each chapter describes the major issues that will be examined in the chapter.
3. *Figures and Tables.* Important points in each chapter are abundantly illustrated with strong visual materials.
4. *Boxed Exhibits.* Some material of unusual interest is set off in specially boxed exhibits.

5. *Summary*. Each chapter ends with a summary that outlines the chapter's major contents.
6. *Review Questions*. Each chapter summary is followed by a list of questions that review the major points made in the chapter.
7. *Case Studies*. The text includes 14 cases for class and/or written discussion. They challenge the reader to apply marketing thinking to actual situations.
8. *Glossary*. The book contains an extensive glossary of terms for quick reference.
9. *Index*. The book contains a subject index to facilitate finding information.
10. *Supplements*. A separate instructor's Manual is available to the instructor along with a Test Bank and a set of Transparency Masters.

ACKNOWLEDGEMENTS

This book is a team effort, reflecting the contributions of many American sources in addition to Professor Kotler's individual input, together with a variety of Australian influences.

The case studies used in this book were prepared with the assistance of Rosalie Gibbs at Monash University and Rodney McColl at Chisholm Institute of Technology, Caulfield campus.

The manuscript of the book was carefully entered into and corrected on a word processor at Monash University by Helen Collens and Margaret Russell, who deserve our sincere thanks.

Many authors and publishers generously allowed us to utilize their material, including: Bernard Holt of Commercial Economic Advisory Service of Australia, data regarding marketing and the law and advertising expenditure; and Philip Ruthven of Ibis Research, economic analysis.

Without the perspicacity of Charles Lucas, editor, and the support of his publishing firm, Prentice-Hall of Australia, this book and its earlier companion volume would not have existed. They deserve special praise for their role in advancing Australian marketing literature. We would also like to acknowledge the tenacious editorial work of Robert Utter and Rina Harber, whose diplomatic and practical skills were amply demonstrated.

This book is dedicated to Trish and Adam Shaw (one of whom was more demanding than the other during the preparation of the manuscript), and to Jill and Christina FitzRoy, whose cheerfulness helped overcome the lost weekends.

Robin N. Shaw
Peter T. FitzRoy
Peter C. Chandler

Part 1

Marketing's Role in the Economy

Marketing and Human Needs

1

Marketing touches all of us every day of our lives. We wake up in the morning to a National radio alarm clock, which plays a Johnny Farnham song followed by a commercial for a Qantas holiday flight to Fiji. We move to the bathroom where we shave with Gillette, shower with Palmolive, and use various other toiletries and appliances produced by manufacturers around the world. We put on our Amco jeans and shirt, and Adidas shoes. We enter the kitchen and pour some Farmland orange juice, and prepare a bowl of Kellogg's Rice Bubbles and sliced SPC peaches in Pura milk. After this, we drink one or two cups of Nescafé coffee with two teaspoons of CSR sugar. We are the personal beneficiaries of oranges grown in South Australia, coffee imported from Papua-New Guinea, a newspaper made from Tasmanian wood pulp, and radio news coming from as far away as New York.

All of these products ended up in our homes. The marketing system made this possible without effort on our part. It has designed and delivered to us a standard of living.

In starting our discussion of marketing, we should recognize that it means different things to different people, affects everyone, and is highly controversial.

Marketing Has Different Meanings

What does the term *marketing* mean? Most people think of it as synonymous with selling

3

and promotion: Australians are bombarded with television commercials, unsolicited mail advertisements, newspaper ads, and sales calls. Someone is always trying to sell us something. It seems that we cannot escape death, taxes or selling.

Therefore it may come as a surprise to many people that the most important part of marketing is not selling. Selling is only the tip of the marketing iceberg; it is only one of several functions that marketers perform, and often not the most important one. If the marketer does a good job of identifying consumer needs, developing appropriate products, and pricing, distributing and promoting them effectively, these goods will sell very easily. The amount of 'hard selling' required will not be intense.

Everyone knows about 'hot' products to which consumers are drawn in droves. When Morris offered the first Mini Minor, when Kodak designed its instamatic camera, and when Victa introduced its rotary lawn-mower, these manufacturers were swamped with orders because they had designed the 'right' product. Not 'me-too' products, but distinct offers that outshone the others. Peter Drucker, a leading management theorist, puts it this way:

- The aim of marketing is to make selling superfluous.[1]

This is not to say that selling and promotion are unimportant, but rather that they are part of a larger 'marketing mix' or set of marketing tools that must be finely orchestrated for maximum impact.

Marketing Affects Everyone

Marketing affects the buyer, the seller and the citizen. This is illustrated in the following examples.

The buyer. Neil Humphreys, a student, wants to buy stereo equipment and he there-fore visits a large stereo retail outlet. He sees many stereo components. As he examines them, the following questions come to his mind:

- Is the brand selection wide enough?
- Is there a brand that has the features I want?
- Is the price fair?
- Is the salesperson helpful, pleasant and honest?
- Is the service good, and is there a warranty?

Neil Humphreys and other buyers want the marketplace to provide good-quality products at convenient locations for reasonable prices. The kind of marketing system found in an economy will make a great difference to people's satisfaction as buyers and consumers.

The seller. Bill Pickett is the marketing manager in a company that manufactures stereo equipment. To do his job well, he must decide on a number of issues:

- What do consumers want in stereo equipment?
- Which consumer groups and needs should my company try to satisfy?
- How should the product be designed and priced?
- What guarantees and service should we offer?
- What types of intermediaries should we use?
- What types of advertising, personal selling, promotion and publicity would be cost-effective in selling this product?

Thus the seller faces a number of challenges when trying to develop an attractive offer. The market is very demanding. The seller must apply the most modern marketing tools available to arrive at an offer that attracts and satisfies customers.

The citizen. Joyce Evans, a member of parliament, has a special interest in business's performance in the marketplace. As a citizen and legislator, she is concerned with the following questions:

- Are manufacturers making safe and reliable products?
- Are they describing their products accurately in their ads and packaging?
- Is competition working in this market to keep quality high and prices low?
- Are the retailers and service people behaving fairly towards consumers?
- Are the manufacturing or packaging activities hurting the environment?

Joyce Evans acts as a watchdog of consumer interests, trying to improve consumer education, information and protection. The marketing system has a major impact on the lives of Australians, and they and their representatives will want to make it work as well as possible.

Marketing Is Controversial

Marketing affects so many people in so many ways that it is inevitably controversial. There are persons who intensely dislike modern marketing activity, accusing it of such sins as ruining the environment, bombarding the public with inane ads, creating unnecessary wants, and teaching greed to youngsters. Consider the following charges:

> For the past 6000 years the field of marketing has been thought of as made up of fast-buck artists, con-men, wheeler-dealers, and shoddy-goods distributors. Too many of us have been 'taken' by the tout or con-men; and all of us at times have been prodded into buying all sorts of 'things' we really did not need, and which we found later on we did not even want.[2]

> What does a man need – really need? A few pounds of food each day, heat and shelter, six feet to lie down in – and some form of working activity that will yield a sense of accomplishment. That's all – in a material sense. And we know it. But we are brainwashed by our economic system until we end up in a tomb beneath a pyramid of time payments, mortgages, preposterous gadgetry, playthings that divert our attention from the sheer idiocy of the charade.[3]

There are others, however, who equally vigorously defend marketing. Consider the following:

> Goods and services are not really produced until they get to the point of consumption. Therefore, marketing is truly a part of production. Transporting, storing, grading, wholesaling, retailing, buying, selling; all constitute parts of marketing. Selling is one of the most vital functions performed, and advertising is a very important part of the selling function. Selling is sometimes given a derogatory connotation and condemned along with advertising, but where would we be if we could not attempt to influence the actions of others, if we could not sell products, if we could not sell ideas?[4]

> Advertising nourishes the consuming power of men. It creates wants for a better standard of living. It sets up before a man the goal of a better home, better clothing, better food for himself and his family. It spurs individual exertion and greater production. It brings together in fertile union those things which otherwise would not have met.[5]

It is clear that various social commentators have vastly different views on the meaning and contribution of marketing. We will consider these issues later in the book after we have gained a better understanding of how marketing works. We will largely deal with marketing from the seller's point of view, since the seller is trying to put together marketing programmes that are profitable and that create value for the consumers. At the same time, no seller can make long-run profits without taking into account the buyers' and citizens' point of view. In fact, the major ideological breakthrough in the last thirty years has been the recognition that sellers not only must take the buyers' wants into account but must start with them.

Business is now going through a further

learning phase, discovering that it must also take the citizens' interests into account. Marketing, at its highest practical level, should balance and serve the combined interests of sellers, buyers and citizens. This book is oriented towards helping sellers see the importance of formulating and carrying out marketing practices that are grounded in consumer and citizen interests as well as self-interest. It is a matter not only of doing what is right but also of ensuring the long-run profitability and survival of business in an increasingly competitive and turbulent marketplace.

THE RAPID ADOPTION OF MARKETING

Many people think that marketing is something practised only by large companies in highly capitalistic countries, companies like Reckitt & Colman, IBM, Kodak, Gillette, McDonald's and Coca-Cola. In fact, marketing is spreading rapidly both within and outside the business sector.

The Business Sector

In the business sector, marketing entered the consciousness of different industries at different times. It spread most rapidly in consumer packaged-goods companies, consumer-durables companies and industrial-equipment companies – in that order. Industrial-commodity companies (steel, chemicals, paper) came later to marketing consciousness, and many still have a long way to go. Within the last decade, service firms – especially in recreational and financial areas – have opened themselves to marketing. Bankers initially showed great resistance to marketing, but in the end they embraced it enthusiastically.

The most recent business groups to encounter marketing have been those providing professional services, such as lawyers, accountants and doctors. Although various professional societies have generally prohibited their members from engaging in price competition, client solicitation, and advertising, trade practices investigators have recently called these restraints illegal.

> The fierce competition engendered by the new limits on corporate growth is forcing accounting firms into aggressive new postures ... The accountants insist on referring to their efforts to drum up business as 'practice development'. But many of the activities that fall under this euphemism are dead ringers for what is called 'marketing' in other fields ... Accountants speak of 'positioning' their firms and of 'penetrating' unexploited new industries. They compile 'hit lists' of prospective clients and then 'surround' them by placing their firms' partners in close social contact with the top executives of the target companies.[6]

The International Sector

Marketing is practised throughout the world. In fact, several European and Japanese multinationals – companies like Nestlé, Siemens, Toyota and Hitachi – have in many cases outperformed their marketing counterparts in the United States.[7] Multinationals, in general, are a continuing force in the introduction and spread of modern marketing practices throughout the world. As a result, management in smaller companies is beginning to ask: What is marketing? How does it differ from plain selling? How can we introduce marketing into the firm? Will it make a difference?

In socialist countries such as the USSR and those of Eastern Europe, marketing has traditionally had a bad name. Today, however, various functions of marketing, such as marketing research, branding, advertising, and sales promotion, are spreading rapidly. In the USSR, for example, there are now more than 100 state-operated advertising agencies and marketing-research firms.[8] Several companies in Poland and Hungary have marketing departments, and several socialist universities teach marketing.

The Non-profit Sector

Marketing's most recent entry has been in the non-profit sector of the economy. Such diverse organizations as colleges of advanced education, hospitals, museums and performing arts groups are currently taking a look at marketing. Consider the following developments:

- Many performing groups cannot attract large enough audiences. Even those that have seasonal sellouts face huge operating deficits at the end of the year.
- Many non-profit organizations that flourished in earlier years – the YMCA, Salvation Army, Girl Guides, and Women's Christian Temperance Union – are now re-examining their missions in an effort to reverse membership declines.

These organizations all have marketplace problems: their administrators are struggling to keep them alive in the face of rapidly changing client attitudes and diminishing financial resources. Many institutions have turned to marketing as a possible answer to their problems. As a sign of the times, the Evanston Hospital of Evanston, Illinois, recently appointed a vice-president of marketing and was the first hospital in the world to do so.

Government agencies are also showing an increasing interest in marketing. Australia Post and Telecom have developed marketing plans for their respective operations; the army has a marketing plan to attract recruits and is one of the top advertising spenders in the country. Other government agencies are becoming involved in marketing energy conservation, 'national pride', and other public causes.

WHAT IS MARKETING?

We have said many things about marketing without defining it. Marketing has been defined in a number of ways. The American Marketing Association's official definition is:

- Marketing is the performance of business activities that direct the flow of goods and services from producer to consumer or user.[9]

This definition, unfortunately, makes marketing sound largely like distribution and fails to indicate its role in determining what goods are to be produced. It does not indicate the specific business activities that constitute marketing. Another way to describe marketing is as follows:

- Marketing is getting the right goods and services to the right people at the right place at the right time at the right price with the right communication and promotion.

This definition does give an idea of the specific activities that marketers carry out. However, it fails to define marketing activity broadly enough, in ignoring the fact that things other than goods and services can be marketed. Furthermore, it defines marketing as a business process rather than a social process. Here is a thought-provoking definition of marketing:

- Marketing is the creation and delivery of a standard of living.[10]

In contrast to the previous definitions, this takes a macro or social view of marketing. However, it does not reveal the fundamental and universal nature of marketing. We would like to propose the following definition:

- *Marketing* is human activity directed at satisfying needs and wants through exchange processes.

To understand this definition, we have to explain the following more basic concepts: needs, wants, demands, products, exchange, transactions and markets.

Needs

The most fundamental concept underlying marketing is that of *needs*. Inanimate objects do not have needs, but living matter does: plants require water and sunlight to survive; animals require air, water and food. Higher animals have emotional as well as biological needs. We define human need as follows:

- A *human need* is a state of felt deprivation in a person.

Human needs are plentiful and complex. They include basic physiological needs for food, clothing, warmth and safety; social needs for belongingness, influence and affection; and individual needs for knowledge and self-expression. These needs are not created by advertising but are a basic part of human make-up.

When a need is not satisfied the person is unhappy, this being greater the more intense and central the need. An unhappy person will do one of two things – undertake steps to obtain an object that will satisfy the need, or try to extinguish the desire. That is, need reduction can occur in two ways:

$$\text{Need reduction} = \frac{\text{Obtaining desired goods or services}}{\text{Extinguishing the desire}}$$

People in Western industrial societies tend to follow the numerator: they manage their needs by trying to find objects that will satisfy them. People in Eastern societies, however, have traditionally followed the denominator: they try to eliminate or reduce their needs whenever possible.

Wants

Human *wants* are the expression of human needs as they are shaped by a person's culture and individual development. Suppose someone is hungry. If that person lives in Bali, the need may be expressed as a want or desire for mangoes, suckling pig and beans. If that person lives in Australia, the same need may

express itself as a want for fish and chips, and some flavoured milk. Wants always have a reference to culturally defined objects. Within the same culture, there will be some variation in individual wants because of individual experience and tastes.

As a society becomes more complex, its members' wants expand. First, the inhabitants are exposed to more objects, some of which pique their curiosity, interest and desire. Second, producers undertake specific actions to build desire for the things they produce. The surest way to do this is to try to form a connection between a given object and people's pre-existing needs: the product is promoted as a satisfier of one or more particular needs. The marketer does not create the need; it is there. If marketers are successful, however, they can create a want.

Sellers often confuse wants and needs. A manufacturer of drill bits may think that the customer needs a drill bit, but what the customer really needs is a hole. In this sense there are no products; only services performed by products. If another product can provide the service better or more cheaply, the customer will have a new want but the same need. Manufacturers who focus only on existing wants, and fail to recognize the underlying need structure, are in danger of one day waking up to no demand. They suffer from 'marketing myopia.'[11] These sellers are so enamoured of their products that they lose sight of the customers' needs. They forget that a physical object is a tool to solve a consumer problem.

Demands

People have numerous wants, many of which they cannot satisfy. Every person has a finite set of resources (income, savings, time, energy) and must decide which things are affordable and will make him or her feel better off. A want becomes a demand when the person is able and willing to buy the object he or she desires.

There is no doubt that modern needs and wants have assumed staggering proportions. In one year alone, Australians purchased 1905 million litres of beer, 926 000 tonnes of beef and veal, 50 000 cremations, 317 million train journeys, 624 000 motor vehicles, and 468 000 life-insurance policies. These and other consumer goods and services led to a derived demand for more fundamental inputs, such as 7 million tonnes of raw steel and 792 000 tonnes of locally produced paper. These are just a few of the wants and needs that are expressed in a $100 billion (thousand million) economy.

A society could plan next year's production by using this year's mix of demand, as is the practice in the USSR and other centrally planned economies. Demands, however, are not very reliable. People tire of some things they are currently consuming; they seek variety for its own sake; and they make new choices in response to changing prices and incomes. Kelvin Lancaster has pointed out that products are really bundles of attributes and people choose the products that give them the best bundle of things they are seeking.[12] Thus a Mini Moke represents a benefit bundle of basic transportation, low purchase price, and fuel economy; and a Mercedes represents a benefit bundle of high comfort, luxury and status. The car that a person chooses is the one that packages the best bundle of attributes

for the money that he or she is willing to spend.

Products

The existence of human needs, wants and demands implies the concept of products. We define product as follows:

- A *product* is something that is viewed as being capable of satisfying a need or want.

All the products that are capable of satisfying a certain need may be called the product choice set. Suppose a woman feels a need to enhance her appearance. This product set includes cosmetics, new clothes, a Gold Coast holiday, a beautician's services, plastic surgery, and so forth. These products are all competitive but are not all equally desirable: the more accessible satisfiers, such as cosmetics, clothing and a new haircut, are more likely to be purchased first.

Another means of illustrating this point is to represent any specific product as a circle and ask how much the product would satisfy the person's want, also represented as a circle. Figure 1-1a indicates that product A has no want-satisfying ability relative to the person's want X. Figure 1-1b shows that product B has partial want-satisfying ability (it may be minimal or substantial). Figure 1-1c shows that product C has virtually complete want-satisfying ability, i.e. it is an ideal product.

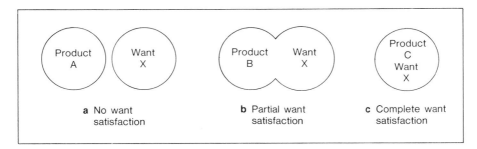

a No want satisfaction **b** Partial want satisfaction **c** Complete want satisfaction

Figure 1-1   Three degrees of want satisfaction

The concept of an ideal product can be made more rigorous. Suppose the product is vanilla ice-cream. We choose a set of important product attributes – say, 'creaminess' and 'sweetness' – and ask the consumer how much of each attribute he or she would ideally want. Suppose the consumer's answer is represented by 'Ideal' in Figure 1-2. Now the consumer is asked to taste various existing brands of vanilla ice-cream and describe their respective levels of creaminess and sweetness (also represented in Figure 1-2). We would thus predict that the consumer would buy brand B, because it comes closer than the other brands to 'packaging' the ideal levels of the two attributes the consumer wants. We are assuming that price and other attributes are not important to the consumer, and that purchase situation factors – e.g. stock conditions, a damaged container, a desire to try something different – play no part.

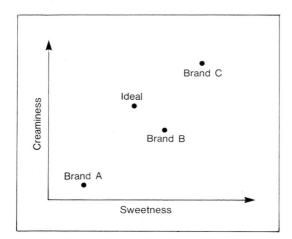

Figure 1-2   Vanilla ice-cream brands in a brand space made up of creaminess and sweetness

It is important not to limit our concept of product to physical objects. The key thing about a product is the service that it renders. Anything capable of rendering a service, i.e. satisfying a need, can be called a product. This includes persons, places, organizations, activities and ideas. A consumer chooses between different entertainers to watch on television, different places to go to for a holiday, different organizations to contribute to, and different ideas to support. From the consumer's point of view, these are alternative products. If the term product seems unnatural at times, we can substitute the term satisfier, resource or offering – all of which describe something of value to someone.

Exchange

The fact that people have needs, wants and demands, and that there are products capable of satisfying them, is necessary but not sufficient to define marketing. Marketing exists when people decide to satisfy needs and wants through exchange.

- *Exchange* is the act of obtaining a desired object from someone by offering something in return.

Exchange is one of four ways in which individuals can obtain a desired object. Let us again suppose that someone is hungry. This person can try to obtain food in the following ways:

1. *Self-production.* The hungry person can relieve this hunger through personal efforts (hunting, fishing, fruit-gathering). There is no necessity to interact with anyone else; there is no market and no marketing.
2. *Coercion.* The hungry person can forcibly wrest or steal food from someone else. No benefit is offered to the other party except the chance not to be harmed.
3. *Supplication.* The hungry person can approach someone and ask or beg for food. The supplicant has nothing tangible to offer except gratitude.
4. *Exchange.* The hungry person can approach someone who has food and offer some resource (money, another good, some service) in exchange.

Of these four ways of satisfying individual needs, exchange has a great deal in its favour. The person wanting a specific product does not have to prey on others or depend on alms. Nor does this person have to produce every necessity, regardless of skill: it is possible to concentrate on producing those things for which he has the greatest comparative advantage, and trade them for needed items produced by others. The members of a society end up specializing in production, thus leading to much more total output than under any alternative.

Specialization in production, however, does not always lead to a society in which exchange is the basis of distributing goods. Goods may be distributed in a society in one of three ways:[13]

1. *Reciprocity.* In some societies, each producer supplies goods or services to whoever wants them and, in turn, goes to others for whatever is needed. A cobbler will repair shoes for others and will in turn go to the butcher, the baker and the candlestickmaker for the things he needs. The modern family works on this principle, each member providing services for other members without formal exchange arrangements.
2. *Redistribution.* In other societies, producers turn over some part of their output to a chief or a central depot. The output is subsequently redistributed to persons according to their needs, status or power.
3. *Exchange.* In most modern societies, producers offer to sell their goods to others in exchange for money. Exchange is the core concept of the discipline of marketing. For exchange to take place, five conditions must be satisfied:

a) There are at least two parties.
b) Each party has something that might be of value to the other party (or parties).
c) Each party is capable of communication and delivery.

d) Each party is free to accept or reject the offer of the other party (or parties).
e) Each party believes it is proper to deal with the other party (or parties) in this way.

These five conditions set up a potential for exchange. Whether exchange actually takes place depends upon the parties' coming to an agreement on the *terms*. If they agree, we conclude that the act of exchange leaves all of them better off (or at least not worse off) because each was free to reject or accept the offer. In this sense, exchange is a value-creating process. Just as production creates value, so does exchange create value through enlarging the consumption possibilities facing any individual.

It should be noted that exchange is a human activity without counterpart in the animal kingdom. Ant colonies and gorilla societies show some division of labour but little evidence of formal exchange. The political economist Adam Smith observed that: 'Nobody ever saw a dog make a fair and deliberate exchange of one bone for another with another dog. Nobody ever saw one animal by its gestures and natural cries signify to another, this is mine, that is yours; I am willing to give this for that.'[14]

Whereas people, according to Smith, have a natural 'propensity to barter, truck, and exchange one thing for another', anthropologists have cast doubt over whether exchange is a natural human propensity or a learned disposition (see Exhibit 1-1). Whatever the case, exchange seems to be a uniquely human activity.

Transactions

If exchange is the core concept of the discipline of marketing, what is the discipline's unit of measurement? The answer is, a transaction. A *transaction* consists of a trade of values between two parties: A gives X to B, and gets Y in return. Thus, in a monetary transaction, Jones gives $400 to Smith and obtains a television set. Not all transactions require money as one of the traded values, however. A barter transaction would consist, for example, of Jones giving a refrigerator to Smith in return for a television set; it may also consist of the trading of services instead of goods, as when lawyer Jones writes a will for physician Smith in return for a medical examination.

A transaction involves several measurable entities: (i) at least two things of value; (ii) conditions that are agreed to; (iii) a time of agreement; (iv) a place of agreement. Transactions can easily give rise to conflicts based on misinterpretations or malice, and thus a legal system usually arises to support and enforce certain behaviour on the part of the transactors. Without a 'law of contracts', people would approach transactions with distrust and everyone would lose.

Business firms keep records of their transactions and sort them by item, price, customer, location and other specific variables: in sales analysis, for example, they try to analyze where the company's sales are coming from by product, customer, territory, and so on.

A transaction should be distinguished from a *transfer*, i.e. where A gives X to B but receives nothing explicit in return (as with gifts, subsidies and altruistic acts). It would seem to follow that marketers should confine their study to transactions and not to transfers. However, a little more thought suggests that transfer behaviour also includes a concept of exchange. The transferrer gives a gift in the expectation of some immediate or eventual benefit, such as gratitude, a good feeling, relief from a sense of guilt, or the wish to put the other party under an obligation. Professional fund-raisers are acutely aware of the 'reciprocal' motives underlying donor behaviour and try to supply the utilities being sought by the givers; if they neglect donors or show no gratitude, they will soon lose them. As a result,

marketers have recently broadened the concept of marketing to include the study of transfer behaviour as well as transaction behaviour.

Markets

The concept of transactions leads to the concept of a market.

- A *market* is the set of all actual and potential buyers of a product.

To understand the nature of a market, let us imagine a primitive economy consisting of four persons: fisher, hunter, potter and farmer. Figure 1-3 shows three different ways in which these tradespeople could meet their needs. In the first case, *self-sufficiency*, each person relies completely upon himself to gather the goods he needs for living. Thus the fisher spends most of his time fishing but also takes time to hunt, make pottery, and farm to obtain the other goods. He is therefore less efficient at fishing, and the same is true of the other tradespeople. In the second case, *decentralized exchange*, each person sees the other three as potential 'buyers' of his product and therefore making up a market. Thus the fisher may make separate trips to exchange his goods for those of the hunter, potter and farmer. In the third case, *centralized exchange*, a merchant appears and sets up in a central area called a marketplace. Each tradesperson brings his goods to the merchant and trades for all the things he needs. Thus the fisher now transacts with only one 'market' to obtain the goods he needs, rather than with three other persons. The emergence of a merchant substantially reduces the total number of transactions required to accomplish a given volume of exchange. In other words, merchants and central marketplaces increase the transactional efficiency of the economy.[15]

As the number of persons and transactions increases in a society, the number of merchants and marketplaces also increases. In

Exhibit 1-1 The Origin of Trade

Since exchange is the idea underlying marketing, we might ask how exchange or trade originated in human society. Exchange is so pervasive in modern society that we may ignore the fact that it is an invention and not inevitable human practice. For example, there is no evidence of trade behaviour among certain groups, such as the Incas, Eskimos and early Polish peasants. Eskimos, in fact, consider the idea of exchange vulgar, believing that a person should give something without expecting anything in return.

Scholars are not in agreement as to the origins of trade. Several years ago, George Robbins summarized seven different theories as to how trade began.

1. *Trading is instinctive*. This theory holds that human beings have an inborn instinct to 'truck and barter'. Although this instinct is not as strong as those of self-preservation and sex, it nevertheless appears in much of human society. A modification of the theory holds that this trait will appear more strongly in certain people than others: every society will spawn individuals who are instinctive traders or 'born' salespeople who get their kicks from swapping goods.

2. *Trading grew out of warfare*. This theory holds that many primitive tribes initially resorted to warfare in order to gain the economic goods they need or want. But the casualties of war led them to search for other ways to obtain those goods, and eventually they hit upon the idea of trading with the other tribes. Trading thus becomes a sublimation of warlike behaviour.

3. *Trading originated in predation*. This theory holds that much of human history is filled with groups and individuals who extracted tribute from others by conquering them. Those collecting tribute eventually offered something in return, such as security or small gifts, to keep the tributees from rebelling. It is held that trading may have picked up some of its negative overtones because it grew out of such practices.

4. *Trading grew out of friendly gift-giving*. The practice of friendly gift-giving has appeared in many societies. Through receiving gifts, people may have learned the utility of exchange. Having become accustomed to giving and receiving gifts, they transformed the principle into trading behaviour.

5. *Trading originated with the 'silent trade'*. Anthropologists have noted many tribes which have engaged in 'silent trade', where one tribe leaves its goods on a promontory and retires from sight to permit another group to come out of hiding to take these goods and leave something in return. Silent trade took place primarily between tribes of very different cultures, who wished to obtain certain goods without resorting to war on the one hand or building friendship on the other.

6. *Trading arose from surpluses*. A popular theory holds that trading developed from an early division of labour, which resulted in certain families or tribes having a surplus of certain goods. They looked for others who had a surplus of needed goods, and proposed to offer some of their goods in exchange.

(continued)

Exhibit 1-1 (continued)

7. *Trading developed from the property concept.* People discover that possession of certain scarce goods gives them power or status, which leads to a concept of ownership and property. Those who want something belonging to another must make a strong offer, hence leading to the concept of trading.

All of these theories have elements of truth and yet none applies to all societies where trading has been observed. Trading can be found in societies that never went to war, that did not practise gift-giving, and that did not have a strong concept of property. The question of how trading originated, like the question of how the solar system was formed, may never be fully answered but nevertheless leads to many interesting speculations.

Source: Adapted from George W. Robbins, 'Notions about the Origins of Trading', *Journal of Marketing*, January 1947, pp. 228–36.

advanced societies, marketplaces need not be physical locations: with the development of modern communications and transport, a merchant can advertise a product on late-evening television, take telephone orders from hundreds of customers, and mail the goods on the following day without any direct contact with the buyer.

A market can grow up around a good, a service, or anything else of value. For example, a labour market exists when there are persons ready to offer their labour to others in return for wages or products. Various institutions will grow up around a labour market to facilitate its functioning, such as employment agencies, job advertising, and job-counselling firms. Similarly, a money market emerges to meet the needs of people who wish to borrow, lend, save or safeguard money. The donor market emerges to meet the financial needs of non-profit organizations so that they can carry out their work.

Marketing

The concept of markets finally brings us full circle, to the concept of marketing. Marketing means human activity that takes place in relation to markets. Marketing means working with markets, which means attempting to actualize potential exchanges for the purpose of satisfying human needs and wants. Thus

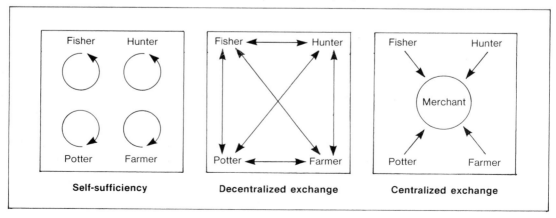

Figure 1-3 Evolution toward centralized exchange

we return to our definition of marketing as human activity directed at satisfying needs and wants through exchange processes.

Exchange processes involve work. The seller has to search for buyers, identify their needs, design appropriate products, promote them, store and transplant them, negotiate, and so on. Such activities as product development, search, communication, distribution, pricing and service are core marketing activities.

Although it is normal to think of marketing as the activities of 'sellers', buyers also carry out marketing activities. The homemaker searches for the goods he needs at prices he is willing to pay; the purchasing agent who needs a commodity in short supply has to track down sellers and offer attractive terms. A sellers' market is one in which the buyer is the more active 'marketer', and a buyers' market is one in which the seller is the more active 'marketer'.

In the early 1950s the growing supply of goods created a buyers' market, and marketing

---

Exhibit 1-2 Various Approaches to the Study of Marketing

Any phenomenon can be studied from several points of view. The following approaches have been prominent in the history of marketing, and they are listed in the rough order of their appearance.

1. *Commodity approach.* The commodity approach focuses on particular commodities and classes of products to determine how they are produced and distributed to intermediate and ultimate consumers. The major product classes studied are farm produce, minerals, manufactured goods, and services.

2. *Institutional approach.* The institutional approach focuses on the nature, evolution and functions of particular institutions in the marketing system, such as producers, wholesalers, retailers and various facilitating agencies. An institutionalist may study a department store, for example, to determine both how it has developed over the years and its likely future direction.

3. *Functional approach.* The functional approach focuses on the nature and dynamics of various marketing functions, such as buying, selling, storing, financing and promoting. A functionalist studies how these functions are carried on in various product markets and by various marketing institutions.

4. *Managerial approach.* The managerial approach focuses on the use of marketing in successfully positioning organizations and products in the marketplace. Managerial marketers are especially interested in marketing analysis, planning, organization, implementation and control.

5. *Social approach.* The social approach focuses on the social contributions and costs created by various marketing activities and institutions. It addresses such issues as market efficiency, product obsolescence, advertising truthfulness, and the ecological impact of marketing.

became identified with sellers trying to find buyers. This book will take such a view, and examine the marketing problems of sellers in a buyers' market. However, it will occasionally allude to the marketing done by buyers to produce desired exchanges.

MARKETING MANAGEMENT

Those who engage in exchange learn how to do it better over time. In particular, sellers learn how to professionalize their marketing management. We define marketing management as follows:

- *Marketing management* is the analysis, planning, implementation and control of programmes designed to create, build and maintain mutually beneficial exchanges and relationships with target markets for the purpose of achieving organizational objectives.

The popular image of the marketing manager is that of someone whose primary task is to stimulate demand for the company's products. This, however, is too limited a view: marketing managers are concerned not only with the creation and expansion of demand, but also with its modification and possible reduction. Marketing management must regulate the level, timing and character of demand in a way that will help the organization achieve its objectives; marketing management is demand management.

The organization forms an idea of a *desired* level of transactions with a market; at any point in time, the actual demand level may be below, equal to or above this, which leads to eight distinguishable marketing tasks:[16]

1. *Conversional marketing.* This is the task of trying to get people who dislike something, to like it (e.g. many people have a fear of flying, and the airline industry tries to convert them into willing flyers). Conversional

marketing is a difficult task, and it is questionable because it tries to change rather than serve people's wants. One's attitude toward conversional marketing depends on whether the 'cause' is seen as worthwhile.

2. *Stimulational marketing.* This is the task of trying to stimulate a want for an object, in people who initially have no knowledge of or interest in it (e.g. trying to get people to buy 'pet rocks').

3. *Developmental marketing.* This is the task of trying to develop new goods or services that meet a clear market need (e.g. the effort to develop an efficient electric car).

4. *Remarketing.* This is the task of trying to rebuild interest in a stable or declining product (e.g. the various steps that church groups are taking to attract followers in the face of growing competition from secular activities).

5. *Synchromarketing.* This is the task of trying to alter the time pattern of demand so that it will better match the time pattern of supply (e.g. where public-transport authorities try to encourage more passengers to travel during off-peak periods and thus reduce the amount of equipment needed during rush hours).

6. *Maintenance marketing.* This is the task of trying to maintain the existing level of sales in the face of competition. The maintenance marketer monitors the environment continuously and is ready to make necessary changes in order to protect the sales level.

7. *Demarketing.* This is the task of trying to reduce the demand for goods or services on a temporary or permanent basis (e.g. the use of pricing and promotion techniques to encourage consumers to reduce their energy consumption). Demarketing calls for using the normal marketing tools in reverse, such as reducing availability, advertising and service, and increasing prices.[17]

8. *Countermarketing.* This is the task of trying to destroy the demand for or interest in a

particular product (e.g. an anti-smoking campaign to persuade people who like smoking to stop smoking). Countermarketing is a difficult marketing task in that the aim is to get people who like something to give it up.

MARKETING-MANAGEMENT PHILOSOPHIES

We have described marketing management as the conscious effort to achieve desired exchange outcomes with target markets. Now the question arises of the philosophy that guides these efforts. Very often the interests of the organization, the customers and society are in conflict: it is desirable that marketing activities be carried out according to a clear concept of both responsive and responsible marketing.

There are five alternative concepts which provide business and other organizations with guidelines for their marketing activity: the production, product, selling, marketing and societal marketing concepts.

The Production Concept

The production concept is one of the oldest concepts guiding sellers.

- The *production concept* assumes that consumers will favour those products that are available and affordable. The major task of management is therefore to improve the efficiency of both production and distribution.

The implicit assumptions of the production concept are:

1. Consumers are primarily interested in product availability and low price.
2. Consumers know the prices of the competing brands.
3. Consumers do not see or attach much im-

portance to non-price differences within the product class.
4. The organization's task is to continue to improve production and distribution efficiency, and lower costs, in order to attract and hold customers.

The production concept is an appropriate management philosophy in two situations. The first is where the demand for a product exceeds supply: here consumers are ready to buy any version of the product they can find. The second is where the product's cost is high and must be brought down by producing it more efficiently. Henry Ford's philosophy was to perfect the production of one car model (the Model T) so that its cost could be brought down; he joked about offering people a car of any colour as long as it was black. Texas Instruments is a prime contemporary practitioner of putting major effort into achieving production volume and lower costs in order to bring down prices. It succeeded in winning a major share of the pocket-calculator market with this philosophy, and is applying it again in the manufacture of digital watches.

Some service organizations also follow the production concept. Many medical and dental practices are organized on assembly-line principles, as are some government agencies such as unemployment offices. While this results in handling many cases per hour, this type of management is open to the charge of impersonality and insensitivity to consumers.

The Product Concept

The product concept is another major concept guiding sellers.

- The *product concept* assumes that consumers will favour those products that offer the most quality for the price, and therefore the organization should devote its energy to improving product quality.

The implicit premises of the product concept are:

1. Consumers buy products rather than solutions to needs.
2. Consumers are primarily interested in product quality.
3. Consumers know the quality and feature differences of the competing brands.
4. Consumers choose between competing brands on the basis of obtaining the most quality for their money.
5. The organization's task is to continue to improve product quality, in order to attract and hold customers.

Many a manufacturer believes that if he can build a better mousetrap, the world will beat a path to his door.[18] But he is often rudely shocked. In the first place, buyers are looking for a solution to a mouse problem and not necessarily a mousetrap – the solution might take the form of a chemical spray, an exterminating service, or something that works better than a mousetrap. In the second place, the inventor of the better mousetrap will get nowhere unless positive steps are taken to design, package and price this new product attractively, place it in convenient distribution channels, bring it to the attention of persons who need it, and convince them that it has superior qualities.

Companies that operate according to a product concept can be found in all fields. Railways management was so sure that it had a superior form of transport that it overlooked the emerging challenge of the airlines, buses, trucks and cars. Historically, universities assumed that high-school students would continue to want their product.

The Selling Concept

The selling concept (also called the sales concept) is another hallowed way in which many producers guide their exchange activity.

- The *selling concept* assumes that consumers will either not buy, or not buy enough of, the organization's products

unless the organization makes a substantial effort to stimulate their interest in its products.

The implicit premises of the selling concept are:

1. Consumers have a normal tendency to resist buying most things that are not essential.
2. Consumers can be induced to buy more through various sales-stimulating devices.
3. The organization's task is to organize a strong sales-oriented department, in order to attract and hold customers.

The selling concept is practised most aggressively in the instance of 'unsought goods', i.e. those goods that buyers do not usually think of buying. Examples include insurance, encyclopaedias, and burial plots; relevant industries have established various techniques of tracking down prospects and hard-selling them on the benefits of their product.

Hard-selling is also practised by manufacturers and resellers when they have a surplus of goods on their hands. Car dealers often are prime practitioners of the selling concept:[19]

> From the moment the customer walks into the showroom, the car salesman will engage in 'psyching him out', and exaggerating the car's virtues. If the customer likes the floor model, he may be told that there is another customer about to buy it and that he should decide on the spot. If the customer balks at the price (which is artificially high to begin with), the salesman offers to talk to the manager to get a special concession. The customer waits ten minutes and the salesman returns with 'the boss doesn't like it but I got him to agree'. The aim is to 'work up the customer' to buy then and there.

The sales concept is also practised in the non-profit area. Consider a political party: having chosen a parliamentary leader and candidates, it will vigorously sell this leader to the voters. The leader and his supporters visit electoral districts from early morning to late evening shaking hands, kissing babies, and making breezy speeches. Countless dollars are spent on radio and television advertising, posters and mailings. Any flaws in the candidates are shielded from the public because the aim is to get the sale, not worry about post-purchase satisfaction.

The Marketing Concept

The marketing concept is a more recent one in the history of exchange relations.[20]

- The *marketing concept* assumes that the key to achieving organizational goals consists of the organization's determining the needs and wants of target markets and adapting itself to satisfying these more effectively and efficiently than its competitors.

The marketing concept has been expressed in more colourful ways, such as 'Find wants and fill them', 'Make what you can sell instead of trying to sell what you can make', 'Love the customer and not the product'. It is evident in advertising slogans such as 'Have it your way' and 'You're the boss'.

The underlying premises of the marketing concept are:

1. Consumers may be grouped into different market segments according to their needs and wants.
2. The consumers in any market will favour the offer of that organization which comes closest to satisfying their particular needs and wants.
3. The organization's task is to research and choose target markets, and develop effective offers and marketing programmes, in order to attract and hold customers.

The selling concept and the marketing concept are frequently confused by business-people and the public alike. Levitt draws the following contrast between the two orientations:

> Selling focuses on the needs of the seller; marketing on the needs of the buyer. Selling is pre-occupied with the seller's need to convert his product into cash; marketing with the idea of satisfying the needs of the customer by means of the product and the whole cluster of things associated with creating, delivering and finally consuming it.[21]

The marketing concept replaces and reverses the logic of the selling concept (see Figure 1-4). The selling concept starts with the firm's existing products, and uses selling and promotion to stimulate a profitable volume of sales. The marketing concept starts with the firm's target customers and their needs and wants, coordinates a set of appropriate products and programmes, and derives profits through satisfying its customers. In essence, the marketing concept is a customer needs and wants orientation backed by integrated marketing effort aimed at generating customer satisfaction as the key to satisfying organizational goals.

The marketing concept is a company's commitment to the time-honoured economic approach known as consumer sovereignty:

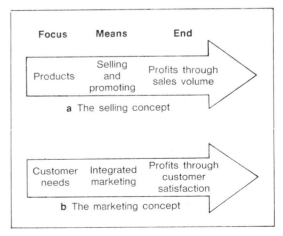

Figure 1-4 **The selling and marketing concepts contrasted**

the determination of what is to be produced should not be in the hands of the companies or in the hands of government but in the hands of consumers. The companies produce what the consumers want, and thus maximize consumer welfare as well as their profits.

Have many countries adopted this approach? We know that the marketing concept is behind the success of such companies as IBM, Avon, and McDonald's; we also know that it is more prevalent in consumer-goods companies than in industrial-goods companies, and in larger companies than in smaller companies.[22] In many cases the marketing concept, although professed, is not practised in any methodical way: the company may have the forms of marketing (such as a marketing manager, product managers, marketing plans, marketing research) but not the substance.[23] It takes several years of top-management determination to turn a sales-oriented company into a truly market-oriented company.

The Societal Marketing Concept

Some people have recently begun to question whether the marketing concept is an adequate philosophy for business in an age of environmental deterioration, resource shortages, explosive population growth, worldwide inflation and neglected social services.[24] The issue is whether the firm that does an excellent job of sensing, serving and satisfying individual consumer needs is necessarily acting in the best long-run interests of consumers and society. The marketing concept sidesteps the conflict between consumer wants, consumer interests and long-run societal welfare.

As a concrete instance, consider the Coca-Cola Company. Its products do an excellent job of meeting the wants of people for tasty soft-drinks. But is it really serving their long-run interests? Here are some criticisms that have been levelled against the company by consumer and environmental groups:

1. Coca-Cola is a product from which customers derive little nutritional benefit.
2. The sugar and phosphoric acid are not beneficial for people's teeth.
3. The brominated vegetable oil in colas has been removed from the American Food and Drug Administration's list of products 'generally recognized as safe'.
4. The caffeine in colas has been found to produce tremor, insomnia, gastrointestinal disorders, and possible cell damage in the drinker or the unborn foetus.
5. Saccharin, used in Coca-Cola's low-calorie drink Tab, may be banned by health authorities.
6. The soft-drink industry has catered to the demand for convenience by the increasing use of one-way (disposable) bottles. The one-way bottle is wasteful of resources, in that one returnable bottle can make seventeen trips before it is no longer usable. Many one-way bottles are not biodegradable, and thus often become litter.

This and similar situations have led to the call for a new concept which goes beyond that of marketing. Among the proposals are the 'human concept', 'intelligent consumption concept' and 'ecological imperative concept',[25] all of which tackle different aspects of the same problem. We would like to propose the 'societal marketing concept', defined as follows:

- The *societal marketing concept* holds that the key task of the organization is to determine the needs, wants and interests of target markets, and to deliver the desired satisfactions more effectively and efficiently than its competitors in a way that preserves or enhances the consumer's and the society's well-being.

The underlying premises of the societal marketing concept are:

Exhibit 1-3 McDonald's Corporation: The Marketing Concept in Practice

Among the prime practitioners of the marketing concept is McDonald's Corporation, the fast-food hamburger retailer. In its short twenty-five years, McDonald's has served Australians, Americans and citizens of several other countries more than 27 billion (thousand million) hamburgers. With over 4200 outlets worldwide, its current annual sales are running at $US4.6 billion. This leading position is the result of a thoroughgoing marketing orientation: McDonald's knows how to serve people well and adapt to changing needs and wants.

Before McDonald's, Americans could buy hamburgers in restaurants or diners but not without problems. In many places, the hamburgers were poor in quality, service was slow, decor was poor, conditions were unclean, and the atmosphere noisy. In 1955 Ray Kroc (then a salesman of malted-milk machines) became interested in a particular restaurant owned and managed by Richard and Maurice McDonald. He liked their concept of a fast-food restaurant and proposed a programme of selling franchises. This was the beginning of the successful McDonald's system, formulated as an alternative whereby the customer could walk into a spotlessly clean outlet, be greeted by a friendly and efficient order-taker, and receive a tasty hamburger a minute after placing the order, with the chance to eat it there or take it away. There were no jukeboxes or telephones to create a teenage hangout and in fact, McDonald's became a family affair, particularly appealing to the children.

As times changed, so did McDonald's. The sit-down sections were enlarged, the decor improved, and new outlets opened in high-traffic parts of the city. McDonald's was clearly being managed to evolve with changing customer needs and profitable opportunities.

McDonald's management also knows how to efficiently design and operate a complex service business. It chooses its locations carefully, selects highly qualified franchise operations, gives complete management training (in the United States, at its Hamburger University), supports its franchises with a high quality national advertising and sales promotion programme, monitors product and service quality through continuous customer surveys, and puts great energy into improving the technology of hamburger production to simplify operations, bring down costs, and speed up service.

1. Consumers' wants do not always coincide with their long-run interests or those of society.
2. Consumers will increasingly favour organizations that show a concern for meeting their wants, long-run interests, and society's long-run interests.
3. The organization's task is to serve target markets in a way that produces not only want satisfaction but long-run individual and social benefit, in order to attract and hold customers.

Societal marketing involves four considerations in marketing decision-making: consumer needs and wants, consumer interests, company interests, and society's interests. The major question facing companies is how societal marketing will affect their profitability, as they cannot be expected to absorb losses or lower profits in its pursuit. Fortunately there are many companies which have increased their profits by practising the societal marketing concept, and thus others can be expected to give it serious consideration.

THE GOALS OF A MARKETING SYSTEM

This brings us to the final question in this chapter: What should society seek from its marketing system? The question is particularly pertinent, as various governments around the world are increasingly regulating the normal marketing activities of firms. Some of the interventions may seem quite extreme:

- Government officials in India are considering prohibiting the branding of certain staple products such as sugar, soap, tea and rice. The allegation is that branding is inevitably accompanied by costly packaging and high advertising and promotional expenditures, which push up prices.
- Government officials in the Philippines are talking about solving the same problem through socialized pricing. Certain staples consumed heavily by the poor would have their prices held down through either subsidy or price control.
- Government officials in Norway are considering proposals to ban certain 'luxury' goods from the market, such as private swimming pools, tennis courts, aircraft and luxury vehicles. They think Norway's resources are too limited to permit their use for these purposes, even where they are affordable by the affluent. These officials want to promote the idea of 'collective consumption' of expensive goods and services.
- To promote 'truth-in-advertising', the US Federal Trade Commission experimented with three new measures in the early 1970s. Advertising substantiation requires firms to be prepared to provide documentary evidence backing any claim they make in an ad. Corrective advertising requires a firm found guilty of a false claim to spend 25 per cent of its subsequent advertising budget to announce that error to the public. Counter advertising encourages groups that have a different view about the social value of some product (such as an anti-smoking

group) to have easy access to the media to voice their opinion.

The recent proliferation of marketing legislation and regulation throughout the world raises a fundamental question: What are the proper goals of a marketing system? Any policy interventions in a marketing system should be guided by a clear image of what marketing is supposed to contribute to that society. (For further discussion of this issue, see Chapter 21.) At least four alternative goals have been suggested: maximize consumption, maximize consumer satisfaction, maximize choice and maximize life quality.

Maximize Consumption

Many business executives view marketing as a business function charged with the task of maximizing the amount of goods and services that the public buys and consumes, which in turn will maximize consumption, production, employment and wealth. This goal can be inferred from typical headlines in the business press: 'Wrigley Seeks Ways to Get People to Chew More Gum'; 'Opticians Introduce Fashion in Glasses to Stimulate Demand'; 'Steel Industry Maps Strategy to Expand Sales'.

The underlying assumption is that the more people buy and consume, the happier they are. This is captured in the phrase 'more is better', and has been a driving force in the Australian economy. Yet some people have begun to doubt that increased material goods mean more happiness; they see too many affluent people leading unhappy lives, and deny that the good life is achieved through continuous and conspicuous consumption. Their personal philosophy is 'less is more' and 'small is beautiful'.

Frederick Pohl, in a science-fiction story called *The Midas Touch*, dramatizes the possible dire consequences of too much consumption. In this story, society has reached a point where factories are completely automated.

Goods roll out continuously, and people are required to consume as much as they can so that they will not be buried under these goods. Ordinary people are given high consumption quotas, while an elite is excused from having to consume so much and its members are furthermore given the few jobs that still exist so that they will not have to face the bleakness of no work.

Maximize Consumer Satisfaction

Most marketers see the goal of marketing as that of maximizing consumer satisfaction rather than consumption. Chewing more gum or owning more cars is significant only if these objects bring about real increases in consumer satisfaction.

Unfortunately, consumer satisfaction as a goal of the marketing system poses some formidable conceptual and measurement problems. First, no welfare economist has worked out a meaningful scale by which the total satisfaction created by a particular product or marketing activity can be assessed. Second, the direct satisfaction that individual consumers obtain from particular 'goods' fails to take into account some of the 'bads' created in the process, such as pollution and environmental damage. Third, the satisfaction that people experience when consuming, for example, status goods, depends precisely on how few other people have these goods. For these and other reasons, it is difficult to evaluate a marketing system in terms of how much satisfaction it delivers.

Maximize Choice

Some marketers believe that the ideal marketing system is one that maximizes consumer choice, i.e. produces a great variety of products and brands and thus enables consumers to precisely satisfy their individual tastes. In such an economy, individual consumers are able to maximize their lifestyles and, therefore, their satisfaction.

Maximizing consumer choice unfortunately also has some flaws. First, goods and services will be more expensive since the great variety of products will call for shorter production runs and higher levels of required inventories. The higher cost of goods will reduce the consumers' real income and their ability to buy a greater quantity of goods. Second, the gain in consumer satisfaction from the great variety of goods will be offset by the greater cost of search time and effort. Consumers will have to spend more time learning about the features of different versions of a product, more time making an evaluation, and possibly more time travelling to the specific dealer carrying the chosen product. Third, an increase in the number of brands will not necessarily mean an increase in the consumers' range of *real* choice: there are, for example, many brands of beer in Australia but most of them have the same basic taste. When a product category features many brands with few differences, this is called product proliferation and the consumer faces 'false choice'. Finally, the presence of great variety will not always be welcomed by all customers as some will feel that too much choice causes frustration and anxiety.

Maximize Life Quality

The aim of a marketing system must transcend a narrow hedonistic view of consumer satisfaction. In a complex technological society, many different forces affect the happiness of its citizens: the concept of 'life quality' appears to be a useful way to encapsulate these various forces.

People everywhere try to improve the quality of their lives. The quality of life is a function of: (i) the quantity, quality, range, accessibility and cost of goods and services; (ii) the quality of the physical environment; and (iii) the quality of the cultural environment. In the future, marketing systems will be judged not only by the degree to which consumer wants

Exhibit 1-4   What is the Difference Between Economics and Marketing?

We might think that the concerns of marketing are the same as those of economics. True, economics is the parent discipline of marketing, but marketing has gone beyond economics in some of the questions it raises and elsewhere has gone into other questions more deeply.

Economics is a 200-year-old science whose core concept is that of scarcity: economists have noted that human beings have infinite needs but that nature is niggardly. Given scarce resources, a society must make decisions on which needs to satisfy. Economists study the following three major problems:

- What goods and services should the society produce?
- How should these goods and services be produced?
- Who should get them?

The answers to these questions differ according to whether the society is organized along capitalist, communist or other principles. All the questions revolve around the issue of economic efficiency in resource allocation, i.e. how to make resources go as far as possible in satisfying wants in a society.

Free-enterprise economists start with the two goals of consumer sovereignty and economic efficiency. They assume that consumers strive to maximize their economic satisfaction, that they have reasonably full information about the quality and price of the available goods, and that they are able to move easily to where the best buys can be found. These economists also assume that producers and sellers maximize their economic profit, know the costs of different resources and technologies at different scales of operation, and know how to put all of this information together to achieve the maximum profit. The free interaction of rational consumers and rational producers is assumed to produce maximum economic output and satisfaction.

Marketing began only seventy-five years ago, with the attempt to understand certain questions that economists had neglected or oversimplified. Whereas economists tried to explain, say, food prices through demand and supply curves, marketers were interested in tracing the complex sequence of activities that led to final price and consumption levels: farmers' decisions to plant certain crops, purchase certain seed fertilizer and equipment; the selling of their crops to grain elevators; the purchase of the grain by food processors, who sold the processed food to wholesalers, who in turn sold it to retailers, who in turn sold it to consumers. During this complicated process, several functions were carried out, including several levels of buying and selling, assembly, sorting, grading, storing, transporting, risk-bearing and financing. The final price reflected these many operations and the overall efficiency of the marketing process. This was a far cry from the economists' oversimplified picture of price setting.

Thus marketing started out as an effort to develop a richer description of distribution institutions and processes. Marketers were interested in exploring the 'whys' of consumer and seller behaviour, and were not willing to explain it merely in terms of utility and profit maximization. This inevitably led to less reliance on economic concepts and more use of the findings of modern psychology, sociology and anthropology. Today marketing is essentially an applied behavioural science rather than a branch of economic science, and its students are interested in three analytical questions:

Exhibit 1-4 (continued)

1. *Consumer behaviour.* What are the needs and wants of consumers, how are they formed and influenced, and how do consumers go about satisfying these needs and wants?
2. *Seller behaviour.* How do providers or sellers go about trying to supply and influence the wants and buying behaviour of consumers?
3. *Market channel behaviour.* What institutions and activities come into being to facilitate exchange and the satisfaction of human wants?

The answers to these questions provide the key to improving the performance of the marketing system and, therefore, consumer welfare. Students of marketing are also interested in the following normative questions:

1. How can consumers be helped to become better buyers?
2. How can providers be helped to become better sellers?
3. How can marketing institutions be improved to increase consumer satisfaction and welfare?

This leads to the normative purpose of the marketing discipline: to help sellers sell better, buyers buy better, and government agencies regulate better in the interest of promoting efficiency, consumer satisfaction, and life quality through the marketplace.

are directly satisfied but also by the impact of marketing activity on the quality of the physical and cultural environment.

SUMMARY

Marketing is a subject that touches everyone. It is the means by which a standard of living is developed and delivered to a people. It involves a large set of activities, including marketing research, product development, distribution, pricing, advertising, personal selling, and a number of other functions. Too many people mistakenly believe that marketing consists of only one or a few of these functions, whereas marketing is actually a high level integration of several functions designed to sense, serve and satisfy consumer needs while meeting the goals of the organization.

Marketing practices have been both praised and criticized because of their major impact on people in their roles as buyers, sellers and citizens. The controversy is likely to continue and possibly intensify as more and more institutions in the business sector, on the international scene and in the non-profit sector apply marketing concepts and techniques in the pursuit of improved performance.

Marketing may be defined as the study of how various parties go about satisfying their needs and wants through exchange and market processes. The key concepts involved are needs, wants, demands, products, exchange, transactions and markets.

Marketing management is the conscious effort of one or both parties to manage the exchange process to secure desired outcomes. It involves analysis, planning, implementation and control of programmes designed to create, build and maintain mutually beneficial exchanges and relationships with target markets for the purpose of achieving organizational objectives. The major marketing tasks are conversional marketing, stimulational marketing, developmental marketing, remarketing, synchromarketing, maintenance marketing, demarketing and countermarketing.

Any one of five alternative philosophies may guide organizations in their exchange activity. The production concept assumes that consumers will readily respond to products that are available and affordable, and therefore management's major task is to improve production efficiency and bring down prices. The product concept assumes that consumers will respond favourably to quality products that are reasonably priced, and therefore little additional marketing effort is required. The selling concept assumes that consumers will not tend to buy enough of the company's products unless substantial selling and promotion efforts are made. The marketing concept assumes that the main tasks of the company are to determine a chosen set of customers' needs, wants and preferences, and to adapt accordingly so that these are satisfied. The societal marketing concept assumes that the main task of the company is to generate customer satisfaction, and long-run consumer and societal well-being, as the key to satisfying organizational goals and responsibilities.

Different goals have been proposed for a marketing system, such as maximizing consumption, consumer satisfaction, consumer choice, or life quality. The orientation of this book is that the goal of the marketing system is to maximize the quality of life.

QUESTIONS FOR DISCUSSION

1. How does marketing differ from selling? Do you think that marketers have succeeded in educating the public as to the difference between the two?

2. Discuss how marketing affects the buyer, the seller and the citizen with regard to the Holden Commodore.

3. Why has marketing been embraced by many non-profit organizations in recent years? Elaborate on a specific example.

4. What distinguishes the definition of marketing used in this text from all others?

5. Compare and contrast needs, wants and demands. How does the consumer reconcile these three concepts? Relate them to a recent purchase of your own.

6. You are planning to go to a fast-food outlet for lunch. Apply the notions of products, exchange and a market to this situation.

7. How may the product concept and the production concept be contrasted? Give an example of each.

8. Why has the societal marketing concept superseded the marketing concept in some organizations?

9. What four alternative goals of a marketing system were discussed? Which one do you feel is the best, and why?

NOTES

1 Peter F. Drucker, *Management: Tasks, Responsibilities, Practices* (New York: Harper & Row, 1973), pp. 64–65.

2 Richard N. Farmer, 'Would You Want Your Daughter to Marry a Marketing Man?', *Journal of Marketing*, January 1967, p. 1.

[3] Sterling Hayden, *Wanderer* (New York: Knopf, 1963).

[4] John Schneider, quoted in R. R. Walker, *Communicators* (Melbourne: Lansdowne Press, 1967), p. 21.

[5] Sir Winston Churchill.

[6] Deborah Rankin, 'How C.P.A.'s Sell Themselves', *New York Times*, 25 September 1977.

[7] Ralph Z. Sorensen II, 'U.S. Marketers Can Learn from European Innovators', *Harvard Business Review*, September–October 1972, pp. 89–99.

[8] Thomas V. Greer, *Marketing in the Soviet Union* (New York: Holt, Rinehart & Winston, 1973).

[9] *Marketing Definitions: A Glossary of Marketing Terms*, Committee on Definitions (Chicago: American Marketing Association, 1960).

[10] This definition was originally proposed by Paul Mazur and was modified by Malcolm McNair. See Malcolm P. McNair, 'Marketing and the Social Challenge of Our Times', Keith Cox & Ben M. Enis (eds), *A New Measure of Responsibility for Marketing* (Chicago: American Marketing Association, 1968), p. 2.

[11] See Theodore Levitt's classic article, 'Marketing Myopia', *Harvard Business Review*, July–August 1960, pp. 45–56.

[12] Kelvin J. Lancaster, 'A New Approach to Consumer Theory', *Journal of Political Economy*, 14 (1966), pp. 132–57.

[13] Cyril S. Belshaw, *Traditional Exchange and Modern Markets* (New York: Prentice-Hall, 1965).

[14] Adam Smith, *The Wealth of Nations*, 1776 (New York: Crowell-Collier and Macmillan, 1909), p. 19.

[15] For further discussion, see Wroe Alderson, 'Factors Governing the Development of Marketing Channels', in Richard M. Clewett (ed.), *Marketing Channels for Manufactured Products* (Homewood, Ill.: Richard D. Irwin, 1957), pp. 211–14.

The number of transactions in a decentralized exchange system is given by $N(N-1)/2$. With four persons, this means $4(4-1)/2 = 6$ transactions. In a centralized exchange system, the number of transactions is given by N, here 4. Thus a centralized exchange system reduces the number of required transactions to accomplish a given volume of exchange.

[16] See Philip Kotler, 'The Major Tasks of Marketing Management', *Journal of Marketing*, October 1973, pp. 42–49.

[17] See Philip Kotler & Sidney J. Levy, 'Demarketing, Yes, Demarketing', *Harvard Business Review*, November–December 1971, pp. 74–80.

[18] See 'So We Made a Better Mousetrap', *President's Forum*, Autumn 1962, pp. 26–27.

[19] See Irwin J. Rein, *Rudy's Red Wagon: Communication Strategies in Contemporary Society* (Glenview Ill.: Scott, Foresman, 1972).

[20] See John B. McKitterick, 'What is the Marketing Management Concept?', *The Frontiers of Marketing Thought and Action* (Chicago: American Marketing Association, 1957), pp. 71–82; Fred J. Borch, 'The Marketing Philosophy as a Way of Business Life', *The Marketing Concept: Its Meaning to Management*, Marketing Series, No. 99 (New York: American Management Association, 1957), pp. 3–5; and Robert J. Keith, 'The Marketing Revolution', *Journal of Marketing*, January 1960, pp. 35–38.

[21] Levitt, 'Marketing Myopia'.

[22] Carlton P. McNamara, 'The Present Status of the Marketing Concept', *Journal of Marketing*, January 1972, pp. 50–57.

[23] Peter M. Banting & Randolph E. Ross, 'The Marketing Masquerade', *Business Quarterly* (Canada), Spring 1974, pp. 19–27. Also see Philip Kotler, 'From Sales Obsession to Marketing Effectiveness', *Harvard Business Review*, November–December 1977, pp. 67–75.

[24] Laurence P. Feldman, 'Societal Adaptation: A New Challenge for Marketing', *Journal of Marketing*, July 1971, pp. 54–60; and Martin L. Bell & C. William Emery, 'The Faltering Marketing Concept', *Journal of Marketing*, October 1971, pp. 37–42.

[25] Leslie M. Dawson, 'The Human Concept: New Philosophy for Business', *Business Horizons*, December 1969, pp. 29–38; James T. Rothe & Lissa Benson, 'Intelligent Consumption: An Attractive Alternative to the Marketing Concept', *MSU Business Topics*, Winter 1974, pp. 29–34; and George Fisk, 'Criteria for a Theory of Responsible Consumption', *Journal of Marketing*, April 1973, pp. 24–31.

The Structure of Marketing Systems

2

Every two minutes an Australian is born. She is a disarming little thing, but she begins to scream loudly in a voice that can be heard for seventy years or more. She is screaming for 7000 litres of milk, 4000 kilograms of sugar, 3500 kilograms of potatoes, 15 000 eggs, 5000 kilograms of flour, 7500 kilograms of meat, and 10 000 litres of beer, plus great storehouses of other foods, drinks and resources. These are lifetime demands on her country and its economy.[1]

When one stops to think about it, the amount of material needs of people during their lives is incredible. If individuals had to produce all the things they needed, they would not get very far; their standards of living would be abysmally low. Modern society, fortunately, has discovered three efficient principles for producing and distributing all the goods and services that people need. The first is the *division of labour*, whereby each person becomes skilled in making one or a few things that can be traded to obtain the other necessities. The second principle involves the *market*, which creates organized arenas for the efficient trading of goods and services. The third principle is the invention of *money*, which becomes a common denominator of value that facilitates the operation of trade and markets.

Modern society consists of many interlinked marketing systems that carry on the work of meeting people's material needs. In this chapter we examine the concept of a marketing system, which is the first step towards understanding the marketing process. We define it as follows:

- A *marketing system* is a set of interacting participants, markets and flows that are involved in an organized arena of exchange.

28

A marketing system comprises three levels: national, industry, and company. We will illustrate each of these, devoting most of our attention to the last.

NATIONAL MARKETING SYSTEMS

Every nation develops a particular set of institutions and practices to bring desired goods into existence and distribute them to consumers. Although the number of national marketing systems is tremendous, they can be classified into three broad groups:

1. *Tradition-directed systems.* In this type of economy, the methods of production and distribution are fairly primitive and are governed by ancient customs. Goods may be distributed on the basis of reciprocity, redistribution, or primitive market systems.
2. *Market-directed systems.* In this type of economy, people freely choose their production and consumption activities on the basis of self-interest. Products and prices are determined by demand and supply. Australia, the United States, Japan and several Western economies operate market-directed systems, although they are experiencing increased government regulation and control.
3. *Command-directed systems.* In this type of economy, relevant activities are planned and managed by a central authority. This system is found in the USSR, mainland China, and other socialist countries.

Structure of a National Marketing System

We will now examine the structure of a national marketing system as it occurs in a market-directed or command-directed economy. The structure in either case is similar, except for the role of government. It consists of three *participants* (consumers, business firms and government), two *markets* (resource markets and product markets), and three *flows* (goods and services, resources, and money). This is shown in Figure 2-1.

The first participant group (consumers) needs a vast amount of goods and services. Instead of producing these themselves, consumers go to product markets and exchange their money for the goods and services they

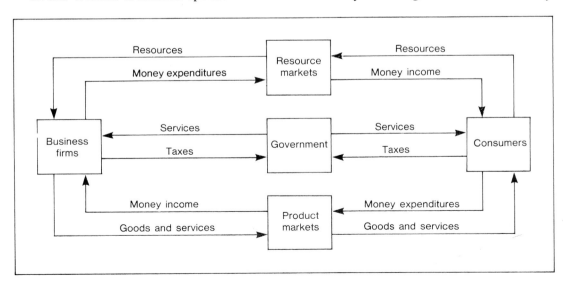

Figure 2-1 Structure of a national marketing system

want. But where do the consumers get their money? They acquire it by going to resource markets and exchanging their resources (labour, land and capital) for income (wages, rent and interest).

Meanwhile, members of the second participant group (business firms) are seeking money income, which they obtain by offering goods and services to the product markets. To produce these goods and services, they first go to the resource markets and buy the proper mix of productive resources.

Thus the marketing system consists of a flow of resources being turned into a flow of goods and services, and a flow of money expenditures being turned into a flow of money income. Another important flow (not shown in Figure 2-1) is the flow of information and communications, which facilitates the exchange processes.

The third participant in the national marketing system is government. In a market-directed economy, government's major role is to provide certain services for consumers and business firms, and to finance these by collecting taxes from the participants. The theory of the system is that consumers are free to buy what they want and business firms are free to sell what they want. Prices on the resource and product markets move up and down with changes in demand and supply. If prices are too high, goods do not sell, inventories pile up, and workers are laid off: this is a signal to business firms to reduce or transfer their resources to other industries. Conversely, if consumers are buying the goods in substantial quantities, it is a signal that further resources could well be transferred into this industry. The whole system is driven by consumers voting on which goods they want and what prices they will pay. The government's tasks are mainly: (i) providing consumer information, education and protection; (ii) preventing anti-competitive behaviour (such as price fixing), where one firm takes unfair advantage of other firms; and (iii) producing certain goods and services that business firms are unable or unwilling to produce.

On the other hand, the government plays the major role in command-directed economies such as the USSR and mainland China. The government owns and operates the business firms, decides what to produce, and sets the prices in the resource and product markets. Consumers usually face a much smaller range of products and have more limited options with respect to the jobs they can take. The marketing system is less responsive to changing consumer needs, because the government moves more slowly and is not necessarily willing to satisfy all classes of needs.

Participants and Forces in a National Marketing System

We will now take a closer look at the major participants and forces in a national marketing system. We should recognize that business firms play different roles in the system, there are various types of consumers, and there are various publics and forces that influence the system (see Figure 2-2).

The task system involves those who play a major role in supplying, exchanging and consuming economic goods and services. One group of participants consists of resource suppliers, such as farmers, miners, timber producers, energy producers, workers and financers. Their resources are purchased by a second group, manufacturers and processors who convert these resources into food and other products. A third group consists of distributors and facilitators, who help bring these goods and services to their proper markets where a fourth group, consumers (such as households, schools, hospitals and governments), proceeds to purchase and consume them. Thus the task system consists of specialized organizations and individuals who are good at carrying out certain economic functions.

Although the basic direction of economic

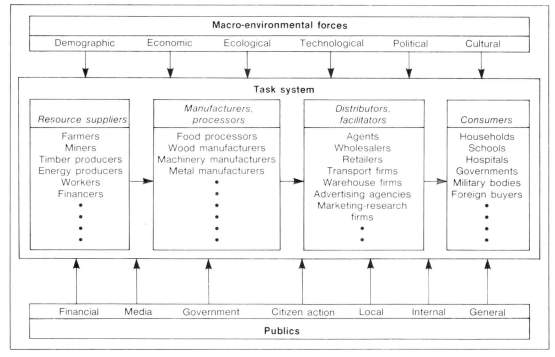

Figure 2-2 Major participants and forces in a national economic system

flow is shown as moving from left to right in Figure 2-2, it should be recognized that the actual flows are multi-directional. For example, manufacturers and processors sell some of their finished goods back to resource suppliers (as when International Harvester sells its farm equipment to farmers). Distributors and facilitators also provide services for resource suppliers selling to each other and to manufacturers, as well as to manufacturers selling to other manufacturers. Finally, consumers are not only consumers but also resource suppliers.

Outside the task system there is another set of participants (known as publics), which watches and influences the performance of the participants within that system. A *public* is any group with an actual or potential interest in, or impact on, other organizations: banks, newspapers, government agencies, citizen action groups and other publics are taking an

increasing interest in evaluating and influencing the participants in the task system. We will discuss their influence on marketing activity later in this chapter.

Finally, all the participants are inescapably affected by major macro-environmental forces that create new threats and opportunities. Every organization must find some way to not only monitor these changing demographic, economic, ecological, technological, political and cultural forces but also interpret and respond to them. We will look at these macro-environmental forces later in the chapter, and discuss their marketing implications in depth in Chapter 7.

How to Research a National Marketing System

Although all modern economies share the general relationships shown in Figures 2-1 and

2-2, major differences in marketing practices and philosophies can be found from country to country. Marketers in one country cannot assume that they will find the same marketing practices in another country. Each country must be freshly researched in terms of its marketing structure and dynamics.

Who would have an interest in researching the marketing system of a particular country? Its government officials would want to examine and evaluate the national marketing system in order to improve its functioning. Domestic firms would want to know how the system operates in order to perform well in the marketplace. Foreign firms which are considering doing business in that country would want to know how its marketing system works. Finally, various international agencies that make loans or provide technical assistance would want to research the nation's marketing system.

As major new markets open in China, the Middle East, South America and other parts of the world, companies looking for opportunities must have a systematic method for quickly and efficiently grasping the major features of any marketing system. To illustrate, suppose SPC Limited wants to expand its market penetration in the Middle East. It studies the various countries in which it is not yet operating and identifies Saudi Arabia, among other countries, as having a high sales potential for its canned fruits, jams and jellies. This is based on a preliminary reading of the market size, purchasing power, fruit consumption, and particular competitors. Additional information would be needed, including the major urban markets, the major channels of distribution, the normal markups given to intermediaries, and the available advertising media.

Table 2-1 outlines the major types of information needed to understand a national marketing system. To get further information, the marketing-research department at SPC would obtain an overseas business report from the Australian Department of Trade and Resources. For example, a 1980 report entitled *Businessman's Guide: Saudi Arabia* supplies valuable information about that country's marketing system, along with a list of additional sources of information. Some of the things SPC will learn about Saudi Arabia are:

- The population is estimated at about 7 million people, which includes more than

Table 2-1   The information required for understanding a national marketing system

Overall Market Characteristics
A. Population
B. Geographic characteristics
C. Urban/rural characteristics
D. Income size, distribution and growth
E. Consumption patterns
F. Cultural values
G. Government role and laws on marketing

Marketing Characteristics
A. Number of people engaged in sales and other marketing activities
B. Major industries
(i)   Size distribution of firms
(ii) Employment
C. Channels of distribution
(i)   Wholesaling (number, size, types, operating characteristics)
(ii) Retailing (number, size, types, operating characteristics)
(iii) Other intermediaries
(iv) Import channels
(v) Export channels
(vi) Agricultural channels
D. Facilitating intermediaries
(i)   Transport (roads, trucks, railways, air, waterways)
(ii) Storage and warehousing
(iii) Communication (mail, telephone and telegraph, newspapers, radio, television, outdoor)
(iv) Banking and credit
(v) Marketing-research agencies
(vi) Advertising agencies
E. Marketing mix
(i)   Product development
(ii) Pricing
(iii) Advertising and sales promotion
(iv) Sales force and sales management
(v) Marketing research
(vi) Physical distribution

1.5 million non-Saudis. The major cities are Jeddah (400 000 people, the major commercial centre and port); Riyadh (400 000 people, the administrative capital); and Dammam (100 000 people, the main port in the Gulf area).

- Saudi Arabia covers four-fifths of the Arabian peninsula, of which only 0.2 per cent is cultivated. Most land is desert, but some is suitable for grazing.
- Exports from Saudi Arabia to Australia, essentially comprising petroleum and its products, are approximately three times the level of imports from Australia, composed principally of food.
- The country depends on imports for almost all its manufactures and most of its food. Most foodstuffs are imported duty-free, and some are even subsidized by more than 20 per cent.
- No known local Saudi companies can carry out a complete market survey on behalf of Australian exporters. The trade commissioner in Jeddah can assist, but a personal visit to the market is recommended.
- Effective local agency representation is essential. Many merchants operate as both retailer and wholesaler, importing directly from suppliers. It is common to find a merchant selling butter, carpets, motor cars and building materials, although specialization is increasing.
- Regulations covering imported foods require that labels in Arabic be fixed to the package stating the name of the food, ingredients, country of origin, net contents, name and address of manufacturer, date produced, and expiry date
- Promotional material, including catalogues, brochures and advertising matter, will not be admitted if it contains photographs of the scantily-clad female form, alcohol or pigs.

This information may be very encouraging to SPC, but the company may decide to dig further by making some field trips to Saudi Arabia and talking to knowledgeable business and government officials. It must also try to get a picture of Saudi consumers and their needs and wants, and the kind of lives they lead. When SPC has enough information, it can decide whether it should enter the Saudi market. The key to this decision is the detailed study of the major characteristics of that nation's marketing system.

INDUSTRY MARKETING SYSTEMS

We now shift our analysis of marketing systems from the national to the industry level. Various participants, markets and flows arise in each industry to facilitate the production, distribution and consumption of its products. Wroe Alderson, one of the leading marketing scholars, saw the role of industries as that of transforming heterogeneous raw materials into meaningful assortments that match the need patterns of consumers: 'The whole economic process may be described as a series of transformations from meaningless to meaningful heterogeneity.'[2]

To understand an industry marketing system a marketer must identify the major participants, markets and flows that interact to transform raw resources into finished goods and services. We will illustrate the marketing system found in a rural-based industry.

Canned-peaches industry marketing system. It is the task of peach-growers to distribute a large quantity of fruit, much of it canned, to the Australian public each year. Figure 2-3 shows the various distribution channels available to these producers, which may be described as the distribution structure.

This system makes it clear that one of the major marketing tasks is channel management. Marketing managers must identify, choose and manage complex relations with a

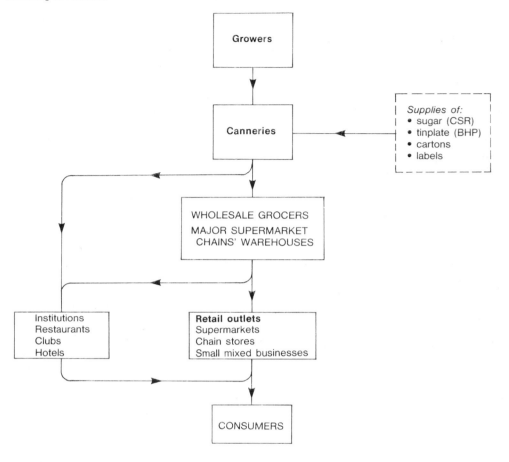

Figure 2-3 Distribution channels for canned peaches

variety of other institutions whose services are needed and whose efficiency ultimately affects the producer's sales and profits.

COMPANY MARKETING SYSTEMS

We may also define a marketing system from the company's point of view:

- A *company marketing system* is the set of major participants, markets and forces that make up the company's marketing environment.

The company may be seen as operating in a marketing environment made up of several levels of complexity, six of which are identified in Figure 2-4. At the centre stands the company. Next to the company are various marketing channel firms that participate in the activities necessary to produce and distribute the company's products. Next are the markets served by the company. Then there are the competitors, which also offer goods and services of potential interest to the same markets. Both the company and its competitors operate under the watchful eye of various

Figure 2-4 Levels in the marketing environment of a company

publics, which have an interest in and a potential impact on their actions. Finally, all of the institutions and markets operate in a macro-environment of major demographic, economic, ecological, political, technological and cultural forces that have a significant and continuous impact on their performance.

We will now examine each level of the company's marketing environment. As an illustration we will discuss them in connection with ACI Fibreglass, a major Australian producer of insulation materials such as 'pink batts'.

The Company

At the centre of any marketing system stands the company. We are concerned with the group within the company called marketing managers. At ACI Fibreglass the marketing department consists of a marketing manager, national and state sales managers and a sales force, a marketing research manager, some market managers, a national projects manager, an advertising coordinator, and some other marketing executives. Not every organization will have these marketing positions; some, especially non-profit organizations, will not even have a marketing department or marketing managers. However, all organizations engage in marketing activities whether or not they are recognized as such or are carried out by people who are called 'marketing managers'.

The marketing managers at ACI Fibreglass

must base their marketing decisions not only on the forces operating in the external environment but also on the forces operating within the company. The main forces in the company's internal environment are shown in Figure 2-5.

The first level of the internal environment to be considered by marketing management comprises the company's other major departments. All the departments cooperate in the development of annual and long-range business plans: marketing management supplies important inputs for the business-planning process, and thereby often provides a starting point, but throughout the process it works with and needs the support of the other departments.

Figure 2-5 A company's internal environment

Four major departments are shown in Figure 2-5. Financial management at ACI Fibreglass is concerned with the availability of funds to carry out the marketing plan, the efficient allocation of these funds to different products and marketing efforts, the likely rates of return that will be realized, and the level of risk in the sales forecast and marketing plan. Research and Development (R & D) management is concerned with the technical problems of designing safe, effective and attractive insulation and developing efficient methods of producing it. Purchasing is concerned with the availability and costs of obtaining needed supplies to produce the quantity of insulation called for in the sales forecast. Finally, manufacturing is concerned with whether there will be sufficient production capacity and labour, and whether marketing has called for an inordinate number of variations to be produced. Other departments not shown – such as accounting, personnel and credit – also have to be contacted by marketing managers for their views and assistance.

A second level of the company's internal environment is top management. Top management at ACI Fibreglass includes the fibreglass-division general manager, the chairman of the board, and the board of directors, plus the top executives and board of Australian Consolidated Industries Ltd, which is the holding company of ACI Fibreglass. These higher levels of management set the company's mission, objectives, broad strategies, and policies. Marketing managers must make their decisions in the larger context defined by top management, and their plans are reviewed by these higher levels of management before they may be implemented.

In developing its plans, marketing management must also take into account the company's internal 'culture'. Every organization is moulded by its history, leading personalities, and accomplishments: culture describes the way in which the company's managers look upon the world and their mission. Many organizations have a traditional business culture, sticking to 'tried-and-true' ways of doing things and avoiding risk. Others have an innovative culture, always looking for new and better ways to perform their tasks. Some companies are dominated by a financial culture, others by a production culture, and still others by a sales culture. One of the greatest challenges to top management is to transform the existing culture of an organization into a marketing culture.

Marketing Channel Firms

No company can perform by itself all the activities involved in the production and distribution of its goods and services to its final markets. It must work with other firms to get the job done. The major types of firms involved are illustrated in Figure 2-6, and can be defined as follows:

1. *Suppliers* are business firms and individuals who supply the necessary resources for the production of the particular good or service.
2. *Merchants* are business firms – such as wholesalers and retailers – that buy, take title to and resell merchandise (often called *resellers*).
3. *Agents* are business firms – such as manufacturers' representatives and brokers – that are hired by producers to find buyers and negotiate sales, but do not take title to the merchandise.
4. *Facilitators* are business firms – such as transport companies, warehouses, banks and insurance companies – that assist in the logistical and financial tasks of distribution, but do not take title to goods or negotiate purchases or sales.
5. *Marketing firms* are business firms – such as advertising agencies, marketing-research and consulting firms – that assist in targeting and promoting the sellers' products to the right markets.

We are now able to define marketing channel:

- A *marketing channel* is the set of all the firms and individuals that cooperate to produce, distribute and consume the particular good or service of a particular producer. It therefore comprises the five

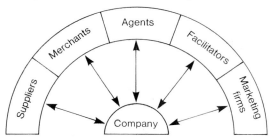

Figure 2-6 Marketing-channel firms

types of marketing-channel firms listed above, plus the producer and the end user.

A distribution channel is a subset of the firms and individuals in a marketing channel:

• A *distribution channel* is the set of all the firms and individuals that take title, or assist in transferring title, to the particular good or service as it moves from the producer to the consumer. Thus it primarily includes the merchants (because they take title) and the agents (because they assist in transferring title). It also includes the producer and the final consumers as starting and ending points. The distribution channel does not include suppliers, facilitators and marketing firms.

We will illustrate the marketing channel in the case of ACI Fibreglass insulation. To produce and distribute insulation, ACI works with a host of firms that make up the marketing channel (see Figure 2-7). First, ACI contracts with various suppliers for resources needed in insulation manufacture: these include materials (sand, soda ash, limestone), components (laminates, plastic sheets), energy (heat, light), labour and funds. Second, ACI sells its insulation directly to merchants (wholesalers and retailers), who thus make up the distribution channel. Third, ACI hires the services of various facilitators (transport companies, warehouse companies, banks and insurance companies) to facilitate and finance the physical distribution of its insulation to final markets. Fourth, ACI hires the services of various marketing firms (marketing research agencies, advertising agencies and

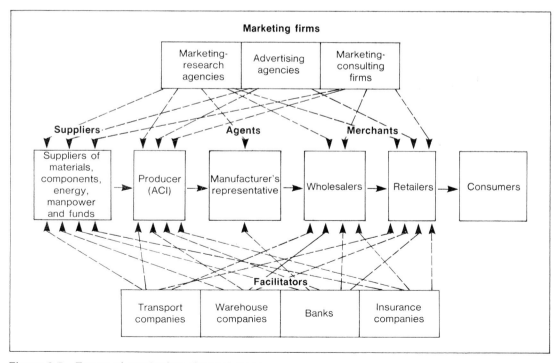

Figure 2-7 Types of marketing-channel firms

consulting firms) to improve its marketing efficiency and effectiveness.

ACI always has the option of performing additional marketing activities internally, instead of through other firms. It faces a number of 'make-or-buy' decisions: Should ACI do its own marketing research or use an agency? Prepare its own advertising or use an agency? Develop its own truck fleet or use a transport firm? Sell directly to retailers or sell through wholesalers? The fact is that marketing intermediaries are usually more efficient in these activities, because of their experience and scale of operations, and thus the company typically finds it cheaper to hire them for such functions. The reason for this may be touched on here, although more will be said about the use of intermediaries in Chapter 14. ACI's insulation will be of little or no use to the customer unless it is in the right form, in the right place, at the right time, and in the customer's possession. Thus the marketing task consists of creating the following utilities:

- *Form*. This necessitates making materials available in the right form: a pink batt has more form utility than a pile of sand, limestone and soda ash.
- *Place*. This necessitates making something available for purchase in the right place: a pink batt in a Perth K-Mart has more utility for a Perth buyer than the same batt in ACI's Melbourne warehouse.
- *Time*. This necessitates making something available at the right time: a pink batt that can be delivered today has more utility than one that could not be delivered until six weeks from today.
- *Possession*. This necessitates taking ownership of a good: a pink batt owned by the consumer has more utility than one that is only on loan to the consumer.

To produce these utilities efficiently, ACI will find it more economical to work with other firms than to do the whole job itself. Let us ask why ACI does not sell its insulation directly to consumers. There are two major reasons. First, ACI produces millions of square metres of insulation annually, whereas each consumer buys less than 200 square metres – i.e. there is a discrepancy in the quantities made by the producer and wanted by the consumer. It would be very costly for ACI to sell each lot of insulation individually, so it becomes preferable for it to sell thousands of square metres at a time to intermediaries who are equipped to sell smaller quantities in their individual trade areas. Second, ACI offers only one brand of insulation, whereas the consumer might want to see and compare various brands – i.e. there is a discrepancy of assortment between ACI's assortment and that desired by the consumer. If all consumers insisted on buying insulation from stores carrying several brands, ACI would be forced to sell to multibrand insulation retailers. Altogether, certain discrepancies between the producer's capabilities and the market's requirements underlie the producer's interest in working with intermediaries to reach and serve its target markets effectively.

Markets

The next level of the company's marketing environment consists of its actual and potential markets. The company can choose to operate in one or more of five basic types of markets. These are illustrated in Figure 2-8, and can be defined as follows:

1. *Consumer markets*: the set of individuals and households that buy products for personal consumption.
2. *Producer markets*: the set of organizations that buy products for use in production to make profits or achieve other objectives.
3. *Reseller markets*: the set of organizations that buy products in order to resell them at a profit.
4. *Government markets*: the set of government agencies that buy products for the creation

of public services, and/or transferring these products to others who need them.

5. *International markets*: the set of buyers found in other countries, including consumers, producers, resellers and governments.

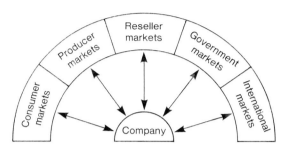

Figure 2-8　Basic types of markets

A company can choose to sell in any of the five types of market. For example, ACI could consider selling its insulation directly to consumers from the factory or via company-owned retail outlets. It could sell to producers who wished to use insulation in their operations to retard heat loss or gain, e.g. manufacturers of domestic appliances and so on. It could sell pink batts to insulation wholesalers and retailers, who in turn would resell them to consumer and producer markets. It could sell insulation to government agencies. And it could sell insulation to foreign consumers, producers, resellers and governments. Each type of market has particular characteristics that call for careful study by the seller. (The buying characteristics of different markets are discussed in Chapters 8, 9 and 20.)

Each market is capable of further subdivision into market segments.

- A *market segment* is a subset of buyers who have similar needs and/or responses to marketing offers.

Thus the consumer market for home insulation can be segmented into the following subgroups: (i) consumers seeking inexpensive insulation, perhaps just in the ceiling; (ii) con-

sumers seeking medium-quality insulation, perhaps only in the ceiling, but wanting safety and thickness; and (iii) consumers seeking thorough insulation, including ceiling and walls, with substantial thickness and safety.

An insulation manufacturer that decides to design insulation for the consumer market has to decide whether to sell in one, two or all three market segments. Small manufacturers generally specialize in one market segment so that they can do a good job in spite of limited resources. Suppose a small manufacturer decides to specialize in the complete-insulation market segment. It will undertake a study of who buys insulation, where they are located, their media habits, and the retailers they patronize. It will then design and produce a complete insulation package, make it available in the right retail outlets, and advertise it in the appropriate media. This small firm can, through concentrating its attention on one market segment, create a high level of consumer satisfaction and loyalty in that market.

A large company such as ACI will normally choose to serve more than one market segment, but it will not try to develop one insulation offering and one marketing programme for the entire market. Instead, it will try to develop different insulation lines and marketing programmes for distinct segments: for example, ACI offers batts and 'blankets' of various thicknesses and in different pack sizes, plus bags of granulated insulation which can be poured according to requirements. We will say more about market segmentation in Chapter 10.

Competitors

Competitors constitute another level of the company marketing environment. The company must identify and monitor its competitors in order to gain and hold a profitable share of the market.

The competitive environment does not consist only of other companies or products:

every company faces four major types of competitors in trying to serve its target markets. These are illustrated in Figure 2-9, and can be defined as follows:

1. *Desire competitors* are other immediate desires that the consumer might want to satisfy.
2. *Generic competitors* are other basic ways in which the buyer can satisfy a particular desire.
3. *Product-form competitors* are other product forms that can satisfy the buyer's particular desire.
4. *Brand competitors* are other brands of the same product that can satisfy the buyer's particular desire.

Let us discuss these four types of competitors in relation to ACI Fibreglass. ACI's marketing manager would like to know who the major competitors are. The best way to do this is to research how people make insulation-buying decisions. Suppose Mike and Kristine Broom, a young married couple, are considering what to do with some discretionary income (see Figure 2-10). Several possibilities come to mind, including spending some money on home improvements, buying a stereo set, and taking a trip to Europe: these are desire competitors, because they represent immediate desires. If the Brooms decide that

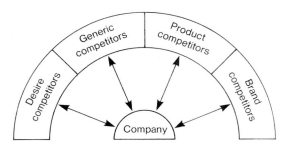

Figure 2-9   Types of competitors

they want to improve their home, they must then consider what they want to buy. Among the possibilities are redecorating, renovating or insulating. This is the set of generic competitors. If insulating turns out to be the most attractive alternative, Mike and Kristine will next think about what type of insulation to buy: this leads to a set of product-form competitors, such as fibreglass, rockwool, sea grass, cellulose, and reflective foil. They might tentatively decide on fibreglass, in which case they will want to examine several brand competitors, such as ACI, Bradford Insulation and Boral Insulwool.

In this way the marketing manager at ACI can determine those competitors standing in the way of selling more ACI insulation. This information will help the manager spot opportunities to improve the appeal of ACI fibreglass in the appropriate areas.

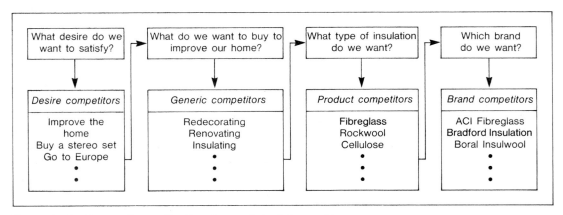

Figure 2-10   Competitors affecting buyers' decision-making

Publics

As discussed earlier in this chapter, the company's marketing environment also involves various publics. We define public as follows:

- A *public* is any group that has an actual or potential interest in or impact on an organization's ability to achieve its objectives.

In general, a company can view any of its publics in one of three ways. A welcome public is one that the company is interested in and that is interested in the company (e.g. donors). A sought public is one that the company is interested in but that does not take a strong interest in the company (e.g. mass media). Unwelcome public is shunned by the company, but it insists on taking an interest in the company (e.g. a citizens' action group).

The company has to market not only to its target customers but often to its major publics. Suppose the company wants some response from a particular public, such as goodwill, favourable word-of-mouth or donations of time or money. This calls for analyzing what the company could offer to elicit the desired response. In other words, the company has to plan a benefit package that will build up the desired relationship with the target public.

The multitude of publics surrounding an organization can be classified into seven generic types (see Figure 2-11):

1. Financial publics. These include all groups which take an interest in and might influence the organization's ability to obtain funds. Banks, investment houses, stockbroking firms and shareholders are the major financial publics. A company like ACI would seek to cultivate the goodwill of these groups by issuing annual reports, answering questions, and satisfying the financial community that its house is in order.

2. Media publics. These include media companies that carry news, features and editorial opinion: specifically, newspapers, magazines, and radio and television stations. A company like ACI is interested in obtaining as much favourable coverage and as little unfavourable coverage as possible. Getting more and better coverage from the press calls for understanding what the press is really interested in. The effective press-relations manager knows most of the news editors and systematically develops a mutually beneficial relationship with them. The manager offers interesting news items, information, and quick access to top management; in return for which media editors are more likely to give the company fair coverage.

3. Government publics. Management is increasingly finding it necessary to take government developments into account when formulating plans and policies on product safety, dealer rights and restraints, truth-in-advertising, and so on. Managers at ACI and other companies are making greater use of the company's lawyers for advice on what they can and cannot do. They are enlarging their government-relations department to anticipate developments, see parliamentarians, express concerns and rally support. They are also joining trade associations to lobby for the common interests of their industry. For example, ACI is a member of the Fibreglass Insulation Manufacturers Association of Australia, pushing for government incentives such as the tax benefits on home insulation introduced in 1980.

4. Citizen action publics. A company's marketing decisions are increasingly affected

Figure 2-11   Types of publics

by consumer organizations, environmental groups, and other vocal minority or public-interest groups. For example, there is periodic concern about glass fibres causing respiratory and dermatological problems, similar to asbestos complaints; ACI works individually and via the manufacturers' association to sponsor research and communicate with affected groups.

5. *Local publics.* Every organization is physically located in one or more areas and comes into contact with local publics such as neighbourhood residents, community organizations and district officials. For example,

people who live near a factory often complain about noise, smoke and parking. Companies usually appoint a community-relations officer whose job consists of keeping close to the community, attending meetings, answering questions and making contributions to worthwhile causes. Instead of waiting for local issues to erupt, the company invests in the community to build a bank of goodwill.

6. *General public.* The company is ultimately concerned with the attitude of the general public towards its products and activities. The general public does not act in an organized way towards the company, as do

---

Exhibit 2-1 Citizen Action Group Calls for Boycott of Nestlé Products

Even the most venerable marketing company can wake up one day and find one of its products under attack by a citizen action group. In fact, the group is likely to call for a boycott of all the company's products, even though only one is under criticism. The publicity from such efforts can damage the goodwill a company has taken years to build.

Nestlé, the Swiss-based multinational which manufactures such well-known products as Nestlé chocolate and Nescafé instant coffee, was singled out as such a target in 1978. Nestlé also produces a powdered-milk formula for infants, and an American citizens' group accused the company of irresponsibly marketing the formula to third-world mothers who may not understand the importance of sterilizing the formula. They further accused Nestlé of underplaying the importance of breast-feeding to the health of the baby. Nestlé's selling effort, according to INFACT (Infant Formula Action Coalition), was carried on by persons who wore nurses' uniforms but were not really nurses. Nestlé counter-argued that the medical representatives were qualified nurses or midwives 'who worked closely with' local government health authorities 'on such topics as the importance of breast-feeding, diet for mothers and proper formula use'.

INFACT pursued the boycott for months through a mail campaign which urged 'more people have to know' and asked for financial help in bringing the message to more people. The INFACT letter named all the brands owned by Nestlé. Nestlé was worried about the future effects of the boycott particularly as the World Health Organization had also urged restrictions on the advertising of breast milk substitute products. Finally, in 1982, Nestlé issued guidelines to its international subsidiaries which stopped marketing activities which discouraged breast-feeding.

Source: Adapted from *Marketing News* (American Marketing Association), 23 March 1979, pp. 1–2, and 'Nestlé Agrees Mother's Milk is Best', *Australian Financial Review*, 19 March 1982, p. 30.

citizen action groups, but its members have a certain image of the company's standing as a corporate citizen and this affects their patronage. To build a good image, a company like ACI will lend its employees to community fund drives and make substantial contributions to charity. It will set up systems to respond to consumer complaints. And it will use institutional advertising to describe what kind of company it is.

7. *Internal publics.* Every organization has internal as well as external publics. These include blue-collar workers, white-collar workers, managers and the board of directors. The larger the company, the more important it is to develop internal newsletters and other forms of communication to inform and motivate the internal publics. Every employee of the company is involved in public relations, from the chief executive who meets the general public, to the finance manager who addresses the financial community, to the field sales representative who calls on customers: if employees feel good about the company, they will show a positive attitude towards these external publics.

Macro-environment

The company and its marketing channel members, customers, competitors and publics all operate in the macro-environment: a larger context of forces which shape opportunities for, and pose threats to, the successful functioning of the company. These forces are generally uncontrollable; in the short run, the company has to adapt through judicious choice of the controllable factors, such as the markets it elects to serve and its marketing programmes. In the long run, however, the company, along with other companies, can have a formative influence on these macro-environmental forces.

The macro-environment consists of six major factors, as shown in Figure 2-12. An insulation company such as ACI would be

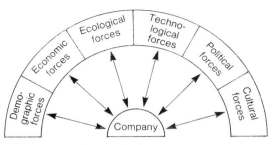

Figure 2-12　Forces in the macro-environment

well advised to monitor each of these in order to stay abreast of possible opportunities as well as emerging threats.

1. *Demographic forces.* This category covers all the main trends and developments in the size and character of the population, particularly birth rates, age distribution, geographical distribution, and marriage and divorce rates. ACI should pay particular attention to the implications of such factors as the stabilizing and ageing population, because fibreglass insulation is non-perishable: once the existing stock of uninsulated homes are retrofitted, the demand for insulation will be closely tied to the slow growth in new households.

2. *Economic forces.* This category covers the major trends and developments in personal disposable income, discretionary income, the cost of living, consumer savings and debt, and changing expenditure patterns. All of these will have an impact on the willingness and ability of consumers to insulate, and on the type of insulation they will buy. Home insulation is a discretionary item, and downward shifts in real income will substantially dampen demand.

3. *Ecological forces.* This category covers trends in the supply and cost of natural resources and energy, and problems of environmental deterioration and pollution control. In the case of insulation, ecological forces are favourable: the high cost of heating fuels and the rise in the price of electricity for airconditioning will increase interest in domestic conservation.

4. Technological forces. This category covers major developments in new products, materials and processes that will have an impact on the industry. ACI has pioneered the technique of compressing pink batts for transport in a way that allows them to resume their expanded form when installed. A major technological threat to ACI is the emergence of a material with less bulk but improved thermal properties.

5. Political forces. This category covers major developments in legislation, government decisions and enforcement, and the impact of public-interest groups on the industry. ACI will need to monitor legislation regarding product safety, occupational safety, truth-in-advertising, truth-in-credit, and other legal and political developments that may affect its marketing planning.

6. Cultural forces. This category covers major developments and shifts in those cultural values and lifestyles which may affect the particular industry and company. ACI will benefit from the growing national interest in home improvements, the DIY (do-it-yourself) trend, and the move toward greater comfort and 'home-centredness'.

We will examine macro-environmental forces in greater detail in Chapter 7, pointing out specific trends and their implications for marketing decision-making.

This concludes our discussion of the *structure* of marketing systems. In the next chapter we will consider the *process* by which companies make strategic planning and marketing decisions in an effort to survive in a rapidly changing marketplace.

SUMMARY

A marketer has to be skilled in analysing marketing systems, which are the sets of interacting participants, markets and flows involved in an organized arena of exchange. Marketing systems exist at three levels.

A *national marketing system* consists of consumers, business firms, product markets, resource markets, and government institutions, and the flows of money, resources, and goods and services that interconnect them. In trying to understand the marketing system of a particular nation, one must examine the nation's characteristics and its major marketing institutions and practices.

An *industry marketing system* describes the participants, markets and flows involved in moving the products of a particular industry to its consumers.

A *company marketing system* describes the set of interacting institutions, markets and forces that make up the company's marketing environment. A company operates in a marketing environment consisting of six levels of complexity. The first level involves the company's internal environment – its several departments and management levels – as it affects marketing management's decision-making. The second level consists of the marketing-channel firms that cooperate to create marketing value for a marketplace: suppliers, agents, merchants, facilitators and marketing firms. The third level consists of the major types of markets in which the company may sell: consumers, producers, resellers, governments and international markets. The fourth level consists of the four basic types of competition facing any company offer: desire, generic, product-form, and brand competitors. The fifth level consists of all the publics with an actual or potential interest in, or impact on, the organization's ability to achieve its objectives: financial, media, government, citizen action, local, general and internal publics. The sixth level consists of the major macro-environmental forces impinging on the organization and its surrounding institutions: demographic, economic, ecological, technological, political, and cultural.

QUESTIONS FOR DISCUSSION

1. What are the three major types of national marketing systems? Into which categories do Uganda and Canada fall?

2. Who are the direct and indirect participants in national marketing systems? Describe those taking part in a decision to stimulate the development of solar energy.

3. Evaluate the Saudi Arabian national marketing system.

4. Discuss the participants, markets and flows for the brewing-industry marketing system.

5. What is the first level in the company marketing system? Specifically, whom must the marketing manager take into consideration in making decisions at this level?

6. Describe the marketing-channel firms that Lever & Kitchen might use when marketing a new laundry detergent.

7. Compare and contrast the consumer, producer and reseller markets, using motor vehicles as an illustration.

8. Discuss the four types of competitor that need to be understood by someone planning to open a new pizza parlour near your university or college.

9. How do publics differ from consumers? Explain by using a specific example.

10. Comment on each of the macro-environmental factors that will have an impact on Ampol's marketing of petrol.

NOTES

[1] Estimated from data on annual births, life expectancy, and apparent consumption of foodstuffs per capita, in Australian Bureau of Statistics, *Yearbook 1980* (Canberra: Australian Bureau of Statistics, 1980), pp. 103, 111, 312.

[2] Wroe Alderson, 'The Analytical Framework for Marketing', *Proceedings – Conference of Marketing Teachers from Far Western States* (Berkeley: University of California Press, 1958).

Part 2

Marketing's Role in the Company

Strategic Planning and the Marketing Process

3

To most Australian businessmen, the words 'stars', 'wildcats', 'cows', and 'dogs' mean nothing at all as commercial terms. But to Mr Jack Davenport, managing director of the building materials and concrete products group, Monier Ltd, these are the words that every chief executive should be thinking of as he plans his company's growth over the next few years. The words are those used by the US-based corporate strategy group the Boston Consulting Group, to sort out a company's good performing areas from its poorly performing areas.

Sitting at his company's Chatswood head office in Sydney with the BCG study of Monier in front of him, Mr Davenport points to a page that is divided into four parts. In the top left-hand corner are the 'stars' (good sales growth, large market share); in the top right-hand corner are the 'wildcats' (good sales growth, small market share); in the bottom left-hand corner are the 'cash cows' (poor sales growth, large market share); and in the bottom right-hand corner are the 'dogs' (poor sales growth, small market share). 'I want to have a few more up here', he says pointing to the area marked 'stars'. 'If you are in the dogs area then you have to watch out', he says.

At Monier, Mr Davenport places a lot of emphasis on the formulation of company strategy both in terms of working out how best to push into new areas where it is not presently operating (the 'wildcats' area) and also in terms of working out how to fend off the competition in areas where it is well entrenched and where potential competitors are trying to break in (the 'stars' and 'cows' area).

In one of the company's main activities, the manufacture of roofing tiles, Monier is actually in both the 'wildcats' and 'cows' areas at the same time. In its overseas expansion, Monier has set up a large number of roofing tile plants in the United States and Japan, and as a 'wildcat' is attempting to break into both these very large markets. On the other hand, within Australia in roofing tiles it is a 'cow' with 65 per cent of the Australian roofing tile market. Here, much of its energy is directed at keeping a jump ahead of the competition from groups such as Humes, BMI, Boral and the CSR-owned Wunderlich group, which would all no doubt love to gain an increased slice of the market at Monier's expense.

In the US, Monier is operating in a market that offers enormous potential for its roofing tiles. 'In the US it is a matter of marketing. A lot of people have tried to introduce roofing tiles to the US market, but most haven't made any money', Mr Davenport said. 'The difference with us in the US is that we are not trying to sell tiles; we are selling roofs. The point is that there is a lot of knowledge and expertise involved in the roofing operation itself, and if the builder doesn't know how to put the tiles on the roof then he won't buy them. So a lot of our effort in the US is concentrated on training people to do the roofing', he said. As a result, in its main area of Southern California it now has 12 per cent of the market, whereas the market share held by concrete roofing tiles was negligible before it began.

In Australia, Monier knows it has to keep at least a step ahead of the opposition if it wants to hang on to its dominant position in the roofing tile market. It jealously guards this position. It doesn't invite anyone in to have a look at its roofing tile factories. No cameras are allowed inside the fence. Employees have to sign an undertaking that they will not reveal the details of its manufacturing processes to anyone else.

Monier has taken out a number of patents for its roofing tile manufacturing process. When it develops a new process, it refers it to a special committee that has to decide whether its competitive position would be better served by putting a patent on it – where it is out in the open but gives Monier exclusive rights to it – or by just keeping it secret.

Another area where Monier is in an even stronger competitive position than roofing tiles is in the operation involving the cleaning and re-lining of water mains, water pipes and oil and slurry pipelines. In the language of the Boston Consulting Group, this activity is another 'cash cow'. Before the 1950s, all the water mains put in in Australia were made of steel or cast iron. Gradually, these pipes have accumulated a growth that attaches to its inner wall. This growth will, given enough time, eventually fill up the inside of the pipe and stop the water from getting through. Monier has a system that – while the pipe is in situ underground – cleans out the muck in the pipe and puts a cement lining in the pipe. This makes the pipe as good as new and is much cheaper than pulling up the pipe and re-laying a new pipe.

Monier has a near monopoly on this business and Mr Davenport says with a smile that 'when a Water Board puts out tenders to clean out and re-line some of its pipes, there is usually just one tender – from us'. The cement lining stays for ever and doesn't collect any muck. So if Monier has a problem here it is that eventually it will have re-lined all the old pipes and will then have done itself out of a job.

Its cement linings operation is of great historical significance to Monier because it is the reason why the company was formed in the first place. The company was originally called Cement Linings Ltd when it was formed in 1936 to patent the rights to the cement lining processes that had been developed by some Water Board engineers. Monier has long protected its virtual monopoly position in this area with a string of patents. In addition, its executives over the years have developed considerable skills and knowledge in pipe re-lining work.

One area where Monier is looking forward with confidence is in oil pipelines. Even today, the oil companies are not putting down pre-lined pipes to carry their oil, and Mr Davenport is pleased because he knows that Monier will eventually get the job to re-line them.

Surprisingly, in its current overseas expansion, Monier has made little attempt to establish its cement re-lining operation as a 'star' or 'wildcat' in other countries. It is roofing tiles that has formed the bulk of the company's overseas expansion. Mr Davenport says that Monier has looked at setting up overseas in this area and at one time had an operation in Germany. But the company found that the German operation turned into a bit of a 'dog', as the marketing of this activity is a very difficult and slow process. It is hard to convince a local council that it should spend some of its limited funds on re-lining its old pipes, when it could be spending the money on much more visible activities such as laying down new pipes to supply outlying housing areas. 'The selling of cement re-linings is an eight- to ten-year job. It takes a long time to get started and convince the councils of the need for it', Mr Davenport said.

Another part of the Davenport strategy is not to reveal too much about the company's various operations, so that Monier's competitors have to keep guessing about just how profitable some of its operations are. For instance, while its 1979 accounts show that its total sales for the year were $219 million and its net profit was $13.3 million there is no sales or profit split-up between its main divisions such as roofing tiles, concrete pipes, contracting, masonry and bricks, raw materials and the overseas operation.

Investment analysts have been trying for years to find out how big each of these is in the Monier group. Their general view is that by far its biggest single money spinner is its roofing tiles, if only because Monier generally mentions it first in its reports and because the group general manager of its roofing division, Mr Clive Nettleton, reports directly to Mr Davenport. But as far as Mr Davenport is concerned, no one is going to find out how big is each of its operations. 'We feel that it is in the interests of our shareholders that this information be not revealed, as it may affect our competitive position', he said.

Monier's reluctance to tell all in this area possibly stems from an experience that the company had some 30 odd years ago just after Mr Davenport had joined the company in the late 1940s. At the time, the company largely had only one activity, the cement re-lining of water mains, in which it was the only operator. But the publication of its accounts enabled its competitors to find out exactly how much profit it was making out of this activity. And the next time there was a tender on the cement re-lining job, it found that it suddenly had a number of competitors, all which under-bid it in order to get the job.

If there was a lesson here, it was that a one-product firm always faces the problem that its competitors know exactly what its cost structure is. Monier rapidly widened its range of activities and to this day has never seen any advantage in giving a split-up of its sales and profits on its operations.[1]

We are now ready to look inside the company to examine the processes it uses to select markets, enter them profitably, and grow in these markets. In trying to cope with an ever-changing and challenging environment, modern companies use two key processes. The first is strategic planning, which enables top management to determine what businesses it wants to emphasize. The second is the marketing process, which enables the company to proceed in a systematic way to identify specific opportunities and turn them into profitable businesses.

Companies will differ considerably in the degree to which they use strategic planning and the marketing process. The most outstanding companies use both; many others fail to use either. As a result, it has been said that 'there are three types of companies: those which make things happen. Those which watch things happen. Those which wonder what happened.'

It should be recognized at the outset that not all organizations have the same characteristics and objectives. In this chapter we will do the following:

1. Distinguish major types of organizations that have strategic marketing problems.
2. Analyze the underlying requirements for successfully adapting any organization to its environment.
3. Describe the major steps involved in company strategic planning.
4. Describe the major steps in the marketing process.

THE AGE OF ORGANIZATIONS

Our society abounds in organizations that stand ready to serve every need, whether large or small, good or bad, elevated or prosaic. With little effort, people can walk down the streets of Sydney and instantly gratify their appetite for chicken, hamburger or pizza – courtesy of Kentucky Fried Chicken, McDonald's or Pizza Hut. If they are interested in buying something to wear, they can drive to an airconditioned shopping centre and rummage through racks of clothes at K-Mart, Target or Venture stores. Their desire for recreation or entertainment can also be satisfied immediately – courtesy of the YMCA or Hoyt's Theatres. If the weather is too cold, they can board a TAA Airbus at Mascot and reach the balmy shores of Queensland one hour later. All said, innumerable organizations stand ready to serve human needs by responding to them as business opportunities. The twentieth century is the age of organizations.

Organizations are so omnipresent that it is difficult to believe that life ever existed without them. Yet throughout most of human history, people have had to satisfy their needs through their own exertions: there were no fast-food outlets or local cinemas available. We define organization as follows:

- A *formal organization* is a social unit which is characterized by explicit goals, definite rules and regulations, a formal status structure and clear lines of communication and authority.[2]

Of the various ways to classify organizations in a society, we are primarily interested in whether the organization is privately or publicly owned and operated, and whether it is organized for profit or non-profit purposes. These two distinctions lead to the four types of organization shown in Figure 3-1.

	Private	Public

Profit	I
	Private companies
	Partnerships
	Sole
	  proprietorships
		II
		State-owned
		  airlines
		State-owned
		  telephone

Non-profit	IV
	Private charities
	Private
	  associations
		III
		Government
		  agencies
		Government
		  schools
		Public hospitals

Figure 3-1   Four types of organization

Quadrant I of the figure shows private-for-profit firms and is known as the first or *private sector* because it has been entrusted with most of society's economic work – producing food, clothing, shelter and so on.

Quadrants II and III make up the second or *public sector* and cover all the government organizations set up to carry on necessary societal functions that normally yield no profit and warrant public control. This includes such classic governmental functions as defence, public works, public education, and justice. Most of the public-sector organizations are in Quadrant III, but the government may also own and operate enterprises for profit (or at least cost recovery) as shown in Quadrant II.

Quadrant IV covers the remaining organizations in society, those operated privately and not for profit. It is called the third or *non-profit sector*, and comprises organizations performing those societal functions that do not yield a profit, are desirable to perform, and need not be under public ownership. The non-profit sector represents a middle way for meeting social needs, without resorting to the profit motive on the one hand or government bureaucracy on the other. It contains thousands of organizations, ranging from the committee for the Defence of Government Schools (DOGS) and Billboard Utilizing Graffitists Against Unhealthy Promotions (BUGA UP) to major foundations, colleges, hospitals, charities, social agencies, and churches.

All these organizations face the problem of survival. Private-for-profit firms survive by continually adapting their product lines and marketing programmes to new opportunities in the marketplace. Government agencies and non-profit firms survive to the extent that they continue to render valued services and maintain the support of constituencies. Every organization must know how to develop exchange values so that it can attract the resources required for its survival.

ORGANIZATIONS AND THE ENVIRONMENT

An organization's performance in the marketplace depends on the degree of its creative alignment with the environment. The ideal organization examines its environment for opportunities, sets appropriate objectives, develops a strategy to achieve them, builds a framework to carry them out, and designs management systems to support the process. This is illustrated in Figure 3-2a.

In practice, however, several factors can prevent this ideal from being realized. The main problem is that the various components alter at different rates, resulting in a less than optimal alignment. A typical company situation is shown in Figure 3-2b. Here the company is operating in a 1983 environment with objectives established in 1981, a strategy developed in 1978, an organizational structure

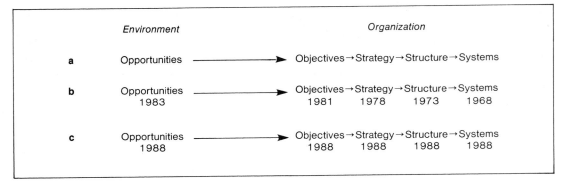

Figure 3-2 The organization and its environment

developed in 1973, and management systems designed in 1968. In other words, the company's existing systems, structure, strategy and objectives are dictating what opportunities it sees and pursues. Instead of modifying itself to take advantage of new opportunities, it looks only for those it can handle with its present arrangements.

Of all the elements in the picture, the environment is the one that changes most rapidly: even bringing everything into alignment with this year's environment is not enough. A sophisticated corporation such as CSR or Westpac will attempt to forecast its business environment in, say, 1988. On the basis of this prediction it will set objectives that describe where it wants to be in that year, and then formulate a strategy to achieve these objectives. It will begin to alter the organization and its systems so that these will support rather than hinder the new strategy. This forward-looking thinking may be summarized as shown in Figure 3-2c.

Environmental Change

Although environments change, not all industries and companies are exposed to the same rate of fluctuation. Some companies operate in a fairly *stable environment*: the future is expected to be pretty much like the present. For example, ice-cream producers expect the consumption of ice-cream to grow at roughly the population growth rate, and they plan accordingly. They foresee neither major threats nor new opportunities in their environmental picture. Other companies operate in a slowly *evolving environment*. Watch manufacturers are seeing the popularity of new types of watches (digital, electronic) gradually superseding that of the older types (spring, pin-lever), and they are able to adapt to these changes – if adapt they will – in an orderly way. Other companies operate in a *turbulent environment*, in which major and unpredictable disturbances are the rule. The operations of oil companies, for example, are affected by sudden price changes, new oil discoveries, oil shortages, and new legislation and regulation. It seems that companies will increasingly find themselves operating in turbulent environments, and this will call for greater strategic flexibility.

Opportunity and Threat Analysis

In a rapidly changing environment, companies need to operate an intelligence system that continually monitors major developments and trends. Management should be alerted to new developments as they occur, and each should be assessed in terms of its implications for company planning and marketing decision-making. Some trends and developments will represent threats to the company; others will represent opportunities; and still others will represent both. It is important that managers in charge of various divisions, products and markets not only recognize the major threats and the major opportunities that surround their business but take steps to deal with them.

Suppose the various cigarette brand-managers working at the Philip Morris Company are alerted to the following trends and developments affecting their business:

1. The Minister for Health is considering asking parliament to pass a law requiring that every cigarette brand include a skull and crossbones on the front of the package and the warning: 'Scientific evidence shows that daily smoking shortens a person's life-span by an average of seven years.'
2. An increasing number of public places are prohibiting smoking, or are setting up separate sections for smokers and non-smokers.
3. A new insect is attacking tobacco-growing areas, leading to the possibility of smaller crops in the future and larger price increases if some means cannot be found to control it.
4. The research laboratory at Philip Morris is on the verge of discovering a way of turning lettuce leaves into benign tobacco. If successful, the new tobacco will be enjoyable and harmless.
5. Cigarette smoking is rapidly increasing in foreign markets, especially in developing nations.
6. Several groups are pressing for the legalization of marijuana so that it can be manufactured openly and sold through standard retail outlets.

Each of these items has implications for the cigarette business. The first three can be classified as environmental threats, which may be defined as follows:

- An *environmental threat* is a challenge posed by an unfavourable trend or specific disturbance in the environment which would lead, in the absence of purposeful marketing action, to the stagnation or demise of a company, product or brand.

Not all threats warrant the same attention or concern. Managers should assess each threat according to two dimensions: its potential severity as measured by the amount of money the company would lose if the threat materialized, and its probability of occurrence. The results of assessing the three threats listed above are shown in the threat matrix in Figure 3-3a: all are high in their potential severity, and two have a high probability of occurring. Cigarette managers should concentrate on major threats (those in the high-severity and high-probability cells) and should have contingency plans ready. These managers should also keep a close watch on threats in the south-west and north-east cells, although contingency plans are less necessary. They can, for all practical purposes, ignore threats in the south-east cell.

The last three trends and developments in the list can be classified as company marketing opportunities, which may be defined as follows:

- A company *marketing opportunity* is an arena of relevant marketing action in which a particular company is likely to enjoy superior competitive advantages.

Not all opportunities, of course, are equally attractive. An opportunity should be assessed in terms of two basic dimensions: its attractiveness as measured by the amount of profit it might yield to an average company, and the probability that this company will be able to outdo its competitors in the venture. The results of assessing the three opportunities are shown in the opportunity matrix in Figure 3-3b: these opportunities fall into two

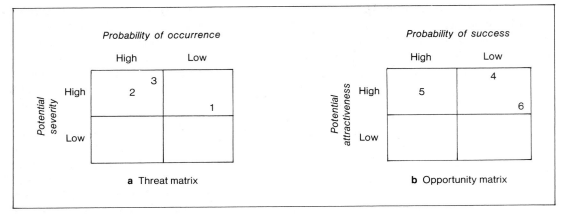

Figure 3-3   Threat and opportunity matrices

different cells, according to the judgment of management. The managers will concentrate on opportunities falling in the north-west cell, pay some attention to those in the south-west and north-east cells, and pay little or no attention to those in the south-east cell. Furthermore, management may want to dismiss certain financially attractive opportunities if they are unattractive on social grounds. The Philip Morris Company may want to pass up opportunities 5 and 6 because of their questionable moral or social character.

Considering the two matrices together, this business faces two major threats and one major opportunity. This makes it somewhat speculative: it is high on opportunity and high on risk. In fact, four outcomes are possible with this analysis, as shown in the

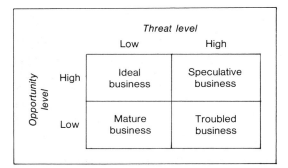

Figure 3-4   Opportunity–threat matrix

opportunity-threat matrix in Figure 3-4. An *ideal* business is one that is high in major opportunities and low in (or devoid of) major threats. A *speculative* business is high in both major opportunities and threats. A *mature* business is low in both major opportunities and threats. Finally, a *troubled* business is low in opportunities and high in threats.

Organizational Response

Each business unit can seek to improve its situation by moving toward its major opportunities and away from its major threats. With respect to opportunities, the firm must carefully appraise their quality: there is a whole profession of 'futurologists' who conjure up wonderful products and services the public needs. Levitt has cautioned business executives to judge opportunities carefully:

> There can be a need, but no market; or a market, but no customer; or a customer, but no salesman. For instance, there is a great need for massive pollution control but not really a market at present. Market forecasters who fail to understand these concepts have made spectacular miscalculations about the apparent opportunities in this and other fields, such as housing and leisure products.[3]

Even when pursuing a marketing opportunity, the firm can control its level of risk-taking. It might make a token investment in marketing research and R & D just to keep up, without getting sidetracked from its main business. It might make a moderate investment in the hope of becoming a leader. Or it might make a substantial investment in the hope of becoming *the* leader, although this may involve great risk to its present business.

In facing a major threat, the firm has three modes of adaptation available:

1. *Opposition.* The firm can try to fight, restrain or reverse the unfavourable development. Thus Philip Morris might lobby for a law requiring all public establishments to permit customers to smoke if they wish.
2. *Modification.* The firm can try to reduce the threat's severity. Philip Morris might advocate separate smoking areas in public establishments as an alternative to a total ban on smoking.
3. *Relocation.* The firm can decide to shift gradually to another business in which it can produce more value. Philip Morris might decide to increase its market share of the beverage and food business and decrease its reliance on the cigarette business.[4] (It has done this, by acquiring wine companies such as Lindemans.)

In general, management must pay attention to the key concepts of market evolution and strategic fit. All markets undergo development marked by changing customer needs, technologies, competitors, channels and laws. The firm should be looking out of a strategic window, watching these changes and assessing the requirements for continued success in each market.[5] There is only a limited period of optimal *fit* between the requirements of a particular market and the firm's competences: at these times the strategic window is open, and the firm should be investing in this market. In some subsequent period, the evolutionary path of this market may be such that the firm can no longer serve it effectively and efficiently: consideration should then be given

to disinvesting and shifting the firm's resources to areas of growing opportunity.

The major processes that a company uses to adapt to its environment are summarized in Figure 3-5. The company gathers information on broad macro-economic forces, publics, competitors, marketing channels, markets and target markets: this information plays an essential role in two major adaptive processes – strategic planning and marketing.

The strategic-planning process takes place at both corporate and divisional levels. Top management sets the pace by defining the company's overall mission, objectives and goals, growth strategy, and portfolio plan. The same steps are repeated by the management in each division, since each division will have its own definitions.

The marketing process both supports the strategic-planning process and involves more detailed analysis and planning for specific marketing opportunities. The marketing process occurs in relation to the company's specific products and markets: it calls for marketing-opportunity analysis, target-market selection, marketing mix strategy, and the development of marketing management systems. The decisions arrived at are executed in the environment, the results are fed back as new information, and further adaptive steps are taken. The following examines the strategic-planning process, after which we will focus on the marketing process.

STRATEGIC PLANNING

We define strategic planning as follows:

- *Strategic planning* is the managerial process of developing and maintaining a strategic fit between the organization and its changing marketing opportunities. It relies on developing a clear company mission, objectives and goals, a growth strategy, and product portfolio plans.

We will now discuss each component of this process.

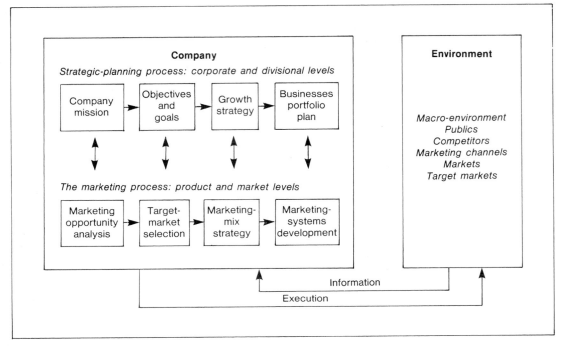

Figure 3-5 Strategic-planning process and the marketing process

Company Mission

An organization exists to accomplish something in the larger environment. Its specific purpose or mission is usually clear at the beginning, but over time one or more things happen. Its mission may become unclear as the organization grows, and develops new products and markets. Alternatively, the mission may remain clear but some managers may no longer be interested in it. Finally, the mission may remain clear but may lose its appropriateness because of new conditions in the environment.

When management senses that the organization is drifting, it is time to renew the search for purpose and ask the following questions:[6] What is our business? Who is the customer? What is value to the customer? What will our business be? What should our business be? These simple-sounding questions are among

the most difficult the company will ever have to answer: successful business firms raise them continually and answer them thoughtfully and thoroughly.

More and more organizations are developing formal *mission statements* to answer these questions. A well-worked-out mission statement provides corporate personnel with a shared sense of opportunity, direction, significance and achievement. It acts as an 'invisible hand' which guides widely scattered employees, and enables them to work independently and yet collectively toward the realization of the organization's potential. Unfortunately, this is not easy to achieve: some organizations will spend a year or two before they come up with a satisfactory statement about the purpose of their firm, and in the process they will discover a lot about themselves and their latent opportunities. An effective mission statement will be market-oriented, feasible, motivating and specific.

Market-oriented. The mission statement should define the business domain(s) in which the organization will operate, in market-oriented terms if possible. Business domains can be defined in terms of product class, technology, customer group, market need, or some combination of these. Companies have traditionally defined their business domain in product terms ('We manufacture slide-rules') or in technological terms ('We are a chemical-processing firm'), but some years ago Theodore Levitt proposed that market definitions are preferable.[7] His main argument was that products and technologies eventually become obsolete, whereas basic market needs generally endure for ever. Thus a slide-rule manufacturer will go out of business as soon as the electronic calculator is invented, unless it defines itself as being in the business of meeting calculation needs rather than that of making slide-rules. A market-oriented mission statement calls for the business to be defined in terms of serving a particular customer group and/or meeting a particular type of market need.

Feasible. A market-based definition of a business should avoid being either too narrow or too broad. A lead-pencil manufacturer which says it is in the business of making 'communication equipment' is stating its mission too broadly. A useful approach is to move from the current product to successively higher levels of abstraction, and then decide on the most realistic level for the company. Figure 3-6 shows the options open to a prune-manufacturing company: it may see itself as a dried-fruit company, a fruit company, or ultimately as a food company; alternatively, it may see itself as a laxative company or ultimately as a pharmaceutical company. Each broadening step opens a vision of new opportunities, but may also lead the company into

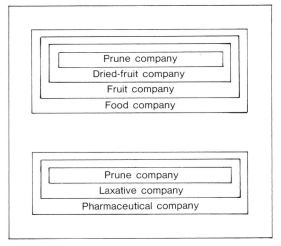

Figure 3-6 Successive expansions of business domains of a prune company

unrealistic business ventures beyond its capabilities.

Motivating. A company mission statement should be inspiring or motivating: employees like to feel that their work is significant and that they are making a contribution to people's lives. If the Wrigley Company says that its mission is to 'sell more chewing gum', this does not offer much inspiration; if it says that its mission is to 'make more money' or to 'be the market leader', these are equally uninspiring. Sales, profits and market leadership should be the result of the company's successful pursuit of its mission, not the mission itself. The mission should be stated, if possible, as something to accomplish outside the firm.

Specific. Too many mission statements are written for the purposes of public relations and lack specific guidelines for choice between alternative courses of action. The statement 'We want to be the leading company in this industry, producing the highest-quality products with the widest distribution and service at the lowest possible prices' sounds good but fails to supply any clear directions. A mission statement should include major policies that the company plans to honour in the pursuit of its mission. Policies convey the value system of the company and the tone of its dealings with customers, suppliers, distributors, competitors and other market participants and publics.

Such a statement should serve the company for many years: its mission is not something that needs to be revised in response to short-term environmental changes or new unrelated opportunities. On the other hand, a company sometimes has to reconsider its mission if this no longer works or fails to define an optimal course.

Company Objectives and Goals

The company's mission should be further defined into a set of supporting objectives for each level of management: each manager should know these objectives and be responsible for their accomplishment. This system is known as *management by objectives*.

As an illustration, the International Minerals and Chemical Corporation is in a number of businesses including that of producing fertilizer. The fertilizer division does not say that its mission is to produce fertilizer, but that it is 'to fight world hunger': this leads to a definite hierarchy of objectives (see Figure 3-7).[8] The mission to fight world hunger leads to a company objective of increasing agricultural productivity. Agricultural productivity, in turn, can be increased by researching new fertilizers that promise higher yields. But research is expensive and requires improved profits to plough back into research programmes – so a major company objective becomes 'profit improvement'.

Profits can be improved by increasing the sales of current products, reducing current costs, or both; sales can be increased by increasing the company's share in the domestic market and entering new foreign markets.

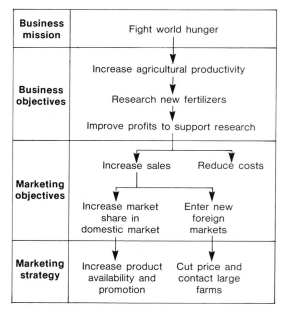

Figure 3-7   Hierarchy of objectives for Fertilizer Division of the International Minerals and Chemical Corporation

These are adopted by the marketing department as its current objectives. The next step is to develop marketing strategies to support the objectives. To increase its domestic market share, the company will increase its product's availability and promotion. To enter new foreign markets, it will cut prices and concentrate on large farms.

Each marketing strategy will be spelled out in greater detail for different specialists within the marketing department (not shown in Figure 3-7). For example, increasing the product's availability will be given as an objective not only to the sales force but also to the advertising department, and both will have to find an appropriate strategy. The increased sales objective will also be turned into manufacturing objectives, financial objectives, and personnel objectives for these respective departments. In this way the mission of the firm is translated into a specific set of objectives for the current period.

To determine whether the department was successful, all the objectives have to be turned into specific *quantitative goals*: the objective 'increase our market share' is not as satisfactory as 'increase our market share to 15 per cent by the end of the second year'. Managers use the term goals to describe an objective that has been made highly specific with respect to magnitude and time. Turning the objective into goals facilitates the process of management planning and control.

Company Growth Strategy

Among the various objectives that companies adopt, growth – in sales, profits and other dimensions – is one of the most common. To accomplish this, they must select a target growth rate and formulate a strategy for achieving it.

Growth comes about in either of two ways: through managing current products for growth, or adding new products. This is shown in Figure 3-8, which illustrates a hypothetical company with three product lines (A, B and C). Product line A produces about 60 per cent of the company's current profits, B about 30 per cent, and C the remaining 10 per cent. Looking ahead, the company expects A's earnings to decline, B's earnings to grow and

then decline, and C's earnings to grow. By the sixth year, C will be contributing most of the profit, followed by B and then A. Together, however, the three product lines will not earn enough to sustain the company's desired profit-growth rate: the figure shows a profit gap that must be filled by improving the performance of the current product lines, and/or adding new product lines.

We will now examine a particular company to determine how it can systematically search for growth opportunities with its current products and possible new products.

> Modern Publishing Company (name disguised) publishes a leading health magazine that has a monthly circulation of 30 000 copies. The company's marketing environment is changing rapidly in terms of consumer interests, new competitors and rising publishing costs. It is attempting to formulate a systematic plan for company growth during the remainder of the 1980s.

A company growth strategy can be generated by applying three levels of analysis. The first level identifies those opportunities available to the company in its current sphere of operations (intensive-growth opportunities). The second level identifies those opportunities available through integration with other parts of this marketing system (integrative-growth

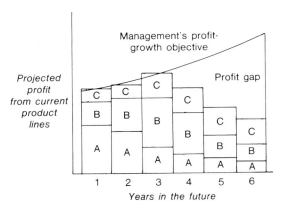

Figure 3-8 Projected profit growth from current products

Table 3-1 Major classes of growth opportunities

| **I Intensive growth** |
| A. Market penetration |
| B. Market development |
| C. Product development |
| |
| **II Integrative growth** |
| A. Backward integration |
| B. Forward integration |
| C. Horizontal integration |
| |
| **III Diversification growth** |
| A. Concentric diversification |
| B. Horizontal diversification |
| C. Conglomerate diversification |

opportunities). The third level identifies those opportunities lying outside the current marketing channels (diversification-growth opportunities). Table 3-1 lists the specific possibilities found in each broad opportunity class.

Intensive growth. Intensive growth makes sense if a company has not fully exploited the opportunities in its current products and markets. Ansoff has proposed a useful device for generating ideas in this regard: a product/market expansion matrix.[9] This matrix, shown in Figure 3-9, focuses on three major types of intensive-growth opportunities:

1. Market penetration. This is where the company seeks increased sales for its current products in current markets, through more aggressive marketing. It includes three possibilities:

a) Modern Publishing can encourage current subscribers to increase their purchase quantity by giving subscriptions to friends.

b) Modern can try to attract competitors' customers by offering lower subscription rates or promoting its magazine as being superior to other health magazines.

c) Modern can try to convert new prospects who do not now read health magazines but have the same profile as current readers.

2. Market development. This is where the company seeks increased sales by taking its current products into new markets. It includes three possibilities:

	Existing products	New products
Existing markets	1. Market penetration	2. Product development
New markets	3. Market development	4. Diversification

Figure 3-9 Product/market expansion matrix

a) Modern can distribute its magazine in new geographical markets – regional, national or international – where it has not hitherto been available.

b) Modern can try to make the magazine attractive to new types of individual readers by developing new features that appeal to these segments.

c) Modern can try to sell its magazine to new types of institutional subscribers, such as hospitals, physicians' offices, and health clubs.

3. Product development. This is where the company seeks increased sales by developing new or improved products for its current markets. It includes three possibilities:

a) Modern can develop one or more new health magazines that will appeal to present readers of its health magazine.

b) Modern can create regional versions of its health magazine to increase its appeal.

c) Modern can develop an abbreviated cassette edition of its existing magazine as an alternative for those who prefer listening to reading.

Integrative growth. Integrative growth makes sense if a company's basic industry has a strong growth outlook, and/or the company can increase its profitability, efficiency or control by moving with the industry. Such movement may be in any of three directions, defined as follows:

1. Backward integration. This is where a company seeks ownership or increased control of its supply systems. Modern Publishing might consider buying a paper company or a printing company to increase its control over supplies.

2. Forward integration. This is where a company seeks ownership or increased control of its distribution systems. Modern might see an advantage in buying some magazine wholesalers or subscription agencies.

3. Horizontal integration. This is where a company seeks ownership or increased control of some of its competitors. Modern might consider acquiring other health magazines or health-magazine publishing companies.

Diversification growth. Growth through diversification makes sense if a company's marketing channels show little opportunity for additional growth or profit, or if there are superior opportunities outside the present marketing system. Diversification does not mean that the company takes up any opportunity that comes along: it will attempt to identify fields that make use of its distinctive competences or help it overcome a particular problem. There are three broad types of diversification:

1. Concentric diversification. This is where a company seeks to add new products which complement or have technological and/or marketing synergies with the existing product line; these products will usually appeal to new classes of customers. Modern Publishing, for example, might consider starting a paperback division to take advantage of its network of magazine distributors.

2. Horizontal diversification. This is where a company seeks to add new products that might appeal to current customers, although technologically unrelated to current product lines. For example, Modern might decide to open a series of health clubs in the hope that readers of its health magazine would become members.

3. Conglomerate diversification. This is where a company seeks to add new products that have no relationship to the company's current technology, products or markets; these products will usually appeal to new customers. Modern might want to enter new business areas such as real estate, hotel management and fast-food services.

Thus we see that a company can systematically identify growth opportunities through applying a marketing-systems framework – looking first at current product/market opportunities, then at opportunities in other parts of the marketing system, and finally at relevant opportunities outside the system.

Company Portfolio Plan

After management has examined the company's various growth opportunities, it is in a better position to make decisions about its current product lines. Management must evaluate all of the company's current businesses so that it can decide which to build, maintain, phase down or phase out: its job is to keep refreshing the company's portfolio of businesses by withdrawing from poorer businesses and adding promising new ones.

Management's first step is to identify the company's key businesses, which may be called the strategic business units (SBUs). An SBU ideally has the following characteristics: (i) it is a single business; (ii) it has a distinct mission; (iii) it has its own competitors; (iv) it has a responsible manager; (v) it controls certain resources; (vi) it can benefit from strategic planning; and (vii) it can be planned independently of the other businesses. An SBU may be one or more company divisions, a product line within a division, or a single product or brand.

The next step calls for all the SBUs to be rated in a way that would reveal how much resource support each one deserves. The two best-known evaluation schemes are those of the Boston Consulting Group and the General Electric Company.

Boston Consulting Group approach. The Boston Consulting Group (BCG), a leading management consulting firm, advises a company to review all of its SBUs and classify them in the growth-share matrix illustrated in Figure 3-10. This matrix comprises two important business indicators. The vertical axis, market growth rate, refers to the annual

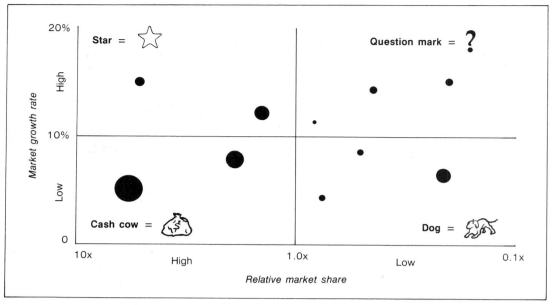

Figure 3-10   The BCG growth-share matrix

growth rate of the market in which the product is located. In Figure 3-10, the market growth rate goes from a low of 0.0 per cent to a high of 20 per cent, although a larger range could be shown: market growth is here arbitrarily divided into high and low growth by a 10 per cent growth line.

The horizontal axis, relative market share, refers to an SBU's market share relative to that of the industry's largest competitor. Thus a relative market share of 0.1 means that the company's SBU stands at 10 per cent of the leader's share; and 10 means that the company's SBU is the leader and has ten times the share of the next-strongest company in the market. Relative market share (drawn in logarithmic scale) is divided into high and low share, using 1.0 as the dividing line.

By dividing the growth-share matrix as indicated, four types of SBUs can be distinguished:

* *Stars.* Stars are high-growth, high-share SBUs. They are often cash using SBUs because cash is necessary to finance their

rapid growth. When their growth eventually slows down, they become major cash generators (cash cows) supporting other SBUs.

* *Cash cows.* Cash cows are low-growth, high-share SBUs. They produce a large amount of cash that the company uses to meet its bills and support other SBUs that are cash-using.

* *Question marks.* Question marks (also called 'wildcats' or 'problem children') are low-share SBUs in high-growth markets. They require a large amount of cash merely to maintain their share, let alone increase it. Management has to think hard about whether to spend more to build these question marks into leaders. If it decides against doing so, the question marks must be phased down or phased out.

* *Dogs.* Dogs (also called 'cash traps') are low-growth, low-share SBUs. They may generate enough cash to maintain themselves, but do not promise to be a large source of cash.

The ten circles in the growth-share matrix represent the company's ten current SBUs: it has two stars, two cash cows, three question marks and three dogs. The areas of the circles are proportional to the SBUs' dollar sales. This company is in fair shape, although not in good shape. Fortunately it has two good-sized cash cows, whose excess cash generation helps to finance the company's question marks, stars and dogs. The company should consider taking some decisive action concerning its dogs and its question marks. (The prospect would be worse if the company had no stars, too many dogs, or only one weak cash cow.)

Having arrived at this picture, the task of company portfolio planning is to determine the future role of each of the company's SBUs. Four alternative objectives can be pursued:

- *Build.* Here the objective is to increase the SBU's market share, even if this means foregoing short-term earnings. Building is especially appropriate for question marks, whose share has to grow if they are to become stars.
- *Hold.* Here the objective is to preserve the SBU's market share. This objective is especially appropriate for strong cash cows, if they are to continue to yield a large positive cash flow.
- *Harvest.* Here the objective is to increase the SBU's short-term positive cash flow, regardless of the long-term effect. This strategy is especially appropriate for weak cash cows, whose future is dim and from which more cash flow is needed. It may also be used with question marks and dogs.
- *Divest.* Here the objective is to sell or liquidate the business because resources can be better used elsewhere. This is especially appropriate not only for dogs, but also for question marks that the company decides it cannot finance for growth.

As time passes, SBUs will change their position in the growth-share matrix. Each SBU has a lifecycle (see Chapter 11): many start out as question marks, move into the star category if they succeed, later become cash cows as market growth falls, and finally turn into dogs toward the end of their cycle. For this reason the company needs to continually add new products and ventures, in the hope that some of them will acquire star status and eventually become cash cows to help finance the other SBUs.[10]

General Electric approach. General Electric (GE) has gone beyond the BCG approach by introducing a more comprehensive portfolio planning tool called a strategic business-planning grid (see Figure 3-11). GE believes that in addition to market growth rate and relative market share, several further factors have to be considered when evaluating an existing or prospective SBU. All of these factors can be combined under two major headings, industry attractiveness and business strength. The best businesses are obviously those that are in highly attractive industries and for which the particular company has high business strength.

In Figure 3-11, industry attractiveness is shown on the vertical axis. Industry attractiveness is a composite index made up of such factors as:

- *Market size.* Large markets are more attractive than small markets.
- *Market growth rate.* High-growth markets are more attractive than low-growth markets.
- *Profit margin.* High-profit-margin industries are more attractive than low-profit-margin industries.
- *Competitive intensity.* Industries with many strong competitors are less attractive than industries with a few weak competitors.
- *Cyclicality.* Highly cyclical industries are less attractive than cyclically stable industries.

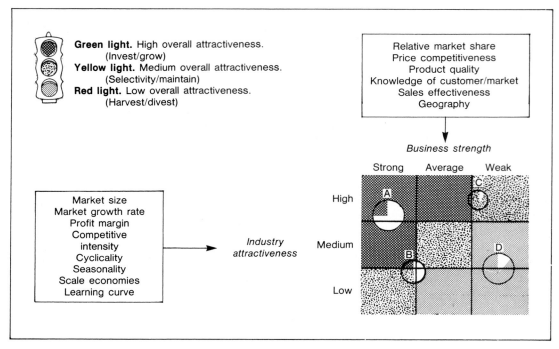

Figure 3-11 GE's strategic business-planning grid

- *Seasonality.* Highly seasonal industries are less attractive than industries which are not affected by seasons.
- *Scale economies.* Industries where unit costs fall with increases in plant size and distribution are more attractive than constant-cost industries.
- *Learning curve.* Industries where unit costs fall as management accumulates experience in production and distribution are more attractive than industries where management has reached the limit of its learning.[11]

Each of these factors is represented by a scale (not shown in Figure 3-11), and each current and prospective industry is rated on all factors. The factors are given different weights, and a weighted average is taken to find the industry attractiveness score. For our purposes, an industry's attractiveness may be broadly described as high, medium or low.

In Figure 3-11, business strength is shown on the horizontal axis. Business strength is a composite index made up of such factors as:

- *Relative market share.* The higher the company's relative market share, the greater its business strength.
- *Price competitiveness.* The higher the company's price competitiveness (that is, the lower its cost relative to those of its competitors), the greater its business strength.
- *Product quality.* The higher the company's quality relative to that of its competitors, the greater its business strength.
- *Knowledge of customers and markets.* The deeper the company's knowledge of customers and their needs and wants, the greater its business strength.
- *Sales effectiveness.* The greater the company's sales effectiveness, the greater its business strength.

- *Geography.* The greater the company's geographic presence and advantages in the market, the greater its business strength.

These factors are also scaled and weighted, and the company can assess its business strength in any existing or prospective market. Its business strength may be broadly described as strong, average or weak.

The grid is divided into three zones – green, yellow and red. The green zone consists of the three cells at the upper left, indicating those industries that are favourable in industry attractiveness and business strength, and suggesting that the company has the green light to 'invest and grow'. The yellow zone consists of the diagonal cells stretching from the lower left to the upper right, indicating industries that are medium in overall attractiveness: the company usually decides to maintain, rather than grow or reduce, the SBU's share. The red zone consists of the three cells at the lower right, indicating those industries that are low in overall attractiveness: here the company gives serious consideration to harvesting or divesting.

The circles represent four current SBUs making up the company. The areas of the circles are proportional to the sizes of the industries in which these SBUs compete, while the pie slices within the circles represent each SBU's market share. Thus circle A represents a company SBU with a 75 per cent market share in a good-sized industry that is highly attractive and in which the company has solid business strength. Circle B represents an SBU in which the company has a 50 per cent market share but the industry is not very attractive. Circles C and D represent two SBUs in which the company has small market shares and not much business strength. Altogether, the company has to build A, maintain B and make some basic decisions about C and D.

A grid should also be plotted showing projected positions of the SBUs if there is no change in strategies. By comparing the current and projected business grids, management can identify the major strategic issues and opportunities it faces.[12] This type of analysis led GE to sort its current mix of SBUs into five investment groups:[13]

1. High-growth products, i.e. those deserving the highest investment support (engineering plastics, medical systems, transport).
2. Steady reinvestment products, i.e. those deserving high and steady investment (major appliances, steam and gas turbines, lamps).
3. Support products, i.e. those deserving steady investment support (meters, specialty transformers).
4. Selective pruning or rejuvenation products, i.e. those deserving reduced investment.
5. Venture products, i.e. those deserving heavy R & D investment ('10-tonne aircraft engine', microwave ovens, synthetic diamonds).

Whatever analysis of the company's current business portfolio is used, the main point is that the company must evaluate its SBUs as a basis for setting objectives and resource-allocation priorities. This analysis enables management to decide on the business objective for each SBU, and on what resources it will be given. The task of the SBU's management and marketing personnel will be to decide on the best way to accomplish that objective. Marketing managers in certain businesses will find that their objective is not necessarily to build that business (somewhat contrary to their traditional mandate, which is to build sales) but rather to hold the existing volume in spite of fewer marketing dollars, or actually to reduce demand. Thus the generic task of marketing management is not to build demand but to manage demand. The cue must be taken from the objective developed for the business in the course of strategic planning at the corporate level: marketing contributes to evaluation of both the business's potential and its position in the matrix, but once an overall objective is set, marketing's task is to carry this out efficiently and profitably.

MARKETING PROCESS

We will now examine the other process which plays a key role in a company's ability to adapt creatively to its changing environment. We define this as follows:

- The *marketing process* is the managerial process of identifying, analyzing, choosing and exploiting marketing opportunities to fulfil the company's mission and objectives. It specifically consists of identifying and analyzing marketing opportunities, segmenting and selecting target markets, developing a competitive marketing-mix strategy, and designing support systems for planning and control, information, and marketing personnel.

The steps in the marketing process are illustrated in Figure 3-5, and are discussed in the following sections.

Marketing Opportunity Analysis

The marketing process begins with the company's effort to find attractive opportunities. In this quest the marketing department plays a major role: although new opportunities may be spotted by various persons in the company, marketers bear the major responsibility for generating, evaluating and selecting attractive opportunities.

Marketers use several techniques to spot new opportunities. They make sure that any ideas arising in the firm flow to the marketing department where they can be evaluated. Marketers often conduct brainstorming sessions to develop new ideas. They make use of systematic techniques such as the product/market expansion matrix (Figure 3-9) for locating growth opportunities; they watch a number of industries, which they rate on their attractiveness by using the GE approach (Figure 3-11).

It is important to distinguish between environmental opportunities and company opportunities. There are attractive environmental opportunities available in any economy as long as there are unsatisfied needs. Currently there are great opportunities to develop new sources of energy, new food products, improved agricultural methods, improved forms of transport, new forms of leisure and improved teaching technology; there are opportunities in garbage disposal, low-cost legal services, containerization, prefabricated housing, water purification, day-care centres, and biomedical instruments. But none of these necessarily represents an opportunity for any specific company. Fast-food restaurants are probably not an opportunity for BHP, nor are biomedical instruments an opportunity for Kentucky Fried Chicken.

To be successful, the company should be concerned with attractive environmental opportunities for which it has the required business strength. We call these company opportunities. The company must be able to bring to an attractive environmental opportunity more business strength than its potential competitors can. We make the following assumptions:

1. Every environmental opportunity has specific success requirements.
2. Each company has distinctive competences, i.e. things that it can do especially well.
3. A company is likely to enjoy a differential advantage in an area of environmental opportunity if its distinctive competences outmatch those of its potential competition.

Suppose McDonald's, Petersville, and Rothmans of Pall Mall all become interested in starting a national network of franchised day-care centres. Which firm would enjoy the greatest differential advantage? First we consider the success requirements, which would include: (i) having a strong public image for trustworthiness; (ii) having the ability to train and motivate people in a service business; and

(iii) having the technical ability to manage a franchising operation. McDonald's has distinctive competence in all three areas. Petersville has a good corporate image, but limited experience in both service businesses and franchising. Rothmans raises mixed feelings in people who dislike cigarette smoking, and it also lacks experience in the other two areas. All things considered, it appears that McDonald's would enjoy a major differential advantage in the operation of a successful national system of day-care centres.

The combination of attractive company marketing opportunities is often called the company opportunity set, and the marketer's task is to evaluate each. Who would buy the product? How much would they pay? What would be the optimal features? How many units would be bought? Where are the buyers located? Who would the competition be? What distribution channels would be needed? The answers to these and other questions will lead to an estimate of the marketing opportunity's sales potential; financial and manufacturing executives would add their estimates of costs. This information will enable the marketers to rank the opportunities and recommend those that should be selected for further development.

Target-market Selection

The second step of the marketing process is called target-market selection. If a company has spotted an especially attractive market, the issue becomes how to enter that market. Every market is filled with many more customer groups and customer needs than one company can normally serve or, at least, serve in a competitively superior fashion. The task calls for market segmentation, i.e. dividing the market into segments that differ in their requirements, buying responses or other critical characteristics. The company can then consider which is the best part of the market to enter, which becomes its target market.

- The *target market* is a well-defined set of customers whose needs the company plans to satisfy.

We will illustrate market segmentation and target-market selection by using the following situation:

A successful manufacturer of trail-bikes is looking for a new product line. Management reviews several opportunities, and finds the idea of manufacturing ride-on mowers to be attractive in terms of market growth, sales potential and company business strength. The marketing manager thoroughly investigates the structure of the ride-on mower industry to determine whether the company could find a viable niche there.

A useful approach to segmentation is to develop a *product/market grid*. Figure 3-12 illustrates such a grid for ride-on mowers: the company can decide to manufacture any of three product types: petrol, diesel or electric; and it can design the mower for either of two markets: consumer or industrial. The marketing manager will proceed to estimate, for each of the six product/market segments, its degree of market attractiveness and the company's degree of business strength. Suppose the segment that looks best is the diesel-driven ride-on mower for the industrial market segment

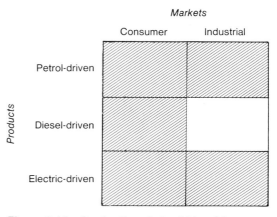

Figure 3-12   Product/market grid for ride-on mowers

(the unshaded box in Figure 3-12). If this market segment proves to be larger than the company can serve, subsegmentation is warranted. Figure 3-13 shows a subsegmentation of this market by customer use and customer size. Ride-on mowers can, for example, be designed for use as slashing equipment (e.g. on farms), as trimming mowers (e.g. on sports grounds) or as maintenance mowers (e.g. on grassed areas in municipalities). Their design will also be affected by whether the company will try to sell them to large, medium or small customers. After evaluating the various subsegments, the marketing manager concludes that the 'large customer, maintenance segment' looks best. Thus management has arrived at a clear idea of its target market.

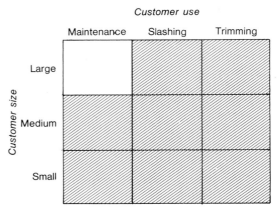

Figure 3-13 **Subsegmentation by customer use and customer size**

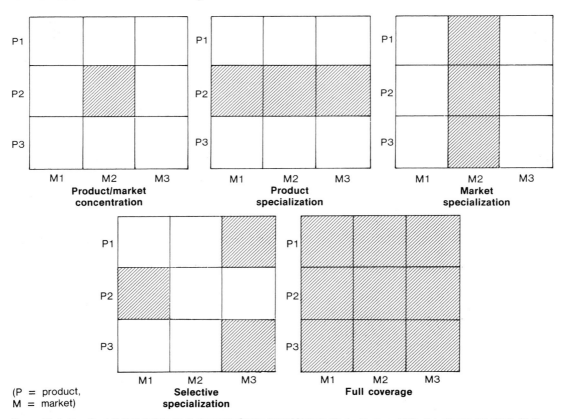

(P = product, M = market)

Source: Adapted from Derek F. Abell, *Defining the Business: The Starting Point of Strategic Planning* (Englewood Cliffs, N.J.: Prentice-Hall, 1980), Ch. 8.

Figure 3-14 **Five patterns of market coverage**

This target market may constitute the total ambition of the company in this market, or be viewed as a launching pad for later expansion to other market segments. Companies will usually consider any one of the five market-coverage strategies shown in Figure 3-14:

1. *Product/market concentration* is where the company niches itself in only one part of the market (here, making only diesel-driven ride-on mowers for industrial buyers).
2. *Product specialization* is where the company decides to produce only diesel-driven ride-on mowers, but for all customer groups.
3. *Market specialization* is where the company decides to make an assortment of ride-on mowers that serve the varied needs of a particular customer group, such as industrial buyers.
4. *Selective specialization* is where the company enters several unrelated product markets which individually provide an attractive opportunity.
5. *Full coverage* is where the company makes a full range of ride-on mowers to serve all the market segments.

Marketing Mix Strategy

The third step in the marketing process consists of developing a marketing-mix strategy which is competitively effective in the target market. Marketing mix is one of the major concepts in modern marketing. We define it as follows:

- *Marketing mix* is the particular blend of controllable marketing variables that the firm uses to achieve its objective in the target market.

There are actually a great number of marketing-mix variables, but fortunately they can be classified into a few major groups. One of the most popular classifications has been proposed by McCarthy and is called 'the four Ps': product, price, place and promotion.[14]

The particular marketing variables under each *P* are shown in Figure 3-15, where it is emphasized that the marketing mix must be adapted to the target market.

Figure 3-15 **The four *P*'s of the marketing mix**

The company arrives at its marketing mix by determining the competitive position it wants to occupy in the target market: it must examine both the wants of that market and the position of competitors, and decide on what it wants to competitively offer to that market. We can illustrate competitive positioning by returning to the company that has decided to produce ride-on mowers for organizations that will use them for maintenance. Suppose this company learns, through marketing research, that business customers are primarily interested in two ride-on mower attributes: size and speed. The company can ask prospective customers and dealers where they perceive competitors' ride-on mowers to be located along these dimensions, and the results can be plotted in the product space map shown in Figure 3-16. Competitor A is seen as producing small, fast ride-on mowers; B, medium-size, medium-speed ride-on mowers; C, small-to-medium-size, slow ride-on mowers; and D, large, slow ride-on mowers. The areas of the circles are proportional to the competitors' sales. Not all customers share the same perceptions, and thus maps showing average perceptions (as in Figure 3-16) must be interpreted with care. Attention should also be paid to the scatter of perceptions.

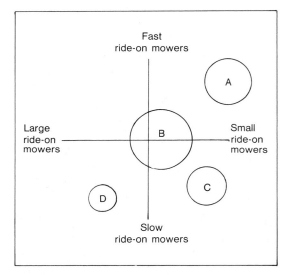

Figure 3-16 A product space map showing perceived offers of four competitors

Given these competitor positions, what position should the new manufacturer seek? The company has two basic choices. One is to take a position next to one of the existing competitors, and fight to obtain the customers who want that type of ride-on mower. The company might choose to do this if it feels that: (i) it can build a better ride-on mower of this type; (ii) the market for this type of ride-on mower is large enough for two competitors; (iii) it has more resources than the existing competitor; and/or (iv) this position is the most consistent with the company's reputation and competence.

The other choice is to develop a ride-on mower that is not currently offered to this market, such as a large, fast ride-on mower (see empty north-west quadrant of Figure 3-16). The company would, of course, gain instant leadership, but before deciding it must be established that: (i) it is technically feasible to build a large, fast ride-on mower; (ii) it is feasible to build a large, fast ride-on mower at the planned price level; and (iii) there are sufficient buyers who would prefer a large, fast ride-on mower to any other kind. If the answers are all positive, the firm has discovered a 'hole' in the market and should quickly move to fill it.

Suppose, however, that the company decides there is more potential profit and less risk in building a small, fast ride-on mower to compete with competitor A. In this case the company would study A's ride-on mower and other aspects of the offer, seeking a way to differentiate its offer in the eyes of potential buyers. Instead of competitive positioning through product/feature differentiation, it might seek competitive positioning through price/quality differentiation. If competitor A's ride-on mower is of average quality and carries an average price, the company could offer a better-quality mower at a somewhat higher price – using the familiar argument 'You pay more and get more'. Alternatively, it could offer a better-quality mower but charge the same as A, arguing 'More quality for the same price'. Or it could design an average-quality mower and charge less, 'Same quality for less money'. Other price/quality strategies are also possible, and the company will have to choose its strategy carefully.

All the decisions on the product's quality, features, price, advertising budget, marketing channels and other variables for this target market make up the company's marketing mix. The marketing mix is the means by which the company defines and supports the competitive position it seeks to occupy in the target market.

The Development of Marketing Management Systems

Once the company has chosen a target market and defined its competitive position, it is ready to develop its marketing management systems. Marketing cannot be carried out effectively unless certain management systems are created to support the effort, and the three principal systems can be described as follows:

1. *Marketing planning and control.* Every company should plan its goals, strategies, marketing programmes, and budgets. Companies vary considerably as to the degree of formal planning they use, although most of them are becoming increasingly methodical. It is the authors' belief that a formal planning system is essential to achieving the maximum results sought in the marketplace. Formal marketing planning also requires a control system for checking on whether marketing goals are being achieved and what corrective actions, if any, are needed to improve performance. (These issues are discussed in detail in Chapter 4.)

2. *Marketing information.* The effective planning and controlling of marketing effort calls for a great amount of continuous information about the macro-environment, customers, marketing intermediaries, competitors and other forces in the company's marketing environment. The gathering, processing and dissemination of this information calls for an information system that is accurate, timely and comprehensive. (These issues are discussed in detail in Chapter 5.)

3. *Marketing organization.* The company must design an organization that is capable of effectively carrying out the many and diverse marketing tasks. First, the organizational structure must foster integrated, innovative and responsible marketing planning and control. This usually means appointing a manager to supervise several marketing executives and coordinate their reports. Second, each marketing position (e.g. advertising manager, prod-

uct manager and sales manager) must be described in terms of the job's purpose, functions, tasks and responsibilities. Third, the jobs must be filled by individuals who have adequate skills and motivation, and a personality that will enable them to do their marketing job effectively. (These issues are discussed in detail in Chapter 6.)

SUMMARY

Every organization must evolve a corporate strategy and marketing process if it is to survive and grow. The environment undergoes rapid change, and the organization must fit its objectives, strategy, structure, and systems into a viable relationship with the environment. The organization must continuously identify and evaluate marketing opportunities and threats, and take the necessary actions.

Management is the entrepreneurial agent that interprets market needs and translates them into satisfactory products and services. To achieve this, the processes of strategic planning and marketing are necessary. The strategic-planning process describes the steps taken at the corporate and divisional levels to develop long-run strategies for survival and growth. This provides the context for the marketing process, which describes the steps taken at the product and market levels to develop viable marketing positions and programmes.

The strategic-planning process consists of defining the company mission, objectives and goals, growth strategy, and portfolio plans. Developing a sound mission statement is a challenging undertaking: it must be market-oriented, feasible, motivating and specific if it is to serve its purpose of directing the firm to its best opportunities.

Strategic planning then calls for developing a set of objectives such as sales and market-share growth, profitability, and innovation to support the company mission. These objectives should be hierarchical, quantitative, realistic and consistent.

To achieve growth, the company must identify market opportunities which offer it a differential advantage over competitors. The company can generate relevant opportunities by considering intensive growth opportunities within its present product/market scope (such as market penetration, market development, and product development), integrative growth opportunities within its marketing channel system (such as backward, forward and horizontal integration), and diversification growth opportunities outside its marketing channel system (such as concentric, horizontal and conglomerate diversification).

Finally, strategic planning must define, for each strategic business unit (SBU) in the company's portfolio, whether it will be built, maintained, harvested or terminated. As aids to doing this, companies can use either the BCG growth-share matrix or the GE strategic business-planning grid.

Within this context, the marketing process can be enacted. The first step consists of generating, evaluating and recommending marketing opportunities. For any sound opportunity, the next step is to examine the product/market structure and identify the best target market. The third step is to decide on the best competitive position and marketing-mix strategy for the company within that target market. The fourth step calls for designing three major marketing management systems – planning and control, information and organization – for effectively carrying out the intended marketing effort.

Exhibit 3-1 Survival Is Not That Easy

Nations (Assyria), species (dinosaurs), industries (horse-drawn carriages), and companies (Mainline) have collapsed because they failed to meet environmental challenges with creative responses. History is filled with the names of products which, despite their size or fame, had their market eroded and eventually became casualties:

- The VW Beetle and the BMC Mini (once leaders in the small-car market), and the Holden Kingswood (once the most popular car in Australia) are rapidly rusting into oblivion.

- *Number 96, Homicide, Blankety Blanks* and many other television shows rose to great heights (in terms of viewing audience, at least), only to be superseded by modified products which are essentially similar but 'packaged' differently.

- Circuses felt the chill wind of substitution when television entered homes and became a principal distraction for children.

- Butter was a 'national dish' bound up in a mixture of rural mythology and national pride. However, the cheaper and 'technologically superior' (spreadable) margarine struck with devastating effect.

- The Bank of Adelaide faltered, and joined the ES&A Bank as an anonymous part of the ANZ Bank.

- On the lighter side, where are Lolly Gobble Bliss Bombs? And Uncle Sam deodorant? And Sherbet?

QUESTIONS FOR DISCUSSION

1. What are the four major types of organization discussed in this chapter? Give an example of each.

2. Is the low birth rate in Australia an environmental threat for Johnson & Johnson? How has (or how should) the company respond?

3. Would you classify the college or university that you attend as a speculative, mature or troubled organization? Why?

4. Why is strategic planning such an important process for organizations moving through the 1980s?

5. Develop a mission statement for a local pop-music recording company. Discuss each of the essential characteristics of this statement.

6. How do the major classes of growth opportunity differ? Into which class(es) would you place the following companies: McDonald's, IBM and CSR?

7. Briefly describe the four types of strategic business unit (SBU) developed by the Boston Consulting Group. Classify Ford's current car models (i.e. LTD, Fairlane, Falcon, Meteor and Laser) into each of the four categories. Defend your choices.

8. Relate the four major steps in the marketing process to a service of your choice.

9. 'If managers do a good job of planning and control, they will be properly accomplishing the marketing-management systems development step in the marketing process.' Comment.

NOTES

1. Malcolm Wilson, 'Monier: In Among the Stars, Wildcats, Cows and Dogs', *Australian Financial Review*, 5 August 1980, pp. 12–13.

2. Based on the discussion in Peter Blau & Richard Scott, *Formal Organizations* (New York: Harper & Row, 1962), Ch. 1.

3. Theodore Levitt, 'The New Markets – Think Before You Leap', *Harvard Business Review*, May–June 1969, pp. 53–67 (esp. pp. 53–54).

4. 'Philip Morris: Turning 7 Up into the Miller of Soft Drinks', *Business Week*, 2 April 1979, pp. 66–67.

5. See Derek F. Abell, 'Strategic Windows', *Journal of Marketing*, July 1978, pp. 21–26.

6. See Peter Drucker, *Management: Tasks, Responsibilities, Practices* (New York: Harper & Row, 1973), Ch. 7.

7. Theodore Levitt, 'Marketing Myopia', *Harvard Business Review*, July–August 1960, pp. 45–56.

8. For a useful discussion of setting objectives, see Charles H. Granger, 'The Hierarchy of Objectives', *Harvard Business Review*, May–June 1964, pp. 63–74.

9. H. Igor Ansoff, 'Strategies of Diversification', *Harvard Business Review*, September–October 1957, pp. 113–24.

10. For additional reading, see Charles W. Hofer & Dan Schendel, *Strategy Formulation: Analytical*

Concepts (St Paul, Minn.: West Publishing, 1978), pp. 30–32; and George S. Day, 'Diagnosing the Product Portfolio', *Journal of Marketing*, April 1977, pp. 29–38.

[11] The learning curve is very important to pricing and marketing strategy. See 'Selling Business a Theory of Economics', *Business Week*, 8 September 1973, pp. 86–88.

[12] For additional reading, see Hofer & Schendel, pp. 32–34. Also see 'General Electric's Stoplight Strategy for Planning', *Business Week*, 28 April 1975, p. 49.

[13] 'GE Growth Plans Outline by Jones', *Bridgeport Telegram*, 8 November 1974.

[14] E. Jerome McCarthy, *Basic Marketing: A Managerial Approach* (Homewood, Ill.: Richard D. Irwin, 4th edn, 1971), p. 44 (1st edn, 1960).

Two alternative classifications are worth noting. Frey proposed that all marketing decision variables could be divided into two factors: (i) the offering (product, packaging, brand, price, and service); and (ii) methods and tools (distribution channels, personal selling, advertising, sales promotion, and publicity). See Albert W. Frey, *Advertising* (New York: Ronald Press, 3rd edn, 1961), p. 30. Lazer and Kelley proposed a three-factor classification: (i) good and service mix; (ii) distribution mix; and (iii) communications mix. See William Lazer & Eugene J. Kelley, *Managerial Marketing: Perspectives and Viewpoints* (Homeward, Ill.: Richard D. Irwin, revised edn, 1962), p. 413.

The Marketing Planning and Control System

A Sydney direct-marketing company is now finalizing a successful direct marketing campaign – but one which began disastrously. Permail Pty Ltd succeeded in its programme to sell the 1976 Montreal Olympic coins, and as a result won from Paramount International Coins of Ohio, US, a marketing contract in Australia to sell Russian Olympic stamps.

Logically enough, Permail advertised the stamps in full-page advertisements in Stamp News and space advertisements in the Australian and the National Times. Total cost was $6000 and Permail sold $5228 worth of stamps – hardly an auspicious opening to the programme. Says Permail's general manager, Eddy Boas: 'We decided to go back to scratch and study the programme as a marketing venture. Clearly this operation was not a simple one of selling stamps to collectors.' Permail found three major problems:

1. That established stamp dealers looked upon Russian stamps with contempt.
2. The dealers were not interested in one-off stamp programmes.
3. Russia, after the invasion of Afghanistan, was not everyone's favourite country and many Australians opposed Australian participation in the Olympics.

Permail was offering seventy-nine different stamps and first-day covers. The seventy-nine stamps consisted of nine issues of sport stamps depicting every Olympic sport and the six issues of city stamps depicted the various Russian cities where competitions were to be held. Permail offered:

- A subscription programme over a fifteen-month period at a given cost per month.
- Story pages about previous Olympics, and about the stamps in the collection. These pages were issued with the special albums.

The company devised strategies to help overcome the sensitive political issues. The 'Russian Olympic Stamp Programme' was renamed 'The 1980 Olympic Stamp Programme'. The services of Dawn Fraser, probably Australia's best-known advocate of Australian participation in the Moscow Olympics, were obtained. Dawn Fraser wrote for Permail a letter endorsing the programme. Additional endorsement was received from the Australian Olympic Federation for consideration of three per cent of the face value of all stamps sold.

The next task was to find the target market since clearly press advertising had failed. 'We decided on direct mail. We knew of only one mailing list of stamp collectors and that was of subscribers to Australia Post's Stamp Bulletin*', says Boas. 'When I first approached Australia Post in November 1977 I received a flat "No". I kept at it, and in February 1979 I received Australia Post's list of 235 000 names. As an insert to the* Stamp Bulletin *we used a four-page four-colour brochure with the heading "Welcome to the 1980 Olympic Stamp Program". The back of the brochure had a cut out coupon saying "YES, send me information on how I may get started on an official 1980 Olympic Collection".' The brochure did not mention price. 'Response was overwhelming with 22 103 enquiry coupons received, a 9.5 per cent response.'*

Every enquiry was then sent an order-generating mailing package which consisted of an eight-page four-colour brochure describing the stamps, a two-page letter from the Olympic Stamp Programme, the Dawn Fraser endorsement letter and an addressed order form setting out various buying methods for either single or first day cover stamps, plus a business reply-paid envelope. The offer was for fifteen issues delivered and paid for over fifteen months with payments varying from $14.95 per issue to $38.90 per issue depending on whether the purchaser bought singles or first-day covers, or both.

From the original enquiry list of 22 103, Permail obtained 2635 orders, a 12 per cent response. The average order was $27.80 per month for 15 months. In December, 1979, the company made a repeat offer through the philatelic mailing list and obtained another 11 142 enquiries and 654 orders. 'We now had total orders from 3289 subscribers with the attrition rate being very low. Only about 200 buyers dropped out of the programme. With each delivery of stamps we enclosed attention-getting and informative information about the Olympics, for example, the Australian Olympian Newsletter *and an Olympic Games programme. Since then a number of orders have drifted in – clearly from word-of-mouth recommendation. We are only now in the process of winding up the programme.'[1]*

Every company is, of course, the scene of continuous decision-making and problem-solving, but this should not be confused with marketing planning and control. The latter is a separate and higher-order activity which often rewards the company with improved sales and profit.

Here we will examine how organizations develop marketing planning and control systems to serve their markets effectively. The relationship between marketing planning and control – a three-step process – is shown in Figure 4-1. The first step requires the company to plan its marketing effort, i.e. identify

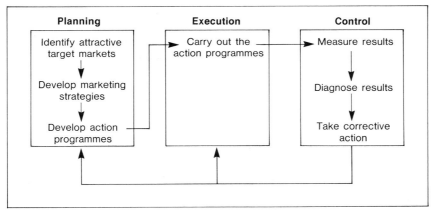

Figure 4-1 Marketing planning and control system

attractive target markets, develop effective marketing strategies and develop detailed action programmes. The second step involves the execution of the action plans, both geographically and over time. The third step calls for controls to make sure that the marketing objectives are being achieved: the measurement of results, analysis of the causes of poor results, and corrective action. Corrective action consists of adjustments in the plan, its execution, or both.

The first part of this chapter will deal with marketing planning, and the second part with marketing control.

MARKETING PLANNING

Sooner or later, all organizations ask themselves whether they need a system of business and marketing planning, what form it should take, and what should be done to make it effective. We will consider these questions in the following sections.

Benefits of Planning

Many companies operate without the benefit of a formal planning system, choosing to solve various problems as they arise. In the case of newer companies, their managers are often so busy solving existing problems that they have no time for planning. In the case of mature companies, many managers argue that they have done well without formal planning and therefore it cannot be too important. They resist the idea of taking time to prepare a written statement of objectives, strategies and action programmes: much preliminary work would be required, and the document itself would be too revealing of both the condition of the business and the quality (or lack of quality) of the responsible person's thinking. Many managers argue that their marketplace changes too fast for a plan to be useful or relevant; many also argue that planning becomes an annual ritual entered into halfheartedly by executives and wasteful of time. For these and other reasons, many companies have not yet introduced formal planning systems.

In spite of these objections, formal planning will yield a number of distinct benefits if sound procedures are used. Melville Branch has listed the following major benefits of a formal planning system:

1. It encourages systematic thinking ahead by management.
2. It leads to a better coordination of company efforts.
3. It leads to the development of performance standards for control.

4. It causes the company to sharpen its guiding objectives and policies.
5. It results in better preparedness for sudden developments.
6. It brings about a more vivid sense, in the participating executives, of their interacting responsibilities.[2]

How Business Planning Evolves in Organizations

An organization is rarely able to install an advanced business-planning system when it first decides to formalize its planning. Such a system tends to evolve in stages – getting better, it is hoped, in the process.

Unplanned stage. When businesses first become established, their managers are so busy hunting for funds, customers, equipment and materials that they have little time for formal planning. Management is totally engrossed in the day-to-day operations required for survival – there is no planning staff and hardly any time to plan.

Budgeting system stage. Management eventually recognizes the desirability of installing a budgeting system for the company's cash flow. Management estimates total sales for the coming year, and the associated costs and cash flows that may be expected. Each departmental manager prepares a budget for the coming year. These budgets are financial only, and do not require the kind of attention that goes into *business* planning. Budgets are not the same as plans.

Annual-planning stage. Management eventually recognizes the need to develop formal annual plans, and adopts one of three possible planning systems.

The first is *top-down planning*, so called because top management sets goals and plans for all the lower levels of management. This model is taken from military organizations, where generals prepare the strategy and the troops carry it out. In commercial organizations this accords with the 'Theory X' view of employees, i.e. that they dislike work and responsibility, and prefer to be directed.[3]

The second system is *bottom-up planning*, so called because the various units in the organization prepare their own goals and plans, based on the best they think they can do, and send them to upper management for approval. This style is based on Theory Y, i.e. that employees like work and responsibility, and are more creative and committed if they participate in planning and running the enterprise.

Most companies use a third system known as *goals-down plans-up* planning. Here top management takes a broad look at the company's opportunities and requirements, and sets corporate goals for the year. The various units of the company are responsible for developing plans to help achieve these goals: these, when approved by top management, become the official annual plans.

Strategic-planning stage. At this stage the planning system of the company is developed in an effort to improve its overall effectiveness.

The major change is the addition of *long-range planning*. Management realizes that annual plans only make sense in the context of a long-range plan. In fact the long-range plan should come first, and the annual plan be a detailed version of its first year. The long-range plan is reworked each year (called rolling planning), because the environment may change rapidly and require an annual review of the original assumptions.

A further development is that the various plans begin to take on a more strategic character. When a company first turns to planning, the planning documents tend to be long on statistics and specific tactical actions, and short on strategy. (One often looks in vain for a clear statement of strategy.) In more advanced planning systems, the plans are constructed so as to require a section on strategy.

As the company gains experience in planning, an effort is made to standardize the plan formats. Plans for different comparable units (such as divisions, product lines, products or brands) that follow the same or a similar format allow higher management to make useful comparisons.

As the planning ethos takes hold in the company, further improvements are introduced. Marketing managers receive more training in the use of financial analysis, and are required to justify their recommendations in terms of contribution margin, cash flow, and rate of return on manageable assets, rather than sales volumes only. Computer programmes are developed to help product managers examine the impact of alternative marketing plans and environmental assumptions on sales and profits.[4] The managers are eventually asked to develop contingency plans, in addition to main plans, showing how they would respond if specific major threats or opportunities were to arise. These and other developments mark the emergence of a true strategic-planning culture in the firm.

Steps in the Business- and Marketing-Planning Process

Business firms vary in the way they use the terms business planning and marketing planning. Some use the two terms interchangeably; others say that they develop their marketing plan first, and then their business plan; still others say that they develop their business plan first, and then their marketing plan.

The proper way to view the process of business and marketing planning is shown in Figure 4-2. First, marketing executives attempt to describe the market, sales and profits that the company could reasonably aim for, and the broad marketing strategies that might be pursued. At best, this can be called a market

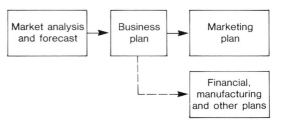

Figure 4-2 Steps in business and marketing planning

analysis and forecast. The marketing executives then work with the executives in charge of manufacturing, finance, personnel and so on, to develop a *business plan*, which might involve revising the market analysis and forecast. Once this has been approved, the marketing department proceeds to develop a detailed plan called the *marketing plan*, which outlines the specific goals, strategies, programmes, budgets and controls that the marketing department will use to support the business plan. (Other key executives will also, of course, develop versions of the business plan pertinent to their operation.) The following plans require strong marketing inputs:

1. *Product line plan.* This describes objectives, goals, strategies and tactics for a specific product line; one is prepared by each product line manager.
2. *Product plan.* This describes objectives, goals, strategies and tactics for a specific product or product category; one is prepared by each product manager.
3. *Brand plan.* This describes objectives, goals, strategies and tactics for a specific brand within the product category; one is prepared by each brand manager.
4. *Market plan.* This is a plan for developing and serving a specific market. If the organization has market managers as well as product managers, the market managers will prepare these plans.
5. *Product/market plan.* This is a plan for marketing a specific product or product line in

a specific industrial or geographical market. An example would be a bank that markets its lending services to the transport industry.

The Components of a Marketing Plan

What does a marketing plan look like? Our discussion will focus on product or brand plans, which should contain the following sections: executive summary, situation analysis, objectives and goals, marketing strategy, action programme, budgets and controls (see Figure 4-3).

Executive summary. The planning document should open with a short summary of the main goals and recommendations to be presented, as in this abbreviated example:

> The 1983 Marketing Plan seeks to generate a significant increase in company sales and profits in comparison with last year's achievements. The sales target is set at $80 million, which represents a 20 per cent sales gain in comparison with last year. This increase is deemed to be attainable because of the improved economic, competitive and distribution picture. The operating margin is forecast at $8 million, which represents a 25 per cent increase in comparison with last year. To achieve these goals, the sales promotion budget will be $1.6 million, which represents 2 per cent of projected sales. The advertising budget will be $2.4 million, which represents 3 per cent of projected sales. . .

The executive summary permits higher management to quickly grasp the major thrust of each plan before seeking the information by which the plan may be evaluated. To facilitate this, a table of contents should follow the executive summary.

Situation analysis. This comprises the first major section of the plan, in which the manager describes the major features affecting his operation. It has four subsections: background, normal forecast, opportunities and threats, and strengths and weaknesses.

Background. This section usually starts with a summary of key sales and profit data for the last few years. An example of five years of past data is shown in Table 4-1. Row 1 of the table shows that the market volume is growing at the rate of 200 000 units a year. Row 2 shows that the company's brand has risen from a 6 per cent share of the market to a fairly stable 10 per cent. Row 3 shows that the product's price of $2 has been increasing. Row 4 shows that variable cost per unit originally declined but has been increasing. Row 5 shows that the gross contribution margin per unit – the difference between price (row 3) and unit variable cost (row 4) – first increased, and then decreased in the most recent year. Rows 6 and 7 show sales volume in both units and dollars, and row 8 shows the total gross contribution margin. Row 9 shows a stable and then a rising level of overhead. Row 10 shows net contribution margin, i.e. gross contribution margin less overhead. Rows 11 and 12 show advertising and distribution expenses, respectively. Finally, row 13 shows net operating profit after marketing expenses. The picture is one of growing sales, with profits growing at a slower rate.

These data are followed by a description of noteworthy facts and trends relating to the market, distribution and competition. The market section should describe market size and trends, major target market segments, and buyer behaviour developments. The distribution section should describe the major

Figure 4-3 Contents of a marketing plan

Table 4-1 Historic product data

Variable	Columns	1978	1979	1980	1981	1982
1. Market (total units)		1 000 000	1 200 000	1 400 000	1 600 000	1 800 000
2. Share (%)		6	8	10	10	10
3. Price per unit ($)		2.00	2.00	2.00	2.20	2.40
4. Variable cost per unit ($)		1.20	1.10	1.10	1.30	1.55
5. Gross contribution margin per unit ($)	(3 − 4)	.80	.90	.90	.90	.85
6. Sales volume in units	(1 × 2)	60 000	96 000	140 000	160 000	180 000
7. Sales ($)	(3 × 6)	120 000	192 000	280 000	352 000	432 000
8. Gross contribution margin ($)	(5 × 6)	48 000	86 400	126 000	144 000	153 000
9. Overhead ($)		20 000	20 000	20 000	30 000	30 000
10. Net contribution margin ($)	(8 − 9)	28 000	66 400	106 000	114 000	123 000
11. Advertising ($)		8 000	12 000	15 000	18 000	20 000
12. Distribution ($)		4 000	8 000	15 000	15 000	20 000
13. Net operating profit ($)	(10 − 11 − 12)	16 000	46 400	76 000	81 000	83 000

trends in marketing channels and physical distribution. The competition section should describe the major competitors and their market shares, strategies and strengths and weaknesses. The factors underlying the most recent sales and profit results should be analysed.

Normal forecast. The background section should be followed by a forecast of market size and company sales under normal conditions, i.e. assuming no major changes in the marketing environment or marketing strategies. This forecast could be obtained in a number of ways. The simplest method is straightforward extrapolation of past growth rates: for example, in Table 4-1 the market volume for the coming year can be forecast as 2 million units, on the assumption that the 200 000 annual increase continues; market share can be assumed to stay at 10 per cent; prices can be expected to rise by, say, 20 cents. Another method is to forecast the economy, and other major variables affecting sales, and then incorporate these estimates in a statistical-demand equation to forecast sales (see Chapter 5). A further method is to gather sales-force estimates of what they expect to sell next year.

Most companies use two or more forecasting methods, and take an average of the estimates.

The forecast will have to be revised if quite different environmental conditions are expected or strategies are planned. If the forecast does not satisfy higher management, the product or brand manager would have to consider alternative strategies that promised a higher level of sales and profits.

Opportunities and threats. The normal forecast should be followed by a section in which the manager identifies the main opportunities and threats in the external environment. Usually the manager is aware of a number of these but should be challenged to put them into words. Higher management can then question details or omissions.

Table 4-2a shows the opportunities and threats faced by the cheque-account business of a trading bank. These are outside factors, and the descriptions suggest some actions that might be warranted. The manager may be asked to rate the opportunities and threats for their potential impact and probability, to indicate which deserve most attention and planning.

Strengths and weaknesses. In this section the manager lists the main internal strengths and weaknesses of the business unit (this is shown for the cheque-account business in Table 4-2b). The list of strengths has implications for strategy formulation, while the list of weaknesses has implications for corrective investments. Each enables higher management to raise important questions about each business unit.

Objectives and goals. Situation analysis points out where the business stands and where it might go. The next task is to develop a statement about where the business *should* go: managers have to set specific objectives and goals that will be accepted by higher management.

Higher management typically defines the company's overall goals for the coming period. The top management of an electronics firm may state that it wants the company to achieve: (i) a 15 per cent growth in sales volume; (ii) a pre-tax profit of 20 per cent on sales; and (iii) a pre-tax profit of 25 per cent on investment. In this context, each manager develops unit goals that will support the company goals. Those business units enjoying strong market positions will be expected to adopt even more ambitious goals than the company goals; those in difficult markets will adopt more modest goals. Top management wants to stretch each business unit to its maximum potential.

Let us assume that the manager of television products in the electronics company sees the key need as increasing the profitability of that line. The line's current return on investment (ROI) is 10 per cent, and higher management wants it to yield 15 per cent. This can be accomplished by: (i) increasing sales revenue; (ii) decreasing the cost (or not increasing it by as much as the higher sales revenue); and (iii) decreasing the investment (or not increasing it by as much as the increase in profit). Any or all of these can be

Table 4-2   Aspects of the cheque-account business of a trading bank

---

a   Opportunities and Threats

Opportunities
1. The level of market penetration suggests that this market may grow at levels faster than population growth.
2. While the bank is well known in Western Australia, we have a limited number of branches there.
3. Cash is increasingly being perceived as a risky medium for exchange.

Threats
1. The government inquiry into financial markets may lead to the entry of overseas banks.
2. Consumer pressure for either interest-bearing accounts or reduced charges could inhibit profitability.
3. Increasing use of credit cards and electronic funds transfer could cause usage to drop substantially.

b   Strengths and Weaknesses

Strengths
1. Awareness of our bank and its services is high (95 per cent).
2. Our branches are generally well sited.
3. We have a large number of corporate customers which are increasingly paying their staff by cheque.

Weaknesses
1. Waiting time for service at a number of branches is far too high.
2. Bank staff, particularly part-time tellers, have an inadequate knowledge of the service.
3. Our recent advertising campaign did not satisfy our objectives. We may have to consider switching to a new advertising agency.

---

adopted as objectives for the coming period.

The objectives that the manager decides to emphasize may be turned into goals, i.e. they can be given magnitudes and target dates. The manager might propose the following goals for attaining a 15 per cent ROI in the television line: (i) attain a 12 per cent increase in sales revenue for the coming year; (ii) increase the expense budget by 8 per cent for the coming year; and (iii) hold the investment level constant for the coming year.

Each of these goals will, in turn, be broken down into subgoals for the various operating units. For example, the overall sales goal will eventually be allocated to the sales units of the company (such as sales regions, sales districts, and, finally, individual salespersons): in this form they are called sales quotas, and will be based on the past performance and estimated potential facing each unit.

Marketing strategy. In this section, marketing management outlines a strategy for attaining its objectives: the 'game plan' by which the business unit hopes to 'win'. More specifically, we can define marketing strategy as follows:

* *Marketing strategy* is the fundamental logic by which the business unit intends to achieve its marketing objectives. Marketing strategy consists of a coordinated set of decisions on target markets, marketing mix, and marketing expenditure level.

Target markets. A sound marketing strategy calls for different degrees of emphasis on the various market segments. These segments differ in their preferences, responses to marketing effort, and profitability; and thus in the degree they may be satisfied by the particular company. Instead of pursuing all the market segments with equal fervour, the company would be sensible to allocate its effort and energy to those it can serve best from a competitive point of view. Here is an example:

The ABC management consulting firm (name disguised) was having difficulty maintaining its billings in a highly competitive market. Various competitors were beginning to specialize in certain industries and were building superior reputations there, whereas ABC operated as a generalist firm and was therefore less in demand. It became clear to ABC's management that its marketing strategy was ill defined with respect to target markets, and that if it did not make some hard choices as to which industries it would concentrate on, it would really be lacking a marketing strategy.

Marketing mix. The company should attempt to develop a cost-effective marketing mix for each target market that it pursues. The marketing mix will consist of a particular set of levels of the four *Ps* – product, price, place and promotion – and there are many options available. Consider the following example:

The Papermate Pen Company (owned by Gillette) recently developed a new ballpoint pen called the Eraser Mate, the first pen developed to use erasable ink. People who prefer pens to pencils can now erase their writing (they are, however, cautioned against using the pen to write cheques).

The company faced the task of devising a marketing-mix strategy for this pen. It considered charging a price of $1.69 or $1.99; setting an advertising budget of $200 000 or $300 000 for the first year; and setting a retailer discount of 20 or 30 per cent off the recommended retail price. Given these three variables, and the two levels of each, the company can choose any of eight marketing mixes (2 × 2 × 2). For example, one marketing mix would be 'high price, high advertising, low retailer discount', and another would be 'high price, high advertising, and high retailer discount'. Each marketing mix has to be analysed for its probable impact on sales and profits, along with its likelihood of attracting competition into the market.

The problem of choosing a marketing mix is thus even more challenging when we begin to recognize additional marketing variables and possible levels of each. Members of the marketing department will differ over the effectiveness of the various marketing variables. The sales manager may want to spend marketing funds on hiring more salespersons; the advertising manager may want to buy more ads; the product manager may want to improve product quality or packaging; and the marketing research manager may want to conduct a deeper study of the market. These differences in opinion are one of the reasons that marketing must be planned in a coordinated way.

Marketing expenditure level. Marketing strategy also calls for a decision on the dollar level of marketing expenditures. Even if the marketing mix is optimal, the company may be spending too much or too little on marketing. Companies typically establish their marketing budget at some conventional percentage of the sales goal. For example, a perfume company might set its marketing budget at 35 per cent of sales, and a fertilizer company at 15 per cent of sales. Companies entering a new market have to spend a fairly high amount in relation to anticipated sales, in the hope of building their market share. Companies know that the more they spend on marketing, the higher their sales will be – what they need to determine is the point where increased sales no longer bring increased profits, but actually cut into profits.

Action programme. The marketing strategy must be turned into a set of specific actions for accomplishing goals, and it is useful to make someone responsible for each strategy element. Suppose the marketing strategy calls for 'developing a substantially improved advertising campaign' and the task is assigned to Richard Bluck, advertising manager. He should list the various actions required to develop an improved advertising campaign, such as 'Gather the names of three highly regarded advertising agencies', 'Listen to competitive proposals', 'Select the best agency', 'Approve the final copy', and 'Approve the media plan'. Each activity, a completion date, is then assigned to someone in the advertising department. This process would be repeated for each strategy element.

The overall action plan may take the form of a table, with the twelve months (or fifty-two weeks) of the year serving as columns, and various marketing activities serving as rows. Dates can be entered to indicate when various activities or expenditures will be started, reviewed and completed. This action plan is subject to change during the year as new prob-

lems and opportunities arise, but it serves as a general framework for implementing tactics.

Budgets. The goals, strategies and planned actions allow the manager to formulate a supporting budget statement for the operation. This is essentially a projection of profits and losses: on the revenue side, it shows the forecast number of sold units and the average net realized price; on the expense side, it shows the costs of production, physical distribution and other marketing areas broken down into finer categories. The difference, or projected profit or loss, is also shown. Management reviews the budget and approves it with or without modifications: this provides the basis for procuring materials, production scheduling, personnel planning and marketing operations.

Controls. The last section of the plan deals with the controls that will be applied to monitor the plan's progress. Normally the goals and budgets are spelled out for each month or quarter, so that higher management can review the results regularly and spot those businesses that are not attaining their goals. The managers of these deficient businesses have to offer an explanation and indicate what actions they plan to take. (The marketing control system will be discussed in greater detail later in this chapter.)

Developing the Marketing Budget

We will now examine more closely the task of constructing a marketing budget to attain a given level of sales and profits. We will first illustrate a common approach to this exercise, and then describe certain improvements suggested by marketing resource-allocation theory.

Target-profit planning. Assume that Peter Link is the ice-cream product manager at Petersville and that it is now time for him to prepare his annual plan. If he is like most managers, he will follow the procedure shown in Table 4-3, called target-profit planning.

Table 4-3   A target-profit-oriented product plan

1	Forecast of total market	25 000 000 cartons
	This year's total market (24.3 million cartons × recent growth rate 3%)	
2	Forecast of market share	0.28
3	Forecast of sales volume (**1** × **2**)	7 000 000 cartons
4	Set the price to distributor	$4.45 per carton
5	Estimated sales revenue (**3** × **4**)	$31 150 000
6	Estimate the variable costs	$2.75 per carton
	Materials ($1.20) + packaging ($0.30) + labour ($1.10) + physical distribution ($0.15)	
7	Estimate the contribution margin to cover fixed costs, profits and marketing ([**4** − **6**] × **3**)	$11 900 000
8	Estimate the fixed costs	$7 000 000
	Fixed charge $1.00 per carton × 7 million cartons	
9	Estimate the contribution margin to cover profits and marketing (**7** − **8**)	$4 900 000
10	Estimate the target profit	$1 900 000
11	Amount available for marketing (**9** − **10**)	$3 000 000
12	Split of the marketing budget	
	Advertising	$2 000 000
	Sales promotion	$900 000
	Marketing research	$100 000

Peter Link first estimates the total market for ice-cream in the coming year (we will consider only the household market). An estimate can be formed by applying the recent growth rate of the market (3 per cent) to this year's market size (24.3 million cartons). This forecasts a market size of 25 million cartons for next year. He then forecasts Petersville sales based on the assumption that its past market share of 28 per cent will continue: thus Petersville sales are forecast to be 7 million cartons.

Next he sets a distributor price of $4.45 per carton for next year, based mainly on expected increases in labour and material costs. Thus the planned sales revenue will be $31.15 million.

He then estimates next year's variable costs at $2.75 per carton. This means that the contribution margin to cover fixed costs, profits and marketing is $11.9 million. Suppose the company charges this brand with a fixed cost of $1 per carton, or $7 million. This leaves a contribution margin of $4.9 million to cover profits and marketing.

At this step Peter Link brings in the target profit goal. Suppose a profit level of $1.9 million will satisfy higher management (it is usually some increase, say 5 to 10 per cent, over this year's profit). He then subtracts the target profit from what remains of the contribution margin to learn that $3 million is available for marketing.

In the final step the product manager splits the marketing budget into its mix elements, such as advertising, sales promotion, and marketing research. This split is normally based on the preceding year's split and the way in which competitors are using their marketing budgets. He decides to spend two-thirds of the money on advertising, almost one-third on sales promotion, and the remainder on marketing research.

Although this method produces a workable marketing plan and budget, several improvements are possible:

1. The product manager estimated market size and market share by straightforward extrapolation of past trends. He should consider possible changes in the marketing

environment that would lead to a different demand forecast.

2. The product manager assumed no change in his marketing strategy. One of the reasons for planning, however, is to consider alternative marketing strategies and their potential impact on company sales and profits: he should estimate the company's market share *after* he has developed a marketing strategy.

3. The product manager set next year's price largely to cover expected cost increases, rather than considering demand and expected competitor's prices. Setting the price mainly on the basis of cost is not a market-oriented pricing method.

4. The product manager developed the marketing mix on the basis of 'more of the same'. His rationale should have considered how each marketing-mix element would support the marketing objectives at this stage in the product's lifecycle.

5. The product manager seems to be guided by the idea of finding a 'satisficing' plan, one that produces satisfactory profits. Instead, he should try to find the optimal profit plan.

Profit optimization planning. We will now consider how to find the optimal profit plan. Profit optimization requires the manager to explicitly recognize the relationship between sales volume and the various elements of the marketing mix. We will use the term sales-response function to describe this relationship:

- A *sales-response function* forecasts the likely sales volume, during a specified time period, associated with different possible levels of one or more marketing-mix elements.

The best-known sales-response function is the demand function, illustrated in Figure 4-4a: the lower the price, the higher the sales in any given period, but a price of $1 would

have led to sales of 10 000 units in that period. The illustrated demand curve is curvilinear, although other shapes are possible.

Suppose that the marketing variable is not price but total marketing dollars spent by the company on sales-force, advertising and other marketing effort. In this case the sales-response function is likely to resemble Figure 4-4b: the more the company spends in a given period on marketing effort, the higher the sales are likely to be. The particular function is S-shaped, although other shapes are possible. The S-shaped function says that low levels of marketing expenditure are not likely to produce high levels of sales – too few buyers will be reached, or reached effectively, by the company's message. Higher levels of marketing expenditure per period will produce much higher levels of sales; very high expenditures, however, might represent marketing overkill.

The occurrence of eventually diminishing returns to increases in marketing expenditure is plausible for the following reasons. First, there is an upper limit to the total potential demand for any particular product: the easier sales prospects are sold almost immediately; the more recalcitrant ones remain. As the upper limit is approached, it becomes increasingly expensive to stimulate further sales. Second, as a company steps up its marketing effort its competitors are likely to do the same, with the net result that each experiences increasing sales resistance. Third, if sales were to increase progressively throughout, natural monopolies would result, i.e. a single firm would tend to take over in each industry because of its greater marketing effort. Yet this is contrary to what we observe in industry.

How can marketing managers estimate the sales-response functions that apply to their businesses? Essentially, three methods are available. The first is the *statistical method*, where the manager gathers data on past sales and levels of marketing-mix variables, and estimates the sales-response functions through

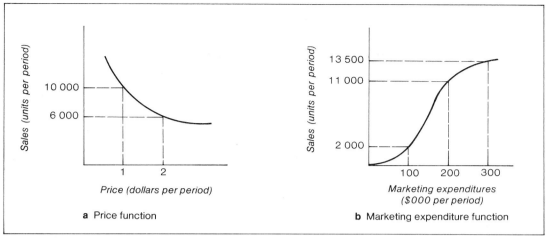

Figure 4-4   Sales-response functions

standard statistical procedures.[5] The second is the *experimental method*, which calls for deliberately varying the marketing expenditure and mix levels in matched samples (of geographical or other units), and noting the resulting sales volume.[6] The third is the *judgmental method*, where experts are asked to make intelligent guesses about the needed magnitudes.[7]

Once the sales-response functions are estimated, how are they used to help optimize profits? Graphically, we must introduce some further curves to find the point of optimal marketing expenditure, as in Figure 4-5. The key function is that of the sales response, which resembles that in Figure 4-4b except for two differences. First, sales response is expressed in dollars instead of units, so that we can find the profit-maximizing marketing expenditure. Second, the sales-response function is shown as starting above zero on the assumption that some sales might take place even in the absence of marketing expenditures.

To find the optimal marketing expenditure, the marketing manager subtracts all non-marketing costs from the sales-response function to derive the gross-profit curve. Next, marketing expenditures are drawn in such a

way that a dollar on one axis is projected as a dollar on the other (this amounts to a 45° line when the axes are scaled at identical intervals). The marketing-expenditures curve is then subtracted from the gross-profit curve to derive the net-profit curve. The net-profit curve shows positive net profits with marketing expenditures between M_L and M_U which could be defined as the rational range of marketing expenditure. The net-profit curve reaches a

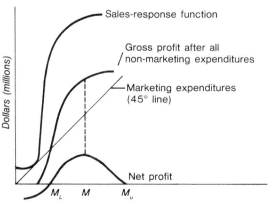

Figure 4-5   Relationship between sales volume, marketing expenditures, and profits

maximum at M, and thus the marketing expenditure that would maximize net profit is M.

The graphical solution may also be carried out numerically or algebraically; indeed, it must be if the sales volume is a function of more than one marketing-mix variable. We will now present a numerical example.

A numerical example. Mary Pender, a product manager, has been selling her product for some years by using a low-price, low-promotion strategy. The current price is $16, and $10 000 is being spent on advertising and another $10 000 on sales promotion. Sales are around 12 400 units, and profits are around $14 000. Higher management consider this unimpressive, and Mary Pender is anxious to find a better strategy to increase profits.

Her first step is to generate a set of alternative marketing-mix strategies. By assuming a high and a low level of each of three variables she formulates the eight strategies shown in the price, advertising and promotion columns of Table 4-4 (the first strategy is the current one). Her next step is to estimate the sales likely to be attained with each alternative, shown in the last column of Table 4-4.

Her final step is to determine which marketing mix maximizes profits, assuming the sales estimates are reliable. This calls for introducing a profit equation, and inserting into it the different marketing mixes. If, for example, fixed costs are $38 000 and unit variable costs are $10, expected profit can be computed for each marketing mix by using the following profit equation:

Profit = Total revenue − Total cost

Profit = (Price × Quantity) − Total variable cost − Fixed cost − Marketing cost

Applying this to the first mix in Table 4-4, we get:

Profit = ($16 × 12 400) − ($10 × 12 400) − $38 000 − ($10 000 + $10 000)

= $16 400

The product manager now estimates the profit with each marketing mix shown in Table 4-4. The resulting profits are:

1	$16 400
2	$13 000
3	− $7 400
4	− $2 400
5	$19 000
6	$16 800
7	− $4 200
8	$2 000

Marketing mix 5, calling for a price of $24, advertising of $10 000, and promotion of $10 000, promises to yield the highest profits ($19 000).

This concludes our discussion of how marketing management can discover and examine the profit-optimizing marketing mix. This mix

Table 4-4 Marketing mixes and estimated sales

Marketing mix	Price	Advertising	Promotion	Sales
1	$16	$10 000	$10 000	12 400
2	16	10 000	50 000	18 500
3	16	50 000	10 000	15 100
4	16	50 000	50 000	22 600
5	24	10 000	10 000	5 500
6	24	10 000	50 000	8 200
7	24	50 000	10 000	6 700
8	24	50 000	50 000	10 000

would be part of the larger marketing plan developed to achieve the company's objectives in a chosen market – to be effective, the plan must be carefully executed, monitored and revised when necessary. This brings us to the subject of marketing control.

MARKETING CONTROL

The purpose of marketing control is to maximize the probability that the company will achieve its short-run and long-run objectives in target markets. There are likely to be many surprises in the marketplace during the execution of the action programmes, and these will call for continuous review and control of performance. Various managers will have to exercise these responsibilities as well as those of planning and implementation.

Marketing control is far from being a single process, and three types of marketing control can be distinguished (see Table 4-5).

Annual plan control refers to the steps taken during the year to check continuing per-

formance against the plan, and the taking of corrective action when necessary. Profitability control consists of efforts to determine the actual profitability of different products, territories, end-use markets and trade channels. Strategic control consists of systematic examination and appraisal of the overall fit of the company to its marketing environment and opportunities. The following sections will deal with each of these processes in turn.

Annual Plan Control

The purpose is to make sure that the company is achieving the sales, profits and other goals established in its annual plan. This calls for the four steps shown in Figure 4-6. First, management must state well-defined goals for each month, quarter or other period during the year. Second, management must have ways to continuously measure performance and developments in the marketplace. Third, management must determine the underlying causes of any serious deviations in performance. Fourth, management must decide on the

Table 4-5 Types of marketing control

Type of control	Prime responsibility	Purpose	Approaches
I. Annual plan control	Top management Middle management	To examine whether the planned results are being achieved	Sales analysis Market-share analysis Marketing expense-to-sales ratios Customer-attitude tracking
II. Profitability control	Marketing controller	To examine where the company is making and losing money	Profitability by: product territory market segment trade channel order size
III. Strategic control	Top management Marketing auditor	To examine whether the company is pursuing its best marketing opportunities and doing this efficiently	Marketing audit

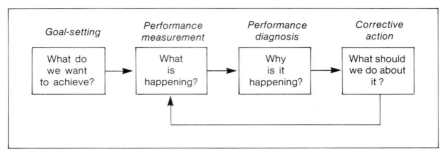

Figure 4-6 The control process

best corrective action to take to close the gaps between goals and performance. This may call for improving the ways in which the plan is being implemented, or even changing the goals.

This system is called *management by objectives*. Top management takes the initiative by developing the sales, profit and other goals for the planning period. These goals are broken down into derived goals for successively lower levels of management. During the period, various managers receive reports that allow them to determine whether goals are being reached and, if not, to take the necessary corrective action.

The four main tools used by management to check on progress are sales analysis, market-share analysis, marketing expense-to-sales analysis, and customer attitude tracking.

Sales analysis. This is the process of measuring and evaluating *actual* sales in relation to the sales goals set for different managers. There are two specific tools in this connection.

Sales variance analysis is an attempt to determine the relative contribution of different factors to a gap in sales performance. Suppose the annual plan called for selling 4000 widgets in the first quarter at $1 a widget, yielding $4000. At the end of the quarter, however, only 3000 widgets have been sold at 80 cents a widget, yielding $2400. The sales performance variance is −$1600, or −40 per cent of

expected sales. The question then arises: How much of this underperformance is due to the price decline and how much due to the volume decline? The following calculation supplies the answer:

Variance due to
price decline $= (\$1.00 - \$0.80)(3000)$
                       $= \$ \ 600$

Variance due to
volume decline $= (\$1.00)(4000 - 3000)$
                       $= \$1000$

Total variance $= \$1600$

Accordingly, almost two-thirds ($1000, or 62.5 per cent) of the sales variance is due to a failure to realize the volume target. Since volume tends to be more controllable than price, the company should look closely into why its expected sales figure was not achieved.[8]

Micro-sales analysis may provide the answer: this is an attempt to determine the specific products, territories and so forth, that failed to produce their expected share of sales. Suppose the company sells in three territories and expected sales were 1500, 500 and 2000 units respectively, adding up to 4000 widgets. The actual sales volume was 1400, 525 and 1075 units respectively. Thus the first territory showed a 7 per cent shortfall in terms of expected sales; the second, a 5 per cent surplus; and the third, a 46 per cent shortfall. It is now clear that the third territory is causing most of the trouble, and the sales manager can check to see which, if any, of the following hypotheses explains its poor performance: (i) the sales representative is loafing or has a personal problem; (ii) a major competitor has entered the territory; (iii) economic activity is depressed in this territory.

Market-share analysis. A company's sales performance does not reveal the company's position in relation to its competitors. A sales increase may be due to a general improvement in the economy, in which all firms are participating, or to improved marketing by this company in relation to its competitors. The normal way to remove the influence of the general environment is to track the company's market share. If the company's market share goes up, it is gaining on its competitors; if its market share goes down, it is probably losing out to its competitors. Conclusions drawn from market-share analysis are, however, subject to certain qualifications:[9]

- *The assumption that outside forces affect all companies in the same way is often not valid.* For example, the combined effects of international recession and escalating fuel costs have disadvantaged local conference venues less than overseas sites.
- *The assumption that a company's performance should be judged against the average performance of all companies is not always valid.* A company with greater than average opportunities should register a growing market share: if the market share remains constant, this may imply deficient rather than average management.
- *If a new firm enters the industry, every existing firm's market share may fall (again, not necessarily equally).* Here is a case where a falling market share does not mean that the company is performing below the average of the industry.
- *Sometimes the decline in a company's market share is the result of a deliberate policy to improve profits.* Management, for example, may drop unprofitable customers or products with a resulting decline in market share.
- *Market share fluctuates for many reasons.* For example, the market share in a particular period can be affected by whether a large sale is made on the last day of the period or at the beginning of the following period. A current shift in market share does not always have a significant marketing implication.

Marketing expense-to-sales analysis. Annual plan control also requires checking on marketing expenses in relation to sales, to make sure that the company is not overspending to achieve its sales goals. In one company the ratio of expenses to sales is normally 30 per cent, made up of five component ratios: sales force to sales (15 per cent); advertising to sales (5 per cent); sales promotion to sales (6 per cent); marketing research to sales (one per cent); and sales administration to sales (3 per cent).

Management's job is to monitor the overall and component marketing expense ratios to detect whether any are getting out of control. Small random fluctuations can be ignored, but those in excess of the normal range of variation are a cause for concern. The period-to-period fluctuations in each ratio can be charted on a control chart, as shown in Figure 4-7. This chart shows that the advertising expense-to-sales ratio normally fluctuates between 8 and 12 per cent; in the fifteenth period, however, it exceeded the upper control limit. One of two opposing hypotheses can explain this phenomenon.

- *Hypothesis A:* The company still has good control over sales, and this represents a chance event.
- *Hypothesis B:* The company has lost control over this cost as a result of some assignable cause.

If hypothesis A is accepted, no investigation is

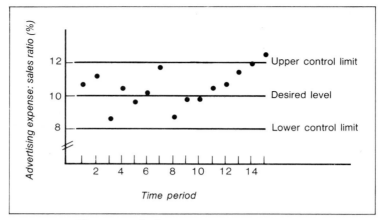

Figure 4-7 The control chart model

made to determine whether the environment has changed. The risk here is, of course, that some real change has occurred and the company will fall behind. If hypothesis B is accepted, the environment is investigated at the risk of uncovering nothing.

Even behaviours within the control limits should be watched for patterns that seem difficult to explain by chance. In Figure 4-7, for example, it should be noted that the level of the expense-to-sales ratio rose steadily from the ninth period onward. The probability of encountering a pattern of six successive increases in what should be a random and independent process is only one out of sixty-four;[10] therefore this unusual pattern should have led to an investigation before the fifteenth observation.

When an expense-to-sales ratio gets out of control, disaggregated data may be needed to track down the source of the problem. To this end an expense-to-sales deviation chart may be used, as shown in Figure 4-8. This shows the performance of different sales districts in terms of their quota and expense attainments (in percentages). For example, district D has accomplished its quota with nearly the expected level of expense. District B has exceeded its quota, and its expenses are proportionately higher. The most troubling districts

are in the north-west quadrant. For example, district J has accomplished less than 80 per cent of its quota and its expenses are disproportionately high.

The next step is to prepare a similar chart for each deviant district, showing sales representatives' standing on percentage of quota and expense attainments. Within district J,

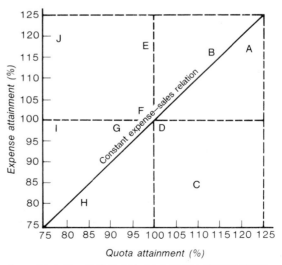

Source: Adapted from D. M. Phelps and J. H. Westing, *Marketing Management* (Homewood, Ill.: Richard D. Irwin, 3rd edn, 1968), p. 754. © 1968 by Richard D. Irwin, Inc.

Figure 4-8 Comparison of expense and quota deviations by district

for example, it may turn out that the poor performance is associated with specific individuals.

Customer attitude tracking. The control measures outlined above are largely quantitative. Alert companies also set up systems to track the changing attitudes of customers, dealers and other participants in the marketing system. The assumption is that attitude changes lead to changes in purchasing behaviour, which management will eventually see in sales reports. However, by monitoring current customer attitudes toward the company and its products, management can take much earlier action. Companies use the following major systems for tracking customer attitudes:

1. Complaint and suggestion. At a minimum, companies should record, analyse and respond to any written or oral complaints that come in from customers. These should be tabulated according to type, and the more serious and frequent ones should be given early attention. Many retailers, such as hotels, restaurants and banks, have gone further and provide suggestion cards to encourage customer feedback. Some companies have organized consumer-affairs departments to handle and anticipate customer problems. It may be argued that market-oriented companies should strive to maximize the opportunity for consumer complaints to provide management with a more complete picture of consumer reactions to their goods and services.

2. Customer panels. Some companies have created panels consisting of a cross-section of customers who have agreed to communicate their attitudes periodically through phone-calls or mail questionnaires coming from the company. These panels are thought to be more representative of the range of customer attitudes than customer complaints and suggestions.

3. Customer survey. This is a feedback system where standardized questionnaires are periodically administered to a random sample of customers. Questions may be asked about the friendliness of the staff, quality of the service, and so on.[11]

Corrective action. Corrective action has already been mentioned several times in this chapter. When actual performance deviates too much from the annual goals, companies go through a well-known cycle of defensive manoeuvres to correct the situation. Consider the following case:

> A large fertilizer producer found itself falling behind in its sales goals for the year. This was happening to its competitors as well, all of which had built excess capacity, and some were beginning to cut prices in order to achieve their planned sales volume.

In attempting to save and reverse the situation, this company was observed to go through a number of increasingly drastic steps:

1. *Production cutting.* The company found its inventories rising and proceeded to order cutbacks in production.
2. *Price cutting.* The company began to cut its prices selectively (higher discounts, freight allowances, and so on) to meet competition and retain its share of the market.
3. *Increased pressure on sales force.* The company put more pressure on its sales force to meet their quotas. The sales representatives in turn started 'beating down' doors, pressuring customers to buy more or buy before the end of the year.
4. *Fringe expenditure cutting.* The company proceeded to cut the budgets for personnel hiring and training, advertising, public relations, charities, and research and development.
5. *Personnel cuts.* The company began to lay off, retire or fire personnel in various departments, particularly staff services such as public relations, marketing research, and operations research.

6. *Bookkeeping adjustments.* The company undertook some fancy bookkeeping to bring about a better picture of profits, including changing the depreciation base, recording purchases (wherever possible) as capital items rather than as expenses, selling some company assets for leaseback in order to increase cash resources, and recording sales to phantom buyers, revising them as returned merchandise in the following year.

7. *Investment cutting.* The company began to cut back on its investment in plant and equipment.

8. *Selling property.* The company started to consider selling some of its product lines or divisions to other companies.

9. *Selling the company.* The final steps this company considered were selling out, or merging with another company that had good finances or some complementary attributes.

Profitability Control

Besides annual plan control, companies carry out periodic research to determine the actual profitability of their different products, territories, customer groups, trade channels and order sizes. This task requires an ability to assign marketing and other costs to specific marketing entities and activities.

Analysis of marketing profitability. The analysis of marketing profitability helps the marketing executive determine whether any current marketing activities should be eliminated, added or altered in scale.[12] The starting point is the company's profit and loss statement, of which a simplified example is shown

---

Exhibit 4-1 A New Marketing Position: Marketing Controllers!

Large companies such as Johnson & Johnson have established job positions known as marketing controllers, to monitor marketing expenses and activities. Marketing controllers are trained in both finance and marketing, and can perform a sophisticated financial analysis of past and contemplated marketing expenditures. They carry out the following activities:

1. Maintain a record of adherence to profit plans.
2. Closely control media expense.
3. Prepare brand managers' budgets.
4. Advise on optimum timing for strategies.
5. Measure the efficiency of promotions.
6. Analyze media production costs.
7. Evaluate customer and geographic profitability.
8. Present sales-oriented financial reports.
9. Assist direct accounts in optimizing purchasing and inventory policies.
10. Educate the marketing area to financial implications of decisions.

Source: Adapted from Sam R. Goodman, *Techniques of Profitability Analysis* (New York: John Wiley, 1970), pp. 17–18. Reprinted by permission of John Wiley & Sons, Inc.

Table 4-6 A simplified profit and loss statement

Sales		$60 000
Cost of goods sold		39 000
Gross margin		$21 000
Expenses		
Salaries	$9 300	
Rent	3 000	
Supplies	3 500	
		15 800
Net profit		$5 200

in Table 4-6. Profits are arrived at by subtracting cost of goods sold and other expenses from sales. The marketing executive would try to develop analogous profit statements by analysing functional marketing areas such as products, customers or territories. To do this, 'natural' expenses (such as salaries, rent, supplies) would have to be reclassified as 'functional' expenses. Consider the following example:

> The marketing manager of a lawn-mower firm wishes to determine the costs and profits of selling through three different types of retail channels: hardware stores, garden supply shops, and department stores. The company produces only one model of lawn-mower. Its profit and loss statement is shown in Table 4-6.

This marketing manager's task would involve the following steps:

1. Identifying the functional expenses. Assume that the salary expenses listed in Table

4-6 are incurred to sell, advertise, pack and deliver the product, and billing and collecting. The first task is to show how much of each natural expense was incurred in each of these activities. Suppose that most of the salaries expense went to sales representatives and the rest went to an advertising manager, packing and delivery help, and an office accountant. Let the breakdown of the $9 300 be $5 100, $1 200, $1 400 and $1 600 respectively (see Table 4-7).

Table 4-7 also shows the rent account of $3 000 allocated to the four activities. Since the sales representatives work away from the office, none of the building's rent expense is assigned to selling. Most of the floor space and rental of equipment arises in connection with packing and delivery; a small portion of the floor space is taken up by the activities of the advertising manager and the office accountant.

Finally, the supplies account lumps together promotional materials, packing materials, fuel purchases for delivery, and home-office stationery. The $3 500 in this account should be reassigned to the functional uses made of the supplies. The result of this and the previous breakdowns is that the total expenses of $15 800 are reclassified from a natural basis into a functional activity basis.

2. Assigning the functional expenses to the marketing entities. The next task is to determine how much of each activity has gone into serving each type of channel. Consider the selling effort: in each channel this is approximated by the number of sales calls made, given in the selling column of Table 4-8.

Table 4-7 Mapping natural expenses into functional expenses

Natural accounts	Total	Selling	Advertising	Packing and delivery	Billing and collecting
Salaries	$ 9 300	$5 100	$1 200	$1 400	$1 600
Rent	3 000	—	400	2 000	600
Supplies	3 500	400	1 500	1 400	200
	$15 800	$5 500	$3 100	$4 800	$2 400

Table 4-8 Bases for allocating functional expenses to channels

Channel type		Selling	Advertising	Packing and delivery	Billing and collecting
		No. of sales calls in period	No. of advertisements	No. of orders placed in period	No. of orders placed in period
Hardware		200	50	50	50
Garden supply		65	20	21	21
Department stores		10	30	9	9
		275	100	80	80
$\frac{\text{Functional expense}}{\text{No. of units}}$	=	$\frac{\$5\,500}{275}$	$\frac{\$3\,100}{100}$	$\frac{\$4\,800}{80}$	$\frac{\$2\,400}{80}$
	=	$20	$31	$60	$30

Altogether 275 sales calls were made during the period, so since the total selling expense amounted to $5 500 (see Table 4-7) the selling expense per call averaged $20.

As for the advertising expense, Table 4-8 shows this allocated on the basis of the number of advertisements addressed to the different trade channels. Since there were 100 advertisements altogether, and a total advertising expense of $3 100, the average advertisement cost $31.

The basis chosen for allocating the expenses of packing and delivery, billing and collections was the number of orders placed by each type of channel.

3. Preparing a profit and loss statement for each marketing entity. It is now possible to prepare a profit and loss statement for each chan-

nel as shown in Table 4-9. Since hardware stores accounted for one-half of total sales ($30 000 out of $60 000), this channel is charged with half of the cost of goods sold ($19 500 out of $39 000), leaving a gross margin of $10 500. From this must be deducted the proportions of the functional expenses that hardware stores consumed. According to Table 4-8, hardware stores received 200 out of 275 total sales calls. At an imputed value of $20 a call, hardware stores have to be charged with $4 000 of the selling expense. Table 4-8 also shows that hardware stores were the target of fifty advertisements: at $31 an advertisement, they are thus charged with $1 550 of the advertising activity. The same reasoning applies in computing the share of the other functional expenses to charge to hardware

Table 4-9 Profit and loss statement for channels

	Hardware	Garden supply	Department stores	Whole company
Sales	$30 000	$10 000	$20 000	$60 000
Cost of goods sold	19 500	6 500	13 000	39 000
Gross margin	$10 500	$ 3 500	$ 7 000	$21 000
Expenses				
Selling ($20 per call)	$ 4 000	$ 1 300	$ 200	$ 5 500
Advertising ($31 per advertisement)	1 550	620	930	3 100
Packing and delivery ($60 per order)	3 000	1 260	540	4 800
Billing ($30 per order)	1 500	630	270	2 400
Total expenses	$10 050	$ 3 810	$ 1 940	$15 800
Net profit (or loss)	$ 450	$ (310)	$ 5 060	$ 5 200

stores, and they are found to have given rise to $10 050 of the total expenses. Subtracting this from the gross margin, the profit from the activities of selling to hardware stores is small ($450).

The same analysis is repeated for the other channels. It is found that the company is losing money selling through garden supply shops, and makes most of its profits from sales to department stores. Clearly, gross sales through each channel are not a reliable indicator of the net profits being made in each.

Determining the best corrective action. The results of analysing marketing profitability do not constitute an adequate basis for deciding on corrective action. It would be naive to conclude that garden supply shops (and possibly hardware stores) should be dropped as channels in order to concentrate on department stores. Answers to the following questions would be needed first:

1. To what extent do buyers buy on the basis of the type of retail outlet versus the brand? Would they seek out the brand in those channels that are not eliminated?
2. What are the future market trends with respect to the importance of these three channels?
3. Have marketing efforts and policies directed at the three channels been optimal?

On the basis of this and other information, marketing management will want to define its major alternatives:

- *Establish a special charge for handling smaller orders to encourage larger orders.* This move is based on the assumption that small orders are the ultimate cause of the relative unprofitability of dealing with garden supply shops and hardware stores.
- *Give more aid to garden supply shops and hardware stores.* This is based on the assumption that the managers of these stores could increase their sales with more training or promotional materials.

- *Reduce the number of sales calls and the amount of advertising going to garden supply shops and hardware stores.* This is based on the assumption that some of these costs can be saved without proportionately reducing the level of sales to these channels.
- *Do nothing.* This is based on the assumption that current marketing efforts are optimal and that either future marketing trends point to an imminent improvement in the profitability of the weaker channels, or dropping any type of channel would reduce rather than improve profits because of repercussions on production costs or on demand.
- *Do not abandon any channel as a whole but only the weakest retail units in each channel.* This is based on the assumption that a more detailed cost study would reveal many profitable garden shops and hardware stores whose profits are concealed by the poor performance of other stores in these categories.

To evaluate these alternatives, each would have to be spelled out in greater detail. Marketing profitability analysis provides information on the relative profitability of different channels, products, territories or other marketing entities. It does not imply that the best course of action is to drop the unprofitable marketing entities, nor does it actually measure the likely profit improvement if these marginal marketing entities are dropped.

Strategic Control

From time to time, companies must stand back and undertake a critical review of their overall marketing effectiveness. This goes beyond carrying out annual plan control and profitability control. Marketing is one of the major areas where rapid obsolescence of objectives, policies, strategies and programmes is a constant possibility. Because of the rapid changes in the marketing environment, each company should periodically reassess its overall approach to the marketplace. A major tool in this connection is the marketing audit.[13]

The marketing audit. Companies are increasingly turning to marketing audits to assess their marketing opportunities and operations. We define marketing audit as follows:

- A *marketing audit* is a comprehensive, systematic, independent and periodic examination of a company's (or business unit's) marketing environment, objectives, strategies and activities. Its aim is to determine problem areas and opportunities, and recommend a plan of action to improve the company's marketing performance.

Let us examine the marketing audit's four characteristics:

1. *Comprehensive.* The marketing audit covers all the major marketing issues in a business, not merely one or a few troublespots. If an examination covered only the sales force, pricing, or some other marketing activity, it would be called a functional audit.
2. *Systematic.* The marketing audit involves an orderly sequence of diagnostic steps covering the organization's marketing environment, internal marketing system and specific marketing activities. The diagnosis is followed by a corrective action plan involving both short-run and long-run proposals to improve the organization's overall marketing effectiveness.
3. *Independent.* The marketing audit is normally conducted by either an inside or outside party who is relatively independent of the marketing department, who has obtained top management's confidence and has the needed objectivity.
4. *Periodic.* The marketing audit should be carried out periodically, not only when there is a crisis. It promises benefits for

apparently successful companies as well as those in deep trouble.

The six major components of a marketing audit are outlined in Table 4-10. First, the marketing auditor would examine pertinent information about the current and future character of the marketing environment in which the company operates. The aim is to identify major opportunities and threats. Second, the marketing auditor would look at the company's marketing mission, objectives and strategy to see if the firm is responding appropriately to its best opportunities. Third, the marketing auditor would analyse whether the marketing organization is well adapted to carrying out the company's marketing objectives and strategy. Fourth, the marketing auditor would check on whether the company's major marketing management systems of information, planning and control are adequate to support its marketing effort. Fifth, the marketing auditor would analyze the company's marketing profitability, particularly to learn where the company is making its profits and whether its marketing activities are cost-effective. Sixth, the marketing auditor would examine one or more major marketing functions – product, price, distribution, sales force, advertising, sales promotion, and publicity – to see whether these are well managed.

Not all of these components need to be reviewed, or reviewed extensively, in a marketing audit. The purpose of the examination is to judge whether the company is performing optimally from a marketing point of view. The auditor will produce some short-run and long-run recommendations: it is up to management to consider this advice carefully and implement those suggestions which, it feels, will contribute to improved marketing performance. The marketing audit is not a plan but rather an independent appraisal by an inside or outside auditor of the main problems and opportunities facing the company and what it can do about them.

Table 4-10 Components of a marketing audit

PART I: MARKETING ENVIRONMENT AUDIT

Macro-environment

A. *Demographic*

1. What major demographic developments and trends will pose opportunities or threats for this company?
2. What actions has the company been taking in response to these developments and trends?

B. *Economic*

1. What major developments and trends in income, prices, savings and credit will have an impact on the company?
2. What actions has the company been taking in response to these developments and trends?

C. *Ecological*

1. What is the outlook for the cost and availability of natural resources and energy needed by the company?
2. What concerns have been expressed about the company's role in pollution and conservation, and what steps has the company taken?

D. *Technological*

1. What major changes are occurring in product technology? In process technology? What is the company's position in these technologies?
2. What major generic substitutes might replace this product?

E. *Political*

1. What laws now being proposed could affect marketing strategy and tactics?
2. What federal, state and local agency actions should be watched? What is happening in the areas of pollution control, equal employment opportunity, product safety, advertising, price control and so forth, that is relevant to marketing strategy?

F. *Cultural*

1. What attitude is the public taking towards business, and towards products such as those produced by the company?
2. What changes now occurring in consumer and business lifestyles and values have a bearing on the company's marketing strategy?

Task environment

A. *Markets*

1. What is happening to market size, growth, geographic distribution, and profits?
2. What are the major market segments? What are their expected rates of growth? Which are high-opportunity and low-opportunity segments?

B. *Customers*

1. How do current customers and prospects rate the company and its competitors, particularly with respect to reputation, product quality, service, sales force and price?
2. How do different classes of customers make their buying decisions?
3. What are the evolving needs of (and satisfactions being sought by) the buyers in this market?

C. *Competitors*

1. Who are the major competitors? What are the objectives and strategy of each? What are their strengths and weaknesses? What are the sizes and trends in market shares?
2. What trends can be foreseen in future competition and substitutes for this product?

Table 4-10 (cont.)

D. *Distribution and Dealers*

1. What are the main trade channels bringing products to customers?
2. What are the efficiency levels and growth potentials of the different trade channels?

E. *Suppliers*

1. What is the outlook for the availability of different key resources used in production?
2. What trends are occurring among suppliers in their pattern of selling?

F. *Facilitators and Marketing Firms*

1. What is the outlook for the cost and availability of transport services?
2. What is the outlook for the cost and availability of warehousing facilities?
3. What is the outlook for the cost and availability of financial resources?
4. How effectively is the advertising agency performing?

G. *Publics*

1. What publics (financial, media, government, citizen, local, general and internal) represent particular opportunities or problems for the company?
2. What steps has the company taken to deal effectively with its key publics?

PART II. MARKETING STRATEGY AUDIT

A. *Business Mission*

1. Is the mission of the business clearly stated in market-oriented terms?
2. Is the mission feasible in terms of the business's opportunities and resources?

B. *Marketing Objectives and Goals*

1. Are the corporate objectives clearly stated, and do they lead logically to the marketing objectives?
2. Are the marketing objectives stated in the form of clear goals to guide marketing planning and subsequent performance measurement?
3. Are the marketing objectives appropriate, given the company's competitive position, resources and opportunities? Is the appropriate strategic objective to build, hold, harvest, or terminate this business?

C. *Strategy*

1. What is the core marketing strategy for achieving the objectives? Is it a sound marketing strategy?
2. Are enough resources (or excessive resources) budgeted to accomplish the marketing objectives?
3. Are the marketing resources allocated optimally to prime market segments, territories, and products of the organization?
4. Are the marketing resources allocated optimally to the major elements of the marketing mix — i.e., product quality, service, sales force, advertising, sales, promotion and distribution?

PART III. MARKETING ORGANIZATION AUDIT

A. *Formal Structure*

1. Is there a high-level marketing officer with adequate authority and responsibility over company activities that affect the customer's satisfaction?
2. Are the marketing responsibilities optimally structured along functional, product, end-user and territorial lines?

Table 4-10 (cont.)

B. *Functional Efficiency*

  1. Are there good communication and working relations between sales and other marketing areas?

  2. Is product management working effectively? Are the product managers able to plan profits or only sales volume?

  3. Are there any groups in marketing that need more training, motivation, supervision or evaluation?

C. *Interface Efficiency*

  1. Are there any problems between marketing and manufacturing that need attention?

  2. Marketing and R & D?

  3. Marketing and financial management?

  4. Marketing and purchasing?

PART IV. MARKETING SYSTEMS AUDIT

A. *Marketing Information System*

  1. Is the marketing intelligence system producing accurate, sufficient and timely information about developments in the marketplace?

  2. Is marketing research being used adequately by company decision-makers?

B. *Marketing Planning System*

  1. Is the marketing planning system well conceived and effective?

  2. Is sales forecasting and market potential measurement soundly carried out?

  3. Are sales quotas set on a proper basis?

C. *Marketing Control System*

  1. Are the control procedures (monthly, quarterly, etc.) adequate to ensure that the annual plan objectives are being achieved?

  2. Is there provision for periodic analysis of the profitability of different products, markets, territories, and channels of distribution?

  3. Is provision made to examine and validate periodically various marketing costs?

D. *New-Product Development System*

  1. Is the company well organized to gather, generate and screen new-product ideas?

  2. Does the company do adequate concept research and business analysis before investing heavily in a new idea?

  3. Does the company carry out adequate product and market testing before launching a new product?

PART V. MARKETING PROFITABILITY AUDIT

A. *Profitability Analysis*

  1. What is the profitability of the company's different products, served markets, territories, and channels of distribution?

  2. Should the company enter, expand, contract or withdraw from any business segments? What would be the short- and long-run profit consequences?

B. *Cost-Effectiveness Analysis*

  1. Do any marketing activities seem to have excessive costs? Can cost-reducing steps be taken?

Table 4-10 (cont.)

PART VI. MARKETING FUNCTION AUDITS

A. *Products*

1. What are the product line objectives? Are these objectives sound? Is the current product line meeting these objectives?
2. Are there particular products that should be phased out?
3. Are there new products that are worth adding?
4. Are any products able to benefit from quality, feature or style improvements?

B. *Price*

1. What are the pricing objectives, policies, strategies and procedures? To what extent are prices set on sound cost, demand and competitive criteria?
2. Do customers see the company's prices as being in or out of line with the perceived value of its offer?
3. Does the company use price promotions effectively?

C. *Distribution*

1. What are the distribution objectives and strategies?
2. Is there adequate market coverage and service?
3. Should the company consider changing its degree of reliance on distributors, sales reps and direct selling?

D. *Advertising, Sales Promotion, and Publicity*

1. What are the organization's advertising objectives? Are they sound?
2. Is the right amount being spent on advertising? How is the budget determined?
3. Are the ad themes and copy effective? What do customers and the public think about the advertising?
4. Are the advertising media well chosen?
5. Is sales promotion used effectively?
6. Is there a well-conceived publicity programme?

E. *Sales Force*

1. What are the organization's sales-force objectives?
2. Is the sales force large enough to accomplish these objectives?
3. Is the sales force organized along the proper principle(s) of specialization (territory, market, product)?
4. Does the sales force show high morale, ability and effort? Are they sufficiently trained and motivated?
5. Are the procedures adequate for setting quotas and evaluating performances?
6. How is the company's sales force perceived in relation to those of competitors?

SUMMARY

The planning and control of marketing is one of three major systems supporting the company's operations in the marketplace. It involves the three steps of planning, execution and control: in this chapter we focused on planning and control.

Companies operate planning systems with various degrees of sophistication – from single budgeting to annual planning to strategic planning. Normally the planning process starts with a preliminary market analysis and forecast, which is used to build the business plan, which in turn leads to development of a detailed marketing plan to be implemented by the marketing department. The marketing plan contains the following sections: executive summary, situation analysis, objectives and goals, marketing strategy, action programme, budgets and controls. The marketing strategy defines the target markets, marketing mix, and marketing expenditure level that will be used to achieve the marketing objectives. The marketing budget may be developed either by setting a target profit or by using sales-response functions to identify the marketing plan which will optimize profits.

Marketing control is the natural sequel to marketing planning. Companies need to exercise at least three types of marketing control.

Annual plan control is the task of monitoring the current marketing effort and results to make sure that annual sales and profit goals will be achieved. The main tools are sales analysis, market-share analysis, marketing expense-to-sales analysis, and customer-attitude tracking. If underperformance is detected, the company can implement a variety of corrective measures including cutting production, changing prices, increasing sales-force pressure and cutting fringe expenditures.

Profitability control is the task of determining the actual profitability of different marketing entities, such as the firm's products, territories, market segments and trade channels. Analysis of marketing profitability reveals the weaker marketing entities, although it does not indicate whether these should be bolstered or phased out.

Strategic control is the task of making sure that the company's marketing objectives, strategies and systems are optimally adapted to the current and forecast marketing environment. It uses the tool known as a marketing audit, which is a comprehensive, systematic, independent and periodic examination of the organization's marketing environment, objectives, strategies and activities. The purpose of the marketing audit is to determine marketing opportunity and problem areas, and recommend a short-run and long-run action plan to improve the organization's overall marketing effectiveness.

QUESTIONS FOR DISCUSSION

1. Do most businesses begin their marketing planning by engaging in the strategic-planning process? If not, what usually happens?

2. A recently hired member of the marketing staff at Kellogg's was helping to put together the marketing plan for Rice Bubbles. She asked, 'Why is the executive summary needed?'. How would you advise her?

3. Briefly discuss those aspects of situation analysis that a marketing planner for Seppelt's wine would have to consider.

4. What major decisions constitute the marketing-strategy phase of the marketing plan? Why is it so essential that they be well coordinated?

5. The idea of having a marketing controller who is well versed in both marketing and finance was discussed in this chapter. Would this individual be helpful in the latter stages of marketing planning? Why?

6. A friend is planning to open a discotheque. He realizes that marketing control is essential for success. How would you advise him on the options relevant to his new venture?

7. What are the relative advantages and disadvantages of customer-attitude tracking when compared with the other annual-plan control approaches?

8. The heart of the strategic control process is the marketing audit. Briefly discuss the characteristics and purpose of this concept.

9. Marketing planning and marketing control are independent and unrelated. Comment.

NOTES

[1] 'Sound Planning Saves Campaign From Disaster', *Rydge's In Marketing*, 7 March 1981, p. 22.

[2] See Melville C. Branch, *The Corporate Planning Process* (New York: American Management Association, 1962), pp. 48–49.

[3] Douglas McGregor, *The Human Side of Enterprise* (New York: McGraw-Hill, 1960).

[4] For an example, see the case 'Concorn Kitchens' in Harper W. Boyd Jr & Robert T. Davis (eds), *Marketing Management Casebook* (Homewood, Ill.: Richard D. Irwin, 1971), pp. 125–36.

[5] For empirical studies using fitted sales-response functions, see Doyle L. Weiss, 'Determinants of Market Share', *Journal of Marketing Research*, August 1968, pp. 290–95; Donald E. Sexton Jr, 'Estimating Marketing Policy Effects on Sales of a Frequently Purchased Product', *Journal of Marketing Research*, August 1970, pp. 338–47; and Jean-Jaques Lambin, 'A Computer On-Line Marketing Mix Model', *Journal of Marketing Research*, May 1972, pp. 119–26.

[6] See Russell Ackoff & James R. Emshoff, 'Advertising Research at Anheuser-Busch', *Sloan Management Review*, Winter 1975, pp. 1–15.

[7] See Philip Kotler, 'A Guide to Gathering Expert Estimates', *Business Horizons*, October 1970, pp. 79–87.

[8] For further discussion, see James M. Hulbert & Norman E. Toy, 'A Strategic Framework for Marketing Control', *Journal of Marketing*, April 1977, pp. 12–20.

[9] See Alfred R. Oxenfeldt, 'How to Use Market-Share Measurement', *Harvard Business Review*, January–February 1959, pp. 59–69.

[10] There is a chance of $\frac{1}{2}$ that any succeeding observation will be higher, and the same chance that it will be lower (excluding the possibility that two successive values are identical). Therefore the probability of finding six successively higher values is given by $\frac{1}{2}$ to the power of six $= \frac{1}{64}$.

[11] For a consumer survey applied to a hotel chain, see Arthur J. Daltas, 'Protecting Service Markets with Consumer Feedback', *Cornell Hotel and Restaurant Administration Quarterly*, May 1977, pp. 73–77.

[12] For a basic text, see Donald R. Longman & Michael Schiff, *Practical Distribution Cost Analysis* (Homewood, Ill.: Richard D. Irwin, 1955).

[13] For details, see Philip Kotler, William Gregor & William Rodgers, 'The Marketing Audit Comes of Age', *Sloan Management Review*, Winter 1977, pp. 25–43. A preliminary marketing audit tool is described in Philip Kotler, 'From Sales Obsession to Marketing Effectiveness', *Harvard Business Review*, November–December 1977, pp. 67–75.

5

The Marketing Information System

Agree creme and conditioner became the Number 1 brand in Australia just six months after launch in February, 1978. The shampoo range took Number 3 position in that much larger market (both in dollar terms and numbers of competitors) after just eight months. Yet SC Johnson's, better known as Johnson Wax, was a household packaged-goods manufacturer which had never ventured into the hair-care market – a market then dominated by heavyweights Sunsilk (Unilever) and Alberto (Alberto Culver) at the conditioner end, and by Sunsilk, Johnson's Baby Shampoo (Johnson and Johnson) and Alberto at the shampoo end.

Agree succeeded because of research – both basic product research and thorough market research – and because the company had the faith and resources to spend blockbuster sums of money on television and magazine advertising, and to carry out extensive free sampling of the product in an innovative manner. Market research showed the main area of dissatisfaction with conditioners was that they left the hair oily after use – largely because most of them contained oil. This was a particular problem in the important market segment, late teens to early 20s when hair is naturally more oily, and of course was of more concern to girls. Johnson initiated a major research and development programme in their US laboratories to produce a product which was virtually oil-free (the claim is 99.75 per cent) yet had desired characteristics such as making hair manageable, combable, soft and shining.

The American campaign was extremely successful, and the brand became the Number 1 seller within a short period. Introduction to Australia was planned for nine months after the US launch, and the local company had the advantage *of access to the final US pack and copy approach for testing in the local market. With the US success behind it, SC Johnson could have launched the product in Australia without delay, and the temptation must have been there to do so in view of the fact that competitors had no doubt monitored the US result.*

Instead, the company decided to test the US pack and copy approach in the local market – a move that proved to be critical. Says Don Holdsworth, product manager, Consumer Products Division of SC Johnson, 'The market research report on the final US pack and copy which had proved so successful there said it was a complete write-off. The market research company recommended we abandon the project.' Double-checking confirmed that the 'greasies' problem was Number 1, and that the age appeal was identical to the US, says Holdsworth. 'That started a rebuilding on the same strategic platform. We still knew it was the Number 1 problem in Australia, but we also knew for certain that wasn't the way to market it.'

One of the problems with the US positioning was that it was too narrow – the Australian research showed that it appealed only to people who thought they had oily hair. The US pack, a solid PVC bottle which did not show the product, was found to be too much like a household product pack for the Australian market. Explains Holdsworth, 'In Australia, conditioners are much more of a cosmetic product, possibly due to the influence of European manufacturers in the past, or the importance of pharmacies.'

In all, SC Johnson spent $50 000 on testing the pack and copy approach to get it right for Australia.[1]

When we discussed marketing planning and control in Chapter 4, we emphasized their form: in this chapter we want to emphasize their *substance*, which is information. At every turn, marketing managers face the need for information. Marion Harper put it this way: 'To manage a business well is to manage its future; and to manage the future is to manage information.'[2] The chapter is divided into four sections, which answer the following questions:

1. What is a marketing information system, and how is it used?
2. What is marketing research, how does it work, and how does it fit into a marketing information system?

3. What information system do companies use to measure current market demand?
4. What information systems do companies use to forecast future market demand?

THE CONCEPT OF A MARKETING INFORMATION SYSTEM

During the nineteenth century, sellers were generally close to buyers and knew their wants firsthand. The owner of a general store knew his customers and their responses; a small manufacturer would personally visit prospective and current customers to gather their reactions. Marketing information was picked up just by being with people, observing them and asking questions.

During the twentieth century, three developments have created a need for more and better marketing information:

1. *The transition from local to national marketing.* As a company's market area expanded, its managers had less firsthand experience with customers and had to rely on formal systems for gathering the needed information.
2. *The transition from buyer needs to buyer wants.* As incomes increased, buyers became more demanding and selective in the goods they bought. Producers found it harder to predict how buyers would feel about different features, styles and other attributes, and they therefore turned to formal systems for researching market preferences.
3. *The transition from price to non-price competition.* As sellers increased their use of competitive weapons (such as branding, product differentiation, advertising, and sales promotion) they required information on the effectiveness of these marketing tools. Not only markets, but also the tools of marketing, had to be researched.

Although the need for marketing information grew geometrically, the supply never seemed sufficient. In many companies today, marketers are still not satisfied with their marketing information. Their complaints include the following:

- There is not enough marketing information of the right kind.
- There is often much marketing information of the wrong kind.
- Marketing information is so dispersed throughout the company that usually a great effort must be made to locate simple facts.
- Important marketing information is sometimes suppressed by subordinates if they believe it will reflect unfavourably on their performance.
- Important information often arrives too late to be useful.
- Information often arrives in a form that leaves no idea of its accuracy, and there is no one to turn to for confirmation.

A growing number of companies are therefore taking a comprehensive look at the marketing information needs of their executives and are beginning to develop a more formal marketing information system (MIS) to meet these needs. A study of 193 major US companies found that 77 per cent either had installed or were in the process of installing an MIS.[3] Among the leaders in this area were General Electric, Coca-Cola, Johnson & Johnson, and RCA.

An MIS is a formal effort to systematize the many information flows needed by marketing managers so that relevant information will be more available and useful to them. We define a marketing information system as follows:[4]

- A *marketing information system* is a continuing and interacting structure of people, equipment and procedures designed to gather, sort, analyse, evaluate and distribute pertinent, timely and accurate information for use by marketing decision-makers to improve their marketing planning, execution and control.

The role and major subsystems of an MIS are illustrated in Figure 5-1. The box at the left side of the figure shows the marketing environment which must be monitored: target markets, marketing channels, competitors, publics and macro-environmental forces. Developments and trends in this environment are picked up in the company through one of four subsystems making up the marketing information system: the internal reports system, marketing intelligence system, marketing research system, and analytical marketing system. The information then flows to the

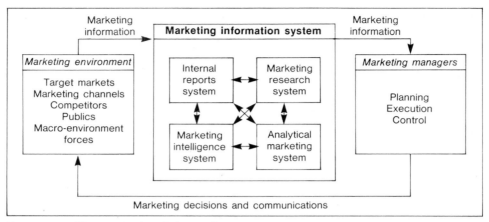

Figure 5-1 The marketing information system

appropriate marketing managers to help them in their marketing planning, execution and control. The resulting actions then flow back to the marketing environment as decisions and communications.

We will now take a closer look at the four major subsystems of the company's MIS.

Internal Reports System

Every company produces periodic internal reports which provide management with current data on sales, costs, inventories, cash flows and accounts. In too many companies, these reports often come too late to satisfy marketing management. It does little good for a marketing manager in a lawn-mower company to learn one month late that sales in Tasmania

are falling sharply. Had the reports come in earlier, the manager could have found out what was happening and taken quick corrective action. In this connection, the computer has been the major force for progress and has permitted companies to build first-rate internal reports systems.

Any company that undertakes to improve its internal reports system should first research the managers who will use it. The goal is to design not the most elegant system but one that will meet the users' needs and abilities.[5] A useful set of questions is listed in Table 5-1. After getting this information, the company should design the marketing information system in a way that reconciles what executives would like to have, what they really need, and what is economically feasible. The

Table 5-1 Questionnaire for determining marketing information needs

1. What types of decisions are you regularly called upon to make?
2. What types of information do you need to make these decisions?
3. What types of information do you regularly get?
4. What types of special studies do you periodically request?
5. What types of information would you like to get that you are not now getting?
6. What information would you want daily? Weekly? Monthly? Yearly?
7. What magazines and trade reports would you like to see routed to you on a regular basis?
8. What specific topics would you like to be kept informed of?
9. What types of data-analysis programmes would you like to see made available?
10. What do you think would be the four most helpful improvements that could be made in the present marketing information system?

Source: Philip Kotler, 'A Design for the Firm's Marketing Nerve Center,' *Business Horizons,* Fall 1966, p. 70.

information to be provided should be tied to the major decisions that the marketing managers make. For example, brand managers, in order to make informed decisions on how much to spend on advertising, should know the degree of awareness and knowledge of the company's brand in the target market, the advertising budgets and strategies of competitors, the relative effectiveness of advertising in the promotional mix, and so on. The MIS should be designed to provide these and other measures needed to make key marketing decisions.

Marketing Intelligence System

Whereas the internal reports system supplies executives with results data, the marketing intelligence system supplies executives with happenings data. We define the marketing intelligence system as follows:

- The *marketing intelligence system* is the set of sources and procedures by which marketing executives obtain their everyday information about developments in the external marketing environment.

Most marketing executives acquire marketing intelligence themselves, by reading newspapers and trade publications, talking to various outsiders and relying on subordinates. To the extent that their intelligence work is casual, important information will often be over-looked – they may learn of a competitive move, a new customer need or a dealer problem too late to make the best response.

A company can take some concrete steps to improve the quality of marketing intelligence received by its managers. First, the company should train and motivate the sales force to do a better job of spotting and reporting new developments. Sales representatives are the eyes and ears of the company, and are in an excellent position to pick up information that would not appear in the usual internal sales reports. Yet they are also very busy and often fail to pass on significant information. The company must 'sell' its sales force on their importance as intelligence gatherers, and emphasize this in their sales bonuses. Their intelligence responsibilities should be facilitated by designing sales call reports that are easy to fill out, and sales representatives should know which managers in their company should receive what information.

Second, the company should also motivate distributors, retailers and other allies to pass along important intelligence. Many companies send out comparison shoppers to learn how various brands are selling and how helpful retail sales personnel are. Interviewing customers and dealers to learn about new opportunities and problems is a legitimate intelligence activity. Much can be learned about competitors through such overt means as: (i) pricing or purchasing competitors' products; (ii) attending 'open houses' and trade shows; (iii) reading competitors' published reports and attending shareholders' meetings; (iv) talking to competitors' former and present employees, dealers, distributors, suppliers and freight agents; (v) hiring a media reporting service (such as a press-clipping service); and (vi) reading the *Australian Financial Review*, major newspapers and trade magazines.

Third, many companies supplement their own intelligence work by purchasing information from outside specialists. The A.C. Nielsen Company sells data from national or regional, continuous or discontinuous, bimonthly retail audits in food, chemist, confectioner/milkbar and take-away liquor outlets, indicating brand shares, retail prices, and proportion of shops in (or out of) stock of a product. The Roy Morgan Research Centre also offers a wide variety of information resources. These include a weekly Australia-wide omnibus survey of 1100 people aged 14 years and over (marketers can pay for a question to be asked), the Morgan Gallup poll, a national panel of 3000 households completing diaries covering purchases in about fifty product categories, the SAMI warehouse withdrawal reports based on products dispatched from warehouses to retail stores, and continuous readership surveys and consumer measurement.

Fourth, the company can establish an office that is specifically responsible for improving the quality and circulation of marketing intelligence. The staff would perform a number of services. It would scan major publications, abstract the relevant news and disseminate it in newsletter form to the appropriate marketing managers. It would develop a master index so that all past and current information could easily be stored and retrieved. The staff would also assist managers in evaluating the reliability of any piece of information. These and other services would greatly enhance the quality of the information available to marketing managers.

Marketing Research System

From time to time, marketing managers need to make a specific study so that they will have enough information to make an intelligent decision. Consider the following situation:

> The publisher of *Playboy* would like to find out more about the incomes, educational levels and lifestyles of the current readers of its magazine, their reading preferences, and their attitudes toward some possible format changes in the magazine.

In such circumstances, managers cannot wait for information to arrive in bits and pieces – a formal project is required. Managers usually do not have the skills or the time to obtain the information themselves in an efficient way. There is a clear need for marketing research. We define marketing research as follows:

- *Marketing research* is the systematic design, collection, analysis and reporting of data and findings relevant to a specific marketing situation facing the company.

The major study of marketing research in Australia is that conducted by Hart in 1971.[6] Others – more current, but also more limited – include those by Cramphorn, Cooley and Kitching.[7] Comprehensive current data are clearly needed.

Hart sent a detailed mail questionnaire to 220 leading Australian marketing companies, receiving usable responses from 137 (57 per cent). Of these respondents, 38 per cent reported having a formal marketing-research department, defined as comprising more than one full-time researcher (i.e. single-person 'departments' were excluded). More than 50 per cent of these departments had been formed within the last ten years, although 2 per cent were established before World War II. Marketing-research departments were most common among advertising agencies (60 per cent), and manufacturers of consumer products (50 per cent) and consumer or industrial products (45 per cent). They were least likely to exist in wholesaling and retailing firms (14 per cent), a finding confirmed and elucidated by Cooley.

The median size of the marketing-research budget, as a percentage of company sales, was larger for consumer-goods manufacturers (0.14 to 0.43 per cent of sales) with industrial-goods manufacturers reporting 0.04 to 0.13 per cent of sales. Hart established that, in 1971, companies spent approximately one-third of their marketing-research budget on outside services. Bradford lists over 350 marketing research firms, falling into three major categories:[8]

1. *Full-line research firms*. These firms offer general marketing-research services. Their clients range from companies that are too small to support their own research department to large firms which subcontract a portion of their work to relieve backlog or to obtain an independent point of view.
2. *Specialty-line research firms*. These firms specialize in particular services, such as

market analysis and forecasting, survey re-search work, packaging research, product research or brand-name testing. They may also specialize in either consumer or industrial goods.

3. *Syndicated information-selling firms.* These firms specialize in gathering continuous trade or consumer data, which they sell to clients on a fee-subscription basis. Well-

known examples include A.C. Nielsen Company, Roy Morgan Research Centre, and McNair-Anderson (which leads in the provision of television and radio 'rating' data).

The scope of marketing research. Marketing-research departments have been steadily expanding their activities and techniques. Table 5-2 lists thirty different

Table 5-2   Research activities of Australian and US companies

Type of research	Companies engaged in research (%)	
	Australia	*USA*
Advertising research		
Motivation research	38	48
Copy research	36	49
Media research	44	61
Studies of ad effectiveness	57	67
Business economics and corporate research		
Short-range forecasting (up to one year)	75	85
Long-range forecasting (over one year)	70	82
Studies of business trends	66	86
Pricing studies	—	81
Plant and warehouse location studies	46	71
Product-mix studies	—	51
Acquisition studies	49	69
Export and international studies	42	51
Internal company employees studies	25	65
MIS (management information system)	—	72
Corporate responsibility research		
Consumers 'right to know' studies	—	26
Ecological impact studies	—	33
Studies of legal constraints on advertising and promotion	—	51
Social values and policies studies	—	40
Product research		
New product acceptance and potential	68	84
Competitive product studies	—	85
Testing of existing products	49	75
Sales and market research		
Measurement of market potentials	70	93
Market-share analysis	79	92
Determination of market characteristics	72	93
Sales analysis	77	89
Establishment of sales quotas, territories	63	75
Distribution channels studies	50	69
Test markets, store audits	33	54
Consumer-panel operations	24	50
Sales compensation studies	27	60
Promotional studies of premiums, coupons, sampling, deals, etc.	18	52

Source: Dik Warren Twedt (ed.), *1978 Survey of Marketing Research* (Chicago: American Marketing Association, 1978), p. 41; Lance R. Hart, 'The Status of Marketing Research in Australia' (M.Admin. thesis, Monash University, 1973), p. 120.

marketing-research activities, and the percentage of firms in Australia and the United States engaging in each. (Some of the gaps in the Australian data result from a lack of comparable definitions of the research activities rather than indicate the absence of these activities, while data were not available on corporate responsibility research.) As this table shows, the nine most common activities are determi-

nation of market characteristics, measurement of market potentials, market-share analysis, sales analysis, competitive-product studies, new-product acceptance and potential, short-range forecasting, long-range forecasting, and studies of business trends. The similarity between the Australian and US data is striking, although there may be less use in Australia of analysis of internal company operations.

These studies have benefited over the years from increasingly sophisticated techniques. Table 5-3 shows the approximate decade when various techniques began to be substantially considered or used in marketing research. Many of them – such as questionnaire construction and area sampling – evolved naturally and were quickly and widely accepted. Others – such as motivation research and mathematical methods – came in uneasily, with prolonged and heated debates among practitioners over their usefulness. But they, too, settled in the corpus of marketing research methodology – or at least the parts that stood the test of time. As for the 1980s, Green has predicted a number of new developments that have already undergone preliminary field tests:

Table 5-3   Evolving techniques in marketing research

Prior to 1910	Firsthand observation Elementary surveys
1910–20	Sales analysis Operating-cost analysis
1920–30	Questionnaire construction Survey technique
1930–40	Quota sampling Simple correlation analysis Distribution-cost analysis Store auditing techniques
1940–50	Probability sampling Regression methods Advanced statistical inference Consumer and store panels
1950–60	Motivation research Operations research Multiple regression and correlation Experimental design Attitude-measuring instruments
1960–70	Factor analysis and discriminant analysis Mathematical models Bayesian statistical analysis and decision theory Multi-dimensional scaling theory Computer data processing and analysis Marketing simulation Information storage and retrieval
1970–	Market structure analysis Product positioning analysis Econometric models Comprehensive marketing planning models Test-marketing laboratories Multi-attribute attitude and choice models

- Optical scanners for tabulating sales data at supermarkets and other retail outlets.
- Cathode ray display devices and computerized questionnaires for carrying out telephone surveys.
- New methods of combining mail surveys with telephone follow-up interviews.
- Interactive consoles (in shopping malls and other high-density locations) for automating self-administered questionnaires.
- Large computer-accessible data tapes of diary-panel members, containing demographics, product usage and other background information for studies involving pre-specified market segments.
- Controlled market testing, as already illustrated by ADTEL's split-cable television series and controlled product distribution.
- Computerized graphics for reducing huge arrays of data to meaningful graphs that can

be readily modified as market assumptions are systematically varied.

- The microprocessor and its potential for providing highly detailed data at the snap of a touch-tone telephone dial.[9]

Analytical Marketing System

The analytical marketing system consists of a set of advanced techniques for analyzing marketing data and problems, providing more findings and conclusions than could be obtained by only commonsense manipulation of the data. Large companies, such as Cadbury Schweppes, tend to make extensive use of such systems, but other companies find them too technical or too academic.

An analytical marketing system contains two sets of tools known as the statistical bank and the model bank (see Figure 5-2). The *statistical bank* is a collection of advanced statistical procedures for learning more about the relationships within a set of data and their statistical reliability. Such procedures allow management to go beyond the frequency distributions, means and standard deviations in the data. Managers often want answers to such questions as:

- What are the major variables affecting my sales, and how important is each one?

- If I raised my price 10 per cent and increased my advertising expenditures 20 per cent, what would happen to sales?
- What are the most discriminating predictors of persons who are likely to buy my brand rather than that of my competitor?
- What are the best variables for segmenting my market, and how many segments will be created?

The statistical techniques themselves are somewhat technical, and the interested reader is advised to consult other sources.[10]

The *model bank* is a collection of models that will help marketers develop better marketing decisions. Each model consists of a set of interrelated variables that represent some real system, process or outcome and can help answer the questions 'what if?' and 'which is best?'. In the last twenty years, marketing scientists have developed a great number of models to help marketing executives do a better job of pricing, designing sales territories and sales-call plans, selecting sites for retail outlets, developing optimal advertising media mixes, developing optimal advertising budgets and forecasting new-product sales. Here are examples of some models in current use:

- A new-product manager can sit down at a computer terminal, dial a new-product programme called Sprinter III, and type in

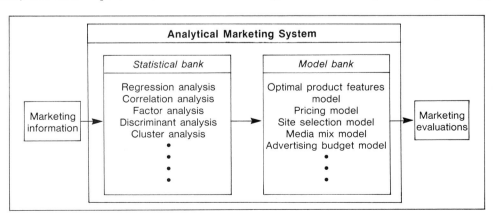

Figure 5-2   Analytical marketing system

various estimates as they are called for by the computer. These may include the estimated size of the target group, recent product-trial rates, repeat-purchase rates, the promotional budget, size of investment, target rate of return, product price, and gross profit margin. The computer will digest this information and print out a monthly forecast for the next few years of the total number of buyers, company market share, period profits, and discounted cumulative profits. The new-product manager can change the estimates to see their effect on sales and profits.[11]

- An advertising manager can dial a media-selection programme called MEDIAC and type in information on the size of the advertising budget, the number and size of important market segments, media exposure and cost data, advertisement size and colour data, sales seasonality and other information. The computer will then recommend a media schedule that is calculated to achieve maximum exposure and sales impact in the customer segments.[12]

- A sales manager can dial a sales-redistricting programme, type in data on workload and/or sales potential of various regions, their distances from each other and the number of desired territories. The computer will digest this information and assign various regions, to make up new sales territories in such a way that: (i) the sales territories are approximately equal in workload and/or sales potential; and (ii) the sales territories are compact in shape, thus cutting down travel costs.[13]

- A marketing executive can dial a dealer site-location programme, type in a proposed location and size for a new dealership in a large city, and receive a forecast of its sales and market share and the loss of sales to other dealerships.[14]

MARKETING RESEARCH PROCEDURE

Almost every marketer will occasionally need marketing research. In a large consumer-packaged-goods company like Reckitt & Colman, a brand manager will probably commission several research studies annually; smaller companies will undoubtedly utilize fewer studies. Administrators of non-profit organizations are increasingly finding that they need marketing research, such as when a hospital wants to know whether people in its service area have a positive attitude toward the hospital, or when a university or college wants to determine its image among secondary-school student advisers, or when a political organization wants to find out what voters think of its policies versus other policies.

The challenge facing managers who need marketing research is to know enough about both its potential and its limitations to obtain the right information at a reasonable cost and use it intelligently. If they know nothing about marketing research, they might allow the wrong information to be collected, or collected too expensively, or interpreted incorrectly. One protection against this is to work only with highly experienced and credible marketing researchers and agencies because it is in their interest to do a good job and produce information that leads to correct decisions. An equally important protection is that managers should know enough about marketing research procedure to assist in its planning and in the interpretation of results.

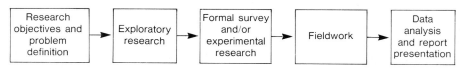

Figure 5-3 The marketing research process

This section will describe the five basic steps involved in good marketing research (see Figure 5-3). We will illustrate these steps in connection with a specific situation.

In November 1980, Australian consumer affairs ministers established an inquiry into computerized supermarket-checkout systems. Of primary concern to the governments was the possible impact on consumers of changes which might occur when Australian Product Number (APN) scanning systems were introduced.

The technological basis of APN scanning systems is the assignment of a unique APN identification number to each consumer product, and the printing of this number in the form of a bar-code symbol on the label or package. At the retail checkout, the shop assistant passes each package over a slot scanner (or built-in light pen). An in-store computer interprets the symbol, looks up the price and item description, and transmits this back to an electronic cash register at the checkout. The price and description are then displayed to the customer and printed on a detailed receipt tape.

APN scanning systems can provide, directly or indirectly, many benefits for consumers, such as faster checkout, fewer errors at the checkout, an elaborated receipt tape, an improved visual display at the checkstand, opportunities for more personalized services, and a better availability of products.

The benefits available to retailers include improved checkout productivity and accuracy. Probably most important in the longer term are the additional benefits derived from the sales data captured by the computer. Manufacturers as well as retailers can track sales more easily than with the previous methods of store audits or warehouse withdrawals.[15]

From a technological viewpoint, it is not necessary to price-mark each individual item if APN scanning is operating and if each product carries an APN symbol. This innovation has obvious economic implications in terms of the resources released from the activity of price-marking. However, questions have arisen from some sources regarding the implications, for consumer behaviour and welfare, of the cessation of item price-marking.

The government inquiry was expected to focus on the importance to consumers of item price-marking, and was empowered to make recommendations about the desirability of legislation to compel retailers to stamp a price on every package. Clearly, mandatory item price-marking would involve unnecessary costs to retailers and hence reduce the economic viability of installing APN scanning systems. This would lead to fewer stores with scanning, and less 'scandata' information being available to manufacturers.

The industry association sponsoring the introduction of APN, the Australian Product Number Association Limited (APNA), decided to make a submission to the government inquiry based on the best available marketing research data. The Roy Morgan Research Centre was retained to assist APNA.

Research Objectives and Problem Definition

The first step in research is to define the research objectives. These may be to learn more about a market, to find a practical way to increase sales, or to find data to support or refute a strongly held viewpoint. Defining the research objectives makes it easier to arrive at a useful definition of the problem. If the problem is stated vaguely, if the wrong problem is defined, or if the uses of the research are not made clear, then the results may prove useless.

The marketing researchers working on the APNA case defined the objective as being able to demonstrate to the government inquiry that APN scanning was a positive innovation with general acceptance, and that item price-marking was not an issue requiring immediate legislation. Coincidentally, the first Australian supermarket with an APN scanning system had opened one month earlier, and the store management had decided not to price-mark most products (relying on shelf price-marking). This store would provide a concrete local example for research, although the vast majority of Australian shoppers would have had virtually no experience of the system.

Exploratory Research

Exploratory research means carrying out a number of informal procedures to learn more about the market before any final research is done. The major procedures at this stage include collecting secondary data, doing observational research, and conducting informal interviews with individuals and groups.

Secondary data research. In seeking information, a researcher can gather secondary data, primary data, or both. Primary data consist of originally collected data for the specific purpose at hand; secondary data are those that already exist somewhere, having been collected for another purpose. If the right secondary data exist, the researcher should prefer them because they can normally be obtained more quickly and less expensively.

In looking for secondary data, the APNA investigators can consult the following seven major sources of secondary data:

1. *Internal company records.* The researchers should check APNA's files for relevant local reports and for studies illustrating international experiences and reactions.
2. *Government.* The major government source of data is the Australian Bureau of Statistics, which publishes thousands of periodic statistical bulletins including the *Year Book*. Retailing data, especially regarding trends in supermarket shopping, would interest APNA.
3. *Trade, professional and business associations.* The researchers should check with the Aus-

tralian Retailers Association and the shop assistants' union to seek information on shopping patterns and employment aspects.

4. *Private business firms.* The suppliers of APN scanning systems (such as NCR and IBM) and other interested organizations should be approached, particularly because of their affiliates' experience overseas, where scanning had begun in 1974.

5. *Marketing firms.* Marketing research firms, advertising agencies and media firms (newspaper and magazine publishers, radio and television broadcasters) may possess useful studies of supermarket consumers, perhaps revealing where shoppers look for price information.

6. *Universities, research organizations and foundations.* These organizations are often a good source of secondary data. For example, grocery shoppers have been studied at Chisholm Institute of Technology[16] and Monash University.[17]

7. *Published sources.* Much marketing information can be found in books, journals, magazines and newspapers. Favoured marketing journals include the *Journal of Marketing, Journal of Marketing Research, Journal of Consumer Research, Journal of Retailing, Australian Marketing Researcher* and *Journal of Australian Marketing, Advertising, Communication.* Useful general business magazines include *Rydge's In Marketing, Rydge's, Business Review Weekly, Australian Business, Advertising News,* and *B & T Weekly.* The APNA researchers will also consult trade magazines such as *Foodweek* and *Retail World,* and newspapers such as the *Australian Financial Review.* Published sources make a library the most rewarding one-stop shopping centre for secondary data, especially those with indexing systems such as the Australian Public Affairs Information Service, and the Business Periodicals Index.

If good ideas and findings come from secondary data, this is fine. However, the researcher must be careful to evaluate the secondary data, since they were collected for a variety of purposes and under a variety of conditions that may limit their usefulness. Marketing researchers should check these data for relevance, impartiality, validity, and reliability.

Observation. Personal observation is another exploratory procedure: APNA researchers, for example, might linger in supermarkets and listen to shoppers talking about the different operations; they might shop at stores with different price-marking and checkout practices to observe any difficulties and the service. These and similar studies may suggest some interesting new ideas for APNA to consider.

Casual interviewing. The researchers can talk casually to various people – consumers, checkout staff and others – about shopping to obtain their impressions of the various approaches. At this stage they can do this by striking up conversation rather than conducting a formal interview.

Focus-group interviewing. This is one of the most useful exploratory research steps. From six to ten persons who are typical of the target market are invited to meet to discuss a product – whether a good or a service, an organization, or other marketing entity. A trained leader probes the group's feelings and behaviour toward the entity, encouraging as much free discussion as possible. The comments are recorded, and subsequently examined by marketing executives. Several focus-group interviews might be held to sample the thinking of different market segments. The findings do not have the validity of a true sample, but they do provide the basis of an effective questionnaire for a subsequent formal survey of the market.[18]

Formal Surveys

The role of exploratory research is to produce a much better understanding of the problem and of what needs to be measured formally. At this stage, various hypotheses can be formed and tested. Suppose the APNA researchers noted, through exploratory research, that many supermarket customers said that their major frustrations were slow checkouts, being overcharged and having difficulty reading the receipt tape, waiting for 'price checks' at the checkout, and finding that the store had run out of products on the shelves. Suppose also that shoppers revealed little tendency to compare the prices of similar products in different parts of the store (e.g. canned beans versus frozen beans). The researchers could see the possibility of consumers appreciating the benefits of APN scanning, and it seemed that the need for portable price information within the store was low. But how would shoppers feel about relying on shelf price-marking only (without item price-marking)? Would they shop at a 'prices-off' store, and would 'price awareness' decrease if they did so?

At this point the marketing researcher can proceed to design a survey research project, an experimental research project, or both. We will describe survey research in this section and experimental research in the next section.

Many managers take an overly simplistic view of survey work. They think that it consists of constructing a few obvious questions and finding an adequate number of people in the target market to answer them. The fact is that amateur research is liable to incur many errors; designing a reliable survey is definitely a job for a professional marketing researcher. However, users of marketing research should know the fundamentals of developing the research instrument, the sampling plan and the fieldwork.

Research instrument. The main research instrument is the questionnaire. The construction of a good questionnaire calls for considerable skill. Every questionnaire should be pre-tested on a pilot sample of persons before being used on a large scale. A professional marketing researcher can usually spot several errors in a casually prepared questionnaire (see Exhibit 5-1).

A common error is that of the *types* of question asked: the inclusion of questions that cannot be answered, would not be answered or need not be answered, and the omission of others that should be answered. Each question should be checked to determine whether it is

necessary in terms of the research objectives. Those that are merely interesting should be dropped because they lengthen the time required and try the respondent's patience.

The *form* of questions can make a substantial difference to the response. An open-ended question is one that the respondent is free to answer in his own words (e.g. 'What is your opinion of supermarket shopping?'). A closed-ended question is one in which the possible answers are supplied: the respondent may be asked to answer in one of two ways (dichotomous questions), to answer in one of several

Exhibit 5-1   A Questionable Questionnaire

Suppose the following questionnaire had been prepared by a beer company brand manager who needed data quickly at a time when the company's marketing researcher was on holiday. How would you feel about each question?

1. What is your income to the nearest hundred dollars?
2. Are you a heavy or light beer-drinker?
3. Do you ever get drunk? Yes (   ) No (   )
4. How much beer did you drink in January last year? In January of this year?
5. What TV programmes did you watch last Monday week?
6. What other concoctions do you favour?
7. Do you think it is right to buy foreign beer and put Australians out of work?

Comments:

1. People do not necessarily know their income to the nearest hundred dollars, nor may they want to reveal their income that closely. Furthermore, a questionnaire should never open with such a personal question.
2. What do 'heavy' and 'light' mean in consumption per week? Would anyone want to admit to being a heavy drinker?
3. 'Drunk' is a relative term. Besides, will people admit it? Furthermore, is yes or no the best way to allow a response to the question? Why is the question being asked in the first place?
4. Who is likely to remember this?
5. Who is likely to remember this? The important point is the programmes the person *normally* watches.
6. What is a 'concoction'? Don't use big words on me.
7. Loaded question. How can one answer yes, given the bias?

ways (multiple-choice questions), to place marks along a scale (scaling questions), and so forth. The choice between open-ended and close-ended questions affects the thoughtfulness of responses, the costs of interviewing and the quality of analysis.

The choice of words also calls for considerable care. The researcher should strive for simple, direct, unambiguous and unbiased wording. It is important that the questions be pre-tested on a sample of respondents before they are used on a wide scale.

Other 'dos' and 'don'ts' arise in connection with the *sequencing* of questions. The lead questions should create interest, if possible (open-ended questions are usually better here). Difficult or personal questions should be used toward the end of the interview, so that an emotional reaction will not affect subsequent answers or cause the respondent to break off the interview. To avoid confusing the respondent, the questions should be asked in as logical an order as possible. Data classifying the respondent are usually asked for last because they tend to be less interesting and are relatively personal.

Sampling plan. Designing formal surveys also includes a sampling plan, which calls for four decisions:

1. *Who is to be surveyed?* The proper sampling unit is not always obvious from the nature of the information sought. In the APNA survey to find out consumer reactions to APN scanning systems, should the sampling unit be the shoppers at the lone scanning store, shoppers at other non-scanning supermarkets in the area, shoppers in other areas, or some combination of the three? Where the roles of instigators, influencers, deciders, users and/or purchasers of a 'product' are not combined in one person, the researcher must determine not only what information is needed but also who is most likely to have it.

2. *How many people should be surveyed?* Large samples obviously give more reliable results than small samples, but it is not necessary to sample the entire target market or even a substantial part of it to achieve satisfactory precision. Samples amounting to less than a small fraction of one per cent of a population can often provide good reliability, given a creditable sampling procedure.

3. *How should the respondents be chosen?* To draw valid and reliable inferences about the target market, a random sample of the population should be drawn. Random sampling allows the calculation of confidence limits for sampling error, e.g. 'The chances are ninety-five in 100 that the interval "five to seven trips per month" contains the true number of shopping trips made by regular customers of the scanning store.' But random sampling is almost always more costly than non-random sampling, and some marketing researchers feel that the extra expenditure for probability sampling could be put to better use, i.e. a larger proportion of a fixed research budget could be spent in designing better questionnaires and hiring better interviewers to reduce response and non-sampling errors, which can be just as fatal as sampling errors. This is a real issue, one that the marketing researchers and marketing executives must weigh carefully.

4. *How should the subject be contacted?* The options are telephone, mail or personal interviews. Telephone interviewing is the best method for gathering information quickly, and permits the interviewer to clarify questions if they are not understood. Its two main drawbacks are that only people with telephones can be interviewed, and only short not-too-personal interviews can be carried out. A mail questionnaire may be the best way to reach persons who would not give personal interviews or who might be biased by interviewers. These do, on the

other hand, require simple and clearly worded questions, and the return rate is usually low and/or slow. Personal interviewing is the most versatile of the three methods, in that more questions can be asked and the interview supplemented with personal observations. Personal interviewing is the most expensive method, however, and requires more technical and administrative planning and supervision.

Fieldwork. After the research design has been determined, the research department must supervise (or subcontract) the task of collecting the data. This phase is generally the most expensive and the most liable to error. There are four major potential problems:

1. *Respondent unavailable.* When the respondent is not at home or at work, the interviewer must either call back later or find a substitute.
2. *Refusal to cooperate.* If this is the case, the interviewer must find ways of encouraging the respondent to assist.
3. *Respondent bias.* The interviewer must encourage accurate and thoughtful answers.
4. *Interviewer bias.* Interviewers are capable of introducing a variety of biases into the interviewing process, through the mere fact of their age, sex, manner or intonation. There is also the problem of conscious interviewer bias or dishonesty.

Experimental Research

We have discussed research design in its most common form, that of designing a survey. An increasing number of marketing researchers are eager to go beyond measuring the opinions and intentions of a target market and are seeking to measure actual cause-and-effect relationships. For example, the APNA researchers might like to know answers to such questions as:

- Are shoppers more aware of prices when

they shop in a store with individual item price-marking rather than shelf price-marking only?
- Do shoppers compare the prices of products in different locations within a supermarket?
- Do shoppers check the prices marked on products against the prices shown on their receipt tapes, after they have left the store?

Each of these questions could be answered by the survey method, but respondents may not give their true opinions or carry them out. Experimental research is more rigorous, in that situations are created where the actual behaviour of the target market can be observed and the causes determined.

Let us apply the experimental method to the first question. We have already established that one supermarket has installed the APN scanning system and has no price-marked items. Suppose APNA identifies a similar supermarket, but one which has no scanning system and thus has 'prices on'. The researchers could now interview shoppers in each store, asking them to estimate the prices of products which they have in their trolleys at the checkout (while covering any price-marks, of course). The researchers could agree that estimates within 10 per cent of the actual prices are taken to be correct, and compare the frequency of this price awareness between the two stores. Any conclusions drawn about the impact of item price-marking would have to be tentative unless all possible alternative hypotheses to explain any differences could be dismissed. For example, one store may have a higher proportion of customers from lower socio-economic groups, who may be more aware of prices.

The experimental method is being increasingly recognized in marketing circles as the most rigorous and conclusive one, if the proper controls can be exercised and the cost is reasonable. The method requires selecting matched groups of subjects, giving them different treatments, controlling extraneous variables, and assessing the statistical significance of observed differences. To the extent that the design and execution of the experiment eliminates alternative explanations of the results, the research and marketing managers can have confidence in the conclusions.[19]

Data Analysis and Report Presentation

The last step in survey research is to extract pertinent information and findings from the data to present to management. The researcher tabulates the data and develops one-way and two-way frequency distributions. Averages and measures of dispersion are computed for the major variables. The researcher will attempt to apply advanced statistical techniques and decision models in the hope of additional findings.

The researcher's purpose is not to overwhelm members of management with numbers and fancy statistical techniques – this will lose them – but to present major findings that are relevant and can resolve the major issues that gave rise to the study.[20] Marketing research should reduce the amount of uncertainty facing marketing executives (see Exhibit 5-2).

MEASUREMENT OF MARKET DEMAND

Marketing research is carried on for the many purposes shown in Table 5-2. Two important research activities will be examined in the remainder of this chapter. One is the recurrent need of marketing managers to measure current market demand for a given product: according to Table 5-2, more than 70 per cent of all companies engage in the measurement of market potentials. The other research activity, which we will look at in the following section, involves market and sales forecasting, which is carried out by over 75 per cent of all companies.

Key Concepts in Market-demand Measurement

Many different terms are used by businesspeople to describe market demand. Before approaching the question of how a manager can estimate market demand, we want to develop a uniform set of definitions for the following terms: market demand, market forecast, market potential, company demand, company sales forecast, and company potential.

Market demand. In evaluating marketing opportunities, the first step is to estimate market demand, which we define as follows:

* *Market demand* for a product is the total volume that would be bought by a defined customer group in a defined geographical area in a defined time period in a defined marketing environment under a defined marketing programme.

There are eight elements in this definition.

Product. Market-demand measurement requires careful definition of the product class boundaries. A company that manufactures steel cans has to specify whether its market consists of metal-can users or all container users. This depends on the degree of substitutability between items in the smaller and larger product class.

Total volume. Market demand can be measured in terms of physical volume, dollar volume or relative volume. The Australian market demand for soft-drinks may be described as either one billion litres or more than $600 million per year; the market demand for soft-drinks in Sydney and Melbourne may be expressed as 40 per cent of the nation's total demand.

Bought. In measuring market demand, it is important to define whether 'bought' means the volume ordered, shipped, paid for, received or consumed. For example, a forecast

Exhibit 5-2 Marketing Managers and Marketing Researchers: A Clash of Cultures?

One would think that marketing managers would flock to marketing researchers to find needed information. But the facts are otherwise. There are too many marketing managers who do not use marketing research, or use it too rarely. Is it that they would rather spend the money on selling and other promotional effort than on knowing more about the market? Clearly, the more they know about the market, the better they can spend their money. Several factors operate to keep the relationship from becoming more productive:

- *Intellectual differences.* Differences in the mental styles of line managers and researchers often get in the way of productive relationships. All too often the marketing researcher's report seems too academic, complicated and tentative, whereas the manager wants concreteness, simplicity and certainty.
- *A narrow conception of marketing research.* Many executives see marketing research as only a fact-finding operation. The marketing researcher is expected to design a questionnaire, choose a sample, carry out interviews and report results, often without being given a careful definition of the problem or of the decision alternatives before management. As a result some of the fact-finding fails to be useful, which reinforces management's idea of the limited good that can come from marketing research.
- *Uneven calibre of marketing researchers.* Some companies view marketing research as little more than a clerical activity and reward it as such. In these cases, less-able individuals are attracted whose deficient training and creativity are reflected in their output. Disappointing output reinforces management's prejudice against expecting too much from marketing research. Management continues to pay low salaries, perpetuating the basic difficulty.
- *Late results.* Marketing research that is carefully designed may take a long time to carry out. Often the report is ready after the decision has had to be made, or when the issue has become less salient to the executives.
- *Erroneous findings by marketing research.* Many executives want conclusive information from marketing research, although the processes do not usually yield more than probabilities. The problem is complicated by the low budgets often given to marketing researchers to get the information. Executives are disappointed, and are apt to think that marketing research is not really worthwhile. Clearly, marketing managers and marketing researchers have to be educated about the other party's needs and capabilities.

of new housing for the next year usually means the number of units that will be ordered, not completed (called housing starts).

Customer group. Market demand may be measured for the whole market or for any segment(s). Thus a steel producer may estimate separately the volume to be bought by the construction industry and by the transport industry.

Geographical area. Market demand should be measured with references to well-defined geographical boundaries. A forecast of next year's car sales will vary depending upon whether the boundaries are limited to Australia or include New Zealand and/or other export markets.

Time period. Market demand should be measured with reference to a stated period of time. Thus market demand could indicate the next calendar year, the next five years, or the year 2000.

Marketing environment. Market demand is affected by a host of uncontrollable factors. Every forecast of demand should explicitly list the assumptions made about the demographic, economic, ecological, technological, political and cultural environment.

Marketing programme. Market demand is also affected by factors controlled by sellers. In most markets it will show some elasticity with respect to industry price, promotion, product improvements and distribution effort and thus a forecast requires assumptions about these factors.

The most important thing to realize about market demand is that it is not a single number, but a *function.* For this reason it is also called the market-demand or market-response function. The functional nature of market demand is shown in Figure 5-4. The market-demand function in Figure 5-4a is shown as a curve that rises with higher levels of industry marketing expenditure. (The curve is defined for a given marketing environment.) It should be noted that this curve is not a picture of market demand over time, but rather shows forecasts of demand associated with possible levels of industry marketing effort in the *current* period.

The shape of the curve has to be determined for each market. The curve in this illustration has the familiar S-shape, suggesting that market demand shows first increasing and then diminishing sales response to increased industry marketing expenditure. Some base sales, the *market minimum*, would take place without any demand-stimulating marketing expenditures by the industry; positive marketing expenditures will yield increasing, then decreasing, returns; still higher expenditures would not stimulate much further demand, thus suggesting an upper limit to market demand (the *market potential*).

The distance between the market minimum and the market potential shows the overall marketing sensitivity of demand in that industry. We can think of two extreme types of market, the expandable and the non-expandable. The total size of an expandable

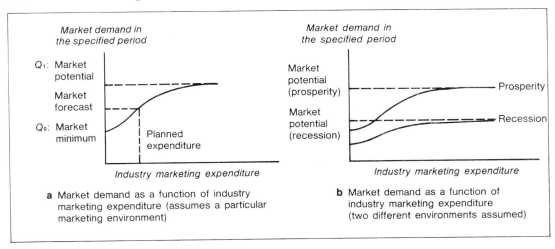

a Market demand as a function of industry marketing expenditure (assumes a particular marketing environment)

b Market demand as a function of industry marketing expenditure (two different environments assumed)

Figure 5-4 Market demand

market (such as one for a new product) is quite affected by the level of marketing expenditure; in terms of Figure 5-4a, the distance between Q_0 and Q_1 is relatively large. A non-expandable market (e.g. cigarettes or steel) is not much affected by the level of marketing expenditures; the distance between Q_0 and Q_1 is relatively small. A firm selling in a non-expandable market can take the market's size (the level of primary demand) for granted and concentrate its marketing resources on getting a desired market share (the level of selective demand).

Market forecast. Only one of the many possible levels of industry marketing expenditure will actually occur. The market demand corresponding to the planned expenditure is called the market forecast. The market forecast shows the expected market demand for the planned marketing expenditure and the given environment.

Market potential. The market forecast shows the expected, not the highest possible, market demand. For the latter, we have to visualize the level of market demand for a 'very high' level of industry marketing expenditure, where further increases in expenditure would do little to stimulate demand. *Market potential* is the limit approached by market demand as industry marketing expenditure increases to infinity, for a given set of competitive prices and a given environment.

Market potential is always defined for a given set of competitive prices. If all prices went to zero, we could ask how many units the market would acquire of the free good. We would call this the market capacity. The market potential is always less than the market capacity. The phrase 'for the given environment' is also crucial in the concept of market potential. The market potential for cars is higher during prosperity than during a recession because market demand is income-elastic. The dependence of market potential on the environment is illustrated in Figure 5-4b.

Company demand. We are now ready to define company demand, i.e. the company's sales resulting from its share of market demand. Company demand, like market demand, is a function – called the company-demand or sales-response function – and is subject to all the determinants of market demand plus whatever influences the company's share of the market.

The company's market share is influenced by the following:

1. The price of its product(s) in relation to competitors.
2. Its total marketing expenditure in relation to competitors.
3. Its marketing mix in relation to competitors.
4. Its allocation of funds to products and territories.
5. Its efficiency in spending marketing funds.

Management scientists have built these factors into mathematical models of market-share determination to be used by companies to help set their marketing strategies.[21]

Company sales forecast. Company demand describes estimated company sales as alternative levels of company marketing expenditure and price. It remains for management to set its marketing decision variables. These variables will imply a particular level of sales: the company sales forecast is the expected level of company sales based on a chosen marketing plan and assumed marketing environment.

Too often the sequential relationship between the company sales forecast and the company marketing plan is confused. One frequently hears that the company should plan its marketing effort on the basis of its sales forecast. This sequence is valid if forecast sales are unaffected (or minimally affected) by company marketing expenditures, but not if market demand is expandable. The company sales forecast is rather the *result* of an assumed blueprint for marketing action: it must be viewed as a dependent variable that is affected, among other things, by the planned marketing activity of the firm.

Two other concepts – sales quota and sales budget – are worth mentioning in relation to the company sales forecast. A sales quota is a sales goal set for a product line, company division or sales representative. It is primarily a managerial tool for defining and stimulating sales effort, and is arrived at through consideration of the sales forecast. In order to stimulate achievement of the forecast, sales quotas are generally at a slightly higher figure.

The other concept is a sales budget. A sales budget is a conservative estimate of the expected volume of sales and is used primarily for making current decisions about purchasing, production, and cash flow. The sales budget takes account of both the sales forecast and the need to avoid excessive investment in case the forecast is not realized, and thus is generally set slightly lower than the forecast.

Company potential. Company sales potential is the limit approached by company demand as company marketing expenditure increases in relation to competitors. The absolute limit of company demand is, of course, the market potential: the two would be equal if the company achieved 100 per cent of the market, i.e. achieved a monopoly. In most cases company sales potential is less than market potential, even when a company's marketing expenditures increase considerably over those of competitors, because each competitor has a hard core of loyal buyers who are not very responsive to other companies' efforts to woo them away.

Methods of Estimating Current Demand

We are now ready to consider practical methods of estimating current demand. There are two types of estimate in which a seller might be interested: total market potential and territorial potential. Total market potential is

of interest when a seller is facing a decision to introduce a new product or drop an existing one, and wants to know whether the total size of the market is sufficient to justify the company's participation.

Total market potential. Total market potential is the maximum amount of sales (in units or dollars) that might be available to all the firms in an industry during a given period under a given level of industry marketing expenditures and given environmental conditions. A common way to estimate this is as follows:

$$Q = n \times q \times p \qquad (5\text{-}1)$$

where Q = total market potential
n = number of buyers in the specific product market under the given assumptions
q = quantity purchased by an average buyer
p = price of an average unit

Thus, if there are 5 600 000 buyers of books each year, whose purchases average three books a year at an average price of $4, then the total market potential for books is approximately $67 200 000 (= 5 600 000 × 3 × 4).

A variation on Formula 5-1 is known as the chain ratio method. This is based on the notion that it may be easier to estimate the separate components of a magnitude than the magnitude directly. Consider the following example.

The Australian navy seeks to attract new male recruits each year, mainly from secondary schools. The question is, what is a reasonable target in relation to the market potential? The market potential has been estimated by using the following chain ratio method:

Total number of male secondary
   school students aged 16 years
   or over   120 000

Percentage who are militarily
qualified (no physical,
emotional or mental
handicaps)   × .50
Percentage of those qualified
who are potentially interested
in military service   × .15
Percentage of those qualified
and interested in joining
the armed forces, who would
prefer the navy   × .30

This chain of numbers shows the market potential to be 2700 recruits. The target would be set lower to recognize the unlikely conversion of all 'prospects' to actual recruits.

Territorial potentials. All companies are concerned with: (i) selecting the markets to sell in; (ii) allocating their marketing budget optimally among these markets; and (iii) evaluating their performance in the different markets. The basis for these decisions lies in competent estimation of the market potential of different territories. The methods used are essentially extensions of Equation 5-1, now applied at the territory level rather than that of the overall market. One common method, used by both industrial and consumer-goods firms, is the market build-up method (discussed below). Another approach is to use either Australian Bureau of Statistics data or such syndicated services as are offered by A.C. Nielsen and Company.

Nielsen. The Nielsen company provides estimates of the current market size, in both units and dollars, for products sold in the following markets: food stores, confectionery, cigarettes and tobacco, take-away package liquor, and pharmacy. In each of these markets, Nielsen gathers data from a selection of outlets held to be a statistically reliable sample of the entire population of outlets. At each outlet sampled, consumer offtake is measured by adding store purchases to net inventory change over a two-month period: aggregating these over all outlets provides a measure of total consumer purchases. In each of the above

five market areas, data are provided on sales of a number of product forms, such as razor blades, cereals, etc.: this information includes size of the market in units and dollars, the market shares of different brands and pack sizes, the levels of distribution of the brands, their retail selling price, and trends. While such an approach focuses on the current market and its trends, it is a useful starting point for estimating market potential.

Market build-up method. The market build-up method calls for identifying all the potential buyers of the product in each market and adding the estimated potential purchases of each. This is a straightforward method if one has a list of all potential buyers and a good estimate of what each will buy; unfortunately, however, one if not both is usually lacking.

Consider the problem faced by the manufacturer of power saws used to cut metal sections, such as steel or aluminium, to length. Suppose it wants to estimate territory potential in New South Wales. The first step is to identify all potential buyers of saws in New South Wales. The saw is too large for home-workshop purchase, so household buyers can be excluded: the market is primarily in manufacturing establishments, in particular, manufacturing fabricators, those establishments which buy steel or aluminium sections in bulk and manufacture steel roof trusses, aluminium doors, and so on.

To estimate the territorial market potential, use can be made of the Australian Standard Industrial Classification (ASIC).[22] This system has been developed by the Australian Bureau of Statistics as a method for classifying establishments by industry. An establishment is defined as an individual unit (shop, factory, etc.) carrying out all its operations at a single physical location: these are then classified on the basis of their major activity, and the classes, in turn, are combined on a number of broader levels. At the highest level, all establishments in Australia are classified into twelve divisions – agriculture, mining, manufacturing, finance, community services, etc. – which are then broken down into subdivisions, groups and finally classes.

For each ASIC class, the Bureau of Statistics provides the number of establishments classified by location, together with data on number of employees, value added, wages and salaries, turnover, fixed capital expenditure, etc.

Our saw manufacturer must then determine the ASIC classes that represent products whose manufacture is likely to require power saws. Suppose these are manufacturing (Division C) sub-division 31 (fabricated metal products), classes 3111 (fabricated structural steel), 3112 (architectural aluminium products) and 3133 (nuts, bolts, screws and rivets). To get a full picture of all ASIC classes that might use saws, the company can use three methods: (i) look at past sales and determine the ASIC codes of the past customers; (ii) go through the ASIC manual and check off all the classes judged to have an interest in saws; (iii) mail questionnaires to a wide range of companies to inquire about their interest in saws.

Once the company identifies the ASIC classes relevant to its product, its next step is to determine an appropriate base for estimating the number of saws likely to be used by the firms in each class. Suppose it decides that customer value added is the most appropriate base. For example, in ASIC classes 3111 and 3133 ten saws are used for every million dollars of value added, while in class 3112 eight saws are used for every million dollars of value added. Once the company is able to establish the rate of saw ownership relative to the customer industry's value added (or number of employees, or turnover, or fixed capital expenditures, or whatever), it can calculate the market potential.

Table 5-4 shows a hypothetical computation for New South Wales involving three ASIC classes. The company can use a similar method to estimate the market potential for other territories. Suppose the market potentials for all markets sum to 3070 saws. In this case the company concludes that the New South Wales market contains 40 per cent of the total market potential. Without further qualification, this might warrant a 40 per cent allocation of marketing effort (sales force, advertising, and so on) to the New South Wales market. In practice, however, the saw manufacturer should determine additional factors such as the extent of market saturation, the number of competitors, the market growth rate and the average age of the equipment in use – before actually deciding on the amount of resources to allocate to each market.

MARKET AND SALES FORECASTING

Having looked at ways to estimate current demand, we are now ready to examine the problem of forecasting future demand. Very few products or services lend themselves to easy forecasting – such cases generally involve a

Table 5-4 **Market build-up method using ASIC codes (hypothetical saw manufacturer, NSW)**

ASIC Code	No. of establishments	Value added ($m)	Potential no. of saws per $1m of value added	Market potential
3111	244	73.8	10	738
3112	108	38.2	8	306
3133	48	18.4	10	184
				1228

product whose absolute level or trend is fairly constant, and a situation where competitive relations are virtually non-existent (public utilities) or stable (pure oligopolies). More commonly neither market demand nor, in particular, company demand is stable from one year to the next, and good forecasting becomes a key factor in company success. Poor forecasting can lead to overly large inventories, costly price mark-downs, or lost sales due to being out of stock. The more unstable the demand, the more critical is forecast accuracy and the more elaborate the procedure. We will examine six major methods of forecasting demand.

Surveys of Buyer Intentions

Forecasting is the art of anticipating what buyers are likely to do under a given set of conditions, which suggests that a most useful source of information would be the buyers themselves. This is especially true if the buyers have clearly formulated intentions, will carry them out, and will describe them to interviewers. In regard to major consumer durables such as cars, new housing and appliances, the University of Melbourne Institute of Applied Economic and Social Research produces quarterly reports on consumer buying intentions.

With rising incomes over the past few decades, consumers have gained a large degree of discretion over how they spend their income. Spending decisions depend not only on ability to buy but also willingness to buy: measures of consumer sentiment and expectations provide advance indications of changes in consumer spending behaviour and, especially, of the turning points in their expenditure on durable goods.

The institute's survey utilizes a sample of about 2200 consumers, Australia-wide, who are selected and interviewed by the Roy Morgan Research Centre. Respondents are asked a series of questions relating to their buying intentions for a range of products (such as colour television, refrigerators, dishwashers, new cars, new houses, etc). For each product, respondents are asked to indicate the probability that they, or their family, will purchase the product during the next twelve months. The scale used for this is:

1. Almost certain.
2. Better than even chance.
3. Even chance.
4. Worse than even chance.
5. Very unlikely.

These results are then aggregated to show the proportion of spending units intending to buy the particular product during the next twelve months. Consumers are also asked about their personal situation and their future expectations on prices, unemployment, inflation, etc., which are summarized in an index of consumer sentiment. Many producers of consumer durables subscribe to the service in the hope of learning in advance of major shifts in buying intentions so that they can adjust their manufacturing and marketing plans accordingly. This survey has proved useful in predicting future demand for these products.

The appropriateness of this survey method increases to the extent that (i) the buyers are few; (ii) the cost of effectively reaching them is small; (iii) they have clear intentions; (iv) they follow their original intentions; and (v) they are willing to disclose their intentions. As a result, it is of value for industrial products, for consumer durables, for product purchases where advanced planning is required, and for new products where past data do not exist.

In the realm of industrial buying, intention surveys regarding plant, equipment and materials have been carried out by various organizations. The best-known capital-expenditure survey is the one conducted by the Australian Bureau of Statistics. Other surveys, such as that conducted by the Confederation of Australian Industry and Westpac, examine the status of operations and the degree of optimism among a sample of several hundred manufacturers.

Composites of Sales-force Opinions

Where is it impractical to make direct buyer inquiries, the company may decide to ask its sales representatives for estimates. Few sales-force estimates are used without some adjustments, however. In the first place, sales representatives are biased observers – they may be congenitally pessimistic or optimistic, or may be influenced by a recent sales setback or success. Furthermore, they are often unaware of larger economic developments and do not know whether their company's marketing plans will influence future sales in their territory; they may understate demand so that the company will set a low sales quota.[23] They may not have the time to prepare careful estimates, or may not consider it worthwhile to do so.

Assuming these tendencies can be countered, a number of benefits may be gained by involving the sales force in forecasting. First, because of their closer contact with customers they may have more knowledge of, or better insight into, developing trends than any other group. This is especially likely where the product is fairly technical and is subject to changing technology. Second, because of their participation in the forecasting process, sales representatives may have greater confidence in the resulting sales quotas and thus greater motivation to achieve them. Finally, grassroots forecasting results in estimates broken down by product, territory, customer and sales representative. (Motor-vehicle companies gather sales estimates directly from their dealers, which are thus subject to the same strengths and weaknesses as sales-force estimates.)

Firms sometimes resort to outside experts for estimates of future demand: these may be general economic forecasts, special industry forecasts, or estimates of probabilities in areas such as new technology or changing business conditions.

There are at least three ways to gather the judgments of a group of experts. They may meet as a committee and come up with a group estimate (group discussion method). They may supply separate estimates to a project leader who merges these into a single estimate (pooled individual estimates method). Or they may supply individual estimates and assumptions that are reviewed and revised by the project leader, followed by a second round of individual estimation, a third round, and so forth, until the assumptions and estimates converge (Delphi method). The third approach is becoming increasingly popular for developing market and technological forecasts.[24]

Market-test Method

In cases where buyers do not plan their purchases carefully, or carry out their intentions erratically, or where experts are not very good guessers, a more direct market test of likely behaviour is desirable. This applies particularly when forecasting the sales of a new product, or the likely sales of an established product in a new channel of distribution or territory. Where a short-run forecast of likely buyer response is desired, a small-scale market test is usually an ideal answer. Market testing is discussed in Chapter 11.

Time-series Analysis

As an alternative to costly surveys or market tests, some firms prepare forecasts on the basis of a statistical-mathematical analysis of past data. The underlying logic is that past data are an expression of enduring causal relations and can thus be used to predict future sales. Here forecasting becomes an exercise in adroit backcasting.

A time series of past sales of a product can be analysed into four major temporal components. The first component, trend (T), is the result of basic developments in population, capital formation, and technology. It is found by fitting a straight or gradually curved line through the time-series data. If the trend turns out to be statistically significant, it becomes central in the preparation of a long-range forecast.

The second component, cycle (C), is seen in the wave-like movement of sales. Many sales are affected by swings in the level of general economic activity, which tends to be somewhat periodic, and isolation of this component can be useful in intermediate-range forecasting.

The third component, season (S), refers to a consistent pattern of sales movements within the year. The term 'season' is broadly used, to describe any recurrent hourly, weekly, monthly or quarterly pattern. The seasonal component may be related to weather factors, holidays, and/or trade customs, and provides the investigator with a norm for forecasting short-range sales.

The fourth component, erratic events (E), includes strikes, fads, riots, fires, war scares, price wars and other disturbances. These factors have the effect of obscuring the more systematic components, and the problem becomes one of starting with the original 'noisy' time series and separating the underlying systematic forces from the erratic.

Classical time-series analysis involves decomposing the original sales series (Y) into the T, C, S and E components. These can then be recombined to produce the sales forecast for a future period. Here is an example:

A medium-sized insurance company sold 12 000 new ordinary life insurance policies last year. It would like to predict this year's December sales. The long-term trend shows a 5 per cent sales growth rate per year, which alone suggests sales this year of 12 600 (= 12 000 × 1.05). However, a business recession is expected this year and will probably result in only 90 per cent achievement of the expected trend-adjusted

sales, i.e. 11 340 (= 12 600 × .90). If sales were the same each month, this would mean monthly sales of 945 (= 11 340 ÷ 12). However, December is an above-average month for insurance sales, with a seasonal index standing at 1.30, and so December sales may be as high as 12 285 (= 945 × 1.3). As no erratic events (strikes, new insurance regulations) are expected, the best estimate of the number of new policies that will be sold this December remains 12 285.

Statistical Demand Analysis

Time-series analysis treats past and future sales as a function of time rather than of any real demand factors. Numerous factors do, however, affect the sales of any product: *statistical demand analysis* is a set of statistical procedures designed to discover and rate the most important of these, i.e. prices, income, population and promotion.

Statistical demand analysis consists of expressing sales (Q) as a dependent variable and trying to explain sales variation as a result of variation in a number of independent demand variables ($X_1, X_2, \ldots, X_n$):

$$Q = f(X_1, X_2, \ldots, X_n) \tag{5-2}$$

Using a technique called multiple-regression analysis, various equation forms can be statistically fitted to the data in the search for the best predicting factors and equation.[25] As an illustration, an American soft-drink company found that the per capita sales of soft drinks by state was well explained by the following equation:[26]

$$Q = -145.5 + 6.46X_1 - 2.37X_2 \tag{5-3}$$

where X_1 = mean annual temperature of the State (in degrees Fahrenheit)
X_2 = annual per capita income in the State (in hundreds of dollars)

For example, New Jersey had a mean annual temperature of 54°F and an annual per capita income of $2400. Using Equation 5-3, we would predict per capita soft-drink consumption in New Jersey to be:

$$Q = -145.5 + 6.46\,(54) - 2.37\,(24)$$
$$= 147$$

Actual per capita consumption was 143: to the extent that this equation predicted equally well for other states, it would serve as a useful sales-forecasting tool. Marketing management would predict next year's temperature and per capita income for each state and use the equation to derive a sales forecast for each state.

Many Australian marketers are using statistical demand analysis. For example, the following equation forecasts the ANZ Bank index of factory production, which is related to product sales:

$$Q = 0.6192$$
$$+\ 0.4816 \text{ (building and construction)}$$
$$+\ 0.1159 \text{ (plant and equipment)}$$
$$+\ 0.2484 \text{ (consumer durables)}$$
$$-\ 0.0964 \text{ (clothing)}$$
$$+\ 0.1911 \text{ (motor vehicles)}$$
$$-\ 0.1651 \text{ (product price/all prices)}$$

When this model was used for forecasting, and subsequently compared with the actual outcomes, a substantial agreement was noted.[27]

Marketing researchers are constantly improving the available forecasting tools – in fact, marketers' demands for solid information on which to base their marketing decisions are being met by an encouraging increase in data and tools that will aid them in their marketing planning, execution, and control.

SUMMARY

To carry out their responsibilities of marketing planning, execution and control, marketing managers need a great deal of information. Too often, however, such information is not available, comes too late or cannot be trusted.

An increasing number of companies have become aware of these deficiencies and are taking concrete steps to improve their marketing information systems.

A well-designed marketing information system consists of four major subsystems. The first is the internal reports system, which provides current data on sales, costs, inventories, cash flows, and accounts receivable and payable. A number of companies have developed advanced computer-based reports systems to allow for speedier and more comprehensive information. The second system is that of marketing intelligence, which supplies marketing executives with everyday information about developments in the external marketing environment. Here a better-trained sales force, special intelligence personnel, data purchased from syndicated sources, and an intelligence office can improve the marketing information available to company executives. The third system is marketing research, which involves collecting information that is relevant to a specific marketing problem. Many large companies operate marketing-research departments to help their executives obtain such information. The fourth system is analytical marketing, where advanced statistical procedures and models are applied to information to help develop more rigorous findings. A small but growing number of companies are building statistical and model banks to improve their analytical capabilities.

Marketing managers who need marketing research can work with professional marketing researchers to design the necessary study. Marketing research is a five-step procedure comprising the definition of research objectives and problems, exploratory research, the design of formal survey and/or experimental research, fieldwork, and data analysis and report presentation.

One of the major tasks of marketing research is to estimate current market demand. A company should use a clear set of concepts for demand measurement and should especially note the distinction between market demand and company demand, and between forecasts and potentials. Current demand may be estimated for the market as a whole or for various territories. In the latter case, the market build-up method is commonly used for industrial goods.

For estimating future demand, the company may use any of at least six different forecasting methods: surveys of buyer intentions, sales-force estimates, expert opinions, market tests, time-series analysis, or statistical demand analysis. These methods vary in their appropriateness with the purpose of the forecast, the type of product, and the availability and reliability of data.

QUESTIONS FOR DISCUSSION

1. How does a marketing information system differ from a marketing intelligence system?

2. What is the overriding objective of the marketing research system at Prentice-Hall, publishers?

3. Briefly describe the meaning of an analytical marketing system. Do you feel that a men's clothing store in a small town would use such a system? Why?

4. Once the research objectives and the problem are defined, the researcher is ready to begin the formal surveying of people. Comment.

5. Which type of research would be most appropriate in the following situations and why?
   a) Sanitarium wants to investigate the effect that children have on the actual purchase of its cereal products.
   b) Your campus bookshop wants to gather some preliminary information on how students feel about the merchandise and service it provides.
   c) McDonald's is considering locating a new outlet in a fast-growing suburb.
   d) Gillette wants to test the effect of two new advertising themes for its Right Guard lime-stick deodorant on sales in two cities.

6. The president of a campus organization to which you belong has asked you to conduct a marketing research project on why membership is declining. Discuss how you would apply the steps in the marketing research procedure to this project.

7. Relate the concepts of market potential and company demand to Tooth LA beer.

8. What are the two major methods of estimating current company demand? Which one do you think Levi Strauss should use?

9. Discuss two market and sales forecasting techniques that Spalding might use for a new line of tennis rackets.

NOTES

1 Abstracted from 'New Product Launches: Why Some Win and Others Flop', *Rydge's In Marketing*, 7 March 1980, pp. 89–92.

2 Marion Harper Jr, 'A New Profession to Aid Management', *Journal of Marketing*, January 1961, p. 1.

3 Richard H. Brien, 'Marketing Information Systems: The State of the Art', *Combined 1972 Conference Proceedings* (Chicago: American Marketing Association, 1973), p. 20.

4 The definition is adapted from 'Marketing Information Systems: An Introductory Overview', in Samuel V. Smith, Richard H. Brien & James E. Stafford (eds), *Readings in Marketing Information Systems* (Boston: Houghton Mifflin, 1968), p. 7.

5 Donald F. Cox & Robert E. Good, 'How to Build a Marketing Information System', *Harvard Business Review*, May–June 1967, pp. 145–54.

6 Lance R. Hart, 'The Status of Marketing Research in Australia' (M.Admin. thesis, Monash University, 1973).

7 Spike Cramphorn, 'Researching the Research Business', *Australian Marketing Researcher*, Summer 1977–78, pp. 54–63; M. B. Cooley, *Market Research in Retailing* (Melbourne: Australian Wool Corporation, 1978); Timothy Kitching, 'Marketing Research in Australia' (unpublished M.Admin. project, Monash University, 1978).

8 Ernest S. Bradford, *Bradford's Directory of Marketing Research Agencies and Management Consultants in the United States and the World* (Middlebury, Vt: Bradford Co., 15th edn, 1973–74). See also, *National Directory of Market Research Services* (Sydney: Market Research Society of Australia; NSW Division, 1979), for a listing of approximately fifty organizations and their claimed competences.

9 Based on Paul E. Green, 'The Future Marketing Researcher' (paper presented at the 61st International Marketing Conference, Philadelphia, Pa., 4–7 June 1978), pp. 5–6.

10 See David A. Acker (ed.) *Multivariate Analysis in Marketing: Theory and Applications* (Belmont, Calif.: Wadsworth, 1971).

11 Glen L. Urban, 'Sprinter Mod III: A Model for the Analysis of New Frequently Purchased Consumer Products', *Operations Research*, September–October 1970, pp. 805–54.

12 See J. D. C. Little & L. M. Lodish, 'A Media Planning Calculus', *Operations Research*, January–February 1969, pp. 1–35.

13 See Sidney W. Hess, 'Realignment of Sales and Service Districts', Working Paper (Philadelphia: Management Science Centre, Wharton School, University of Pennsylvania, July 1968).

14 T. E. Hlavac Jr & J. D. C. Little, 'A Geographic Model of an Automobile Market', Working Paper No. 186–66 (Cambridge: Massachusetts Institute of Technology, Alfred P. Sloan School of Management, 1966).

15 For details see Robin Shaw's 'APN Scandata – A New Numbers Game', *Journal of Australian Marketing, Advertising, Communication*, July 1981, pp. 22–27; and 'Will Code Scanning Revolutionize Research?', *Australian Marketing Researcher*, Summer 1979, pp. 22–27.

16 A. M. Sutherland & T. Davies, *Supermarket Shopping Behaviour – an Observational Study* (Caulfield: Department of Marketing, Caulfield Institute of Technology, 1978).

17 Robin N. Shaw & Rosalie Gibbs, 'Shopper Behaviour, Price Information, and New Technology', *Australian Marketing Researcher*, March 1981, pp. 25–33.

18 See Keith K. Cox et al., 'Applications of Focus Group Interviews in Marketing', *Journal of Marketing*, January 1976, pp. 77–80; and Bobby J. Calder, 'Focus Groups and the Nature of Qualitative Marketing Research', *Journal of Marketing Research*, August 1977, pp. 353–64.

19 For more reading on experimental research, see Seymour Banks, *Experimentation in Marketing* (New York: McGraw-Hill, 1965).

20 For a progress report, see Ian Cannon, 'Shoppers in Favour of Laser Scans', *Australian*, 15 September 1981, p. 23.

21 See Philip Kotler, *Marketing Decision Making: A Model Building Approach* (New York: Holt, Rinehart & Winston, 1971), especially Ch. 4.

22 Australian Bureau of Statistics, *Australian Standard Industrial Classification, Volume 1 – The Classification* (Canberra: Australian Bureau of Statistics, 1975).

23 However, see Jacob Gonik, 'Tie Salesmen's Bonuses to Their Forecasts', *Harvard Business Review*, May–June 1978, pp. 116–23.

24 See Normal Dalkey & Olaf Helmer, 'An Experimental Application of the Delphi Method to the Use of Experts', *Management Science*, April 1963, pp. 458–67.

25 See William F. Massy, 'Statistical Analysis of Relations between Variables', in David A. Acker (ed.), *Multivariate Analysis in Marketing: Theory and Applications* (Belmont, Calif.: Wadsworth, 1971), pp. 5–35.

26 See 'The DuPort Company', in Harper W. Boyd Jr & Ralph Westfall (eds), *Marketing Research: Text and Cases* (Homewood, Ill.: Richard D. Irwin, 3rd edn, 1972), pp. 576–81.

27 See Lance Robertson, 'The Econometric Model and Industrial Marketing', *Rydge's In Marketing*, 7 November 1981, pp. 40–42.

The Marketing
Organization

In 1975, the former Postmaster-General's Department was split into two
statutory authorities: The Australian Postal Commission and The Australian
Telecommunications Commission. This development resulted from government
acceptance of recommendations made by a Commission of Inquiry into the
Australian Post Office. The Commission of Inquiry recognized that the nature
of the two businesses was significantly different and warranted separate
management.

From the new charter of the Postal Commission incorporated application of the
'user pays' concept to postal services. The Inquiry's report had pointed out that
if services were provided at less than cost, the unrecovered costs would need to
be met by the Australian taxpayers, who do not coincide, as a group, with users
of the services. The report also cautioned that where goods and services are
provided at less than cost, distortions in usage would inevitably result. By
recommending that the Commission operate under authority status, it was
intended to allow the normal market forces to determine the level of postal
services sought by the Australian community.

From having operated as a Department steeped in traditional practices and
heavily subsidized, the Australian Postal Commission, with its new trading name
'Australia Post', was charged with the responsibility of providing a fast and
efficient postal service at the least possible cost at standards which reasonably
meet the needs of the Australian community. Australia Post was also required

to raise sufficient revenue to cover its operating costs and fund at least 50 per cent of its capital requirements.

Clearly the need was for a change from a highly operationally-oriented organization – the mail must get through (at any price) – to a more marketing-oriented organization. Some half of the Commission's revenue is derived from its monopoly letter service and the other half from competitive markets such as parcels, time-critical articles, money-transfer services and agency business.

Change in any form brings with it casualties. Bearing in mind that the postal service is a highly labour-intensive operation with more than 80 per cent of its total operating costs being labour-related, it should come as no surprise to learn that there were many staff who found the new directions and charter difficult to accept. Much operational expertise was lost due to premature retirements in those early years of Australia Post.

To make matters even more difficult, the price of its basic product, the standard article, had to increase by 80 per cent in 1975–76 in order that Australia Post could meet its new financial obligations. The basic postal article was not a new product, it offered no new advantages, it simply cost more! Australia Post's new marketing team went quickly into action. In the face of an immediate 12 per cent loss of business following the substantial price increase, several new services were introduced. By 1976 Australia Post was operating its own courier service, had introduced special charges for bulk local mail and was offering discounts for bulk quantities of advertising mail.

Late in 1976 a special campaign titled 'Get the Business' was conducted. It involved a team of trained sales people selling Australia Post's services. The strategy adopted was principally a chain-reaction strategy whereby the training was passed on by those sales people to others in the field. Ultimately, every post office in Australia (some 6000) played some part in improving Australia Post's business.

In subsequent years, Australia Post continued to introduce products and services making better use of existing facilities and continually reviewing the viability of those facilities. After six years of operation on its new basis, Australia Post had more than regained the quantity of mail lost in 1975–76. Having made productivity gains, the rate of increase in postal charges has been, on average, less than the rate of cost increases in the community generally. Australia Post had also achieved an accumulated trading surplus of $84 million. Nevertheless, as a national postal service, it has not, as would be expected, been free of community pressure and political influence. Nor has it (some six years since its creation) completed the transition to a marketing-oriented organization.

A degree of uncertainty about Australia Post's future arises from a current Committee of Inquiry into the functions and duties of the Postal Commission, including a review of whether its monopoly in respect to the carriage of letters should be reduced or abolished. Depending upon government decisions following the report of that inquiry, and as Australia Post addresses its opportunities in respect to advertising markets (i.e. promotion of use of the mail as an effective advertising medium) and meets the challenges of electronic communications, it will clearly need to adopt an even more responsive marketing orientation.[1]

In this chapter we turn our attention to the marketing function within an organization and how it should be arranged for maximum effectiveness. The form of this arrangement – the number of marketing staff, what their responsibilities are, what their authority is – will depend on the marketing philosophy adopted by the organization.

If an organization adopts the marketing concept the marketing function takes on greater prominence and becomes a more powerful managerial group. This is frequently resisted by other organizational entities, who perceive such increased power as being associated with a diminution in their own.

With the slowdown in economic growth in Australia, increased competition from within and outside their industry, and greater levels of import competition, many organizations are finding that they have to understand their markets better. BHP, for example, despite its virtual monopoly in steel, is being challenged by steel imports as well as substitute products; recently a new competitor (Smorgons) has established a mini-mill for reprocessing scrap steel, enabling it to compete with BHP in selected markets. This has meant a greater commitment to the marketing concept on BHP's part, and also that marketing has increased its relative importance with respect to other functions, particularly manufacturing.

Australia Post has also had to appoint a number of marketing staff because its custom has declined: it now actively promotes direct-mailing as a cost-effective method to communicate with their actual and potential users. Telecom has undertaken research to demonstrate the effectiveness of telephone selling for both consumer and industrial products. Today, many organizations have realized the necessity for more accurate knowledge of their markets and customers, and have increased the magnitude and sophistication of their marketing effort. This has meant hiring more marketing staff and successfully integrating these into the organization.

Here we want to look at designs for the marketing organization. Planning, control and information systems only become effective when a marketing organization knows how to use them. This chapter answers the following questions:

1. How do marketing departments evolve in the typical company?
2. How should the marketing department be organized?
3. What is the relationship between the marketing department and the other company departments?
4. What steps are involved in producing a company-wide marketing orientation?

THE EVOLUTION OF THE MARKETING DEPARTMENT

The modern marketing department is the product of a long evolution. From very humble beginnings it has passed through five stages, each of which is recognizable in companies today.

Simple Sales Department (Stage 1)

All companies start out with four simple functions. Someone must raise and manage capital (finance), produce the product or service (operations), sell it (sales), and keep the books (accounting). The selling function is headed by a sales manager or sales director, who supervises a sales force and also does some selling. When the company needs some occasional marketing research or advertising, the sales manager also handles this because it supports the objective of obtaining more sales. The sales force remains his prime concern, however, and other assignments are often handled halfheartedly. This stage is illustrated in Figure 6-1a.

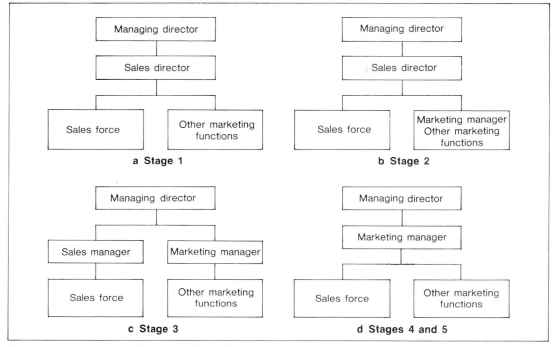

Figure 6-1   Stages in the evolution of a marketing department

Sales Department with Ancillary Functions (Stage 2)

As the company expands, it finds that it needs marketing research, advertising, and customer service on a more continuing and expert basis. The sales manager hires a few specialists to perform these functions, and may hire a marketing manager to plan and control the nonselling functions (see Figure 6-1b).

Separate Marketing Department (Stage 3)

The continued growth of the company inevitably increases the importance of other marketing functions – research, new-product development, advertising and promotion, customer service – relative to sales-force activity. Nevertheless, the sales manager continues to give disproportionate time and attention to the sales force. The marketing manager will argue that sales could be facilitated by greater financial investment in these other marketing activities, and the managing director or divisional general manager will eventually see the advantage of establishing a marketing department that is relatively independent of the sales manager (see Figure 6-1c). The marketing department will be headed by a marketing manager who will report, with the sales manager, to the managing director. At this stage, sales and marketing are seen as separate and equal but cooperating functions in the organization.

Modern Marketing Department (Stage 4)

Although the sales manager and the marketing manager are supposed to work in harmony, their relationship is often characterized by rivalry and distrust. The sales manager sees a conspiracy to make the sales force less important in the marketing mix; and the marketing manager seeks to gain power over all the customer-impinging functions. The sales manager tends to be preoccupied with achieving current sales; the marketing manager tends to be preoccupied with planning the right products and marketing strategy to meet the customers' long-run needs.

At times it seems that the sales and the marketing people represent two different cultures in the organization. Salespeople usually have less education, are more practical and 'streetwise', whereas the marketing people are younger, better educated, and less experienced in selling. Often the salespeople do not trust or believe the marketing people's findings; some companies arrange for the marketing people to get more selling experience, and even assign them a few customers to keep them close to the selling situation.

If there is too much conflict between sales and marketing, the managing director may: (i) eliminate the position of marketing manager and place marketing activities back under the sales director; (ii) take it on himself to handle conflicts that arise; or (iii) place the marketing manager in charge of everything, including the sales force. The last solution is eventually chosen in many companies, and forms the basis of the modern marketing department – headed by a marketing manager or director with subordinates reporting from every marketing function, including sales management (see Figure 6-1d).

Modern Marketing Company (Stage 5)

A company may have a modern marketing department and yet not operate as a modern marketing company. This depends upon how the officers of the company view the marketing function: if they view marketing as primarily a selling function, they are missing the point. The director of marketing, no matter how well he runs the marketing department, meets frequent resistance from other executives in attempting to carry out a company-wide customer orientation. The manufacturing director holds to the logic of cost minimization and resents interrupting production schedules to please customers. The financial director is not sure about the return from investments in marketing research, communication and promotion, and normally reacts to sales declines by recommending cuts in these expenditures. Other departments may also resist cooperating to produce satisfied customers. Ultimately the job may call for increasing the power and authority of the marketing director over the other business functions. Only a few companies have attained the stature of true marketing companies.

ORGANIZING THE MODERN MARKETING DEPARTMENT

An examination of modern marketing departments reveals numerous arrangements. All marketing organizations must somehow accommodate to four basic dimensions of marketing activity: functions, geographical units, products, and end-use markets.

Functional Organization

The most common form of marketing organization has various functional specialists reporting to a marketing manager, who coordinates all of their activities. Figure 6-2 shows five such specialists: marketing administration manager, advertising and sales promotion manager, sales manager, marketing research manager, and new-products manager. Additional functional specialists might include a customer-service manager, a marketing-planning manager, and a physical distribution manager.

The main advantage of a functional marketing organization is its administrative simplicity, but there may be disadvantages as the

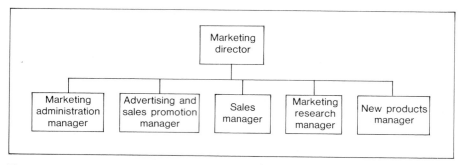

Figure 6-2   Functional organization

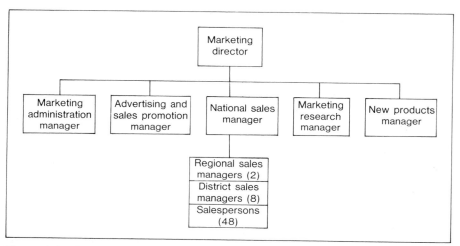

Figure 6-3   Geographical organization

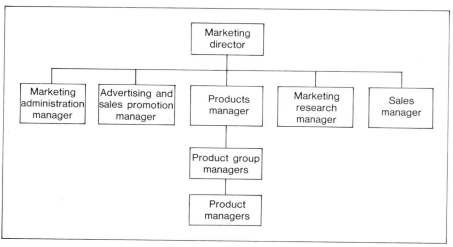

Figure 6-4   Product management organization

company's product line or number of markets increases. First, there is inadequate detailed planning for specific products and markets, since no one is assigned full responsibility for any one of these. Products that are not favourites with various functional specialists tend to get neglected. Second, each functional group develops its own subgoals, which include trying to gain more budget and status vis-a-vis the other functions. The marketing director has to constantly sift the claims of competing specialists and faces a difficult problem in coordination.

Geographical Organization

A company selling in the national market often organizes its sales force (and sometimes other functions) along geographical lines, typically States. Figure 6-3 shows one national sales manager, two regional sales managers, eight district sales managers and, finally, forty-eight salespersons. The span of control increases as we move from the national sales manager down toward the district sales managers. Shorter spans allow managers to give more time to subordinates and are warranted when the sales task is complex, the salespersons are highly paid, and the salesperson's impact on profits is substantial.

Product Management Organization

Companies producing a variety of products and/or brands often establish a product management organization (also called brand management). This does not replace functional management organization, but rather serves as another layer of management: the organization is headed by a products manager, who supervises several product-group managers, who in turn supervise product managers in charge of specific products (see Figure 6-4).

The decision to establish a product management organization is influenced by both product heterogeneity and numbers. If the company product lines can benefit from specialized marketing programmes, or if the sheer number of products is beyond the capacity of a functional marketing organization, a product management organization is a natural recourse.

Product management first made its appearance in the Proctor & Gamble Company in the United States in 1927. A new company soap, Camay, was not doing well, and one of the young executives, Neil H. McElroy (later president of P&G), was assigned to give his exclusive attention to developing and promoting this product. This he did successfully, and the company soon added other product managers.

Since then a large number of firms, especially those in the food, soap, toiletries and chemical industries, have established similar organizations. Gillette (Australia) has a product manager for each different type of business – toiletries, razor blades and writing instruments – and each is responsible for a range of products in that area. Product managers report to a brand supervisor, who in turn reports to the marketing manager.

The product management organization creates a focal point of planning and responsibility for individual products. The product manager's role is to create strategies and plans, see that they are implemented, monitor the results, and take corrective action. This responsibility breaks down into the following six tasks:

1. Develop a long-range and competitive strategy for the product.
2. Prepare an annual marketing plan and sales forecast.
3. Work with advertising and merchandising agencies to develop copy, programmes and campaigns.
4. Stimulate interest in, and support of, the product among the sales force and distributors.

5. Gather continuous intelligence on the product's performance, customer and dealer attitudes, and new problems and opportunities.
6. Initiate product improvements to meet changing market needs.

These basic functions are common to managers of both consumer and industrial products. Yet there are some important differences in their jobs and emphases.[2] Consumer product managers tend to manage fewer products than their industrial counterparts; they spend considerably more time dealing with advertising and sales promotion; they spend most of their time working with others in the company and various agencies, and little time in direct contact with customers; they tend to be younger and better educated. Industrial product managers, by contrast, think more carefully about the technical aspects of their product and possible improvements in design; they spend more time with laboratory and engineering personnel in the company; they work more closely with the sales force and key buyers; they tend to pay less attention to advertising, sales promotion, and promotional pricing; they emphasize rational product factors, not emotional ones.

Product management introduces several advantages in the management of the firm's marketing activity. First, the product manager can balance and harmonize the various functional marketing inputs needed by a product. Second, the product manager is in a position to react quickly to problems in the marketplace without involving several different people in lengthy meetings. Third, because they have a champion, smaller brands are less neglected in this system than they tend to be in functional marketing organizations. Fourth, product management is an excellent training ground for promising young executives, because it involves them in almost every area of company operations (see Figure 6-5).

A price is paid for these advantages, however. First, the product management organiz-

ation introduces many sources of conflict and frustration that might not otherwise be present.[3] Product managers are typically not given enough authority to carry out their responsibilities effectively, and have to rely on their persuasive skills when seeking the cooperation of various resource managers. They spend so much time trying to get the support of advertising, sales and manufacturing managers that they have little time for planning. They have been told by their superior that they are 'mini-directors', but they are often treated like low-level coordinators. They solicit the help of specialists but often do not follow their advice. Sometimes they are forced to go over the heads of others. They are bogged down by a great amount of paperwork. If such frustrations lead to a rapid turnover of product managers, it can damage the sound long-range planning of products.

Second, product managers become experts in their product but can rarely become experts in any of the functions for which they are responsible. This is particularly unfortunate when the product basically depends on a specific type of expertise, such as advertising, and in such cases it would almost make more sense to put the product in the hands of an appropriate specialist.

Third, the product management organization often turns out to be more costly than anticipated. Initially, one person is appointed to manage each major product. Soon thereafter, product managers are appointed to manage even minor products. Each product manager, usually overworked, pleads for and receives an assistant brand manager. Later, both the product manager and the assistant brand manager, still overworked, persuade management to give them a brand assistant. Product managers who supervise the more important company products, in their frustration at having to coax time from advertising, packaging and other specialists, next pressure to hire their own specialists. With all these personnel, payroll costs climb. Meanwhile, the company

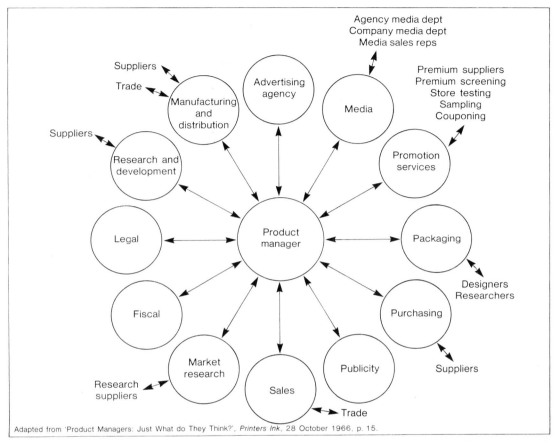

Adapted from 'Product Managers: Just What do They Think?', *Printers Ink*, 28 October 1966, p. 15.

Figure 6-5 The product manager's interactions

continues to increase its number of functional specialists in copy, packaging, media, promotion, market surveys, statistical analysis, and so on: it soon finds itself stuck with a costly superstructure of product management people and a superstructure of functional specialists.

When a company has a product management organization that breeds too much conflict or cost, it should think about possible improvements. Although P&G eventually managed to achieve an effective product management organization, many of its imitators have not been as successful. Pearson and Wilson have suggested the following steps to make the product management system work better.

1. Clearly delineate the limits of the product manager's role and responsibility for the management of a product ... [Product managers are essentially proposers, not deciders.]
2. Build a strategy development and review process to provide an agreed-to framework for the product manager's operations ... [Too many companies allow product managers to get away with shallow marketing plans featuring a lot of statistics but little strategic rationale.]

3. Take into account areas of potential conflict between product managers and functional specialists when defining their respective roles . . . [Clarify which decisions are to be made by the product manager, which by the expert, and which will be shared.]

4. Set up a formal process that forces to the top all conflict-of-interest situations between product management and functional line management . . . [Both parties might be expected to put all issues in writing and forward them to general management for settlement.]

5. Establish a system for measuring results that is consistent with the product manager's responsibilities . . . [If product managers are to be held accountable for profit, they should be given more control over the factors that affect their operations' profitability.][4]

The position of product manager is undergoing several important changes; in many companies these managers are assuming greater responsibility for brand profitability. Cost inflation has resulted in companies being less satisfied with the sheer volume they sell and more concerned with the profits they make. The product manager is becoming more of a profit centre and must put a profit test to the various items in his or her line and to the various marketing expenditures. Some companies are even holding their product managers responsible for excessive costs of inventory and receivables.

Product managers are also working more closely with other managers in the company to find ways of securing scarce supplies, developing substitute ingredients, engineering product economies, smoothing production and keeping total costs down. Another trend is that higher levels of marketing management are exercising greater control over brand managers – they now realize that there is a need for more coordinated planning of whole product lines rather than brands alone, and that brand managers should be more responsive to

consumer concerns about advertising truthfulness and product safety.[5]

Market Management Organization

Many companies will sell one product to a highly diverse set of markets. For example, Dulux sells paint to individual consumers and contract painters; BHP sells steel to the car, railway, construction and engineering industries. Where the company sells to customers who fall into distinct user groups according to their buying practices or product preferences, some market specialization is desirable in the marketing organization.

The general structure of a market management organization is similar to that of the product management shown in Figure 6-4. As well as functional managers, there is a markets manager who supervises several market managers (also called market-development managers, market specialists or industry specialists). Market managers are responsible for developing long-range and annual plans for the sales and profits in their markets. They have to draw resource help, such as marketing research or advertising, from the functional specialists in the organization. This system's strongest advantage is that the company is organized to monitor and focus on the needs of distinct customer groups.

An increasing number of companies are reorganizing their management structures along market lines. Hanan calls these *marketing-centred* organizations, and argues that 'the only way to ensure being market-oriented is to put a company's organizational structure together so that its major markets become the centres around which its divisions are built'.[6]

Product/Market Management Organization

Companies that produce multiple products for multiple markets face a real dilemma. They could utilize a product management organiz-

Exhibit 6-1 The Heinz Company Moves Toward a Market Management System

One of the most dramatic shifts to market-centredness has occurred at the Heinz Company in the United States. Heinz was primarily organized around a brand management system, with separate brand managers for soups, condiments, puddings and so on. Each brand manager was responsible for both grocery sales and institutional sales. Then, in 1964, Heinz created a separate marketing organization for institutional sales. Thus ketchup sales to institutions would be the responsibility of the institutional product managers rather than the brand managers. Recently Heinz split the marketing organization into three broad groups: groceries, commercial restaurants, and institutions. Each group contains further market specialists (e.g. the institutional division contains separate market specialists for schools, colleges, hospitals and prisons). The market manager positions are as follows:

Groceries	**Commercial restaurants**	**Institutions**
Supermarkets Market Manager Wholesale Co-ops Market Manager Wholesalers Market Manager	Drug and Variety Stores Market Manager Drive-ins Market Manager Coffee Shops Market Manager Fine Restaurants Market Manager	Schools Market Manager Colleges Market Manager Hospitals Market Manager Prisons Market Manager

ation, which requires product managers to be familiar with highly divergent markets, or they could utilize a market management organization, which means that market managers would have to be familiar with highly divergent products. Alternatively, they could install both product and market managers, i.e. a product/market organization.

Although it may appear that product/market management is desirable in a multiple-product, multiple-market company, such a system is not only costly but also generates conflict. There is the cost of supporting a three-dimensional matrix organization (i.e.

two layers of programme management and one layer of resource management), and there are also serious questions as to where authority and responsibility should reside. Here are two of the many dilemmas:

1. *How should the sales force be organized?* In the Du Pont example (see Exhibit 6-2), should there be separate sales forces for rayon, nylon and each of the other fibres? Or should the sales forces be organized according to men's wear, women's wear and other markets? Or should the sales force not be specialized?

Exhibit 6-2   Du Pont Uses a Product/Market Management System

Du Pont's textile fibres division consists of both product managers and market managers:

Market Managers

	Men's wear	Women's wear	Home furnishings	Industrial markets
Rayon				
Acetate				
Nylon				
Orlon				
Dacron				

Product Managers (label at left of Nylon row)

The product managers are responsible for planning the sales and profits of their respective fibres and focus primarily on short-run performance and uses of their fibre. Their job is to contact each market manager and ask for an estimate of how much material can be sold in each market. The market managers, on the other hand, are responsible for developing profitable markets for existing and potential Du Pont fibres. They take a long-term view of market needs, and care more about evolving the right products for their market than pushing specific fibres. In preparing their market plan, they contact each product manager to learn about planned prices and availabilities of different materials. The final sales forecasts of the market managers and the product managers should add to the same grand total.

2. *Who should set the prices for a particular product or market?* In the Du Pont example, should the nylon product manager have final authority for setting nylon prices in all markets? What happens if the men's-wear market manager feels that nylon will lose out in this market unless special price concessions are made on nylon?

Some companies are adopting a product/market organization, and others already using it are having second thoughts; most agree that only the more important products and markets would justify separate managers. Some observers argue that such a system gives the company the benefit of both the short-run and the long-run view, and that conflict is in itself healthy.[7]

Corporate Divisional Organization

As multiproduct companies grow, they have a tendency to turn their larger product groups into separate divisions. The larger divisions often set up their own marketing departments, on the grounds that this will give them more knowledgeable and controllable marketing resources. This poses the question of which marketing services and activities should be retained as the corporate headquarters. Divisionalized companies have reached different answers to this question, and seem to follow any of four models:[8]

1. *No corporate marketing.* Some companies do not have a corporate marketing staff. They do not see any useful function for marketing at the corporate level, and thus each division has its own marketing department.

2. *Minimal corporate marketing.* Some companies have a small corporate marketing staff that performs a few functions. These generally include assisting top management with overall opportunity evaluation; providing divisions with consulting assistance on request; helping divisions that are without marketing or that have weak marketing, and attempting to promote the marketing concept to other departments in the company.

3. *Moderate corporate marketing.* Some companies have a corporate marketing staff that, in addition to the preceding activities, provides various marketing services to the divisions. These may include specialized advertising services, sales promotion services, and sales administration services.

4. *Strong corporate marketing.* Some companies have a corporate marketing staff that, in addition to the preceding activities, has the authority to participate strongly in the planning and control of divisional marketing activities.

MARKETING'S RELATIONS WITH OTHER DEPARTMENTS

In principle, business functions should mesh harmoniously to achieve the overall objectives of the firm. In practice, however, departmental relations are often characterized by rivalries and misunderstandings that impede progress. Some interdepartmental conflict stems from differences of opinion as to what is in the best interests of the firm; some from real trade-offs between departmental and company well-being; and some from unfortunate stereotypes and prejudices.

The Question of Marketing's Importance in the Organization

There is much confusion about marketing's relative importance in the firm. In some firms it is just another function, no more and no less important than others: all functions influence corporate strategy, and none takes precedence. This view is illustrated in Figure 6-6a.

If the company faces slow growth – or, even worse, a sales decline – the marketers start arguing for a larger budget in order to build market demand. They claim that marketing is a more important function than the others (see Figure 6-6b).

Some marketers go further and say that marketing is the central function of the firm. They quote Drucker's statement: 'The aim of the business is to create customers.' They say it is marketing's responsibility to define the company's mission, products and markets, and to direct all the other functions in the task of serving customers (see Figure 6-6c).

This view incenses the other department heads, who do not want to think of themselves as subordinate to marketing. Enlightened marketers respond by putting the customer at the centre of the company: they argue for a customer orientation in which all functions work together to sense, serve and satisfy the customer (see Figure 6-6d).

Finally, some marketers say that marketing still needs to command a central position in the firm if customers' needs are to be correctly interpreted and efficiently satisfied (see Figure 6-6e). This argument may be summarized as follows:

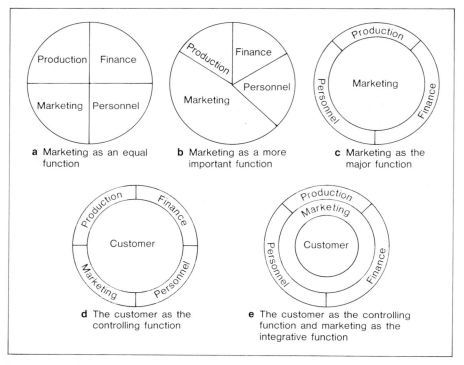

a Marketing as an equal function

b Marketing as a more important function

c Marketing as the major function

d The customer as the controlling function

e The customer as the controlling function and marketing as the integrative function

Figure 6-6   Evolving views of marketing's role in the company

1. The assets of the firm have little value without the existence of customers.
2. The key task of the firm is therefore to create and hold customers.
3. Customers are attracted through promises and held through satisfaction.
4. Marketing's task is to define an appropriate promise to the customer and to ensure the delivery of satisfaction.
5. The actual satisfaction delivered to the customer is affected by the performance of the other departments.
6. Marketing needs influence or control over these other departments if customers are to be satisfied.

Types of Interdepartmental Conflict

In a typical organization, each department has an impact on customer satisfaction. Under the marketing concept, it is desirable to coordinate individual activities and decisions, because the satisfaction gained by the customer is a function of *all* relevant stimuli.

The marketing department is very willing to accept this responsibility and use its influence. There are two reasons for appointing a marketing director: (i) to integrate and coordinate the formal marketing activities of the company, such as sales forecasting, marketing research, advertising, sales force, promotion, and customer service; and (ii) to deal with the directors of finance, manufacturing, and so on, on a regular basis so that they will better appreciate the benefits of a customer orientation.

There is little unanimity, however, on how much influence and authority marketing should have over other departments to bring about coordinated marketing. Other departments resent having to bend their efforts to the will of the marketing department. Just as marketing stresses the customer's point of view, other departments wish to stress the importance of their tasks; inevitably, self-interest influences the definition of company problems and goals. The reason is that both departments and individuals deal continuously with problems in a local portion of the overall system. The major organizational conflicts between marketing and other departments are summarized in Table 6-1. We will briefly describe the typical concerns of each department.

R & D. The R & D manager is interested in making new discoveries, and expects marketing people to be able to find markets for them. This executive focuses attention on functional product features, and tends to overlook the market's psychology of buying.

Engineering. The product engineer is interested in designing a product that meets engineering standards of simplicity and economy. This executive tends to concentrate on these attributes at the expense of those that may increase the product's marketability.

Table 6-1 Summary of organizational conflicts between marketing and other departments

Department	Their emphasis	Marketing's emphasis
R & D	Basic research	Applied research
	Intrinsic quality	Perceived quality
	Functional features	Sales features
Engineering	Long design lead time	Short design lead time
	Few models	Many models
	Standard components	Custom components
Purchasing	Narrow product line	Broad product line
	Standard parts	Nonstandard parts
	Price of material	Quality of material
	Economical lot sizes	Large lot sizes to avoid stockouts
	Purchasing at infrequent intervals	Immediate purchasing for customer needs
Manufacturing	Long production lead time	Short production lead time
	Long runs with few models	Short runs with many models
	No model changes	Frequent model changes
	Standard orders	Custom orders
	Ease of fabrication	Aesthetic appearance
	Average quality control	Tight quality control
Inventory	Fast-moving items, narrow product line	Broad product line
	Economical level of stock	High level of stock
Finance	Strict rationales for spending	Intuitive arguments for spending
	Hard and fast budgets	Flexible budgets to meet changing needs
	Pricing to cover costs	Pricing to further market development
Accounting	Standard transactions	Special terms and discounts
	Few reports	Many reports
Credit	Full financial disclosures by customers	Minimum credit examination of customers
	Low credit risks	Medium credit risks
	Tought credit terms	Easy credit terms
	Tough collection procedures	Easy collection procedures

Purchasing. The purchasing agent's main concern is to keep down the costs of acquiring the company's required inputs. This executive's material and design recommendations often conflict with qualities that marketing would like to build into the product.

Manufacturing. The production officer is interested in keeping down manufacturing costs. But manufacturing economies are achieved in ways often incompatible with the goal of high customer satisfaction.

Inventory. The executive responsible for inventory management wants to keep down inventory costs. This executive is typically more concerned with holding down carrying costs than with the less-tangible costs of stockout.

Finance. The financial officer likes to keep a tight rein on company expenditures, and wants to see profit on each transaction. This often conflicts with the need to take initial losses in order to develop loyal customers.

Accounting. The accountant's natural interest is in keeping down the costs of the company's reporting operation. Therefore this executive is apt to resent nonstandard marketing transactions, and to resist requests by the marketing department for a multitude of sales and cost analyses.

Credit. The credit officer looks on the bad debt as a blot on his own performance. To minimize losses, this executive tends to set higher standards for customer credit than seems reasonable to the salesperson who is working so hard to find customers.

It is no wonder that many departments resent the marketing concept. Marketing, in trying to mobilize the company's resources to develop customer satisfaction, often causes other departments to do – in their terms – a poorer job. Requests and pressures by the marketing department can increase product-design and material-purchasing costs, disrupt production schedules, increase accounting costs, and create budget headaches.

STRATEGIES FOR BUILDING A COMPANYWIDE MARKETING ORIENTATION

Only a handful of Australian companies are truly marketing-oriented. A much larger number of companies are sales-oriented, which they confuse with being marketing-oriented. At some point in a company's history, something happens to create a disturbing awareness of the lack of a true marketing orientation. Among the most common triggers are the following:

1. Sales decline. The company starts experiencing falling sales and recognizes the need to improve its marketing research, advertising and sales promotion. In the newspaper business, for example, circulation is falling. Publishers are beginning to realize that they know very little about why people read newspapers. As a result they are commissioning consumer research and are redesigning formats so that their newspapers will be more contemporary, relevant and interesting.

2. Slow growth. The company's growth may slow down and inspire a search for new markets. The company then recognizes the need for marketing know-how if it is to successfully identify, evaluate, select and enter new markets. BHP had to acquire new marketing talent when it decided to enter the house construction marketing with slab-on-ground.

3. Changing buying patterns. The company may find that its customers' tastes and preferences are changing. During the 1960s, car manufacturers failed to understand why people were switching to smaller Japanese cars. After seeing their market share drop substantially, they began to recognize the need to replace their sales orientation with a marketing orientation.

4. Increased competition. The company may suddenly find its market invaded by a sophisticated marketer, and be forced to improve its marketing to meet the challenge. Banks in Australia have been exposed to increased competition in two of their main areas of business. On the retail level, building societies offer higher interest rates to depositors. In terms of corporate customers, merchant banks – generally with overseas affiliations – have been very aggressive. As a result the trading banks have had to substantially improve their marketing strength.

5. Increasing sales expenditures. The company may find that its expenditures on adver-

tising, sales promotion, marketing research and customer service are increasing without rhyme or reason. When this happens, the company may decide to reorganize and consolidate its marketing functions.

In any of these circumstances, top management's problem is how to convert the company from a traditional sales company to a modern marketing company. The issue is how to get all departments to think 'customer'. A companywide customer orientation has been expressed in many different ways:

- 'We're not the boss; the consumer is. What the consumer wants, the consumer gets.'
- 'Under the marketing concept, the customer is at the top of the organization chart.'

Exhibit 6-3   Banks Learn Their Marketing Slowly

Thirty years ago, few banks either understood or practised marketing. Bankers simply assumed that customers needed them. In the mid-1960s, however, competition increased to the point where some banks aggressively turned to marketing (although still not quite understanding it). Marketing has evolved through five stages in the banking industry:

1. *Marketing is advertising, sales promotion, and publicity.* At first the banks thought marketing simply amounted to the use of some advertising, sales promotion, and publicity to attract new customers.
2. *Marketing is providing a friendly atmosphere.* Banks then realized that keeping the new customers required a pleasant manner and an attractive environment.
3. *Marketing is innovation.* Then some banks realized that marketing consists of developing new services to meet new needs and wants. The marketing department would research customer needs, design new services and develop plans for marketing them.
4. *Marketing is positioning.* Many banks soon found themselves going after the same customers and looking very much alike. A few banks started to concentrate on certain target markets in order to develop a distinct position in the market.
5. *Marketing is analysis, planning and control.* Banks are currently realizing that effective marketing requires certain forms of organization, and advanced systems of marketing analysis, planning and control.

All sorts of institutions that turn to marketing seem to go through a period of 'slow learning' before they fully grasp the revolutionary character of marketing.

- 'A company should prefer a franchise over a market to a franchise over a plant.'
- 'Look at the company through the customer's eyes.'
- 'Instead of trying to market what is easiest for us to make, we must find out much more about what the customer is willing to buy. In other words, we must apply our creativeness more intelligently to people, and their wants and needs, than to products.'[9]

To acquire a modern marketing orientation, the company must consider the following measures.

Top management leadership. The managing director's enthusiasm for marketing is a prerequisite to establishing a modern marketing company. The managing director must understand the difference between marketing and sales, believing that marketing is the key to company growth and prosperity, and build marketing into both speeches and decisions.

Marketing task force and outside marketing consultant. The managing director should appoint a marketing task force to examine the need for modern marketing, set objectives and anticipate problems, i.e. develop a strategy. Such a team would probably benefit from including an experienced outside marketing consultant to offer guidance and assistance.

A corporate marketing department. A key step is that of establishing a corporate marketing department and hiring a capable and experienced marketing director. The company should try to attract marketing talent from leading marketing companies, and hire recent graduates with an MBA degree in marketing.

In-house marketing seminars. The new corporate marketing department should develop a programme of in-house marketing seminars for top corporate management, divisional general managers, marketing and sales personnel, manufacturing personnel, R & D personnel, and so on. The seminars should start with the higher levels of management and move to lower levels, the aim being to bring about changes in the marketing knowledge, attitudes and behaviour of various executive groups.

Promotion of market-oriented executives. The company should favour market-oriented individuals when selecting new division managers. Large public-accounting firms are currently trying to become market-oriented, giving preference to market-oriented rather than financially oriented individuals in promoting staff members to managing partners.

Installation of a modern marketing-planning system. An excellent way to train an organization to think marketing is to install a modern market-oriented planning system. Managers will start their planning with market opportunities, and formulate marketing strategies to capitalize on these. Other departments will plan around the resulting strategies and forecasts.

The implementation of a marketing orientation throughout the company is an uphill and never-ending battle. The purpose is not to resolve every issue in favour of the customer, no matter what the cost; but rather to remind others that customers are the foundation of the company's business.[10]

SUMMARY

The modern marketing department evolved through several stages to reach its contemporary form. It started as a simple sales department consisting of only a sales force. Later the sales department took on some ancillary functions, such as advertising and marketing research. As the ancillary functions grew in importance, many companies created a separate marketing department to manage these activities. But the heads of sales and marketing often disagreed on company marketing policy, and eventually the two departments were merged into a modern marketing department headed by the marketing director. A modern marketing department, however, does not automatically create a modern marketing company unless the other officers accept a customer orientation as the hub of the enterprise.

Modern marketing departments are organized in a number of ways. The most common form is the functional organization, where the various marketing functions are headed by separate managers who report to the marketing manager. Another common form is the product management organization, where major products are the responsibility of product managers who work with the various functional specialists to develop and achieve their plans for the product. Another, less common, form is the market management organization, where major markets are the responsibility of market managers who work with the various

functional specialists to develop and achieve their plans for the market. Some large companies use a product/market management organization, which combines both systems. Finally, multidivision companies normally utilize corporate management, developing a marketing staff and separate marketing department for each division.

Marketing must work in harmony with other company functions. In its pursuit of the customer's interests, marketing frequently comes into conflict with R & D, engineering, purchasing, manufacturing, inventory, finance, accounting, credit, and other functions that stress a cost-minimization logic. These conflicts can be reduced when the managing director commits the company to a customer orientation, and when the marketing director learns to work effectively with the other officers. Acquiring a modern marketing orientation requires top management support, a marketing task force, outside marketing-consulting help, a corporate marketing department, in-house marketing seminars, new marketing personnel, promotion of market-oriented executives, and a market-oriented planning system.

QUESTIONS FOR DISCUSSION

1. Discuss how the marketing department probably evolved in Australian Consolidated Industries Ltd.

2. What are the major advantages and disadvantages of organizing by function, geography or end-use markets?

3. Discuss the pros and cons of instituting the product management organization for International Harvester's line of farm equipment (i.e. tractors, combines, implements such as plows and harrows).

4. How does product/market management organization differ from corporate-divisional organization?

5. Marketing is the most important function in any firm. Comment.

6. What do you think would be the area of strongest interdepartmental conflict with marketing in the following organizations:
   - ICI
   - Jantzen (swimwear)
   - ANZ Bank
   - Cadbury Schweppes?

7. If a local museum was experiencing declining attendance, what strategies for a marketing orientation would you suggest?

NOTES

[1] This vignette has been prepared by (and is reproduced by kind permission from) Barry J. Beilby, General Manager, Marketing Services, Australia Post.

[2] See Elmer E. Waters, 'Industrial Product Manager . . . Consumer Brand Manager: A Study in Contrast', *Industrial Marketing*, January 1969, pp. 45–49.

[3] See David J. Luck, 'Interfaces of a Product Manager', *Journal of Marketing*, October 1969, pp. 32–36.

[4] Andrall E. Pearson & Thomas W. Wilson Jr, *Making Your Organization Work* (New York: Association of National Advertisers, 1967), pp. 8–13.

[5] For further reading, see Richard M. Clewett & Stanley F. Stasch, 'Shifting Role of the Product Manager', *Harvard Business Review*, January–February 1975, pp. 65–73; Victor P. Buell, 'The Changing Role of the Product Manager in Consumer Goods Companies', *Journal of Marketing*, July 1973, pp. 3–11; 'The Brand Manager: No Longer King', *Business Week*, 9 June 1973; and Joseph A. Morein, 'Shift from Brand to Product Line Marketing', *Harvard Business Review*, September–October 1975, pp. 56–64.

[6] Mark Hanan, 'Reorganize Your Company around Its Markets', *Harvard Business Review*, November–December 1974, pp. 63–74.

[7] See B. Charles Ames, 'Dilemma of Product/Market Management', *Harvard Business Review*, March–April 1971, pp. 66–74.

[8] See Watson Snyder Jr & Frank B. Gray, *The Corporate Marketing Staff: Its Role and Effectiveness in Multi-Division Companies* (Cambridge, Mass.: Marketing Science Institute, April 1971).

[9] This last quote is from Charles G. Mortimer, 'The Creative Factor in Marketing', Fifteenth Annual Parlin Memorial Lecture (Philadelphia Chapter, American Marketing Association, 13 May 1959).

[10] For further discussion, see Edward S. McKay, *The Marketing Mystique* (New York: American Management Association, 1972), pp. 22–30.

Part 3

Target Market Analysis

The Marketing Environment

7

The Australian caravan industry seems to have ended its five-year rationalization with last week's demise of Franklin's Caravans and the major producer Vicarr Industries Ltd expecting to increase its production by 20 per cent in the next year. The industry, from parks to van-finishers, is attempting a bigger comeback based on public boredom with petrol-pricing publicity and because of bigger, more powerful four-cylinder cars.

The market leader, Vicarr, holds a 60 per cent share, and is the result of a merger between the ailing Millard company and Viscount. The company has released a 78-model range under the title of Grand Tourer with prices ranging from $4700 to $12 925, where most industry hopes for continued revitalization centre.

But the news has not been good for Franklin's Caravans, which was closed down last week by its parent Escor Ltd. The company had a loss of $1 534 000 for the year, which prompted the decision. The caravan market has been in the process of rationalization for some time, and the Franklin's closure means the stranglehold of Vicarr will be extended in the next two years.

The caravan in many ways complements the motor vehicle market, and with the slump in six-cylinders there have not been the powerful cars to pull a caravan according to Franklin's. It had a basic five-model range with prices starting at $3500.

The comeback in the use of caravans is at the expense of motels and hotels, which have dropped from 16.2 to 15.2 per cent of the NSW visitor market in the last two years. At the same time caravan and camping grounds have increased their share of the market by 1.4 per cent to 14.9 per cent. There are now more *than 3000 caravan parks across Australia, with increases in numbers and value at around 15 per cent each year. Most of the new proprietors are professionals or wealthy businessmen able to outlay $500 000 to $1 million for a small to medium-sized park. The future is apparently in the creation of total entertainment complexes for the whole family, retaining the tourist's disposable income within the grounds through such things as water slides, electronic amusements, swimming pools, squash courts and laundromats. Reg Grundy's new leisure division plans a chain of parks between Adelaide and Brisbane – all a day's drive apart.*

There is a move away from families parking in rest areas because of the number of violent crimes on major highways. This might also encourage the use of parks in the future. Police, as well as a number of driver groups, are also unimpressed with the way the high-speed caravan on major highways sways like a drunk at a picnic. New caravans, including the Grand Tourers, are claimed to have smoother, wedged profiles, reducing wind resistance and saving petrol. Vicarr also claims its new models have a new suspension system, making caravans easier to tow.

The petrol crisis has passed in the mind of the Australian motorist, according to the executive administrator of the Caravan and Camping Industry Association, Mr John Stingemore. He said: 'People have been forced back to vans because of the lack of disposable income at the moment as well as the substantial increases in prices of holiday accommodation.'

The rent spiral has also affected many park owners, and most are paying between $10 000 and $50 000 in rates each year. As well as rents, electricity and water, which make the cost of each caravan space between $5000 and $6000 a year, the proprietor is continually faced with blocked drains, breakages and complaints from frustrated Charles Sturts who want the real outdoors with plumbing.

Caravan production figures have wavered disconcertingly over the past three years, with 18 157 made in 1978–79, 10 607 in 1979–80 and an improvement to 13 000 forecast for 1980–81. Companies which are buying only between 5 and 10 per cent of caravan production, are expected to increase this share in the next few years because of the mining and real estate booms.[1]

Marketing planning begins with a company's analysis of its marketing environment. The marketing environment is in continual flux, spinning off new opportunities and new threats. Instead of changing in a slow and predictable way, the environment is capable of causing major surprises and shocks. In 1971, which oil companies would have predicted the end of cheap energy in the following years? How many managers at H.J. Heinz foresaw the end of the 'baby boom'? Drucker has called this an age of discontinuity,[2] and Toffler has described it as future shock.[3]

The key to an organization's success is its

ability to spot and adapt to changes in the marketing environment. Every company needs to establish a monitoring system that continually tracks the changing environment: a major company may employ several professionals; smaller companies must settle for simply being alert and occasionally using an outside consultant (see Exhibit 7-1).

In this chapter we focus on the macro-environment – all the external, major institutions and forces that are potentially relevant to the firm. The macro-environment has six major components: demographic, economic, ecological, technological, political and cultural. We will examine the current trends occurring in each and consider their implications for company marketing strategy.

DEMOGRAPHIC ENVIRONMENT

The demographic environment is of major interest to marketers because people make up markets. Some major demographic trends are reviewed below.

World Population Growth

Perhaps the major fact about world population has been its recent explosive growth:

> In 1970 the population totalled 3.6 billion and the rate of growth was 2.1 per cent per year. The doubling time at this growth rate is thirty-three years. Thus, not only has the population been growing exponentially, but the rate of growth has also been growing.[4]

Exhibit 7-1 Environmental Forecasting

A local organization which is achieving a great deal of exposure in the forecasting area is IBIS Research Services which sells predictions to Kodak, GE, ICI and others, and enlivens many business conventions with its provocative scenarios. Some recent divinations include:

- By the mid-1980s the number of over 30-year-olds will exceed the under-30s for the first time in our Caucasian history.
- We can expect more conservatism, less noise and a more reflective society.
- We will have the feeling of being the lucky country again.
- We may assume a degree of brashness, even mild arrogance, as Australians develop a belief that they live in the 'Middle East' of the region.
- We can expect to be more religious and more married.
- The 1980s will have fewer industrial disputes.
- A 32-hour working week can be expected for some before 1990, and a 28-hour week soon after the turn of the century.
- Labor or a socialist party is likely to win two elections between 1980 and 2000, the non-socialists four or five.
- A strong return to home entertainment is likely, reminiscent of the 1930s and 1940s.
- We will debate immigration fiercely, finally accepting very high levels in the late 1980s.
- We will be deeply concerned with the economy and unemployment in the first half of the 1980s, but more buoyant and cocky in the second half.

Source: Steve Harris, 'The Future Without a Crystal Ball', *Age*, 27 July 1978, p. 9.

The 'population explosion' has been a major concern of many governments and groups throughout the world. Two factors underlie this concern. First, the earth's resources may not be able to support this much human life, particularly at levels that represent the aspiration of most people. Second, the rate of population growth is highest in the countries and communities that can least afford it.

Some relief may be in sight. Various students of world population have estimated that although global population may reach 5.8 billion by the year 2000, the rate of growth may have declined to about 1.7 per cent per annum.[5] The world's population was estimated to be 4.495 billion in September 1981, compared with 4.415 billion one year earlier.[6]

The rate of increase of the world's population has great importance for business. A growing population means growing human needs, and thus growing markets if there is sufficient purchasing power. On the other hand, if there is insufficient purchasing power, it means recession and vigorous attacks against business institutions.

Australian Demographics

In 1970, the Australian government initiated the National Population Inquiry chaired by Professor W. D. Borrie of the Australian National University. In 1975 the first report was tabled in the House of Representatives.[7] Many of its findings were not previously known or recognized, especially in the areas of population growth and its relevance to immigration policy, fertility rates and consequent effects on planned growth centres. A supplementary report was issued in 1978, clarifying and updating many of the areas covered by the first report. Several other publications have also appeared from various sources, some of which will reappear as revised editions each year.[8]

Some demographic elements of key rel-evance to the formulation of marketing policies are discussed below.

1. Age at marriage. In contrast to previous patterns (before 1971, about three out of four women married by age 24 and all but 5 per cent married by age 34), the average age of marriage is no longer declining, and may in fact be increasing in line with some overseas trends. This will slow down the sales of engagement and wedding rings, bridal outfits and life insurance.

2. High rates of marriage and household formation. Nearly 95 per cent of men and women have been marrying in recent times. This proportion represents a considerable increase since the early twentieth century, when economic constraints prevented many people from marrying. The slight drop in the current number of registered marriages may be the result of an increase in de facto unions. It seems, however, that household formation, and the associated demand for housing and related products, will grow by roughly stable increments in the near future, yielding progressively slower rates of growth as the population becomes larger.

3. Decline in marital fertility. Age-specific fertility rates (i.e. births per 1000 female population in each age group) have shown a general decrease since 1961. The major cause of this has been the declining fertility of married women.

4. Decrease in births. Although 224 000 births were registered in 1979–80 compared with 223 000 in 1978–79, the actual number of births decreased in the 1970s. This was clearly indicated in the 1976 census, which revealed 1 279 200 persons in the 5–9 age group but only 1 235 000 in the 0–4 age group. The net reproduction rate fell to 1.05 in 1975 and in 1976 to below 1.00 – at which point the birth rate is below the 'replacement rate'. In the absence of increased net migration, a stage of zero population growth may be reached in the twenty-first century.

The decline in birth rate is a threat to some industries and a boon to others. It has produced anxiety attacks in the boardrooms of companies dealing in children's toys, clothes, furniture, food and accessories. Reactions have varied; however: Johnson & Johnson is trying to interest adults in using their baby products; others offer travel, eating out and other recreations to young couples with fewer children and more time and income.

5. *Number of children per family.* By the 1940s, as a result of a long-term trend, the small family system had emerged, dominated by the family of two and three children. Since then a further shift has occurred away from childlessness and with reduced proportions of one-child families, towards higher proportions of two- and three-child families, and lower proportions of families with four or more children. The index of current marriage fertility declined from the equivalent of 2.7 children per marriage in 1956–60 to 1.8 in 1975.

Early completion of childbearing. About four out of five women now complete their families by the age of 30, i.e. long before fecundity begins to diminish. This results in the need to avoid unwanted pregnancies, and is obviously linked with changing attitudes to birth control and contraception, including abortion, and the concomitant advances in relevant technology. Also important is the increasing delay by couples in having their first child, leading to a 'bunching' effect in the years approaching the age of 30 for women, if they do have children.

7. *Divorce and remarriage.* The Family Law Act of 1975 altered the grounds for dissolution of marriage in such a way that the comparison of post-1975 divorce activity with early statistics can be misleading. It does seem, however, that Australia has an accelerating divorce rate, with about 20 per cent of marriages ending in divorce and with one in nine being dissolved by its tenth year. This has led to the establishment of thousands of additional housing units. More than 50 per cent of divorcees remarry leading to the phenomenon of the 'blended' family.

8. *Mortality and ageing.* In Australia, the average expectation of life from birth has risen from about 57 years in 1901–11, to 71 years for males and 78 years for females. This is largely due to the control of infectious diseases and improved education in preventative health care. As a result of this longevity an increasing proportion of adults now live to and beyond the age of retirement. This usually means an extension of married life, although the differential life expectancies generates a growing preponderance of widows. Coupled with the declining birth rate, this decrease in mortality has meant an ageing of the population; the median age is now about 30 and is expected to reach 35 by the year 2011.

9. *Education and dependence.* Approximately 20 per cent of Australians aged between 17 and 22 are engaged in tertiary education. This high participation rate greatly exceeds that of even ten years ago, and generally means that children are dependent on their parents for longer.

10. *Working women.* There has been a trend towards increased participation of women in the labour force before they bear children. The reduction of sex discrimination in employment, and the smaller number of years occupied with childbearing, have also contributed to increasing labour-force participation of women. Today more than 43 per cent of all married women hold a job.

These working women have increased the market for better clothing, child-care services, home cleaning services and convenience foods; and reduced that for television soap operas and domestic women's magazines. Their incomes contribute substantially to the household income and influence the purchase of more costly goods and services.

11. *Non-family households.* Approximately 16 per cent of all households comprise a lone person – the SSWD group (single, separated, widowed, divorced). These individuals

generally need small dwellings, inexpensive and smaller appliances, furniture, and furnishings, and food that is packed in smaller quantities. Some constitute a market for various services seeking to create social opportunities such as singles bars and discos, tours and cruises.

Two other non-family households are prominent today. The co-habitors (living together) include both heterosexual and gay couples, and since their arrangements may be temporary they tend to look for inexpensive household furnishings. Another set of people in the market for economic products comprise group households: three or more people of the same or different sexes share expenses by sharing accommodation. It is a common pattern amongst students, religious groups and, increasingly, young people on the dole.

12. Immigration patterns. Approximately 20 per cent of Australians were not Australian-born, perhaps one-third have neither parent born here, and close to one-half have at least one parent born elsewhere. The proportion of migrants and their immediate families is considerably higher in major metropolitan areas than in the country. More than 100 dialects or languages are now spoken in Australia; broadcasting occurs in thirty languages, and seventy newspapers are printed in a dozen languages. Yet of the 20 per cent of Australians born overseas, more than 40 per cent were born in Britian or Ireland and three out of four of the remaining 60 per cent were European-born, (primarily Italian, Greek and Yugoslav). Thus, Australia's 'ethnicity' is mainly Anglo-Saxon, which itself is heterogeneous, although recent moves to reduce discrimination in migration may increase the diversity further.

13. Geographic distribution. With 861 000 inhabitants, Victoria was the most populous Australian State in 1881. However, by 1901 New South Wales had regained the title with 1 354 000 of Australia's 3 773 000 people. Since then the dominance of the two States has been overwhelming, comprising 62 per cent of the national population in 1979. Not only is there regional concentration of population, but the level of urbanization is also extremely high by world standards. For example, 70 per cent of Australia's population resides in the eleven capital cities (excluding Darwin) and major towns of 100 000 persons or more (Newcastle, Wollongong, Geelong and the Gold Coast).

During the 1970s the drift from Sydney and Melbourne continued, both to Western Australia and more particularly to the south-eastern coast of Queensland. Similarly, concentration persisted in the seaboard areas of the nation and in the major growth corridors of the two larger capital cities. Some inland cities, such as Albury-Wodonga and Campbelltown, continued to grow. There was an acceleration of outer-suburban growth in major cities, and a widening of the area of population decline moving from the centre of cities outwards. City growth was retarded by the reduction in migrant intakes, and also by the lack of job opportunities which traditionally attract country youth. One in every six Australians over the age of 15 changes residential address each year, with approximately half of these 'internal migrants' remaining in the same capital city.

Marketers should be alert to the opportunities suggested by these geographic shifts. For example, those moving to Queensland and Western Australia will need less warm clothing and air-conditioners. Many suburban dwellers who have wealth and mobility are attracted to retailers in regional shopping complexes. On the other hand, many young people are renewing inner-city housing, which creates a market for renovation requisites and compact amenities.

14. Population projections and age distribution. An average annual growth rate of approximately 1.15 per cent in total population was presented in the Borrie report. This projection applied to 1986, and was based on a net reproduction rate of 1.0 and net immigration of 50 000 per year. Thus a population of 15.2 million was expected, rising to about 17.6 million in 2001 when the rate of growth was predicted to be less than 1.00 per cent and falling. A 'stationary state' population may not directly affect marketers, occurring around 2030 or later if at all, but the appropriate responses to a 'decelerating' state with marked distributional shifts should be carefully explored.

Various projections of population have appeared since the Borrie Report, and estimates of the population in 2001 are now between 18.4 and 19.6 million. It is thus possible to estimate the likely age distribution of the population for the remainder of the century. Some key age cohorts or groups are examined next.

The number of 5-year-olds should increase each year, while the number of 12-year-olds is likely to decrease in the later 1980s but increase substantially from the mid-1990s. As a proportion of the total population, the 0–14 age group will probably decrease from the current 25.0 per cent level to 22.8 per cent in 2001.

The number of 18-year-olds is expected to fluctuate substantially between now and the end of the century, with a peak around 1984 and a trough in 1989, followed by sustained growth. The 15–24 age group will generally decrease from 17.3 per cent of the total population to 13.5 per cent in 2001. This may foretell sagging sales of cricket and football equipment, records and other youth goods. It also suggests enrolment problems for educational institutions, which are already experiencing overcapacity and have to think about attracting new groups to the campus such as homemakers and retired people.

The 25–44 age group comprised only 25.3 per cent of the total population in 1971, but should rise to 30.8 per cent by 1991 and then decline to 29.6 per cent in 2001. With childbearing completed, and the resumption of two incomes in many cases, this market can look beyond household basics to more discretionary purchases of goods, services and 'experiences'.

The age group 45–64 years will increase slightly until the second half of the 1980s, when it will enter a period of rapid growth. This is the 'empty-nest' group whose children leave home and who thus find themselves with increased time and income. This group is a major market for eating out, travel, expensive clothes, and golf and other recreations.

The over-65 group will increase substantially from 8.4 per cent of the total population in 1971 to 12.2 per cent in 2001. This foretells a burgeoning demand for retirement homes and communities, quieter forms of recreation (fishing, golf, bowls), single-portion food packaging, and medical goods and services (medicines, spectacles, canes, hearing aids and convalescent homes). This group, and indeed the general ageing of the population, also means a slowing down in the adoption of new cultural ideas, more conservative politics, and new rights demanded by senior citizens to protect their standard of living.

These demographic trends are highly reliable in the short and medium term. There is little excuse for a company's being surprised by a demographic development: the alert firm can list the major trends, spell out their implications for a particular industry, and classify these from very positive to very negative. This process is applied in Table 7-1 for twelve major industries – in the case of airlines, for example, each population trend is expected to have a positive sales and profit impact.

ECONOMIC ENVIRONMENT

Markets require purchasing power as well as people. Total purchasing power is a function of current income, prices, savings, and credit availability. Marketers should be aware of four main trends in the economic environment.

Table 7-1 The changing population mix and which industries are likely to profit

Industry	Baby boom generation matures	More elderly persons	More working women	Smaller family units
Airlines	Many will have more money for travel as they get older ✓✓✓	They have the time to travel but inflation may rob them of the means ✓	Second income allows more families to take trips; more single women have money ✓✓✓	More disposable income per member; more economical to fly than drive ✓✓
Apparel	Will spend more on clothes as they age; shift from casual to higher quality ✓✓✓	Older people spend less on clothing ×	Career women need more clothing and have the money to buy it ✓✓✓	A shift toward higher-quality, higher-margin merchandise ✓✓
Cosmetics	This group is moving through prime cosmetic-usage years ✓✓✓	Elderly women often spend less on cosmetics ×	Career women use more cosmetics, and can better afford them ✓✓	More income, more divorced women, more single women ✓✓
Electronics (consumer)	Rising incomes provide means to buy better-quality stereos, TVs, etc. ✓✓	Little demand from this group; often forced to make do with older products ×	Can buy more and higher-priced merchandise ✓✓	More income per capita; electronic entertainment replaces family activities ✓✓
Machinery (agricultural)	No significant effect □	No significant effect □	No significant effect □	Need for mechanized equipment as substitute for manual labour ✓
Pollution control	No significant effect □	Driving less; will lessen demand for exhaust-control equipment ×	Slightly increased use of packaging materials adds to waste problems ✓	Slightly increased use of packaging materials adds to waste problems ✓
Health care	Little effect □	Largest consumers of health-care products and services ✓✓✓	Working women are having fewer children ✓	No significant effect □
Home furnishings	Will want to improve home environments ✓✓✓	Very small factor in this market □	With two paychecks can afford better furnishings ×	More households, all needing basic furnishings ✓✓✓
Leisure time	With rising incomes, they will spend more on travel and recreation ✓✓✓	Has most leisure time of all; if inflation abates, will be heavier spenders □	Single or married, they have money to spend on leisure activities ✓	More money per person, and with fewer children, more time for leisure ✓✓✓
Restaurants	This large group will have more money to eat out ✓✓✓	The elderly tend to eat out less ×	Little time or energy to cook at home ✓	Smaller families visit restaurants more frequently ✓✓✓
Retailing	As affluence increases, group will trade up in merchandise purchases ✓✓✓	Very price-conscious ×	Likely to spend more on high-margin merchandise ✓✓✓	High demand stemming from more disposable income per capita ✓✓✓
Textiles	Likely to expand wardrobes and spend heavily on home furnishings ✓✓✓	The elderly buy less clothing and home furnishings ×	Good for both apparel and furnishings ✓✓✓	A shift toward higher-priced fabrics ✓

✓✓✓ Very positive ✓✓ Positive ✓ Mildly positive □ Neutral × Negative

Source: Chicago Tribune, 8 April 1979, Section 5, p. 1. Copyright © 1979 by Standard & Poor's Corp., 345 Hudson St., New York, N.Y. 10014. Reproduction by permission.

Slowdown in Real Income Growth

Australian per-capita gross national product stood at $5368 in 1976, ranking fourteenth on a world list behind such countries as the United States ($6943) and Sweden ($7629), but ahead of Japan ($4320) and New Zealand ($3740).[9] Average household income (with 3.09 persons in the average household) stood at $11 000 in 1975–76.

Although money income per capita keeps rising, there has been little or no growth in *real* income per capita since 1975. This is the result of several factors – an inflation rate exceeding the money income growth rate, an unemployment rate between 5 and 8 per cent, and an increase in the tax burden – which have reduced disposable personal income (i.e. the amount people have left after taxes). Furthermore, many people have experienced reduced discretionary income, i.e. the amount they have left after paying for basic food, clothing, shelter, insurance and other necessaries. Reductions in discretionary income hurt sellers of discretionary goods and services, such as cars, large appliances, and holidays. On the positive side, however, there has been a rise in the number of two-income families, which has increased average family earnings. Many companies have introduced 'economy' versions of their products and have turned to price appeals in their advertising messages. Some consumers have postponed their purchase of durable items, while others have purchased out of fear that prices will be 10 per cent higher next year. Many families have begun to feel that a large home, two cars, foreign travel, and private education are now beyond their reach. Of course, for many people this ideal has always been beyond their reach – for example, the 270 000 permanent residents of caravan parks, the 16 per cent of households with no car at all and the social security recipients who exist below the poverty line.

Therefore, marketers should also pay attention to income differences as well as average income trends. Income distribution in Australia is still pronouncedly skewed: 50 per cent of aggregate family income is received by the top 30 per cent of families, while only 13 per cent is received by the lowest 30 per cent of families. Even more striking is the assertion that 22 per cent of all personal wealth is held by just one per cent of Australia's adult population.[10] At the top are upper class consumers, whose expenditure patterns have not been affected by current economic events; such consumers still represent a major market for luxury goods (Rolls Royces at up to $150 000) and services (round-the-world cruises starting at $10 000). There is a comfortable middle class that exercises some expenditure restraint but is able to afford 'luxuries' (expensive clothes, minor antiques, a small boat, a second home). The working class must stick closer to the basics of food, clothing and shelter, and husband their resources. Finally, there is the 'underclass' (persons on social security benefits) and retirees, who have to count their pennies carefully when making purchases of even the most basic kind.

Income levels and growth rates also vary regionally. They are affected by the level of local economic activity and employment, the rate of migration, and wage rates. For example, average income tends to be higher in the Australian Capital Territory and lower in Tasmania and South Australia. Such differences must be taken into account when planning marketing programmes.

Continued Inflationary Pressure

A high rate of inflation continues to push up the prices of cars, house construction, furniture, medical care, and food. Inflation leads consumers to search for opportunities to save money, such as buying cheaper brands in large economy sizes, buying from less-expensive retail outlets, performing more of their own services, and bartering services with others.

In an advertisement for an investment newsletter, the following prices have been forecast for 1990: milk, $2.50 per litre; bread, $2.30 per loaf; beer, $3.60 per bottle; newspapers 60 cents each; postage, $1.00 per local letter; petrol, $1.20 per litre; and $30 000 for an average four-cylinder car.[11]

Changing Savings and Debt Patterns

Consumer expenditures are also affected by consumer savings and debt patterns. Australians hold their savings in the form of bank savings accounts, building-society and credit-union deposits, bonds and shares, real estate, insurance and other assets. These savings are a major source of finance for major durable purchases.

Consumers can also increase their purchases through borrowing. Consumer credit has been a major contributor to the rapid growth of the Australian economy, enabling people to buy more than their current income or savings permitted and thus creating more jobs and still more income and more demand. In June 1981, bankcard holders had total debts of $1168 million, although their authorized limits were $3392 million. A CBC Bank survey showed that the average worker owes more than $5000, and uses 43 per cent of his disposable income to pay off debts compared to 23 per cent in 1960.[12] Clearly credit is costly, with interest rates of up to 20 per cent or even higher. This retards the further growth of housing and other durable-goods markets that are heavily dependent on credit.

Changing Consumer Expenditure Patterns

As people's incomes change, marketers can expect pronounced shifts in the relative demand for different categories of goods and services. Such shifts were noted as early as 1875 by the German statistician Ernst Engel, who compared the budgets of individual working-class families. Engel observed that while rising family income tended to be accompanied by increased spending in all categories, the percentage spent on food tended to decline, the percentage spent on housing and household operations tended to remain constant, and the percentage spent on other categories (clothing, transport, recreation, health and education) and savings tended to increase. This 'law' has generally been validated in subsequent budget studies. At the same time, a company involved in a particular product category will want to look more closely at how expenditures there vary with income. For example, a higher income may lead to the purchase of higher-quality food rather than more food, thus causing food expenditures to remain proportionately constant for a while. In general, however, as incomes rise people will spend a higher proportion of their incomes on major durables, luxury goods, and services.

Changes in major economic variables – money income, cost of living, interest rates, savings and borrowing patterns – have an immediate impact on the marketplace. Some industries are particularly income-sensitive, and companies in these industries would be well advised to invest in sophisticated economic forecasting. Businesses need not be wiped out by a downturn in economic activity: with adequate forewarning, they can take the necessary steps to tighten their sales and ride out the economic storm.

ECOLOGICAL ENVIRONMENT

The 1960s witnessed growing public concern over whether the natural environment was being irreparably damaged by the industrial activities of modern nations. Kenneth Boulding pointed out that the planet Earth was like a spaceship in danger of running out of fuel if it failed to recycle its materials. The Meadowses and others, in *The Limits to Growth*, raised concern about the adequacy of future natural resources to sustain economic growth. Rachel Carson, in *The Silent Spring*, pointed out the environmental damage to water, earth and air caused by industrial activity of certain kinds. These warnings led to the formation of various watchdog groups such as the Australian Conservation Foundation and Friends of the Earth, as well as various proposals to regulate the impact of industrial activity on the natural environment. (This is discussed further in Chapter 21.)

Marketers should be aware of the challenges and opportunities created by four trends in the ecological environment.

Impending Shortages of Certain Raw Materials

The earth's materials fall into three groups: the infinite, the renewable finite, and the non-renewable finite. Infinite resources such as water and air pose no immediate problem, although it is argued that there is too high a level of pollution. Environmental groups have lobbied for the banning of aerosol cans because of their potential damage to the ozone layer of the atmosphere, and they have fought against the pollution of water bodies and various streams by unregulated industrial wastes.

Renewable finite resources such as forests and food pose no immediate problem, but may be a concern in the longer term. Companies in the forestry business are increasingly required to re-afforest timberlands, in order to protect the soil and to ensure a sufficient level of wood supply to meet future demand. Food supply may be a major problem in that the amount of arable land is relatively fixed and urban areas are constantly expanding to absorb farmland.

Non-renewable finite resources such as oil, coal and various minerals do pose a serious problem:

> ... it would appear at present that the quantities of platinum, gold, zinc, and lead are not sufficient to meet demands ... silver, tin, and uranium may be in short supply even at

higher prices by the turn of the century. By the year 2050, several more minerals may be exhausted if the current rate of consumption continues.[13]

The marketing implications are many. Firms that rely on these minerals face substantial cost increases even if the materials remain available, and they may not find it easy to pass these cost increases on to the consumer. There is a need to find substitute minerals. Firms engaged in research and development and exploration have an immense opportunity to develop valuable new sources and materials.

Increased Cost of Energy

One finite and non-renewable resource – oil – has created the most serious problem for future economic growth. The major industrial economies of the world are heavily dependent on oil, and until substitute forms of energy can be developed on a practical basis it will continue to dominate the world political and economic picture. The shortage of oil and consequent price manipulation have created a frantic search for alternative forms of energy. Coal is once again popular, and companies are investigating practical schemes to harness solar, nuclear, wind and other forms of energy. In the solar-energy field alone, hundreds of firms are putting out first-generation products to harness solar energy for heating homes and other uses. Other firms are searching for ways to make a practical electric car, with a vast potential prize going to the winner.

Increased Levels of Pollution

Some portion of modern industrial activity will inevitably damage the quality of the natural environment. One has only to think of the disposal of chemical and nuclear wastes, the dangerous mercury levels in the ocean, the quantity of DDT and other chemical pollutants in the soil and food supply, and the littering of the environment with non-biodegradable bottles, plastics and other packaging materials.

Public concern in this regard constitutes a marketing opportunity in two ways. First, it creates a large market for pollution-control solutions such as recycling centres. Second, it invites the discovery of alternative ways to produce and package goods that do not cause environmental damage.[14]

Increasing Government Intervention in Natural-resource Management

Growing concern about the deterioration of the natural environment has led various government agencies to regulate and enforce conservation and pollution-control behaviour. Ironically, this effort to protect the environment often runs counter to attempts to increase employment and economic growth, such as when business is forced to buy expensive pollution cleanup equipment instead of investing in capital-producing goods. From time to time, conservation politics takes a back seat to economic-growth politics. Marketing management must be alert to regulatory developments and to the opportunities afforded by efforts to protect the natural environment.

Marketing management will have to pay increasing attention to ecological issues, in terms of both obtaining needed resources and avoiding damage to the natural environment. Business may expect to face increasing controls from both government and pressure groups. Instead of opposing all forms of regulation, companies should try to find socially acceptable solutions to the materials and energy problems facing the nation.

TECHNOLOGICAL ENVIRONMENT

The most dramatic force shaping people's destiny is technology. Technology has released such wonders as penicillin, open-heart surgery, and the birth-control pill; it has released such horrors as the hydrogen bomb, nerve gas, and the submachine gun; it has released such mixed blessings as the car, television set, and white bread. One's response to these determines one's attitude toward technology.

Every new technology has the potential to spawn a major industry. One has only to think of transistors, xerography, computers and antibiotics. These industries not only create but destroy: transistors hurt the vacuum-tube industry, and xerography hurt the carbon-paper business; the car hurt the railways, and television hurt the cinemas. The economist Schumpeter saw technology as a force for 'creative destruction'. Every enterprise must watch what is new in the environment, for this might eventually destroy it – if it has imagination, the new might save it. It is discouraging that most phonograph companies did not enter the radio field, wagon manufacturers did not enter the motor-vehicle business, and steam locomotive companies did not enter the diesel locomotive business.

The growth rate of the economy is intimately tied to how many major new technologies arise in the coming years. Unfortunately, technological discoveries are not generally regular: the railway industry created a lot of investment and then there was a dearth until the car industry emerged; the same applied in the case of radio and television. In the absence of major innovations which open up great markets and opportunities, an economy can stagnate.

There are of course usually small innovations filling such gaps. Freeze-dried coffee probably made no one happier and antiperspirant deodorants probably made no one wiser, but they meet certain daily needs in an improved manner.

New technology creates some major long-run consequences that are not always foreseeable. The contraceptive pill, for example, led to smaller families, more working wives, and larger discretionary incomes – resulting in higher expenditures on holiday travel, among other things. Little did the airlines foresee that the pill would increase their traffic. The pill also led to the enlargement of the average size of brassieres, something that the women's lingerie industry had missed entirely.

Following are some of the main trends in technology that the marketer should watch.

Accelerating Pace of Technological Change

Most of the technological products we take for granted today were not available even 100 years ago. In the 1850s, people celebrating the naming of the colonies Victoria, Tasmania and Queensland did not know of cars, aeroplanes, record-players, radio or the electric light. In 1901, Australians experiencing the federation of the former colonies did not know of television, aerosol cans, home freezers, automatic dishwashers, room air-conditioners, antibiotics or electronic computers. The victims of World War II did not know of xerography, synthetic detergents, tape-recorders, birth-control pills or earth satellites. And Prime Minister Harold Holt knew little of the following recent innovations:

- Rotary engines
- Fuel-injection engines
- Electronic pocket calculators
- Felt-tipped and nylon-tipped pens
- Digital wristwatches
- Videotape machines for home use
- Garbage compactors
- Microwave ovens
- Freeze-dried coffee
- Polaroid movie cameras
- Four-channel stereo
- Water beds
- Noncholesterol egg substitutes
- Sugar substitutes

People – even well-qualified experts – have usually greeted new ideas with scepticism.

Consider the following major forecasting blunders:

Cars: 'The ordinary "horseless carriage" is at present a luxury for the wealthy; and although its price will probably fall in the future, it will never, of course, come into as common use as the bicycle.'

Literary Digest, 14 October 1899

Commerical television: 'While theoretically and technically television may be feasible, commercially and financially I consider it an impossibility, a development of which we need waste little time dreaming.'

Lee DeForest, 1926

Moon landing: 'Landing and moving around the moon offers so many serious problems for human beings that it may take science another 200 years to lick them.'

Science Digest, August 1948

Alvin Toffler, in his book *Future Shock*, sees things quite differently – namely, an accelerative thrust in the successful invention, exploitation and diffusion of new technologies.[15] More ideas are being worked on; the time lag between idea and successful implementation is falling rapidly; and the time between introduction and peak production is shortening considerably. Toffler sees technology as feeding on itself. As someone has observed, 90 per cent of all the scientists who ever lived are still alive.

Unlimited Innovational Opportunities

There seems to be no dearth of ideas for needed new products and services, only a delay in bringing them to economic and technical fruition.[16] Among the most important needed innovations being worked on today are:

- Practical solar energy
- Cancer cures
- Electric cars
- Desalination of seawater
- Home computer systems

- Lung and liver pills
- Household robots to do cleaning and cooking
- Non-fattening, tasty, nutritious foods
- Happiness pills
- Chemical control of mental illness
- Electronic anaesthetic for pain killing
- Totally safe and effective contraception

- Small flying cars
- Single-person rocket belts
- Three-dimensional television
- Commercial space shuttle
- Space colonies
- Human clones

Scientists are also working on more 'far-out' fantasy products, including the following:

The challenge in each case is not technical but commercial, i.e. to command the marketing skills to present new technological products to target markets in a highly attractive and affordable manner.

Exhibit 7-2 The Home of the Future

Ring . . . 'Oh, hello, Sue,' said Jill as her Picturephone screen came into focus. 'Would you hold on for one moment while I instruct the computer not to let my French gourmet dinner overcook? You know how temperamental these gourmet dishes are if you let them cook more than five minutes.' As Jill attends to her dinner, Sue types a few code words into her computer terminal and receives her facsimile newspaper, with the lead story describing a giant transparent bubble being put over Hobart to keep the city at 20°C all year round. Jill returns. 'Say, Jill, did you see the marvellous movie on three-dimensional TV last night?' 'No, I didn't, but I preprogrammed my computer to have it videotaped before I left in my new electric car for an evening out on the town.'

Is this the future — where home entertainment, cooking, and news reports are controlled by mini-computers in the home? Not exactly. As a matter of fact, the dialogue of Sue and Jill only scratches the surface of the home of the future.

Many envisage a day when the home computer will act as a central control device for functional as well as entertainment purposes in the home. For example, the computer will act as a monitor and control for efficient air-conditioning and heating, dishwashing, security control, and personal budget management. It will direct a home robot to carry out cleaning activities.

In the entertainment domain, the computer will provide a basis for developing computer 'art' and 'music' along with an expansive array of games to be played. It will also serve as a learning centre for children and adults alike and allow home access to any document in the public library.

What is the marketing challenge posed by the home computer? Marketers will have to learn how to market a whole new lifestyle centred on an extremely automated environment. As all chores are handled and pleasures provided by the flick of a switch, people will have an increased appetite for new experiences. The day of marketing 'experiences' rather than products will have arrived.

Source: Adapted from an unpublished paper by Rob Philiotis, by permission.

Fluctuating R & D Budgets

Australian expenditure on industrial research and development declined during the 1970s from approximately 1.2 per cent of gross domestic product in 1973–74, to about one per cent in 1976–77, and is now probably somewhat less than one per cent. Thus, approximately $1 billion is spent annually, with governments providing about 60 per cent of the funds and undertaking approximately 40 per cent (in terms of expenditure) of the overall national R & D effort.[17]

In the early 1970s, some 4500 technical people were employed in industry in R & D; towards the end of that decade the figure was less than 3000.[18] It seems that few manufacturing firms have concerted research programmes, and that most of these are overseas-controlled;[19] it may be that much of the R & D carried out in Australia consists of modifying foreign developments for the local market.

The Commonwealth Scientific and Industrial Research Organization (CSIRO) is a statutory body which was established in 1949. It is the largest research organization in Australia, with an annual budget of approximately $200 million. Much of its research effort focuses on aspects of primary industry, although increasing attention is being devoted to areas of secondary industry.

The Australian government has various incentive schemes to encourage R & D, including the Industrial R & D Grants scheme which dispensed $24 million to industry in 1978–79. Payments of 50 per cent of project costs, up to a maximum of $500 000 per annum per company, are made to approved firms.

Most of today's research is carried out by scientific teams working in research laboratories, rather than by independent inventors of the breed of Thomas Edison, Samuel Morse or Alexander Graham Bell. Managing scientific personnel poses major challenges: these people are professionals who resent too much cost control, and many of them are more interested in solving scientific problems than in coming up with marketable products. Yet companies are making some progress in convincing their scientific personnel that there is a need for a stronger marketing orientation.

Concentration on Minor Improvements Rather Than Major Discoveries

Tight money in recent years has led many companies to concentrate on pursuing major product improvements rather than gambling on major innovations. In the past, such major foreign companies as Du Pont, Bell Laboratories, and Pfizer would invest heavily to make major breakthroughs and were successful in many cases. Even these companies seem to be pursuing more modest goals today. Most companies are content to put their money into improving such things as antiperspirant deodorants, car styles, and soft-drink flavours. Some part of every R & D budget is spent simply on watching or copying competitors' products rather than striving to surpass them.

Increased Regulation of Technological Change

Technological change is encountering more regulation and opposition than ever before. As products become more complex, the public needs to be assured of their safety. Government agencies have responded by expanding their powers to investigate and ban new products that might be directly harmful or have questionable side effects. The Department of Health, for example, has issued elaborate regulations governing the scientific testing of new drugs, resulting in: (i) much higher research costs; (ii) longer intervals between idea and introduction (now about nine years) and (iii) the migration of much drug research to other parts of the world, where regulations are less stringent. Safety and health regulations have substantially increased in other areas, including food, motor vehicles, clothing, electrical appliances, and construction. Marketers must be aware of these regulations and take them seriously when proposing, developing and launching new products.

Technological change is also meeting opposition from those who see large-scale technology as a threat to nature, privacy, simplicity and even the human race. They have opposed the construction of new power plants, high-rise buildings, and recreational facilities in national parks. They have clamoured for assessment of new technologies before permitting them to be commercialized in this society (see Exhibit 7-3). A sign of this increased awareness was the appointment of a committee of inquiry into technological change in Australia, which presented its report in 1980.[20]

Marketers must understand the technological environment and the nuances of technology. They must be able to foresee how technology may be connected with human needs. They must work closely with R & D people to encourage more market-oriented research. They must be alert to the possible negative aspects of any innovation.

POLITICAL ENVIRONMENT

Developments in the political environment are increasingly affecting decisions on the market-

---

Exhibit 7-3 Technology Assessment

At a recent seminar, participants from government, industry and education agreed that Australia needs some system of technology assessment and futures studies, but many participants were sceptical that this could be effectively incorporated into Australia's existing political system.

Of a list of 20 possible studies for corporate and national planning in Australia to the year 2000, those ranked as having top priority were:

- Implications of developing relations with South-East Asian countries for Australian economy and society.
- Alternative energy supply/demand scenarios for Australia.
- Changing world trade relations and structural adjustment in the Australian economy.
- Youth unemployment and socio-economic change in Australian society.
- Technology, productivity and employment in Australian manufacturing industries.
- Growth prospects for the mineral and metal processing industries in Australia.
- Research and development priorities and innovation opportunities and needs in Australian industry.
- Petroleum energy conservation options in transport to the year 2000.
- Alternative economic, social and technological futures for Australia.
- Socio-economic impacts of new computer information and communication technologies.

Source: 'How Australia Should Plan for Year 2000', *Australian Financial Review*, 14 July 1978, p. 10.

ing of goods and services. A political system covers the rules and institutions by which a nation is governed, consisting of an interacting set of laws, government agencies, and pressure groups that influence and constrain the conduct of various organizations and individuals in the society.

We will now examine the main political trends and their implications for marketing management.

Increasing Regulation of Business

In Australia and various other countries, the basic political model is that of a democratic, regulated capitalist market economy. Consumers and business firms are generally free to pursue their self-interest, except where this is clearly harmful to others or to the larger society. Government is to play a minor role, limiting itself to activities such as war and defence, public works (roads, public monuments), public services (fire, police, schools, justice), and regulation to maintain competition and protect public health. Over the years the government sector has steadily increased its power and is now the major employer in Australia, accounting for 32 per cent of the labour force and spending approximately 30 per cent of the gross national product. Its growth has been abetted by the demands of pressure groups for favours or protection. While many nations have adopted a socialist model of society, with government ownership and operation of major industries, most Australians seem to prefer government in the role of regulator, not initiator, of economic activity.

Legislation affecting business has steadily increased over the years, partly in reaction to the growing complexity of technology and business practices. Such legislation seeks to accomplish any of three purposes. The first is to protect companies from each other. Business executives all praise competition in the abstract, but try to neutralize it when it

touches them. If threatened, they show their teeth:

> A Rockhampton-based merchant recently called for the licensing of new shopping centres. Aghast at the apparent prospect of 'overstoring', the company's chief executive told its annual meeting that television and radio stations, hotels and service stations all had to apply for and receive a licence to operate before setting up business. The time had come, he said, for an extension of this procedure to the developers of shopping complexes.[21]

So laws are passed to define and prevent unfair competition. These laws are enforced by the Trade Practices Commission and other national and State authorities. Sometimes, unfortunately, these regulations end up protecting the inefficient rather than promoting the efficient but, by and large, they help discourage business executives from dishonourable competitive practices. It is difficult to imagine that the economy would be more efficient if competition were not supervised.

The second purpose of government regulation is to protect consumers from business firms. A few firms are willing to adulterate their products, mislead through their advertising, deceive through their packaging, and bait through their prices. Unfair consumer practices must be defined, and agencies established to protect consumers. Many business executives see red with each new consumer law, and yet a few have said that 'consumerism may be the best thing that has happened . . . in the past 20 years'.[22]

The third purpose of government regulation is to protect the larger interests of society against unbridled business behaviour. Gross national product may rise but the quality of life deteriorates at the same time. Most firms are not charged with the social costs of their production or products. Their prices are artificially low and their sales artificially high until agencies such as the Environmental Protection Agencies shift the social costs back to these firms and their customers. As the environment continues to deteriorate, new laws and their enforcement will continue or increase. Business executives have to watch these developments in planning their products and marketing systems.

Marketing executives cannot plan intelligently without a good working knowledge of the major laws and regulations that exist to protect competition, consumers and the larger interests of society. They should know why national laws were passed, and how they are being interpreted in the courts. And they should know the many State and local laws affecting the conduct of the marketing activity.

It seems that, apart from eight voluntary industry codes, there are at least nine national and thirty-nine State Acts (plus more than fifty regulations) directly concerned with the control of marketing practices.[23] An excellent source of information in this area is a publication by the Commercial Economic Advisory Service of Australia, entitled *Marketing and the Law*. Other leading publications include the *Trade Practices Reporter* published by CCH Australia. These manuals provide a continuous update service covering recent developments.[24]

The paramount piece of legislation affecting Australian business is the Trade Practices Act 1974, as amended in 1977 and later.[25] Of twelve parts, the provisions relating to restrictive trade practices (part IV) and consumer protection (part V) are the most important to marketers, although familiarity with the other parts is also desirable.

Restrictive trade practices. Under the restrictive trade practices provisions the following are prohibited:

1. Agreements restricting dealings or affecting competition, i.e. contracts, arrangements or understandings that have the purpose or effect (or likely effect) of substantially lessening competition, or that are between competitors and restrict or limit the supply of goods or services.
2. Agreements in relation to prices, i.e. contracts, arrangements or understandings that have the purpose or effect (or likely effect) of fixing, controlling or maintaining prices.
3. Covenants running with land affecting competition.
4. Covenants running with land fixing prices.
5. Secondary boycotts.
6. Monopolization.
7. Exclusive dealing.
8. Resale price maintenance.
9. Price discrimination.
10. Mergers involving control or domination of a market.

Consumer protection. The major consumer protection provisions are contained in two divisions. In relation to unfair practices, there are provisions for the following:

1. Misleading or deceptive conduct.
2. False representations.
3. Offering gifts and prizes.
4. Bait advertising.
5. Referral selling.
6. Accepting payment without intending to supply as ordered.
7. Misleading statements about certain business activities.
8. Coercion at place of residence.
9. Pyramid selling.
10. Product safety standards.
11. Information standards.
12. Unsolicited credit cards.
13. Payment for unsolicited goods and directory entries.
14. Liability of recipients of unsolicited goods.

The conditions and warranties division deals with:

1. Hire-purchase and other contracts.
2. Supply by sample and description.
3. Implied undertakings as to quality and fitness.
4. Liability in case of breach of contract.
5. Warranties in relation to the supply of services.

Under a 1978 amendment to the Act, consumers may have up to ten years from the date of purchase in which to bring an action following the discovery of an inherent defect in an article.

The Trade Practices Commission, established under the Act, has three main functions: (i) research into aspects of law reform relevant to consumers, and the dissemination of information relating to the rights and obligations of persons under the provisions of the Act; (ii) authorization or clearance of contracts or arrangements which could otherwise be prohibited under the Act; (iii) enforcement of the Act via the Industrial Court, by instituting proceedings for the recovery of pecuniary penalties and the obtaining of injunctions restraining offences. The function of the Trade Practices Tribunal (set up under earlier legislation) is to hear applications for review of determinations by the Commission granting or revoking authorizations.

In addition to the laws mentioned above, new bills to regulate business are proposed in parliament each year. Not all of them, however, are passed, or passed in the form intended – lobbying has in many cases compromised bills until they are only a shadow of the original proposal, and thus has become a major marketing tool for an increasing number of Australian firms. Sorely lacking in the whole area of business legislation is a mechanism for formally evaluating the full effects of the law's enforcement upon both business and consumers, which would encourage the formulation of more effective legislation.

Growth of Public-interest Groups

Another political development is the rapid growth in recent years of groups lobbying for increased consumer protection and business regulation. These various pressure groups – concerned with issues such as the environment, advancement of women, Aborigines, senior citizens, the handicapped – may represent a new and dynamic form of public representation capable of challenging conventional party politics.

Various developments (new laws, more active enforcement, growing pressure groups) have severely constrained business, and marketers have increasingly had to clear their planned moves with the company's legal and public relations departments. Private marketing transactions have gradually moved into the public domain, the marketers can no longer follow the simple credo of meeting consumer wants. Salancik and Upah put it this way:

There is some evidence that the consumer may not be king, nor even queen. The consumer is but a voice, one among many. Consider how General Motors makes its cars today. Vital features of the motor are designed by the government; the exhaust system is redesigned by certain state governments; the production materials used are dictated by suppliers who control scarce material resources. For other products, other groups and organizations may get involved. Thus, insurance companies directly or indirectly affect the design of smoke detectors; scientific groups affect the design of spray products by condemning aerosols; minority activist groups affect the design of dolls by requesting representative figures. Legal departments also can be expected to increase their importance in firms, affecting not only product design and promotion but also marketing strategies. At a minimum, marketing managers will spend less time with their research departments asking 'What does the consumer want' and more and more time with their production and legal people asking 'What can the consumer have'.[26]

CULTURAL ENVIRONMENT

Another major component of the macro-environment is culture. People grow up in a particular society that shapes their basic beliefs, values and norms. They absorb, almost unconsciously, a world view that defines their relationship to themselves, others, institutions, society at large, nature and the cosmos. The following cultural characteristics can affect marketing decision-making.

Core Cultural Values Persist

People in a given society hold many beliefs and values, not all of which are equally important. Those that are most central can be called core beliefs and values, and have a high degree of persistence. For example, most Australians believe in work, marriage, giving to charity, and being honest. These beliefs shape and colour everyday attitudes and behaviours: they are passed on from parents to children, and are reinforced by the major institutions of society (schools, churches, business, government).

People also hold secondary beliefs and values that are more open to change in the wake of new social forces. Believing in the institution of marriage is a core belief; believing that people ought to get married early is a secondary belief. Debates about whether cultural change is slow or fast in this society often fail to distinguish between core and secondary beliefs and values.

Marketers who would like to change core beliefs and values would be wise not to try. A women's-clothing designer who wants to sell women on the idea of going topless would be attacking a core value held by both men and women. The same designer, however, may succeed in selling women on wearing shorter skirts or lower necklines, because this does less violence to their core beliefs.

Each Culture Consists of Subcultures

Although a society is characterized by particular core beliefs and values, there are always groups who deviate from the accepted norms (e.g. criminals). Furthermore, there can be much variation in secondary beliefs and values, giving rise to subcultures. For example, immigrants, the super-rich and the intelligentsia, because they have had different life experiences and face different issues, will exhibit different systems of beliefs and values. This will be reflected in different patterns of consumer wants and behaviour.

One also finds cultural differences between generations. In a modern Australian family, the grandparents are conservative in their tastes and careful in their expenditures; the parents work and play hard and purchase many things on credit; their 18-year-old son may show little interest in either work or consunption.

Secondary Cultural Values Undergo Shifts

Although core cultural values are fairly persistent, there are always more transient cultural events that are worth monitoring. Consider the impact that such culture heroes as the 'hippies', the Beatles and Elvis Presley, as well as *Playboy* magazine, have had on young people's hairstyles, clothing, and sexual norms.

The measurement and forecasting of cultural change is still highly speculative. Occasionally some major companies, marketing research firms, and futures research firms issue reports that summarize cultural trends. One of the best known of these is the *Australian Social Barometer* produced by a division of the Roy Morgan Research Centre. The output is usually in the form of a 'state of the nation' document, plus brand or product usage profiles. Each year approximately 400 respondents throughout Australia are asked a wide variety of questions, including their opinions on more than 200 social and political issues, and their consumption of over 100 goods and services.

A distinction should be drawn between the dominant value system and trends in the value system. Most people in this society see themselves as 'happy, home-loving, clean and traditional' (the dominant value system); and although there is a slight trend toward less conventional behaviour (e.g. open marriage, cohabitation) this is never practised by more than a small percentage of the population despite the undue emphasis given to it by the news media. Thus major producers will want to cater to dominant value groups, and minor producers may see less-conventional groups as a market niche opportunity.

The major cultural values and shifts in people's relationship to themselves, others, institutions, society, nature and the cosmos can be summarized as follows.

People's relation to themselves. People vary in how much emphasis they put on gratifying their own needs versus serving others. Today more people focus on self-fulfilment, seeking to do the things they want to do rather than follow conventions or please other people. Some are pleasure-seekers, wanting to have fun, change, and escape from the humdrum; others are pursuing self-realization by joining therapeutic or religious groups.

The marketing implications of this trend are many. People seek self-expression through the product, brand and service choices they make. They are more willing to buy their 'dream cars' and take 'dream holidays'; they will spend more time in the wilderness, in health activities (jogging, tennis, yoga) and introspection, and will be interested in arts and crafts. The leisure industry (camping, boating, arts and crafts, sports) has a good growth outlook as a result.

People's relation to others. People choose to live their lives with different degrees of sociability – from seclusion to gregariousness. One trend seems to be a desire for more open and easy relationships with others – people want to be able to say things on their mind without causing offence, they want to 'tell it like it is'.

For marketers, this means several things. People may prefer products such as furniture to be more casual and less pretentious. They may want packaging to provide more complete and honest information. They may want advertising messages to be more realistic. They may want salespersons to be more honest and helpful.

People's relation to institutions. People vary in how they feel about major institutions such as big companies, government agencies, trade unions, universities and hospitals. By and large, people are willing to work in major institutions and rely on them to carry out society's work. There is, however, a trend towards declining loyalty to institutions: people are inclined to give them a little less, and to trust them a little less. The work ethic has gradually been eroding.

The marketing implications of this trend are several. Companies will be challenged to find new ways to build consumer confidence in themselves and their products. They will have to review advertising communications to make sure that their messages do not raise the question: Can you trust this company? They will have to review their various interactions with the public to make sure that they are coming across as 'solid citizens'. More companies are turning to social audits and enlightened public relations to maintain a positive relationship with their publics.[27]

People's relation to society. People vary in their attitudes toward the society in which they live – there are patriots who defend it, reformers who want to change it, and discontents who want to leave it. There is, however, a trend toward declining patriotism, with stronger criticism and cynicism about where the country is going.

People's orientation to their society will influence their consumption patterns, levels of savings, and attitudes toward the marketplace.

People's relation to nature. People vary in their relation to nature. Some feel subjugated by it, others are in harmony with it, and still other seek mastery over it. One of the major long-term trends in Western society has been people's growing mastery over nature through technology. Co-existing with this has been the attitude that nature is bountiful and that nature's riches are infinite. More recently there has been a growing awareness of nature's fragility and a desire to preserve its magnificence. People are becoming aware that nature can be destroyed or spoiled by human activities.

Consumers are increasingly participating in such activities as camping, hiking, boating and fishing. Business is responding by producing a large assortment of equipment for nature enthusiasts; tour operators are packaging more trips to Australia's wilderness areas; food producers have found growing markets for 'natural' products, such as 100 per cent natural cereal, natural ice cream, and health foods; marketing communicators are using beautiful natural backgrounds in advertising many of their products.

People's relation to the universe. People vary in their belief system about the origin of the universe and their place in it. Most Australians are monotheistic, although their religious conviction and practice has been waning through the years. Church attendance has been falling steadily, with the exception of certain evangelical movements. Some of the religious impulse has been translated into a growing interest in Eastern religions, mysticism and the occult.

The marketing implications are several. As people lose their religious orientation, they in-crease their efforts to enjoy life as fully as possible. Their interest centres on earthly possessions and experience: secularization and materialism go hand in hand. 'Enjoy yourself' becomes the dominant theme, and people gravitate to those goods and services that offer them fun and pleasure. Religious institutions face a continuing decline in membership and support, and they are turning to marketers for help in competing against the secular attractions of modern society.

SUMMARY

Those who plan and manage products operate in a complex and rapidly changing environment, which the firm must continuously monitor and adapt to if it is to survive and prosper. The marketing macro-environment consists of all the major external institutions and forces that are potentially relevant to the firm. It has six components: the demographic, economic, ecological, technological, political and cultural environments.

The demographic environment is characterized by a slowdown in the birth rate, the ageing of the population, changing family structures, the rise of non-family households, geographical shifts in population, and a better-educated populace.

The economic environment shows a slowdown in real income growth, continued inflationary pressure, changing savings and debt patterns, and changing consumption expenditure patterns.

The natural environment is marked by impending shortages of certain raw materials, increased cost of energy, increased levels of pollution, and increasing government intervention in natural-resource management.

The technological environment exhibits an accelerating pace of change, unlimited innovational opportunities, modest local R & D budgets, concentration on minor improvements rather than major discoveries, and increased regulation of technological change.

The political environment shows an increasing amount of legislation regulating business, and the growth of public-interest groups.

Finally, the cultural environment shows long-run trends toward self-fulfilment, immediate gratification, the easy life, informal and open relationships, and a more secular orientation.

QUESTIONS FOR DISCUSSION

1. Discuss how demographic changes are likely to affect the following marketers in the next twenty years:
   - suppliers of children's toys
   - motel operators in South Australia
   - retirement communities
   - marriage-guidance counsellors.

2. It is the year 2000. The price of petrol is $3 per litre, the price of minced meat is $20 per kilogram, the average home costs $300 000, and the annual rate of inflation has been 10 per cent for the last twenty years. Given this information, what might you speculate about the market size or potential for luxury products?

3. It has been said that 'technology will solve our ecological problems and marketing need not worry about them'. Respond to this statement.

4. What major factors are currently inhibiting significant technological innovations in Australia? Do you think this situation will change soon?

5. The political environment has become increasingly volatile in recent years. How have consumer action groups, the Trade Practices Commission, consumer affairs bureaus and the actions of governments affected marketing decision-making?

6. What current cultural values do you see having the strongest long-run impact on marketing in Australia?

7. Discuss in some depth how the six macro-environmental forces discussed in this chapter may affect the marketing of Coca-Cola in 1990.

NOTES

[1] Tim Allerton, 'Caravan Industry Poised for Growth After Rationalization', *Australian Financial Review*, 18 March 1981, p. 27.

[2] Peter Drucker, *Age of Discontinuity* (New York: Harper & Row, 1969).

[3] See Alvin Toffler, *Future Shock* (New York: Bantam, 1970), p. 28.

[4] Donella H. Meadows, Dennis L. Meadows, Jorgen Randers & William W. Behrens III, *The Limits to Growth* (New York: New American Library, 1972), p. 41.

[5] See, for example, 'World Population Growth Declines', *Age*, 16 February 1978, p. 7.

[6] 'Population Up', *Age*, 4 September 1981, p. 9.

[7] National Population Inquiry (W. Borrie, Chairman), *Population and Australia – A Demographic Analysis and Projection* (Canberra: Australian Government Publishing Service, 1975).

[8] *Population and Australia – Recent Demographic Trends and Their Implications* (Canberra: Australian Government Publishing Service, 1978). See also, *Social Indicators No. 3* (Canberra: Australian Bureau of Statistics, 1980); *Year Book Australia No. 65* (Canberra: Australian Bureau of Statistics, 1981); *Review of Australia's Demographic Trends* (Canberra: Australian Government Publishing Service, 1981).

[9] 'Arabs Well Up On Rich Scale', *Age*, 18 February 1978, p. 25.

[10] Paul Malone, '22pc of Personal Wealth in Aust. Owned by 1pc – Survey', *Australian Financial Review*, 3 August 1978, p. 9.

[11] *Australian Financial Review*, 16 September 1981, p. 25.

[12] Peter Ellingsen, 'Australians Spend 40 per cent of Income on Credit', *Age*, 8 September 1981, p. 3.

[13] *First Annual Report of the Council on Environmental Quality* (Washington D.C.: Government Printing Office, 1970), p. 158.

[14] See Karl E. Henion II, *Ecological Marketing* (Columbus, Ohio: Grid, 1976).

[15] Toffler, pp. 25–30.

[16] For an excellent and comprehensive list of future possible products, see Dennis Gabor, *Innovations: Scientific, Technological, and Social* (London: Oxford University Press, 1970).

[17] *Year Book Australia No. 62* (Canberra: Australian Bureau of Statistics, 1978), p. 677. See also, *Science and Technology Statement 1980-81* (Canberra: Australian Government Publishing Service, 1981).

[18] 'Industry's Research Gap Shows', *Australian Financial Review*, 14 June 1978, p. 48.

[19] 'Our CSIRO Research Gap is Showing', *Australian Financial Review*, 3 January 1978, p. 24.

[20] Committee of Inquiry into Technological Change in Australia (Sir Rupert Myers, Chairman), *Technological Change in Australia* (Canberra: Australian Government Publishing Service, 1980).

[21] 'New Shopping Centres Should be Licensed', *Australian Financial Review*, 19 December 1978, p. 22.

[22] Leo Greenland, 'Advertisers Must Stop Conning Consumers', *Harvard Business Review*, July–August 1974, p. 18.

[23] R. R. Walker, 'With Friends Like These . . .', *Age*, 8 November 1978, p. 23.

[24] See also, Paul Latimer, *Australian Business Law* (North Ryde, NSW: CCH Australia, 1981), especially Chs 6 and 7.

[25] For a helpful overview, prepared by the Trade Practices Commission, see *Advertising and Selling* (Canberra: Australian Government Publishing Service, 1981).

[26] These are extracts from Gerald R. Salancik & Gregory D. Upah, 'Directions for Inter-organizational Marketing' (unpublished paper, School of Commerce, University of Illinois, Champaign, August 1978).

[27] See Raymond A. Baurer & Dan H. Fenn Jr, 'What Is a Corporate Social Audit?', *Harvard Business Review*, January–February 1973, pp. 37–48; and Leonard L. Berry & James S. Hensel, 'Public Relations: Opportunities in the New Society', *Arizona Business*, August–September 1973, pp. 14–21.

Consumer Markets and Buying Behaviour

⑧

In the overcrowded shampoo and hair conditioner market quite a few new products have gone down the drain. One of the more recent casualties is an upmarket range called Floreal, which was introduced into selected pharmacies and department stores by the L'Oréal company last year. A lack of advertising support led to its demise, according to some Sydney pharmacists, while the manufacturer claims the fault lies in their failure to actively go out and sell the product.

Attractively packaged and displayed in imitation wood-grain hopper bins, the Floreal range was unusual in that it came in four different perfumes – Apple, Peach, Plum and Camomile Blossom. It was also more expensive than average retailing for $3.95 per 250 ml bottle.

Positioned like a cosmetic, the aim behind it according to L'Oréal managing director, John Conrads, was to offer pharmacists a distinctive product they could actively promote to their customers. Pharmacies have been gradually losing their share of the shampoo and conditioner market to supermarkets so it was decided to offer them a prestige product with a higher profit margin. Depending on how much a pharmacist buys, the profit margin on shampoos and conditioners is normally around 20–25 per cent but in the case of Floreal it averaged between 35–40 per cent.

Mr Conrads argues that if the company had supported the brand with heavy advertising, the high profit margin it was able to offer pharmacists would have been whittled away. Only around $40 000 was spent on promotion, which paid for the in-store display units and a limited amount of advertising in glossy magazines.

By offering pharmacists a high profit margin the onus was placed squarely on them to sell it but, as far as Mr Conrads is concerned, very few of them demonstrated the art of effective salesmanship. Some Sydney pharmacists are going all out to get rid of it with one even offering free posters with each purchase. One attributes its failure to the lack of consumer acceptance of the perfumes and the fact that there was nothing brilliant about the product. 'While they might buy one they did not come back for more', he says. The pharmacist, who claims to have no trouble selling more expensive shampoos, says it was the consumers in the end who killed the product. He summed up the situation as a case of an overseas-directed firm telling the Australian company what to sell. The Floreal range has been successfully sold in France where the L'Oréal company is headquartered. The pharmacist claims there is not the same choice of shampoos in Europe and that Australians are more particular because shampoos here are better than anywhere else in the world.

Disappointed that the marketing strategy failed to work, Mr Conrads claims it is not a major disaster because the company's targets for the brand were not very high. Its potential share of the market was only 2–3 per cent compared with around 10 per cent for the company's Elsève range, he claims.[1]

This example highlights how careful marketers have to be in analyzing consumer markets. The best assumption to make is that consumers' buying behaviour is never simple. Consumers often turn down what appears to be a winning offer – if they do not vote for a product, the product is dead.

The market is the sovereign force in the economy, and therefore has to be the starting point in company planning. A company must begin its thinking not with its products but with customer groups and customer needs. What the company finds out about the market affects and determines its product development, pricing, distribution channels, advertising messages and media, and other elements of the marketing mix.

What Is a Market?

At the outset we should clarify how the term market is being used. The term has acquired many usages over the years.

1. In one of the earliest usages a market consisted of a physical place where buyers and sellers gathered to exchange goods and services. Medieval towns had market squares where sellers brought their goods and buyers shopped for goods. Most Australian cities at one time had market areas where owners of goods set up carts and buyers came from all over the city to look for bargains. Today, transactions occur all over the city in what are called shopping centres rather than markets.

2. To an economist, a market describes all the buyers and sellers involved in actual or potential transactions with respect to some good or service. Thus the soft-drink market consists of major sellers such as Coca-Cola, Cadbury-Schweppes, and Amatil and all the consumers who buy soft-drinks. The economist is interested in describing and evaluating the structure, conduct and performance of the market.

3. To a marketer, a market is the set of all

actual and potential buyers of a product. Thus the marketer limits market to mean the buyer side of the economist's definition of a market, with the seller side being called the industry or competition. The marketer wants to know several things about the market, such as its size, purchasing power, needs and preferences.

We will adopt the last definition of market. The definition hinges on the definition of the term buyer, which means a person or organization who might have: (i) a latent interest in the product; and (ii) the means to acquire it. A buyer is someone who is potentially 'willing and able to buy'.

Let us apply this to the market for microwave ovens, which consists of both individual households and organizations such as restaurants. Focusing on households, not all will be in the market: their kitchens are too small, they feel that these machines are too complex, they fear that they are dangerous. Of the interested consumers, many are unwilling to pay $400 or more for this appliance.

This means that the size of a market at a given time is a function of existing parameters such as consumer beliefs and product prices. A seller can expand the size of a market by recognizing this relationship: a manufacturer of microwave ovens may sponsor an educational campaign to convince consumers that microwave ovens are safe, or lower its prices below $400 and thus increase the number of consumers who can afford one.

The job of a marketer is to know the market. To understand a specific market, one needs a working knowledge of the operating characteristics of four generic types of markets: consumer market, producer market, reseller market, and government market. These are distinguished on the basis of the buyers' role and motives rather than the characteristics of the purchased product. Consumers are individuals and households buying for personal use; producers are individuals and organizations buying for the purpose of producing; resellers are individuals and organizations buying for the purpose of reselling; governments are governmental units buying for the purpose of carrying out governmental functions.

Because markets are complex, we need a common framework to define their character. The marketer can develop a good understanding of any market by asking the following five questions:

- Who is in the market? (buying population)
- What buying decisions do buyers make? (buying decisions)
- Who participates in the buying process? (buying participants)
- What are the major influences on the buyers? (buying influences)
- How do the buyers make their buying decisions? (buying process)

We will examine these questions for consumer markets in this chapter, and for organizational markets in Chapter 9.

WHO IS IN THE CONSUMER MARKET?
(buying population)

The consumer market consists of all the individuals and households who buy or acquire goods and services for personal consumption. The Australian consumer market consists of approximately 15 million persons who yearly consume about $100 billion worth of goods and services – the equivalent of more than $6600 worth for every man, woman and child. Each year this market grows by another 150 000 persons and another $10 billion, in current dollar terms, representing a most lucrative consumer market.

Marketers have found it worthwhile to distinguish different consumer groups, and develop products and services tailored to their needs. If a market segment is large enough, some companies may set up special marketing programmes to serve it. As we saw in Chapter 7, market segments may be distinguished on the basis of age, work status (working women, etc.), ethnicity, geographic location and mobility, educational status (tertiary students, etc.), marital status, household size and many other variables.

Australian consumers buy an immense variety of goods and services. These goods and services can be classified in different ways to throw light on their marketing characteristics (see Chapter 12). Here we will concentrate on trying to understand consumer behaviour.

WHAT BUYING DECISIONS DO CONSUMERS MAKE? (buying decisions)

We are now ready to consider the buying decisions that consumers make. At first glance this appears to be a simple case of 'to buy or not to buy', but closer scrutiny reveals an elaborate process involving many decisions along the way. The marketer can ill afford to look at only the final decision to buy. All these – from the decision to seek information to the decision on style, method of payment and other aspects of the purchase – must be studied by marketers to see where they could influence the final buying decision.

Three Classes of Buying Situation

The number of subdecisions involved in buying anything varies with the complexity of the product and buying situation. There are great differences between buying toothpaste, a tennis racket, an expensive camera and a new car. Howard and Sheth have suggested that consumer buying can be viewed as a problem-solving activity, and have distinguished three classes of buying situation.[2]

Routinized response behaviour. The simplest type of buying behaviour occurs in relation to low-cost, frequently purchased items. Buyers have very few decisions to make – they

are well acquainted with the product class, know the major brands and have fairly clear preferences. The choice of brand may of course be influenced by stockouts, special deals and a wish for variety, but generally buyers' operations are routinized, and they are not likely to give much thought, search or time to the purchase. The goods in this class are often called low-involvement goods.

The marketer's task in this situation is two-fold. With respect to current customers, the marketer should provide positive reinforcement: the brand's quality, stock level, and value must be maintained. With respect to non-customers, the marketer must break their normal buying habits by cues that call attention to the brand and its value in relation to usually preferred brands. These cues include new features or benefits, point-of-purchase displays, price specials, and premiums.

Limited problem-solving. Buying is more complex when buyers confront an unfamiliar brand in a familiar product class. For example, persons thinking about buying a new tennis racket may hear of a new oversized brand called the Prince. They may ask questions and look at ads to learn more about the new brand concept before choosing. This is described as limited problem-solving because buyers are fully aware of the product class and the qualities they want, but are not familiar with all the brands and their features.

The marketer recognizes that consumers are trying to reduce risk through information gathering, and must therefore design a communication programme that will increase the buyer's brand comprehension and confidence.

Extensive problem-solving. Buying reaches its greatest complexity when buyers face an unfamiliar product class and do not know what criteria to use. For example, a person may contemplate buying a citizen-band transceiver for the first time. He has heard brand names such as AWA Clarion, National and

Philips, but lacks clear brand concepts; he does not even know what product-class attributes to consider in choosing a good citizen-band receiver. He is faced with extensive problem-solving.

The marketer of products in this class must understand the information gathering and evaluation activities of prospective buyers. The marketer's task is to facilitate the buyer's learning of the attributes of the product class, their relative importance, and the high standing of the brand on the more important attributes.

Major Subdecisions Involved in the Buying Decision

We are now ready to examine the various subdecisions involved in a particular buying decision. We will consider the following case:

Betty Smith is a brand manager in a leading consumer-packaged-goods company. She is currently interested in finding a new leisure activity that will offer some contrast to her working day, and this need culminated in her buying a Nikon camera. Betty was asked to reconstruct the decisions which she made, that ultimately led to the purchase (these are shown in Figure 8-1).

The buying process started with Betty feeling a need for some new activity. She tried to clarify the nature of her need and decided that she wanted some new form of self-expression (need-class decision). She considered various alternatives and decided that photography would be fun to try (generic-class decision). In considering the different classes of photographic equipment, she concluded that she wanted a camera (product-class decision). She decided that a complex 35 mm camera would be best (product-form decision). Among the brands she saw, Nikon gave her the most

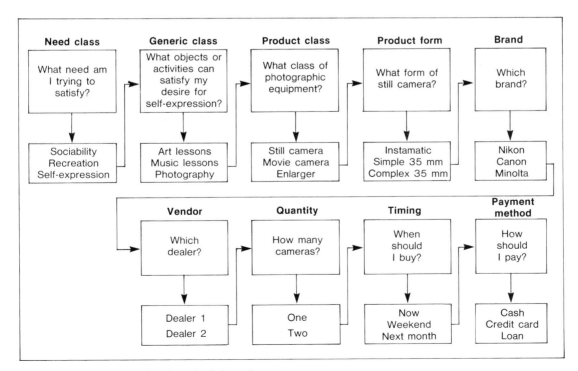

Figure 8-1   Consumer buying decisions for a camera

confidence (brand decision). She decided to go to dealer 2, who was reputed to run the best camera shop in town (vendor decision). She also thought of suggesting that her girlfriend buy a camera and take up photography but dropped the idea (quantity decision). She decided to buy the camera on the weekend (timing decision). Finally, she decided to pay for it using her credit card (payment-method decision).

This mapping of the consumer's sub-decisions provides many clues for the camera marketer. Let us return to Figure 8-1. Each box contains a decision facing the consumer and a set of alternative solutions that are or could be considered (called an *evoked set*).[3] Marketers have a strong interest in the size and contents of the evoked set at each decision point. Nikon would not have sold a camera to Betty Smith if she had not moved through that particular decision chain, i.e. Self-expression → Photography → Cameras. Thus, in selling cameras, the Nikon Company could gain from promoting the value of self-expression, and the role of cameras in photographic self-expression.

Given that Betty became interested in a camera, Nikon needed to be one of the brands included in the evoked set of brands. If Betty had not known about Nikon, Nikon would not have made the sale. Therefore we start with the concept of the *total set*, which represents all the brands of camera that are available to this consumer (i.e. sold in the local area), whether or not the buyer knows about them (see Figure 8-2).[4] The total set can be divided into the consumer's *awareness set* (those brands that she recalls) and the *unawareness set*. We can see that Nikon is one of four brands in Betty's awareness set: of these, three meet her buying criteria and constitute her *consideration set*; the other is relegated to an *infeasible set*. As she learns about or considers these brands, two remain strong choices and constitute her *choice set*, the other being relegated to a *non-choice set*. She carefully evalu-

ates the brands in the choice set and then makes her final decision, in this case choosing a Nikon camera.

The company's task is to work hard to get its brand included in the buyer's awareness set, and to remain in the successive consideration and choice sets. The marketer must research other brands that are likely to be included, and the criteria used by the buyer as she moves to successively smaller sets in making her decision.

WHO PARTICIPATES IN THE CONSUMER BUYING PROCESS?
(buying participants)

In consumer marketing there is a strong temptation to identify the buyer (also called the customer or decision-making unit) and focus most of the effort on influencing that buyer. For some products, this seems logical because their purchase is relatively simple and involves primarily one decision-maker. Thus men are normally the decision-making unit for pipe tobacco, and women are the decision-making unit for pantyhose, with little influence coming from the other. On the other hand, the decision-making unit for a family car or trip is likely to consist of husband, wife and older children. In these cases the marketer must take steps to identify the various participants and the roles they play.

Let us look more closely at this problem. Suppose the Parmelia Hilton Hotel in Perth is anxious to attract more wedding parties to its facilities. Its promotion programme will be more efficient if it can identify the major buying participants, and select appropriate and effective messages and media. The most frequent participants in this particular selection decision are the bride and groom, the bride's and groom's families, friends of the families, and friends of the bride and groom.

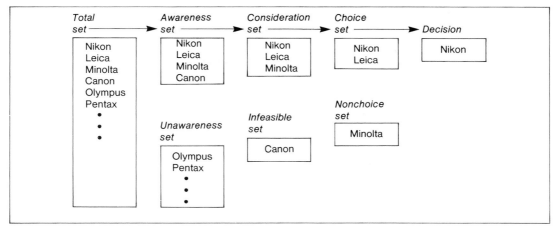

Figure 8-2 Successive sets involved in consumer decision-making

The next thing to note is that these participants may play up to five different roles in the buying process:

1. *Initiator.* The initiator is the person who first suggests or thinks of the idea of buying the particular good or service.
2. *Influencer.* An influencer is a person whose views or advice carry some weight in making the final decision.
3. *Decider.* The decider is a person who ultimately determines any part of or the entire buying decision: whether to buy, what to buy, how to buy, when to buy, where to buy.
4. *Buyer.* The buyer is the person who makes the actual purchase.
5. *User.* The user is the person(s) who consumes or uses the good or service.

For example, a friend of the bride may have initiated the question of where the wedding party would be held. The bride may then have consulted several persons to obtain their opinions. The actual decision may be made jointly by the bride and groom, with the bride being slightly dominant. The bride and her mother might act as the buyer by signing the contract with the hotel. The users consist of the bride and groom and their entire wedding party.

The hotel should therefore identify and sort out the roles played by these different participants and direct most of its publicity at the deciders. If brides do most of the deciding, then the hotel should research the typical criteria used by brides in selecting venues. A bride may be particularly interested in the elegance of the ballroom and the quality of the food; her father may be particularly interested in the cost. Knowing who are the main buying participants and what attributes they look at most helps the marketer to fine-tune the marketing programme.

WHAT ARE THE MAJOR INFLUENCES ON CONSUMER BUYERS?
(buying influences)

A multitude of influences shape the behaviour of the various participants in a buying decision. Returning to the earlier illustration of Betty Smith's purchase of a camera, we can sort the various influences on her decision into four major groups. There are influences associated with the buyer (here Betty Smith), the product, the seller and the situation:

1. Buyer characteristics. We would need to know several things about Betty Smith to understand how she came to buy a Nikon camera. These factors could be grouped into cultural, social, personal and psychological characteristics (see Figure 8-3), and will be discussed in the next section.

2. Product characteristics. Various product characteristics will influence the buying outcome, in this case the camera brand's features, styling, quality, price and backup services. The marketer has control over these attributes, and can design them in such a way that they will maximize the product's appeal to the target market.

3. Seller characteristics. Various seller characteristics will influence the buying outcome. In this case Betty Smith will form an opinion about the manufacturer, Nikon, and the retail outlet, say the ABC Camera Company. Betty will have a certain image of Nikon's reliability and service as a manufacturer; she will also form an impression of the retailer's knowledgeability, friendliness and service. Both should therefore consider the seller characteristics that make a difference to whether Betty buys the camera.

4. Situational characteristics. Various situational factors also influence the buying decision. One such factor is time: under great time pressure, Betty Smith might make the decision with less information and rely more on the salesperson than she would if she could investigate at her leisure. Other factors include the time of year, the weather, chance meetings with friends who have opinions about cameras, the current economic outlook, and so on.

All these components interact to produce the buying outcome. We will have much to say about the product, seller and situation in the following chapters. Here we will concentrate on the buyer characteristics shown in Figure 8-3. We want to understand how the buyer's cultural, social, personal and psychological characteristics influence the final decision.

Cultural Characteristics

The broadest influence on buyers is their cultural characteristics. We will look at the role played by the most important of these.

Culture. As we discussed in Chapter 7, culture is the most fundamental determinant of a person's wants and behaviour. Whereas the

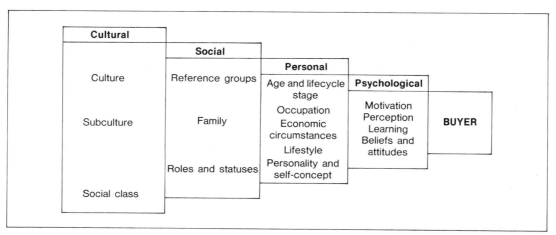

Figure 8-3   Characteristics influencing consumer buying behaviour

behaviour of lower creatures is largely governed by instinct, human behaviour is largely learned: the child growing up in a society learns a basic set of values, perceptions, preferences and behaviours through a process of socialization involving the family and other key institutions.

Betty Smith's knowledge of and interest in cameras is a function of being raised in a modern society where camera technology and a related set of consumer learnings and values have developed. Betty is able to consider a camera because she knows what cameras are; she knows how to read their operating instructions; and her society has accepted the idea of women photographers. In another culture, say remote backward tribe in South America, a camera has no significance. International marketers know that cultures are at different stages of development and interest with respect to various consumer goods, and must consider this when choosing target markets and preparing marketing programmes.

Subculture. Each culture contains smaller groups or subcultures, and each of these provides more specified identification and socialization for its members. Four types of subcultures may be distinguished: nationality groups, religious groups, racial groups, and geographical groups – all of which have distinct tastes, preferences, taboos and/or lifestyles.

Betty Smith's interest in various goods will obviously be influenced by her nationality, religion, race and geographical background. This would probably be true of her food preferences and might also influence her clothing choices, recreations and career aspirations. Her subculture identifications may have played a prominent role in her wanting to buy a camera and choosing a Nikon. We can imagine that subcultures attach different meanings to picture taking, and this could have influenced her interest.

Social class. Virtually all human societies exhibit social stratification. This may take the form of a caste system, where the members of different castes are reared for certain roles and cannot change their caste membership. More frequently, stratification takes the form of social classes. Social classes are relatively homogeneous and enduring divisions in a society which are hierarchically ordered and whose members share similar values, interests and behaviour and which form part of a hierarchy.

Social classes have several characteristics: (i) persons within a given social class tend to behave more alike; (ii) persons are ranked as occupying inferior or superior positions according to their social class; (iii) social class is not indicated by any single variable but is measured as a weighted function of one's occupation, income, wealth, education, value orientation, and so on; and (iv) social class is continuous rather than discrete, with individuals able to move into a higher social class or drop into a lower one.

The American research tradition in social class distinguishes six social classes.[5]

1. Upper uppers (less than one per cent). Upper uppers are the social elite who live on inherited wealth and come from well-known families. They give large sums to charity, run the debutante balls, maintain more than one home, and send their children to the most expensive schools. They are a market for costly jewellery, antiques, homes and holidays. While small as a group, they serve as a reference group for others to the extent that their consumption decisions trickle down and are imitated by other social classes.

2. Lower uppers (about 2 per cent). Lower uppers are persons who have earned high income or wealth through exceptional ability in professions or business. They usually come from the middle class. They tend to be active in social and civic affairs, and seek to buy the symbols of status for themselves and their children, such as expensive homes, schools, yachts, swimming pools and cars. They include the nouveaux riches, whose pattern of conspicuous consumption is designed to impress those with less wealth. The ambition of this group is to be accepted in the upper-upper stratum, which is more likely to be achieved by their children than themselves.

3. Upper middles (12 per cent). Upper middles are concerned with 'career': they have attained positions as lawyers, doctors, scientists and university professors. They believe in education, and want their children to develop professional or administrative skills so that they do not drop into a lower stratum. This class likes to deal in ideas and 'culture'. They are a market for good homes, clothes, furniture and appliances. They seek to run a gracious home entertaining friends and clients. The home, the car and even the wife are used as symbols of the husband's success.

4. Lower middles (30 per cent). Lower middles are concerned with 'respectability'. They are conscientious workers and adhere to culturally defined norms and standards, including church attendance and obeying the law. The home is important, and lower middles like to keep it neat and 'pretty'; they buy conventional furnishings and do many of their own household tasks. The lower-middle wife spends much of her shopping time looking for bargains. Although white-collar workers make up a large part of this group, so do postal and fire-brigade personnel and 'aristocrat blue collars' (plumbers, factory foremen).

5. Upper lowers (35 per cent). Upper lowers lead an unchanging day-to-day existence. They live in small houses and flats in dull areas of the city; the men work at manual jobs and have only a moderate education. The wife spends most of her time in the house cooking, cleaning and caring for her children. She sees motherhood as her main vocation, and has little time for organizations and social activity. She tends to buy the same brands from week to week, and occasionally buys items impulsively.

6. Lower lowers (20 per cent). Lower lowers are at the bottom of society and viewed by the other classes as slum dwellers. Some lower lowers try to rise above their class but often fall back and ultimately stop trying. They tend to be poorly educated. They often reject middle-class standards of morality and behaviour. They buy more impulsively. They often do not evaluate quality, and they pay too much for products and buy on credit. They are a large market for food, television sets and used cars.

Marketers in many countries have found social class to be a useful variable for segmenting markets. Products, messages and atmospheres can be designed to appeal to specific classes, each of which tends to show distinct tastes in such areas as clothing, home furnishings, leisure activity and cars. There is also evidence that social classes differ in their purchase-decision processes.

The Australian perception of social class appears to be somewhat different from that in other countries. For example, when more than 8000 Australians were asked to assign themselves to a social class, most people rated themselves as middle class (63 per cent), only 37 per cent of respondents considered themselves to be working class, with virtually nobody claiming to be upper class.[6] While there are undoubted methodological problems in comparing self-assignment with researcher-assignment to classes, such results may in fact represent a less class-conscious or class-structured society, which has important implications for the use of social class as a variable in marketing strategy.

Social Characteristics

A consumer's behaviour is also influenced by social factors such as reference groups, family, and social roles and statuses.

Reference groups. Reference groups are those that influence a person's attitude, opinions and values. Some are primary groups (also called face-to-face groups, such as family, close friends, neighbours and fellow workers), and others are secondary (clubs, professional associations). People are also influenced by groups of which they are not members, called aspirational groups (such as sports heroes and movie stars).

A person is significantly influenced by his reference groups in at least three ways. These groups expose the person to possible new behaviours and lifestyles; they also influence attitudes and self-concepts, because each person usually wants to 'belong'; and they create pressures for conformity that may affect the person's actual product and brand choices.

A company would like to know whether a consumer's decisions to purchase its product and brand are importantly influenced by reference groups, and if so, which. With regard to some products, such as soap and canned peaches, the buyer normally makes choice without any such influence. Betty Smith's friends are not a factor in her decision to buy soap or a particular brand of soap. Where product or brand choice is not subject to reference-group influence, the seller's marketing communications should stress the product's attributes, price and quality, or other differential advantages.

There are other products where reference-group influence tends to be a strong factor in product and/or brand choice, particularly where the product may be visible to people whom the buyer respects.[7] Betty Smith's decision to buy a camera, and her brand choice, may be strongly influenced by some of her reference groups – such as friends who belong to a photography club – but her girlfriends, for example, will probably have no influence on either decision. The more cohesive the reference group, the more effective its communication process and the higher the person esteems it, the more influential it will be in shaping the person's product and brand choices.

If sellers sense that certain reference groups have a big impact on consumer behaviour, their task is to calculate how to reach the group opinion leaders. At one time sellers thought that opinion leaders were primarily community social leaders whom the mass market imitated because of 'snob appeal'. Today it is recognized that they are found in all strata of society and that a specific person may be an opinion leader in certain product areas and an opinion follower in other areas. The marketer tries to reach opinion leaders by identifying certain personal characteristics associated with such a role, determining the media they read and thus developing messages that they are likely to pick up.

Family. Among the groups who most directly influence individual buying decisions are members of the buyer's family. Actually, we can distinguish between two families in every person's life. The family of *orientation* consists of one's parents, from whom are acquired a mental set involving not only religion, politics and economics but also personal ambition, self-worth and love. Even if the buyer no longer interacts very much with his parents, their influence on unconscious behaviour can be significant; in countries where parents continue to live with their children, this influence can be crucial.

Even more important as an influence on everyday buying behaviour is one's family of *procreation*. The family is the most important consumer-buying organization in society, and it has been researched extensively.[8] Marketers are interested in the roles and relative influence of the husband, wife and children in the purchase of a large variety of products and services.

Husband-wife involvement varies widely by product category. The wife has traditionally been the main purchasing agent for the family, especially in the areas of food, sundries and basic clothing. This is changing with the increased number of working wives and the willingness of husbands to do more of the family purchasing, and marketers of such items should therefore adjust their thinking accordingly.

In the case of more expensive and less frequently purchased products and services, the decision-making process tends to be a joint one. The issue that arises is whether the husband or wife has greater influence on the decision to purchase, or whether they have equal (syncretic) influence. Certain products and services fall into each category.

- *Husband-dominant:* life insurance, cars, television.
- *Wife-dominant:* washing machines, carpeting, non-living-room furniture, kitchenware.
- *Syncretic:* living-room furniture, travel, housing, outside entertainment.

At the same time, the dominance of a family member varies for different subdecisions within a product category. For example, Davis found that the decision of 'when to buy a car' was influenced primarily by the husband in 68 per cent of the cases, primarily by the wife in 3 per cent of the cases, and equally in 29 per cent of the cases.[9] On the other hand, the decision of 'what colour car to buy' was influenced primarily by the husband in 25 per cent of the cases, by the wife in 25 per cent of the cases, and equally in 50 per cent of the cases. A car manufacturer would take these varying decision roles into account when designing and promoting its cars.

In the case of Betty Smith buying a camera, her husband will be an influencer – he will have an opinion about her buying a camera and the kind of camera to buy – but she will be the primary decider, purchaser and user.

Roles and statuses. A person participates in many groups throughout life: family, other reference groups, organizations and institutions. The specific position that a person has in each group can be defined in terms of role and status. For example, with her parents, Betty Smith plays the role of daughter; in her family, she plays the role of wife; in her company, she plays the role of brand manager. A *role* consists of a set of activities that the individual is supposed to perform, according to the definition and expectations of the individual and the persons around him or her. Each of Betty's roles will influence some of her buying behaviour.

Each role has a *status* attached to it, which reflects the general esteem accorded to that role in society or in the eyes of the immediate group. The role of brand manager has more status in this society than the role of daughter. As a brand manager, Betty will buy the kind of clothing that reflects both her role and her status.

Personal Characteristics

A buyer's decisions are also influenced by external personal factors, notably the age and lifecycle stage, occupation, economic circumstances, lifestyle, personality and self-concept.

Age and lifecycle stage. There is no question that the goods and services that people buy change during their lifetime. Their food, for example, will consist of baby fare in the early years, a broad diet in the growing and mature years, and finally special regimes and food taboos in the later years. People's tastes in clothes, furniture and recreation are also age-related.

Not only does age affect one's buying decisions, it also affects one's marital status, presence or absence of children, and one's children's ages. Marketers have distinguished nine relevant stages of the family lifecycle. They are listed in Table 8-1, with the financial situation and typical product interests of each group. Marketers are increasingly defining their target markets in these terms and are

Table 8-1   An overview of the lifecycle and buying behaviour

Stage in lifecycle	Buying or behavioural pattern
1. *Bachelor stage:* Young single people not living at home	Few financial burdens. Fashion opinion leaders. Recreation-oriented. Buy: basic kitchen equipment, basic furniture, cars, equipment for the mating game, vacations.
2. *Newly married couples:* Young, no children	Better off financially than they will be in near future. Highest purchase rate and highest average purchase of durables. Buy: cars, refrigerators, stoves, sensible and durable furniture, vacations.
3. *Full nest I:* Youngest child under six	Home purchasing at peak. Liquid assets low. Dissatisfied with financial position and amount of money saved. Interested in new products. Like advertised products. Buy: washers, dryers, TV, baby food, chest rubs and cough medicines, vitamins, dolls, wagons, sleds, skates.
4. *Full nest II:* Youngest child six or over	Financial position better. Some wives work. Less influenced by advertising. Buy larger-sized packages, multiple-unit deals. Buy: many foods, cleaning materials, bicycles, music lessons, pianos.
5. *Full nest III:* Older married couples with dependent children	Financial position still better. More wives work. Some children get jobs. Hard to influence with advertising. High average purchase of durables. Buy: new, more tasteful furniture, car travel, non-necessary appliances, boats, dental services, magazines.
6. *Empty nest I:* Older married couples, no children living with them, head in labour force	Home ownership at peak. Most satisfied with financial position and money saved. Interested in travel, recreation, self-education. Make gifts and contributions. Not interested in new products. Buy: vacations, luxuries, home improvements.
7. *Empty nest II:* Older married couples, no children living at home, head retired	Drastic cut in income. Keep home. Buy: medical appliances, medical-care products that aid health, sleep, and digestion.
8 *Solitary survivor*, in labour force	Income still good but likely to sell home.
9. *Solitary survivor*, retired	Same medical and product needs as other retired group; drastic cut in income. Special need for attention, affection, and security.

Source: William D. Wells & George Gubar, 'Life Cycle Concept in Marketing Research', *Journal of Marketing Research*, November 1966, p. 362.

developing appropriate products and marketing plans.

Recent attempts have also been made to identify *psychological lifecycle stages,* i.e. certain passages or transformations that adults experience as they go through life.[10] Thus Betty Smith may change from being a satisfied brand manager and wife to being an unsatisfied person searching for a new way to fulfil herself. This may have contributed to her currently strong interest in photography. Marketers should therefore pay more attention to the changing needs for goods and services that might be associated with these adult passages.

Occupation. A person's occupation will lead to certain needs and wants for goods and services. A blue-collar worker will buy work clothes, work shoes, lunchboxes and football tickets. A company manager will buy expensive blue serge suits, air travel, club membership and a large boat. In general, marketers may study the level of interest likely to be shown by certain occupational groups in the company's products and services; a company may even choose to specialize in the products and services needed by a particular occupational group.

Economic circumstances. A person's economic circumstances will of course greatly affect the goods and services he considers and buys. There are several factors involved: *spendable income* (its level, stability, and time pattern), *savings and assets* (including the percentage that is liquid), *borrowing power,* and *attitude* (towards spending versus saving). Thus Betty Smith can only consider buying an expensive Nikon if she has enough spendable income, savings or borrowing power, and places a higher importance on spending than saving. Marketers of various income-sensitive goods and services constantly monitor trends in personal income, savings, and interest rates. If indicators predict a worsening economic climate, marketers can take positive steps to redesign, reposition and reprice their product, reduce their production and inventories, and otherwise protect their financial solvency.

Lifestyle. A person's buying behaviour is also affected by his chosen lifestyle. People coming from the same subculture, social class and even occupational group may have quite different lifestyles. Betty Smith, for example, can choose to be a homemaker, a career woman, or a free spirit. As it turns out, she plays several roles and her way of reconciling them becomes her lifestyle. If she gravitates towards becoming a professional photographer this has further lifestyle implications, such as keeping odd hours and doing a considerable amount of travelling.

Marketers believe that particular product and brand choices are a key indicator of lifestyle. The implications of this concept are well stated by Boyd and Levy:

> Marketing is a process of providing customers with parts of a potential mosaic from which they, as artists of their own life styles, can pick and choose to develop the composition that for the time seems the best. The marketer who thinks about his products in this way will seek to understand their potential settings and relationships to other parts of consumer life styles, and thereby to increase the number of ways they fit meaningfully into the pattern.[11]

Personality and self-concept. Another characteristic influencing a person's buying behaviour is personality, i.e. distinguishing character traits, attitudes and habits. Each person has a distinct personality marked by his or her degree of extroversion versus introversion, creativity versus conventionality, activeness versus passiveness, and so on. Suppose Betty Smith is extroverted, creative and active. This would explain to some extent her interest in photography, and also implies that she would be active in searching for a camera, talking to people, asking them questions, and buying when it felt right.

Marketers of various products search for potential personality traits revealed by their target market. For example, a beer company might discover that heavy beer drinkers are more outgoing, aggressive and dogmatic, and decide to develop an appropriate brand image for its beer (e.g. feature in its ads a real person who has these traits, with whom heavy beer drinkers can identify and feel that this is their brand). Personality variables do not show up strongly in all product areas, but some companies have been able to use personality segmentation to advantage (see Chapter 10).

Many marketers use a related concept – a person's *self-concept* or self-image. All of us carry around a complex mental picture of ourselves. For example, Betty may see herself as extroverted, creative and active, and thus favour a camera that expresses these qualities. If the Nikon is promoted as a camera for extroverted, creative and active persons, then its brand image would match her self-image. The implication is that marketers should develop brand images that match the self-image of the target group in the market.

The theory, however, is not that simple. What if Betty's actual self-concept (how she views herself) differs from her ideal self-concept (how she would like to view herself), and from her others-self-concept (how she thinks others see her). Which of her selves will she try to satisfy with the choice of a camera? Marketers generally differ over the answer to this question, and as a result, self-concept theory has had a mixed record of success in predicting consumer responses to brand images.[12]

Psychological Characteristics

A person's buying choices are also influenced by four major psychological processes – motivation, perception, learning, and beliefs and attitudes.

Motivation. We know that Betty Smith became interested in buying a camera. Why? What was she really seeking? What needs was she trying to satisfy?

A person will have all kinds of needs at any point in time. Some are biogenic: they arise from physiological states of tension such as might be caused by the need for food, drink, sex, and bodily comfort. Other needs are psychogenic: they arise from psychological states of tension such as the need for recognition, response, or variety of experience. Few of these needs will be intense enough to motivate the person to act at a given point in time. A need becomes a *motive* when it is aroused to a sufficient level of intensity. A motive (or drive) is a stimulated need which is sufficiently pressing to direct the person towards the goal of satisfying the need. After the need is satisfied, the person's tension is discharged and he returns to a state of equilibrium.

Psychologists have proposed various theories of human motivation. Three of the most popular are those of Sigmund Freud, Abraham Maslow and Frederick Herzberg; each has interesting implications for consumer marketing.

Freud's theory of motivation. Freud asserted that people are not likely to be conscious of the real motives guiding their behaviour, because these have been shaped in early childhood and are often repressed. Children enter the world with strong self-gratification drives. Very quickly and painfully they learn that instant gratification is not possible, and repeated frustration leads them to perfect more subtle means of satisfaction.

The child's psyche grows more complex as the child grows older. One part, the id, remains the reservoir of strong drives and urges. Another part, the ego, becomes the child's conscious centre for planning to obtain satisfactions. A third part, the superego, causes the instinctive drives to be channelled into socially approved outlets to avoid the pain of guilt or shame.

The guilt or shame a person feels about some urges, especially sexual urges, leads to repression of them. Through such defence mechanisms as rationalization and sublimation, these urges are denied or transformed into socially acceptable behaviour. They are never eliminated or under perfect control, however; they emerge in dreams, in slips of the tongue, in neurotic and obsessional behaviour, or ultimately in mental breakdowns when the ego can no longer maintain the delicate balance between the impulsive power of the id and the oppressive power of the superego.

Human behaviour, therefore, is never simple. A person does not fully understand his motivational wellsprings, nor are they obvious to a casual observer. If Betty is about to purchase an expensive camera, she may describe her motive as wanting a hobby or career. At a deeper level, she may be purchasing the camera to impress others with her creative talent. At a still deeper level, she may be buying the camera to feel young and independent again.

An important marketing implication of Freudian motivation theory is that buyers are motivated by psychological as well as functional product concerns. When Betty looks at a camera, she will not only process information about the camera's performance but also react to other cues – the camera's shape, size, weight, material, colour and case are all capable of triggering certain emotions. A rugged-looking camera may arouse Betty's feelings about being independent, which she can either manage or try to avoid. The manufacturer, in designing the camera's features, should be aware of the impact of visual and tactile elements on consumer emotions that may stimulate or inhibit purchase.

The leading exponent of Freudian motivation theory in marketing is Ernest Dichter, who for more than two decades has been interpreting buying situations and product choices in terms of unconscious motives. Dichter calls this *motivational research*: it consists of 'in-depth interviews' with a few dozen target buyers to uncover their deeper motives triggered by the product. Various 'projective techniques' (such as word association, sentence completion, picture interpretation, and role playing), are used to throw the respondents' egos off guard.[13]

Motivation researchers have produced some interesting and occasionally bizarre hypotheses about the buyer's state of mind regarding certain purchases. They have suggested the following:

- Consumers resist prunes because they are wrinkled-looking and remind people of old age.
- Men smoke cigars as an adult version of thumbsucking. They like their cigars to have a strong odour in order to prove their masculinity.
- Women prefer vegetable shortening to animal fats because the latter arouse a sense of guilt about killing animals.
- A woman is very serious when baking a cake because unconsciously she is going through the symbolic act of giving birth. She dislikes easy-to-use cake mixes because the easy life evokes a sense of guilt.

Maslow's theory of motivation. Abraham Maslow's interest lay in identifying the relationships *between* various human needs. His theory of motivation can be stated as follows:[14]

1. A person has many needs. In the order of importance, they are physiological needs, safety needs, social needs, esteem needs, and self-actualization needs.
2. A person will try to satisfy the more important needs first.
3. When a person succeeds in satisfying an important need, it will cease being a motivator for the present time, and attention will be directed to the next most important need.

For example, a starving man (need 1) will not take an interest in the latest events in the art world (need 5), nor in how he is seen or esteemed by others (need 3 or 4), nor in whether he is breathing clean air (need 2). But as each important need is satisfied, the next one will come into play.

What light does Maslow's theory throw on Betty Smith's interest in buying a camera? We will assume that Betty has satisfied her physiological, safety and social needs, in which case they are not motivators of her interest in cameras. We may consider the possibility that her camera interest comes from a strong need for more esteem from others. If this need is satisfied, we would guess that her camera interest is meeting her need for self-actualization, i.e. she wants to actualize her potential as a creative person and express herself through photography.

Herzberg's theory of motivation. Frederick Herzberg is also interested in the role that different needs play in a person's motivation.[15] He has developed a 'two-factor theory' of motivation, which distinguishes between dissatisfiers (factors that cause dissatisfaction) and satisfiers (factors that cause satisfaction). For example, if the Nikon camera did not come with a warranty, this would be a dissatisfier. Betty would like a product warranty, but the presence of one would not be a satisfier or motivator of her purchase since it is not an intrinsic source of satisfaction with the Nikon camera. The Nikon camera's capacity to photograph at one-thousandth of a second *would* be a satisfier, because faster camera speeds would increase Betty's ability to enjoy photography.

The marketing implications of this theory of motivation are twofold. First, sellers should do their best to eliminate dissatisfiers from affecting the buyer – such as insufficient printed information on how the camera is operated, an arrogant salesperson, and a poorly designed carrying case. While these things will not sell the camera, they might easily unsell it. Second, the manufacturer should carefully identify the major satisfiers or motivators of purchase in the camera market, and be sure to include them: they will make the major difference as to which camera brand the customer buys.

Perception. A motivated person is ready to act; *how* that person decides to act is influenced by his perception of the situation. Two people in the same motivated state and objective situation may act quite differently because they perceive the situation differently: Betty Smith might see a fast-talking camera salesperson as aggressive and insincere; another camer buyer might see the same salesperson as intelligent and helpful.

Why do people have different perceptions of the same situation? We start with the notion that all of us apprehend a stimulus object through *sensations*, i.e. flows of information through one or more of our five senses: sight, hearing, smell, touch and taste. However, each of us organizes and interprets this sensory information in an individual way: perception may be defined as 'the process by which an individual selects, organizes and interprets information inputs to create a meaningful picture of the world'.[16] Perception depends not only on the character of the physical stimuli, but also on both the relation of the stimuli to the surrounding field (the Gestalt idea) and conditions within the individual.

People can have quite different perceptions of the same stimulus object or situation because of three perceptual processes: selective exposure, selective distortion and selective retention.

Selective exposure. People are exposed to a tremendous number of stimuli every moment of their lives (e.g. the average person may encounter more than 1500 ads a day). It is impossible to attend to all of these stimuli, and thus most are screened out. The real challenge is to explain which stimuli people will heed:

1. People are more likely to notice stimuli that bear on a current felt need of theirs. Betty Smith will notice all kinds of camera ads because she is motivated to buy one; she will probably not notice ads about stereophonic equipment.
2. People are more likely to notice stimuli that they anticipate. Betty Smith is more likely to notice cameras in the camera store than a line of radios also carried by the store, because she did not expect the store to carry radios.
3. People are more likely to notice stimuli whose change level is large in relation to the normal size of the stimuli. Betty Smith is more likely to notice an ad offering $100 off the list price of a Nikon than one offering $5 off.[17]

Selective exposure means that marketers must work especially hard to gain the attention of consumers in the marketplace. Their message will be lost on most people who are not in the market for the product, and even those who are in the market may not notice the message unless it stands out from the surrounding sea of stimuli. Ads that are larger in size, use four colours where most ads are black and white, or are novel and provide contrast, are more likely to be noticed.

Selective distortion. Even stimuli noted by consumers do not necessarily come across in the intended way. Each person has an organized mind set and attempts to fit incoming stimuli into this pre-existing mode of thought: selective distortion describes this tendency of people to twist information into personal meanings. Thus Betty Smith may hear the salesperson mention some good and bad points about a competing camera brand. Since she already has a strong leaning toward Nikon, she is likely to distort the points she hears in order to conclude that Nikon is the better camera. People tend to interpret information in a way that will support rather than challenge their preconceptions.

Selective retention. People tend to forget much that they learn, and retain information that supports their attitudes and beliefs. Because of selective retention, Betty is likely to remember good points mentioned about the Nikon and forget good points mentioned about competing cameras. She remembers Nikon's good points because she 'rehearses' them more whenever she thinks about her decision to buy a camera.

These three perceptual factors mean that marketers have to work hard to break through very strong filters. This explains why marketers have to buy so much message repetition, and why they place such an emphasis on message dramatization.

Learning. When people act, there are direct and indirect effects which influence their future behaviour. Learning describes those changes in an individual's behaviour arising from experience. Most behaviour is learned; the exception is behaviour based on instinctive responses, growth, or temporary physiological states of the organism, such as hunger or fatigue. Learning theorists hold that a person's learning is produced through the interplay of drives, stimuli, cues, responses and reinforcement.

A *drive* is a strong internal stimulus impelling action. It appears that Betty Smith has a drive toward self-actualization. Her drive becomes a motive when it is directed toward a particular drive-reducing *stimulus object* (in this case, a camera). Betty's response to the idea of buying a camera is conditioned by the surrounding configuration of *cues*, i.e. the

minor stimuli that determine when, where and how the person responds. Her husband's opinion on buying a camera, the economic outlook and the season of the year are all cues that may affect her *response* to the impulse to buy a camera.

Suppose Betty buys the camera. If the experience is rewarding, she will probably use the camera more and more. Her response to cameras will be *reinforced.*

Later on, Betty may also want to buy a tape-recorder, and may experience cues similar to those that existed when she bought a camera. If she responds in the same way, buys the tape recorder and is satisfied, this reinforces her response to similar stimuli and drives in the future, i.e. she has generalized her response to similar stimuli.

A countertendency to generalization is discrimination. When Betty has the opportunity to use two similar cameras on a trial basis and finds one more rewarding than the other, her future ability to discriminate between fairly similar cue configurations will be improved. Discrimination means she has learned to recognize differences in sets of stimuli and can adjust her responses accordingly.

For marketers, the practical import of learning theory is that they can build up demand for a product by associating it with strong drives, using motivating cues, and providing positive reinforcement. A new company can enter the market by appealing to the same drives as competitors and providing similar cue configurations, because buyers are more likely to transfer loyalty to similar brands than to dissimilar brands (generalization). Alternatively, the company may aim its brand to appeal to a different set of strong drives and offer cue inducements to switch.

Beliefs and attitudes. Through learning, people acquire beliefs and attitudes which in turn influence their buying behaviour.

A *belief* is a descriptive thought that a person holds about something. Betty Smith may believe that a Nikon takes wonderful pictures, stands up well under rugged usage, and costs $550. These beliefs may be based on real knowledge, opinion or faith, and may or may not carry an emotional charge. For example, Betty Smith's belief that a Nikon camera is black may or may not matter to her decision.

Manufacturers, of course, are very interested in the beliefs people have about their products and services. These beliefs make up product and brand images, and people's behaviour will partly be a function of their beliefs. If some of the beliefs are wrong and inhibit purchase, the manufacturer would probably launch a campaign to correct these beliefs.

An *attitude* describes a person's enduring favourable or unfavourable cognitive evaluations, emotional feelings, and action tendencies towards some object or idea.[18] People have attitudes regarding almost everything: religion, politics, clothes, music, food, and so on. Attitudes put people into a frame of mind of liking or disliking things, moving towards or moving away from them. Thus Betty Smith may hold such attitudes as 'Buy the best', 'The Japanese make the best products in the world' and 'Creativity and self-expression are among the most important things in life'. The Nikon camera is therefore salient to Betty because it fits well into her pre-existing attitudes. A company would benefit greatly from researching the various attitudes that might bear on its products.

Attitudes enable people to have fairly consistent behaviour toward similar classes of objects: they do not have to interpret everything afresh. Attitudes economize on energy and thought. For this very reason, however, they are very difficult to change. A person's various attitudes have settled into a consistent pattern, and to change one may require painful adjustments in many others. Thus a company would be well advised to try to fit its products into existing attitudes rather than try to change them. There are exceptions, of course, where

the greater cost of doing so might pay off – the recent campaigns involving flavoured milk (Big M, Moove, etc.) are interesting examples.

We are now in a position to appreciate the complexity of buying, the final choice being the result of the interplay of cultural, social, personal and psychological factors. Many of these factors are beyond the influence of the marketer, but they are useful for identifying those buyers who might be more interested than others in the product. Other factors are subject to marketer influence and clue the marketer on how to develop certain product, price, place and promotion elements for optimum impact on the marketplace.

HOW DO CONSUMERS MAKE THEIR BUYING DECISIONS? (buying process)

We are now ready to examine the actual stages passed through to reach a buying decision and outcome. Although we will focus on one person, it should be realized that there may be not only a changing set of buying participants in the different stages, who have different influences on the buyer, but also other influential factors. The purpose of distinguishing different stages in the buying process is to identify what marketers can do to facilitate and influence favourable buying outcomes.

The model in Figure 8-4 shows the consumer passing through five stages: problem recognition, information search, information evaluation, purchase decision, and post-purchase behaviour. This model emphasizes that the buying process starts long before the actual purchase and has consequences long afterwards. It encourages the marketer to focus on the buying process rather than the purchase decision.[19]

Problem Recognition

As discussed at the beginning of this chapter, the buying process starts with the buyer

Figure 8-4   Five-stage model of the consumer buying process

recognizing a problem or need. This need may be triggered by internal or external stimuli. In the former case, one of the person's normal needs – hunger, thirst, sex – rises to a threshold level and becomes a drive. From previous experience, the person has learned how to cope with this drive and is motivated toward a class of objects that he knows will satisfy it.

An external stimulus can also lead to recognition of a problem or need: a woman passes a bakery, and the sight of freshly baked bread stimulates her hunger; she admires a neighbour's new car; or she watches a television commercial for a Fijian vacation.

The challenge to the marketer at this stage is to determine the circumstances usually triggering the consumer's recognition of a problem. The marketer should research consumers to find out: (i) what kinds of felt needs or problems arose; (ii) what brought them about; and (iii) how they led to this particular product. Betty Smith might answer that she felt a need for a new hobby; this happened when her 'busy season' at work slowed down; and she was led to think of cameras as a result of a friend's talking to her about photography. By gathering such information, the marketer will have a chance to identify the more frequent stimuli that give rise to interest in the product category, and then develop marketing plans that capitalize on these stimuli.

Information Search

An aroused consumer may or may not search for more information. If the consumer's drive is strong and a well-defined gratification object is near at hand, the consumer is likely to buy it then. If not, the need may simply be stored in memory, and the consumer undertake no further search, some further search or very active search for appropriate information.

Assuming that the consumer undertakes some search, we distinguish between two levels. The milder search state is called heightened attention. Here Betty Smith simply becomes more receptive to information about cameras. She pays attention to ads about cameras, notices cameras that are used by friends, and listens more to camera conversation.

Or Betty may go into active information search, where she will look for reading materials, phone friends, and engage in other search activities. How much search she undertakes depends upon the strength of her drive, the amount of information she has initially, the ease of obtaining additional information and the value she places on it and the satisfaction she gets from search. Normally the amount of consumer search activity increases as the consumer moves from situations of limited problem-solving to those of extensive problem-solving.

Of key interest to the marketer are the major information sources that the consumer will turn to, and the relative influence each will have on the subsequent purchase decision. These sources fall into four groups:

- Personal sources (family, friends, neighbours, acquaintances).
- Commercial sources (advertising, salespersons, dealers, packaging, displays).

- Public sources (mass media, consumer-rating organizations).
- Experiential sources (handling, examining, using the product).

The relative influence of these varies with both the product category and the consumer's personal characteristics. Generally speaking, the consumer receives the most information about a product from commercial sources, i.e. marketer-dominated sources. On the other hand, the most effective exposures tend to come from personal sources. Each type of source may perform a somewhat different function in influencing the buying decision. Commercial information normally informs, and personal sources legitimize or evaluate. For example, physicians normally learn of new drugs from commercial sources but turn to other doctors for evaluation information.

The marketer will find it worthwhile to study consumers' information sources whenever a substantial percentage of the target market engages in active search, and when the target market shows some stable patterns of using the respective sources. Identifying the information sources and their respective roles and importance calls for interviewing consumers and asking them how they happened to hear about the product, what sources of information they turned to, and what influence each source of information had. The marketer can use the findings to plan effective marketing communications and stimulate favourable word of mouth.

Information Evaluation

The incoming information helps the consumer clarify and evaluate the alternatives in the evoked set. The marketer needs to know how the consumer processes this information to arrive at product judgments. Unfortunately there is no simple and single evaluation process used by all consumers, or even by one consumer in all buying situations.

Certain basic concepts help us to understand the various consumer evaluation processes. The first is that of *product attributes*. We assume that each consumer perceives a product as a bundle of attributes. The consumer perceives each competing product in terms of where it stands on these attributes. The attributes usually of interest to buyers in some familiar product classes are:

- Cameras: picture sharpness, camera speeds, range, camera size, ruggedness, price.
- Hotels: location, cleanliness, atmosphere, cost.
- Mouthwash: colour, effectiveness, kills germs, price, taste, flavour.
- Brassieres: comfort, fit, life, price, style.
- Lipstick: colour, container, creaminess, prestige, flavour.
- Tyres: safety, tread life, ride quality, price.

Individual consumers will vary as to which attributes they consider relevant. The market for a product can often be segmented according to the attributes that have primary interest to different customer groups.

Second, the consumer is likely to attach different importance weights to the relevant attributes. A distinction can be drawn between the importance of an attribute and its salience.[20] Salient attributes are those that come to the consumer's mind when he or she is asked to think of a product's attributes. The marketer must not conclude that these are necessarily the most important attributes. Some may be salient because the consumer has just been exposed to a commercial message mentioning them, or has had a problem involving them, hence making these attributes 'top-of-the-mind'. Furthermore, in the class of nonsalient attributes may be some that the consumer forgot but whose importance would be recognized when they are mentioned. Marketers should be more concerned with attribute importance than attribute salience.

Third, the consumer is likely to develop a set of brand beliefs about where a brand stands in terms of each attribute; the set of these beliefs is known as the *brand image*. The consumer's beliefs or perceptions may not accord with the brand's true attributes, because of both personal experience and the effect of selective perception, selective distortion and selective retention.

Fourth, the consumer is assumed to have a *utility function* for each attribute, i.e. how the consumer expects product satisfaction to vary with alternative levels of each attribute. For example, Betty Smith may expect her satisfaction from a camera to increase with the speed of its lens, to peak with a medium-weight camera as opposed to very light or heavy one, to be higher for a 35 mm camera than for a 135 mm camera. If we combine the attribute levels where the utilities are highest, they make up Betty's ideal camera. The camera would also be her preferred camera if it were available and affordable.

Fifth, the consumer arrives at attitudes (judgments, preferences) toward the brand alternatives through some *evaluation procedure*. Consumers have been found to apply different evaluation procedures to make a choice among multi-attribute objects,[21] and we will describe these using the following illustration.

Bob Jones wants to buy a new car. He has seen ads and visited some dealer showrooms, and his current information about the buying situation is summarized in Table 8-2. He is interested in four brands (i.e. the evoked set) and the five

product-class attributes shown in the columns. The figures in the attribute columns describe his brand beliefs: he perceives the first three attributes in terms of real numbers (although his perception may not be accurate), and the last two reflect his subjective ratings on a scale of 1 to 10.

Which car will Bob buy? Much depends upon his utility function for the various attributes: we will assume that Bob prefers a lower price to a higher price, lower petrol consumption to higher petrol consumption, a car length ideally of 4.6 metres, more style to less style, and better handling to poorer handling. The utility function can be further specified regarding its actual shape, but we will assume linearity. His choice is still not able to be determined. In fact, at least six different models can explain how consumers form a preference ordering of objects.

1. Conjunctive model. Here the consumer sets minimum attribute levels that he will consider, and drops those brands that fall short on any attribute. Bob Jones might decide that he will only consider cars with a price less than $9000 and a handling greater than 8. Only car 4 will satisfy him in this case.

2. Disjunctive model. Here the consumer will consider objects that meet at least one minimum attribute level. Bob might decide that he will only consider cars with petrol consumption less than 19 litres per 100 kilometres *or* a style greater than 8. Here cars 1, 2 and 4 will remain in the consideration set.

Table 8-2   A buyer's beliefs about alternative brands

			Product-class attributes			
	Car	Price	Petrol consumption (litres/100 km)	Car length (metres)	Style*	Handling*
Evoked set	1	$12 000	28.0	5.6	10	10
	2	10 000	17.5	4.9	9	10
	3	8 000	20.0	5.3	5	6
	4	7 000	14.0	4.6	4	9

*A score of 10 represents the highest rating

3. Lexicographic model. Here the consumer will rank the attributes in order of importance. He will compare the objects on the first ranked attribute and choose the superior one. If two objects are tied, he repeats the process with the second attribute. Bob might decide that price is the most important attribute. In this case, he will choose car 4.

4. Expectancy-value model. Here the consumer assigns importance weights to the attributes and chooses the object that maximizes the expectancy value. Suppose Bob feels that only two attributes, style and handling, are important in the selection of a car (the other three attributes have a zero weight); and furthermore feels that style is three times as important as handling. This would lead to the following expectancy values:

Car 1 = 3(10) + 1(10) = 40
Car 2 = 3(9) + 1(10) = 37
Car 3 = 3(5) + 1(6) = 21
Car 4 = 3(4) + 1(9) = 21

We would therefore predict that Bob, given his weights, will favour car 1.[22]

5. Ideal object model. Here the consumer decides on the ideal level of each attribute. Suppose Bob would most prefer a car 4.6 metres in length and which yields 100 kilometres per 19 litres. The further a car is from these levels, the more Bob would dislike it. According to this information, Bob would prefer cars 2, 4, 3 and 1 in this order.

6. Determinance model. Here the consumer ignores attributes that may be important but are at pretty much the same level for all brands. Suppose the four cars all have reasonable safety features. In spite of the fact that Bob may attach high importance to safety, it will have no determinance on his car choice, since all cars in his set are equal on this attribute. Determinant attributes are those that are both important and highly variable.[23]

Marketers can gain useful insights by interviewing a sample of buyers to find out how most of them form their evaluations in that

product. Suppose the marketer discovers that most of the buyers form their preferences by comparing actual objects with their ideal object. Suppose also that the marketer's brand is brand 3, which is less appealing to this market segment than brand 2. What can this marketer do to improve sales of brand 3 to this market segment? The ideal product model suggests at least seven alternative strategies:[24]

1. *New product development.* The marketer may choose to design and introduce another brand that is closer to this segment's ideal product.
2. *Product modification.* The marketer may choose to add to or alter the attributes of the existing brand to bring it closer to this segment's concept of an ideal brand.
3. *Altering beliefs about the company's brand.* The marketer may try to alter consumers' perceptions about the existing brand's standing on different attributes. The marketer may feel that his brand has, for example, better handling and fuel consumption than are recognized by consumers, and resort to a communication campaign to shift their perceptions closer to the ideal product. This is called brand repositioning.
4. *Altering beliefs about the competitors' brands.* The marketer may try to alter consumers' perceptions about where competitors' brands stand on different attributes. This is called competitive depositioning, and can be accomplished by comparative advertising, and in extreme cases by talking down the other brands.
5. *Altering the attribute importance weights.* The marketer may try to persuade consumers to attach more importance to those attributes that the company brand happens to excel in. Thus the manufacturer of car 4, which has high fuel economy, may promote the importance of fuel economy to consumers who have attached less importance to this.
6. *Promoting attention to new attributes.* The

marketer may try to convince consumers to recognize an attribute, say car-safety design, that the consumers were unaware of or indifferent to.

7. *Shifting the ideal product.* The marketer may try to persuade consumers to change their ideal levels for one or more attributes. For example, the manufacturer of car 4 may try to persuade consumers to prefer a fuel efficiency of 14 litres per 100 km rather than 19.

Purchase Decision

Evaluation leads the consumer to form a ranked set of preferences among the alternatives in the evoked set. Normally the consumer will move towards the purchase of the most preferred object, i.e. form a purchase intention. However, at least three factors may intervene before a purchase decision is made (see Figure 8-5).[25]

The first is the attitudes of others. If Bob Jones prefers car 1 but his wife prefers car 2, Bob's 'purchase probability' for car 1 will be somewhat reduced. The extent to which the attitude of another buying participant will reduce one's preferred alternative depends upon both the intensity of that attitude and the consumer's motivation to comply with the other person's wishes.[26] The more intense the other person's negativism, and the closer the other person is to the consumer, the more the consumer will revise downward his or her purchase intention.

Purchase intention is also influenced by anticipated situational factors such as expected family income, expected total cost of the product, and expected benefits from the product. Even when the consumer is about to act, unanticipated situational factors may prevent the carrying out of the purchase intention. Bob Jones may learn that he cannot get a loan to purchase car 1, he may not like the looks of the salesperson when he visits the chosen dealer, he may be turned off by the delay expected in delivery. Marketers believe that unanticipated factors in the critical contact situation can have a great influence on the final decision. Thus preferences and even purchase intentions are not completely reliable predictors of actual buying behaviour. They give direction to purchase behaviour but fail to include a number of additional factors that may intervene.

The decision to modify, postpone or avoid a purchase decision is also heavily influenced by perceived risk; and marketers have devoted a lot of effort to understand buying behaviour as risk-taking.[27] Consumers cannot be certain about the performance and psychosocial consequences of their purchase decision, and

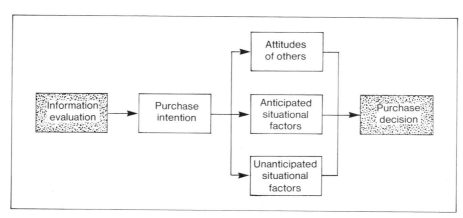

Figure 8-5 Steps between information evaluation and a purchase decision

this produces anxiety. The amount of perceived risk varies with the amount of money at stake, the amount of attribute uncertainty, and the amount of consumer self-confidence. A consumer develops certain routines for reducing risk, such as avoiding decisions, gathering information from friends, and preferring national brand names and warranties. The marketer must understand the factors that provoke a feeling of risk in the consumer, and attempt to provide information and support that will help reduce it.

Postpurchase Behaviour

After purchasing and trying the product, the consumer will experience some level of satisfaction or dissatisfaction. The resulting actions have implications for the marketer.

Postpurchase satisfaction. What determines whether the buyer is highly satisfied, somewhat satisfied, somewhat unsatisfied or highly unsatisfied with a purchase? There are two major theories about this.

The expectations-performance theory holds that a consumer's satisfaction is a function of his expectations and the product's perceived performance.[28] If the product matches expectations, the consumer is satisfied; if it exceeds them, the consumer is highly satisfied; if it falls short, the consumer is dissatisfied.

Consumers form their expectations on the basis of messages and claims sent out by the seller and other sources. If the seller makes exaggerated claims for the product, buyers of that product will experience disconfirmed expectations, which lead to dissatisfaction. Thus if car 1 fails to perform in the way that Bob Jones was led to expect, Bob will revise downward his attitude toward car 1 and may sell it or speak out against the brand. On the other hand, if the car meets his expectations he will tend to be a satisfied owner.

The larger the gap between expectations and performance, the greater the consumer's dissatisfaction. Here the consumer's coping style also comes in: some consumers will tend to magnify the gap when the product is not perfect, and will be highly dissatisfied; others will tend to minimize the gap and feel less dissatisfied.[29]

This theory suggests that the seller should make claims that faithfully represent the product's likely performance – some might even understate performance levels so that consumers would experience higher-than-expected satisfaction with the product.

The other theory of postpurchase satisfaction is called the cognitive dissonance theory. It holds that almost every purchase is likely to lead to some postpurchase discomfort, and the issues are how much discomfort and what will the consumer do about it. As stated by Festinger and Bramel:

> When a person chooses between two or more alternatives, discomfort or dissonance will almost inevitably arise because of the person's knowledge that while the decision he has made has certain advantages, it also has some disadvantages. That dissonance arises after almost every decision, and further, that the individual will invariably take steps to reduce this dissonance.[30]

The amount of dissonance will be a function of the following factors:

1. The more attractive the rejected alternative, the greater the magnitude of the dissonance.
2. The more important the decision, the stronger will be the dissonance.
3. The intensity of dissonance becomes greater as the number of negative characteristics increases.
4. As the number of rejected alternatives increases, the greater will be the dissonance.
5. The greater the perceived similarity of alternatives (cognitive overlap) the greater the dissonance.
6. The more recent the decision between alternatives, the greater will be the magnitude

of dissonance because of the phenomenon of forgetting.

7. A decision that violates a strongly held attitude produces greater dissonance than a decision that rebuts a weaker belief.[31]

Applying this theory, we can expect Bob Jones to feel some postpurchase dissonance. Problems with leaks, rattles, poor performance or sloppy maintenance are likely to stir doubts in his mind as to whether he made the right choice of car; and he will undertake certain actions to reduce this dissonance.

Postpurchase actions. The consumer's satisfaction or dissatisfaction with the purchase choice will affect his subsequent behaviour. If the consumer is satisfied, he will be more likely to purchase the same product next time and will also tend to say good things about the product to others. According to marketers: 'Our best advertisement is a satisfied customer.'

A dissatisfied consumer will of course respond differently, and seek to reduce the dissonance because of a natural human drive 'to establish internal harmony, consistency, or congruity among his opinions, knowledge, and values'.[32] Dissatisfied consumers will resort to one or two courses of action. They may try to reduce the dissonance by abandoning or returning the product, or by seeking information that might confirm its high value (or avoiding information that might disconfirm it). Bob Jones might sell the car, or he might seek information that would lead him to feel better about it.

Marketers can take positive steps to help buyers feel good about their choices. Motor-vehicle companies often send a cordial letter to new car owners, congratulating them on having selected such a fine car. They place ads showing satisfied owners with their new cars.[33] They solicit customer suggestions for improvements and list the location of available services. They write instruction booklets that are dissonance-reducing. They send owners a magazine that contains articles describing the pleasures of owning that car. Postpurchase communications to buyers have been shown to result in fewer product returns and order cancellations.[34]

Thus we see that understanding the buying process is the foundation of successful marketing. By understanding how buyers go through the stages of problem recognition, information search, information evaluation, purchase decision and postpurchase behaviour, the marketer can pick up many clues as to how to meet their needs. By understanding the various participants in the buying process, and the major influences on their buying behaviour, the marketer can develop an efficient marketing programme to support an attractive offer to the target market.

SUMMARY

Markets have to be understood before marketing can be planned. A market is the set of all the individuals and organizations who are actual or potential buyers of a good or service. To understand a market, we ask five questions: (i) Who is the market? (ii) What buying decisions do buyers make? (iii) Who participates in the buying process? (iv) What are the major influences on the buyers? and (v) How do the buyers make their buying decisions? In this chapter we examined these questions for consumer markets.

The consumer market buys goods and services for personal use and consumption. It is the ultimate market for which economic activities are organized, and itself consists of many submarkets (such as ethnic consumers, young adult consumers, and elderly consumers).

The consumer buying decision is made up of many subdecisions. The buyer decides on the need class, generic class, product class, product form, brand, vendor, quantity, timing, and method of payment. The number of conscious decisions made by the consumer depends upon whether the purchase situation is one of routinized response behaviour, limited problem-solving, or extensive problem-solving.

Buying decisions are typically influenced by other participants, who play such roles as initiator, influencer, decider, buyer and user. The marketer's job is to identify these participants, their buying criteria and their level of influence on the buyer. The marketing programme should be designed to appeal to and reach the other key participants as well as the buyer.

The many factors influencing buying participants can be grouped into buyer characteristics, product characteristics, seller characteristics and situational characteristics. Of these, we examined most closely the buyer character-

istics. The buyer's behaviour is influenced by four major variables: cultural (culture, subculture and social class), social (reference groups, family, and roles and statuses), personal (age and lifecycle stage, occupation, economic circumstances, lifestyle, and personality and self-concept), and psychological (motivation, perception, learning, and beliefs and attitudes). All of these offer clues about how to reach and serve the buyer more effectively.

In buying anything, the buyer goes through problem recognition, information search, information evaluation, purchase decision, and postpurchase behaviour. The marketer's job is to understand the buyer's behaviour, and influences operating, at each stage. This understanding allows the marketer to develop a significant and effective marketing programme for the target market.

QUESTIONS FOR DISCUSSION

1. Using the definitions of a market adopted in this text, are you part of the market for a single-family home? Why?

2. Who makes up the consumer market for women's jewellery?

3. Explain which of the three classes of buying situations would probably apply to the purchase decision for:
   - a European vacation
   - a six-pack of beer
   - a new suit
   - a museum to attend

4. Consider the five different roles in the decision process in relation to your choice of a tertiary education institution.

5. Discuss the influence of cultural characteristics (culture, subculture and social class) on the patronage of department stores.

6. Which social characteristics have the greatest effect on an individual's record-album purchases?

7. Based on recent demographic trends, are there any stages of a family lifecycle that are not included in Table 8-1? Discuss the marketing implications.

8. The self-concept is synonymous with personality. Discuss.

9. What level of Maslow's hierarchy of needs are marketers of the following products primarily attempting to satisfy?
   - smoke alarms/detectors
   - STD long-distance dialling
   - American Express Card
   - life insurance
   - transcendental meditation

10. Attitudes are a central concept to understanding an individual's consumer behaviour. Why?

11. Relate the stages of the consumer buying process to your latest purchase of a pair of shoes.

12. Why is the postpurchase behaviour stage included in the model of the buying process?

NOTES

1 Pam Mawbey, 'Sweet Smell of Success Evaded This Product', *Australian Financial Review*, 30 June 1981, p. 17.

2 John A. Howard & Jagdish N. Sheth, *The Theory of Buyer Behaviour* (New York: John Wiley, 1969), pp. 27–28.

3 Howard & Sheth, p. 26.

4 See Chem L. Narayana & Rom J. Markin, 'Consumer Behaviour and Product Performance: An Alternative Conceptualization', *Journal of Marketing*, October 1975, pp. 1–6.

5 Based on the discussion of social class in James F. Engel, Roger D. Blackwell & David T. Kollat, *Consumer Behaviour* (New York: Holt, Rinehart & Winston, 3rd edn, 1978), Ch. 5.

6 'How You Rate In The Social Stakes', *Age*, 28 December 1977, p. 5.

7 See Francis S. Bourne, *Group Influence in Marketing and Public Relations* (Ann Arbor, Mich.: Foundation for Research on Human Behaviour, 1956).

8 See Harry L. Davis, 'Decision Making within the Household', *Journal of Consumer Research*, March 1976, pp. 241–60; Harry L. Davis & Benny P. Rigaux, 'Perception of Marital Roles in Decision Processes', *Journal of Consumer Research*, June 1974, pp. 51–60; and Harry L. Davis, 'Dimensions of Marital Roles in Consumer Decision-Making', *Journal of Marketing Research*, May 1970, pp. 168–77.

9 See Davis, 'Dimensions of Marital Roles'.

10 Gail Sheehy, *Passages: Predictable Crises in Adult Life* (New York: Dutton, 1974); and Roger Gould, *Transformations* (New York: Simon & Schuster, 1978).

11 Harper W. Boyd Jr & Sidney J. Levy, *Promotion: A Behavioural View* (Englewood Cliffs, N.J.: Prentice-Hall, 1967), p. 38.

12 For more reading, see Edward L. Grubb & Harison L. Grathwohl, 'Consumer Self-Concept, Symbolism, and Market Behaviour: A Theoretical Approach', *Journal of Marketing*, October 1967, pp. 22–27; Ira J. Dolich, 'Congruence Relationships between Self-Images and Product Brands', *Journal of Marketing Research*, February 1969, pp. 40–47; and E. Laird Landon Jr, 'The Differential Role of Self-Concept and Ideal Self-Concept in Consumer Purchase Behaviour', *Journal of Consumer Research*, September 1974, pp. 44–51.

13 See Ernest Dichter, *Handbook of Consumer Motivations* (New York: McGraw-Hill, 1964).

14 Abraham H. Maslow, *Motivation and Personality* (New York: Harper & Row, 1954), pp. 80–106.

15 See Frederick Herzberg, *Work and the Nature of Man* (Cleveland: William Collins, 1966); and Robert J. Hourse & L. Widgor, 'Herzberg's Dual-Factor Theory of Job Satisfaction and Motivation: A Review of the Empirical Evidence and a Criticism', *Personnel Psychology*, 20 (1967), pp. 369–80.

[16] Bernard Berelson & Gary A. Steiner, *Human Behaviour: An Inventory of Scientific Findings* (New York: Harcourt Brace Jovanovich, 1964), p. 88.

[17] This relationship is known as Weber's law and is one of the main laws in psychophysics. See Ch. 12.

[18] See David Krech, Richard S. Crutchfield & Egerton L. Ballachey, *Individual in Society* (New York: McGraw-Hill, 1962), Ch. 2.

[19] Several models of the consumer buying process have been developed by marketing scholars. The most prominent models are those of John A. Howard & Jagdish N. Sheth, *The Theory of Buyer Behaviour* (New York: John Wiley, 1969); Francesco M. Nicosia, *Consumer Decision Processes* (Englewood Cliffs, N.J.: Prentice-Hall, 1966); and James F. Engel, Roger D. Blackwell & David T. Kollat, *Consumer Behaviour* (New York: Holt, Rinehart & Winston, 3rd edn, 1978).

[20] James H. Myers & Mark I. Alpert, 'Semantic Confusion in Attitude Research: Salience vs. Importance vs. Determinance', *Advances in Consumer Research* (Proceedings of the Seventh Annual Conference of the Association of Consumer Research, October 1976), IV, pp. 106–10.

[21] See Paul E. Green & Yoram Wind, *Multiattribute Decisions in Marketing: A Measurement Approach* (Hinsdale, Ill.: Dryden Press, 1973), Ch. 2.

[22] If more attributes were included from Table 8-2, it would be necessary to scale them all on a scale (say, 1–10) before applying this formula. It should be recognized that what is meaningful is not the absolute attitude scores but the relative values, because the metric scaling of the importance weights and beliefs is an arbitrary method. For an excellent review of this model, see William L. Wilke & Edgar A. Pessemier, 'Issues in Marketing's Use of Multi-Attribute Attitude Models', *Journal of Marketing Research*, November 1973, pp. 428–41.

[23] See James H. Myers & Mark I. Alpert, 'Determinant Buying Attitudes: Meaning and Measurement', *Journal of Marketing*, October 1968, pp. 13–20.

[24] See Harper W. Boyd Jr, Michael L. Ray & Edward C. Strong, 'An Attitudinal Framework for Advertising Strategy', *Journal of Marketing*, April 1972, pp. 27–33.

[25] See Jagdish N. Sheth, 'An Investigation of Relationships among Evaluative Beliefs, Affect, Behavioural Intention, and Behaviour', in John U. Farley, John A. Howard, and L. Winston Ring (eds), *Consumer Behaviour: Theory and Application* (Boston: Allyn & Bacon, 1974), pp. 89–114.

[26] See Martin Fishbein, 'Attitude and Prediction of Behaviour', in Martin Fishbein (ed.), *Readings in Attitude Theory and Measurement* (New York: John Wiley, 1967), pp. 477–92.

[27] See Raymond A. Bauer, 'Consumer Behaviour as Risk Taking', in Donald F. Cox (ed.), *Risk Taking and Information Handling in Consumer Behaviour* (Boston: Division of Research, Harvard Business School, 1967); and James W. Taylor, 'The Role of Risk in Consumer Behaviour', *Journal of Marketing*, April 1974, pp. 54–60.

[28] See John E. Swan & Linda Jones Combs, 'Product Performance and Consumer Satisfaction: A New Concept', *Journal of Marketing Research*, April 1976, pp. 25–33.

[29] See Rolph E. Anderson, 'Consumer Dissatisfaction: The Effect of Disconfirmed Expectance on Perceived Product Performance', *Journal of Marketing Research*, February 1973, pp. 38–44.

[30] Leon Festinger & Dana Bramel, 'The Reactions of Humans to Cognitive Dissonance', in Arthur J. Bachrach (ed.), *Experimental Foundations of Clinical Psychology* (New York: Basic Books, 1962), pp. 251–62.

[31] See Rom J. Markin Jr, *Consumer Behaviour: A Cognitive Orientation* (New York: Macmillan, 1974), pp. 145–47.

[32] Leon Festinger, *A Theory of Cognitive Dissonance* (Stanford, Calif.: Stanford University Press, 1957), p. 260.

[33] Research shows that new car owners read significantly more advertisements about the car they have just purchased than they do about other cars. See D. Ehrlich, I. Guttman, P. Schonback & J. Mills, 'Post-Decision Exposure to Relevant Information', *Journal of Abnormal and Social Psychology*, January 1957, pp. 98–102.

[34] See James H. Donnelly Jr & John M. Ivancevich, 'Post-Purchase Reinforcement and Backout Behaviour', *Journal of Marketing Research*, August 1970, pp. 399–400.

Organizational Markets and Buying Behaviour

The following advertisement appeared in the Australian Financial Review.

HOW TO BUY A BUSINESS JET

The makers of Cessna Citation offer some objective help in selecting the right aircraft for your needs – whether you are stepping up from a prop plane, or replacing an older, fuel-thirsty jet.

Buying a business jet makes more sense now than ever before.

Using the time of your people most effectively is key to giving you a competitive edge. And evidence is piling up that the corporate jet is a business tool that can help you sustain that edge.

Among the five hundred and twenty-two Fortune 1000 companies currently operating their own aircraft, net income per employee is 37% greater than among companies who don't operate aircraft. These same companies are buying significantly more jets than turboprops today – primarily for their greater speed and comfort.

Then there are the growing costs of business travel. Commercial air fares have risen considerably over the last two years. And cutbacks in service have increased the need for more overnight stays and related travel costs.

If you think the above factors will affect your company, now is the time to make your plans. Practically every business jet on the market has a backlog of 12 to 24 months, or more. Delaying your decision to buy may mean paying a premium for the jet of your choice, or being far down the waiting list.

Start by Evaluating Your Transportation Needs

We suggest you begin with this rule of thumb: If you have at least five key people, who travel more than five times a month, on trips that average from 300 to 500 miles (480–800 km), you almost certainly need a business jet and can justify its cost.

The next step is to determine your company's present transportation costs. How many people in your firm fly regularly? Where do they fly? How often? What are the monetary costs? And even more important, the cost of valuable executive time wasted?

Check your destinations against the latest schedules. Service to many cities has been cut back dramatically. Some smaller cities are no longer even serviced by scheduled airlines.

The Economics of Planning Ahead

For many purchasers, the 12 to 24 month lead time for most business jets can actually work to their advantage in planning cash flow.

Of course, it's no advantage if the price you are quoted today disappears under the pressures of inflation. Be specific in your questions about pricing policies when talking to manufacturers:

- *Will the prices you are quoted now be guaranteed prices upon delivery?*
- *Do they have built-in escalation clauses?*
- *What effect will changing interest rates have on your contract?*

And if you have a company airplane and plan to dispose of it upon delivery of your new jet, find out now which companies offer assistance in marketing your used aircraft.

Two Dozen Business Jets — Which Is Right for You?

If you are looking at business jets for the first time, you may be amazed at the differences.

Some are designed for pure speed. Others travel slightly slower, but deliver much better fuel economy. Business jets vary in payload from five passengers plus crew, to 12 to 15 passengers and crew. And they vary in price from just over a million and a half dollars to nearly $US12 million. Surprisingly, the larger turboprops can cost more than some jets, even though their performance is less. Fuel efficiency is a good place to start your comparisons. Check thoroughly. Some jets will consume nearly twice as much fuel as others with the same payload and in the same price range.

Here is a comparison in actual dollars between two jets of similar cabin size on a typical 600 hour a year flying schedule: one, using 155 US gallons an hour, the other 285 US gallons an hour. At an average $US1.90 a gallon for jet fuel – you could save $US148 000 in fuel alone, just by choosing the right jet.

Don't buy a jet that is larger than you realistically need. Some business jets burn over 600 US gallons of fuel an hour. As fuel approaches two and perhaps *even three US dollars a gallon, flying empty seats around could cost you as much as $US750 000 a year in added fuel costs.*

The length of runway various jets require for takeoff is also a vital point. Some business jets take as little as 765 metres, while others need runways over 1.5 kilometres long. The difference can open up – or close – thousands of airfields to you. Note: one popular turboprop requires 1430 metres for takeoff – nearly twice that of the best short field performance jet.

Make sure engine noise will not close you out of the cities you want to fly to. Fanjets are much quieter than turbojets. As a result, many airports are beginning to prohibit turbojets during certain hours.

Finally, look at safety records of the aircraft you are considering. Ask to see the records from an unbiased source, such as the National Transportation Safety Board in the US, or the Accident Investigation Board in your country.

Fly It Before You Buy It

Once you've narrowed down your choices, arrange demonstration rides on actual business trips.

This is your chance to experience what the different jets feel like. Look for such things as seating comfort, low noise levels, and smooth operation.

Don't underestimate the importance of passenger comfort in the long run. After all, sparing your executives the wear and tear of travel is one of the reasons you're buying a business jet in the first place.

Ask the Man Who Owns One

Have the manufacturer's representatives put you in contact with other companies in your area who have purchased their jets? Maybe even someone you know. Get their opinion from an unbiased viewpoint.

They may well be willing to give you their actual cost breakdowns, as well as their experiences in dealing with the manufacturers, and availability of parts and service.

Look at the *Total* Costs

The first thing everyone asks about a jet is 'What will it cost?' An important question. But you should look beyond that – at costs of ownership and costs of operation. This includes comparisons of maintenance costs of the planes under consideration.

The Next Step Is Yours

The kind of straightforward help Cessna offers doesn't stop on this page. If you think that buying a business jet may make sense for your company, give us a call now. Our sales engineers will help you with the points discussed above, plus detailed feasibility studies, cost comparison versus present travel methods, cost projections, variable costs of use, and fixed costs of ownership.[1]

This advertisement illustrates some of the things involved in organizations selling goods and services to other organizations. These sellers, called industrial marketers, must do their best to understand the buying organization's needs, resources, policies and buying procedures. They must take into account several considerations not usually relevant in marketing directly to consumers:

1. Organizations buy goods and services for the purpose of making profits, reducing costs, serving their internal clienteles' needs, and meeting social and legal obligations.
2. More persons tend to participate formally in organizational buying decisions than in consumer buying decisions. The decision participants usually have different organizational responsibilities and apply different criteria to the purchase decisions.
3. The buyers must heed formal policies, constraints and requirements established by their organizations.
4. The buying instruments (such as request for quotations, proposals, and purchase contracts) add another dimension not found in consumer buying.

Organizations make up a vast market for a multitude of goods and services such as raw materials, manufactured parts, installations, accessory equipment, supplies and business services. (The classification of industrial products is discussed in Chapter 12.) Sellers who specialize wholly or partly in selling their products to other organizations need to understand organizational buying behaviour. Webster and Wind define *organizational buying* as 'the decision-making process by which formal organizations establish the need for purchased products and services, and identify, evaluate, and choose among alternative brands and suppliers'.[2]

THE PRODUCER MARKET

Who Is in the Producer Market?
(buying population)

The producer market (also called the industrial or business market) consists of all the individuals and organizations who acquire goods and services that enter into the production of other products or services to be sold, rented or supplied. The major types of industry making up the producer market are: agriculture, forestry and fisheries; mining; manufacturing; construction; transport; communication; public utilities; banking, finance, and insurance; and services. There are over 250 000 different industrial units, and each is a market for specific types of goods and services. They employ approximately two million workers, generate an annual national income of over $30 billion, and constitute a buying market for the goods of most firms.

More dollars are involved in sales to industrial buyers than to consumers. To bring a simple pair of shoes into existence, hide dealers (mainly meat suppliers) must sell the hides to tanners, who sell the leather to shoe manufacturers, who sell the shoes to wholesalers, who in turn sell the shoes to retailers. Each party in the chain of production and distribution pays more than the previous party. The transactions based on one pair of finished shoes may have been $4 (hide dealer to tanner), $5 (tanner to shoe manufacturer), $20 (shoe manufacturer to wholesaler), and $24 (wholesaler to retailer), making a total of $53, whereas the shoes were sold to the consumer for $30. We can appreciate why there is more industrial marketing going on than consumer marketing.

Industrial markets have certain characteristics that contrast sharply with consumer markets.

Fewer buyers. The industrial marketer normally deals with far fewer buyers than does the consumer marketer. Dunlop Olympic's fate in the industrial-tyre market depends entirely on orders from one of five motor-vehicle companies: General Motors-Holden's, Ford, Mitsubishi, Toyota or Nissan. But when Dunlop Olympic sells to consumers, it has a potential market of several million Australian car owners.

Larger buyers. Even in industrial markets consisting of many firms, a few usully account for most of the purchasing. In such industries as motor vehicles, cigarettes, confectionery, glass, soap, edible oils, and tyres, the top five manufacturers account for over 70 per cent of total production.

Geographically concentrated buyers. While New South Wales and Victoria contain 62 per cent of Australia's consumers, they contain 57 per cent of the total number of agricultural establishments, and 72 per cent of manufacturing establishments. But these broad statistics tend to mask the dominance or unusual level of activity in various States in various industries. For example, Victoria is the leading dairying State, New South Wales leads in wheat production, and Queensland leads in sugar production. Similarly, Tasmania shows a high level of activity in wood and paper industries, Western Australia in mineral and metals extraction, and South Australia in fabricated metal products and transport equipment. This geographic concentration of producers helps to reduce the costs of selling to them. Industrial marketers should watch any pronounced trends towards or away from further geographic concentration.

Derived demand. The demand for industrial goods is ultimately derived from the demand for consumer goods. Thus animal hides are purchased because consumers buy shoes, purses and other leather goods. If the demand for these consumer goods slackens, so will the demand for all the industrial goods relating to their production.

Inelastic demand. The total demand for industrial goods and services is not much affected by price changes. Shoe manufacturers are not going to buy much more leather if the price of leather falls unless: (i) leather is a major cost in shoe manufacture; (ii) the manufacturers will cut their prices of leather shoes drastically; (iii) shoe buyers will buy more shoes. Nor are shoe manufacturers going to buy much less leather if the price of leather rises unless they can find ways to economize on the amount of leather used in shoes, or find leather substitutes. Demand is especially inelastic in the short run because producers cannot make any changes in their production methods. Demand is also inelastic for industrial goods that represent a small percentage of the item's total cost. For example, an increase in the industry price of metal eyelets will barely affect the level of demand for shoes. At the same time producers will use price to decide which supplier to buy from, although it will have less effect on the amount bought.

Fluctuating demand. The demand for industrial goods and services tends to be much more volatile than for consumer goods and services. This is especially true of major installations of plant and equipment. Swings in these goods in turn accelerate the swings in raw materials such as metals and other minerals. Thus a small change in consumer demand can lead to a large increase in industrial demand – economists refer to this as the accelerator principle. Sometimes a rise (fall) of only 10 per cent in consumer demand can cause as much as a 200 per cent rise (fall) in industrial demand in the next period. This phenomenon has led many industrial marketers to diversify their product lines to achieve some cyclical balance.

Professional purchasing. Industrial goods are purchased by trained professionals who spend their lives learning how to buy better. Consumers, on the other hand, are much less trained in the art of careful buying. The more complex the industrial purchase, the more likely it is that several persons will participate in the formal decision-making process; buying committees made up of technical experts and top management are common in the purchase of major goods. This means that industrial marketers have to rely heavily on well-trained sales representatives to deal with the well-trained buyers. Although advertising, sales promotion, and publicity also play an important role in the industrial promotional mix, personal selling is the main tool for producing sales.

Miscellaneous characteristics. Several other characteristics tend to distinguish industrial buying from consumer buying:

1. *Direct purchasing.* Industrial buyers more often buy directly from the producers rather than through intermediaries (whereas consumers most often buy from intermediaries). This is especially true of items that are technically complex and expensive.
2. *Reciprocity.* Industrial buyers often select suppliers who also buy from them. An example of reciprocity would be a paper manufacturer who decides to buy needed chemicals from a chemical company that is buying a considerable amount of its paper. Reciprocity is a dangerous game to play – and may be forbidden by the Trade Practices Act, especially Sections 45 and 49 – because it can unfairly shut out competition. A buyer can choose a supplier that it also sells something to, but it should be able to show that it is getting competitive prices, quality and service from that supplier.[3]
3. *Leasing.* Industrial buyers are increasingly turning to leasing equipment instead of outright purchase. This happens with computers, shoe machinery, packaging equipment, heavy construction equipment, deliv-

ery trucks, machine tools, and sales-force vehicles. The lessee gains a number of advantages, such as having more available capital, getting the seller's latest products, receiving better servicing, and gaining some tax advantages. The lessor often ends up with a larger net income and the chance to get its goods into markets that might not have been able to afford outright purchase.[4]

What Buying Decisions Do Producers Make? (buying decisions)

The industrial buyer, like the consumer buyer, makes a whole set of decisions when making a purchase. The number of these depends on the type of buying situation.

Major types of buying situations. Robinson and others distinguish three types of buying situations, called *buyclasses*,[5] which are analogous to the three consumer buying situations discussed in Chapter 8 (routinized response behaviour, limited problem-solving, and extensive problem-solving).

Straight rebuy. The straight rebuy describes the simplest buying situation, where the buying organization reorders something without any modifications. It is usually handled on a routine basis by the purchasing department. The buyer chooses from suppliers already on its 'list', giving much weight to its past buying experience with the various suppliers. The 'in' suppliers make an effort to keep up product and service quality, and may propose automatic reordering systems so that the purchasing agent will save time. The 'out' suppliers attempt to offer something new or create some dissatisfaction so that the buyer will reconsider the buying assumptions; they may attempt to get their foot in the door with a small order and then try to enlarge their 'purchase share' over time.

Modified rebuy. The modified rebuy is where the buyer is seeking to modify product specifications, prices, other terms, or suppliers in connection with something it purchases. The modified rebuy usually expands the number of decision participants. The 'in' suppliers become nervous and have to put their best foot forward to protect the account. The 'out' suppliers see it as an opportunity to make a better offer to gain some new business.

New task. The new task faces a company buying a product or service for the first time. The greater the cost and/or risk, the larger the number of decision participants and the greater their search for information. This situation is the marketer's greatest opportunity and challenge: he must plan to reach as many key buying influences as possible, and provide information to help them solve their problem (preferably in favour of the marketer's product). Because of the complicated selling involved, many companies use a specialized 'missionary sales force' to carry out this type of task.

Major subdecisions involved in the buying decision. The number of decisions involved in a particular buying project varies with the type of buying situation – fewest in the case of a straight rebuy, and most numerous in the new-task situation. In the latter case, the buying centre will have to determine: (i) product specifications; (ii) price limits; (iii) delivery terms and times; (iv) service terms; (v) payment terms; (vi) order quantities; (vii) acceptable suppliers; and (viii) the selected supplier. Different participants will influence each decision, and the order in which the decisions will be made will vary.

The marketer's task is to anticipate the full range of decisions facing the buyer and offer an attractive and convenient total solution if possible. Suppose, for example, that the buyer wants to build a fertilizer plant. At one extreme, the buyer can make all the separate decisions and hire its own architects, engineers, contractors, legal staff and so on. At the other extreme, the buyer can hire one company that will put together the whole package – this is

called a turnkey operation, because all the buyer has to do is turn the key when the plant is ready to start operating. The underlying idea is that the marketer should try to sell a system rather than a single component, because buyers find this more convenient and attractive. 'Systems selling' is a key industrial marketing strategy for winning and holding accounts.[6]

Who Participates in the Producer Buying Process? (buying participants)

Who does the buying of the billions of dollars' worth of products and services needed by the industrial market? Buying organizations vary tremendously, from small firms with one or a few purchasing executives to huge corporations with large purchasing departments headed by a director of purchasing. The purchasing executives may be responsible for the entire decision (product specifications and supplier), for supplier selection only, or may make neither decision but simply place the order. Typically, they make the decisions regarding smaller items and carry out the wishes of others regarding major capital items.

Webster and Wind call the decision-making unit of a buying organization the buying centre, defined as 'all those individuals and groups who participate in the purchasing decision-making process, who share some common goals and the risks arising from the decisions'.[7] The buying centre includes all members of the organization who play any of five roles in the purchase decision process:[8]

1. *Users.* Users are the members of the organization who will use the good or service. In many cases, the users initiate the buying project and play an important role in defining the purchase specifications.
2. *Influencers.* Influencers are those inside and outside the organization who directly or indirectly influence the buying decision. They often help define specifications and

also provide information for evaluating alternatives. Technical personnel are particularly important as influencers.

3. *Buyers*. Buyers are members of the organization authorized to select the supplier and arrange the terms of purchase. They may help shape product specifications, but they play their major role in selecting vendors and negotiating within the purchase constraints. In more complex purchases, the buyers might include high-level officers of the company.

4. *Deciders*. Deciders are members of the organization who have formal or informal power to select or approve the final suppliers. In the routine buying of standard items, the buyers are often the deciders; in more complex buying, the officers of the company are often the deciders.

5. *Gatekeepers*. Gatekeepers are members of the organization who control the flow of information regarding buying alternatives. For example, purchasing agents often have authority to prevent salespersons from seeing users or deciders; other gatekeepers include technical personnel and even switchboard operators.

Within the organization, the buying centre will vary in size and composition for different classes of products. More decision participants will be involved in buying a computer, for example, than in buying paperclips. The challenge to the industrial marketer is to identify the major decision participants, the decisions in which these exercise influence, their relative degree of influence, and the evaluation criteria used by each. Consider the following example:

> The Hospital Supply Corporation is one of several competitors selling non-woven disposable surgical gowns to hospitals. Its first task is to identify those persons in a hospital who normally participate in the buying decision for surgical gowns. The decision participants turn out to be the hospital's purchasing manager, the

operating-room administrator, and the surgeons. Each party plays a different role. The purchasing manager analyzes whether the hospital should buy disposable gowns or re-usable gowns. If the analysis shows that it is less expensive to buy re-usable gowns and re-launder them, the suppliers of disposable gowns are closed out of this market. If the findings favour buying disposable gowns, then the operating-room administrator is responsible for comparing and choosing between various competitors' products and prices. This administrator considers such qualities as the gown's absorbency, antiseptic quality, design and cost, and usually buys the brand that meets the functional requirements at the lowest cost. Finally, surgeons influence the decision retroactively by reporting their satisfaction or lack of satisfaction with the particular brand (e.g. its style and comfort).

Since a buying centre may include anywhere from one to a dozen persons, the industrial marketer may not have the time or resources to reach them all. Smaller companies try to determine the key buying influences, and concentrate their limited advertising and personal selling resources on them. Larger companies go for multilevel in-depth selling to reach as many decision participants as possible; their salespeople virtually 'live' with the customer when it is a major account with recurrent sales.

What Are the Major Influences on Producer Buyers? (buying influences)

Industrial buyers are subject to many influences when they make their buying decisions, and the marketer must understand these. Some marketers assume that the most important influences are rational. They view the organization as a rational buyer pursuing economic objectives in an efficient way, i.e. making its decisions in favour of the supplier who offers the minimum price or the best product, buys things from the company in return (reciprocity), or is the most ready to accommodate. This view implies that industrial marketers should primarily concentrate on offering strong economic benefits to buyers.

Other marketers emphasize the role of personal motives in the buying process, such as buyers responding to personal favours (self-aggrandizement), attention (ego-enhancement), or to personal risk containment (risk avoiders). A study of buyers in ten large companies concluded that:

> ... corporate decision-makers remain human after they enter the office. They respond to 'image'; they buy from companies to which they feel 'close'; they favour suppliers who show them respect and personal consideration, and who do extra things 'for them'; they 'over-react' to real or imagined slights, tending to reject companies which fail to respond or delay in submitting requested bids.[9]

This suggests that industrial marketers should concentrate on the human and social factors in the buying situation, and that they could overcome offer deficiencies by being more manipulative of emotional and interpersonal factors.

Industrial buyers actually respond to both rational and personal factors. Where there is substantial similarity in what suppliers offer in the way of products, price and service, industrial buyers have little basis for rational choice. Since they can meet organizational goals with any one of a number of suppliers, buyers can bring in personal factors. On the other hand, where competing products differ substantially, industrial buyers are more accountable for their choice and pay more attention to objective factors. Short-run personal gain becomes less motivating than the long-run gain that comes from serving their organization well.

Webster and Wind have proposed that the various influences on industrial buyers be classified into four main groups: environmental, organizational, interpersonal and individual.[10] Figure 9-1 shows the main influences in each group that industrial marketers should focus on in trying to understand the buying situation.

Environmental factors. Industrial buyers are heavily influenced by their company's current and expected environment. Of particular interest are economic factors, such as changes in the level of primary demand, the economic outlook, and the cost of money. As the level of such risk or uncertainty rises, industrial

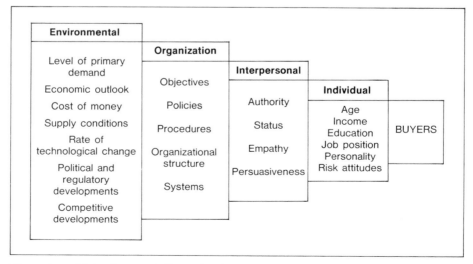

Figure 9-1   Major factors influencing industrial buying behaviour

buyers cease making new investments in plant and equipment and refrain from adding raw materials to their inventories. There is little that the industrial marketer can do to stimulate purchases except cut prices to a level where the buyers are willing to take some risk.

An environmental factor of increasing importance is imminent shortages in key materials. Companies are showing a greater willingness to buy and hold larger inventories of scarce materials, to sign long-term contracts to guarantee the supply of these materials. Several major companies have established supply planning as a major responsibility of their purchasing executives.[11]

Industrial buyers also watch technological, political and competitive developments in the environment. It is the job of the industrial marketer to monitor these factors, determine how they will affect the buyer and prepare to turn them into opportunities.

Organizational factors. Each buying organization has its own objectives, policies, procedures, organizational structure and systems. It is the job of the marketer to know these as well as possible. Such questions arise as: How many people will be involved in the buying decision? Who will they be? What are their evaluative criteria? What are the company's policies and constraints on the buyers? Suppliers are limited in how much they can find out and must work patiently to accumulate information.

The industrial marketer should be aware of the following organizational developments occurring in the purchasing area.

1. Purchasing department upgrading. Purchasing departments have typically occupied a low position in the management hierarchy, in spite of often being responsible for managing more than half of the typical organization's costs. The recent combination of inflation and shortages has led many companies to upgrade their purchasing departments, and several have elevated the heads of purchasing to direc-

tor levels. Caterpillar and some other companies have combined several functions – such as purchasing, inventory control, production scheduling, and traffic – into a high-level function called materials management. Many companies are looking for top talent, hiring MBAs, and offering higher compensation. This means that industrial marketers must correspondingly upgrade their sales personnel to match the calibre of the new buyeres.

2. Centralized purchasing. In multidivisional companies, much purchasing is carried out by the separate divisions because of their differing needs. In recent years, however, there has been a tendency towards recentralizing this function: headquarters is identifying those materials that are purchased by several divisions and is buying them centrally. This gives the buyer more purchasing clout. The individual plants can buy from another source if they can get a better deal, but in general, centralized purchasing produces substantial savings for the company.[12] For the industrial marketer, this development means dealing with fewer and higher-level buyers, e.g. a national account sales force rather than separate regional accounts. National account selling is more complex and demands a more sophisticated sales force and marketing effort.

3. Long-term contracts. More industrial buyers are seeking long-term contracts with suppliers as opposed to single-purchase orders for a definite amount and date of delivery. These contracts call for much more skilful negotiation, and buyers are adding negotiating specialists to their staffs. Industrial marketers, in turn, will have to add skilled negotiators to their staffs.

4. Purchasing performance evaluation. Some buying organizations are setting up incentive systems to reward purchasing managers for especially good performance, in much the same way that sales personnel receive bonuses. These systems will lead purchasing managers to further increase their efforts to seek the best terms.

Interpersonal factors. Industrial buying takes place within a context of interpersonal influences that go beyond the formal organizational characteristics. The buying centre usually includes several participants with different status, authority, empathy and persuasiveness. The industrial marketer is not likely to be able to predict the group dynamics during the buying process, although any information about the personalities involved would be useful.

Individual factors. Each buying participant brings into the buying situation personal motivations, perceptions and preferences influenced by the participant's age, income, education, professional identification, personality, and attitudes toward risk. Buyers definitely have different buying styles. Some of the younger, higher-educated buyers are 'computer freaks' and make rigorous analyses of competitive proposals before making a choice; other buyers are from the 'old school' and play off the sellers against each other.

The point is that industrial marketers must know their customers and thus adapt their tactics not only to known environmental, organizational and interpersonal factors but also to the quirks of individuals involved in the buying process.

How Do Producers Make Their Buying Decisions? (buying process)

We now come to the issue of how industrial buyers move through the buying process (also called procurement process). We could describe the industrial buying process as consisting of the same five stages as the consumer buying process – problem recognition, information search, information evaluation, purchase decision, and postpurchase behaviour. However, there are certain features of industrial buying that call for a more elaborate model. Robinson and others have proposed eight stages of the industrial buying process called 'buyphases'[13]: problem recognition, general need description, product specification, supplier search, proposal solicitation, supplier selection, order routine specification, and performance review.

Problem recognition. The buying process begins when someone in the company recognizes a problem or need that can be met by acquiring a good or a service. This may occur as a result of internal or external stimuli. Internally, the most common events leading to problem recognition are the following:

- The company decides to launch a new product, and needs new equipment and materials to produce this product.
- A machine breaks down and requires replacement or new parts.
- Some purchased material turns out to be unsatisfactory, and this raises the question of finding another supplier.
- A purchasing manager senses an opportunity to obtain better prices or quality.

Externally, the buyer may be exposed to new ideas (e.g. at a trade show, in an advertisement) or receive a visit from a sales representative who offers a better product or a lower price. Industrial marketers cannot sit back and wait for buyers to contact them. When they have a superior offer, they develop promotions and make calls on buyers. Often they help buyers recognize a latent need. For example, manufacturers of flavours and fragrances will often develop new food or cosmetic products that use their ingredients and then offer the 'recipes' to consumer goods marketers for their own usage.

General need description. Having recognized a need, the buyer proceeds to determine the general characteristics and quantity of the needed item. For standard items, this is not much of a problem. For more complex items, the buyer will work with others in the company – engineers, users, and so on –

to define the general characteristics they are seeking. They will want to rank the importance of reliability, durability, price and other desired attributes.

The industrial marketer can assist the buying company in this phase, e.g. by explaining the value of a product's different characteristics, or by helping the buyer define the company's needs.

Product specification. Here the buying organization proceeds to develop the technical specifications for the item. *Value analysis*, which General Electric pioneered in the late 1940s, is an approach to cost reduction in which components are carefully studied to determine if they can be redesigned or standardized or made by cheaper methods of production. An engineering team will carefully examine the high-cost components in a given product – usually 20 per cent of the parts will constitute about 80 per cent of the costs – and then decide on the product specifications and spell them out in the clearest and most technically accurate manner possible. In this way the buyer, who may be unsure, can be protected against making an error. Furthermore, accurately written specifications will allow the buyer to legally refuse to accept merchandise that only roughly approximates the intended items.

Supplier search. The buyer now proceeds to identify the most appropriate vendors, making use of trade directories or computer search, or phoning other companies for their recommendations. Some vendors will be dropped from consideration because they are not large enough to supply the needed quantity, or have a poor credit standing or a poor reputation for delivery and service. The buyer will end up with a small list of qualified suppliers. The newer the buying task, and the more complex and expensive the item, the greater the amount of time spent in searching for and qualifying suppliers. The supplier's job is

thus to make sure of being listed in major directories, and being well known and well thought of by opinion leaders.

Proposal solicitation. In this stage the buyer will invite qualified suppliers to submit proposals. Some suppliers will only send a catalogue or a sales representative; where the item is complex or expensive, the buyer will require detailed written proposals which will be reviewed and the weaker ones dropped. The buyer may request formal presentations by the remaining suppliers. All this implies that industrial marketers must be skilful in researching, writing and presenting proposals – these should be marketing documents, not just technical documents. Their oral presentations should inspire confidence in a way that goes beyond the quality of the written proposals: they should portray the capabilities and resources of the company and position it so that it stands out from the competition.

Supplier selection. The members of the buying centre will then review the proposals and move towards making a selection. They will consider not only the formal competence of the various suppliers to make the specified item, but also their ability to deliver it on time and provide necessary services. The buying centre will often draw up a list of the desired supplier attributes and their relative importance. In selecting a chemical supplier, a buying centre listed the following attributes in order of importance:

1. Technical support services.
2. Prompt delivery.
3. Quick response to customer needs.
4. Product quality.
5. Supplier reputation.
6. Product price.
7. Complete product line.
8. Sales representatives' calibre.
9. Extension of credit.
10. Personal relationships.
11. Literature and manuals.

The members of the buying centre will then rate the candidates against these attributes and identify the most attractive suppliers. They may use an evaluation model similar to one of the consumer evaluation models described in Chapter 8.

The buyers may attempt to negotiate with the favoured suppliers for still better prices and terms before making the final selection. In the end, they may select a single supplier or a few suppliers. Many buyers prefer multiple sources of supply so that they have alternative sources if something goes wrong, and they can compare prices and performance. The buyer will normally place most of the order (say, 60 per cent) with one supplier, and less (30 per cent and 10 per cent) with the other suppliers. The prime supplier will make an effort to protect its position, while the others will try to expand their share. Out-suppliers may also try to get a foot in the door by making an especially good price offer, hoping thereafter to work their way up to being a more major supplier.

Order routine specification. The buyer now writes the final order with the chosen supplier(s) listing the technical specifications, quantity needed, expected time of delivery, return policies, warranties, and so on. In the case of maintenance, repair and operating items (MRO), buyers are increasingly tending to favour blanket contracts rather than periodic purchase orders. It is expensive to write a new purchase order each time stock is needed, and fewer and large purchase orders means carrying more inventory. A blanket contract consists of the supplier's promise to resupply the buyer as needed, on agreed price terms over a specified period of time. The stock is held by the seller (hence the name 'stockless purchase plan'), and the buyer's computer automatically prints out or teletypes an order when stock is needed. Blanket contracting tends to lead to more single-source buying and the buying of more items from

that source. This locks the supplier in tighter with the buyer and makes it difficult for out-suppliers to break in unless the buyer experiences strong dissatisfaction with the supplier.[14]

Performance review. In this stage the buyer reviews the results of dealing with the particular supplier(s). The buyer may contact users and request a rating of satisfaction with various aspects of the order, and accordingly continue, modify or end the relationship with the seller. The seller must monitor the same variables to make sure that it is delivering the expected satisfaction.

We have described the buying stages that would operate in a new-task buying situation. In the modified rebuy or straight rebuy situation, some of these stages would be compressed or bypassed. Each stage represents a narrowing by the buyer of the number of supplier alternatives, with the clear implication that sellers should try to become part of the process as early as possible.

The eight-stage buyphase model represents the essential steps of the industrial buying process. Further steps and idiosyncrasies can of course occur in practice, and the industrial marketer therefore has to model each situation more specifically. Each buying situation involves a particular flow of work (the *buyflow*) which can provide many clues to the marketer. A buyflow map for the purchase of a test-stand for automotive engines is shown in Figure 9-2. The map shows the five different company personnel involved in the buying decision process at one time or another. Two suppliers also were involved, as well as other outside influences (e.g. the Dun & Bradstreet credit reference service). Finally, thirteen different events led to the order being placed with one of the suppliers.

Thus we see that marketing to industrial buyers is a challenging area. The key step is to know the customer's needs and buying patterns. Using this knowledge, the industrial

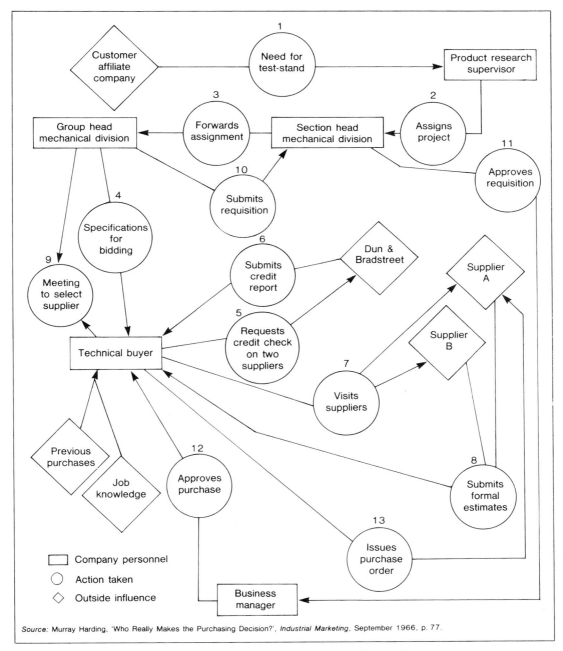

Source: Murray Harding, 'Who Really Makes the Purchasing Decision?', Industrial Marketing, September 1966, p. 77.

Figure 9-2   Map of company purchase of test-stand for automotive engines

marketer can proceed to design an effective plan for selling and servicing the customer.

THE RESELLER MARKET

Who is in the Reseller Market?
(buying population)

The reseller market consists of all the individuals and organizations who acquire goods for the purpose of reselling or renting them to others at a profit. Instead of producing form utility, the reseller market produces time, place and possession utility. In Australia, this market includes over 30 000 wholesaling establishments employing 300 000 persons, and 120 000 retailing establishments employing 750 000 persons; both sectors account for about 15 per cent of the national income. Resellers are more geographically dispersed than producers but more concentrated than consumers.

Resellers purchase both goods for resale, and goods and services for conducting their operations. The latter are bought by resellers in their role as producers, so we shall confine the discussion here to the goods they purchase for resale.

Resellers handle a vast variety of products, indeed everything produced except the few classes of goods that producers choose to sell directly to final customers, such as heavy or complex machinery, customized products, and products sold on a direct-mail or a door-to-door basis. With these exceptions, most products are sold to the final buyer through one or more selling intermediaries.

What Buying Decisions Do Resellers Make? (buying decisions)

Resellers have to make three major types of decision: (i) what assortment to carry; (ii) what vendors to buy from; and (iii) what prices and terms to negotiate. Of these, the assortment decision is the key. The assortment represents the combination of goods and services that the reseller will offer to the market, and it positions the reseller in the marketplace. Wholesalers and retailers can choose one of four assortment strategies:

1. *Exclusive assortment*, i.e. the line of one manufacturer only.
2. *Deep assortment*, i.e. a homogeneous product family, in depth, drawing on many producers' outputs.
3. *Broad assortment*, i.e. a wide range of product lines that still fall within the natural coverage of the reseller's type of business.
4. *Scrambled assortment*, i.e. many unrelated product families.

Thus a camera store can decide to sell only Kodak cameras (exclusive assortment); many brands of camera (deep assortment); cameras, tape-recorders, radios and stereo equipment (broad assortment); or the last plus stoves and refrigerators (scrambled assortment). The assortment the reseller ultimately chooses will influence its customer mix, marketing mix and supplier mix.

The buying decisions facing resellers vary with the type of buying situation. Three buying situations can be distinguished.

1. The *new-item situation* describes the case where the reseller has been offered a new item and will give a 'yes/no' answer, depending on how good the item looks. This differs from the new-task situation faced by producers, who must definitely purchase the needed item from someone.

2. The *best vendor situation* faces the reseller who knows what is needed but must determine the best supplier. This occurs either when the reseller has sufficient space to carry more than a subset of the available brands, or when the reseller wants to sponsor a private brand and is seeking a willing and qualified producer. Resellers such as Coles and Woolworths sell a substantial number of

items under their own name; therefore much of their buying operations consists of vendor selection.

3. The *better-terms situation* arises when the reseller wants to obtain a better set of terms from current suppliers. The buyer is not eager to change the supplier but does want more advantageous treatment. The Trade Practices Act prevents sellers from giving different terms to different resellers in the same reseller class, unless these reflect corresponding cost differences, distress sales, or a few other special conditions. Nevertheless, individual resellers and classes of resellers (discounters, mass merchandisers) do press their suppliers for preferential treatment and this can take many forms, such as more supplier services, easier credit terms, and higher volume discounts.

Who Participates in the Reseller Buying Process? (buying participants)

Who does the deciding and buying for wholesale and retail organizations? In small family firms, the merchandise selection and buying functions may be carried out by the owner or by persons who also carry out other functions in the firm. In large firms, buying is a specialist function and often a full-time job. It is carried out in different ways by department stores, supermarkets, pharmacy wholesalers, and so on, and differences can even be found within each type of distributive enterprise.

Much of the flavour of reseller buying practices can be sensed by examining the particular case of supermarket chains and the respective roles played by corporate-headquarter buyers, storewide buying committees and individual store managers. In the corporate headquarters of a supermarket chain will be found specialist buyers (sometimes called merchandise managers) for different product lines carried by the supermarket. These buyers have the responsibility for developing brand assortments and listening to presentations by salespersons offering new brands. In some chains these buyers have great latitude with respect to accepting or rejecting new items; elsewhere their scope is limited to screening 'obvious rejects' (and sometimes 'obvious accepts'), and most of the new-item proposals must be presented to a buying committee at its weekly meetings.

There is some evidence that buying committees serve as a check rather than a decision-maker. Borden found that the buyer's recommendation is highly important and influential to the committee decision:[15] in deciding what to communicate to the committee, the buyer exerts considerable influence on the decision. Buying committees exert some important indirect effects on product evaluations and decisions, such as serving as a buffer between buyers and salespersons and thus providing buyers with an excuse for rejecting a seller's proposition.

Even if an item is accepted by a chain-store buying committee, it will not necessarily appear in a large number of chain's outlets. According to one supermarket-chain executive: 'No matter what the sales representatives sell or buyers buy, the person who has the greatest influence on the final sale of the new item is the store manager.' In the nation's independent supermarkets, many of the new items accepted at the warehouse are ordered on the individual store manager's own decision, and only in corporate chains is forced distribution the norm.

This picture of the reseller organization's procedure for buying new items points to the formidable problem faced by the producers of new items. Industry offers the nation's supermarkets about fifty new items each week, but store space does not permit more than 20 per cent of these to be accepted.

Several studies have attempted to rank the major criteria used by buyers, buying committees and store managers. A.C. Nielsen Company conducted a study in which store managers were asked to rank on a three-point scale – with three being the highest – the importance of different elements in influencing their decision to accept a new item.[16] The final ranking was as follows:

Evidence of consumer acceptance	2.5
Advertising/promotion	2.2
Introductory terms and allowances	2.0
Why item was developed	1.9
Merchandising recommendations	1.8

Other studies also report the first three items to be the most important criteria.[17] A set of prerequisites established by Australian Safeway Stores for assessing new products, appropriately entitled a 'life assurance policy', appears in Table 9-1. They suggest that sellers stand the best chance when they can report strong evidence of consumer acceptance,

Table 9-1 New product life assurance policy

1. Must be backed by reliable manufacturer
   - Reputation for quality
   - Stands behind product
   - Has history of good trade relations
   - Provides complete information
2. Must fulfil consumer needs
   - Market potential
   - Improvement on existing products
   - Attracts new customers
   - Timely introduction
   - Conforms to stocking policies
3. Must be properly packaged
   - Attractive to consumer
   - Handling convenience
   - Sizes
4. Must evidence sales success
   - Test markets
   - Consumer panels
   - Sold in competitive stores
5. Must be adequately advertised
   - Appropriate media
   - Local trading area concentration
   - Frequency and duration
   - Starting dates
   - Sales promotion and display assistance
6. Must be profitable
   - Proper pricing
   - Special introductory offers
   - Year round profit-margin
   - Volume
   - Repeat sales

Source: Australian Safeway Stores Pty Ltd.

present a well-designed and extensive introductory advertising and sales promotion plan, and provide incentive to the retailer.

These respective roles of buyers, buying committee and store manager generally characterize the buying organizations of distributive enterprises other than supermarket chains. Large department stores or chains rely on buyers for merchandise lines, and usually they have a lot of authority and latitude. The buyers are aided by assistant buyers, who carry out preliminary search as well as clerical tasks involved in ordering. The buyers may report to buying committees, or perform other functions such as demand forecasting, stock control, and merchandising. Individual store managers or their staff usually have some freedom concerning which goods to order and display prominently.

What Are the Major Influences on Reseller Buyers? (buying influences)

Resellers are influenced by the same set of environmental, organizational, interpersonal and individual factors that affect industrial buyers (see Figure 9-1). The seller must note these influences and develop strategies that help the resellers make money or reduce costs.

The role of the individual buyer's style should be taken into account. Dickinson has distinguished the following types in reseller organizations:

1. *Loyal buyer.* This type remains loyal to a resource, or group of resources, year after year for reasons other than that he obtains the best deal.
2. *Opportunistic buyer.* This type selects mainly from a preselected list of those vendors who will further his long-term interests. Within this list, he will pursue the best arrangement possible.
3. *Best-deal buyer.* This type looks for and selects the best deal available in the market at a given point in time.

4. *Creative buyer.* This type tries not to accept the marketing mixes offered by any of the vendors, but rather attempts to sell his offers to the market. This may or may not involve a change in the physical product.
5. *Advertising buyer.* This type attempts primarily to obtain advertising money, which must be a part of every deal.
6. *The chiseller.* This type of buyer constantly negotiates extra price concessions at the time of the offering. He tends to accept the vendor offer carrying the greatest discount from the price he feels that other accounts might pay.
7. *Nuts-and-bolts buyer.* This buyer selects the merchandise that is best constructed, assuming that the merchandise policies of the vendor are acceptable within a very broad range. He is more interested in the thread count than in the number that will sell.[18]

How Do Resellers Make Their Buying Decisions? (buying process)

For new items, reseller buyers apply approximately the same steps as those described for the industrial buyer. For more standard items, the buying process is largely a matter of reordering goods when the inventory levels get low. This may be done by writing new purchase orders, or may be accomplished automatically by computer inventory control systems. The order will be placed with the same suppliers as long as their terms, goods and services are satisfactory. Buyers will, however, try to renegotiate prices from time to time as their margins are eroded by rising operating costs. In many retail lines the profit margin on sales is so low (for example, 1 to 2 per cent in supermarkets) that a sudden decline in demand or rise in operating costs will drive profits into the red.

The buying procedures used by resellers are becoming more sophisticated. Buyers are mastering the principles of demand forecasting, merchandise selection, stock control, space allocation, and display; they are learning to measure return on a profit-per-cubic-metre basis rather than a product-by-product basis only.[19] Major changes in purchasing operations are being made possible by advances in computers and telecommunications. Computers are increasingly used to keep current inventory figures, compute economic order quantities, prepare purchasing orders, develop requests for vendor quotations or expediting of orders, and generate printouts of dollars spent on vendors and products. Through telecommunications, the buyer can feed punched cards describing needed items and quantities into a transmitter which is linked to the supplier's receiving equipment. The supplier's equipment prepares cards or tapes which become the input for mechanized preparation of shipping tickets, invoices and other documents. Many resellers have moved over to stockless purchasing of reorder items, which means that the suppliers are responsible for carrying the inventory and delivering goods at short notice.

All this means that sellers are facing increasingly sophisticated buyers and buying systems in reseller organizations. They need to understand the resellers' changing requirements, and develop competitively attractive offers and services that fit the buyers' evaluative criteria in choosing suppliers.

THE GOVERNMENT MARKET

Who Is in the Government Market? (buying population)

The government market consists of all governmental units (federal, state, and local) which purchase or rent products for carrying out the main functions of government. Each year, Australian governmental units purchase about $25 billion of goods and services (approximately 25 per cent of the gross national product), making it the nation's largest customer.

The federal government accounts for approximately one-third of the total spent by government at all levels.

One reason for the high share of gross national expenditure attributable to governments in Australia is the significant degree of public (i.e. non-private) ownership of trading enterprises. At the national level, major institutions run by the government include Australia Post, Telecom, Qantas, TAA, the ABC, the Overseas Telecommunications Commission, the Australian National Line (shipping), statutory authorities in agriculture such as the Wool Commission, Medibank Private, and the railways. At State level the railways are again involved, plus electricity supply, State insurance, housing and other public transport facilities.

Although substantial government purchasing takes place in Canberra, State capitals and major cities, it also occurs in every municipality. The federal government operates a set of geographically dispersed buying information offices; local goods and services may be bought by local government offices, military bases, and so on.

What Buying Decisions Do Government Buyers Make? (buying decisions)

The fundamental objective of government buying differs from that found in the other sectors of the economy. Apart from operations such as Qantas, government buying is not concerned with personal consumption or profit-making but rather with a level and mix of goods and services that it or the voters establish as necessary or desirable for the maintenance of society.

The result is that government agencies buy an amazing range of products and services. They buy jet fighters, sculpture, chalkboards, furniture, toiletries, clothing, materials-handling equipment, fire engines, mobile equipment, and fuel. All government spends approximately $2.5 billion for defence, $6 billion for education, $5 billion for health and

hospitals, and smaller sums for housing, and so on. The mix of expenditures varies considerably with the particular type of governmental unit, with defence looming large in the federal budget (29 per cent of total expenditure on goods and services) and education looming large in the State budgets (36 per cent). No matter how one feels about government marketing, it represents a tremendous opening for any producer or reseller.

Each product that the government decides to buy requires further decisions on how much to buy, where to buy it, how much to pay, and what other services are required. These decisions are made, in principle, on the basis of trying to minimize costs to the taxpayer, and in normal circumstances, government buyers will favour the lowest-cost bidders that can meet the stated specifications.

Who Participates in the Government Buying Process? (buying participants)

Who does the buying of the billions of dollars' worth of goods and services required by government? Every government agency has some influence or authority, each of which represents a potential target for marketing influence.

Government buying organizations are found on the national, State and local levels. The Department of Administrative Services plays a major role in purchasing many products for use by many Australian government departments and instrumentalities, but various government organizations engage in direct buying, often depending on the value and nature of the goods and services involved. At the State level there are Supply and Tender Boards, whose functions, affiliated departments and government bodies differ from State to State. General activities of these boards include the supervision of contract arrangements (e.g. the calling of tenders). At each level of government, the procurement authorities and the products for which they are responsible seem to change according to evolving administrative and political tendencies. Thus, the reader is urged to contact the relevant central purchasing authority for redirection to the currently responsible organization. The Scott report provides a useful overview of arrangements in the near past, as do briefer but more recent publications.[20]

What Are the Major Influences on Government Buyers? (buying influences)

Like those of other organizations, government buyers are influenced by environmental, organizational, interpersonal and individual factors. Perhaps the unique thing about government buying is that it is monitored carefully by outside publics, such as Parliament and the Auditor General (who seeks to constantly improve public spending efficiency). There are also many private groups which watch different agencies to see how they spend the public's money.

As a result of making spending decisions subject to public review, government organizations tend to be involved in much more paperwork than is considered necessary in private industry. Elaborate forms must be filled out and carry several signatures before purchases are approved – the level of bureaucracy is higher, and marketers have to either find ways to cut the 'red tape' or live with it.

Another influence on government buying is the growing role of non-economic criteria, such as preferences for locally produced products, or discrimination in favour of decentralized producers or others deemed worthy of encouragement. Sellers should keep these factors in mind when deciding whether to go after a particular government business.

How Do Government Buyers Make Their Buying Decisions? (buying process)

Government buying practices appear complex to the uninitiated supplier because of the many agencies and procedures that characterize the market. Most of this can be mastered in a short time, however, and the government is generally helpful in providing information about its buying needs and procedures. In fact, government is often as anxious to attract new suppliers as the suppliers are to find customers.

Australian governments generally subscribe to a competitive procurement system with public tendering as a basic feature. As mentioned earlier, there is a general principle that the 'lowest suitable tender' should be accepted. The lowest price is not, however, a guarantee of acceptance: after-sales service or delivery plans may be unacceptable, or doubts arise about meeting technical specifications or being able to otherwise perform a contract satisfactorily.

For contracts to supply goods and services above minimum 'threshold' amounts ($10 000 for the federal government), public advertising for tenders is required in newspapers and government gazettes, and direct mail of applications to likely interested parties is also undertaken. However, public tender may be avoided if a 'certificate of inexpediency' is issued on the grounds of urgency or secrecy, a standardized item or sole supplier, or the prior establishment of 'qualified product listings' based on public invitations. This bypassing of public tender seems to be quite common.

Government contracts won by large companies give rise to substantial subcontracting opportunities (as much as 50 per cent) for small companies. Thus government purchasing activity in turn creates derived demand in the producer market. Subcontracting firms must, however, go after this business with a willingness to place performance bonds with the prime contractor and thereby assume some of the risk.

By and large, many companies that have served the government have not manifested much of a marketing orientation – for a number of reasons. Total government spending is determined by elected officials rather than by marketing effort; procurement policies have emphasized price, leading the suppliers to invest all their effort in a technological orientation to bring costs down. Where the product's characteristics are carefully specified, product differentiation is not a marketing factor; nor is advertising and personal selling of much consequence in an open-bid competition.

More companies are now establishing marketing departments to guide government-directed marketing effort. They realize that it is necessary to coordinate bids and prepare them more scientifically, to propose projects to meet government needs rather than just to respond to government initiatives, to gather competitive intelligence, and to prepare better communication programmes to describe the company's competence.

SUMMARY

The organizational market consists of all the organizations that buy goods for purposes of further production, resale or distribution to others. Organizations are a market for raw and manufactured materials and parts, installations and accessory equipment, as well as supplies and services.

Producer organizations buy goods and services for the purpose of increasing sales, cutting costs or meeting social and legal requirements. Compared with consumer buyers, the producer market consists of fewer buyers, larger buyers, and more geographically concentrated buyers; the demand is derived, relatively inelastic, and more fluctuating; and the purchasing is more professional. Industrial buyers have to make a number of decisions that vary with the type of buying situation or buyclass. Buyclasses comprise three types: straight rebuys, modified rebuys and new tasks. The decision-making unit of a buying organization (the buying centre) consists of individuals who play any of five roles: users, influencers, buyers, deciders and gatekeepers.

The industrial marketer needs to know the major decision participants, the decisions in which they exercise influence, their relative degree of influence, and the evaluation criteria used by each participant. The industrial marketer also needs to understand the major environmental, organizational, interpersonal and individual influences operating in the buying process. The buying process itself consists of eight stages called buyphases: problem recognition, general need description, product specification, supplier search, proposal solicitation, supplier selection, order routine specification, and performance review. As industrial buyers become more sophisticated, industrial marketers must upgrade their own marketing capabilities.

The reseller market consists of individuals and organizations who acquire and resell goods produced by others. Resellers have to decide on their assortment, suppliers, prices and terms. They face three types of buying situations: new items, new vendors and new terms. In small wholesale and retail organizations, buying may be carried on by one or a few individuals; in larger organizations, by a whole purchasing department. In a modern supermarket chain, the major decision participants include headquarters buyers, storewide buying committees and individual store managers. With new items, the buyers go through a process similar to the one shown for industrial buyers; and with standard items, the buying process consists of routines for reordering and renegotiating contracts.

The government market is a vast one that annually purchases $25 billion of goods and services to fulfil defence, education, welfare and other public needs. Government buying practices are highly specialized and specified, usually characterized by open bidding and/or negotiated contracts. Government buyers operate under the watchful eye of parliament and other monitoring groups. Hence they tend to fill out more forms, obtain more signatures, and move more slowly in placing orders.

QUESTIONS FOR DISCUSSION

1. It has been argued that a school of business administration is an industrial marketer. What characteristics of an industrial market does the demand for students (i.e. industrial products) exhibit?

2. Into which of the major types of buying situation would you classify the following?
   - TAA's purchase of an additional Airbus
   - Caterpillar's purchase of diesel engine parts
   - a State Electricity's Commission's purchase of solar energy panels.

3. How would the participants in the producer buying process differ between a small machine-tool shop and BHP?

4. Discuss the major environmental factors that would influence Ansett Pioneer's purchase of buses.

5. Apply the buyphases to an industrial product with which you are familiar.

6. How do the two major types of reseller differ in the way they make their buying decisions?

7. The government market is not a significant one for most products. Comment.

8. How do the influences on the government buyer differ from those on the producer or reseller buyer?

NOTES

[1] Advertisement, *Australian Financial Review*, 8 December 1980, p. 21.

[2] Frederick E. Webster Jr & Yoram Wind, *Organizational Buying Behaviour* (Englewood Cliffs, N.J.: Prentice-Hall, 1972), p. 2.

[3] See Reed Moyer, 'Reciprocity: Retrospect and Prospect', *Journal of Marketing*, October 1970, pp. 47–54.

[4] See Leonard J. Berry & Kenneth E. Maricle, 'Consumption without Ownership: Marketing Opportunity for Today and Tomorrow', *MSU Business Topics*, Spring 1973, pp. 33–41.

[5] Patrick J. Robinson, Charles W. Faris & Yoram Wind, *Industrial Buying and Creative Marketing* (Boston: Allyn & Bacon, 1967).

[6] See Chapter 12.

[7] Webster & Wind, p. 6.

[8] Webster & Wind, pp. 78–80.

[9] See Murray Harding, 'Who Really Makes the Purchasing Decision?', *Industrial Marketing*, September 1966, p. 76. This point of view is further developed in Ernest Dichter, 'Industrial Buying Is Based on Same "Only Human" Emotional Factors That Motivate Consumer Market's Housewife', *Industrial Marketing*, February 1973, pp. 14–16.

[10] Webster and Wind, pp. 33–37.

[11] See 'The Purchasing Agent Gains More Clout', *Business Week*, 13 January 1975, pp. 62–63.

[12] ibid.

[13] Robinson, Faris & Wind, *Industrial Buying*.

[14] See Leonard Groeneveld, 'The Implications of Blanket Contracting for Industrial Purchasing and Marketing', *Journal of Purchasing*, November 1972, pp. 51–58; and H. Lee Mathews, David T. Wilson & Klaus Backhaus,

'Selling to the Computer Assisted Buyer', *Industrial Marketing Management*, 6 (1977), pp. 307–15.

[15] Neil H. Borden Jr, *Acceptance of New Food Products by Supermarkets* (Boston: Division of Research, Graduate School of Business Administration, Harvard University, 1968).

[16] Robert W. Mueller & Franklin H. Graf, 'New Items in the Food Industry, Their Problems and Opportunities' (Special report to the Annual Convention of the Supermarket Institute, Cleveland, 20 May 1968), p. 5.

[17] 'Merchandising New Items at Retail: The Payoff at Point of Purchase', *Progressive Grocer*, June 1968; and Borden, p. 203. Also see David B. Montgomery, *New Product Distribution: An Analysis of Supermarket Buyer Decisions* (Cambridge, Mass.: Marketing Science Institute, March 1973). Montgomery found the two most important variables to be company reputation and the perceived newness of the product.

[18] Roger A. Dickinson, *Buyer Decision Making* (Berkeley, Calif.: Institute of Business and Economic Research, 1967), pp. 14–17.

[19] See Robert D. Buzzell, *Product Profitability Measurement and Merchandising Decisions* (Boston: Harvard University Press, 1965). For some interesting Australian research, see Michael J. S. Collins & B. Lyon, *Buying The Merchandise – A Study of How the Smaller Apparel Retailers Buy Their Merchandise* (Caulfield, Victoria: Department of Marketing, Caulfield Institute of Technology, 1980).

[20] See *Committee of Inquiry Into Government Procurement Policy – Report May 1974* (Canberra: Australian Government Publishing Service, 1975); *How to do Business with the Commonwealth Government* (Canberra: Australian Government Printing Service, 1980); *Commonwealth Government Purchasing – Report of the House of Representatives Standing Committee on Expenditure* (Canberra: Australian Government Publishing Service, 1981).

Market Segmentation and Targeting

10

Enormous opportunities exist for the wool industry to sell more product to the 16–24 age group – opportunities which are not perceived simply because the manufacturers and retailers of wool products do not understand the target market. This is essentially the finding of Action Wool Associates, an organization established by final year marketing management students at Sydney Technical college. As their final year project, Action Wool Associates undertook, on behalf of the Australian Wool Board, to examine the possibilities of improving sales of woollen products to young people.

The 142-page report points out – though mainly by implication – that while most young people have certain perceptions about wool, these perceptions are not appreciated by either manufacturers or retailers. Research of 25 manufacturers showed 'a very negative attitude to manufacturing products for this market'. Typical of the sort of discrepancies found were:

- Consumers rank comfort as second most important feature for wool in order of importance but manufacturers think comfort least important.
- Manufacturers would advertise to young people in media of only marginal interest to the young.
- Manufacturers are not interested in making new products, but the target market wants new products such as woollen windcheaters and track suits.
- Retailers think young people want wool alternatives whereas they want woollen products.
- Retailers have a negative view, bordering on apathy, toward marketing woollen products to the young.

'Apart from a promotional campaign 10 years ago, there appears to be little evidence of any significant campaign to the 15–24 year age group', says the report. 'The consumers have limited knowledge of wool's attributes and a significant number perceived wool as a product for an older group. The significant difference (between wool and competitors such as cotton and synthetics) is in promotion and production. Wool's competitors emphasize the final products creating their own personality and in some cases unique brand image, without particular reference to the fibre content of the products. Appeal is made to the "lifestyle" of the market. The effectiveness of brand, or personality, marketing is evident in the sales figures for wool alternatives in this age group. The evidence of the success of wool's competitors is before us each day – the high penetration of jeans worn by this age group as well as the definite trend to more casual and bright clothing and accessories.'

The report outlines some of the marketing problems:

Manufacturers' conservatism. *'Most manufacturers under-estimate the opportunities in this market mainly due to a lack of research material on the needs and attitudes of consumers.'*

Industry is product oriented. *'There is a definite emphasis towards product oriented selling and little evidence of consumer oriented marketing.'*

Limited product range. *'Woollen products do not compete with other fibres in a variety and style that would appeal to this age group.'*

Poor-quality merchandise affects wool's image. *'Some retailers offer a range of woollen garments which are very inexpensive but of poor wearing quality which has an adverse effect on long term attitudes.'*

New generation, new attitudes. *'The current generation is experiencing considerable change in lifestyle, fashion and technological advances. Consequently attitudes to wool and its place in Australia's economic development are not understood.'*

Seen for winter. *'Again this reveals lack of knowledge of product attributes which severely limits it in the eyes of the consumer, the uses for wool and woollen products.'*

Competition from 'look-alikes'. *'Competitive fibres have the ability to be processed to provide a similar appearance and texture to woollen products, such that consumers do not recognise readily the genuine woollen product.'*

Itchiness and prickly feeling remains a problem.

Cost of production. *'In comparison with competitive fibres, wool has more handling processes and is consequently labour intensive. Transport is a cost factor.'*

Reducing disposable income. *'This should be seen in context and is not a major problem for the immediate future since wool has not a large share of the market.'*

But several marketing opportunities exist for woollen products:

Benefits of wool/woolblends. *'Educate and promote these benefits. Consumers, by being more aware of the benefits of wool, would be more likely to purchase woollen products. Identify other unique selling propositions of woollen fibre.'*

Market segmentation.

- *More selective marketing – identify specific target markets: age, occupation, lifestyle, sex. Consider 15–19 and 20–24 age groups as two separate markets with different needs and wants.*
- *Middle price products – between high priced luxury woollen products and the cheaper, poor quality.*

Provide wider applications for wool.

- *Product innovations.*
- *Sporting and leisure clothing taking advantage of wool's special characteristics.*
- *Replace vinyl as an upholstery for furnishings – seat covers, etc.*
- *Educate manufacturers to the wider application of wool and identify for them the opportunities that exist.*
- *Make greater use of blending techniques.*

Market positioning. *'Use peer group to influence purchasing decisions – this is an area the competition have been most successful in exploiting. The use of "grand image" advertising offers many opporunities for this age group, or sub-sections of it, to identify with woollen/woolblend products.'*

Product development.

- *Wool blending with other fibres, including those which presently compete against wool.*
- *Research and development offer opportunities to add to the already unique selling properties of wool.*
- *Constantly be on the look-out for new market opportunities with product improvements especially where they offer some real benefit over a competitor's product.*

Tomorrow's market.

- *Initiate education and public relations programmes for pre-15-year-olds, using education system.*
- *Stimulate educationists to take an interest in and learn more about wool.*
- *Promote the sale of woollen/woolblend clothes to the child market.*
- *Become aware of likely buyer behaviour patterns of young people. They are the customers of the future.*[1]

An organization that decides to operate in the clothing or any other market soon recognizes that it cannot serve and appeal to all buyers. The buyers may be too numerous, widely scattered, and varied in their buying requirements and buying practices. Different companies will be in the best position to serve particular segments of the market – instead of competing everywhere, each should identify the most attractive parts of the market that it could serve effectively.

Sellers have not always adhered to this philosophy. In deciding how to operate in a market, they have gone through three stages:

- *Mass marketing.* Mass marketing is where the seller mass-produces and mass-distributes one product and attempts to attract all kinds of buyers. At one time Coca-Cola, for example, produced only one drink for the whole market, hoping it would become everyone's favourite drink. The argument for mass marketing is that it should lead to the lowest costs and prices and therefore create the largest potential market. The mass marketer pays little or no attention to differences in demand.
- *Product-differentiated marketing.* Product differentiation is where the seller produces two or more products designed to appear different both from each other and from competitors' products. The products may exhibit different features, styles, quality, sizes, and so on. Today Coca-Cola produces many different-flavoured soft-drinks in many sizes and types of containers; most are designed not to meet differing needs of specific groups in the market but rather to offer variety.
- *Target marketing.* Target marketing is a style of marketing where the seller distinguishes between different groups (segments) making up the market, chooses one or more of these segments to focus on, and develops products and marketing mixes tailored to meet the needs of each target market. For example, Coca-Cola developed Tab specifically to meet the needs of the group of soft-drink consumers who want to keep their weight down.

Companies may be found today practising each style of marketing, but there is a strong movement away from mass marketing and product-differentiated marketing towards target marketing. At least three benefits of this approach can be identified:

1. *Sellers are in a better position to spot market opportunities.* They are able to notice market segments whose needs are not being fully met by current product offers.

2. *Sellers can make finer adjustments to their products to match the desires of the market.* They are able to interview members of the target market and get a better picture of their specific needs and desires.
3. *Sellers can make finer adjustments to their prices, distribution channels and promotional mixes.* Instead of trying to draw in all potential buyers with a 'shotgun' approach, sellers can create separate marketing programmes aimed at each target market (called a 'rifle' approach).

Target marketing comprises two major steps (see Figure 10-1). The first is market segmentation, the act of dividing a market into distinct and meaningful groups of buyers who might merit separate products and/or marketing mixes. Here the company must identify different bases for segmenting the market, develop profiles of the resulting segments, and develop measures of each segment's attractiveness. The second step is target marketing, the act of selecting one or more of the market segments and developing a positioning and market mix strategy for each. This chapter will

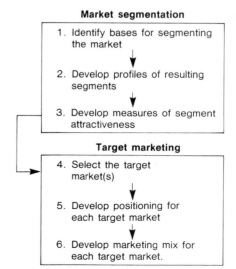

Figure 10-1   Steps in market segmentation and target marketing

describe the major concepts and tools involved in market segmentation and target marketing.

MARKET SEGMENTATION

Markets consist of buyers, and buyers are likely to differ in their desires, resources, geographical locations, buying attitudes, buying practices, and so on. Any of these variables may be used to segment a market, but we will first illustrate the general approach.

The General Approach to Segmenting a Market

Figure 10-2a shows a market consisting of six buyers before it is segmented. The maximum number of segments that a market can contain is the total number of buyers making up that market – each buyer is potentially a separate market because of the unique nature of needs and desires. Ideally, a seller might study each buyer in order to tailor the best marketing programme to that buyer's needs; where there

are only a few major customers, this is done to some extent. For example, the major supplier of car windscreens is Pilkington-ACI which faces only a few buyers and treats them as separate markets. This ultimate degree of market segmentation is illustrated in Figure 10-2b.

Most sellers, however, will not find it worthwhile to 'customize' their product to satisfy each buyer's specific wants. Instead, the seller identifies broad classes of buyers who differ in their product requirements and/or marketing responses. For example, the seller may discover that income groups differ in their product requirements and marketing responses. In Figure 10-2c, a number (1, 2 or 3) is used to identify each buyer's income class and lines are drawn around buyers in the same class. This approach provides three segments, the largest being income class 1 in the illustration.

On the other hand, the seller may find pronounced differences in buyer behaviour between younger and older buyers. In Figure 10-2d the same individuals are shown, but a

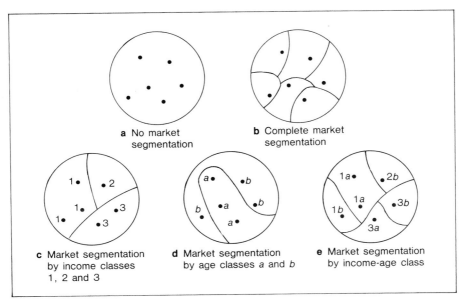

a No market segmentation

b Complete market segmentation

c Market segmentation by income classes 1, 2 and 3

d Market segmentation by age classes *a* and *b*

e Market segmentation by income-age class

Figure 10-2   Different approaches to market segmentation

letter (*a* or *b*) is used to indicate the buyer's age class. This results in two segments, both equally numerous.

It may turn out that income and age both count heavily in differentiating the buyer's behaviour toward the product, and the seller may therefore find it desirable to partition the market according to those joint characteristics. In terms of the illustration, the market can be broken into the following six segments: *1a*, *1b*, *2a*, *2b*, *3a* and *3b*. Figure 10-2e shows that segment *1a* contains two buyers, segment *2a* contains no buyers (a null segment), and each of the other segments contains one buyer. In general, as the market is segmented on the basis of a larger set of joint characteristics the seller achieves finer precision, but at the price of multiplying the number of segments and thinning out the populations in the segments. If the seller segmented the market using all conceivable characteristics, the market would again look like Figure 10-2b, where each buyer would be a separate segment.

Segmenting the market by income and age resulted in different demographic segments. Suppose, instead, that buyers are asked how much they want of each of two product attributes (say, 'bitterness' and 'lightness' in beer). This results in identifying different preference segments in the market, and three different patterns may emerge:

1. *Homogeneous preferences.* Figure 10-3a reveals a market where all the consumers have roughly the same preferences, i.e. there are no natural segments as far as the two attributes are concerned. We would predict that sellers would all go after the same customers and offer highly similar products.
2. *Diffused preferences.* At the other extreme, consumer preferences may be scattered fairly evenly throughout the space with no concentration (Figure 10-3b). Here we would predict that sellers would seek footholds in different parts of the market and

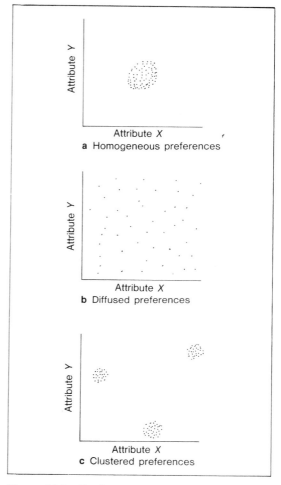

Figure 10-3   Basic market preference patterns

offer products that would satisfy those customers.

3. *Clustered preferences.* An intermediate possibility is the appearance of distinct preference clusters called natural market segments (Figure 10-3c). We would predict that each seller would seek leadership in a particular market segment by designing products and marketing programmes that would appeal to that segment.

Thus segmentation procedures can indicate the existence of natural market segments, be used to construct artificial market segments, or reveal the lack of any market segments. We will now examine specific variables that may be used in the process itself.

Bases for Segmenting Consumer Markets

There is no one way, or right way, to segment a market, for different variables may be introduced which reveal the different market opportunities. Sometimes the marketer merely has to try out the various segmentation variables, singly and in combination, before hitting on an insightful way to view the market structure. Here we will review the major geographic, demographic, psychographic and behaviouristic variables used in segmenting consumer markets (see Table 10-1).

Geographic segmentation. Here the market is divided into different geographical entities (e.g. nations, states, regions, cities or neighbourhoods) on the assumption that consumer needs or responses vary geographically. The company decides either to operate in one or a few parts of the country as a specialist, or to operate broadly but pay attention to variations in geographic needs and preferences. For example, the *Australian* newspaper and the *Australian Women's Weekly* are sold nationally but as regional editions, especially in terms of television programme listings and some sports coverage.

Table 10-1   Major segmentation variables for consumer markets

Variables	Typical breakdowns
Geographic	
Region	Queensland, New South Wales, Victoria, South Australia, Tasmania, Western Australia, Northern Territory
City size	Capital city, provincial city, other
Density	Urban, suburban, rural, remote
Demographic	
Age	under 6, 6–14, 15–24, 25–34, 35–49, 50–65, 65 +
Sex	Male, female
Household size	1, 2, 3, 4, 5 +
Family lifecycle	Single 14–34; married 14–34, no child; married 14–34, child; married 35 + , child; married, 35 + no child; single 35 +
Income	under $10 000, $10 000–$15 000, $15 000–$20 000, over $20 000
Occupation	Professional, manager, small-business owner, white-collar worker, skilled worker, semi-skilled worker, unskilled worker, housewife, unemployed
Nationality	Australian born, UK, German, Italian, Greek, Chinese, Middle Eastern
Psychographic	
Social class	Lower lowers, upper lowers, lower middles, upper middles, lower uppers, upper uppers
Lifestyle	Older conservatives, active organizers, experience-seekers, community active females, sophisticated women, conscientious housewives
Personality	Compulsive, gregarious, authoritarian, ambitious
Behaviouristic	
Purchase occasion	Regular occasion, special occasion
Benefits sought	Economy, convenience, prestige
User status	Non-user, ex-user, potential user, first-time user, regular user
Usage rate	Light user, medium user, heavy user
Loyalty status	None, medium, strong, absolute
Readiness stage	Unaware, aware, informed, interested, desirous, intending to buy
Marketing-factor sensitivity	Quality, price, service, advertising, sales promotion

Companies also distinguish their geographic markets according to market potential and other bases. For example, a food company sorts the various markets for its yoghurt into three groups based on the number of years since the brand was introduced: embryonic markets (one to five years), growth markets (six to ten years), and mature markets (eleven or more years). The firm allocates different resources and uses different marketing strategies in each market.

Demographic segmentation. Here the market is divided into different groups on the basis of demographic variables such as age, sex, family size, family lifecycle, income, occupation, education, religion and nationality. Demographic variables have long been the most popular bases for distinguishing customer groups. One reason is that consumer wants, preferences and usage rates are often highly associated with such factors; another is that these are easier to measure than most other types of variables. Even when the target market is described in non-demographic terms (say, a personality type), the link back to demographic characteristics is necessary in order to know the size of the target market and how to reach it efficiently. Here we will illustrate how certain demographic variables have been applied creatively to market segmentation.

Age and lifecycle state. Consumer wants and capacities change with age. Even children who are six months old differ in their consumption potential, from those who are three months old. Alabe Products, a toy manufacturer, realized this and designed twelve different toys to be used by babies sequentially between the ages of three months and one year. Crib Jiminy is to be used when babies begin to reach for things, Talky Rattle when they first grasp things, and so on.[2] This segmentation strategy means that parents and gift-givers can more easily find the appropriate toy by simply considering the baby's age.

At the other extreme of the age-and-lifecycle continuum, a great deal of attention has been focused on people over 50 and those receiving social security benefits. Publishers have introduced a variety of products such as *Prime Time*, a monthly magazine from the Herald & Weekly Times; *Leisure Life*, also a monthly magazine but aimed up-market with a price of $3.50 per copy; and *Australian Pensioner*, a newspaper from the publishers of the *Age* and priced at 40 cents.[3]

Sex. Sex segmentation has been a long-standing practice in such product categories as clothing, hairdressing, cosmetics and magazines. From time to time, marketers of other goods and services will notice an opportunity for sex segmentation, an excellent example being the motor-vehicle industry. In the past, cars were designed to appeal to both male and female family members: with increases in the number of working and car-owning women, however, some manufacturers are seizing the opportunity to design 'feminine' cars to meet the preferences of women drivers, and to stress those features attractive to women in their current cars when advertising.

Income. Income segmentation is another longstanding practice in such product categories as cars, boats, clothing, cosmetics and travel. Other industries occasionally recognize its possibilities. For example, Suntory, the Japanese liquor company, has introduced a scotch whisky selling for $75 to attract the people who want 'the very best'.

At the same time, income can sometimes incorrectly predict who will buy certain products. Members of the working class were among the first purchasers of expensive colour-television sets; it was cheaper for them to buy these sets than go out to movies and restaurants. Coleman suggested that a distinction should be drawn between the 'underprivileged' and 'overprivileged' segments of each social class: the cheapest, most economical cars are not bought by the really poor, but rather by 'those who think of themselves as poor relative to their status aspirations and to their needs for a certain level of clothing, furniture, and housing which they could not afford if they bought a more expensive car'. On the other hand, medium-priced and expensive cars tend to be purchased by the overprivileged segments of each social class.[4]

Multivariable segmentation. Very often an organization will segment a market by combining two or more variables. The Charles Home for the Blind (name disguised) serves the needs of partially and totally blind persons for care, psychological counselling, and vocational training. However, it is not able to serve all types of blind people, because facilities are limited and other institutions can more easily handle some needs. A multiple segmentation is shown in Figure 10-4, where blind persons are distinguished according to age, sex and income. The Charles Home has decided to concentrate on serving low-income males of working age. It feels that it can do the best job for these persons and has created special programmes to meet their needs.

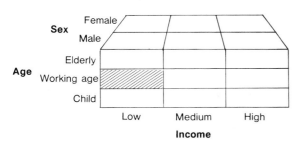

Figure 10-4   Segmentation of blind persons by three demographic variables

Psychographic segmentation. In psychographic segmentation, buyers are divided into different groups on the basis of their social class, lifestyle, or personality characteristics. People within the same demographic group can exhibit very different psychographic profiles. The fact that demographics do not necessarily reveal anything about attitudes and

living styles has led to psychographic segmentation.

Social class. In discussing social class in Chapter 8, we suggested that it may have an influence on a person's preferences in cars, clothes, home furnishings, leisure activities, reading habits, retailers, and so on. Many consumer companies design goods and/or services for specific social classes, building in those features that are clearly appealing to the target market.

Lifestyle. Every person has a lifestyle and there are a limited number of lifestyles. Researchers have found that they can identify these by interviewing people about their activities, interests and opinions and then clustering them into groups sharing common activities, interests, and opinions. Using this approach, one study distinguished eight male lifestyles and reported on the percentages in the population: older conservatives (21 per cent); active organizers (8 per cent); money-oriented males (8 per cent); alienated young bargain-seekers (14 per cent); average successful (on way up) males (18 per cent); experience-seekers (7 per cent); young single actives (13 per cent); intellectual activists (11 per cent). The same study distinguished nine female lifestyle groups and reported their percentages in the sample: young miss libbers (11 per cent); community active females (12 per cent); money-oriented females (9 per cent); bargain-conscious housewives (11 per cent); uninvolved dolly birds (15 per cent); sophisticated women (13 per cent); liberated-equals women (9 per cent); older mundane-life housewives (16 per cent); conscientious housewives (4 per cent).[5] Each of these types is characterized by specific activities, interests and opinions as well as product and media preferences.

In preparing a marketing strategy for a product, the marketers will use this generalized information to attempt to determine which lifestyle groups are likely to find the product most appealing. For example, experience-seekers would be the prime candidates for exotic wines. Knowing this, it is possible to develop advertising copy and media mixes more exactly: the advertising copywriter imagines their lifestyle and develops a wine commercial with which they can identify.

Some researchers are less convinced that these general lifestyle types are useful and prefer more product-specific lifestyle studies. For example, three Sydney researchers identified the following seven lifestyles regarding health care (percentage of each in the Australian population shown in parentheses):

- *Dependents* (8 per cent): old, less educated people whose health is poor. They feel under stress, already use a lot of professional medical care and drugs, and feel incapable of doing much about their health themselves.
- *Rustics* (18 per cent): old, neither affluent nor well-educated people whose health is fairly good. They are likely to be rural dwellers, use the health systems judiciously and be open to advice on preventative care.
- *Modern Millies* (19 per cent): young, educated and independent-minded females with average health and good and growing health knowledge. They use the health systems conservatively and take a lot of vitamins.
- *Independents* (12 per cent): younger, educated people who are physically and mentally healthy. They emphasize preventative and home-remedy solutions, and would be selectively responsive to health advice.
- *Worriers* (14 per cent): younger, blue-collar types probably living in outer suburbs and smoking heavily. They are hypochondriacal but not particularly unhealthy and worry about their health as part of a general syndrome of high stress and feelings of powerlessness.
- *Young executives* (17 per cent): affluent young males with average health. They use

non-prescription medicines heavily but have little health knowledge and their health behaviour could be greatly improved.
- *Machos* (12 per cent): young healthy males who drink copiously and smoke. They are sceptical of a whole range of preventative health-care measures, but will become 'at risk' if their current lifestyles continue into middle age.[6]

If each of the above groups exhibits distinct demographic characteristics and media preferences, pharmaceutical companies can increase their efficiency in reaching target markets.

Personality. Marketers have also used personality variables to segment markets. They try to endow their products with brand personalities (brand image, brand concept) designed to appeal to corresponding consumer personalities (self-images, self-concepts). Westfall found some evidence of personality differences between the owners of convertible cars and nonconvertibles, the former appearing to be more active, impulsive and sociable.[7] Gottlieb found compulsive people to be heavier users of aspirin.[8] Tucker and Painter found some statistically significant but weak personality correlations for nine products in their study.[9]

Behaviouristic segmentation.

In behaviouristic segmentation (also called product-related segmentation), buyers are divided into groups on the basis of their knowledge, attitude, use or response to an actual product or its attributes. Many marketers believe that behaviouristic variables are the best starting point for constructing effective market segments.

Purchase occasion. Buyers can be distinguished according to the particular occasion of their purchases. For example, air travellers include those whose flying relates to business, vacation or family. An airline may decide to specialize in serving people for whom one of these reasons dominates: thus charter airlines often serve people for whom a vacation is the occasion for flying; other airlines might specialize in serving people for whom business is the occasion for flying.

Occasion segmentation is often used by firms seeking to build up product category usage. For example, orange juice is frequently consumed at breakfast and thus an orange-juice company may try to promote drinking orange juice as part of the evening meal. Certain national observances – Mother's Day and Father's Day, for example – were promoted indirectly to increase the sale of such products as confectionery and flowers.

Benefits sought. Buyers can be segmented according to the particular benefit(s) that they are seeking through a product. The task here is to determine the major benefits that people might be looking for in the product class, the kinds of people who might be looking for each benefit, and the existing brands that come close to delivering each benefit.

One of the most successful benefit segmentations was reported by Haley, who studied the toothpaste market (see Table 10-2). Haley's research uncovered four such segments, i.e. those seeking economy, protection, cosmetic and taste benefits. Each benefit-seeking group had a heavy representation of a particular demographic, behaviouristic and psychographic group. For example, decay prevention seekers consisted of a higher number of large families, heavy toothpaste users, and people with conservative lifestyles. The table also shows that certain brands were well positioned in each benefit segment.

A toothpaste company can use these results to clarify which benefit segment it is appealing to, its characteristics, and the major competitive brands. The same company can also search for a new benefit that is not currently being served (such as 'better breath') and launch a brand dedicated to delivering this benefit.

User status. Many markets can be segmented into non-users, ex-users, potential users, first-time users, and regular users of a product. High-market-share companies such as Kodak (in the film market) are particularly interested in going after potential users, whereas a small competitor will concentrate on trying to attract regular users to its brand. Potential users and regular users require different kinds of communication and marketing efforts.

In the social marketing area, agencies such as anti-drug campaigners pay close attention to user status. They direct most of their effort at young people who might be potential users, and try to prevent them developing an interest in hard drugs; they sponsor rehabilitation

Table 10-2 Benefit segmentation of the toothpaste market

Benefit segments	Demographics	Behaviouristics	Psychographics	Favoured brands
Economy (low price)	Men	Heavy users	High autonomy, value-oriented	Brands on sale
Medicinal (decay prevention)	Large families	Heavy users	Hypochondriac, conservative	Crest
Cosmetic (bright teeth)	Teens, young adults	Smokers	High sociability, active	Macleans, Ultra Brite
Taste (good tasting)	Children	Spearmint lovers	High self-involvement, hedonistic	Colgate, Aim

Source: Adapted from Russell J. Haley, 'Benefit Segmentation: A Decision Oriented Research Tool', *Journal of Marketing*, July 1963, pp. 30–35.

programmes to help regular users who want to break their habit; they utilize ex-users to lend credibility to various programmes.

Usage rate. Many markets can be segmented into light-, medium- and heavy-user groups of the product (called volume segmentation). Heavy users may constitute only a small percentage of the numerical size of the market, but consume a major percentage of the unit volume. Some consumer-panel data on usage rates for popular products are shown in Table 10-3. From a marketing point of view, it is obviously critical to know who the heavy buyers are; the hope is that they have certain common demographic, personal or media habits and are homogeneous in their product requirements. With coffee, for example, some heavy buyers appear to look for a quality product while others make their purchases on a price basis.

In the area of social marketing campaigns, agencies often face a heavy-user dilemma. The heavy users are often the most resistant to the selling proposition. A family-planning agency, for example, would normally target its marketing effort to those families who would have the most children; but these are also the most resistant to birth-control messages. Road-safety organizations should target their marketing effort primarily to the unsafe drivers; but these drivers are also the most resistant to safe-driving appeals. The agencies must consider whether to use their limited budget to go after a few heavy users who are highly resistant, or many light users who are less resistant.

Table 10-3 Importance of heavy buyers

Product field	Per cent of buyers	Per cent of sales
Toilet rolls	19	42
Facial tissues	25	62
Packaged ice-cream	19	50
Butter	36	65
Dog food	24	60

Source: Heavy Buyer Profiles (Sydney: Audits and Panels of Australia, 1977).

Loyalty status. A market can also be segmented according to loyalty patterns of consumers. Consumers can be loyal to brands (Tooth LA), stores (Myer) and other entities. We will deal here with brand loyalty. Suppose there is a market with five brands: A, B, C, D and E. Buyers can be divided into four groups according to their loyalty status:[10]

- *Hard-core loyals.* These consumers buy only one brand all the time. Thus a buying pattern over six periods of A, A, A, A, A, A, would represent a consumer with undivided loyalty to brand A.
- *Soft-core loyals.* These show a loyalty to two or three brands. The buying pattern A, A, B, B, A, B would represent a consumer with a divided loyalty between brands A and B.
- *Shifting loyals.* These consumers are shifting their favour from one brand to another. The buying pattern A, A, A, B, B, B would suggest a consumer who is shifting brand loyalty from A to B.
- *Switchers.* These consumers buy a number of brands and show no loyalty to any. The buying pattern A, C, E, B, D, B would suggest a consumer who is either deal-prone (responds to the brand on sale) or variety-prone (wants something different).

Each market is made up of different degrees of these four types. A brand-loyal market is one with a high percentage of the buyers showing hard-core brand loyalty – the toothpaste market and the beer market seem to be fairly high brand-loyal markets. Companies selling in a brand-loyal market have a hard time gaining more market share, and companies trying to enter such a market have a hard time doing so.

A company can learn a great deal by analysing loyalty patterns in its market. First it should study the demographic and psychographic characteristics of its own hard-core loyals. Thus, if the hard-core loyals using Colgate toothpaste are more middle class, have larger families and are more health-conscious, this specifically defines the target for Colgate.

By studying its soft-core loyals, the company can determine which brands are most competitive with its own. If many Colgate buyers also buy Aim, Colgate can attempt to develop improved positioning against Aim, even possibly using direct comparison advertising.

By looking at those customers who are moving away from its brand, the company can learn about marketing deficits that it needs to correct. The company can attract non-loyals (if it wants to) simply by putting its brand on sale or providing special trial incentives.

In classifying consumers, the company has to be aware that what appear to be brand-loyal purchase patterns may in some cases reflect habit, indifference, a low price, or the non-availability of other brands. The concept of brand loyalty has some ambiguities and must be used with care.

Stages of buyer readiness. At any specific time, there is a distribution of people in various stages of readiness to buy the product. Some members of the potential market are unaware of the product; some are aware; some are informed; some are interested; some are desirous; and some intend to buy. The particular distribution of people over stages of readiness makes a big difference in designing the marketing programme. Suppose a health agency wants to attract women to take an annual pap test for the detection of cervical cancer. At the beginning, most of the potential market is unaware of the concept and thus the marketing effort should go into high-reach advertising and publicity using a simple message. If successful, more of the market will be aware of the test and the advertising should be changed to dramatize the benefits of annual examination and the risks of not taking it, so as to move more people into a stage of desire. Facilities should also be readied for handling the large number of women who may be motivated to take the examination. In general, the marketing programme must be adjusted to the changing distribution of buyer readiness.

Marketing factors. Markets can often be segmented into groups responsive to different marketing factors such as price and price deals, product quality, and service. This information can help the company allocate its marketing resources.[11] The marketing variables are usually proxies for particular benefits sought by buyers; a company that specializes in a certain marketing factor will build up hard-core loyals seeking that factor or benefit. Thus Avon, which sells cosmetics on a door-to-door basis, appeals to women who like personal attention and service.

Bases for Segmenting Industrial Markets

In segmenting industrial markets, we can use some of the variables used in consumer market segmentation and add a few new ones. Industrial buyers can be segmented geographically and by several behaviouristic variables: benefits sought, user status, usage rate, loyalty status, readiness stage, and marketing factor sensitivity. Rather than reviewing these, however, we will look at some other variables.

The most common way to segment industrial markets is by end users. Different users often seek different benefits and can be approached with different maketing mixes. This can be illustrated for the transistor market, which consists of three industrial submarkets: defence, industrial and commercial. The defence buyer attaches the utmost importance to the producer's quality standards and the adequacy of plant facilities. Firms selling transistors to the defence market must make a considerable investment in R & D, use sales representatives who know defence buying procedures, and specialize in limited-line products. Industrial buyers, such as electronic-equipment manufacturers, look for high quality and good service. Price itself is not a critical matter unless it becomes exorbitant. In this market, transistor manufacturers must make a modest investment in R & D, use sales representatives who have technical knowledge about the product, and offer a broad line. Commercial buyers, such as pocket-radio manufacturers, buy their components largely on the basis of price and delivery. Transistor manufacturers selling in this market need little or no R & D effort, use high-pressure sales representatives who are relatively non-technical, and offer the most common lines that can be mass-produced.

Customer size is another key segmentation variable. Many companies have found it useful to set up separate systems for dealing with major and minor customers. For example, a major manufacturer of office furniture divides its customers into two groups. Major accounts, such as large insurance companies, are singled out and handled by national account managers who work in conjunction with field district managers. Dealer accounts are handled through field sales personnel working with franchised dealers.

Most industrial companies do not stop at single-variable segmentation but define their target market opportunities with a succession of variables. This is illustrated in Figure 10-5 for an aluminium company.[12] The aluminium company first undertook macrosegmentation consisting of three steps.[13] It looked at which end-use market to serve: motor vehicle, residential, or beverage containers. Choosing the residential market, it determined the most attractive product application: semi-finished material, building components, or aluminium caravans. Deciding to specialize in producing building components, it next determined the best customer size to serve, and this turned out to be large customers. The second stage consisted of forming microsegments within the macrosegment of large customers buying building components. The company realized that large customers fell into three groups – those who considered price, service or quality first. Because the aluminium company had a high service profile, it decided to concentrate on the service-motivated microsegment of the market.

Requirements for Effective Segmentation

Clearly, there are many ways to segment a market; not all resulting segments are effective, however, from a marketing point of

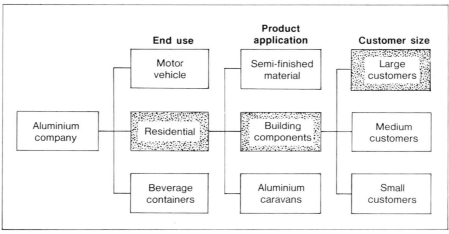

Source: Based on an example in E. Raymond Corey, 'Key Options in Market Selection and Product Planning', *Harvard Business Review*, September–October 1975, pp. 119–28.

Figure 10-5 Three-step segmentation of the aluminium market

view. The buyers of table salt, for example, could be subdivided into blond and brunette customers, but this is hardly relevant to the purchase of salt. In fact, salt buyers may not be segmentable: if all salt buyers wanted to buy the same amount of salt each month, believed all salt was the same, and wanted to pay the same price, this market would be minimally segmentable from a marketing point of view. To be useful, market segments must exhibit the following characteristics:

- *Measurability.* This describes the degree to which the size and purchasing power of the resulting segments can readily be measured. Certain segmentation variables are difficult to measure, e.g. the size of the segment of teenage smokers who smoke primarily to rebel against their parents.
- *Accessibility.* This describes the degree to which the resulting segments can effectively be reached and served. Suppose a perfume company finds that heavy users of its brand are single women who are out late at night and frequent bars. Unless this group lives or shops at certain places and watches certain media, there is no way to reach them efficiently.
- *Substantiality.* This describes the degree to which the resulting segments are large and/ or profitable enough to be worth pursuing. A segment should be the largest possible homogeneous group of buyers that it pays to go after with a specially designed marketing programme. Segmental marketing is expensive, as we shall see. It would not pay, for example, for a motor-vehicle manufacturer to develop a line of cars designed for persons who are more than two metres tall.

Evaluating the Attractiveness of Different Market Segments

Given a set of market segments that have the characteristics of measurability, accessibility and substantiality, the marketer's next task is to evaluate the attractiveness of each segment.

A useful analytical approach is illustrated in Figure 10-6.[14] The market is that for the mechanical products of a steel-fabricating company. Stage 1 shows a segmentation of this market, using the customer-prospect mix and the product-service mix as two variables. The customer-prospect mix consists of contractors in the electrical, general and plumbing lines respectively. The product-service mix consists of three products sold to these contractors: pipe hangers, concrete inserts, and electrical supports. Nine cells result from this joint segmentation, each cell representing a distinct submarket, or product-market segment. A dollar figure is placed in each cell, representing the company's sales in that submarket.

Relative company sales in the nine submarkets provide no indication of their relative profit potential as segments. The latter depends upon market demand, company costs, and competitive trends in each submarket. Stages 2 and 3 show how a particular product submarket, the general-contractor market for concrete inserts, can be analyzed in depth.

Stage 2 appraises present and future sales in the selected submarket. The vertical axis accommodates estimates of industry sales, company sales, and company market share. The horizontal axis is used to project future sales in these categories and market share. The company sold in this submarket last year $200 000 worth of goods, or one-fourth of total estimated industry sales. Looking ahead, the company expects industry sales in this submarket to rise by 6 per cent and its own sales to rise by 15 per cent.

Stage 3 probes deeper into the marketing thinking behind the sales forecasts of Stage 2. The horizontal axis shows the promotional mix that the company is using (or plans to use) to stimulate the sales of concrete inserts to general contractors. The vertical axis shows the distribution mix that the company is using

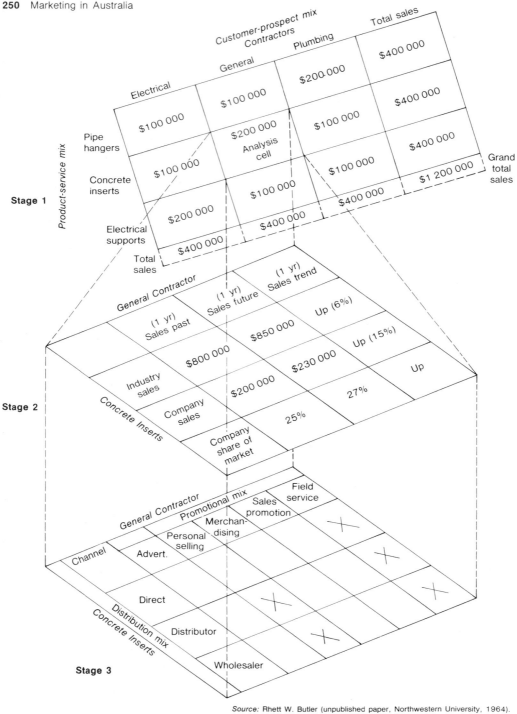

Source: Rhett W. Butler (unpublished paper, Northwestern University, 1964).

Figure 10-6 Analyzing the worth of different market segments for steel-fabricated products

(or plans to use) to move concrete inserts into the hands of general contractors. The actual promotion-distribution mix could be detailed by placing budget figures in the relevant cells. The company will use all three types of distribution and rely mainly on personal selling and field service for stimulating sales to general contractors.

By carrying out this analysis, the seller is led to think systematically about each segment as a distinct opportunity. Analysing the profit potential of each segment will help the seller decide on the appropriate target markets to serve.

TARGET MARKETING

Market segmentation reveals the market segment opportunities facing the firm. At this point the firm has to decide between three broad market selection strategies (see Figure 10-7):

1. *Undifferentiated marketing.* The firm might decide to go after the whole market with one offer and marketing mix, trying to attract as many customers as possible (i.e. mass marketing).
2. *Differentiated marketing.* The firm might decide to go after several market segments, developing an effective offer and marketing mix for each.
3. *Concentrated marketing.* The firm might decide to go after one market segment and develop the ideal offer and marketing mix.

Here we will describe the logic and merits of each of these strategies.

Undifferentiated Marketing

In undifferentiated marketing, the firm chooses not to recognize the different market segments making up the market.[15] It focuses on what is common in the needs of people rather than on what is different: it tries to de-

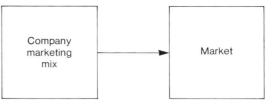

a Undifferentiated marketing

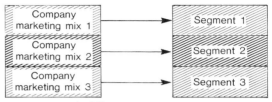

b Differentiated marketing

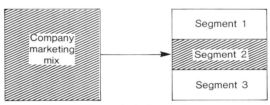

c Concentrated marketing

Figure 10-7 Three alternative market selection strategies

sign a product and a marketing programme that will appeal to the broadest number of buyers; it relies on mass channels, mass advertising media, and universal themes; it aims to endow the product with a superior image in people's minds. An excellent example of undifferentiated marketing was the traditional one-pint bottle of milk, which was virtually the only way to buy milk.

Undifferentiated marketing is primarily defended on the grounds of cost economies. It is thought to be 'the marketing counterpart to standardization and mass production in manufacturing'.[16] The fact that the product line is kept narrow minimizes production, inventory and transport costs. An undifferentiated advertising programme enables the firm to enjoy media discounts through large usage. The absence of segmental marketing research and planning lowers the costs of marketing research and product management. On the whole, undifferentiated marketing results in keeping down several costs of doing business.

Nevertheless, an increasing number of marketers have expressed strong doubts about the effectiveness of this strategy. Gardner and Levy, for example, admitted that 'some brands have very skilfully built up reputations of being suitable for a wide variety of people' but added:

> In most areas audience groupings will differ, if only because there are deviants who refuse to consume the same way other people do . . . It is not easy for a brand to appeal to stable lower middle-class people and at the same time to be interesting to sophisticated, intellectual upper middle-class buyers . . . It is rarely possible for a product or brand to be all things to all people.[17]

When several firms in the industry aim at the largest segment of the market the result is intense competition for the largest segment(s) and undersatisfaction of the smaller ones. The 'majority fallacy', as this has been called by Kuehn and Day, describes the fact that the larger segments may be less profitable because they attract disproportionately heavy competition.[18] Recognition of this has led many firms to re-evaluate the opportunities latent in pursuing smaller segments of the market.

Differentiated Marketing

Under differentiated marketing, a firm decides to operate in two or more segments of the market but designs separate product and/or marketing programmes for each. Thus Ford tries to produce a car for every 'purse, purpose and personality'. By offering product and marketing variations, it hopes to attain higher sales and a deeper position within each market segment; it hopes that the latter will strengthen the customers' overall identification of the company with the product field. Furthermore, it hopes for greater loyalty and repeat purchasing because its offerings have been bent to the customer's desire rather than the other way around.

In recent years an increasing number of firms have moved toward a strategy of differentiated marketing, reflected in multiple-product offerings and multiple-trade channels and media. For example, Johnson and Johnson launched its Reach toothbrush although the company already held 50 per cent of the market with its Tek toothbrush. Reach was priced at three times the price of Tek, and was aimed at the quality-seeking, preventative medicine 'fanatics'.[19]

The net effect of differentiated marketing is to create more total sales than undifferentiated marketing. 'It is ordinarily demonstrable that total sales may be increased with a more diversified product line sold through more diversified channels.'[20] However, it also tends to be true that differentiated marketing increases the costs of doing business in the following ways:

- *Product modification costs.* Modifying a product to meet different market segment requirements usually involves some R & D, engineering, and/or special tooling costs.
- *Production costs.* Generally speaking, it is more expensive to produce, say, ten units of ten different products than 100 units of one product. This is especially true the longer the production setup time for each product and the smaller its sales volume. On the other hand, if each model is sold in sufficiently large volume, the higher costs of setup time may be quite small per unit.
- *Administrative costs.* Under differentiated marketing, the company has to develop separate marketing plans for the separate segments of the market. This requires extra marketing research, forecasting, sales analysis, promotion, planning, and channel management.
- *Inventory costs.* It is generally more costly to manage inventories of differentiated

products than an inventory of only one product, because more records must be kept and more auditing must be done. Furthermore, each product must be carried at a level that reflects basic demand plus a safety factor to cover unexpected variations, and the sum of safety stocks for several products will exceed the safety stock required for one product.

- *Promotion costs.* Differentiated marketing involves trying to reach different segments of the market through advertising media most appropriate to each case. This leads to lower usage rates of individual media and thus forfeiture of quantity discounts. Furthermore, since each segment may require separate creative advertising planning, promotion costs are increased.

Since differentiated marketing leads to higher sales and higher costs, nothing can be said in advance regarding the optimality of this strategy. Some firms are finding, in fact, that they have overdifferentiated their market offers and would like to manage fewer brands, each appealing to a broader customer group. Called 'reverse line extension' or 'broadening the base', they seek a larger volume for each brand. Johnson and Johnson, for example, managed to attract adults to use its baby shampoo.

Concentrated Marketing

Both differentiated marketing and undifferentiated marketing imply that the firm goes after the whole market. However, many firms see a third possibility, one that is especially appealing when the company's resources are limited. Instead of going after a small share of a large market, the firm goes after a large share of one or a few submarkets, i.e. it concentrates its forces to gain a good market position in a few areas.

Many examples of concentrated marketing can be cited. Volkswagen has concentrated on the small-car market; Hewlett-Packard on the high-priced calculator market; and Richard D. Irwin on the economics and business texts market. Through concentrated marketing the firm achieves a strong market position in the particular segments it serves because of its greater knowledge of the segments' needs and the special reputation it acquires. Furthermore, it enjoys many operating economies because of specialization in production, distribution and promotion. If the segment of the market is well chosen, the firm can earn high rates of return on its investment.

At the same time, concentrated marketing involves higher than normal risks. The particular market segment can suddenly turn sour; for example, a competitor may decide to enter the same segment, such as happened to VW when the Japanese focused on small cars. Thus, many companies prefer to diversify in several market segments.

Choosing Among Market Selection Strategies

Particular characteristics of the seller, the product and the market serve to constrain and narrow the actual choice of a market selection strategy.[21]

The first factor is company resources. Where the firm's resources are too limited to permit complete coverage of the market, its only realistic choice is concentrated marketing.

The second factor is product homogeneity. Undifferentiated marketing is more suited for homogeneous products such as grapefruit or steel. Products that are capable of great variation, such as cameras and cars, are more naturally suited to differentiation or concentration.

The third factor is product stage in the lifecycle. When a firm introduces a new product into the marketplace it usually finds it practical to introduce one or, at the most, a few product versions. The firm's interest is to develop primary demand, and undifferentiated marketing seems the suitable strategy; or it might concentrate on a particular segment. In the mature stage of the product lifecycle, firms tend to pursue a strategy of differentiated marketing.

The fourth factor is market homogeneity. If buyers have the same tastes, buy the same amounts per period, and react in the same way to marketing stimuli, a strategy of undifferentiated marketing is appropriate.

The fifth factor is competitive marketing strategies. When competitors are practising active segmentation, it is difficult for a firm to complete through undifferentiated marketing. Conversely, when competitors are practising undifferentiated marketing, a firm can gain by practising active segmentation if some of the other factors favour it.

SUMMARY

Sellers can take three different approaches to a market. Mass marketing is the decision to mass-produce and mass-distribute one product and attempt to attract all kinds of buyers. Product differentiation is the decision to produce two or more products differentiated in terms of style, features, quality, sizes, and so on, thus offering variety to the market and distinguishing the seller's products from competitors' products. Target marketing is the decision to distinguish the different groups that make up a market and develop appropriate products and marketing mixes for each.

Sellers today are moving away from mass marketing and product differentiation toward target marketing, because the latter is more helpful in spotting market opportunities and developing more effective products and marketing mixes.

The key step in target marketing is market segmentation, which is the act of dividing a market into distinct and meaningful groups of buyers who might merit separate products and/or marketing mixes. The investigator tries different variables to see which reveal the best segmentation opportunities. For consumer marketing, the major segmentation variables are broadly classified as geographic, demographic, psychographic and behaviouristic. Industrial markets may be segmented by such variables as end use, customer size, geographic location, and product application. The effectiveness of such an exercise depends upon arriving at segments that are measurable, accessible and substantial. The resulting segments can then be evaluated for their profit potential and other measures of attractiveness.

The seller then has to choose a market selection strategy, either ignoring segment differences (undifferentiated marketing), developing different products and marketing programmes for each segment (differentiated marketing), or going after only one or a few segments (concentrated marketing). No particular strategy is superior in all circumstances. Much depends on company resources, product homogeneity, product stage in the lifecycle, market homogeneity, and competitive marketing strategies.

QUESTIONS FOR DISCUSSION

1. What three stages do sellers move through in their approach to a market? Relate these to the Ford Motor Company.

2. After the market segmentation process is completed, the organization should begin developing the marketing-mix factors. Comment.

3. Besides age and sex, what other demographic segmentation variables are used in the brewery industry? Explain. Also, identify major benefit segments in the beer market.

4. Discuss the lifestyle or lifecycle segments that you will occupy between now and the year 2000.

5. If you were manager of a particular form of public transport, how would you use benefit segmentation to appeal to potential passengers?

6. Give specific examples of marketers who have been successful in segmenting their markets on each of the following bases:
   - low price
   - high quality
   - service.

7. In what ways do you think that IBM has segmented its market?

8. Has the Kentucky Fried Chicken chain met the requirements for effective segmentation? Why?

9. Differentiated marketing is always the best approach to target marketing. Comment.

10. If Levi Strauss were considering a new line of women's skirts for casual wear, how would it go about market segmentation and target marketing?

NOTES

[1] 'Wool Marketers Miss Opportunity in Youth Segment', *Rydge's In Marketing*, 7 December 1980, pp. 16–17.

[2] 'Can the Baby Toy Market Be Segmented 12 Ways?', *Business Week*, 14 February 1977, p. 62.

[3] Judith Hoare, 'Over 50s to have Second Magazine', *Australian Financial Review*, 20 November 1981, p. 26.

[4] Richard P. Coleman, 'The Significance of Social Stratification in Selling', in Martin L. Bell (ed.), *Marketing: A Maturing Discipline* (Chicago: American Marketing Association, 1961), pp. 171–84.

[5] *The Age Lifestyle Study* (Melbourne: David Syme, 1975).

[6] See David Darby, Stan Glaser & Ian Wilkinson, *Health Care and Lifestyle*, quoted in Deborah Smith, 'Treating Yourself', *The National Times*, 14–20 June 1981, p. 47.

[7] Ralph Westfall, 'Psychological Factors in Predicting Product Choice', *Journal of Marketing*, April 1962, pp. 34–40.

[8] Maurice J. Gottlieb, 'Segmentation by Personality Types', in Lynn H. Stockman (ed.), *Advancing Marketing Efficiency* (Chicago: American Marketing Association, 1959), p. 154.

[9] W. T. Tucker & John J. Painter, 'Personality and Product Use', *Journal of Applied Psychology*, October 1961, pp. 325–29.

[10] This classification was adapted from George H. Brown, 'Brand Loyalty – Fact or Fiction?', *Advertising Age*, June 1952 – January 1953, a series.

[11] See Ronald Frank, William Massy & Yoram Wind, *Market Segmentation* (Englewood Cliffs, N.J.: Prentice-Hall, 1972), Part IV.

[12] This example is based on E. Raymond Corey, 'Key Options in Market Selection and Product Planning', *Harvard Business Review*, September–October 1975, pp. 119–28.

[13] Wind and Cardozo suggest that industrial segmentation should proceed by first developing macrosegments and then microsegments. See Yoram Wind & Richard Cardozo, 'Industrial Market Segmentation', *Industrial Marketing Management*, 3 (1974), pp. 153–66.

14 The general approach is described in William J. Crissy & Frank H. Mossman, 'Matrix Models for Marketing Planning: An Update and Expansion', *MSU Business Topics*, Autumn 1977, pp. 17–26. The example was developed elsewhere.

15 See Wendell R. Smith, 'Product Differentiation and Market Segmentation as Alternative Marketing Strategies', *Journal of Marketing*, July 1956, pp. 3–8; and Alan A. Roberts, 'Applying the Strategy of Market Segmentation', *Business Horizons*, Autumn 1961, pp. 65–72.

16 Smith, p. 4.

17 Burleigh Gardner & Sidney Levy, 'The Product and the Brand', *Harvard Business Review*, March–April 1955, p. 37.

18 Alfred A. Kuehn & Ralph L. Day, 'Strategy of Product Quality', *Harvard Business Review*, November–December 1962, pp. 101–2.

19 Tim Allerton, 'Reach For your Latest J. & J. Toothbrush', *Australian Financial Review*, 1 October 1980, p. 14.

20 Roberts, p. 66.

21 R. William Kotrba, 'The Strategy Selection Chart', *Journal of Marketing*, July 1966, pp. 22–25.

Part 4

Marketing-mix Strategy

New-product Development and Product Lifecycle Strategies

11

The rise and fall of the Valiant parallels that of the big car on the Australian market. Mitsubishi Motors Australia Ltd recently stopped making the Valiant CM, although there was a steady, if small, market for it in some rural areas. Its production line was needed for Mitsubishi for the small, front-drive hatchback Mitsubishi Colt which is as much in the motoring mainstream as the Valiant was drifting into a backwater.

Many will mourn the passing of the Valiant. It is easy to blame spiralling petrol prices and the swing to the resultant smaller, more economical cars for the Valiant's demise. But the improvements in modern cars sliced at the Valiant's roots just as effectively as fuel prices bit into motoring budgets.

Chrysler Australia did a good job of squeezing more kilometres out of its Valiants in the last years of the car. Clever modern electronics from the United States were grafted to the home-grown, efficient but harsh six-cylinder engine. Chrysler dubbed the move 'Electronic Lean Burn' in a way all car advances are given catchy, easy-to-grasp labels. Shorn of its title, the device did produce up to 25 per cent better fuel economy, which has resulted in the strong re-sale prices of some of the last CM model Valiants.

As well as improved economy, the small car promised, in the latest form, not only easy driving but little loss of comfort. Buyers were becoming accustomed to expecting secure agility from small cars; at least as good road holding as once could be had only with bulk. Cars destined for the country, for example, once had to be 'heavy'. The mass was thought to provide a worthwhile combination of strength and grip on the road. The short life of some cars in the country – not all of them small – lent some weight to the theory. But the latest *stress analysis programmes can tell if a new model is strong enough before it leaves the drawing board. Some jiggling with the specification is sometimes needed but basic problems can be fixed early in a car's development.*

The Valiant stems from an era when six seats and six cylinders often were thought prerequisites for value. Power to propel the bigger car also was desirable. The biggest appeal of the original R-series Valiant, in 1962, apart from its individual style was its powerful 'Slant Six' engine. It shaded the new Falcons and Holdens of the time. Only 1008 of the R-series were sold before the sleeker S series was introduced in the same year. Still, only 10 009 of the S series were sold.

The AP5 Valiant, which sold 49 440 units in 1963 and 1964, assured the Valiant of its place in Australian motoring. Cleverly marketed with a price premium for its power edge, the next models, the AP6 and the VC, continued to sell well. As well as more power, the Valiant had a smoother, three-speed automatic transmission when the Holdens and Falcons were struggling on two speeds. But while the Valiant was ahead of its rivals in the 1960s, it fell steadily behind in the 1970s.

Entering the 1980s, the Valiant faced a shrinking market and a huge development bill. So its replacement from Europe was arranged – a plan since foundered on the reefs of Mitsubishi's takeover of Chrysler Australia.[1]

Sales of the Valiant had passed through the classic product lifecycle of introduction, growth, maturity and decline. A company has to be good at developing new products. It also has to be good at managing them in the face of changing tastes, technologies and competition. Every product appears to go through a lifecycle.

Figure 11-1 illustrates the hypothetical course of sales and profits over the life of a product. During product development, the company accumulates increasing costs; after the product is launched, its sales pass through an introduction period, then one of strong growth, followed by maturity and, eventually, decline. Meanwhile its profits go from negative to positive, peak in the growth or mature stages, and then decline.

The existence of a product lifecycle means that the firm faces two major challenges. The first is to find new products to replace those in a declining stage (the problem of new-product development). The second is to know how to manage existing products optimally in each stage (the problem of lifecycle strategies). Some companies concentrate mostly on developing and launching new products, sometimes to the detriment of skilfully managing their existing products. Other companies put most of their effort into current-product management and fail to provide enough new products on which to base their future. Somehow companies must try to strike a balance between these two extremes.

This chapter first looks at the problem of developing new products and then discusses the problem of managing them successfully during their lifecycle.

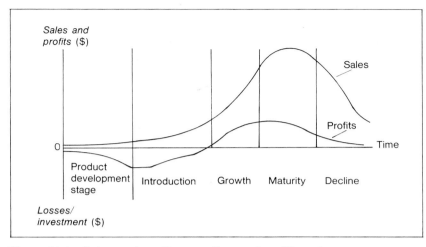

Figure 11-1   Sales and profits over the product lifecycle

NEW-PRODUCT DEVELOPMENT STRATEGY

Under modern conditions of competition, it is risky for a company to rely only on its existing products. Customers want and expect a stream of new and improved products, and competition will do its best to meet these desires. A company programme that includes searching for new products is a necessity.

The company can obtain new products in two basic ways. It can obtain them through acquisition, i.e. by buying a whole company, a patent, or a licence to produce someone else's product. Alternatively it can practise new-product development, setting up its own research and development department. We will concentrate on new-product development: by 'new products' we mean original products, product improvements, product modifications and new brands that the firm brings into existence through its own or others' R & D efforts. We will also be concerned with whether the consumer sees the items as 'new', although this will not be our primary focus.

In Australia, many large firms – e.g. ICI, Shell, BP, IBM, GMH, Ford, GE and Bosch – are subsidiaries of overseas multinationals.

Multinationals, in turn, are increasingly moving towards the concept of world products, i.e. developing a product which can serve the various national markets in which the company operates. Local subsidiaries have a manufacturing and marketing responsibility, but this frequently does not include product development. Instead the Australian subsidiary has a stream of new products available to it from the corporate research laboratories. In some cases it can choose which product it will market, in other cases that decision is also taken at the corporate level. If the local company has some discretion, then its major decisions are which new products are appropriate for the Australian market and what product modifications are required.

The car companies have virtually all adopted the concept of a 'world car', with production being specialized by country. GMH, in line with this policy, suggested that it would be willing to establish a world-scale engine plant in Australia to serve GM's entire world production requirements of a given engine type; on the other hand, the Commodore is based on an international design concept, modified to suit Australian conditions.

In the early 1970s, GMH began the search

for a new car to supplement the Kingswood line. There was a demand for a more compact, fuel-efficient and lighter car, yet one that retained a large measure of interior space. Competition in the Australian market was increasing, particularly from Japanese cars, and Kingswood buyers were beginning to trade-down to smaller cars with lower running costs. At the same time, European styling was beginning to be the basis for style comparisons, and consumers wanted good handling and comfort coupled with more equipment and luxury features.

With these data, GMH looked for alternatives and finally settled on the Opel 'V' car which was then in its early stages of development. The original design was too small for the Holden six-cylinder engine, but Opel subsequently developed a larger version with a longer bonnet. In November 1975, three years before the new car was due to be launched, a small number of consumers (1400 in total) were invited to inspect two versions of the new model. They provided comments on details of the car together with their preferences relative to competing makes. One model came out a firm favourite, with 30 per cent of first preferences.

Extensive work was then required to adapt the car to Australian conditions. The steering system was altered – a design change subsequently adopted on overseas versions. New suspension systems were developed to handle the rough conditions of Australian roads, springs were relocated to provide for greater vertical wheel movement, and so on.

The end result was the Commodore, a car that is still basically the original Opel, yet substantially modified for Australian conditions. GMH has claimed that ultimately 65 per cent of the Commodore's parts were Holden designed, developed and produced. This may be higher than for other firms, but it indicates that extensive modification to overseas designs is frequently required.

So, in Australia, new product development can take a number of forms. For some firms, product development is essentially an adaptation of products developed overseas – these firms typically have technical agreements which give them access to both product and process development by an overseas firm. For others, the Australian firm is responsible for the entire new product development activity; if it also happens to be a subsidiary, new products developed here may, at a future date, be taken up by the parent company and marketed elsewhere in the world.

Innovation can be very risky. Computicket, the computerized booking service sponsored by Myer and other firms, lost millions of dollars. The Australian Leisure Club, which offered a catalogue of 'bargains' in travel and indoor and outdoor leisure products, failed miserably although it was backed by Ampol, National Mutual, and Bullen's. Despite the successes associated with the Packer name, including the best-selling *Women's Weekly*, Australian Consolidated Press misread the market with the magazines *You and Yours* (fitness, nutrition, etc.) and *Solitaire* (for singles and separates). Overseas, and on a grander scale, ICI lost $20 million on its tobacco substitute and the Anglo-French aircraft Concorde will probably never recover its investment. Here are a number of consumer-packaged-goods products that were launched by well-known companies but failed:

- Pro-Vita Cookies (Nabisco)
- Murray River canned dog food (Uncle Ben's)
- Mighty Dog canned dog food (Carnation)
- Wizard drink base (Heinz)
- Dycel paper briefs for women (Reckitt & Colman)
- Caresta milk-based drink (Cadbury-Schweppes)
- Virginia Slims cigarettes (Philip Morris)
- Casserole for Dogs (Arnott-Spillers)

Various estimates of the new-product failure rate have been made, putting it anywhere from 20 to 80 per cent. One of the more careful studies indicated that new-product failure rate at that time was 40 per cent for consumer products, 20 per cent for industrial products, and 18 per cent for services.[2] The failure rate for new consumer products is especially alarming.

In the future, successful new-product development may even be more difficult to achieve, for several reasons:

- *Shortage of important ideas.* Some scientists think there is a shortage of important new technologies of the magnitude of the car, television, computers, xerography and antibiotics.
- *Fragmented markets.* Keen competition is leading to increasingly fragmented markets. Companies have to aim new products at smaller market segments rather than the mass market, and this means lower sales and profits.
- *Growing social and governmental constraints.* New products have to increasingly satisfy public criteria such as consumer safety and ecological compatibility. Government requirements have slowed down the rate of innovation in the pharmaceutical industry, and have considerably complicated product design and advertising decisions in such industries as industrial equipment, chemicals, cars and toys.
- *Costliness of the process.* A company typically has to develop a great number of new-product ideas in order to finish with a few good ones. Booz, Allen and Hamilton studied this question in regard to fifty-one companies, and summarized its findings in the form of a decay curve of new-product ideas (see Figure 11-2). Of every fifty-eight ideas, about twelve pass the initial screening test, which shows them to be compatible with company objectives and resources. Of these, some seven remain after a thorough evaluation of their potential. About three survive the product development stage, two survive the test-marketing stage, and only one is commercially successful. Thus, about fifty-eight new ideas must be generated to find one good one; this one successful idea must then be priced to cover all the money lost by the company in researching the fifty-seven that failed.

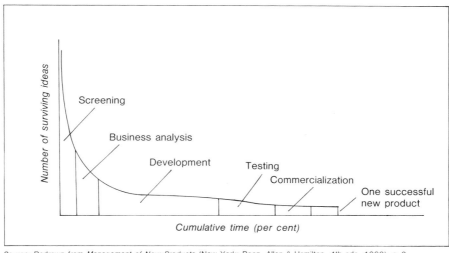

Source: Redrawn from *Management of New Products* (New York: Booz, Allen & Hamilton, 4th edn, 1968), p. 9.

Figure 11-2 **Decay curve of new-product ideas (51 companies)**

- *Capital shortage.* The high cost of new-product development is no longer affordable by many companies because of the high cost of money. Many companies therefore tend to emphasize product modification and imitation rather than true innovation.
- *Shorter life-spans of successful products.* Even when a new product turns out to be a commercial success, rivals are so quick to follow suit that the new product is typically fated for only a short happy life. The race to be first on the market sometimes assumes grotesque proportions. One firm was so eager to beat a competitor's new shampoo to the market that it devised a name and filmed a television commercial before it had even developed its own product.

Thus management faces a dilemma: it should develop new products, but the odds weigh heavily against their success. The answer lies in knowing why new products fail and designing a development process that reduces the most common risk of failure.

There are a number of reasons behind the failure of new products. Too often a high-level executive pushes a favourite idea through in spite of insufficient or even negative marketing research findings. Or the idea is good, but the market size is overestimated. Or the actual product is not designed as well as it should be. Or it is incorrectly positioned in the market, not advertised effectively, or overpriced. Sometimes the costs of product development are higher than expected, or the competitors respond with more ammunition than expected.

To prevent these errors, the company must improve its organizational arrangements for handling the new product development process. Companies use up to five different organizational arrangements for handling the development of new products.[3]

1. Product managers. Many companies leave new product development up to their product managers. In practice, this system has several faults. The product managers are usually too busy managing their product lines to give much thought to new products other than brand modifications or extensions; they also lack the specific skills and knowledge needed to successfully develop new products.

2. New-product managers. Rosella Foods and Johnson & Johnson have established positions of new-product managers (also called product planners) who report to group product managers. This position adds professionalism to the new-product function; on the other hand, new-product managers tend to think in terms of product modifications and line extensions limited to their product market. The position often does not have sufficient authority or top-level support.

3. New-product committees. Most companies have a high-level management committee charged with reviewing new-product proposals. Consisting of representatives from marketing, manufacturing, finance, engineering, accounting and other functional areas, its role is less to develop or coordinate developments than to review and approve new-product plans. These committees tend to be conservative; their members are very busy and too far removed from the actual details of the new product areas. They are not a total solution to the new-product development problem.

4. New-product departments. Large companies often establish a new-product department headed by a manager who is given substantial authority and access to top management. He normally reports to the chief executive, marketing manager, or research and development director. The department's major responsibilities include generating and screening new ideas, directing and coordinating research and development work, and carrying out field testing and pre-commercialization work.

5. New-product venture teams. A venture team is a group specifically brought together

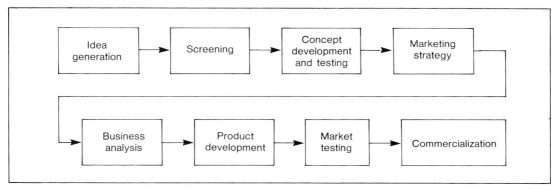

Figure 11-3   Major stages in new-product development

from various operating departments and charged with the responsibility of bringing a specific product to market or a specific new business into being.

The new-product development process itself consists of the eight steps shown in Figure 11-3. We are now ready to examine these steps.

Idea Generation

The first stage in the new-product development process is the generation of new-product ideas. The search should be systematic rather than haphazard, otherwise the company will find scores of ideas, most of which are inappropriate to its type of business. In one company a new product came all the way up to final approval at a cost of more than a million dollars, only to be killed by members of top management who decided they did not want to get into that type of business.

Top management can avoid this by carefully defining its business domains, objectives and strategies for the new-product development programme. Its business domains should state which business areas the company wants to emphasize and how far afield it will go. The objectives should state what the company wants to accomplish with its new products, whether it is high cash flow, market-share domination or some other objective. The strat-

egy should state the relative effort that should be devoted to developing original products, modifying existing products, and imitating competitors' products.

In looking for new-product ideas, there are many excellent sources. Customers, according to the marketing concept, are a logical starting point in the search for ideas. Their needs and wants can be monitored through direct surveys, projective tests, focused group discussions, and their letters and complaints. Scientists are another source, in so far as they may discover or identify new materials or features that could lead to original products or product improvements. Companies should also watch competitors' products to see which are attracting customers. The company's sales force and dealers are another good source of ideas because they are in daily contact with customers. Other sources are inventors, patent offices, university and commercial laboratories, industrial consultants, management consultants, advertising agencies, marketing research firms, trade associations, and industrial publications; many will be non-Australian, and may warrant a personal visit.

Whatever the source of the idea, at least one of four general processes is responsible for producing it – inspiration, serendipity, customer request or formal techniques. Other than maintaining as creative an atmosphere as possible, and being alert to the occasional lucky accident, companies have little control over the first two processes. Moreover, they seldom have significant input into what a customer might request, although a perceptive salesperson might sometimes work with a customer to help clarify needs the manufacturer can satisfy. Companies, however, can train their executives to use certain 'creativity techniques', three of which are now summarized.[4]

1. *Customer problem analysis.* This calls for interviewing customers and asking them to name problems they have with the product. Thus the owners of movie projectors might say that they would like to be able to speed up their movie projectors when they come to boring stretches of film. This then becomes an idea for a new-product feature that a projector manufacturer can adopt.
2. *Product modification analysis.* Here the investigator looks at the various attributes of the product and thinks about opportunities to modify, magnify, minify, substitute, rearrange, reverse or combine one or more features.[5] The same movie-projector manufacturer can consider making a very small projector, substituting a new material, or developing a new rewinding device.
3. *Brainstorming.* Here a group of six to ten people (who may or may not be company personnel) are given a specific problem, such as 'Think of new ways to show movies in the home', and a few days later meet to generate ideas. The rules governing brainstorming sessions are fourfold: (i) criticism is prohibited; (ii) freewheeling is welcomed; (iii) quantity is wanted; and (iv) the group seeks to combine and improve ideas suggested. The participants agree not to criticize any ideas until after the idea generation stage.[6]

Idea Screening

Having generated a number of good ideas, the main purpose of all succeeding stages is to reduce this number. The first idea-pruning stage is screening.

At this stage the company must seek to avoid two types of errors. A drop-error occurs when the company dismisses an otherwise good idea because it fails to recognize its potential. Some companies still shudder when they think of some of the ideas they dismissed:

> Xerox saw the novel promise of Chester Carlson's copying machine; IBM and Eastman Kodak did not see it at all. RCA was able to envision the innovative opportunity of radio; the Victor Talking Machine Company could not. Henry Ford recognized the promise of the automobile; yet only General Motors realized the need to segment the automobile market into price and performance categories, with a model for every classification, if the promise was to be fully achieved.[7]

Even the potential of the Australian Cafe-Bar was not seen by those firms originally offered the concept. If a company makes too many drop-errors, its standards are obviously too conservative.

A go-error occurs when the company lets a poor idea proceed to development and commercialization. We can distinguish at least three types of product failures which ensue. An absolute product failure loses money and its sales do not cover variable costs; partial failure loses money but the product's sales cover all the variable costs and some of the fixed costs; relative failure yields a profit that is less than the company's normal rate of return.

The purpose of screening is to spot and drop poor ideas as early as possible. The rationale is that product development costs rise substantially at each successive stage of the process: when products reach later stages, management often feels that so much has been invested in developing the product that it ought to be launched in the hope of recouping some of the investment. But this is letting good money chase bad money, and the real solution is to not let poor product ideas get this far.

Most companies require their executives to write up each new-product idea on a standard form for review by a new-product committee. At this stage the ideas are rough, and the form simply requires a description of the product, the target market, competition, and some rough guesses as to market size, product price, development time and costs, manufacturing costs, and level of return.

Even if the idea looks good, the question arises: Is it appropriate, i.e. does it mesh well with the company's objectives, strategies and resources? Table 11-1 shows a common type of rating form for this question. The first column lists factors required for successful launching of the product in the marketplace; in the next column, management assigns weights to these factors according to their importance. Thus management believes marketing competence will be very important (0.20), and purchasing and supplies competence will be of minor importance (0.05). The next task is to rate the company's degree of competence on each factor on a scale from 0.0 to 1.0: here management feels that its marketing competence is very high (0.9) and its location and facilities competence is low (0.3). The final

step is to multiply the relative importance of the success requirements by the corresponding levels of company competence to obtain a single overall rating of the company's fitness to carry this product successfully into the market. Thus, if marketing is an important success requirement and the company is very good at marketing, this will increase the overall rating of the product idea. In this example the product idea scored 0.72 which, in the company's experience, places it at the high end of the 'fair idea' level.[8]

A checklist is a means of promoting systematic evaluation and discussion of the product idea among members of management – it is not designed to make the important decision for them.

Concept Development and Testing

Those ideas that survive screening must then be developed into full product concepts. It is important to distinguish between a product idea, a product concept and a product image. A product idea is a *possible* product, described in objective and functional terms, that the company can see itself offering to the market. A product concept is a particular subjective consumer meaning that the company tries to

Table 11-1 Product-idea rating device

Product success requirements	(A) Relative Weight	(B) Company competence level											Rating (A × B)
		0.0	0.1	0.2	0.3	0.4	0.5	0.6	0.7	0.8	0.9	1.0	
Company personality and goodwill	0.20							✓					0.120
Marketing	0.20										✓		0.180
Research and development	0.20								✓				0.140
Personnel	0.15							✓					0.090
Finance	0.10										✓		0.090
Production	0.05									✓			0.040
Location and facilities	0.05				✓								0.015
Purchasing and supplies	0.05										✓		0.045
Total	1.00												0.720*

Source: Adapted from Barry M. Richman, 'A Rating Scale for Product Innovation', *Business Horizons*, Summer 1962, pp. 37–44.
* Rating scale: 0.00–0.40 poor; 0.41–0.75 fair; 0.76–1.00 good. Present minimum acceptance rate: 0.70

build into the product idea. A product image is the particular subjective picture that consumers actually acquire of the product.

Concept development. Suppose that a motor-vehicle manufacturer develops the technology that enables an electric car to travel up to 80 kilometres an hour and cover 200 kilometres before needing to be recharged. The manufacturer estimates that this car's operating costs would be about half of those of a conventional car.

This is a product idea. Customers, however, do not buy product ideas; they buy a product concept. The marketer's task is to develop this idea into some alternative product concepts, evaluate their relative appeal to customers, and choose the best one. Among the product concepts that might be created for the electric car are the following:

- *Concept 1.* An inexpensive small car designed as a second family car to be used by the homemaker for short shopping trips, and so forth. The car is styled in such a way that it is easy to enter, load with groceries, and transport children in.
- *Concept 2.* A medium-cost, medium-sized car designed as an all-purpose family car.
- *Concept 3.* A medium-cost sporty small car appealing mainly to young people.
- *Concept 4.* An inexpensive small car designed to appeal to the conscientious citizen who wants basic transport, low fuel cost, and low pollution.

Concept testing. Concept testing calls for developing these concepts and presenting them to an appropriate group of target consumers for their reactions. The concepts may be presented symbolically or physically – at this stage a word and/or picture description suffices, although the reliability of the test increases the more concrete and physical the stimulus. Here is concept 1 in an elaborated form:

> An efficient, fun-to-drive, electric-powered car in the small-car class that seats four. Great for shopping trips and visits to friends. Costs half as much to operate as similar petrol-driven cars. Goes up to 80 kilometres an hour and does not need to be recharged for 200 kilometres. Priced at $8000.

Consumers will be asked to answer questions similar to those shown in Table 11-2, and their responses will enable the company to determine which of several alternative concepts has the strongest appeal. For example, the last question in Table 11-2 investigates the consumer's intention to buy. If 10 per cent of the consumers said 'definitely' and another 5 per cent said 'probably', the company would project these figures to find the corresponding population size of this target group to estimate whether the sales volume would be sufficient. Such an estimate must, however, be considered tentative at best, because people do not always carry out their stated intentions.

Table 11-2 Major questions in a concept test for an electric car

1. Is the concept of an electric car clear to you?
2. What do you see as distinct benefits of an electric car compared with a conventional car?
3. Do you find the claims about the electric car's performance believable?
4. Would an electric car meet a real need of yours?
5. What improvements can you suggest in various features of the electric car?
6. Who would be involved in a possible purchase decision, and who would use the car?
7. What do you think the price of the electric car should be?
8. Would you prefer an electric car to a conventional car? For what uses?
9. Would you buy an electric car? (Definitely, probably, probably not, definitely not.)

Marketing Strategy Development

Suppose the first-listed concept for the electric car tests out best. The next step is to develop a preliminary concept of the marketing strategy for introducing the electric car: this is necessary in order that the full product and marketing concept can be evaluated from a business point of view in the next stage.

The marketing strategy statement has three parts. The first describes the size, structure and behaviour of the target market, the intended positioning of the new product in this market, and the sales, market share and profit being sought in the first few years. Thus:

> The target market is households which need a second car for short shopping trips and visits to friends. The car will be positioned as more economical to buy and operate, and more fun to drive, than cars currently available to this market. The company will aim to sell 25 000 cars in the first year, at a loss not exceeding $300 000. The second year will aim for sales of 35 000 cars with a planned profit of $500 000.

The second part of the marketing strategy statement outlines the product's intended price, distribution strategy, and marketing budget for the first year:

> The electric car will be offered in three colours and will have optional air-conditioning and power-drive features. It will sell at a retail price of $8000, with 15 per cent off the list price to dealers. Dealers who sell over ten cars per month will get an additional discount of 5 per cent on each car sold that month. An advertising budget of $600 000 will be set. Advertising copy will emphasize the car's economy and fun. During the first year, $50 000 will be spent on marketing research to monitor who is buying the car and their satisfaction levels.

The third part of the marketing strategy statement describes the intended long-run sales, profit and marketing-mix strategy:

> The company intends to ultimately capture 10 per cent of the total car market and realize an after-tax return on investment of 15 per cent.

To achieve this, product quality will start high and be further improved over time through technical research. Price will be raised in the second and third years if competition permits. The total advertising budget will be boosted each year by about 10 per cent. Marketing research will be reduced to $40 000 per year after the first year.

Business Analysis

Once management has developed a satisfactory product concept and marketing strategy, it is ready to undertake a hardheaded analysis of the business attractiveness of the proposal. Management must review the future sales, costs and profit estimates to determine whether they satisfy the company's objectives. If they do, the product concept can be moved to the product development stage.

Estimating sales. The key to whether a product should be developed is whether its sales will be high enough to return a satisfactory profit to the firm. The sales history of similar products, and surveys of market opinion, will provide useful criteria; at the very least, management should have estimates of minimum and maximum sales to provide some indication of the risk involved.

Sales forecasting methods were described in Chapter 5. In predicting the future sales of a product, much depends on whether it is a one-time purchased product, an infrequently purchased product, or a frequently purchased product.

Figure 11-4a illustrates the product lifecycle sales that may be expected for one-time purchased products. Sales rise at the beginning, peak, and later approach zero as the number of potential buyers is exhausted. If new buyers keep entering the market, the curve will not quite go down to zero.

Typical infrequently purchased products are durable goods such as cars, toasters and industrial equipment. These goods exhibit replacement cycles, because either they wear out

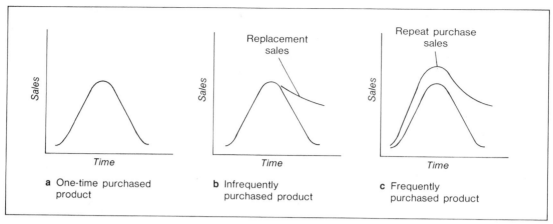

Figure 11-4   Product lifecycle sales for three types of products

or become obsolete as a result of changing styles, features or tastes.[9] Sales forecasting for this category of products consists of separately estimating first-time sales and replacement sales (see Figure 11-4b).

Frequently purchased products, such as consumer and industrial non-durables, have lifecycle sales resembling Figure 11-4c. The number of first-time buyers initially increases and then decreases as there are fewer left (assuming a fixed population). Repeat-purchase sales occur soon, providing that the product satisfies some fraction of people who become steady customers. The sales curve eventually plateaus, representing a level of steady repeat-purchase volume; by this time the product is no longer in the class of new products.

Estimating costs and profits. After preparing a long-range sales forecast, management can proceed to estimate the expected costs and profits of this venture over the same period of time. The costs are gathered through discussions with R & D, manufacturing, accounting and financial personnel, and include the expected sales and net profits listed in the marketing strategy statement. The next step is to calculate the financial attractiveness of the proposal, using techniques such as break-even analysis, payout period analysis, rate-of-return analysis, or discounted cash flow analysis, which are described in standard finance text-books.

Product Development

If the product concept scores highly in the business analysis, it can be turned over to the R & D department and/or the engineering department to be developed into a physical product. Up to now it has existed only as a word description, a drawing, or a very crude mock-up. Development of the concept calls for a large jump in investment, which dwarfs the costs incurred in the earlier stages. This stage will determine whether the product idea can be translated into a technically and commercially feasible product. If not, the company's accumulated investment will be lost except for any useful byproduct information gained in the process.

The R & D department undertakes the development of one or more physical versions of the defined product concept. It succeeds if it finds a prototype that satisfies the following criteria: (i) the prototype is seen by consumers as successfully embodying the key attributes described in the concept statement; (ii) the prototype performs safely under normal use and conditions; (iii) the prototype can be produced for the budgeted manufacturing costs.

The work of developing a successful product prototype can take days, weeks, months or even years. The R & D people must know not only how to design the required functional characteristics but also how to convey the psychological aspects of the concept through physical cues. In the case of the electric car, they may want to convey the idea that it is well-built and safe – which calls for a rugged-looking car. Management must investigate how consumers inspect a car to decide how well built it is. One common practice consists of slamming a car door; if the car does not have 'solid-sounding' doors, then consumers will think that it is not well built.

When the prototypes are ready, they must be put through a series of rigorous functional and consumer tests. Under laboratory and field conditions, the car is tested to make sure that it starts well, its tyres do not fall off, and it can manoeuvre around corners without overturning. A sample of consumers are then brought in to test-drive the prototype and rate their reactions to the car and each of its attributes.

Market Testing

After management is satisfied with the prototype's functional performance and the consumers' initial response, it will arrange for a certain number to be manufactured for use in further market testing. Market testing is where the product and the marketing programme are introduced into more authentic settings to learn how consumers and dealers react to handling, using and repurchasing the product, and how large the market is.

The amount of market testing is influenced by the amount of investment cost and risk on the one hand, and the time pressure and research cost on the other. Products involving substantial investment and risk deserve to be market-tested – the cost of these tests will be an insignificant percentage of the cost of the project itself.

Methods of market testing vary with the type of product (see Table 11-3). For example, companies testing frequently purchased consumer packaged goods will want to estimate four components of sales: trial, first repeat, adoption, and frequency of purchase. From these, total sales can be forecast.[10] The company hopes to find all of these at high levels. Too often, however, it will find many consumers trying the product but not rebuying it; find high first-time repurchase but little repeat purchase; or find high adoption but low frequency of purchase (as in the case of many gourmet frozen foods) because the buyers use the product only on special occasions.

Commercialization

Market testing presumably gives management enough information to make a final decision about whether to launch the new product. If the company goes ahead, it will face its largest costs to date: a full-scale manufacturing facility will need to be built or rented, and (in the case of a new consumer packaged good) between $500 000 and $1 million will be required for advertising and sales promotion alone in the first year.

In deciding to launch the new product, the company must make four basic decisions. Let us see how these decisions would apply to an electric car.

When (timing). The first decision concerns the right time to introduce the new product. If the electric car will cannibalize another car made by the company, its introduction might be delayed until the other car's stock is drawn down through normal sales.[11] If the electric car can still be improved, the company may prefer to miss the selling season in order to come out with a better car in the following year. If the company decides to go ahead, it

Table 11-3 Methods of market testing

Consumer packaged goods	Industrial durable goods

Consumer packaged goods

Sales wave research. Here a sample of consumers are given a free trial of the new product in their homes. They are then reoffered the product or competitive brands as many as three to five times (sales waves) at a reduced cost, with the company noting each time how many consumers selected its product again and what comments they reported about satisfaction.

Simulated store technique. Here a sample of consumers are invited to a brief screening of some television commercials. One of the commercials advertises the new product, but it is not singled out for attention. The consumers are given a small amount of money and are invited into a store: they may use the money to buy any items or keep the money. The company notes how many consumers buy the new product and competing brands. This provides a measure of trial and the commercial's effectiveness against competing commercials. The consumers reconvene and are asked the reasons for their purchase or nonpurchase. Some weeks later they are reinterviewed by phone to determine product attitudes, usage, satisfaction, and repurchase intention, as well as being offered an opportunity to repurchase any products.

Controlled test marketing. Several research firms have arranged a controlled panel of stores which have agreed to carry new products for a certain fee. The company with the new product specifies the number of stores and geographical locations it wants. The research firm takes responsibility for delivering the product to the participating stores and controlling shelf location, number of facings, displays and point-of-purchase promotions, and pricing according to pre-specified plans. Sales results can be tracked to determine the impact of various factors on demand.

Test markets. Test markets are the ultimate form of testing a new consumer product in a situation resembling the one that would be faced in a full-scale launching of the product. The company locates a small number of representative test cities in which the company's sales force will try to persuade the trade to carry the product and give it good shelf exposure. The company will put on a full advertising and promotion programme in these markets similar to the one that would be used in national marketing. Test marketing is undertaken to achieve a more reliable forecast of future sales and pre-test alternative marketing plans.

Industrial durable goods

Product-use tests. The manufacturer selects a small group of potential customers who agree to use the new product for a limited period. The manufacturer's technical people observe how the customers' workers use the product. This clues the manufacturer about customer training and servicing requirements. After the test, the customer is given an opportunity to express purchase intent and other reactions.

Trade shows. Trade shows draw a large number of buyers who view new exhibits in a few days. The manufacturer can see how much interest buyers show in the new product, how they react to various features and terms, and how many orders or purchase intentions they indicate.

Distribution and dealer display rooms. The new industrial product can also be tested in distributor and dealer display rooms, where it may stand next to the manufacturer's other products and possibly competitors' products. This method yields preference and pricing information in the normal selling atmosphere for the product.

Controlled or test marketing. Some manufacturers will produce a limited supply of the product and give it to the sales force to sell in a limited set of geographical areas that will be given promotional support, printed catalogue sheets, and so on.

Source: For methods of testing consumer products, Edward M. Tauber, 'Forecasting Sales Prior to Test Market', *Journal of Marketing*, January 1977, pp. 80–84; for methods of testing industrial products, Morgan B. MacDonald Jr, *Appraising the Market for New Industrial Products* (New York: Conference Board, 1967), Ch. 2.

should time its introduction for the right season.

Where (geographical strategy). The next decision is whether the company should launch the new product in a single locality, a region, the national market or the international market. Few companies have the confidence, capital and capacity to put new products into full national distribution from the start, and will instead develop a planned market rollout over time. Small companies, in particular, will select an attractive city, undertake a blitz campaign to win a market share, and spread out to other cities after having gained a foothold. Medium-sized companies will generally introduce their product into a state or region and then move nationally. Large companies with national distribution networks, such as car companies, will launch their new models in the national market unless there are production shortages.

To whom (target market prospects). Within the rollout markets, the company must target its distribution and promotion to the best prospect groups. Presumably the company has already profiled the prime prospects on the basis of data gathered during market testing or earlier. Prime prospects for a new consumer product would ideally have four characteristics:[12] (i) they would be early adopters of the product; (ii) they would be heavy users of the product; (iii) they would be looked upon as opinion leaders and give the product good word of mouth and influence others to buy it; (iv) they could be reached at a low cost.

How (introductory marketing strategy). The final step is to develop the marketing strategy for introducing the new product into the rollout markets. It calls for allocating the marketing budget among the marketing-mix elements, and sequencing the various activities. Thus the electric car's launch might be preceded by a major publicity campaign several weeks before the car arrives in the showrooms, then by a major advertising campaign once it arrives in the showrooms, and then by offers of gifts to draw more people to the showrooms.

In making these various commercialization decisions, management should be guided by the useful findings in the field known as innovation diffusion and adoption theory (see Table 11-4). These findings clearly point out the high risks involved in new-product development and the careful planning that is needed. In the case of the electric car, it turns out that Ford Motor Company has made the largest investment among the big multinational car makers, but has become pessimistic about early market acceptance. Ford has been endeavouring to perfect a sodium-sulphur battery with a twenty-year life. Until this happens and it can produce a car up to the market's standard, it would rather wait than have another failure on its hands like the infamous Edsel. It is also unlikely that Australia will be selected as the initial market for electric vehicles, although some new products are marketed here prior to international release. For example, Chloride Batteries test-marketed its Torque Starter battery (sealed, no water added, immobilized acid) in Townsville and then the rest of Australia before considering the United Kingdom and United States.[13]

PRODUCT LIFECYCLE STRATEGIES

Once a new product is launched, management crosses its fingers and hopes that the product will enjoy a long and happy life. While under no illusion that the product will last for ever, the company does want a decent profit considering all the effort and risk that went into the product's development. Management hopes that its 'question mark' will become a 'star', and expects that it will eventually settle

Table 11-4 Major findings in innovation diffusion and adoption

In launching a new product, a firm should be guided by researchers' major findings in the field of innovation diffusion and adoption theory. These findings can be summarized as follows:

Stages of adoption. Individual consumers go through a series of stages of acceptance in the process of adopting a new product. The stages are awareness, interest, evaluation, trial and adoption. Thus the manufacturer of a new electric car must think about what can be done to efficiently move people through each stage. For example, if people have awareness and interest but are not coming into a dealer's showrooms, the manufacturer must develop promotional incentives to attract people into the showrooms.

Consumer adopter types. People differ markedly in their penchant for trying new products. There are innovators (the first 2.5 per cent to adopt a new product), early adopters (the next 13.5 per cent), early majority (the next 34 per cent), late majority (the next 34 per cent), and laggards (the last 16 per cent). The electric-car manufacturer should try to identify the characteristics of people who are likely to be early adopters, such as having a high income and being active in the community, and should then focus its promotion on this group.

Role of personal influence. Personal influence plays a large role in the adoption of new products. The statements of other people about a new product carry heavy weight with a prospective buyer, especially if the product is risky or costly. The electric-car manufacturer will want to research what opinion leaders and early buyers say to others about the new electric car and to correct any product features that give rise to complaints as soon as possible. The manufacturer may also want to use a 'testimonial advertising' approach in which some attractive sources assure other people that the electric car is reliable and fun to drive.

Innovation characteristics. Certain characteristics of the innovation strongly affect the rate of adoption. The main ones are the innovation's relative advantage over other products, its compatibility with the person's lifestyle, its complexity, its divisibility into small trial units, and its communicability. Thus an electric car will be more appealing to the extent that it saves buyers a lot of money, fits their lifestyle, is simple to operate, can be test driven, and is easy to understand.

Source: These and other ideas are elaborated in Everett M. Rogers & F. Floyd Shoemaker, *Communication of Innovations* (New York: Free Press, 1971).

into being a 'cash cow'; when it becomes a 'dog', this will be the time to drop it.

Portfolio theory, which we reviewed in Chapter 3, has 'product lifecycle theory' (PLC) as one of its major underpinnings. The lifecycle of a typical product exhibits an S-shaped sales curve marked by four distinct stages beyond that of product development (see Figure 11-1).

1. *Introduction* is a period of slow sales growth as the product is introduced in the market. The profit curve in Figure 11-1 shows profits as being almost non-existent in this stage because of the heavy initial expenses.
2. *Growth* is a period of rapid market acceptance and substantial profit improvement.
3. *Maturity* is a period of slowdown in sales growth because the product has achieved acceptance by most of the potential buyers. Profits peak in this period, and then start to decline because of increased marketing outlays to maintain the product's position against competition.
4. *Decline* is the period when sales show a strong downward drift and profits erode.

Not all products pass through the idealized S-shaped product lifecycle illustrated in Figure 11-1. Some products show a rapid growth from the very beginning, thus skipping the slow sales period implied by the introductory stage. Others, instead of going through a rapid-growth stage, go directly from introduction to maturity; some products move from maturity to a second point of rapid growth. Cox studied the lifecycles of 754 ethical-drug products and found six different patterns.[14] The most typical form was 'cycle-recycle' (see Figure 11-5a): Cox explained the second hump in sales as being caused by a traditional promotional push in the decline stage. Some investigators have reported a 'scalloped' pattern (see Figure 11-5b), which represents a succession of lifecycles based on the discovery of new product characteristics, new uses or new markets. The history of nylon's sales

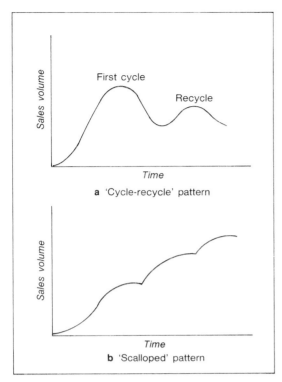

Figure 11-5 Some anomalous product lifecycle patterns

shows a scalloped pattern because of the many new uses – parachutes, hosiery, shirts, carpeting – discovered over time.

The PLC concept should be defined with respect to product class (petrol-powered cars), product form (station wagons), or a brand (Kingswood). The PLC concept has a different degree of applicability in these three cases. Product classes have the longest lifecycles: in many cases their sales can be expected to continue in the mature stage for an indefinite duration, since they are highly population-related (cars, perfume, refrigerators, and steel). Product forms, on the other hand, tend to exhibit the standard PLC histories more faithfully: those such as the 'dial telephone' and 'cream deodorants' seem to pass through a regular history of introduction,

rapid growth, maturity and decline. A brand's sales history can be erratic because changing competitive strategies and tactics can produce substantial ups and downs in sales and market shares, even to the extent of causing a mature brand to suddenly exhibit another period of rapid growth.

The PLC concept can also be applied to what are known as styles, fashions and fads; their special features are described in Exhibit 11-1.

The PLC concept is useful mainly as a framework for developing effective marketing strategies in different stages of the product lifecycle. We now turn to the major stages and consider appropriate marketing strategies.

Introduction Stage

The introduction of a new product into one or more markets takes time, and sales growth is apt to be slow. Such well-known products as instant coffee and tea-bags lingered for many years before they entered a stage of rapid growth. Buzzell identified four causes for the slow growth of many processed food products: (i) delays in expanding production capacity; (ii) technical problems ('working out the bugs'); (iii) delays in making the product available to customers, especially in obtaining adequate distribution through retail outlets; (iv) customer reluctance to change established behaviour patterns.[15] In the case of expensive new products, sales growth is retarded by additional factors such as the small number of buyers who are attuned to innovations and the high cost of the product.

In the introductory stage, profits are negative or low because of low sales and heavy distribution and promotion expenses. Much money is needed to attract distributors and 'fill the pipelines'; promotional expenditures are at their highest ratio to sales 'because of the need for a high level of promotional effort to (i) inform potential consumers of the new and unknown product; (ii) induce trial of the

Exhibit 11-1 Style, Fashion and Fad Cycles

In product markets where style and fashion are influential, cycles can also be observed, and it is important that marketers understand and try to predict them.

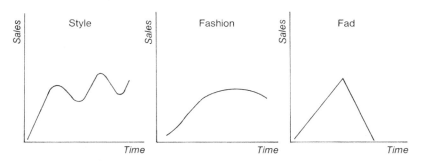

A *style* is a basic and distinctive mode of expression. For example, there are styles in homes (colonial, Spanish, Cape Cod), clothing (formal, casual), and art (realistic, surrealistic, abstract). Once a style is invented it may last for generations, coming in and out of vogue. A style exhibits a cycle of several lives of renewed interest.

A *fashion* is a currently accepted or popular style. For example, jeans are a fashion in today's clothing, and disco is a fashion in today's dance. Fashions tend to pass through four stages. In the distinctiveness stage, some consumers take an interest in something new to set themselves apart from other consumers; the products may be custom-made or produced in small quantities by some manufacturers. In the emulation stage, other consumers take an interest out of a desire to emulate the fashion leaders, and additional manufacturers begin to produce larger quantities of the product. In the mass fashion stage, the fashion has become extremely popular and manufacturers have geared up for mass production. Finally, in the decline stage, consumers start moving toward other incipient fashions that are beginning to catch their eye.

Thus fashions tend to grow slowly, remain popular for a while, and decline slowly. The length of a fashion cycle is hard to predict. Wasson believes that fashions come to an end because they represent an inherent purchase compromise and the consumer eventually starts looking for the missing attributes elsewhere. For example, as cars get shorter, they get less comfortable and a growing number of buyers start wanting longer cars. Furthermore, if too many consumers adopt a fashion this can turn others away. Reynolds suggests that the length of a particular fashion cycle depends on the extent to which the fashion meets a genuine need, is consistent with other social trends, norms and values, and does not meet technological limits as it develops. Robinson, however, sees fashions as living out inexorable cycles regardless of economic, functional or technological changes in society.

Fads are particular fashions that come quickly into the public eye, are adopted with great zeal, peak early, and decline very fast. Their acceptance cycle is short, and they tend to attract only a limited following. They often have a novel or capricious aspect, as with 'pet rocks' or Rubik's cubes, or when people run naked and 'streak'. Fads appeal to people who are searching for excitement, or want to distinguish themselves from others or have some-

Exhibit 11-1 (continued)

thing to talk about. Fads do not survive because they normally do not satisfy a strong need or do not satisfy it well. It is difficult to predict whether something will only be a fad, and if so, how long it will last — a few days, weeks or months. The amount of media attention it receives is one of several factors that will influence its duration.

Source: Prepared from various sources including Chester R. Wasson, 'How Predictable Are Fashion and Other Product Life Cycles?', *Journal of Marketing*, July 1968, pp. 36–43; William H. Reynolds, 'Cars and Clothing: Understanding Fashion Trends', *Journal of Marketing*, July 1968, pp. 44–49; and Dwight E. Robinson, 'Style Changes: Cyclical, Inexorable, and Foreseeable', *Harvard Business Review*, November–December 1975, pp. 121–31.

product; and (iii) secure distribution in retail outlets.'[16]

There are only a few competitors, and they produce basic versions of the product since the market is not ready for individual refinements. The firms direct their selling effort to those buyers who are the readiest to buy, usually higher-income groups. Prices tend to be on the high side because: '(i) costs are high due to relatively low output rates; (ii) technological problems in production may have not yet been fully mastered; and (iii) high margins are required to support the heavy promotional expenditures which are necessary to achieve growth.'[17]

Growth Stage

If the new product satisfies the market, sales will start climbing substantially. The early adopters will continue to purchase and a large number of conventional consumers will begin to follow their lead, especially if there is favourable word of mouth. New competitors, attracted by the opportunities for large-scale production and profit, will enter the market and introduce new-product features, thus expanding the market. The increase in the number of competitors leads to an increase in the number of distribution outlets, and factory sales jump just to fill the pipelines.

Prices tend to remain where they are, or fall only slightly, during this period, in so far as demand is increasing quite rapidly. Com-

panies maintain their promotional expenditures at the same or at a slightly raised level, to meet competition and continue educating the market. Sales rise much faster, causing a decline in the promotion-sales ratio. Profit margins peak, as promotion costs are spread over a larger volume and unit manufacturing costs fall faster than price declines due to the 'experience curve' effect (i.e. the rate at which costs fall as a result of production experience).[18] During this stage the firm tries to sustain rapid market growth as long as possible, which is accomplished in several ways:

1. The firm undertakes to improve product quality and add new-product features and models.
2. It vigorously searches out new market segments to enter.
3. It keeps its eyes open for new distribution channels to gain additional product exposure.
4. It uses less advertising copy for building product awareness, and more to bring about product conviction and purchase.
5. It decides when the time is right to lower prices to attract the next layer of price-sensitive buyers into the market.

The firm that aggressively pursues any or all of these market-expanding strategies will increase its competitive position. This comes at additional cost, however, because the firm in the growth stage faces a trade-off between high market share and high current profit. By spending a lot of money on product improvement, promotion and distribution, it may come to dominate the market; but it forgoes maximum current profit in the hope, presumably, of making up for this in the next stage.

Maturity Stage

At some point the rate of sales growth will slow down and the product will enter a stage of relative maturity. This stage normally lasts much longer than the previous stages, and it poses some of the most formidable challenges to marketing management. Most products are in the maturity stage of the lifecycle, and therefore most of marketing management deals with the mature product.

The beginning of a slowdown in sales growth has the effect of producing over-capacity in the industry, which leads to intensified competition. Competitors engage more frequently in markdowns and off-list pricing; there is a strong increase in promotional budgets, in the form of trade and consumer deals; other firms increase their R & D budgets to find better versions of the product. These steps, to the extent that they do not stimulate adequate sales increases, mean some profit erosion and weaker competitors start dropping out. The industry eventually consists of a set of well-entrenched competitors whose basic orientation is towards gaining competitive advantage.

The product manager of a mature product should not be content to simply defend its current position – a good offence will provide the best defence. The company should consider the three possible strategies.

Market modification. Here the product manager looks for opportunities to find new buyers for the product. First the manager looks for new markets and market segments that have not yet tried the product. Next the manager looks for ways to stimulate increased usage among present customers. Then the manager may want to consider repositioning the brand to appeal to a larger or faster-growing part of the market.

Product modification. A product manager can also try to change product characteristics – such as product quality, features or style – in order to attract new users and more usage.

A strategy of quality improvement aims at increasing the functional performance of the product in such aspects as durability, reliability, speed and taste. This strategy is effective to the extent that the product is capable of quality improvement, buyers believe the claims about improved quality, and a sufficient number of buyers are highly responsive to improved quality.

A strategy of feature improvement aims at adding new features that expand the product's versatility, safety or convenience. Stewart outlines five advantages flowing from such a strategy:[19]

1. The development of new functional features is one of the most effective means of building a company image of progressiveness and leadership.
2. Functional features are an extremely flexible competitive tool because they can be adapted or dropped quickly, and can often be made optional at very little expense.
3. Functional features allow the company to gain the intense preference of preselected market segments.
4. Functional features often bring the innovating company free publicity.
5. Functional features generate a great amount of enthusiasm from the sales force and distributors.

A strategy of style improvement aims at increasing the aesthetic appeal of the product – the periodic introduction of new-car models is an example of style competition rather than quality or feature competition.

Marketing-mix modification. The product manager should consider the possibility of stimulating sales through altering one or more elements of the marketing mix. One tactic is to cut prices in order to attract new triers and competitors' customers; another is to develop a more effective advertising campaign to attract attention and interest. A more direct way to attract other brand users is through aggressive sales promotion – trade deals, cents-off, gifts and contests. The company can also consider moving into higher-volume market channels, particularly discount channels, if these are in a growth stage. The company can also offer new or improved service to the buyer.

Decline Stage

Most product forms and brands eventually enter a stage of sales decline. The decline may be slow, as in the case of porridge; or rapid, as in the case of pinball machines. Sales may plunge to zero and the product may be withdrawn from the market, or they may reach a low level and remain there for many years.

Sales decline for a number of reasons. Technical advances may give birth to new-product classes and forms, which become effective substitutes. Changes in fashion or tastes lead to buyer erosion. The lower costs of imported products hurt the domestic producers. All of these have the effect of intensifying overcapacity and price competition, leading to a serious diminution of profits.

As sales and profits decline, a number of firms withdraw from the market in order to invest their resources in more profitable areas. Those remaining in the industry tend to reduce the number of product offerings, withdraw from smaller market segments and marginal trade channels, and reduce promotion budgets and even prices.

Carrying a weak product is usually very costly to the firm, and not simply in terms of uncovered overhead and profit. No financial accounting can adequately convey all the hidden costs: the weak product tends to consume a disproportionate amount of management's time; it often requires frequent price and inventory adjustment; it generally involves short production runs in spite of expensive setup times; it requires both advertising and salesforce attention that might better be diverted to making 'healthy' products more profitable; its very unfitness can cause customer misgivings and cast a shadow on the company's image. The biggest cost, however, may well lie in the future. By not being eliminated at the proper time, these products delay the aggressive search for replacement products; they create a lopsided product mix, long on 'yesterday's breadwinners' and short on 'tomorrow's breadwinners'; they depress current profitability and weaken the company's grasp on the future.

A company faces a number of tasks and decisions to ensure the effective handling of its aging products.

Identifying weak products. The first task is to establish a system that will identify those products that are in a declining stage. Six steps are involved:

1. A product-review committee is appointed, which includes representatives from marketing, manufacturing, and the financial controller's office.
2. This committee meets and develops a set of objectives and procedures for reviewing weak products in the company's mix.
3. The functional representatives provide data for each product showing trends in market size, market share, prices, costs and profits.
4. This information is run against a computer programme that identifies the most dubious products. The criteria include the number of years of sales decline, market-share trends, gross profit margin, and return on investment.
5. Products on the 'dubious' list are then reported to those managers responsible for

them. The managers fill out forms showing where they think sales and profits will go both with no change in the current marketing programme and with their recommended changes.

6. The review committee examines the rating for each dubious product, and makes a recommendation to leave it alone, modify its marketing strategy, or drop it.[20]

Determining marketing strategies. In the face of declining sales, some firms abandon the market earlier than others; those that remain enjoy a temporary increase in sales as they pick up the customers of the withdrawing firms. Thus any particular firm faces the issue of whether it should be the one to stay in the market until the end.

If it decides to stay in the market, the firm faces further strategic choices. First, the firm could adopt a continuation strategy, in which case it continues its past marketing strategy: some market segments, channels, pricing and promotion. Second, it could follow a concentration strategy, in which case it concentrates its resources only in the strongest markets and channels while phasing out its efforts elsewhere. Finally, it could follow a harvesting strategy, in which case it sharply reduces its expenses to increase its current profits, know-ing that this will accelerate the rate of sales decline and ultimate demise of the product. In some situations, hard-core buyer loyalty may remain strong enough to allow the product to be marketed at a greatly reduced level of promotion, and at the old or even a higher price, both of which mean good profits.

The drop decision. When a product has been singled out for elimination, the firm faces some further decisions. First, it has the option of selling or transferring the product to someone else or dropping it completely. Second, it has to decide whether the product should be dropped quickly or slowly. Third, it has to decide on the necessary level of inventory and service of parts to maintain to cover existing units.

The key characteristics of each of the four stages of the product lifecycle are summarized in Table 11-5; also included are the typical responses made by business organizations in each stage.[21]

SUMMARY

More and more organizations are recognizing the advantages of developing new goods and services. Their current offerings are facing

Table 11-5 Product lifecycle: characteristics and responses

	Introduction	Growth	Maturity	Decline
Characteristics				
Sales	Low	Fast growth	Slow growth	Decline
Profits	Negligible	Peak levels	Declining	Low or zero
Cash flow	Negative	Moderate	High	Low
Customers	Innovative	Mass market	Mass market	Laggards
Competitors	Few	Growing	Many rivals	Declining number
Responses				
Strategic focus	Expand market	Market penetration	Defend share	Productivity
Marketing expenditures	High	High (declining %)	Falling	Low
Marketing emphasis	Product awareness	Brand preference	Brand loyalty	Selective
Distribution	Patchy	Intensive	Intensive	Selective
Price	High	Lower	Lowest	Rising
Product	Basic	Improved	Differentiated	Rationalized

Source: Peter Doyle, 'The Realities of the Product Life Cycle', *Quarterly Review of Marketing*, Summer 1976, p. 5.

shortening life spans and must be replaced by newer products.

New-product development, however, can lead to costly failures. The risks of innovation are as great as the rewards. A large percentage of new products fail in the marketplace, and a still larger percentage have to be dropped before commercialization. They key to successful innovation lies in developing better arrangements for handling new-product ideas, and sound research and decision procedures at each stage of the development process.

The new-product development process consists of eight stages: idea generation, idea screening, concept development and testing, marketing strategy and development, business analysis, product development, market testing, and commercialization. The purpose of each is to decide whether the idea should be further developed or dropped. The company seeks decision criteria for each stage, to minimize the chances of poor ideas moving forward and good ideas being rejected. The last stage, commercialization, is that of introducing the products that have passed the previous tests; it is benefited by marketing planning and strategy based on an understanding of the consumer-adoption process.

Every new product that is launched enters a product lifecycle marked by a changing set of problems and opportunities. The sales history of the typical product is commonly thought to follow an S-shaped curve made up of four stages. The introduction stage is marked by slow growth and minimal profits as the product is pushed into distribution. If successful, the product enters a growth stage marked by rapid sales growth and increasing profits. During this stage the company attempts to improve the product, enter new market segments and distribution channels, and reduce its prices slightly. There follows a maturity stage in which sales growth slows down and profits stabilize. The company seeks innovative strategies to renew sales growth, including market, product and marketing-mix modification. Finally, the product enters a stage of decline in which little can be done to halt the deterioration of sales and profits. The company's task during this period is to identify the truly declining products, develop for each one a strategy of continuation, concentration or harvesting, and finally phase out the product in a way that minimizes hardship to company profits, employees and customers.

QUESTIONS FOR DISCUSSION

1. Discuss what you believe to be the two most important reasons why successful new-product development may be even more difficult in the future.

2. The guiding principle in the idea-generation stage is to limit the number of new-product ideas that are proposed. Comment.

3. At what stage in the new-product development process is the consumer first contacted? Explain briefly.

4. Once the marketing strategy development stage is completed the firm then begins actual product development. Comment.

5. What type of market testing would you suggest for the following new products?
   - Clairol hair-care products
   - Mitsubishi line of trucks
   - Samsonite plastic suitcases.

6. Is the first stage in the product lifecycle simply an extension of the final stage in the new-product development process?

7. Discuss the role and importance of promotional expenditures in each stage of the product lifecycle.

8. Which one of the strategies discussed in the maturity stage did the following utilize?
   - Johnson & Johnson baby shampoo
   - flavoured-milk marketers (Big M, Moove, etc.)
   - marketers of wet-shaving systems (razors, blades).

9. There is nothing the manager can do once a product reaches the decline stage. Comment.

NOTES

1 Christopher De Fraga, 'Vale to the Bulky Valiant', *Age*, 15 September 1981, p. 21.

2 David S. Hopkins & Earl L. Bailey, 'New Product Pressures', *Conference Board Record*, June 1971, pp. 16–24.

3 See *Organization for New-Product Development* (New York: The Conference Board, 1966); and David S. Hopkins, *Options in New Product Organization* (New York: The Conference Board, 1974).

4 For a useful discussion of creativity techniques, see Sidney J. Parnes & Harold F. Harding (eds), *Source Book for Creative Thinking* (New York: Scribner's, 1962), p. 255.

5 See Alex F. Osborn, *Applied Imagination* (New York: Scribner's, 3rd edn, 1963), pp. 286–87.

6 Osborn, p. 156.

7 Mack Hanan, 'Corporate Growth through Venture Management', *Harvard Business Review*, January–February 1969, p. 44.

8 Refinements of this technique can be found in John T. O'Meara Jr, 'Selecting Profitable Products', *Harvard Business Review*, January–February 1961, pp. 83–89; and John S. Harris, 'New Product Profile Chart', *Chemical and Engineering News*, April 1969, pp. 110–18.

9 The physical life expectancies (in years) of some major appliances are: freezer, 20.4; refrigerator, 15.2; electric range, 12.1; colour television, 12.0; automatic washing machine, 10.8. See M. D. Ruffin & K. J. Tippett, 'Service Life Expectancy of Household Appliances: New Estimates from the USDA', *Home Economics Research Journal*, 3 (1975), pp. 159–70.

10 See Edward M. Tauber, 'Forecasting Sales Prior to Test Market', *Journal of Marketing*, January 1977, pp. 80–84. Also see Robert Blattberg & John Golanty, 'Tracker: An Early Test Market Forecasting and Diagnostic Model for New Product Planning', *Journal of Marketing Research*, May 1978, pp. 192–202.

11 See Roger A. Kerin, Michael G. Harvey & James T. Rothe, 'Cannibalism and New Product Development', *Business Horizons*, October 1978, pp. 25–31.

12 Philip Kotler & Gerald Zaltman, 'Targeting Prospects for a New Product', *Journal of Advertising Research*, February 1976, pp. 7–20.

13 'Chloride Avoids Glamour of Television', *Rydge's In Marketing*, 7 October 1981, p. 7.

14 William E. Cox Jr, 'Product Lifecycles as Marketing Models', *Journal of Business*, October 1967, pp. 375–84.

15 Robert D. Buzzell, 'Competitive Behaviour and the Product Life Cycle', in John S. Wright & Jac L. Goldstucker (eds), *New Ideas for Successful Marketing* (Chicago: American Marketing Association, 1966), p. 51.

16 ibid.

17 Buzzell, p. 52.

18 See 'Selling Business a Theory of Economics', *Business Week*, 8 September 1973, pp. 86–88.

19 John B. Stewart, 'Functional Features in Product Strategy', *Harvard Business Review*, March–April 1959, pp. 65–78.

20 This system is spelled out in detail in Philip Kotler, 'Phasing Out Weak Products', *Harvard Business Review*, March–April 1965, pp. 107–18.

Also see Paul W. Hamelman & Edward M. Mazze, 'Improving Product Abandonment Decisions', *Journal of Marketing*, April 1972, pp. 20–26.

21 For further reading on the product lifecycle concept, see Theodore Levitt, 'Exploit the Product Life Cycle', *Harvard Business Review*, November–December 1965, pp. 81–94; and Nariman K. Dhalla & Sonia Yuspeh, 'Forget the Product Life Cycle Concept!', *Harvard Business Review*, January–February 1976, pp. 102–12.

Product, Branding, Packaging and Service Strategy

12

When is a lipstick more than a lipstick? When an Avon lady sits in your living room and sells it to you. The world's largest seller of cosmetics, whose Australian sales of $100 million contribute to total annual sales of well over two billion dollars, knows that when the customer buys lipstick, she is buying much more than lip colour. No doubt a crucial element of Avon's success is a high-quality product. But why buy Avon and not Revlon, which also makes a high-quality product?

The Avon lady is one of the reasons. The Avon lady's call brings to the buyer a bundle of benefits: convenience, a break from routine, conversation, personal attention, help on how to look better, and even a friend. Avon's product is all of these things, and no other major cosmetics firm makes a similar offer.

Avon markets its wares through an army of one million Avon representatives who call on households in thirty-three countries. The majority of the reps are married women with families who work part time to supplement their husband's incomes. They sell their products to other homemakers whose needs they understand. Suburban housewives in the upper-, lower- and middle-income brackets are the majority of Avon's customers.

Avon maintains strong morale among its sales force through sales training, sales meetings to demonstrate new products, and internal promotions such as prizes and contests. The Avon ladies are paid by a percentage of sales. If orders they put in over three weeks are more than $300, they earn 35 per cent ($105). Anything under $300 worth of orders earn them 25 per cent. There is a great turnover of salespeople because many Avon representatives work only until they can accumulate enough cash to make some major purchases.

Avon's product line is highly diversified – thirteen hundred products, including jewellery and household items. If a customer says that she already uses Revlon lipstick, the representative can turn to jewellery or household items and make a sale. Another very strong support for purchase is the Avon money-back guarantee, which offers a full refund if the customer is not satisfied with the product.

Avon also supplies its salespeople with a handsome colour catalogue. The customer can browse through this catalogue, which lists a few hundred products. The company also runs specials throughout the year to stimulate sales and reduce inventories.

One of the most interesting features of the Avon product is the packaging. The packaging of the product is so important that one-third of Avon's items are repackaged every year. The packages are attractive and often double as reusable containers such as mugs or salt and pepper shakers. Many Avon containers have become collector's items.

Avon's salespeople provide continuous feedback to Avon's management about the satisfaction or complaints or needs of their customers. And when Avon tests new products, these products are first tested in clinics with Avon's own representatives.

Clearly a lipstick is more than a lipstick when Avon sells it.[1]

Avon's exceptional success in the rough-and-tumble cosmetics world is based on developing an original and attractive product concept for its target market. Avon is not just selling cosmetics, but an augmented product that has won a worldwide market following. Marketers do not believe that 'a product is a product is a product'. Constructing the product concept is the most important first step in marketing-mix planning.

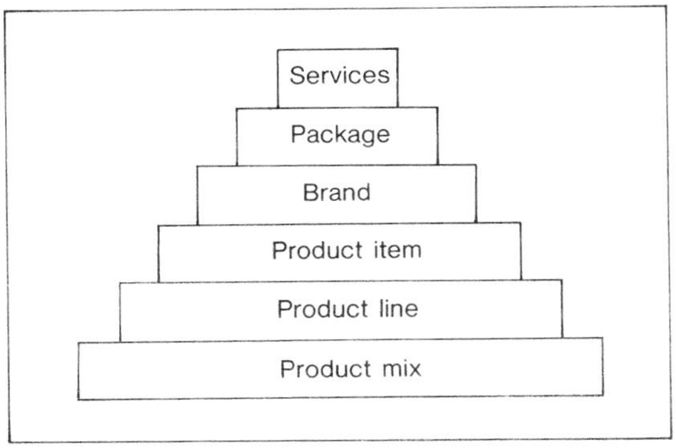

When we examine 'product', the first P of the marketing mix, we find that it is a complex multidimensional concept (see Figure 12-1). An organization's offer to a target market consists of a product mix that is made up of product lines. Each product line contains product items. Each product item is a physical product plus branding plus packaging plus services. The organization has to make decisions and develop strategies for all of these components.

Figure 12-1 Components of 'product'

PRODUCT MIX DECISIONS

Every organization has a product mix. We define product mix as follows:[2]

- A *product mix* (also called product assortment) is the set of all product lines and items that a particular seller offers for sale to buyers.

This definition requires definition of product lines and product items:

- A *product line* is a group of products that are closely related, either because they function in a similar manner, are sold to the same customer groups, are marketed through the same types of outlets, or fall within given price ranges.

- A *product item* is a distinct unit within a product line, that is distinguishable by size, price, appearance or some other attribute. The item is sometimes called a stock-keeping unit, product variant, or subvariant.

Avon's product mix consists of three major product lines: cosmetics, jewellery, and household items. Each of these lines consists of several sublines: for example, cosmetics breaks down into lipstick, powder, and so on. Each line and subline has many individual items.

Altogether, Avon's product mix includes 1300 items. A large supermarket handles as many as 10 000 items; a typical K-Mart stocks 15 000 items; and General Electric manufactures as many as 250 000 items worldwide.

A company's product mix can be described as having a certain width, depth and consistency. These concepts are illustrated in Table 12-1 in connection with selected Unilever consumer products.

The width of Unilever's product mix refers to how many different product lines are carried by the company. If Unilever only carried the four lines shown, then its product mix width would be four. (In fact, Unilever produces many additional lines, including tomato sauce, margarine, canned fish, tea-bags, and so on.)

The depth (also called length) of Unilever's product mix refers to the total number of items or brands. If Table 12-1 represented Unilever's entire product mix, its depth would be eleven. We can also talk about the depth of an average product line at Unilever. This is obtained by dividing the total depth (here 11) by the number of lines (here 4), i.e. the average product line at Unilever consists of 2.8 brands.

The consistency of the product mix refers to how closely related the various product lines are in end use, production requirements, distribution channels or in some other ways. Unilever's product lines are consistent in being consumer goods that go through the same distribution channels (food stores); they are less consistent in so far as they present quite different benefits to buyers.

All three dimensions of the product mix have marketing strategy implications. By increasing the width of the product mix, the company can try to capitalize on its good reputation and skills in present markets. By increasing the depth of its product mix, the company can try to attract the patronage of buyers of widely differing tastes and needs. By increasing the consistency of its product mix,

Table 12-1 Product mix width and product line depth for some Unilever products

	Product mix width			
	Detergents	*Soap*	*Soup*	*Ice-cream*
Product line depth	Drive Omo Surf Wisk Rinso	Lux Pears Lifebuoy	Rosella Continental	Streets

the company can try to acquire an unparalleled reputation in a particular area of endeavour.

PRODUCT LINE DECISIONS

Each product line of a company needs a marketing strategy. Many companies assign a specific person to manage each line and develop a marketing plan. This product-line manager will have to make a number of tough decisions, before which he will analyse the sales, profits and competition facing each item in the line.

The various items in a product line normally contribute different amounts to sales and profits; it is frequently said that the top 20 per cent of the items contribute 80 per cent of the profits (known as the 20-80 rule). A product-line manager should examine the percentage of total sales and profits contributed by each item in the line.

A product line with five items is illustrated in Figure 12-2. The first item contributes 50 per cent of the product line's sales and 30 per cent of its profits. The first two items contribute 80 per cent of the product line's sales and

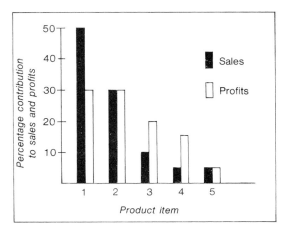

Figure 12-2 **Product item contributions to a product line's total sales and profits**

60 per cent of its profits – if these two items were hit hard by a competitor, the product line's sales and profitability would decline drastically. These items must therefore be carefully monitored and defended. On the other hand, the last item only contributes 5 per cent of the product line's sales and profits. The manager should think about dropping this slow seller.

The manager should also review how the product line is positioned against competitors' product lines.[3] Consider a paper company with a product line consisting of paperboard. Two of the major attributes of paperboard are its weight and the finish quality: paper weights are usually offered at standard levels of 90, 120, 150 and 180; finish quality is offered at three standard levels. The product map in Figure 12-3 shows the location of the various items in the product lines of four competitors (A, B, C and D) as well as company X. For example, competitor A offers two product items in the extra-high-weight class with variable finish quality.

Mapping the product line is useful for designing marketing strategy, in showing which competitors' items are competing with each of company X's items. For example, company X's 90-weight/medium-quality paper competes with competitor D's paper; but its 150-weight/medium-quality paper has no direct competitor. The map reveals locations for possible new-product items: for example, no manufacturer offers a 150-weight/low-quality paper.

Another benefit of the product map is that it is possible to identify market segments and even specific customers according to their paper-buying preferences. Figure 12-3 shows the types of paper, by weight and quality, preferred by the general printing industry, the point-of-purchase display industry, and the office supply industry, respectively. The map shows that company X is well positioned to serve the needs of the general printing industry, but on the borderline of serving the other

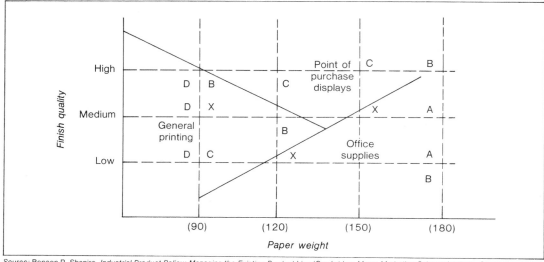

Source: Benson P. Shapiro, *Industrial Product Policy: Managing the Existing Product Line* (Cambridge, Mass: Marketing Science Institute, September 1977), p. 101.

Figure 12-3   Product map for a paper product line

two industries unless it brings out more paper types that meet their needs.

Product-line Length

A major issue facing product line managers is what should be the length of the product line. The line is too short if the manager can increase profits by adding items; it is too long if the manager can increase profits by dropping items.

The question of the optimal length of the product line goes back to the company's objectives. Companies that want to be positioned as full-line companies, and/or are seeking high market share and market growth, will tend to have longer lines. They are less concerned when some items fail to contribute an adequate amount of profit. Companies that are keen on high profitability, on the other hand, will carry shorter lines consisting of 'cherry-picked' (selected) items.

Product lines have a strong tendency to lengthen over time, in an almost unplanned fashion. Several forces are at work:[4]

1. Excess manufacturing capacity puts pressure on the product-line manager to dream up new items.
2. New items are easy to design because they are variations on the existing items.
3. Sales personnel and distributors put pressure on the product-line manager for a more complete product line to satisfy their customers.
4. The product-line manager sees opportunities for additional items in specific products and markets.

As a result, the product-line manager gradually adds items to the product line in the search for more volume and profits. But as items are added, costs go up in the following areas: designing and engineering, inventory-carrying, manufacturing changeover, order-processing, transport and promotion for the new items.

Eventually something happens to call a halt to the mushrooming of the product line. Manufacturing capacity may be in short supply, and top management may refuse to let the line grow any further; or the controller may raise questions about the line's profitability and a study be undertaken to determine how to improve margins. In the latter case the study will show a large number of money-losing items, and they will be pruned from the line in a major effort to increase profitability. This pattern of gradual line growth followed by sudden retrenchment will repeat itself many times, resulting in an undulating 'lifecycle' pattern.

In managing a product line, management must make the following decisions: (i) Should the line be stretched? (ii) Should the line be filled? (iii) Should the line be modernized? (iv) Which item(s) in the line should be featured? These decisions are discussed in the following paragraphs:

Line-stretching Decision

Every company product line stretches over a certain range of the total range offered by the industry as a whole. For example, the Ford LTD is located in the high range of the passenger-car market, the Falcon in the middle range, and the Laser in the low range. Line stretching means lengthening the company's product line beyond its current range, in any of three directions.

Downward stretch. Many companies establish themselves initially at the high end of a market and subsequently add products to the lower end. Beech Aircraft has historically produced expensive private aircraft, whereas Piper has designed less-expensive and smaller private planes. A few years ago Piper decided to design some larger planes; Beech responded by designing some smaller planes. A company may decide to stretch towards the lower end of the market for any of the following reasons:

1. The company is attacked at the high end and decides to counterattack by invading the low end.

2. The company finds that slower growth is taking place at the high end and decides to stretch its product line downwards.
3. The company originally entered the high end in order to establish an image of quality, and always intended to roll downwards.
4. The company adds a low-end unit to fill a hole that would otherwise attract a new competitor.

In making a downward stretch, the company faces some risks. First, the new low-end item might 'cannibalize' higher-end items, leaving the company worse off. Second, the low-end item might provoke competitors to counteract by moving into the higher end. Third, the company's dealers may not be willing or able to handle the lower-end products.

Upward stretch. Companies that are positioned at the low end of the market may want to enter the higher end of the market for either of the following reasons:

1. The company may be attracted by a faster growth rate or higher margins at the upper end of the market.
2. The company may want to position itself as a full-line manufacturer.

When the New South Wales Dairy Promotion Council introduced 'Good One' flavoured milk, it was concerned that sales of its Moove flavoured milk would be cannibalized. However, Good One was positioned as a luxury product with a nutritional emphasis, appealing to an older age-group segment, and was generally accepted with low substitution for Moove.[5]

An upward-stretch decision is accompanied by several risks. The higher-end competitors may not only be well entrenched but the move may tempt them to enter the lower end of the market. Prospective customers may not believe that the company has the wherewithal to produce quality products for the higher end of the market. Finally, the company's sales representatives and distributors may not have the talent or training to serve the higher end of the market, thus requiring intensive training or new sales reps and distributors.

Two-way stretch. Companies that are strongly positioned in the midrange of a market may decide to go after market dominance by stretching their line in both directions. Texas Instruments' strategy in the electronic hand-calculator market provides an excellent illustration of a two-way stretch. Before Texas Instruments (TI) entered this market, the market was dominated primarily by Bowmar at the low-price/low-quality end and Hewlett-Packard at the high-price/high-quality end (see Figure 12-4). TI introduced its first calculators in the medium-price/medium-quality end of the market, gradually adding more machines at each end. It offered better calculators at the same price as, or at lower prices than, Bowmar, ultimately destroying it; and it designed high-quality calculators selling at a much lower price than Hewlett-Packard calculators, taking away a good share of HP's sales at the higher end. This two-way stretch won TI indisputable leadership in the hand-calculator market.

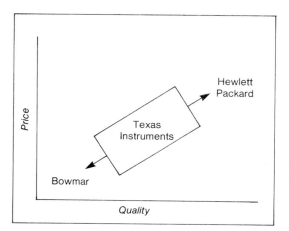

Figure 12-4 Two-way product line stretch, hand calculator market

Line-filling Decision

A product line can also be lengthened by adding more items within the present range. There are five main motives for line filling: (i) reaching for incremental profits; (ii) trying to satisfy dealers who complain about lost sales because of missing items in the line; (iii) trying to utilize excess capacity during slow times; (iv) trying to be the leading full-line house; and (v) trying to keep the competitors from finding holes in the market and filling them.

Line filling can be overdone, resulting in cannibalization and customer confusion. The company should strive to make each item differentiable in the consumer's mind, i.e. each should possess a just-noticeable difference. According to Weber's law, customers are more attuned to relative than to absolute differences[6] – they will perceive the difference between boards two metres long and twenty metres long, but not boards nineteen and twenty metres long. The company should make sure that product item differences within its line are at least as large as just-noticeable differences.

Line Modernization Decision

In some cases the product line is adequate in length but needs to be modernized. For example, a company's line of machine tools may have a 1920s look and lose out to competitors' better-styled lines.

When a company recognizes that its line needs modernization, the issue is whether to overhaul the line piecemeal or in one fell swoop. A piecemeal approach allows the company to test how customers and dealers feel about the new style before committing the whole line; and poses less of a drain on the company's cash flow. A major disadvantage of piecemeal modernization is that it allows competitors to see what the company is doing and gives them time to redesign their own lines.

Line-featuring Decision

The product-line manager typically selects one or a few items for special featuring to draw attention to the line. Sometimes managers promote items (promotional models) at the low end of the line to serve as 'traffic builders'. Thus Myer may announce a special low-priced sewing machine to bring people into the sewing-machine department; once the customers arrive, some salespeople will try to influence them to buy at the higher end of the line.

At other times, managers will feature a high-end item to give the product line 'class' – this practice is common in the advertising of cars displaying various attractive options.

There are other decisions facing product-line managers. They have to set prices on the various items in the line (see Chapter 13), they have to be good at pruning weaker items in the product line (see Chapter 11), and they have to be skilled in planning and managing each individual product in the line. We now turn to the marketing of the individual product line.

PRODUCT ITEM DECISIONS

A pair of skis, a haircut, a television show featuring Bert Newton, and a holiday in Hawaii are all examples of individual product items. We define product as follows:

- A *product* is anything that can be offered to a market for attention, acquisition, use or consumption that might satisfy a need. It includes physical objects, services, persons, places, organizations and ideas. Other names for a product would be the offer, value package, or benefit bundle.

Core, Tangible and Augmented Product

In developing a product to offer to a market, the product planner should distinguish three conceptual levels of a product. At the most fundamental level is the *core product*, which answers the question: What is the buyer really buying? Every product is really the packaging of a problem-solving service. The woman purchasing lipstick from Avon is not simply buying lip colour; she is buying an emotion. Avon's competitor, Charles Revson of Revlon, recognized this early: 'In the factory, we make cosmetics; in the store we sell hope.' Theodore Levitt pointed out that 'purchasing agents do not buy quarter-inch drills; they buy quarter-inch holes.' And supersalesperson Elmer Wheeler would say: 'Don't sell the steak – sell the sizzle.' The marketer's job is to uncover the need hiding under every product and to sell benefits, not features. The core product stands at the centre of the total product, as illustrated in Figure 12-5.

The product planner has to make the core product tangible to the buyer. At this level, it is called the *tangible product*. Lipsticks, computers, educational seminars, political candidates, are all tangible products. If it is a physical object, it may have up to five characteristics: a quality level, features, styling, a brand name, and packaging. If it is a service, it may have some or all of these characteristics in an analogous manner.

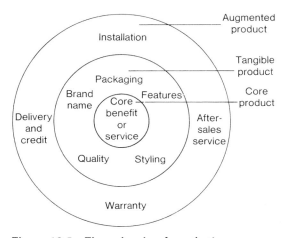

Figure 12-5 Three levels of product

Finally, the product planner has to decide on additional services and benefits that will be offered along with the tangible product. They make up the *augmented product*. We saw how Avon's augmented product – personal attention, delivery, money-back guarantee, and so on – has been a key factor in Avon's success. IBM is another example of a company whose success is traceable to its skilful augmentation of its tangible product – the computer. While the other computer companies were busy telling potential buyers about the features of their computers, IBM recognized that the customer was actually interested in buying solutions, not hardware. What customers wanted was instruction, canned software programmes, programming services, quick repairs, guarantees, and so on. IBM sold a system, not just a computer.[7]

The augmented-product notion leads the seller to look at the buyer's total consumption system, i.e. 'the way a purchaser of a product performs the total task of whatever it is that he or she is trying to accomplish when using the product'.[8] Doing this, the seller should be able to recognize many opportunities for augmenting its product offer in a competitively effective way. According to Levitt:

> The new competition is not between what companies produce in their factories, but between what they add to their factory output in the form of packaging, service, advertising, customer advice, financing, delivery arrangements, warehousing, and other things that people value.[9]

The firm that develops the right augmented product will thrive on this competition.

Classification of Goods

In trying to develop marketing strategies for individual products, marketers have looked at product characteristics and have classified products in ways that would suggest appropriate strategies. A comprehensive classification of goods is shown in Figure 12-6. We will discuss the three major breakdowns shown in the figure.

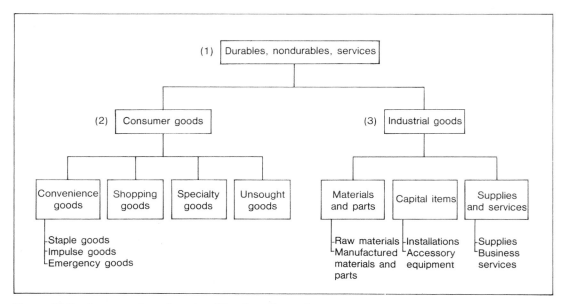

Figure 12-6 A comprehensive classification of goods

Durable goods, nondurable goods, and services. Marketers have suggested that marketing strategies should have some relation to the durability and tangibility of a product. On this basis, three types of product can be distinguished:[10]

- *Nondurable goods* are tangible goods that normally are consumed in one or a few uses. Examples would include beer and soap. Since these goods are consumed fast and purchased frequently, the appropriate strategy is to make them available in many locations, charge only a small markup, and use a lot of advertising to induce trial and provide post-purchase reinforcement.

- *Durable goods* are tangible goods that normally survive many uses. Examples would include refrigerators and clothing. Durable products are likely to need more personal selling and service, command a higher margin, and require more seller guarantees.

- *Services* are activities, benefits or satisfactions that are offered for sale. Examples would include haircuts and repairs. Services are intangible, inseparable, variable and perishable. As a result, they are likely to require more quality control, supplier credibility, and adaptability. Because of the growing importance of services in our society, their marketing will be examined in detail in Chapter 20.

Consumer goods. Consumers buy a vast number of goods. A useful way to classify these goods is on the basis of consumer shopping habits, because they have implications for marketing strategy. We can distinguish convenience, shopping, specialty and unsought goods.[11]

- *Convenience goods* are those consumer goods that the customer usually purchases frequently, immediately and with minimum effort in comparison and buying. Examples would include tobacco products, soap and newspapers.

Convenience goods can be further subdivided into staples, impulse goods, and emergency goods. Staples are goods purchased on a regular basis, and brand loyalty is a factor that helps the customer choose quickly. For example, for one buyer the routinely purchased soft-drink is Coke, the aspirin is Aspro, the petrol is Ampol. The impulse good is purchased without any planning or search effort and must therefore be available in many places, because once the current need is satisfied the consumer does not normally look for the product. Thus confectionery and magazines are placed next to cash register checkouts because shoppers may not have thought of buying them. The emergency good is purchased when a need is urgent – umbrellas during a storm, and suntan lotion during a heatwave. Manufacturers of emergency goods will try to place them in many outlets so they will not lose the sale when the customer needs these goods.

- *Shopping goods* are goods that the customer, in the process of selection and purchase, characteristically compares on such bases as suitability, quality, price and style. Examples would include furniture, clothing, used cars, and major appliances.

Shopping goods can be divided into homogeneous goods and heterogeneous goods. The buyer sees homogeneous shopping goods as being essentially similar in quality but different enough in price to justify shopping comparisons. Thus consumers might shop for the best buy in a washing machine or a toaster, assuming that the various brands are essentially similar; the seller must be prepared to 'talk price' to the buyer. But in shopping for clothing, furniture, and more heterogeneous goods, other qualities may be more important to the consumer than the price. If the buyer wants a pin-striped suit, the cut, fit and look are likely to be more important than small price differences. The seller of heterogeneous shopping goods must therefore carry a good assortment to satisfy individual tastes and must have well-trained sales personnel who can meet the customer's needs for information and advice.

- *Specialty goods* are goods with unique characteristics and/or brand identification, for which a significant group of buyers are habitually willing to make a special purchasing effort.

Examples would include specific brands and types of cars, hi-fi components, photographic equipment, and men's suits. For example, a Mercedes is a specialty good if buyers who want it are willing to travel to the only Mercedes dealer, who might be kilometres away. Specialty goods do not involve shopping comparisons; the buyer only invests shopping time to reach the outlets carrying these goods. The seller of a specialty good does not necessarily have to be established in a convenient location; however, it is important that prospective buyers receive information as to this location.

- *Unsought goods* are goods the consumer either does not know about or knows about but does not have an interest in purchasing. New products, such as smoke-detectors and food processors are unsought goods until the consumer is made aware of them through advertising. The classic examples of known but unsought goods are life insurance, burial plots, gravestones and encyclopaedias.

By their very nature, unsought goods require a lot of marketing effort in the form of advertising and personal selling. Some of the most important modern techniques in personal selling have developed out of the challenge of selling unsought goods.

Industrial goods. The industrial market buys a vast variety of goods and services. An effective industrial-goods classification would suggest appropriate marketing strategies in the industrial market. It is of little use to classify industrial goods according to the shopping habits of the producers, as we did in consumer-goods classification, because producers do not 'shop' in the same sense. More often suppliers seek them out. Industrial goods are more usefully classified in terms of how they enter the production process and their relative costliness. We can distinguish between materials and parts, capital items, and supplies and services.

- *Materials and parts* are those industrial goods that enter the manufacturer's product completely. They fall into two classes: raw materials and manufactured materials and parts.

Raw materials are exemplified by farm products (e.g. wheat, wool, livestock, fruit and vegetables) and natural products (e.g. fish, timber, crude petroleum, iron ore). Each is marketed somewhat differently. Farm products are supplied by many small producers and require intermediaries to provide assembly, grading, storage, transport and selling services. The supply of farm products is somewhat expandable in the long run, but not in the short run. Farm products' perishable and seasonal nature gives rise to special marketing practices; their homogeneity results in relatively little advertising and promotional activity.

Natural products are highly limited in supply. They usually have great bulk and low unit value, and require substantial forms of transport to move them from producer to user. There are fewer and larger producers, who tend to market their products directly to industrial users; because of user dependency on these materials, long-term supply contracts are common. The homogeneity of natural materials limits the amount of demand-creation activity. Price is the major factor in supplier selection.

Manufactured materials and parts are exemplified by component materials (e.g. iron, yarn, cement, wires) and component parts (e.g. small motors, tyres, castings). Component materials are usually fabricated further – for example, pig iron going into steel, yarn being woven into cloth. The standardized nature of component materials usually means that price and vendor reliability are the most important purchase factors. Component parts enter the finished product completely, with no further change in form, as when small motors are put into vacuum cleaners and tyres are added on cars. Most manufactured materials and parts are sold directly by their producers to industrial users, with orders often placed a year or more in advance. Price and service are the major marketing considerations, and branding and advertising tend to be unimportant.

- *Capital items* are those industrial goods that enter the finished product partly. They include two groups: installations and accessory equipment.

Installations consist of buildings (e.g. factories and offices) and fixed equipment (e.g. generators, drill presses, computers). Installations represent major purchases and determine the scale of operation of the firm. They are usually sold directly by the producer to the industrial user, with the typical sale being large and preceded by a long negotiation period. A top-notch sales force is needed, which often includes sales engineers. The sellers have to be willing to design to specification and to supply postsale services. Advertising is used but is much less important than personal selling.

Accessory equipment comprises portable factory equipment and tools (e.g. hand tools, lift trucks) and office equipment (e.g. typewriters, desks). These types of equipment do not become part of the finished product, nor do they influence the scale of production. They simply aid in the production process. They have a shorter life than installations but a longer life than operating supplies. Although some manufacturers of accessory equipment may sell direct, more often they use intermediaries because the market is geographically dispersed, the buyers are numerous, and the orders are small. Quality, features, price and service are major considerations in vendor selection. The sales force tends to be more important than advertising, although the latter can be used effectively.

- *Supplies and Services* are items that do not enter the finished product at all. Supplies are of two kinds: operating supplies (e.g. lubricants, coal, typing paper, pencils) and maintenance and repair items (paint, nails, brooms).

Industrial supplies are the equivalent of convenience goods in the consumer field, because they are usually purchased with minimum effort on a straight rebuy basis. They are normally marketed through intermediaries because of the great number of customers, their geographical dispersion, and the low unit value of these goods. Price and service are important considerations because supplies are quite standardized and brand insistence is not high.

Business services include maintenance and repair services (e.g. window cleaning, typewriter repair) and business advisory services (e.g. legal, management consulting, advertising). Maintenance and repair services are usually supplied under contract. Maintenance services are often provided by small producers, and repair services are often available from the manufacturers of the original equipment. Business advisory services normally occur in new-task buying, and the industrial buyer will choose the supplier on the basis of reputation and personnel.

The preceding discussion of product classifications makes it clear that a product's characteristics will have a major influence on the marketing strategy. At the same time, marketing strategy will also depend on such factors as the product's stage of the lifecycle, the number of competitors, the degree of market segmentation, and the condition of the economy.

BRAND DECISIONS

In developing a marketing strategy for individual products, the seller has to confront the issue of branding. Branding can add value to a product and is therefore an intimate aspect of product strategy.

First, we should become familiar with the language of branding. Here are some key definitions:[12]

- *Brand* is a name, term, sign, symbol or design, or a combination of these, which is intended to identify the goods or services of one seller or group of sellers and differentiate them from those of competitors.
- *Brand name* is that part of a brand which can be vocalized – the utterable. Examples are Avon, Holden, Bankcard, NSW Institute of Technology, and the Liberal Party.
- *Brand mark* is that part of a brand which can be recognized but is not utterable, such as a symbol, design, or distinctive colouring or lettering. Examples are the Playboy bunny and Chesty Bond.
- *Trademark* is a brand or part of a brand that is given legal protection because it is capable of exclusive appropriation. A trademark protects the seller's exclusive rights to use the brand name and/or brand mark.
- *Copyright* is the exclusive legal right to reproduce, publish and sell the matter and form of a literary, musical or artistic work.

Branding poses a number of challenging decisions to the marketer. The key decisions are described in Figure 12-7 and are discussed in the following paragraphs.

Branding Decision

The first decision is whether the company or its dealers should put a brand name on specific products. Historically, most products went unbranded: producers and intermediaries sold their goods directly out of barrels, bins and cases without any supplier identification. The earliest signs of branding were in the efforts of mediaeval guilds to require craftsmen to put trademarks on their products to protect the tradesmen, and to protect the consumer against inferior quality by allowing producers to be traced. In the high arts, too, branding began with great artists and not-so-great artists signing their names to their works.

In Australia, branding increased rapidly from about 1850, with the various pre-federation parliaments enacting trademark laws by the 1880s. Terms associated with the gold rushes, such as 'digger' and 'nugget' were popular, with the word 'Australia' and maps of the country increasing around the time of federation. Some of the early brands which are still with us include Nugget polish, Vegemite, Rosella, Minties and Taubmans; some less apparent today are Go-Poof deodorant, Kure-ettes medicine, Bobby Dazzler clothing, Diggaburra tea, Kangarooster flour, and Blo-Fli-Di insecticide.[13]

The growth of brand names has been so dramatic that today, in Australia, hardly anything is sold unbranded. Salt is packaged in distinctive manufacturers' containers, oranges are often stamped with growers' names, nuts and bolts are packaged in cellophane with a distributor's label, and various parts of a car – spark plugs, tyres, filters – bear visible brand names different from the name of the car.

At the same time, there has been some indication of a return to no branding of certain staple consumer goods and pharmaceuticals. These 'generics' are packaged plainly with little or no manufacturer identification, the obvious aim being to bring down the cost to the consumer by saving on packaging and

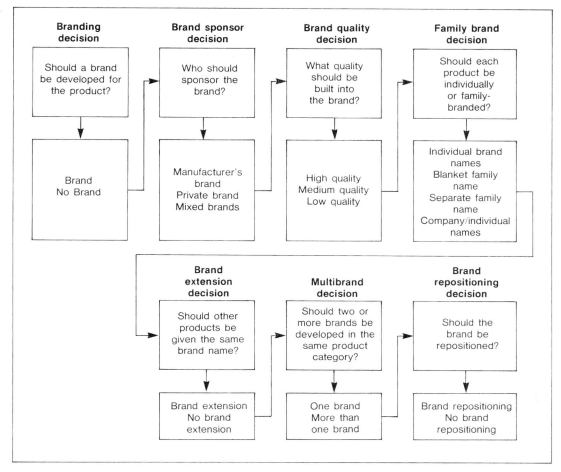

Figure 12-7 An overview of branding decisions

advertising. Thus the issue of branding versus no branding is very much alive today.

This raises the question of why have branding in the first place. Who benefits? How do they benefit? At what cost? We have to look at branding from the buyer's viewpoint, the seller's viewpoint, and society's viewpoint.

Buyer's viewpoint. It is commonly thought that branding is an invention of sellers to serve primarily their own interests. The truth is that buyers in most cases want branding because it is an important information source and creates a number of buyer benefits.

First, a brand tells the buyer something about the product's quality. Suppose a buyer goes shopping for a television set and sees several different sets, none of them carrying brand names. The buyer could tell very little about the quality and reliability of the various sets. In the USSR, where television sets are produced in different factories and not branded, consumers look for factory identification marks on the sets because the factories have different reputations for reliability. The Soviet consumer would welcome branding as a way to determine the quality of different products.

Second, brand names contribute to increased shopping efficiency. Imagine the homemaker going into a supermarket and finding thousands of unlabelled products. The homemaker would probably want to touch, taste or smell many of the products to be sure of their quality, which could vary from week to week. On asking another member of the family to do the shopping, the homemaker would have to communicate the quality desired in each product. It is far more efficient to communicate in brand names than in general product descriptions.

Third, brand names help call consumers' attention to new products that might benefit them. They become the basis upon which a whole story can be built about the new product and its special qualities.

Seller's viewpoint. But why should sellers resort to branding when it clearly involves a cost – packaging, labelling, legal protection – and a risk if the product should prove unsatisfying to the user? It turns out that branding gives the seller several advantages.

First, the seller's brand name makes it easier for the seller to handle orders and track down problems. Thus Carlton & United Breweries receives an order from a retailer for a hundred cartons of Crown Lager beer instead of an order for 'some of your better beer'. Furthermore, the seller finds it easier to trace the order if it is mis-shipped, or to find out why the beer was rancid if consumers complain.

Second, the seller's brand name and trademark give it legal protection when there are unique product features which would otherwise be easy to copy.

Third, branding gives the seller the opportunity to attract a loyal set of customers whose regular purchases give it more sales stability and long-run profit. This is accomplished by supporting the brand with good product quality and promotion. The degree to which the brand name works to give the seller more profit depends on the seller's success in moving customers through the states of brand recognition, brand preference and, ultimately, brand insistence.

Society's viewpoint. The question arises as to whether branding benefits society as a whole, and how much branding is necessary or desirable in particular product categories. Those who favour branding offer the following arguments:

1. Branding leads to higher and more consistent product quality. A brand essentially makes a promise to consumers about delivering certain satisfactions. The seller cannot easily tamper with the brand's quality or be careless about quality control because the consumers have developed certain expectations. Branding also makes it advantageous for some sellers to go after the high-quality end of the market.
2. Branding increases the rate of innovation in society. Branding gives producers an incentive to seek distinctive product features that could be protected against imitating competitors, and this results in much more product variety and choice for consumers.
3. Branding increases shopper efficiency, since it provides much more information about the product and where to buy it.

Others criticize branding for reasons including the following:

1. Branding leads to false and unnecessary differentiation of goods, especially in homogeneous product categories.
2. Branding leads to higher consumer prices, since the brands have to be supported by a lot of advertising, packaging and other costs which are ultimately passed on to consumers.
3. Branding increases the status consciousness of people who buy certain brands to impress others.

Overall, it is probably safe to say that branding adds net value to consumers and society, but it can be overdone in some categories and lead to higher costs. The societal issues posed by branding will be examined in Chapter 21.

Brand Sponsor Decision

After the branding decision has been made, the manufacturer has three options with respect to brand sponsorship. First, the product may be launched as a manufacturer's brand (also called a national brand), where the manufacturer is recognized as the producer. Second, the manufacturer may sell the product in bulk to intermediaries which apply a private brand (also called house brand, distributor brand or dealer brand). Third the manufacturer may decide to produce some output under its own name and some that is sold under private labels. For example, Kellogg, International Harvester and IBM produce virtually all of their output under their own brand names. Ensign Laboratories produces virtually all of its output under various distributors' names. Drug Houses of Australia produces output both under its own name and under distributors' names.

Manufacturers' brands tend to dominate the Australian scene. Consider such well-known brands as Heinz soup and Cadbury chocolate. In recent times, however, large retailers and wholesalers have turned to developing their own brands. For example, Coles has Embassy, Farmland, K-Mart and other private labels, which account for a substantial proportion of its total sales.

Why do intermediaries bother to sponsor their own brands? They have to hunt down qualified suppliers to make sure that they deliver the specified quality. They have to order in fairly large quantities, tie up their capital in inventories, and be exposed to the risks of fire, theft, obsolescence and deterioration. They have to do some promotion of the private label. They have to take the risk that if the product is not good, the customer will develop a negative image about their other products.

In spite of these possible disadvantages, intermediaries are turning to private brands because they can make money on them. They can often find manufacturers which have excess capacity and will produce the private label at a low cost; other costs, such as advertising and physical distribution, may also be low. This means that the private brander is able to charge a lower price and often make a higher profit margin. Furthermore, the private brander may be able to develop brand preference or brand insistence, and this will draw traffic into its stores for brands that other retailers cannot duplicate.

The competition between manufacturers' and intermediaries' brands is often called the battle of the brands. In this confrontation, intermediaries have many advantages. Retail shelf-space is scarce, and many manufacturers, especially newer and smaller ones, cannot introduce products into distribution under their own name. Intermediaries take special care to maintain the quality of their brands, thus building consumers' confidence. Many buyers know that the private-label brand is often manufactured by one of the larger manufacturers anyway. Intermediaries' brands are often priced lower than comparable manufacturers' brands and thus appeal to budget-conscious shoppers, especially in times of inflation. Intermediaries give more prominent display to their own brands and make sure they are better stocked. For these and other reasons, the former dominance of the manufacturers' brands is weakening. Indeed, some marketing commentators predict that intermediaries' brands will eventually knock out all but the strongest manufacturers' brands.

Manufacturers of national brands are in a very trying situation. Their instinct is to spend a lot of money on consumer-directed advertising and promotion to maintain strong brand preference. Their price may be somewhat higher to cover this promotion. At the same time, the mass distributors exert considerable pressure on them to put more of their promotional money toward trade allowances and deals if they want adequate shelf-space. Once manufacturers start giving in, they have less to spend on consumer promotion and their brand leadership starts slipping. This is the national brand manufacturers' dilemma.[14]

Brand Quality Decision

In developing a brand, the manufacturer has to establish the brand's quality level and other attributes that will support its targeted position in the marketplace. Quality is one of the major positioning tools of the marketer: it stands for the rated ability of the brand to perform its functions, an overall measure reflecting the product's durability, reliability, precision, ease of operation and repair, and other valued attributes. Some of these attributes can be measured objectively; from a marketing point of view, quality should be measured in terms of buyers' perceptions of quality.

Most brands are established initially at one of four quality levels: low, average, high and superior. In one study investigators found that profitability rose with brand quality (see the curve in Figure 12-8a).[15] This suggests that a company should aim at delivering high quality; superior quality increases profitability only slightly over high quality, whereas inferior quality hurts profitability substantially. At the same time, if all competitors tried to deliver high quality, this would not be as effective – quality must be chosen with a target market segment in mind.

Another issue is how a company should manage brand quality through time. The three options are illustrated in Figure 12-8b. The first option, where the manufacturer invests in continuous research and development to improve the product, usually produces the highest return and market share. Mercedes-Benz is a major practitioner of product improvement strategy, which, combined with the high initial product quality, helps explain

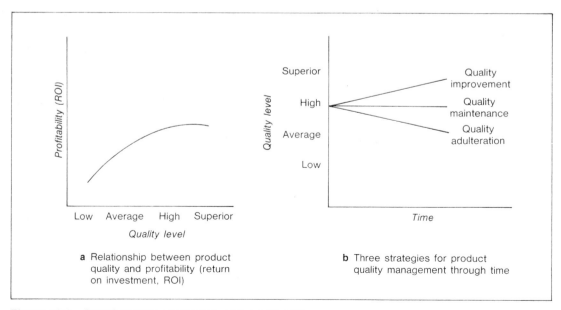

a Relationship between product quality and profitability (return on investment, ROI)

b Three strategies for product quality management through time

Figure 12-8 Brand quality strategies and profitability

its leading position. The second option is to maintain product quality – many companies leave their quality unaltered after its initial formulation unless glaring faults or opportunities occur. The third option is to reduce product quality through time. A few companies will adulterate their products quite deliberately as a way to increase profits, at least in the short run.

Family Brand Decision

Manufacturers who choose to produce most of their output under their own name still face several choices. At least four brand-name strategies can be distinguished:

1. *Individual brand names.* This policy is followed by Unilever (Omo, Drive, Surf, etc.).
2. *A blanket family name for all products.* This policy is followed by such companies as General Electric.
3. *Separate family names for all products.* This policy is followed by Coles (Farmland, Embassy, etc.).
4. *Company trade name combined with individual product names.* This policy is followed by Kellogg (Kellogg's Rice Bubbles and Kellogg's Raisin Bran).

What are the advantages of the first strategy? A major advantage of individual brand names is that the company does not tie its reputation to the product's acceptance. If the product fails, it is not a bad mark for the manufacturer; if the new product is of lower quality, the company does not dilute its reputation.

The opposite policy, that of using a blanket family name for all products, also has some advantages. The cost of introducing the product will be less, because there is no need for 'name' research, or for expensive advertising to create brand-name recognition and preference. Furthermore, sales will be strong if the manufacturer's name is good. Thus Heinz is able to introduce new soups under its brand name with extreme simplicity and instant response.

Where a company produces or sells quite different types of products, it may not be appropriate to use one blanket family name. Thus when Mead Johnson developed a diet supplement for gaining weight, it created a new family name (Nutriment) to avoid confusion with its family brand for weight-reducing products (Metrecal). Companies will often invent different family brand names for different quality lines within the same product class, or for other reasons of distribution. Thus Electrolux sells its appliances directly to consumers under its own name, but uses the Volta name for appliances sold via traditional retail outlets.

Finally, some manufacturers will want to associate their company name with an individual brand for each product. In these cases, the company name legitimizes and the individual name individualizes the new product. Thus the Peters in 'Peters Eskimo Pie' allows the new product to benefit from the company's reputation in the ice-cream field and Eskimo Pie allows room to individualize and dramatize the product.

The brand name chosen should not be a casual afterthought, but an integral reinforcer of the product concept. Among the desirable qualities for a brand name are: (i) it should suggest something about the product's benefits (e.g. Frigidaire, Beautyrest, Craftsman, Accutron); (ii) it should suggest product qualities such as action, colour or whatever (e.g. Wisk, Sunkist, Spic and Span, Pure and Simple); (iii) it should be easy to pronounce, recognize and remember. Short names help (e.g. Ajax, Fab); (iv) it should be distinctive (e.g. Moke, Kodak).

Some marketing research firms have developed elaborate name-research procedures including association tests (what images come to mind), learning tests (how easily is the name pronounced), memory tests (how well is the name remembered), and preference tests (which names are preferred).

The goal of many firms is to build a unique brand name that will eventually become identified with the generic product. Such brand names as Hoover, Thermos, Kleenex, Levis, Biro, Scotch (tape) or Durex, and Esky have succeeded in this way. However, their very success has threatened some of the companies with the loss of exclusive rights to the name. Cellophane and shredded wheat are now names in the common domain, as are linoleum and aspirin.

Brand Extension Decision

A brand extension strategy is any effort to use a successful brand name to launch product modifications or additional products. After Nestlé's success with Milo milk additive, it used the brand name to launch a line of confectionery bars. In general, brand extension saves the manufacturer the high cost of promoting new names and confers instant brand quality on the new product. At the same time, if the new product fails to satisfy consumers it might have a negative effect on their attitudes toward other products carrying the same name.[16]

Multibrand Decision

In a multibrand strategy, a seller develops two or more brands that compete with each other. The technique was pioneered by soap companies, and Colgate-Palmolive now produces at least five different detergent brands.

There are several reasons why manufacturers turn to multibrand strategy. First, there is the severe battle for shelf-space in the nation's supermarkets: each brand that the distributors accept gets some allocation of shelf-space. Second, few consumers are so loyal to a brand that they will not try another. The only way to capture the 'brand switchers' is to offer several brands. Third, creating new

brands develops excitement and efficiency within the manufacturer's organization. Companies such as Unilever and Cadbury-Schweppes see their individual managers competing to outperform each other. Fourth, a multi-brand strategy enables the company to take advantage of different market segments. Consumers respond to various benefits and appeals, and even marginal differences between brands can win a large following.[17]

Brand Repositioning Decision

However well a brand is initially positioned in a market, a number of circumstances may call for repositioning thinking: (i) a competitor may have placed its brand next to the company's brand, thus cutting into its market share in that segment; (ii) customer preferences may have shifted, leaving the company's brand less in the centre of a preference cluster; and (iii) new preference clusters may have formed that represent attractive opportunities.

A classic example of repositioning was provided by the Adelaide Milk Supply Cooperative Limited (AMSCOL).[18] AMSCOL produced a wide range of dairy products, but the main contributor to company profits was ice-cream. In the late 1960s, sales of ice-cream plateaued, although the overall market was still growing; competition had increased in the Adelaide market with new eastern entrants such as Streets and Peters. Based on some qualitative research conducted in 1972, AMSCOL was seen as old-fashioned and dull compared with its competitors, although the product was perceived highly and worth a price premium.

This research was supplemented by quantitative research on distribution methods. More ice-cream was being sold in supermarkets than in milkbars and small-goods shops. Based on Nielsen data, the company's market share had declined from 42 per cent to 35 per cent between December 1972 and June 1973, and its share through supermarkets was very low.

Based on this analysis, the company decided to act to reverse the current trend. A marketing manager and a product manager were hired, and other areas of the company were restructured. A new packaging concept was developed, with a theme to incorporate both tradition and modernity, to appeal to homemakers with children under 12 – the heavy user segment. New plastic, one- and two-litre packs were developed; closer attention was paid to the detailing and servicing of the larger supermarket chains; a new advertising strategy was launched. The result was that in the two-litre market segment, which accounted for 76 per cent of ice-cream sales through supermarkets, the company lifted its market share from 30 per cent in April 1974 to 50 per cent by January 1975, despite a declining market. With an average price above industry average, profits of AMSCOL also significantly improved.

PACKAGING DECISIONS

In the case of many products that are offered to the market, the marketer has to confront the issue of packaging. Packaging can vary from a very minor element (e.g. inexpensive hardware items) to a major marketing element (e.g. cosmetics); some packages – such as the Coca-Cola bottle – are world-famous. Many marketers have called packaging a fifth *P* (along with price, product, place and promotion) but most treat packaging as another aspect of product.

We can define packaging as the activities involved in designing and producing the container or wrapper for a product. The container or wrapper is called the package, and may include up to three levels of material. The primary package is the product's immediate container: the bottle holding Old Spice after-shave lotion is the primary package. The secondary package refers to additional layers of material that protect the primary package and which are discarded when the product is about to be used: the cardboard box containing the bottle of after-shave lotion is a secondary package, and provides additional protection and promotion opportunity. The shipping packaging refers to further packaging necessary for storage, identification or transportation: the corrugated boxes carrying six dozen boxes of Old Spice after-shave lotion are shipping packaging. Finally, labelling is part of the language of packaging and refers to any printed information appearing on or with the packaging that describes the product.

Packages go all the way back to the dawn of history. Primitive peoples had to carry wild berries and other fruit from the forests to caves, and they used animal skin and grass baskets as containers. Earthenware was developed eight thousand years ago in China and was shaped into a variety of containers for holding solid and liquid items. Glass appeared in ancient Egypt and became a major container for liquids. By the Middle Ages packaging materials included leather, cloth, wood, stone, earthenware and glass. For centuries, packaging's main role was to hold, protect and transport goods.

In more recent times, packaging has taken on the additional role of a potent marketing tool. Well-designed packaging can create convenience value for the consumer and act as an effective promotional medium for the producer. Various factors have contributed to the potency of packaging as a marketing tool:

1. *Self-service.* An increasing number of products are sold on a self-service basis as a result of the growth of supermarkets and discount stores. The package must now perform many of the sales tasks. It must attract attention, describe the product's features, give the consumer confidence, and make a favourable overall impression.
2. *Consumer affluence.* The rise in consumer

affluence has meant that consumers are willing to pay a little more for the convenience, appearance, dependability and prestige of better packages.

3. *Company and brand image.* Companies are recognizing the power of well-designed packages to contribute to instant consumer recognition of the company or brand. There is hardly a film buyer who does not immediately recognize the familiar yellow packaging of Kodak film.

4. *Innovational opportunity.* Innovative packaging can bring about large benefits to consumers and profits to producers. Uneeda Biscuit's innovation in 1899 of a new type of stay-fresh packaging (paperboard, inner paper wrap, and paper overwrap) was a great success, keeping biscuits in much better condition for a longer period of time than the old boxes, bins and barrels could. Kraft's development of processed cheese in tins helped extend cheese's shelf-life and earned Kraft a reputation for reliability. The first companies to put their wines in casks, their soft-drinks in cans and their sprays in aerosol packs attracted many new customers. Today plastic cooking bags are an area of innovational opportunity.

Developing the package for a new product requires a large number of decisions. The first task is to establish the packaging concept, i.e. a definition of what the package should basically be or do for the particular product. Should the main function(s) of the package be to offer superior product protection, introduce a novel dispensing method, suggest certain qualities about the product or the company, or something else?

A host of further decisions must be made on the component elements of package design – size, shape, materials, colour, text and brand mark. Decisions must be made between much text or little text, between cellophane and other transparent films, a plastic or a laminate tray, and so on. Each packaging element must harmonize with the other packaging elements; size suggests certain things about materials, materials suggest certain things about colours, and so forth. The packaging elements also must be guided by decisions on pricing, advertising and other marketing elements.

After the packaging is designed, it must be put through a number of tests. Engineering tests are conducted to ensure that the package stands up under normal conditions; visual tests, to ensure that the script is legible and the colours harmonious; dealer tests, to ensure that dealers find the packages attractive and easy to handle; and consumer tests, to ensure favourable consumer response.

In spite of these precautions, a packaging design occasionally gets through with some basic flaw that is discovered belatedly. When Arnott-Spillers introduced Casserole for Dogs, the major supermarket operators were prepared to accept the product – except that the packages were too big for many shelves. Consequently, the product was withdrawn and repackaged in a smaller pack.

It should be clear why developing the packaging for a new product may cost thousands of dollars and take from a few months to a year to put into final form. The importance of packaging cannot be overemphasized, considering the several functions it performs in consumer attraction and satisfaction. Companies, at the same time, must pay attention to the growing societal concerns about packaging and make decisions that serve society's interests as well as immediate customer and company objectives (see Exhibit 12-1).

SERVICE DECISIONS

A company's offer to the marketplace usually includes some service component. The service component may be a minor or a major part of the total offer – in fact, the offer can range

Exhibit 12-1 Packaging and Public Policy

Packaging is attracting growing public interest, and marketers who make packaging decisions must be conscious of societal concerns that will affect their packaging decisions. The following four issues should be noted.

1. *Fair packaging and labelling.* The public has traditionally been concerned with packaging and labelling that might be false and misleading. Consumers have also been concerned with the confusing sizes and shapes of packages, which make price comparisons difficult. In response, voluntary industry-wide packaging standards, and packaging regulations in specific industries, have emerged. Consumers have pressed for open dating (to describe the freshness of the product) and continue to lobby for nutritional labelling, ingredient labelling, unit pricing, and item price-marking.

2. *Excessive cost.* Critics have called packaging excessive in many cases, claiming that it raises prices. They point to secondary 'throwaway' packaging and raise the question of its value to the consumer. They point to the fact that the package sometimes costs more than the contents; for example, Evian moisturizer consists of 150 ml of natural spring-water packaged in an aerosol spray selling for $5.50. Marketers retort that critics do not understand all the functions being performed by the package and that marketers, as much as anyone, want to keep packaging costs down.

3. *Scarce resources.* The growing concern over shortages of paper, petroleum and other materials raises the question of whether industry should try harder to reduce its packaging. For example, the growth of nonreturnable glass containers has resulted in using up to seventeen times as much glass as with returnable containers. The throwaway bottle is also an energy waster, which can be ill afforded in this time of energy shortages. South Australia has passed a law imposing deposits on nonreturnable containers.

4. *Pollution.* As much as half of the total solid waste in this country is made up of package material. Many packages end up in the form of broken bottles and bent cans littering the streets and countryside. All of this packaging creates a major problem in solid-waste disposal that is a huge consumer of labour and energy.

All of these questionable aspects of packaging have mobilized public action and interest in new laws that might further affect marketing decision-making as regards packaging. Marketers must be equally concerned, and must attempt to take an ecologically responsible approach when they develop packaging concepts for their products.[19]

from a pure good on the one hand to a pure service on the other. Four categories of offer can be distinguished.

1. A pure tangible good. Here the offer consists primarily of a tangible good such as soap, toothpaste or salt. No explicit services accompany the product.

2. A tangible good with accompanying services. Here the offer consists of a tangible good accompanied by one or more services to enhance its consumer appeal. For example, a motor-vehicle manufacturer sells a car with a warranty, service and maintenance instructions, and so on. Levitt observes that:

> . . . the more technologically sophisticated the generic product (e.g. cars and computers), the more dependent are its sales on the quality and availability of its accompanying customer services (e.g. display rooms, delivery, repairs and maintenance, application aids, operator training, installation advice, warranty fulfillment). In this sense, General Motors is probably more service intensive than manufacturing intensive. Without its services, its sales would shrivel.[20]

3. A major service with accompanying minor goods and services. Here the offer consists of a major service with some additional services and/or supporting goods. For example, airline passengers are essentially buying transportation; they arrive at their destinations without anything tangible to show for their expenditure. However, the trip includes some tangibles, such as food and drinks, a ticket stub and an airline magazine. The service requires a capital-intensive good called an aircraft for its realization, but the primary item is a service.

4. A pure service. Here the offer consists primarily of a service. Examples include psychotherapy and massages. The client of a psychoanalyst receives a pure service, the only tangible elements being an office and a couch.

Thus the company's product can be a good or a service, and additional services might be included. Here we shall focus on customer services accompanying the main offer; services are discussed further in Chapter 20. The marketer faces three decisions with respect to customer service: (i) What elements of customer service should be included in the customer services mix? (ii) What level of service should be offered; (iii) In what forms should the services be provided?

The Service Elements Decision

The marketer's first task is to survey customers to identify the main service elements in the industry and their relative importance. For example, Canadian buyers of industrial equipment ranked thirteen service elements in the following order of importance: (i) delivery reliability; (ii) prompt quotation; (iii) technical advice; (iv) discounts; (v) after-sales service; (vi) sales representation; (vii) ease of contact; (viii) replacement guarantee; (ix) wide range of manufacturer; (x) pattern design; (xi) credit; (xii) test facilities; and (xiii) machining facilities.[21] These rankings suggest that the seller should at least match competition on those elements deemed most important by the customers.

But the issue of which service elements to emphasize is more subtle than this. A customer service element may be highly important and yet not be a determinant of customer preference if all the suppliers are perceived to be equal on this attribute. Consider the following example:

> The Monsanto Company was seeking a way to improve its customer services mix. Purchasing agents were asked to rate Monsanto and two competitors on several attributes. All three companies, it turned out, were seen by customers as offering high delivery reliability and having good sales representatives. However, none was viewed as rendering sufficient technical service. Monsanto then carried out a study to determine how important technical service is to chemical buyers, and found out it had high importance. Monsanto then hired and trained additional technical people and launched a campaign describing itself as the leader in technical service. This discovery gave Monsanto an opportunity to develop a valued difference in the minds of buyers.

The Service Level Decision

Customers not only expect important service elements to be included in the product offer, but they also want the right amount and quality of service. If bank customers face lengthy waits or confront frowning tellers, they will be inclined to switch their business to another bank.

Companies must maintain a constant check on their own and competitors' service levels in relation to customers' expectations. The company can monitor service deficiencies through a number of devices: comparison shopping, periodic customer surveys, suggestion boxes, and complaint-handling systems. The task is not to minimize complaining behaviour but to maximize it so that the company can really know how it is doing and the disappointed customers can obtain satisfaction.

A useful device is to periodically survey a sample of customers to find out how they feel about each service element. Figure 12-9a shows how fourteen service elements (attributes) of a car dealer's service department were rated by customers as to importance and performance. The importance of a service ele-

ment was rated on a four-point scale of 'extremely important', 'important', 'slightly important' and 'not important'. The dealer's performance was rated on a four-point scale of 'excellent', 'good', 'fair' and 'poor'. For example, the first service element, 'Job done right the first time', received a mean importance rating of 3.83 and a mean performance rating of 2.63, indicating that customers felt it was highly important but not being performed particularly well by this service department. The ratings of the fourteen elements are displayed in Figure 12-9b. The figure is divided into four sections. Quadrant A shows the important service elements that are not being offered at the desired performance levels; they include elements 1, 2 and 9. The dealer should concentrate on improving the service department's performance on these elements. Quadrant B shows important service elements where the department is performing well; its job is to maintain the high performance. Quadrant C shows minor service elements

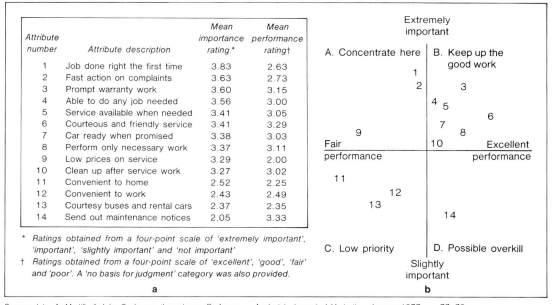

Source: John A. Martilla & John C. James, 'Importance–Performance Analysis', *Journal of Marketing*, January 1977, pp. 77–79.

Figure 12-9 Importance and performance ratings for car dealer's service department

that are being delivered in a mediocre way, but which do not need any attention since they are not very important. Quadrant D shows that a minor service element, 'Send out maintenance notices', is being performed in an excellent manner – a case of possible overkill. This classification of service elements according to their importance and performance provides marketers with guidelines as to where they should concentrate their effort.

The Service Form Decision

Marketers must also decide on the forms in which to offer various service elements. First there is the question of how to price the service element. Consider, for example, what Rank Arena should do in offering repair services on its television sets. Rank Arena has three pricing options:

1. It could offer free television repair service for a year with the sale of its set.
2. It could offer the customer an option to buy a service contract.
3. It could decide not to offer any repair service, leaving this to independent television-repair specialists.

Second there is the question of how the repair service should be provided. Rank Arena has three choices:

1. It could hire and train its own repair people and locate them throughout the country.
2. It could make arrangements with distributors and dealers to provide the repair services.
3. It could leave it to independent companies to provide the necessary repair services.

For each such service element, various options exist as to how it could be provided to customers. The company's decision depends very much on customers' preferences as well as competitors' strategies.

The Customer-service Department

Given the importance of customer service as a competitive weapon, companies would do well to consider developing a strong customer-service department reporting to the marketing manager. Customer-service departments are found in many companies, although their scope and authority vary widely. Ideally, they should integrate and be responsible for a number of customer services, including the following:[22]

1. Complaints and adjustments. The company should establish procedures for facilitating and handling complaints (e.g. some companies have set up 'hot lines'). By keeping statistics on the types of complaints, the customer-service department can recognize and press for changes in product design, quality and control, high-pressure selling, and so on. It is much less expensive to preserve the goodwill of existing customers than to attract new customers or woo back lost ones.

2. Credit service. The company should offer customers a number of options in financing their purchase, including instalment-credit contracts, loans and leasing options. The costs of extending credit are usually more than made up by the gross profit on the additional sales and the reduced cost of marketing expenditures to overcome the customers' objection of not having enough money.

3. Maintenance service. The company should make provision for supplying customers with a parts and service system that is effective, speedy, and reasonable in cost. Although maintenance service is often run by the production department, marketing should monitor customers' satisfaction with this service.

4. Technical service. The company should make sure that customers who buy complex materials and equipment are provided with technical services such as custom design work, installation, customer training, applications research, and process improvement research.

Exhibit 12-2 Product Decisions and Public Policy

Additions to a product mix may be constrained or enhanced by patent laws as well as the merger provisions of the Trade Practices Act. Under the *patent* laws the internal design and development of a similar product which would infringe the rights of an external patent holder is prevented, but an innovative firm can enjoy the benefits of patent protection of a novel product. The *mergers* section of the Trade Practices Act can be raised as an obstacle to product addition via acquisition, if control or domination of a market is likely.

Deletions of a product must be made with an awareness that the firm has legal obligations (written or implied) to its suppliers, dealers and customers which have a stake in the discontinued product.

The Trade Practices Act (section 62) provides for regulations to be prescribed regarding *safety standards* of consumer products in respect to performance, composition, contents, design, construction, finish or packaging of goods, and the form and content of markings, warnings or instructions to accompany the goods. Similarly, section 63 relates to *information requirements* for a product, as are reasonably necessary to give persons using the goods accurate information as to the quantity, quality, nature or value of the goods. As the regulations may also provide for the manner and form in which the information is to be disclosed, the knowledge of these regulations is of paramount importance in the design of packages, labelling and literature accompanying products.

A further important condition implied when goods are supplied is that they are of *'merchantable' quality*, i.e. the goods must be as fit for the purpose or purposes for which goods of that kind are commonly bought as it is reasonable to expect having regard to any description applied to them, the price, and all other relevant circumstances.

Source: Developed from sources including Department of Industry and Commerce, *Marketing a New Product* No. 9 in the Managing the Small Business Series (Canberra: Australian Government Publishing Service, 2nd edn, 1980); and Robin Edwards, *Issues in Marketing Law* (Kensington, NSW: New South Wales University Press, 1982). Also, the Trade Practices Commission, *Packaging and Labelling Laws in Australia* (Canberra: Australian Government Publishing Service, 1977) provides a comprehensive overview of the myriad national and State laws affecting product development, including trade description laws, weights and measures, health and agricultural laws.

5. Information service. The company should consider setting up an information unit that is responsible for answering customer inquiries and providing information on new products, features, processes, expected price changes, order backlog status, and new company policies. The information can be disseminated through company newsletters and selectively to specific customers.

All of the preceding services should be co-ordinated and used as tools in creating customer satisfaction and loyalty.

Thus we see that product strategy is a multidimensional subject calling for decisions on product mix, product-line strategy, and branding, packaging and service strategy. These decisions must be made not only with a full understanding of consumer wants and competitors' strategies, but also with increasing attention to the growing public policy affecting product decisions (see Exhibit 12-2).

SUMMARY

Product is the first and most important element of the marketing mix. Product strategy calls for making coordinated decisions on the product mix, product lines, individual product items, brands, packaging and services.

Product mix describes the set of products offered to customers by a particular seller. The product mix can be described as having a certain width, depth and consistency. All three dimensions of the product mix can be used for strategic positioning.

Each product line in the product mix requires its own strategy. Management should first examine the current items in the line in terms of their relative sales and profit contribution, and how they are positioned against competitors' items. Based on these findings, management can consider various line decisions. Line stretching involves the question of whether a particular line should be extended downward, upward, or both ways. Line filling raises the question of whether additional items should be added within the present range of the line. Line modernization raises the question of whether the line needs a new look, and whether the new look should be installed piecemeal or all at once. Line featuring raises the question as to which end of the line should be featured in promoting the line.

Each product item offered to customers can be looked at on three levels. The core product is the essential service that the buyer is really buying. The tangible product comprises the features, styling, quality, brand name, and packaging of the core product. The augmented product is the tangible product plus the various services accompanying it, such as warranty, installation, service maintenance, and free delivery.

Companies also have to develop brand policies for the product items in their lines. They must decide whether to brand at all, whether to do manufacturing or private branding, what quality they should build into the brand, whether to use family brand names or individual brand names, whether to extend the brand name to new products, whether to put out several competing brands, and whether to reposition any of the brands.

Physical products require packaging decisions that create benefits such as protection, economy, convenience and promotion. Marketers have to develop a packaging concept and test it functionally and psychologically to make sure it achieves the desired objectives and is compatible with public policy.

Finally, companies have to develop a set of customer services that are desired by customers and effective against competitors. The company has to decide on the most important service elements to consider, the level at which each element should be offered, and the form in which each element should be provided. The service mix can be coordinated by a customer-service department that is responsible for complaints and adjustments, credit, maintenance, technical service, and information.

QUESTIONS FOR DISCUSSION

1. Relate the concepts of product mix, product line, and product item to General Motors-Holden's.

2. Discuss the core, tangible and augmented product for your favourite brand of perfume or after-shave lotion.

3. What distinguishes a durable good from a nondurable good? Give an example of each.

4. In how many retail outlets must each type of consumer good (i.e. convenience, shopping, specialty, unsought) be distributed in a particular geographic area? Explain why.

5. Industrial goods always become part of the finished product. Comment.

6. Who benefits from the use of brand names? Explain briefly.

7. National brands are always of higher quality than private brands. Comment.

8. Two of the most expensive and widely discussed brand-name changes in recent years have been Chrysler to Mitsubishi and Bank of New South Wales (and CBA) to Westpac. Why do you think these companies went to this expense?

9. What three factors have contributed to packaging's importance as a strategic tool for marketers? Provide a specific company example for each factor.

10. Describe some of the service decisions that the following marketers must make:
- women's dress shop
- credit union
- sporting goods store.

11. If the Arrow shirt company were planning to develop a customer-service department, what services should the company test?

NOTES

1 See Ross Greenwood & Douglas Aiton, 'How the Other Half Sells', *Business Review Weekly*, 10–16 October 1981, pp. 22–24.

2 This and the following two definitions are (with some modifications) taken from *Marketing Definitions: A Glossary of Marketing Terms*, Committee on Definitions of the American Marketing Association (Chicago: American Marketing Association, 1960).

3 See Benson P. Shapiro, *Industrial Product Policy: Managing the Existing Product Line* (Cambridge, Mass.: Marketing Science Institute, September 1977), pp. 3–5, 98–101. Also see Barbara B. Jackson & Benson P. Shapiro, 'New Way to Make Product Line Decisions', *Harvard Business Review*, May–June 1979, pp. 139–49.

4 See the discussion in Shapiro, pp. 9–10.

5 Pam Mawbey, 'Dairy Council Product Proves to be Good One', *Australian Financial Review*, 7 April 1981, p. 18.

6 See Steuart Henderson Britt, 'How Weber's Law Can Be Applied to Marketing', *Business Horizons*, February 1975, pp. 21–29.

7 Systems selling really originated as systems buying, to describe government practices in buying major weapons and communication systems. Instead of purchasing and putting all the components together, the government would solicit bids from prime contractors who would be willing to assemble the package or system. The winning prime contractor would then buy or bid for the subcomponents. Sellers have increasingly recognized that buyers like to purchase in this way and have responded with augmented product offerings.

8 See Harper W. Boyd Jr & Sidney J. Levy, 'New Dimensions in Consumer Analysis', *Harvard Business Review*, November–December 1963, pp. 129–40.

⁹ Theodore Levitt, *The Marketing Mode* (New York: McGraw-Hill, 1969), p. 2.

¹⁰ The three definitions can be found in *Marketing Definitions*.

¹¹ The first three definitions that follow can be found in *Marketing Definitions*. For further readings on this classification of goods, see Richard H. Holdton, 'The Distinction between Convenience Goods, Shopping Goods, and Specialty Goods', *Journal of Marketing*, July 1958, pp. 53–56; Louis P. Bucklin, 'Retail Strategy and the Classification of Consumer Goods', *Journal of Marketing*, January 1963, pp. 50–55; Leo V. Aspinwall, 'The Characteristics of Goods Theory', in William Lazer & Eugene J. Kelley (eds), *Managerial Marketing Perspectives and Viewpoints* (Homewood Ill.: Richard D. Irwin, rev. edn, 1962), pp. 633–43; and Gordon E. Miricle, 'Product Characteristics and Marketing Strategy', *Journal of Marketing*, January 1965, pp. 18–24.

¹² The first four definitions can be found in *Marketing Definitions*.

¹³ For a fascinating review of the evolution of branding see Mimmo Cozzolino & G. Fysh Rutherford, *Symbols of Australia* (Ringwood, Vic: Penguin, 1980).

¹⁴ See E. B. Weiss, 'Private Label?', *Advertising Age*, 30 September 1974, pp. 27ff. For an excellent example of decision theory applied to a national bakery facing this dilemma, see Robert D. Buzzell & Charles C. Slater, 'Decision Theory and Marketing Management', *Journal of Marketing*, July 1962, pp. 7–16.

¹⁵ Sidney Schoeffler, Robert D. Buzzell & Donald F. Heany, 'Impact of Strategic Planning on Profit Performance', *Harvard Business Review*, March–April 1974, pp. 137–45.

¹⁶ See Theodore R. Gamble, 'Brand Extension', in Lee Adler (ed.), *Plotting Marketing Strategy* (New York: Simon & Schuster, 1967), pp. 170–71.

¹⁷ See Robert W. Young, 'Multibrand Entries', in Adler, pp. 143–64.

¹⁸ Adelaide Milk Supply Co-operative Limited, in Roger A. Layton (ed.), *Australian Marketing Projects 1975-76* (Sydney: Hoover, 1977).

¹⁹ For an overview of relevant issues and authorities see Trade Practices Commission, *Packaging and Labelling Laws in Australia* (Canberra: Australian Government Publishing Service, 1977).

²⁰ Theodore Levitt, 'Production-Line Approach to Service', *Harvard Business Review*, September–October 1972, pp. 41–42.

²¹ Peter G. Banting, 'Customer Service in Industrial Marketing: A Comparative Study', *European Journal of Marketing*, 10, No. 3 (1976), p. 140.

²² See Ralph S. Alexander & Thomas L. Berg, *Dynamic Management in Marketing* (Homewood, Ill.: Richard D. Irwin, 1965), pp. 419–28.

Pricing Strategy

<!-- chapter number graphic: 13 -->

The Staley Company manufactures a recreational vehicle – specifically a caravan – called the Travel-Way, which it sells through franchised dealers at a retail price of $10 000. The dealers have been pressuring the company to add a second caravan, more luxuriously appointed, to expand the line at the higher end. In response, the company has designed the Deluxe and is about to set its price to dealers and customers. Here are the major facts:

1. The company has enough plant capacity to produce up to 500 units per year of the new model. Any more than this would require investing in new plant capacity.
2. The fixed costs of producing the Deluxe are estimated at $500 000. The direct costs are estimated at $10 000 per unit.
3. There is one major competitor producing a high-quality caravan which is retailing for $14 000. The competitor charges its dealers $11 200, which is a 20 per cent dealer discount off the list price. The company estimates that the competitor's profit margin is approximately $1400 per unit. The competitor sells about 600 units per year.
4. The company would like its Deluxe to sell at retail for at least $2200 more than its Travel-Way.
5. The company displayed the Deluxe at the Motor Show, and over two-thirds of the visitors reported that the Deluxe seemed better designed than the competitor's model.

With this information, what dealer and retail price should the Staley Company establish for the Deluxe? If the company is cost-oriented, it could simply start with the fact that each unit costs $10 000 to manufacture and add a markup for the profit it wants per unit. If the company wants $1400 gross profit per unit, the dealers would pay $11 400 and in turn mark it up for the profit they want per unit. The fault with this approach is that it ignores the competitor's price and the consumers' perceived value of the Deluxe.

A market-oriented approach would start with where potential buyers see the value of the Deluxe. For example, if market testing indicates that potential buyers think that the Deluxe is worth at least $500 more than the competitor's caravan, then the company might consider a retail price of $14 500. It might decide to offer its dealers a 22 per cent discount to motivate them at a higher level than the competitor's dealers, which means that dealers would pay $11 310 and the company would make a gross profit of $1310 per unit.

The company should also consider other pricing alternatives. The Deluxe's retail price might be set at $14 499 instead of $14 500 because odd pricing makes the price sound a little lower. Or the Deluxe might be priced at the competitor's price of $14 000 so that the companies are left to fight for market share on the basis of nonprice competition. Or the company might price the Deluxe below the competitor's price, to grab for a higher market share. However, this defeats their wish to price the Deluxe at $2200 or more than the Travel-Way; it could also lead to a higher volume of orders than the company could fill, and thus require increased investment. On the other hand, the company might want to consider pricing the Deluxe higher than $14 500 to suggest a really distinctive vehicle (called prestige pricing).

The Staley Company's pricing problem is even more complicated. The company can produce the Deluxe with optional features (better heating, lighting, bedding, and so on) and will have to figure out a price structure for the different options. Price will also depend on the size of the planned promotion budget because this will affect the company's ability to convince the market to pay a high price. The Deluxe could cannibalize some of the sales of the Travel-Way, depending on how close their prices are. Conversely, the Deluxe could increase the sales of the Travel-Way, since the dealers will be able to attract more traffic with the longer product line.[1]

Many considerations must be taken into account in attempting to set a price on a product. Price will be a major direct determinant of demand, and a major influence on the setting of the other marketing-mix variables. If the Staley Company sets a high price on its new caravan, it must also build in high product quality and plan an expensive promotion programme.

All profit organizations and many non-profit organizations face the task of setting a price on their products or services. Price goes by many names:

Price is all around us. You pay rent for your flat, tuition for your education, and a fee to your doctor or dentist. The airline, railway, taxi and bus companies charge you a fare; the local utilities call their price a tariff; and the local bank charges you interest for the money you borrow. The price for driving your car on the Sydney Harbour bridge is a toll, and the company that insures your car charges you a premium. The guest lecturer charges an honorarium to tell you about a government official who took a bribe to help a shady character steal dues collected by a trade association. Clubs or societies to which you belong may make a special assessment to pay unusual expenses. A lawyer you use regularly may ask for a retainer to cover his services. The 'price' of an executive is a salary, the price of a salesperson may be a commission, and the price of a worker is a wage. Finally, although economists would disagree, many of us feel that income taxes are the price we pay for the privilege of making money![2]

Historically, sellers considered price to be one of the key influences on buyer choice behaviour. In the 1950s and 1960s, however, non-price factors became relatively more important. Table 13-1 shows how US marketing managers ranked twelve marketing activities in 1964; pricing was not named among the five most important factors in marketing success. But by 1980, because of worldwide inflation, many marketers believed that price was the most important element in the marketing mix.

Price is the only element in the marketing mix that creates sales revenues; the other elements are costs. In spite of the importance of setting the right price, most companies do not handle pricing well. The most common mistakes can be summarized as follows: pricing is too cost-oriented, in that companies fail to take sufficient account of demand intensity and customer psychology; price is not revised enough to capitalize on changed conditions in the marketplace; price is all too often set independently of the rest of the marketing mix rather than as an intrinsic element of market-positioning strategy; and price is not varied enough for different product items and market segments.

The pricing function is handled in a variety of ways in different companies. In some companies, pricing is often a decision of top management rather than the marketing or sales department. In large companies, price determination is typically in the hands of divisional and product-line managers. Even here, top management sets the general pricing objectives and policies, and generally has to approve the prices proposed by lower levels of management. In industries where pricing is a key factor (aerospace, electricity, oil)

Table 13-1 Rankings of marketing activities, 1964 and 1975

Marketing activity	1975 rank order of importance	1964 rank order of importance
Pricing	1	6
Customer services	2	5
Sales personnel management	3	3
Product research and development	4	1
Marketing cost budgeting and control	5	9
Physical distribution	6	11
Market research	7	2
Marketing organization structure	8	7
Advertising and sales promotion planning	9	4
Distribution channel control	10	8
Extending customer credit	11	10
Public relations	12	12

Source: Robert A. Robicheaux, 'How Important Is Pricing in Competitive Strategy?' in Henry W. Nash & Donald P. Robin (eds) *Proceedings: Southern Marketing Association* January 1976, pp. 55–57. Robicheaux conducted the 1975 study. The 1964 study was conducted by Jon G. Udell, 'How Important Is Pricing in Competitive Strategy?', *Journal of Marketing*, January 1964, pp. 44–48.

companies will often establish a separate pricing department to set prices or assist others in the determiniation of appropriate prices; this department then reports to either the marketing department or top management. Others who exert an influence on pricing include sales managers, production planners and managers, and finance specialists and accountants.

In this chapter we will consider the following major pricing problems:

1. What price should be set on a product for the first time?
2. When should a company initiate a change in price?
3. How should a company respond to a competitor's change in price?
4. How should prices be set on several interrelated items in a product line?

SETTING PRICE

Pricing is a problem when a company develops new or different products, when it sells existing products to new middlemen or customers, and when it regularly enters bids on new contract work. The setting of price is rarely a simple matter. It is only simple in a price-taking market, i.e. a market where each seller must charge the going price. As conditions approach perfect competition (homogeneous product, high information, and high mobility of resources), as is the case in several raw material markets, suppliers have to charge roughly the same as their competitors. If they charge more (without offering any extra ser-

vices), no one will buy; and there is no reason to charge less as long as buyers are paying the going price.

An example of a market which approaches perfect competition is the sale of beef cattle. Australia is a major exporter of beef, with over 50 per cent of all production being exported. The price of beef in Australia is strongly influenced in the long term by price levels in the United States. In the short term, factors such as seasonality and the size of the herd will also have an effect on prices.

Table 13-2 shows the price obtained for cattle sold at auction in Melbourne for the years 1977–80. The price fluctuates widely from month to month and changes from year to year. The individual farmer cannot affect the prices he receives for his stock: his only decision is whether to sell or not, which may involve an attempt to try to predict prices in this fluctuating market.

Most markets, however, do not meet the conditions of perfect competition and call for price making. The pricing decision can be very complex, as we saw in the case of Staley Company. Marketing executives need to consider all the major factors; a pricing methodology is shown in Figure 13-1, and is discussed in the following paragraphs.

Target-market Objectives

Before a price can be set, management must clarify the target market(s) for the product and the company's marketing objectives. Thus the Staley Company has to decide whether its

Table 13-2 Average monthly prices (cents/kg) of cattle sold at auction

	Jan.	Feb.	Mar.	Apr.	May	June	July	Aug.	Sept.	Oct.	Nov.	Dec.	Average
1977	49	49	56	62	60	65	56	55	53	52	44	43	54
1978	41	51	56	—	66	78	72	86	91	94	95	96	75
1979	103	113	138	171	186	204	190	175	171	168	167	163	162
1980	161	165	172	163	170	183							

Source: Australian Meat and Livestock Corporation, *Statistical Review of Livestock and Meat Industries* (1981).

target market is young people with modest incomes, full-nest families with high incomes, or retirees with declining incomes. This will make a difference not only to the price but also to the design and promotion of the caravan.

The company must also decide on its marketing objectives in that market. The following alternative objectives are the most common.

Current-profit maximization. Economists have worked out a simple yet elegant model for pricing to maximize current profits. The model assumes that the firm can estimate the demand level and therefore the total revenue and its total cost at each possible price. The firm then locates the price that produces the greatest difference between total revenue and total cost, i.e. the highest total profit. This is the optimal price (see Exhibit 13-1).

Market-share leadership. An increasing number of companies believe that long-run profitability is associated with achieving a dominant market share. Texas Instruments and other companies will set out to achieve a high market share by setting prices as low as possible (called market penetration pricing). They will build a large capacity plant to produce a high volume, set the price at or below that of competitors to win a large market share, and keep bringing their price down as their costs fall. They may lose money for the first few years, but will make it up later when they dominate the market and have the lowest cost.

Any of several conditions might favour setting a low price:[3] (i) the market appears to be highly price-sensitive, and therefore a low price will stimulate more rapid market growth; (ii) the unit costs of production and distribution fall with accumulated production experience; or (iii) a low price would discourage actual and potential competition.

Market skimming. Firms may want to take advantage of the fact that some buyers are willing to pay a much higher price than others because the product has high current value to them. These firms will set a high initial price to yield a high profit margin per unit sold, although this will mean fewer units sold.

Market skimming makes sense under the following conditions: (i) a sufficient number of buyers have a higher current demand; (ii) the unit production and distribution costs of producing a smaller volume are not so much higher that they cancel the advantage of charging what some of the traffic will bear; (iii) the high initial price will not attract more competitors; (iv) the high price creates an impression of a superior product.

As time passes, the firm will lower its price to draw in the more price-elastic segments of the market. Du Pont is a prime practitioner of market skimming, particularly on new patent-protected discoveries such as cellophane and nylon. It will charge a high initial price and only lower it gradually to bring in new price-sensitive segments. Polaroid is another practitioner: it will introduce an expensive version of a new camera and gradually introduce

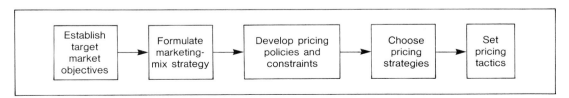

Figure 13-1 Methodology for setting prices

Exhibit 13-1   Finding the Optimal Price

The Supersound Company is preparing to introduce a new tape recorder into the market to be priced somewhere between $100 and $200. It first estimates the demand function – the estimated quantity (Q) that would be purchased this year at various prices (P) that might be charged. The demand equation is:

$$Q = 1000 - 4P$$

This equation illustrates the 'law of demand', i.e. less will be bought at high prices. If the price is, say, $100, demand will be 600 units; if the price is raised to $200, demand will be 200 units.

Supersound next estimates the cost function, which describes the estimated total cost (C) for alternative quantities per period (Q) that might be produced. Suppose the cost equation is:

$$C = 6000 + 50Q$$

Here $6000 represents the fixed cost of production (salaries, overhead, etc.), and $50 represents the cost per unit (labour, material, etc.). Thus it will cost the company $26 000 to produce 400 units.

Then it estimates total revenue (R), which is the price times the quantity sold:

$$R = PQ = P(1000 - 4P) = 1000P - 4P^2$$

Finally it estimates total profits (Z) as the difference between total revenue and total cost:

$$Z = R - C$$
$$Z = (1000P - 4P^2) - (6000 + 50Q)$$
$$Z = 1000P - 4P^2 - 6000 - 50(1000 - 4P)$$
$$Z = -56\,000 + 1200P - 4P^2$$

Total profits turn out to be a second-degree function of price. It is a hatlike figure (a parabola), and profits reach their highest point, $34 000, at a price of $150. No other price would yield a higher profit.

The economist's model has value in showing the role played by the demand and cost function in setting price. But it also has several limitations in practice: (i) it assumes that the other marketing-mix variables are held constant, when in fact they would have to be adjusted for different price settings; (ii) it assumes that competitors do not change their prices, when in fact they will react with different prices to different price settings of the company; (iii) it ignores the reaction of other parties in the marketing system — government, suppliers, dealers, and so on — to various prices that might be charged; and (iv) it assumes that the demand and cost functions can be reliably estimated, when in fact great difficulties exist.

lower-priced models in a bid for the mass market.

Product-quality leadership. A company might adopt the objective of being the product-quality leader in the market. This normally calls for charging a high price to cover the high quality and high cost of research to improve the product.

The Eversun/Aquasun range of sun-care products by Roche demonstrates that users will often value a high-quality product. Up to 1977, the sun-care market had been dominated by Coppertone and Sea & Ski, each with a market share of about 25 per cent. Eversun was developed to allow sun tanning with a reduced risk of skin cancer and skin ageing. Roche launched the product in 1977, with an integrated marketing strategy. The product was distributed through pharmacists, where consumers could obtain professional advice regarding usage, and an educational programme for pharmacists and consumers was launched. An innovative advertising campaign was also developed; the television commercial used won second prize at the Cannes Advertising Film Festival with 1832 commercials from thirty-two countries. By 1980, the product

had a market share of over 35 per cent, which was achieved with a price 31 per cent above competition.[4]

Marketing-mix Strategy

Management must now develop a marketing-mix strategy that will help it achieve its marketing objectives. For example, if the Staley Company adopts a product-leadership objective, this will normally call for high product quality, a high price, high R & D, and high promotion. The appropriate marketing mix, however, is not always so straightforward, and trade-offs will occur between the various marketing variables. Consider, for example, the various combinations possible with any two elements of the marketing mix, such as price and product quality. Suppose each can be set independently at a high, medium or low level. Figure 13-2 shows nine resulting marketing-mix strategies. Sometimes more than one marketing mix can support a given marketing objective: the Staley Company can pursue product-quality leadership by using any of the three strategies in the first row. The difference is that lower prices will normally bring about more market share as well as product-quality

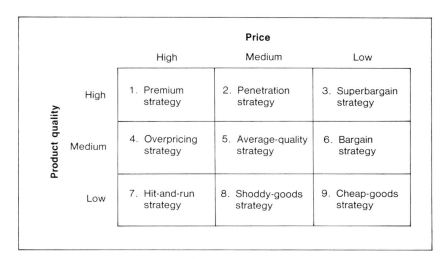

Figure 13-2 Nine marketing mix strategies on price/quality

leadership. The main point is that price cannot be set independently of the question of overall marketing mix strategy.

Pricing Policies and Constraints

Management must scrutinize the contemplated price and other elements of the marketing mix for their compatibility with company policies and external constraints. Many companies have pricing policies that define such things as the price image that the company wants, its position on price discounts, and its philosophy of meeting competitors' prices. Any price being considered must be compatible with the price policies of the company.

In determining prices, the decision-maker has to consider the possible reactions of various parties affected by the pricing decision: distributors, competitors, suppliers, government, and company executives (see Exhibit 13-2).

Pricing Strategy

Pricing strategy is the task of defining both the initial price range and the planned price movement that the company will use to achieve its marketing objectives in the target market. In developing such a strategy, management must anticipate the movements of cost, demand and competition over time, and decide how price should be adapted to them. Although all three elements should always be considered, many pricing strategies in practice lean heavily on one of the three elements. As a result, various pricing strategies have been described as being heavily cost-oriented, demand-oriented, or completion-oriented. We will now explore these strategies.

Cost-oriented pricing strategies. Many firms set product prices largely on the basis of product costs. Typically, all costs are in-

cluded, including an arbitrary allocation of overhead made on the basis of the expected sales level.

Mark-up pricing. The most elementary examples of cost-oriented pricing are mark-up pricing and cost-plus pricing. In both cases, price is determined by adding some fixed percentage to the unit cost. Mark-up pricing is widely used in the retail trades, a predetermined amount being added to the cost of various goods. Cost-plus pricing is most often used to describe the pricing of jobs that are nonroutine and difficult to 'cost' in advance, such as construction and military-weapon development.

Mark-ups vary considerably among different goods. In department stores, mark-ups may be 15 per cent for cameras, 50–80 per cent for clothing, 80–100 per cent for jewellery, and 33 per cent for books. In the retail food industry, mark-ups are generally lower, ranging from 8 per cent to 20 per cent. Mark-ups also vary by level of distribution, wholesaler or retailer: a product may be sold to a wholesaler by a manufacturer for $2, he in turn sells it to a retailer for $2.50 (a 25 per cent mark-up), who in turn sells it to a consumer for $3.30 (a 32 per cent mark-up). Mark-ups also may vary by channel of distribution: the mark-up on a shampoo is generally higher in a pharmacy than it is in a supermarket.

Many hypotheses have been advanced to explain the variations in mark-up within selected product groups. Preston conducted a study to determine how much of this variance within common grocery-product groups could be explained by differences in unit costs, turnover, and manufacturers' versus private brands. The principal finding was that over 40 per cent of the variation remained unexplained in most product categories, and was probably due to erratic decisions, random factors and, frequently, better adaptations to the current market than could be provided by these factors.[5]

Exhibit 13-2 Price Decisions and Public Policy

Pricing is a marketing decision area where knowledge of the law is essential. Management must avoid price fixing, resale price maintenance, price discrimination, charging less than the minimum legal price, or advertising deceptive prices.

Price fixing. Price fixing – i.e. an agreement by two competitors to charge the same price – is generally illegal, whether the agreed prices are 'fair' or not. The Trade Practices Act prohibits price fixing on the grounds that it inhibits competition. Identical prices for standardized products is not necessarily evidence of price fixing; in the case of two manufacturers of electric motors it was found that parallel pricing was based on issues other than anti-competitive behaviour. These horizontal price agreements (agreements between competitors) have in some circumstances been held to be legal, e.g. a recommended price list by the Milk Board in Victoria. In addition, partners in a joint venture can agree on the price of a product to be made by their firm.

Resale price maintenance. A supplier cannot fix the price at which a product will be sold at subsequent levels of distribution. Central price agreements, or resale maintenance as it is commonly called, is illegal whatever the demonstrated effect on competition. Further, suppliers may not attempt to induce resellers not to sell below a specified price, nor may they refuse to supply firms who sell below a recommended price. Stihl Chain Saws (Australia) was fined $25 000 for inducing a retailer not to advertise chainsaws at less than specified prices, and a further $45 000 for withholding chainsaws from the retailer.[6]

Price discrimination. Suppliers are prohibited from discriminating between purchasers of goods of like grade and quality in respect to prices, discounts, allowances, payment terms and other services if discrimination is likely to result in lessened competition. Price discrimination is legal provided it reflects reasonable differences in the cost of manufacture or delivery, or if the supplier can show that the lower discriminatory price was made in good faith to meet competitive prices.

Loss leadering. Goods can be withheld from a reseller who has engaged in loss leadering – selling goods at less than their cost to the reseller. Loss leadering is sometimes undertaken by resellers to attract people to the outlet in the hope that they will purchase other goods. However, goods cannot be withheld if they have been specifically obtained to be sold at a loss, e.g. at a clearance sale.

Deceptive pricing. The Trade Practices Act prohibits deceptive pricing. For example, a reseller can not use an artificially 'normal' selling price in an advertisement ('Was $15, now $10', when the normal selling price is $10). In addition, price reductions cannot be stated solely in percentage terms ('30 per cent off') but must clearly state the former price.

Does the use of a fixed customary mark-up over cost make logical sense in the pricing of products? Generally, no; any model that ignores current demand elasticity in setting prices is not likely to lead, except by chance, to the achievement of maximum profits in either the short or the long run. As demand elasticity changes, as it is likely to do seasonally, cyclically, or over the product lifecycle, the optimal mark-up will also change.

Still, mark-up remains popular for a number of reasons. First, there is generally less uncertainty about costs than about demand.

By pinning the price to unit costs, sellers simplify their own pricing task considerably; they do not have to make frequent adjustments as demand conditions change. Second, where all firms in the industry use this approach, their prices are likely to be similar if their costs and mark-ups are similar. Price competition is therefore minimized, which it would not be if firms paid attention to demand variations when they priced. Third, it is felt that mark-up pricing is fairer to both buyers and sellers: sellers do not take advantage of buyers when the latter's demand becomes acute, but still earn a fair return on their investment.

Target pricing. Another cost-oriented pricing approach is that of target pricing, in which the firm tries to determine the price that would give it a specified target rate of return on its total costs at an estimated standard volume. Target pricing has been most closely associated with General Motors (United States), which prices its cars so as to achieve a long-run average rate of return of 15 to 20 per cent on its investment. This approach is also closely associated with the pricing policies of public utilities such as the State Electricity Commissions, which have a large investment and, in view of their monopoly position, are constrained to seek a fair rate of return on their costs.

Target pricing can be illustrated in terms of the break-even chart in Figure 13-3. Management's first task is to estimate its total costs at various levels of output; the curve is shown rising at a constant rate until capacity is approached. Management's next task is to estimate the percentage of capacity at which it is likely to operate in the coming period. If the company expects to operate at 80 per cent of capacity, this means that it expects to sell 800 000 units if its capacity is one million units; the total cost of producing this volume, according to Figure 13-3, is $10 million. Management's third task is to specify a target rate of return. If the company aspires to a 20 per cent profit over costs, it would like absolute profits of $2 million. Therefore one point on its total-revenue curve will have to be $12 million (at a volume of 80 per cent capacity), and another will be at $0 (zero per cent of capacity). The rest of the total-revenue curve can be drawn between these two points.

Where does price come in? The slope of the total-revenue curve is price. In this example, the slope is $15 per unit: thus if a company charges $15 per unit and manages to sell

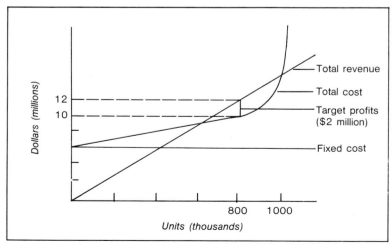

Figure 13-3   Break-even chart for determining target price

800 000 units, it will attain the target rate of return of 20 per cent, or $2 million.

Target pricing, however, has a major conceptual flaw. The company used an estimate of sales volume to derive the price, but price is a factor that influences sales volume – a price of $15 may be too high or too low to move 800 000 units. What is missing is a demand function, showing how many units the firm could expect to sell at different prices. With an estimate of the demand curve and with the requirement to earn 20 per cent on costs, the firm could calculate those prices and volumes that would be compatible and thus avoid setting a price that failed to generate the estimated level of output.

Demand-oriented pricing strategies. Demand-oriented pricing calls for setting a price based on consumer perceptions and demand intensity, rather than on cost.

Perceived-value pricing. An increased number of companies are basing their price on the product's perceived value to the buyer rather than the seller's level of cost. They use the non-price variables in the marketing mix to build up a perceived value and then set prices accordingly.

A perceived-value approach is in line with modern market-positioning thinking. A company develops a product for a particular target market, with a particular market position in mind as to price, quality and service. It then estimates the volume it can see at this price, which in turn suggests the needed plant capacity, investment and unit costs. Management then calculates whether the product will yield a satisfactory profit at the chosen price

---

Exhibit 13-3 How Caterpillar Uses Perceived-value Pricing

Caterpillar uses perceived value to set prices on its construction equipment. It might price a tractor at $24 000 although a competitor's similar tractor is priced at $20 000, and when a prospective customer asks a dealer why he should pay $4000 more for the Caterpillar tractor, the dealer answers:

> $20 000 would be the tractor's price if it were equivalent to the competitor's tractor
> $3 000 is the price premium for superior durability
> $2 000 is the price premium for superior reliability
> $2 000 is the price premium for superior service
> $1 000 is the price premium for the longer warranty on parts
> ───────
> $28 000 is the price to cover the value package
> $4 000 discount
> ───────
> $24 000 final price

The stunned customer learns that although he is being asked to pay a $4000 premium for the Caterpillar tractor, he is in fact getting a $4000 discount! He ends up choosing the Caterpillar tractor because he is convinced that its lifetime operating costs will be smaller.

and cost; if the answer is yes, product development goes ahead; if not the idea is dropped.

The key to perceived-value pricing is accurate determination of the market's perception of the relative value of the company's offer versus competitors' offers. Sellers with an inflated view of the value of their offer may be overpricing their product; others may underestimate the perceived value and charge less than they could. Market research has to be carried out to establish the market's perceptions.[7]

Price discrimination. Another form of demand-oriented pricing is price discrimination (also called demand differential pricing) where a product or service is sold at two or more prices that do not reflect a proportional difference in marginal costs. Price discrimination takes various forms:

1. *Customer basis.* Here different customers pay different amounts for the same product or service. One car buyer pays the full list price, another bargains and pays a lower price.
2. *Product-form basis.* Here different versions of the product are priced differently, but not proportionately to their respective marginal costs. An electric dishwasher with a $5 formica top might be priced at $260, and the same dishwasher with a $10 wooden top might be priced at $280.
3. *Place basis.* Here different locations are priced differently, even though there is no difference in the marginal costs involved. A theatre varies its seat prices because of the different intensities of demand for the various locations.
4. *Time basis.* Here different prices are charged seasonally, by the day, and even by the hour. Public utilities typically vary their prices to commercial users by time of day and weekend versus weekday.

For price discrimination to work, certain conditions must exist.[8] First, the market must be segmentable and the segments show different intensities of demand. Second, there should be no chance that the members of the segment paying the lower price could turn around and resell the product to the segment paying the higher price. Third, there should be little chance that competitors will undersell the firm in the segment being charged the higher price. Fourth, the cost of segmenting and policing the market should not exceed the extra revenue derived from price discrimination. Fifth, the practice should not breed customer resentment and thus a switch to competitors' products.

Competition-oriented pricing strategies.

When a company sets its prices chiefly on the basis of what its competitors are charging, its pricing strategy may be described as competition-oriented. It is not necessary to charge the same price as the competition – prices may be lower or higher than the competition by a certain percentage. The distinguishing characteristic is that the firm does not seek to maintain a rigid relation between its price and its own costs or demand: the latter may change but the firm maintains its price because competitors maintain their prices, or the same prices may be changed when competitors change theirs even if costs or demand have not altered.

Going-rate pricing. The most popular type of competition-oriented pricing is where a firm tries to keep its price at the average level charged by the industry. This going-rate pricing is popular for several reasons. Where costs are difficult to measure, it is felt that the going price represents the collective wisdom of the industry concerning the price that would yield a fair return. It is also felt that conforming to a going price would be least disruptive of industry harmony. The difficulty of knowing how buyers and competitors would react to price differentials is still another factor.

Going-rate pricing primarily characterizes pricing practice in a homogeneous product market, although the market structure itself many vary from pure competition to pure

---

Exhibit 13-4 Airlines Move to Demand Differential Pricing

Passengers on a Melbourne–Sydney flight may be paying as many as nine different fares for essentially the same flight. First-class passengers receive superior inflight treatment, but other categories of passenger receive a set standard of service, despite the price differential. As of mid-1981, the possible one-way fares were $128.30 for first class, $88.40 for economy, $66 for standby, $57.45 for APEX, $55.20 for children 3–15 years of age, $55.20 for full-time students 15–19 years of age, $66.30 for students less than 26, $79.56 for group travel with a common interest, and $75.14 for group travel with a sporting interest.

---

oligopoly. The firm selling a homogeneous product in a highly competitive market has actually very little choice but to set the going price. In pure oligopoly, where a few large firms dominate the industry, the firm also tends to charge the same price as the competition but for different reasons. Since there are only a few firms, each is quite aware of the others' prices and so are the buyers; the slightest price difference would attract business to the lower-price firm. The individual oligopolist's demand curve has a kink in it at the level of the present prices; the demand curve tends to be elastic above the kink because other firms are not likely to follow a rise in prices; it tends to be inelastic below the kink because other firms are likely to follow a price cut. An oligopolist can gain little by raising its price when demand is elastic or lowering its price when demand is inelastic.

In markets characterized by product differentiation, the individual firm has more latitude in its price decision because the buyer is desensitized to existing price differentials. Firms try to establish themselves in a pricing zone with respect to their competitors, i.e. high-price, medium-price or low-price. Their product and marketing programme are made compatible with this chosen pricing zone, or

vice versa, and they respond to competitive changes in price to maintain their position.

Sealed-bid pricing. Competition-oriented pricing also dominates in those situations where firms compete for jobs on the basis of bids, such as original equipment manufacture and government authorities. The bid is the firm's offer price, and it is a prime example of pricing based on expectations of how competitors will price rather than on a rigid relation based on the firm's own costs or demand. The objective of the firm is to get the contract, and it hopes to set its price lower than that of any of the other bidding firms.

Yet the firm does not ordinarily set its price below a certain level. Even when it is anxious to get a contract in order to keep the plant busy, it cannot quote a price below marginal cost without worsening its position. On the other hand, as it raises its price above marginal cost, it increases its potential profit but reduces its chance of getting the contract.

The net effect of the two opposite pulls can be described in terms of the expected profit of the particular bid. Suppose a bid of $9500 would yield a high chance of getting the contract, say 81 per cent, but only a low profit, say $100. The expected profit with this bid is therefore $81. If the firm bid $11 000 its profit would be $1600, but its chance of getting the contract might be reduced, say to one per cent, and the expected profit would be only $16. One logical bidding criterion would be to state the bid that would maximize the expected profit. According to Table 13-3, the best bid would be $10 000, for which the expected profit is $216.

The use of the expected-profit criterion makes sense for a large firm that makes many bids and is not dependent on winning any particular contract. In playing the odds, it should achieve maximum profits in the long run. The firm that bids only occasionally, and/or may need a particular contract badly, will probably not find it advantageous to use the expected-profit criterion. This does not, for example, distinguish between a $1000 profit with a 10 per cent probability and a $125 profit with an 80 per cent probability. Yet the firm that wants to keep production going is likely to prefer the second contract to the first. In other words, the dollar value of expected profits may not reflect the utility value.

Pricing Tactics

Management ultimately has to establish specific prices within the context of the chosen pricing strategy, and two forms of pricing tactics are of particular interest: psychological pricing and discount pricing.

Psychological pricing tactics. The final price set on a product must take the psychology of the buyer into account. Four different pricing psychologies can be distinguished.[9]

Odd-even pricing. Many sellers believe that buyers favour odd prices over even prices. Instead of pricing a stereo amplifier at $300, the seller will price it at $299.95 or $295 – presumably the customer sees this as a $200 price rather than a $300 price, or sees it as a discount from the full price. This type of pricing has become customary, and newspaper ads are dominated with prices ending in odd numbers. Some psychologists have gone further and argue that each digit has symbolic and visual qualities that should be considered in pricing. Thus 8 is symmetrical and should be used for a soothing effect; 7 is angular and should be used when a jarring effect is desired.

Pricing lining. Many sellers believe that buyers are not sensitive to small differences in price but only to large differences in price. The sellers will establish a limited number of prices for selected lines of merchandise. Thus a men's clothing store carries men's suits selling at three price levels: $150, $220 and $310. The customers will associate low-, average- and high-quality suits with the three price 'points'. Even if the three prices are moderately changed, men will continue to buy suits at the price point they are used to.

Prestige pricing. Buyers often take price to be a sign of product quality, especially for products that they cannot easily evaluate. Bayer aspirin, although the highest-priced aspirin, continues to outsell lower-priced brands, suggesting that people take its price to be a sign of higher quality. A person who is shown two fur coats with different prices will almost always assume that the higher-priced coat has higher quality. Thus price has

Table 13-3 Effect of different bids on expected profit

Company's bid	Company's profit	Assumed probability of getting award with this bid	Expected profit
$ 9 500	$ 100	.81	$ 81
10 000	600	.36	216
10 500	1 100	.09	99
11 000	1 600	.01	16

symbolic connotations that the seller must consider. At the same time, if the price is set too high, it can strain the buyer's credibility and create distrust of the retailer.

Promotional pricing. Buyers love to respond to special or low prices that indicate they are receiving a bargain. Supermarkets and department stores will often price a few of their products below their normal mark-up or even below cost. As discussed earlier, loss leaders are used to attract customers to the store in the hope that they will buy other things at normal mark-ups. Sellers will also use special-event pricing in conjunction with sales seasons and special situations to draw in more customers. Thus summer fashion clothes are sold at especially low prices every January as a means of attracting shopping-weary customers into the stores after Christmas. Discounts from normal prices are a legitimate form of promotional pricing.

Discount pricing tactics. Pricing tactics call for establishing a list price (the official price) and a set of discounts and allowances that might be offered to dealers and customers as special incentives. The major forms of discounts and allowances are described below.

Cash discounts. A cash discount is an offer of a price reduction to buyers who pay their bill promptly. A typical example would be '2/10, net 30', which means that payment is due within thirty days but the buyer can deduct 2 per cent from the cost by paying the bill within ten days. The standard discount must be granted to all buyers. Such discounts have become customary in many industries, improving the seller's liquidity and reducing credit-collection costs and bad debts.

Quantity discounts. A quantity discount is an offer of a price reduction to buyers who buy larger volumes. A typical example would be '$10 per unit for less than 100 units; $9 per unit for 100 or more units'. Quantity discounts must be offered to all customers, and

are not supposed to exceed the cost savings to the seller associated with selling in large quantities (e.g. reduced expenses of selling, inventory, and transportation). They may be offered on a non-cumulative basis (on each order placed) or a cumulative basis (on the number of units ordered over a given period). Discounts are an incentive to the buyer to buy more from a given seller rather than buying from multiple sources.

Functional discounts. Also called trade discounts, functional discounts are payments to channel members for performing marketing functions required by the seller, such as selling, storing and record-keeping. A typical example would be when a manufacturer quotes a retail list price of $100 and discounts of 40 and 10 per cent to retailers and wholesalers respectively. Manufacturers may offer different functional discounts to different trade channels because of the varying services they provide, but must offer the same functional discounts within each trade channel.

Seasonal discounts. A seasonal discount is an offer of a price reduction to buyers who buy merchandise or services out of season. Seasonal discounts allow the seller to maintain steadier production during the year. Ski manufacturers will offer seasonal discounts to retailers in the spring and summer in order to stimulate earlier ordering and keep their production going. Hotels, motels and airlines will offer seasonal discounts in their slower selling periods. A typical two-bedroom flat on the Gold Coast will cost $25 per day in the low season and $40 per day during the high season.

Allowances. Allowances are other types of reductions from the list price. For example, trade-in allowances are price reductions granted for turning in an old item when buying a new one (most common in the car industry). Promotional allowances are payments or price reductions to reward dealers for participating in advertising and sales-support programmes.

This completes our review of a methodology for setting prices. Once the strategy is achieved, however, changes occurring in the environment will require the seller to consider altering the price. We now turn to this problem.

INITIATING PRICE CHANGES

Circumstances will often lead the seller to investigate the merits of a price cut or increase. We will examine both moves, and also consider how to estimate the likely reactions of various parties, particularly buyers and competitors.

Price Cuts

Several circumstances may lead a firm to consider reducing its price, even though this may threaten industrial harmony and provoke a price war. One circumstance is excess capacity, where the firm needs additional business and presumably has failed to generate it through increased sales effort, product improvement, and other normal means of sales expansion. In the late 1970s various companies began to break ranks with 'follow-the-leader pricing' and turned to flexible pricing to gain as much business as they could.[10]

Another circumstance is falling market share in the face of vigorous price competition. Faced with increasing competition from high-quality Japanese products, manufacturers in many countries in the world have had to revise their price strategy. In Australia, BHP has found that it must be selective in its approach to raising prices: it can raise the prices on some products, but others are under severe threat of import substitution and price rises must be kept to a minimum. Woolworths food-market share has remained stable in Victoria over the last decade, probably one explanation for the dramatic price war which erupted in that State in early 1981. It was reported that Woolworths cut prices on over 3000 lines in an attempt to improve their position; once the price war started, it proved difficult to contain and soon spread to Western Australia.

Still another circumstance provoking price cutting is a drive for dominance through lower costs. Either the aggressive pricer starts with lower costs than its competitors, or it initiates price cuts in the hope of gaining market share which would lead to falling costs through larger volume.

Price Increases

Many companies have had to raise prices in recent years. They do this even though the price increases will be resented by not only customers and dealers but also the company's own sales force. A successful price increase can increase profits considerably: if a company's profit margin is 3 per cent of sales, for example, a one per cent price increase will increase profits by 33 per cent if sales volume is unaffected.

A major reason for upward price revision is the persistent worldwide cost inflation.[11] Rising costs unmatched by productivity gains squeeze profit margins and lead companies to regular rounds of price hikes; prices are often raised by more than the cost increases in anticipation of further inflation or government price controls. Companies hesitate to make price commitments in long-term contracts for fear that cost inflation will erode their profit margins. They have become adept at inflation pricing through such measures as: (i) adopting delayed quotation pricing; (ii) writing escalator clauses into contracts; (iii) unbundling goods and services, and pricing them separately; (iv) reducing cash and quantity discounts and off-list pricing by sales force; (v) increasing minimum acceptance order sizes; (vi) putting more sales power behind higher margin products and markets; and (vii) reducing product quality, features or service.[12]

The other major circumstance leading to

price increases is overdemand. When a company cannot supply all of its customers, it may either raise its price or use allocation quotas, or both. Prices may be raised relatively invisibly by dropping discounts and adding high-priced units to the line; or they may be pushed up boldly.

Price increases should be accompanied by a well-thought-out communication programme in which the customers are told why the prices are being increased, and how they might economize. The company's sales force should make regular calls on the customers and attempt to help them solve their problem.

Buyers' Reactions to Price Changes

Whether the price is to be moved up or down, the action is sure to affect buyers, competitors, distributors, suppliers and, possibly, government. Here we will look at buyers' reactions.

Price elasticity of demand. The traditional analysis of buyers' reactions to price change utilizes the concept of price elasticity of demand. This is given by:

$$\text{Price elasticity of demand} = \frac{\text{\% change in quantity demanded}}{\text{\% change in price}}$$

A price elasticity of -1 means that sales rise (fall) by the same percentage as price falls (rises). In this case, total revenue is unaffected. A price elasticity greater than -1 means that sales rise (fall) by more than price falls (rises) in percentage terms; in this case, total revenue rises. A price elasticity less than -1 means that sales rise (fall) by less than price falls (rises) in percentage terms; in this case, total revenue falls.

Price elasticity of demand gives precision to the question of whether the firm's price is too high or too low. From the point of view of maximizing *revenue*, price is too high if demand is elastic and too low if demand is inelastic. Whether this is also true of maximizing *profits* depends on the behaviour of costs.

Perceptual factors in buyers' response. Perceptual factors are an important intervening variable, for customers will not always put the most straightforward interpretation on a price change when it occurs.[13] A price reduction may mean a number of things to buyers: (i) the item is about to be superseded by a later model; (ii) the item has some fault and is not selling well; (iii) the firm is in financial trouble and may not stay in business to supply future parts; (iv) the price will come down even further and it pays to wait; or (v) the quality has been reduced.[14]

A price increase may also carry a variety of different meanings to buyers: (i) the item is very 'hot' and may be unobtainable unless it is bought soon; (ii) the item represents an unusually good value; or (iii) the seller is greedy and is charging what the traffic will bear.

Competitors' Reactions to Price Changes

A firm contemplating a price change has to worry about competitors' as well as customers' reactions. Competitors' reactions are particularly important where the number of firms is small, the product is homogeneous, and the buyers are discriminating and informed.

In the example quoted earlier of the retail-grocery price war in Victoria, competitors reacted swiftly and vigorously. Prices were cut by competitors such as Coles and Safeway on a wide range of products. These price cuts often resulted in goods being sold at below wholesale replacement cost, as Table 13-4 demonstrates.

To help finance the cost of this price war, it was claimed that Coles had approached suppliers with a view to increasing their promotion charges.[15]

A reaction to a price cut may be in terms of non-price variables. During this price war, grocery retailers were reported to be spending an additional $100 000 a week on advertising;

Table 13-4   Effects of a price war on item retail costs

	Cost per carton ($)	Items per carton	Cost per item (c)	Special price (c)	Above/below cost
Meadow Lea margarine (500 g)	18.42	20	92.1	79	− 13.1
Nescafé (150 g)	31.65	12	264	259	− 5.0
CSR sugar (2 kg)	7.11	8	88.9	89	.1
Pal dog food (680 g)	10.33	20	51.7	49	− 2.7

Source: Retail World, 4 March 1981, p. 1.

in Perth, one competitor addressed shoppers through a loudspeaker outside a new store opened by an opposition chain, indicating comparative prices.

How can the firm estimate the likely reactions of its competitors? Let us assume that the firm has only one large competitor. The likely behaviour of this competitor can be approached from two quite different starting points. One is to assume that the competitor has a set policy for reacting to price changes, the other is to assume that the competitor treats each price change as a fresh challenge and reacts according to self-interest at the time.

The problem is complicated because the competitor is capable of putting different interpretations on the company's price change: (i) the company is trying to steal the market; (ii) the company is not doing well and is trying to improve its sales; or (iii) the company is hoping that the whole industry will reduce its prices in the interests of stimulating total demand.

When there is more than one competitor, the company must estimate the likely reaction of each. If all competitors behave alike, this amounts to analyzing only a typical competitor. If the competitors cannot be expected to react uniformly because of critical differences in size, market shares, or policies, then separate analyses are necessary. If it appears that a few competitors will match the price change, there is good reason to expect the rest will also match it.

RESPONDING TO PRICE CHANGES

Let us reverse the previous question and ask how a firm should respond to a price change initiated by a competitor. The firm should first consider the following: (i) Why did the competitor change the price – to steal the market, to utilize excess capacity, to meet changing cost conditions, or to evoke a calculated industry-wide price change to take advantage of total demand? (ii) Is the competitor intending to make the price change temporary or permanent? (iii) What will happen to the company's market share and profits if it ignores the price change? Are the other companies going to ignore the price change? (iv) What is the competitor's (and other firms') response likely to be to each possible reaction?

The best response requires an analysis of the particular situation. The company under attack has to consider the product's stage in the lifecycle, its importance in the company's portfolio, the intentions and resources of the competitor, the price sensitivity versus value sensitivity of the market, the behaviour of costs with volume, and the company's alternative opportunities.

An extended analysis of company alternatives is not always feasible at the time of a price change. The competitor who initiated the price change may have spent considerable time preparing for this decision, but the company may have to react decisively within hours or days. About the only way to place such a decision on a sure footing is to

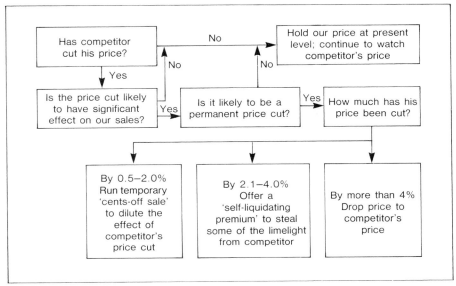

Source: Redrawn from Raymond J. Trapp (unpublished paper, Northwestern University, 1964).

Figure 13-4   Decision programme for meeting a competitor's price cut

anticipate price changes and prepare an advanced programme to guide managers' responses (see Figure 13-4). Such programmes are likely to find their greatest application in industries where price changes occur with some frequency and where it is important to react quickly.

PRICING THE PRODUCT LINE

The logic of setting or changing a price on an individual product has to be modified when the product is a member of a product line. Here the quest is for a set of mutual prices that maximizes the profits of the line, but this is made difficult because various company products are interrelated in demand and/or cost and are subject to different degrees of competition. We will consider two different situations.

The first has to do with a product line that consists of main products and satellite products. The satellite products take two forms.

The first consists of related-option products, i.e. the buyer of the main product is free to buy none, one, or more optional products. The person buying a car can order such options as electric window controls, air-conditioners, and light dimmers; the restaurant customer can order or skip liquor with the main course. The seller's task is to decide on prices for the related optional items. If the prices are too high, customers will either forgo purchase of the options or switch to sellers who price these options lower. Management can choose between pricing these options high, as an independent profit source, and pricing them low to act as a traffic builder. Many restaurants choose to price their liquor high and their food low: the food revenue covers the cost of the food and operating the restaurant, and the liquor produces the profit. Others will price their liquor low and food high to draw in a crowd that likes to drink.

The other type of satellite product is a captive product (or after-market product), such as razor blades, camera film, and copier supplies.

Exhibit 13-5 How Heublein Inc. Protected its Smirnoff Vodka Brand Against a Price Cutter Through Strategic Pricing

Heublein Inc. produces Smirnoff vodka, the leading brand (with 23 per cent of the American vodka market). In the 1960s it was attacked by another brand, Wolfschmidt, priced at one dollar less a bottle and claiming to be of the same quality. Heublein saw a real danger of customers switching to Wolfschmidt, and considered the following possible reaction:

1. Lower the price of Smirnoff by one dollar or less to hold on to market share. This would reduce Smirnoff's profits.
2. Maintain the price of Smirnoff but increase advertising and promotion expenditures. This would reduce Smirnoff's profits.
3. Maintain the price of Smirnoff and let its market share fall. This would reduce Smirnoff's profits.

It seemed that Heublein could not win.

At this point a fourth strategy suddenly occurred to management, and it was brilliant. Heublein *raised* the price of Smirnoff by one dollar, introduced a new brand (Reiska) to compete with Wolfschmidt at the original price, and still another brand (Popov) at a lower price than Wolfschmidt. This strategy positioned Smirnoff as the elite brand and Wolfschmidt as just another ordinary brand. The moves resulted in an increase in Heublein's total profits.

Manufacturers of the main products (razors, cameras, and copiers) often price them low in order to stimulate purchase and then make their profit through a high mark-up on the supplies. Thus Kodak prices its cameras low because it makes its money on the film; those camera makers who do not sell film have to price their cameras higher than Kodak in order to make the same overall profit.

The other interesting line-pricing situation arises in connection with by-products. In the production of processed meats, petroleum products and other chemicals, there will often be by-products. If these have no value and in some cases a cost of disposal, this will have to be considered in pricing the main product. The manufacturer will normally attempt to find a market for the product in its raw state or process it into a valued product where the processing cost is less than its value. The manufacturer should be willing to accept any price for the by-product that covers more than its cost of processing and delivery, since this will enable the seller to reduce the price of the main product and thus make it more competitive in the market.

SUMMARY

In spite of the increased role of non-price factors in the modern marketing process, price remains an important element and is especially challenging in certain situations.

In setting an original price on a product, the company should follow a methodology consisting of five steps. First, the company should carefully identify the target market and establish its marketing objective, such as current-profit maximization, market-share leadership, market skimming, or product quality leadership. Second, the company should consider the contemplated price in relation to the company's established pricing policies and the attitudes of important publics such as distributors, competitors, suppliers, government, and company executives. Fourth, the company should select a pricing strategy in the light of its possible orientation to cost (mark-up pricing, target pricing), demand (perceived-value pricing, differential demand pricing), or competition (going-rate pricing, sealed bidding). Fifth, the company should consider determining the price by paying attention to psychological pricing tactics (odd-even pricing, price lining, prestige pricing, and promotional pricing) and to discount pricing tactics (cash, quantity, functional and seasonal discounts and allowances).

When a firm contemplates changing its price, it must carefully consider customers' and competitors' reactions. The probable reaction of customers is described in the price elasticity of demand; competitors' reactions must be anticipated on the assumption that they either flow from a set policy or from a fresh appraisal of the challenge each time. The firm initiating the price change must also consider the probable reactions of suppliers, middlemen and government.

The firm that faces a competitor's price change must try to understand the competitor's intent and the likely duration of the change. If swiftness of reaction is desirable, the firm should preplan its reactions to different possible pricing developments.

Pricing is complicated when various products in a line have important demand and/or cost interrelationships. Then the objective is to develop a set of mutual prices that maximize the profits on the whole line.

QUESTIONS FOR DISCUSSION

1. In setting prices it is essential only to establish target-market objectives. Comment.

2. Do the following companies practise market penetration or market skimming in pricing their products?
   - McDonald's
   - Bang and Olufsen Hi Fi
   - Bic Corporation
   Why?

3. Relate the essential parties in developing pricing policies and constraints, to Adidas' decision to price a new line of shoes.

4. What are the major types of cost-oriented pricing strategies? Provide a company example of each.

5. Which psychological pricing tactics do you think the following marketers utilize?
   - Country Road
   - Safeway
   - K-Mart
   - Florsheim Shoes

6. Discuss two major discount-pricing tactics that Dynastar Skis might employ in dealing with its retail outlets.

7. In recent years the majority of price changes made by marketers have been price increases. Why?

8. If a company is to respond accurately to price changes, it must thoroughly understand its competitors. Comment.

9. Public policy makers are charged with overseeing what three major pricing issues?

NOTES

1 Based on an example in David J. Schwartz, *Marketing Today: A Basic Approach* (New York: Harcourt Brace Jovanovich, 2nd edn, 1977), pp. 542–44.

2 Ibid., p. 520.

3 See Joel Dean, *Managerial Economics* (Englewood Cliffs, N.J.: Prentice-Hall, 1951), pp. 420*ff*.

4 *The Australian Journal of Pharmacy*, August 1980, pp. 502–8.

5 Lee E. Preston, *Profits, Competition, and Rules of Thumb in Retail Food Pricing* (Berkeley: University of California Institute of Business and Economic Research, 1963), pp. 29–40.

6 Paul Latimer, *Australian Business Law* (Sydney: CCH, 1981), p. 374.

7 See Daniel A. Nimer, 'Pricing the Profitable Sale Has a Lot to Do with Perception', *Sales Management*, 19 May 1975, pp. 13–14.

8 See George Stigler, *The Theory of Price* (New York: Macmillan, rev. edn, 1952), pp. 215*ff*.

9 For further discussion, see Edward R. Hawkins, 'Price Policies and Theory', *Journal of Marketing*, January 1954, pp. 233–40.

10 See 'Flexible Pricing', *Business Week*, 12 December 1977, pp. 78–88.

11 See 'Pricing Strategy in an Inflation Economy', *Business Week*, 6 April 1974, pp. 43–49.

12 Norman H. Fuss Jr, 'How to Raise Prices – Judiciously – to Meet Today's Conditions', *Harvard Business Review*, May–June 1975, pp. 10*ff*.

13 For an excellent review, see Kent B. Monroe, 'Buyers' Subjective Perceptions of Price', *Journal of Marketing Research*, February 1973, pp. 70–80.

14 See Alfred R. Oxenfeldt, *Pricing for Marketing Executives* (San Francisco: Wadsworth, 1961), p. 28.

15 *Food Week*, 24 March 1981.

Marketing-channel and Physical-distribution Strategy

14

Kevin Weldon is rather well known in the book trade. In the late 1960s, members accused him of ruining the industry; in 1973, he was at the centre of a wrangle which embarrassed then Prime Minister Gough Whitlam – he had Gough promoting a publication printed in Japan. And now, Weldon has published the Macquarie Dictionary. It has received heavy promotion and been hailed by critics as the most important Australian cultural event of the year. But you can't buy it in a bookshop – not yet anyway.

Kevin Weldon is proprietor of the new publishing company, Macquarie Library, which he operates from a small office in St Leonards, Sydney. But today's appearances are misleading. Up until two years ago Weldon was one of the more important forces in Australian publishing. He was the founding managing director of the Paul Hamlyn group in Australia (now known as the Rigby Group).

In his eleven years with the company, Weldon headed up the push into low-cost LP records through Music for Pleasure and Summit Records; he launched Australia's Heritage, a mammoth 105-part series which broke new marketing ground and was the largest single publishing investment in Australia's history with eventual sales topping six million; he oversaw the publication of Australia: The Greatest Island with sales at the respectable 50 000 mark; led the push into direct mail with the eventual handling of 2.5 million pieces a year; saw the takeover of Rigby Publishers and the purchase of 51 per cent of Hanna Barbera.

Weldon successfully pushed the Hamlyn formula of selling books like soap with the accompanying techniques of television advertising, point-of-sale material, packaging, and zany sales promotion campaigns. Weldon was in *charge of several hundred employees and a turnover in the tens of millions. Now he has three employees and he wants it to 'stay that way until I die'. As far as he is concerned the book trade can relax – the* Macquarie Dictionary *does not mark the launch of another giant in the publishing industry. But when questioned on the rationale behind the distribution of the* Macquarie Dictionary, *Weldon claims, 'I have never failed in something big' – and the way it is uttered you know it has been said before, with equal conviction.*

The decision to distribute the Macquarie Dictionary *as a privilege offer through newspapers such as the* Sydney Morning Herald *and the* Advertiser, Adelaide, *was based on sound economic calculations. 'Doing your sums prior to production, each dictionary would have had to sell for at least $50 with an initial print run of 10 000 – this way we can sell it for $30 with a 50 000 print run. It is cheaper through the newspapers – they handle all promotion and distribution costs', Weldon claimed. 'If we had released it through the book trade, we would have had to sell the rights to a wholesaler because we have no reps and no agency set up. This would have meant a sale at a 50 to 60 per cent discount on retail price. The Macquarie is different from other dictionaries. We only have Australia as a market, not the whole English speaking world, yet we have the same establishment and production costs.'*

The Macquarie Dictionary *had already been rejected by most publishers on financial grounds before Weldon took it up. He had followed it in his days with Hamlyn, knew it would be a quality publication, and wanted to be associated with it. 'Hamlyn declined to take it up, and, in retrospect, that's the best thing that has ever happened to me. The newspaper solution was staring me in the face – I had done it before with the Hamlyn* Encyclopedia World Dictionary. *We sold 75 000 through that channel.'*

Weldon admits that the book trade is upset at the moment – people are coming in and asking for the Macquarie Dictionary *and they can't get it for them. 'We are not trying to be smart and say we don't need book outlets. They said I would ruin the book trade years ago – but by God, I helped them sell more books.'*

The first edition of the Macquarie Dictionary *will be released to the trade in time – Gordon and Gotch has agreed to distribute a certain number. The concise version has been pre-sold to Doubleday; the primary and secondary pocket rights have been sold to Jacaranda Wiley.*[1]

Marketing-channel decisions are among the most critical decisions faced by management. The channels chosen for the company's product intimately affect every other marketing decision. The firm's pricing decisions depend upon whether it seeks large and high-quality dealers or medium-sized and medium-quality dealers. The firm's sales-force decisions depend upon how much selling and training the dealers will need. In addition, the channel decisions involve the firm in relatively long-term commitments to other firms. When a truck manufacturer signs up independent dealers, it cannot easily replace them with company-owned branches if conditions change. Therefore management must choose its channels carefully with an eye on tomorrow's likely selling environment as well as today's.

In this chapter we will examine the following issues: (i) What is the nature of marketing channels and what trends are taking place? (ii) What are the major decisions facing marketers with respect to designing, managing and modifying their channels? (iii) What role do physical-distribution decisions play in attracting and satisfying customers? In the following chapter we will shift our focus and examine marketing issues and decisions from the perspective of retailers and wholesalers.

THE NATURE OF MARKETING CHANNELS

Every producer seeks to link the marketing institutions that will help it best accomplish its objectives, i.e. the distribution channel. In Chapter 2, we defined distribution channel as the set of all the firms and individuals that take title, or assist in transferring title, to the particular good or service as it moves from the producer to the consumer. We also distinguished between four groups: merchants, agents, facilitators and marketing firms. Further classifications and definitions of intermediaries will be given in Chapter 15.

Why Are Marketing Intermediaries Used?

Why is the producer generally willing to delegate some of the selling job to intermediaries? This usually means relinquishing some control over how and to whom the products are sold – the producer appears to be placing the firm's destiny in the hands of intermediaries. Since producers are free in principle to sell directly to final customers, there must be cer-

tain advantages in or needs for using intermediaries. Some of these are described below.

Many producers lack the financial resources to embark on a programme of direct marketing. Even the largest manufacturers would be hard pressed to raise the cash to buy out all their dealers.

Direct marketing would require many producers to become intermediaries for the complementary products of other producers in order to achieve mass distributional efficiency. For example, the Wrigley Company would not find it practical to establish small retail chewing-gum shops throughout the country or to sell gum door to door or by mail order. It would have to tie gum in with the sale of many other small products and end up in the foodstore business. It is much easier for Wrigley to work through the existing and extensive network of privately owned distribution institutions.

Those producers who have sufficient capital to develop their own channels can often earn a greater return by increasing their investment in other parts of their business. If a company is earning a 20 per cent rate of return on its manufacturing operation and foresees only a 5 per cent return from direct marketing, it would not make sense to make such an investment.

The use of intermediaries largely boils down to their superior efficiency in making good widely available and accessible to target markets. Marketing intermediaries, through their contacts, experience, specialization and scale of operation, offer the firm more than it can usually achieve on its own.

From the point of view of the economic system, the basic role of marketing channels is to transform the heterogeneous supplies found in nature into meaningful goods assortments desired by people:

> The materials which are useful to man occur in nature in heterogeneous mixtures which might be called conglomerations since these mixtures have only random relationship to human needs

and activities. The collection of goods in the possession of a household or an individual also constitutes a heterogeneous supply, but it might be called an assortment since it is related to anticipated patterns of future behaviour. The whole economic process may be described as a series of transformations from meaningless to meaningful heterogeneity.[2]

Alderson has summarized this as follows: 'The goal of marketing is the matching of segments of supply and demand.'[3]

Figure 14-1 shows just one source of the economics effected by the use of intermediaries. Figure 14-1a shows three producers using direct marketing to reach each of three customers, a system which requires nine different contacts. Figure 14-1b shows the three producers working through one distributor who in turn contacts the three customers, requiring only six contacts and thus reducing the amount of work that must be done.

Marketing-channel Functions

A marketing channel is essentially a method of organizing the work that has to be done to move goods from producers to consumers. The purpose of the work is to overcome various gaps that separate the goods and services from those who would use them. The work of intermediaries is designed to create form, time, place and possession utilities. The following major marketing-channel functions or tasks are involved in this work:[4]

1. *Research*, i.e. gathering the information necessary for planning and facilitating exchange.
2. *Promotion*, i.e. the development and dissemination of persuasive communications about the offer.
3. *Contact*, i.e. searching out and communicating with prospective buyers.
4. *Matching*, i.e. shaping and fitting the offer to the buyer's requirements. This includes such activities as manufacturing, grading, assembling and packaging.
5. *Negotiation*, i.e. the attempt to reach final agreement on price and other terms of the offer so that transfer of ownership or possession can be effected.
6. *Physical distribution*, i.e. transporting and storing the goods.
7. *Financing*, i.e. the acquisition and dispersal of funds to cover the costs of the channel work.
8. *Risk-taking*, i.e. the assumption of risks in connection with carrying out the channel work.

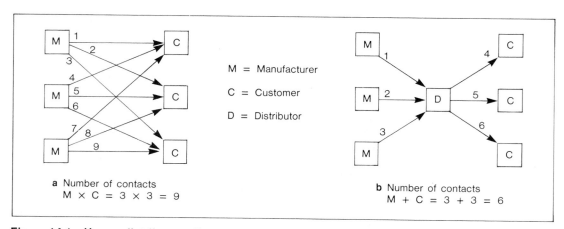

a Number of contacts
M × C = 3 × 3 = 9

M = Manufacturer

C = Customer

D = Distributor

b Number of contacts
M + C = 3 + 3 = 6

Figure 14-1 How a distributor effects an economy of effort

The first five functions deal primarily with consummating transactions; the last three deal with facilitating transactions.

It is not a question of whether these functions must be performed – they must be – but rather who is to perform them. All of the functions have three things in common: they use up scarce resources, they can often be performed better through specialization, and they are shiftable. To the extent that the manufacturer performs them, its costs go up and its prices have to be higher; when some of these tasks are delegated to intermediaries, the producer's costs and prices are lower but the intermediaries must add a charge to cover the use of scarce resources. The issue of who should perform various channel tasks is largely one of relative efficiency and effectiveness.

Marketing functions, then, are more basic than the institutions that appear to perform them. Changes in channel institutions largely reflect the discovery of more efficient ways to combine or separate economic functions that must be carried out to provide useful assortments of goods to target customers.

Number of Channel Levels

Marketing channels have a number of levels. Each intermediary that performs some work to bring the product and its title closer to the point of consumption constitutes a channel level. Since both the producer and the ultimate consumer perform some work, they are part of every channel. We will use the number of intermediary levels to designate the length of a channel. Figure 14-2 illustrates several marketing channels of different lengths.

A *zero-level channel* (a direct marketing channel) consists of a manufacturer selling directly to a consumer. Avon's sales representatives sell cosmetics directly to homemakers on a door-to-door basis; IBM's sales representatives sell computer equipment directly to user firms; and Bell Apple Orchard invites the public to pick their own apples at a flat price per case.

A *one-level channel* contains one selling intermediary. In consumer markets this intermediary is typically a retailer; in industrial markets it is often a sales agent or a broker.

A *two-level channel* contains two intermediaries. In consumer markets they are

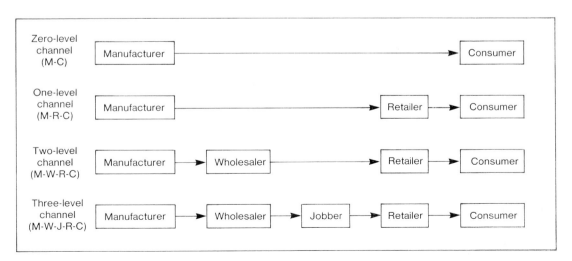

Figure 14-2 Examples of different-level channels

typically a wholesaler and a retailer; in industrial markets they may be a sales agent and a wholesaler.

A *three-level channel* contains three intermediaries. For example, a jobber may intervene between the wholesalers and the retailers. The jobber buys from wholesalers and sells to the smaller retailers, who generally are not serviced by the large wholesalers.

Higher-level marketing channels are also found, but with less frequency. From the producer's point of view the problem of control increases with the number of levels, even though the manufacturer typically deals only with the adjacent level.

Types of Channel Flow

The various institutions that make up a marketing channel are connected by several types of flow, which are illustrated in Figure 14-3 for the marketing of forklift trucks.

The *physical flow* describes the actual movement of physical products, including raw

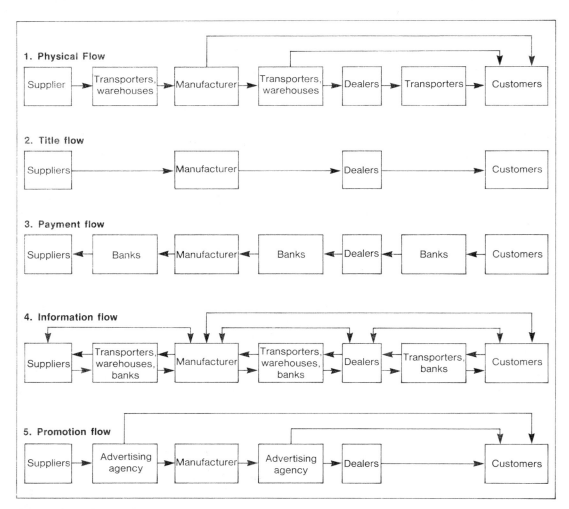

Figure 14-3   Five different marketing flows in the marketing channel for forklift trucks

materials, to final customers. In the case of a forklift-truck manufacturer, such as Hyster or Clark Equipment, raw materials, subassemblies, parts and engines flow from suppliers via transport companies (transporters) to the manufacturer's warehouses and plants. The finished trucks are warehoused and later shipped to dealers in response to their orders. The dealers in turn sell and ship them to customers. Large orders may be supplied directly from the company warehouses or even from the plant itself. At each stage of movement, one or more modes of shipment may be used, including railways, trucks, and airfreight.

The *title flow* describes the actual passage of title (of ownership) from one marketing institution to another. In the case of forklift trucks, title to the raw materials and components passes from the suppliers to the manufacturer. Title to the finished trucks passes from the manufacturer to the dealers and then to the customers. If the dealers only held the trucks on consignment, they would not be included in the diagram.

The *payment flow* shows customers paying their bills (through banks and other financial institutions) to the dealers, the dealers remitting payment to the manufacturer (less the commission), and the manufacturer making payments to the various suppliers. There will also be payments made to transporters and independent warehouses (not shown in the figure).

The *information flow* describes how information is exchanged between the institutions in the marketing channel. A two-way information exchange takes place between each successive stage in the channel, and there are several information flows between non-adjacent institutions.

Finally, the *promotion flow* describes directed flows of influence (advertising, personal selling, sales promotion and publicity) from one party to other parties in the system. Suppliers promote their name and products to the manufacturer. They may also promote their names and products to final customers in the hope of influencing the manufacturer to prefer products embodying their parts or materials. A promotion flow is also directed by the manufacturer to dealers (trade promotion) and final customers (end-user promotion).

If all of these flows were superimposed on one diagram, they would emphasize the tremendous complexity of even simple marketing channels. This complexity goes even further, once we start distinguishing among different types of retailers, wholesalers and others (see Chapter 15).

Channels in the Service Sector

The concept of marketing channels is not limited to the distribution of physical goods. Producers of services and ideas also face the problem of making their output available and accessible to target populations. Current talk about 'educational dissemination systems' and 'health delivery systems' is simply another way of describing marketing channels that distribute services in the non-profit sector. The producers' problem is one of developing and locating a set of agencies and facilities to provide services to a spatially distributed population:

> Hospitals must be located in geographic space to serve the people with complete medical care, and we must build schools close to the children who have to learn. Fire stations must be located to give rapid access to potential conflagrations, and voting booths must be placed so that people can cast their ballots without expending unreasonable amounts of time, effort or money to reach the polling stations. Many of our states face the problem of locating branch campuses to serve a burgeoning and increasingly well educated population. In the cities we must create and locate playgrounds for the children. Many overpopulated countries must assign birth control clinics to reach the people with contraceptive and family planning information.[5]

Channels of distribution are also used in 'person' marketing. Before 1940 seven different channels were available to a professional comedian seeking an audience: vaudeville houses, special events, nightclubs, radio, movies, carnivals, and theatres. In the late 1950s television emerged as a strong channel and vaudeville disappeared. Politicians also must find cost-effective channels – mass media, rallies, pamphlets – for distributing their ideas to the voters.

Channels are normally thought to describe routes for the forward movement of products, but increasingly there is talk of backward channels. According to Zikmund and Stanton:

> The recycling of solid wastes is a major ecological goal. Although recycling is technologically feasible, reversing the flow of materials in the channel of distribution – marketing trash through a 'backward' channel – presents a challenge. Existing backward channels are primitive, and financial incentives are inadequate. The consumer must be motivated to undergo a role change and become a producer – the initiating force in the reverse distribution process.[6]

The authors go on to identify several types of intermediary that can play a role in the 'backward channel', including manufacturers' redemption centres, 'clean-up days' by community groups, traditional intermediaries such as soft-drink distributors, refuse-collection specialists, recycling centres, modernized 'rag and bone men', waste-recycling brokers and central-processing warehousing.

Growth of Vertical Marketing Systems

One of the most significant channel developments in recent years has been the emergence of vertical marketing systems to challenge and supplant conventional marketing channels. Conventional channels are 'highly fragmented networks in which loosely aligned manufacturers, wholesalers and retailers have bargained with each other at arm's length, nego-

tiated aggressively over terms of sale, and otherwise behaved autonomously'. By contrast, vertical marketing systems (VMSs) are 'professionally managed and centrally programmed networks, pre-engineered to achieve operating economies and maximum market impact'.[7] Vertical marketing systems offer effective competition to conventional marketing channels because they achieve impressive scale economies through their size, bargaining power, and elimination of duplicated services. In fact, they have emerged in the consumer-goods sector of the Australian economy as the preferred mode of distribution.

Corporate VMS. Three types of vertical marketing systems are shown in Figure 14-4. A corporate vertical marketing system has as its distinguishing characteristic the combining of successive stages of production and distribution under a single ownership. Australian Safeway manufactures much of its own ice-cream and bakery products; Shell is increasingly operating its own self-service outlets rather than utilizing lessees.

Contractual VMS. A contractual vertical marketing system is where independent firms at different levels of production and distribution integrate their programmes on a contractual basis to obtain more economies and/or sales impact than they could achieve alone. Contractual VMSs constitute one of the most significant developments in the economy. There are three major types of contractual VMSs.

Wholesaler-sponsored voluntary chains. These originated when wholesalers attempted to save the independent retailers they served from the competition of large chain organizations. The wholesaler develops a programme in which independent retailers join together to standardize their practices and/or achieve buying economies that enable them as a group to withstand the inroads of the chains.

Retailer cooperatives. These arose through

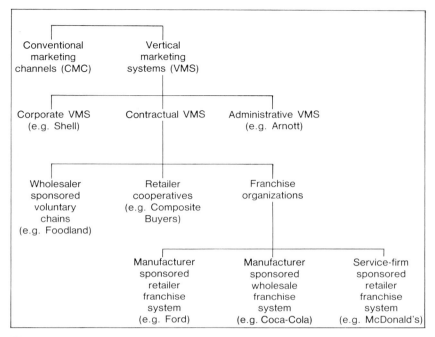

Figure 14-4   Conventional and vertical marketing channels

the efforts of groups of retailers to defend themselves against the corporate chains. The retailers organize a new business entity to carry on wholesaling and possibly production. Members are expected to concentrate their purchases through the retailer cooperative and plan their advertising jointly. Profits are passed back to members in the form of patronage refunds; non-member retailers may also be allowed to buy through the co-op but do not receive patronage funds.

Franchise organizations. Here several successive stages in the production-distribution process are linked under an agreement with one channel member called the franchiser. Franchising has been the fastest-growing and most interesting retailing development in recent years. Although the basic idea is an old one, some forms of franchising are quite new. Three forms of franchises can be distinguished.

The first is the manufacturer-sponsored re-

tailer franchise system, exemplified by the motor-vehicle industry. A car manufacturer such as Ford licenses dealers to sell its cars, the dealers being independent businesspeople who agree to meet various conditions of sales and service.

The second is the manufacturer-sponsored wholesaler franchise system, which is found in the soft-drink industry. Coca-Cola, for example, licenses bottlers (wholesalers) in various markets who buy its syrup concentrate and then carbonate, bottle and sell it to retailers in local markets.

The third is the service-firm-sponsored retailer franchise system. Here a service firm organizes a whole system for bringing its service efficiently to consumers. Examples are found in the car rental business (Hertz, Avis), and fast-food service business (McDonald's, Kentucky Fried Chicken). This type of franchising system is discussed further in Chapter 15.

Administered VMS. An administered vertical marketing system, by contrast, achieves coordination of successive stages of production and distribution not through common ownership but through the size and power of one of the parties within the system. Thus manufacturers of a dominant brand are able to secure strong trade cooperation and support from resellers. Such companies as General Electric, Arnott, Kraft, and Heinz are able to command unusual cooperation from their resellers and retailers in connection with displays, shelf space, promotions, and price policies.

Many independents, if they have not joined VMSs, have become specialty-store operators, serving segments of the market that are not available or attractive to the mass merchandisers. Thus there is a polarization in retailing, with large vertical marketing organizations at one extreme and specialty independent stores at the other. This development creates a problem for independent manufacturers, as they are strongly aligned with independent intermediaries whom they cannot easily give up. At the same time, they must eventually realign themselves with the high-growth vertical marketing systems and will probably have to accept less-attractive terms from these large buying organizations. Vertical marketing systems can always decide to bypass large manufacturers and set up their own manufacturing. The new competition in retailing is no longer between independent business units but rather between whole systems of centrally programmed networks (corporate, administered and contractual) competing against each other to achieve the best economies and customer response.

Growth of Horizontal Marketing Systems

Another significant development is the readiness of two or more companies to form alliances to jointly exploit an emerging marketing opportunity. None of these companies is able to amass the capital, know-how, production, or marketing facilities to venture alone; or it prefers not to because of the high risk; or it sees a substantial synergy in the proposed relationship. The companies may set up temporary or permanent arrangements to work with each other, or to create another entity owned by the parents. Such developments in horizontal marketing systems have been described by Adler as 'symbiotic marketing'.[8] For example, Reckitt & Colman established a joint venture with Cerebos, called the Menu Master Company, to market the products of both parent-companies in the expanding food service or catering industry. Menu Master also distributes for Nabisco in this area.

Growth of Multichannel Marketing Systems

Companies are increasingly adopting multichannel systems to reach the same or different markets. For example, Myer operates department stores, mass-merchandising stores (called Target) and supermarkets (also Target). Tillman has labelled large retailing stores with diversified retailing channels 'merchandising conglomerates' or 'conglomerchants', and has defined them as 'a multiline merchandising empire under central ownership, usually combining several styles of retailing with behind-the-scenes integration of some distribution and management functions'.[9]

A growing number of companies are operating multichannels that serve two different customer levels. This dual distribution can be a source of many conflicts for the sponsoring company.[10] For example, Ansett and TAA sell airline tickets directly to the public and also via travel agents; clearly, there are advantages to the airlines if direct reservations and ticketing cost less than the agents' commissions.[11]

Roles of Individual Firms in a Channel

Our discussion of vertical, horizontal and multichannel marketing systems underscores the dynamic and changing nature of channels. Each firm in an industry has to define its relationship to the dominant channel type. McCammon has distinguished five types of relationships:[12]

1. *Insiders* are the members of the dominant channel who enjoy continual access to preferred sources of supply and high respect in the industry. They have an interest in perpetuating the existing channel arrangements, and are the main enforcers of the industry code.
2. *Strivers* are those firms which are seeking to become insiders but have not yet arrived. They have less regular access to preferred sources of supply, which can handicap them in periods of short supply. They adhere to the industry code because of their desire to become insiders.
3. *Complementors* neither are nor seek to be part of the dominant channel. They perform functions not normally performed by others in the channel, serve smaller segments of the market, or handle smaller quantities of merchandise. They usually benefit from the present system and tend to respect the industry code.
4. *Transients*, like complementors, are outside the dominant channel and do not seek membership. They go in and out of the market, or move around as opportunities arise, but they are really members of another channel. They have short-run expectations and little incentive to adhere to the industry code.
5. *Outside innovators* are the real challengers and disrupters of the dominant channels. They come with an entirely new system for carrying out the marketing work of the channel; if successful, they cause major channel realignments. They are companies like McDonald's and Avon, which doggedly develop a new system to challenge the old.

Another important role is that of channel captain – the dominant member of a particular channel, who organized and leads it. For example, General Motors-Holden's is the channel captain of a system consisting of a huge number of suppliers, dealers and facilitators. The channel captain is not always a manufacturer, as the examples of McDonald's and Coles indicate. Some channels do not have an acknowledged captain, in that the various firms do not even recognize that they are acting as part of a system.

Channel Cooperation, Conflict and Competition

It should be clear that within and between marketing channels there are different degrees of cooperation, conflict and competition. Cooperation is usually the dominant theme among members of the same channel, as the channel represents a coalition of dissimilar firms that have banded together for mutual advantage. Manufacturers, wholesalers and retailers complement each other's needs, and their partnership normally produces greater profits for each participant than could have been secured by individual efforts. The need for channel cooperation is a natural extension of the marketing concept, in that firms are trying to effectively sense, serve and satisfy the needs of the target market.

Conflict, nevertheless, also tends to occur within each channel system. Horizontal channel conflict refers to conflict between firms at the same level of the channel: some Ford dealers in Sydney may complain that other Ford dealers in the city are being too aggressive in their pricing and advertising, and are stealing sales from them; some Pizza Hut franchisees may complain about others cheating on the ingredients, maintaining poor service, and hurting the overall Pizza Hut image. In cases of horizontal channel conflict, the responsibility lies with the channel captain to set clear and enforceable policies, and to see that information about intralevel channel conflict flows upward to management. Quick and decisive action is required to reduce or control this type of conflict, which, if left unchecked, could hurt the channel's image and cohesiveness.

Vertical channel conflict, i.e. between different levels of the same channel, is even more common. Consider the following examples:

- Commercial television stations initially rejected advertisements for home videocassette recorders because it was felt that inadequate warnings on copyright restrictions were given, thereby encouraging illegal recording of programmes and depriving stations of revenue.[13]
- Stihl Chain Saw (Australia) was fined for several breaches of the Trade Practices Act, in particular its attempt to impose resale price maintenance on a retailer-customer.[14]
- In response to many previously 'chemist-only' products going to open sale in supermarkets and elsewhere, retail pharmacists have been urged to substitute similar but restricted products or to carry only non-comparable package sizes to those appearing in supermarkets.[15]

Some amount of vertical channel conflict is healthy, and the problem is mainly to manage it better. The channel captain should attempt to develop superordinate goals for the system, from which everyone would gain: trying to minimize the total cost of moving the product through the system, improving information flows within the system, and cooperating to increase consumer acceptance of the product. Administrative mechanisms should also be developed that increase participation and trust, and help to resolve conflicts, such as dealer and distributor councils, and various conciliation, mediation and arbitration mechanisms.[16]

Channel competition describes the normal competition between firms and systems trying to serve the same target markets. Horizontal channel competition occurs between firms at the same channel level competing for sales in the same target market, as where various appliance retailers (such as department stores, discount specialty stores, discount department stores) all compete for the consumer's appliance dollar. This competition is healthy and should result in consumers' enjoying a wider range of choice in the way of products, prices and services. Channel system competition describes the competition between different whole systems serving a given target market: are food consumers better served by conventional marketing channels, corporate chains, wholesaler-sponsored voluntary chains, retailer-cooperatives, or food franchise systems? While each system will have some loyal followers, the share of the different systems in the total food business will shift over time in favour of those best able to meet changing consumer needs.

CHANNEL-DESIGN DECISIONS

We will now look at channel decisions from the producer's point of view. In Chapter 15, we will examine channel management decisions facing resellers.

In selecting channels of distribution, producers have to struggle with what is ideal and what is available. In the typical case a new firm starts as a local or regional operation selling to a limited market; since it has limited capital, it usually utilizes existing intermediaries. The number of intermediaries in any local market is apt to be limited: a few manufacturer's sales agents, a few wholesalers, an established set of retailers, a few transport companies, and a few warehouses. Deciding on the best channels may not be an issue – the problem may be to convince one or a few available distributors to handle the line.

If the new firm is successful, it may branch out to new markets. The producer will again tend to work through the existing intermediaries, although this may mean using different types of marketing channels in different areas. In the smaller markets the firm may sell directly to the retailers; in the larger markets it may work only through distributors. In rural areas it may work with general-goods merchants; in urban areas, with limited-line merchants. In one part of the country it may grant exclusive franchises because the merchants are accustomed to work this way; in another, it may sell through any and all outlets willing to handle the merchandise. Thus the producer's channel system evolves in response to local opportunities and conditions, as well as other factors.

Identifying the Major Channel Alternatives

Let us assume that a company has defined its target market and desired positioning. It should next attempt to identify its major channel alternatives: the types of business intermediaries, the number of intermediaries, and the terms and mutual responsibilities of the producer and intermediaries.

Types of intermediary. The firm should first identify the types of intermediary available to carry on its channel work. Consider the following example:

A manufacturer of test equipment for public utilities developed an audio device for detecting poor mechanical connections in any machinery with moving parts. The company executives felt that this product would have a market in all industries where electric, combustion or steam engines were either used or manufactured. This meant such industries as aviation, motor vehicle, railways, food canning, construction, and oil. The existing sales force was small, and the problem was how to reach these diverse industries effectively. The following channel alternatives came out of management discussion:

1. *Company sales force.* Expand the company's direct sales force. Assign sales representatives to territories and give them responsibility for contacting purchasing agents in the relevant industries. Or specialize the company sales force by end-use industries.

2. *Manufacturer's agency.* Hire manufacturer's agencies, operating in different regions or end-use industries, to sell the new test equipment.

3. *Industrial distributors.*[17] Find distributors in the different regions and/or end-use industries who will buy and carry the new line. Give them exclusive distribution, adequate margins, product training and promotional support.

As well as conventional channel arrangements, more innovative possibilities sometimes suggest themselves. This happened when the organ companies decided to merchandise organs through department and discount stores, thus drawing more attention to organs than they had ever enjoyed in the small shops where they had traditionally been merchandised. A daring new channel was exploited when K-Tel decided to merchandise records through television; other sellers, perceiving the success of K-Tel, developed their own television marketing operations, such as Summit and Starcall (RCA).

Sometimes a company is forced to choose or invent a channel other than its preferred one, because of the difficulty or cost of breaking into the preferred channel. The decision, may, however, turn out extremely well; the experience of the Macquarie Dictionary, outlined at the beginning of this chapter, is a case in point.

Number of intermediaries. The number of intermediaries used at each stage is influenced by the degree of market exposure sought by the company. Three degrees of market exposure may be distinguished.

Intensive distribution. Producers of convenience goods and common raw materials generally seek intensive distribution, i.e. as many outlets as possible. The dominant factor in the marketing of these goods is their place utility. The producers of cigarettes, for example, try to enlist every possible retail outlet and device to create maximum brand exposure and convenience. This policy has culminated in the use of over one million outlets in the United States, which is about as intensive as distribution can get.

Exclusive distribution. Some producers deliberately limit the number of intermediaries handling their products. The extreme form of this is exclusive distribution, the policy of granting a limited number of dealers the exclusive right to distribute the company's products in their respective territories; it often goes hand in hand with exclusive dealing, where the manufacturer requires the dealers not to carry competing lines. Exclusive distribution is found at the retail level with respect to the distribution of new cars, some major cosmetics, and some brands of women's apparel. Through granting exclusive distribution, the manufacturer hopes to gain a more aggressive selling effort and be able to exercise more direct controls over intermediaries' policies on prices, promotion, credit and various services. Exclusive distribution also tends to enhance the image of the product and allow higher mark-ups.

Selective distribution. Between intensive and exclusive distribution stands an intermediate arrangement called selective distribution, i.e. the use of more than one but less than all of the willing intermediaries. It is used both by established companies with good reputations, and by new companies seeking to obtain distributors. The company does not have to dissipate its efforts over a lot of outlets, many of which would be marginal, but can develop a good working understanding with the selected intermediaries and expect a better-than-average selling effort. Selective distribution enables the producer to gain adequate market coverage with more control and less cost than intensive distribution.

Terms and responsibilities of channel members. The producer must determine the mix of conditions and responsibilities to be assumed by different channel members. The main elements in this 'trade-relations mix' are the price policies, conditions of sale, territorial rights, and specific services to be performed by each party.

Price policy is one of the major elements in the trade-relations mix. The producer usually establishes a list price, and then allows discounts to various types of intermediaries and possibly for various quantities purchased. In developing the schedule of discounts, the producer must proceed carefully because intermediaries have strong feelings about the discounts they and others are entitled to.

Conditions of sale refer to payment terms and producer guarantees. Most producers grant cash discounts to their distributors for early payment, and may also extend certain guarantees to distributors regarding defective merchandise or price declines. The offer of a guarantee against price declines may be necessary to induce distributors to buy in large quantities rather than on an as-needed basis.

Distributors' territorial rights are another element in the trade-relations mix. Distributors want to know where the producer intends to enfranchise other distributors, and would also like to receive full credit for all sales taking place in their territory, whether or not these were stimulated through their personal efforts.

Mutual services and responsibilities must be carefully spelled out, especially in franchised and exclusive-agency channels. For example, the Pacific Seven company provides its '7-Eleven' franchisees with the store, rental of equipment, utilities, bookkeeping, some financial control, general administrative and technical assistance, and promotional support. In turn, the franchisee meets company standards of presentation and operation, and provides required information.[18]

Evaluating the Major Channel Alternatives

Suppose a producer has identified several major channel alternatives and wants to decide which would best satisfy the long-run objectives of the firm. Each alternative should be rated against economic, control and adaptive criteria. Suppose a company wishes to reach a large number of retailers in a certain region. One alternative is to hire and train three sales representatives, who would operate out of a sales office in the region and be paid a base salary with the opportunity for further earnings through commissions. The other alternative is to use a manufacturers' agency in the region that has developed extensive contacts with retailers; the agency has eight sales representatives who would receive a commission on the goods sold.

Economic criteria. Each channel alternative will produce a different level of sales and costs. The first issue is whether more sales will be produced through a company sales force or a sales agency. Most marketing managers believe that a company sales force will sell more: company representatives concentrate entirely on the company's products, are better trained to sell the company's products, are more aggressive because their future depends on the company, and are more successful because customers prefer to deal directly with the company.

But these are abstract arguments. It is possible that the sales agency could produce as many or more sales. First, the producer is considering hiring three new company sales representatives versus using eight agency sales representatives. The sheer difference in the size of the sales force would lead to more sales through the agency. Second, the agency's sales force may be just as aggressive as a direct sales force, depending on how much commission the line offers them in relation to others they represent. Third, some customers may prefer

dealing with agents who represent a large number of manufacturers rather than dealing with salespersons from one company. Fourth, one of the chief assets of an agency is the extensive contracts it has built up over the years, which a company sales force would have to cultivate from scratch.

The next step calls for estimating the costs associated with selling different volumes under each system (see Figure 14-5). The fixed costs of engaging a sales agency are lower than those of establishing a company sales office; on the other hand, costs rise faster with additional sales through a sales agency because agents get a larger fixed percentage of sales than do company salespeople who are only on part commission.

Looking at the chart, there is one sales level (S_B) at which selling costs would be the same for the two channels. The sales agency would constitute a superior channel at any volume of sales below S_B, and the company sales branch would constitute a superior channel at any higher volume. This analysis accords with common observations of the circumstances under which the two channels are used: sales agents tend to be engaged by smaller firms, or by larger firms in their smaller territories,

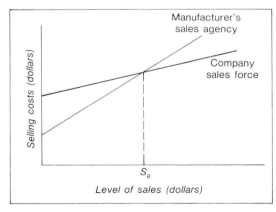

Figure 14-5 Break-even cost chart for the choice between a company sales force and a manufacturer's sales agency

because in both cases the sales volume is too low to justify a company sales force.

Control criteria. The evaluation must now be broadened by considering the control aspects of the channel alternatives. The use of sales agents can give rise to a number of control problems, because an agency is essentially an independent business interested in maximizing its own profits. The agent may not cooperate with the client's agent in an adjacent territory; the agent concentrates calls on the customers that are most important to the agency in terms of the total assortment of goods, rather than those most important to the client. The agent's sales force may not take the time to master the technical details concerning the client's product or use the client's promotion materials carefully.

Adaptive criteria. Each channel alternative involves some commitment and loss of flexibility. A manufacturer who decides to use a sales agency may have to offer a five-year contract; during this period other means of selling, such as direct mail, may become more efficient, but the manufacturer is not free to drop the sales agency. A channel alternative involving a long commitment should show evidence of being greatly superior on economic or control grounds in order to be considered.

CHANNEL-MANAGEMENT DECISIONS

After a company has determined its basic channel design, individual intermediaries must be selected, motivated and evaluated.

Selecting Channel Members

Producers differ in their ability to recruit qualified intermediaries. Some have no trouble finding specific business establishments to join the channel, because of the firm's high prestige or because the specific product or line appears to be a good money-maker. For example, some of Australia's leading retailers agreed to participate in the ill-fated Computicket venture. In some cases the promise of exclusive or selective distribution will influence a sufficient number of distributors to join the channel. The main problem for the producer who can attract enough intermediaries is one of selection, i.e. a decision as to which distributor characteristics provide the best indication of competence.

At the other extreme are producers who have to work hard to line up the desired number of qualified intermediaries. In its early days, Polaroid could not get photographic-equipment stores to carry its new cameras and was forced to go to mass-merchandising outlets. Often small producers of new food products find it difficult to get shelf-space in food outlets.

Whether producers find it easy or difficult to recruit intermediaries, they should determine what characteristics distinguish the better distributors from the poorer ones. They should evaluate the intermediaries' number of years in business, the other lines carried, growth and profit record, solvency, co-operativeness and reputation. If the intermediaries are sales agents, producers should also evaluate the number and character of other lines carried, and the size and quality of the sales force. If the intermediary is a department store being considered for exclusive distribution, the producer should evaluate the store's location, growth potential, and type of clientele.

Motivating Channel Members

Intermediaries must be motivated to do their best job. The factors and terms that lead them to join the channel provide some incentive, but these must be supplemented by continuous supervision and encouragement from the producer. The producer must sell not only through the intermediaries but to them.

The manufacturer must begin by attempting to understand the needs and wants of the particular intermediaries. According to McVey, the intermediary is often criticized by manufacturers:

... for failure to stress a given brand, or for the poor quality of his salesman's product knowledge, his disuse of supplier's advertising materials, his neglect of certain customers (who may be good prospects for individual items but not for the assortment), and even for his unrefined systems of record keeping, in which brand designations may be lost.[19]

However, shortcomings from the manufacturer's point of view may be quite justifiable from the distributor's point of view. McVey listed the following four propositions to help understand intermediaries:

The middleman is not a hired link in a chain forged by a manufacturer, but rather an independent market ... After some experimentation, he settles upon a method of operation, performing those functions he deems inescapable in the light of his own objectives, forming policies for himself wherever he has freedom to do so ...

[The middleman often acts] primarily as a purchasing agent for his customers, and only secondarily as a selling agent for his suppliers ... He is interested in selling any product which these customers desire to buy from him ...

The middleman attempts to weld all of his offerings into a family of items which he can sell in combination, as a packaged assortment, to individual customers. His selling efforts are directed primarily at obtaining orders for the assortment, rather than for individual items ...

Unless given incentive to do so, middlemen will not maintain separate sales records by brands sold ... Information that could be used in product development, pricing, packaging, or promotion-planning is buried in nonstandard records of middlemen, and sometimes purposely secreted from suppliers.[20]

These propositions are a provocative departure from stereotyped thinking about the performance of intermediaries. The first step in motivating others is to see the situation from their viewpoint.

Producers vary in their level of sophistication with respect to handling distributor relations. We can distinguish between three approaches: cooperation, partnership, and distribution programming.[21] Most producers see the problem of motivation as one of determining how to gain *cooperation* from independent and sometimes difficult intermediaries who 'aren't loyal' or 'are lazy'. A common response is to use the carrot-and-stick approach: dream up positive motivators such as higher margins, special deals, premiums, cooperative advertising allowances, display allowances, and sales contests; and if these do not work, apply negative sanctions such as threatening to reduce the margins, slow down service, or terminate the relationship. The basic problem with this approach is that the producer has not really studied the needs, problems, strengths and weaknesses of the distributors, but has instead put together a miscellaneous set of devices based on crude stimulus-response thinking. McCammon notes that many programmes developed by the manufacturer 'consist of hastily improvised trade deals, uninspired dealer contests, and unexamined discount structures ... this traditional attitude toward distributor programming is a luxury that can no longer be easily afforded.'[22]

More sophisticated companies try to forge a long-term *partnership* with their distributors. This calls for the manufacturer's developing a clear sense of what it wants from its distributors, and what its distributors may expect from the manufacturer in terms of market coverage, product availability, market development, account solicitation, technical advice and services, and market information. The manufacturer seeks an agreement from its distributors on these policies, and may set up compensation based on their adhering to these policies.

Distribution programming is a further stage

in the possible relation between manufacturers and their distributors. McCammon defines it as building a planned, professionally managed, vertical marketing system that incorporates the needs of both the manufacturer and the distributors.[23] The manufacturer sets up a special department within the marketing department (called distributor relations planning), whose job is to identify the distributors' needs and build up programmes to help each distributor operate as optimally as possible. This department and the distributors jointly plan the merchandising goals, inventory levels, space and visual merchandising plans, sales-training requirements, and advertising and other promotion plans. The aim is to convert the distributors from thinking that they make their money primarily on the buying side (through an adversary relation with the supplier) to seeing that they make their money on the selling side by being part of a sophisticated vertical marketing system.

Evaluating Channel Members

The producer must periodically evaluate intermediaries' performance against certain standards such as sales-quota attainment, average inventory levels, customer delivery time, treatment of damaged and lost goods, cooperation in company promotional and training programmes, and distributor services owed to the customer.

The producer typically issues sales quotas to define current performance expectations, and may list the sales of various intermediaries after each sales period and send the rankings out. This device is intended to motivate intermediaries at the bottom of the list to do better for the sake of self-respect (and continuing the relationship), and those at the top to maintain their performance out of pride. A more useful measure is to compare each intermediary's sales with performance in the preceding period, using the average percentage improvement as a norm. Another useful measure is to compare each intermediary's performance with assigned quotas based on an analysis of the sales potential in the respective territories. After each sales period, intermediaries are ranked according to the ratio of their actual sales to their sales potential, and diagnostic and motivational effort can then be focused on the underachievers.

CHANNEL-MODIFICATION DECISIONS

Every so often, the market channel requires modification to meet new conditions in the marketplace. This fact struck a large manufacturer of major household appliances, which had been marketing exclusively through franchised dealers: a relative loss in market share led it to take stock of several recent developments including: (i) an increasing share of major brand appliances were being merchandised through discount houses; (ii) an increasing share of major appliances were being sold on a private-brand basis through large department stores; (iii) a new market was developing in the form of volume purchases by project-home builders who preferred to deal directly with the manufacturers; (iv) door-to-door and direct-mail solicitation of orders was being undertaken by some dealers and competitors; (v) the only strong independent dealers were those in small towns, and rural families were increasingly making their purchases in large cities. These and other developments in the ever-changing distribution scene led this manufacturer to undertake a major review of possible channel modifications.

Adding or Dropping Individual Channel Members

The decision to add or drop a particular intermediary usually requires a straightforward economic analysis of the firm's potential profits both with and without this intermediary.

The analysis could be complex if, for example, the decision is made to grant another franchise: the analysis will have to take into account not only the new dealer's probable sales, but also the possible losses or gains in the sales of the manufacturer's other dealers.

Adding or Dropping Particular Marketing Channels

Sometimes a producer contemplates adding or dropping a marketing channel. For example, International Harvester might find that in

---

Exhibit 14-1 Distribution Decisions and Public Policy

Marketers have a choice in the way goods and services move from the point of production to the ultimate consumer. Once the channel is selected, producers and distributors set the conditions that will govern their relationship. These include, inter alia, definition of territories, minimum quantity of purchases, stocks to be held, purchasing and selling price, promotion methods and expenditure, and relations with competitors.

However it has been recognized that one of the parties may abuse a position of power to impose terms that will restrain the freedom of the other party and be detrimental to competitive enterprise and the public interest. Such contracts are governed by the restraint of trade provisions in the Trade Practices Act. For instance, Associated Drug Companies of Australia, owned by pharmacist wholesale cooperatives, tried to demand minimum terms relating to operating margins and sought to boycott manufacturers attempting to reduce margins. Their agreement was refused clearance by the Trade Practices Commission. Attempts to supply only selected distributors, or to supply with specific conditions of sale or minimum purchase requirements, may also be considered as being in restraint of trade; as in the case of Australian Fibreglass Pty Ltd, which sought to supply one of its products only to members of the Federation of Wall and Ceiling Contractors of Australia and New Zealand.

Naturally enough, suppliers wish their products to receive the maximum selling effort from the resellers. The easiest way to achieve this would be to induce the reseller to cease handling competitive products, e.g. by granting discounts or finance or providing special services. A supplier could also facilitate the sale of its products by supplying one type of product on condition that the customer bought other types of goods or services supplied by itself or a related company. The control of distributors could also be made easier by restricting them to a definite geographic market. Such arrangements may, however, severely restrict the freedom of the reseller in terms of the goods offered for sale, or deprive customers of choice in a range of goods, with the result that competition would be lessened.

It is not unexpected, therefore, to find such types of arrangements strictly limited by law. 'Exclusive dealing' is expressly prohibited by section 47(1), if it is likely to have the effect of substantially lessening competition in a market for goods and services. Applications by suppliers for authorization to engage in potentially exclusive dealing may be granted by the Commission, however, but only if it is concluded that this is likely to result in a substantial benefit to the public.

There are numerous cases where the Commission has denied authorization because of exclusive dealing. The Ford Motor Company tried to prevent its dealers handling other makes of new motor vehicles on the grounds of efficiency and product development; Tooth and Tooheys would not allow their retailers to sell competitive products.

using the same dealers to sell heavy trucks, light trucks, and recreational vehicles, the dealers prefer to spend their energy selling trucks to fleet owners rather than selling single recreational vehicles to consumers. To improve the sale of its recreational vehicles, International Harvester would then consider establishing a new marketing channel, in the form of recreational vehicle dealerships.

Modifying the Whole Channel

The most difficult decision involves revising the company's overall system of distribution. For example, a motor-vehicle manufacturer may consider replacing independent dealers with company-owned dealerships; a soft-drink manufacturer may consider replacing local franchised bottlers with centralized bottling and direct sales. These decisions must be made at the top-management level, because they would necessitate revising most of the marketing mix and policies to which the firm is accustomed. Such decisions have so many ramifications that any quantitative modelling of the problem can only be a first approximation.

PHYSICAL-DISTRIBUTION DECISIONS

Up to now, we have examined how companies select channels of distribution to carry their products to the final markets. We have not examined, however, the physical side of distribution, i.e. how companies arrange for the efficient storing, handling and moving of goods so that they will be in the place needed at the time needed. Customer attraction and satisfaction are deeply affected by the seller's physical-distribution capabilities. Here we will examine the nature, objectives, systems and organizational aspects of physical distribution.

Nature of Physical Distribution

Physical distribution involves planning and implementing the physical flows of materials and final goods from points of origin to points of use or consumption to meet the needs of customers at a profit. The main elements of the physical-distribution mix are shown in Table 14-1. Inventory carrying is the major cost of physical distribution, followed by transportation, order processing, warehousing, packaging and storage, receiving and dispatch, and administration. Management is becoming increasingly concerned about these costs, which amount to 14.1 per cent of sales.[24] Authorities hold that substantial savings can be effected in relation to physical distribution, which has been described 'the last frontier for cost economies'[25] and 'the economy's dark continent'.[26] Physical-distribution decisions, when uncoordinated, result in profit suboptimization. Not enough

Table 14-1   Comparative distribution costs (percentage of sales)

	USA	UK	Japan	Australia
Transportation	6.4	5.5	13.5	2.5
Receiving and dispatch	1.7	2.5		1.4
Warehousing	3.7			1.8
Packaging and storage	2.6	2.0		1.7
Inventory	3.8	3.0	13.0	3.6
Order processing	1.2	1.0		2.1
Administration	2.4	2.0		1.0
Total	21.8	16.0	26.5	14.1

Source: P. Gilmour and P. J. Rimmer, 'Business Logistics in the Pacific Basin', *Columbia Journal of World Business*, Vol. 11, No. 1, Spring 1976, p. 65.

use is being made of modern decision tools for blending economic levels of inventories, efficient modes of shipment, and sound plant, warehouse and store locations.

Physical distribution is, of course, a potent tool for creating demand. Companies can attract additional customers by offering better service, or by cutting prices through reducing distribution costs; they can lose customers when they fail to make their goods available on time.

Traditional physical-distribution thinking starts with goods at the plant and tries to find low-cost methods to get them to customers. Marketers have argued for market logistics thinking that starts with market considerations and works backwards. In at least one case, such a viewpoint led to a creative distribution breakthrough. In Germany, consumers typically purchase soft-drinks by the bottle. A soft-drink manufacturer, looking for an advantage, decided to design a six-pack. The manufacturer tested the idea with consumers, who responded positively to the convenience of such a pack. The retailers also responded positively because the bottles could be loaded faster on the shelves and could lead to more bottles being purchased per occasion. The manufacturer designed the six-packs to fit on the shelf in a way that maximized utilization of the shelf-space; then it designed cases and pallets that would bring these packs efficiently to the store's receiving rooms. The plant operations were redesigned to produce the new bottles and six-packs. The purchasing department let out bids for the new needed materials. Once implemented, this new way of packaging soft-drinks was an instant hit with consumers and the manufacturer's market share increased substantially.

The Physical-distribution Objective

Many companies state their physical-distribution objective as getting the right goods to the right places at the right time for the least cost. Unfortunately, this provides little actual guidance – no physical-distribution system can simultaneously maximize customer service and minimize distribution cost. Maximum customer service implies such policies as large inventories, premium transportation, and many warehouses; whereas minimum distribution cost implies such policies as slow and cheap transportation, low stocks, and few warehouses.

A company cannot achieve physical-distribution efficiency by letting physical-distribution managers simply keep down their own costs. Various physical-distribution costs interact, often in an inverse way:

> The transport manager favours rail shipment over air shipment whenever possible. This reduces the company's freight bill. However, because the railways are slower, this ties up company capital longer, delays customer payment, and may cause customers to buy from competitors offering more rapid service.
>
> The shipping department uses cheap containers to minimize shipping costs. This leads to a high damage rate of goods in transit and the loss of customer goodwill.
>
> The inventory manager favours holding low inventories to reduce total inventory cost. However, this results in many stockouts, backorders, accompanying paperwork, special production runs, and high-cost fast-freight shipments.

The point is that since physical-distribution activities are highly interrelated, decisions must be made on a total system basis.

Before designing the physical-distribution system it is necessary to study what the customers want in the way of service and what the competitors are offering. Customers are interested in several things: (i) on-time delivery, (ii) the supplier's willingness to meet the customer's emergency merchandise needs; (iii) the care with which merchandise is delivered in good condition; (iv) the supplier's readiness to take back defective goods and resupply them quickly; and (v) the supplier's willingness to carry inventory for the customer.

The company has to research the relative importance of the various services to the target customers. Table 14-2 shows the results of an Australian study into the relative importance of these in the scientific instrument and supplies market. Each of the market sectors in this industry, together with the suppliers of these products, were asked to rank in order of importance (1 = most important to 9 = least important) the nine aspects of customer service. From the table it can be seen that not only do the requirements vary for different segments, but that generally the suppliers are unaware of what their customers' needs actually are. Agreement was generally expressed on the importance of availability; but suppliers thought that efficient telephone handling of orders was second in importance, while none of the customer segments ranked it higher than fourth.

The company must also look at competitors' service standards in setting its own, and should normally offer at least the same level of service as competitors. But the objective is to make profits, not necessarily maximize sales. The company has to look at the costs of providing different levels of service. Some companies will decide to offer less service, but will charge a lower price and bear lower physical-distribution costs. Other companies will decide to offer more service than competitors and will charge a premium price to cover their higher service costs.

In the end the company will have to establish specific objectives to guide its physical-distribution system planning. For example, Coca-Cola wants 'to put Coke within an arm's length of desire', and this has clear implications. Companies go further and define standards for each service factor. One appliance manufacturer has established the following service standards: (i) to deliver at least 95 per cent of the dealer's orders within seven days of order receipt; (ii) to fill the dealer's orders with 99 per cent accuracy; (iii) to answer dealer inquiries on order status within three hours; and (iv) to ensure that damage to merchandise in transit does not exceed one per cent.

Given a set of physical-distribution objectives, the company is ready to design a system that will minimize the cost of achieving these objectives. The major decision issues are:

- How should orders be handled? (order processing)

Table 14-2 Ranking of customer service by supplier and customer grouping

Customer service element	Suppliers	All customers	Private companies	Government instrumentalities	Secondary schools	Universities and CAEs	Hospitals
Availability of item	1	1	1	5	1	1	1
After-sales service and back-up	5	2	5	1	7	2	2
Efficient telephone handling of orders and queries	2	6	4	6	4	7	7
Ordering convenience	7	7	8	9	2	6	8
Competent technical representatives	3	5	5	2	8	5	3
Delivery time	5	4	2	6	5	3	5
Reliability of delivery	4	3	3	4	3	4	4
Demonstrations of equipment	8	7	7	3	9	7	5
Availability of published material	9	9	9	8	6	9	8

Source: P. Gilmour et al., 'Customer Service: Differentiating by Market Segment', *International Journal of Physical Distribution*, Vol. 7, No. 3, 1977, p. 146.

- Where should stocks be located? (warehousing)
- How much stock should be kept on hand? (inventory)
- How should goods be shipped? (transportation)

We will now examine these four major elements and their implication for marketing.

Order Processing

Physical distribution starts with the receipt of a customer order. Sales representatives, dealers and customers dispatch orders to the firm; the order department prepares multicopy invoices and dispatches them to various departments. Items that are out of stock are back-ordered. Items that are shipped are accompanied by shipping and billing documents that are also multicopied and go to various departments.

The company has a strong interest in carrying out these steps as quickly and accurately as possible. Sales representatives are supposed to send in their orders every evening, in some cases phoning them in when obtained. The order department should process these quickly, the warehouse should send the goods out as soon as possible, and bills should go out as soon as possible; the computer should be harnessed to expedite the order-shipping-billing cycle.

Industrial engineering studies of how sales orders flow through the company may help to shorten this cycle substantially. Some of the key questions are: What happens after the receipt of a customer purchase order? How long does the customer credit check take? What procedures are used to check inventory and how long does this take? How soon does manufacturing hear of new stock requirements? How long does it take for sales executives to learn of current sales?

Ringer and Howell reported a study of one company's order routine, which resulted in cutting down the time between the receipt and issuance of an order, from sixty-two hours to thirty hours without any change in costs.[27] General Electric operates a computer-oriented system which, upon receipt of an order, checks the customer's credit standing and whether and where the items are in stock. If the answers are positive, the computer system issues an order to ship, bills the customer, updates the inventory records, sends a production order for new stock, and relays the message back to the sales representative that the customer's order is on its way – all in less than fifteen seconds.

Warehousing

Every company must make provision for stocking its goods at various locations while they wait to be sold, because production and consumption cycles rarely match (e.g. many agricultural commodities are produced continuously, but demand is often seasonal). The storage function overcomes discrepancies in timing and in quantities desired.

The company must determine the number of stocking locations to maintain. With more stocking locations, it can deliver goods to customers more quickly. This is favoured by the marketers. However, warehousing costs go up with the number of locations that have to be managed. The number of stocking locations must be chosen with an eye to balancing customer delivery service and distribution costs.

Some of the company's stock will be kept at or near the plant, and the rest will be located in major warehouses throughout the country. The company may have its own warehouses and/or rent space in public warehouses. Companies have more control in private warehouses, but at the same time they tie up their capital and have less flexibility to change to more desirable locations. Public warehouses, on the other hand, charge only for the space being rented and provide additional services such as inspecting goods, packaging them, shipping them to customers, invoicing customers, and even providing desk space and telephone service for company salespeople. In using public warehouses, companies have a wide choice of locations and warehouse types, including those that specialize in cold storage, commodities only, and so on.

The storage warehouse is designed to store goods for moderate to long periods of time. Companies also use distribution warehouses (sometimes called distribution centres), which receive goods from many company plants on a daily basis, assemble them, and move them out to customers as soon as possible. The alternative would have required each plant to send less than full-load quantities to each customer as orders come in, which would be very costly.

Older multistoreyed warehouses with slow lifts and inefficient materials-handling arrangements are now facing competition from single-storeyed automated warehouses with advanced materials-handling systems under the control of a central computer. These have reduced worker injuries, labour costs, and pilferage and breakage, and have improved inventory control.

Inventory

Inventory levels represent another major type of physical-distribution decision affecting customer attraction and satisfaction. The marketer would like the company to carry enough stock to fill all customer orders immediately, but this amount of inventory is not cost-effective. Inventory cost increases at an increasing rate as the customer service level approaches 100 per cent, and the company needs to know whether sales and profits would increase enough to justify this higher investment.

Inventory decision-making is a two-step process which requires knowledge of both when and how much to order. As inventory is drawn down, management must decide when a new order should be placed. The stock level at which this is desirable is called the order (or re-order) point, i.e. an order point of 20 would mean that when the supply of an item falls to twenty units, it should be re-ordered.

The determination of the order point depends upon the order lead time, the usage rate and the service standard. The higher these are, the higher the order point, and if the order lead time and customer usage rate are variable, the order point would have to be higher by an amount of safety stock. The final order point is set on the basis of balancing the risks of stockouts against the costs of overstock.

The other decision is how much to order: obviously, the larger the quantity ordered, the less often an order has to be placed.

Much depends on determining order-processing costs versus inventory carrying costs. Order-processing costs for a manufacturer consist of set-up and running costs for the item. If set-up costs are very low, the manufacturer can produce the item often and the cost per item is pretty constant and equal to the running costs. However, if set-up costs are high, the manufacturer can reduce the average cost per unit by producing a long run and carrying more inventory.

Order-processing costs must be compared with inventory carrying costs (i.e. storage charges, the cost of capital, taxes and insurance, and depreciation and obsolescence). The larger the average stock carried, the higher the inventory carrying costs, which may run as high as 30 per cent of the inventory value. This means that marketing managers who want their companies to carry larger inventories must be able to convince top management that these will yield additional sales with an incremental gross profit that would more than cover the incremental carrying costs.

The optimal order quantity can be determined by observing how order-processing costs and inventory carrying costs sum up at different possible order levels. Figure 14-6 shows that the order-processing cost per unit decreases with the number of units ordered, because the order costs are spread over more units; inventory carrying charges per unit increase with the number of units ordered, because each unit remains longer in inventory. The two cost curves are summed vertically into a total-cost curve: its lowest point is projected down on the horizontal axis to find the optimal order quantity Q^*.

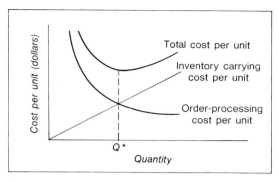

Figure 14-6 Determining optimal order quantity

Transport

Marketers take an interest in their company's choice of transportation, which will affect the price of products, on-time delivery performance, and the condition of the goods when they arrive. These things will affect customers' interest in buying from this company and their postpurchase satisfaction.

In shipping goods from its plants to its warehouses, or from its warehouses to dealers or customers, the company can choose among four major transportation modes – rail, road, sea and air – which are discussed briefly in the following paragraphs, and tabulated in Table 14-3.

Rail. Railways are one of the most cost-effective modes of transport for shipping quantities of bulk products – coal, sand, minerals, farm and forest products – over long land distances. The rate costs for rail shipping are quite complex. To meet competition, especially road transport, railways have designed new kinds of equipment to handle merchandise more effectively, and provide flatcars to permit the carrying of truck trailers by rail.

Road. Trucks are a highly flexible means of transport in their route opportunities and time schedules. They can move merchandise door to door, thus saving shippers the need to transfer goods from truck to rail and back again at a loss of time and risk of theft or

damage. Trucks are an efficient mode of transport for short hauls of high-value merchandise. Their rates are competitive with railway rates in many cases, and trucks can usually offer faster service.

Sea. A substantial amount of goods is carried by ship on coastal waterways. This form of transport is very low in cost for shipping bulky, low-value, non-perishable products such as sand, coal, grain, oil, and metallic ores. It is, on the other hand, the slowest transport mode.

Air. Air carriers transport less than one per cent of the nation's goods but are becoming an increasingly important form of transport. Although airfreight rates are considerably higher than rail or road rates, airfreight is ideal where speed is essential and/or distant markets have to be reached. Among the products frequently shipped by air are high perishables (e.g. fresh fish, cut flowers) and high-value, low-bulk items (e.g. technical instruments, jewellery). Airfreight reduces required inventory levels, number of warehouses, and costs of packaging.

In choosing a transportation mode for a particular product, shippers may consider as many as six different criteria, as illustrated in Table 14-4. If a shipper is trying to achieve speed, the table shows that air and truck are the prime contenders for consideration. If the

Table 14-3 Freight transport, Australia, by mode

Year ending 30 June	Public rail	Private rail*	Road	Sea	Air	Total
		Thousand million tonne-kilometres				
1950	10.9	0.4	8.2	16.1	0.03	35.6
1960	12.9	0.5	13.3	30.3	0.05	57.1
1965	18.0	0.6	17.4	41.5	0.06	77.6
1970	23.6	9.2	24.9	65.0	0.09	122.8
1975	29.0	26.0	33.0	74.0†	0.11	162.1
1976	31.0	26.0	35.0	101.0	0.11	193.1
		Percentage				
1950	30.6	1.0	23.1	45.2	0.1	100.0
1960	22.6	0.9	23.1	53.1	0.1	100.0
1965	23.1	0.8	22.4	53.6	0.1	100.0
1970	19.2	7.5	20.3	52.9	0.1	100.0
1975	17.9	16.0	20.4	45.6†	0.1	100.0
1976	16.1	13.4	18.1	52.3	0.1	100.0
		Million tonnes				
1965	59.3	4.7	440.0	23.4	0.1	527.5
1970	75.5	37.2	700.0	32.5	0.1	845.2
1975	87.0	104.4	950.0	42.0	0.1	1183.5
1976	95.0	117.0	960.0	48.0	0.1	1220.1
		Percentage				
1965	11.2	0.9	83.4	4.5	0.0	100.0
1970	8.9	4.4	82.8	3.9	0.0	100.0
1975	7.4	8.8	80.2	3.6	0.0	100.0
1976	7.8	9.6	78.7	3.9	0.0	100.0

*Includes only iron-ore railways in South Australia and Western Australia and the Emu Bay Railway in Tasmania
†New series commencing 1971–72; not strictly comparable with earlier estimates

Source: P. J. Rimmer, 'The Australian Transport Industry: Its Changing Structure, Conduct, and Performance', in P. Gilmour (ed.), *Proceedings of 1977 Physical Distribution Seminar* (Melbourne: Monash University, 1977); Department of Transport, *Australian Transport, 1977–78* (Canberra: Australian Government Publishing Service, 1978), p. 8.

Table 14-4 Transportation modes ranked according to major shipper criteria*

	Speed (door-to-door delivery time)	Frequency (scheduled shipments per day)	Dependability (meeting schedules on time)	Capability (ability to handle various products)	Availability (no. of geographic points served)	Cost (per tonne km)
Rail	3	4	3	2	2	3
Water	4	5	4	1	4	1
Road	2	2	2	3	1	4
Pipeline	5	1	1	5	5	2
Air	1	3	5	4	3	5

Source: Adapted from James L. Heskett, Robert J. Ivie & Nicholas A. Glaskowsky, *Business Logistics* (New York: Ronald Press, 1964), pp. 71ff.

*1 = highest rank

goal is low cost, then water and pipeline are the prime contenders if appropriate for the specific products. It should be noted that trucks appear to embody the most advantages, and this explains their domination.

In addition to using single modes of transportation, the shipper will often combine two or more modes. This is due largely to containerization, i.e. putting the goods in boxes or trailers that can easily be transferred. Piggyback describes the use of rail and trucks; fishback, water and trucks; trainship, water and rail; and airtruck, air and trucks. Each coordinated mode of transportation offers specific advantages to the shipper, e.g. piggyback is cheaper than road transport alone, but provides flexibility and convenience.

Decisions about transportation must take into account not only the complex trade-offs between various transportation modes, but also between the chosen mode and its implications for other distribution elements such as warehousing and inventory. As relative costs change over time, companies need to reconsider their options in the search for optimal physical-distribution arrangements.

Organizational Responsibility for Physical Distribution

By now it should be clear that decisions on warehousing, inventory and transportation require the highest degree of coordination. A growing number of companies have set up a permanent committee, composed of managers responsible for different physical distribution activities, which meets periodically to develop policies for improving overall distribution efficiency. Other companies have centralized their physical-distribution activities under a manager who may or may not be responsible to the marketing manager.

The location of the department within the company is a secondary concern. The important thing is the company's recognition that it needs to coordinate its physical-distribution and marketing activities in order to achieve high market impact at a reasonable cost.

SUMMARY

Marketing-channel decisions are among the most complex and challenging decisions facing the firm. Each channel system has a different potential for creating both sales and costs. Once a particular marketing channel is chosen, the firm must usually adhere to it for a substantial period. The chosen channel will significantly affect and be affected by the rest of the marketing mix.

Each firm usually has a number of alternative ways to reach the market: from direct selling, to the use of one or more intermediary channel levels. The firms making up the marketing channel are connected in different ways by physical, title, payment, information and promotion flows. Marketing channels are characterized by continuous and sometimes dramatic change. Three of the most significant trends are the growth of vertical, horizontal and multichannel marketing systems. These trends have important implications for channel cooperation, conflict and competition.

Channel design calls for identifying the major channel alternatives in terms of the type and number of intermediaries, and the channel terms and responsibilities. Each alternative has to be evaluated according to economic, control and adaptive criteria.

Channel management calls for selecting particular intermediaries and motivating them with a cost-effective trade-relations mix. Individual channel members must be periodically evaluated against their own past sales and other channel members' sales.

Channel modification at the individual member level, particular channel level, or whole channel level will be required from time to time as the environment changes.

Just as the marketing concept is receiving increasing recognition, a growing number of business firms are beginning to heed the physical-distribution concept. Physical distribution is an area of high potential cost savings, improved customer satisfaction and competitive effectiveness. When order processors, warehouse planners, and inventory and transportation managers make decisions in isolation they affect each other's costs and demand-creation capacity but do not take them into consideration. The physical-distribution concept calls for treating all these decisions within a unified framework. Then the important task becomes that of designing physical-distribution arrangements that minimize the total cost of providing a given customer service.

QUESTIONS FOR DISCUSSION

1. Why are marketing intermediaries used? Explain by using a concrete example.

2. What major channel functions are labelled facilitating functions? Discuss these in relation to the sale of milk.

3. How many channel levels are commonly used by the following companies?
   • Myer
   • Electrolux
   • Coles supermarkets.

4. Channels of distribution do not differ for services and physical products. Comment.

5. Distinguish between the three major types of vertical marketing systems. Give an example of each.

6. There is no way to alleviate channel conflict. Comment.

7. Which of the following products would be intensively, exclusively and selectively distributed, and why?
   • Rolex watches
   • Volkswagen cars
   • Gillette blades
   • Estée Lauder perfume.

8. After the channel design is determined, what three activities must the marketers undertake? Explain each briefly.

9. How do physical-distribution decisions differ from channel decisions? What is the overriding objective of physical distribution?

10. In what ways has the computer facilitated physical distribution?

11. Which mode of transportation would probably be used to distribute the following products?
    • beer
    • expensive jewellery
    • natural gas
    • farm machinery.

NOTES

[1] Colleen Ryan, 'Relax – Kevin Weldon Intends to Stay Small', *Australian Financial Review*, 9 October 1981, p. 52.

[2] Wroe Alderson, 'The Analytical Framework for Marketing', *Proceedings – Conference of Marketing Teachers from Far Western States* (Berkeley: University of California Press, 1958).

[3] Wroe Alderson, *Marketing Behaviour and Executive Action: A Functionalist Approach to Marketing Theory* (Homewood, Ill.: Richard D. Irwin, 1957), p. 199.

[4] For other lists, see Edmund D. McGarry, 'Some Functions of Marketing Reconsidered', in Reavis Cox & Wroe Alderson (eds), *Theory in Marketing* (Homewood Ill.: Richard D. Irwin, 1950), pp. 269–73; and Louis P. Bucklin, *A Theory of Distribution Channel Structure* (Berkeley: Institute of Business and Economic Research, University of California, 1966), pp. 10–11.

[5] Ronald Abler, John S. Adams & Peter Gould, *Spatial Organization: The Geographer's View of the World* (Englewood Cliffs, N.J.: Prentice-Hall, 1971), pp. 531–32.

[6] William G. Zikmund & William J. Stanton, 'Recycling Solid Wastes: A Channels-of-Distribution Problem', *Journal of Marketing*, July 1971, p. 34.

[7] Bert C. McCammon Jr, 'Perspectives for Distribution Programming', in Louis P. Bucklin (ed.), *Vertical Marketing Systems* (Glenview, Ill.: Scott, Foresman, 1970), pp. 32–51.

[8] Lee Adler, 'Symbiotic Marketing', *Harvard Business Review*, November–December 1966, pp. 59–71.

[9] Rollie Tillman, 'Rise of the Conglomerchant', *Harvard Business Review*, November–December 1971, pp. 44–51.

[10] See Robert E. Weigand, 'Fit Products and Channels to Your Markets', *Harvard Business Review*, January–February 1977, pp. 95–105.

[11] Ali Cromie, 'Agents Fighting for Ticket Sales Commissions', *Australian Financial Review*, 7 July 1981, p. 14.

[12] Bert C. McCammon Jr, 'Alternative Explanations of Institutional Change and Channel Evolution', in Stephen A. Greyser (ed.), *Toward Scientific Marketing* (Chicago: American Marketing Association, 1963), pp. 477–90.

[13] 'Philips' Video Advert Canned', *Age*, 18 March 1978, p. 29.

[14] 'Stihl Fined $75 000 for Resale Price Offences', *Australian Financial Review*, 11 December 1978, p. 11.

[15] Ian Davis, 'TPC Watch on Boycott Action by Pharmacy Guild', *Australian Financial Review*, 17 January 1978, p. 5.

[16] For an excellent summary of interorganizational conflict and power in marketing channels, see Louis W. Stern & Adel I. El-Ansary, *Marketing Channels* (Englewood Cliffs, N.J.: Prentice-Hall, 1966), Ch. 7.

[17] For further reading on industrial distributors, see Frederick E. Webster Jr, 'The Role of the Industrial Distributor', *Journal of Marketing*, July 1976, pp. 10–16.

[18] Julianne Schultz, 'Now the Drive-In Milk Bar', *Australian Financial Review*, 28 February 1978, pp. 1, 3.

[19] Phillip McVey, 'Are Channels of Distribution What the Textbooks Say?', *Journal of Marketing*, January 1960, pp. 61–64.

[20] Ibid.

[21] See Bert Rosenbloom, *Marketing Channels: A Management View* (Hinsdale, Ill.: Dryden Press, 1978), pp. 192–203.

[22] McCammon, p. 32.

[23] McCammon, p. 43.

[24] For an excellent overview of this topic, and an extensive local reading list, see Peter Gilmour, *The Management of Distribution: An Australian Framework* (Melbourne: Longman Cheshire, 1979).

[25] Donald D. Parker, 'Improved Efficiency and Reduced Cost in Marketing', *Journal of Marketing*, April 1962, pp. 15–21.

[26] Peter Drucker, 'The Economy's Dark Continent', *Fortune*, April 1962, pp. 103ff.

[27] Jurgen F. Ringer & Charles D. Howell, 'The Industrial Engineer and Marketing', in Harold Bright Maynard (ed.), *Industrial Engineering Handbook* (New York: McGraw-Hill, 2nd edn, 1963), pp. 10, 102–3.

Retailing and Wholesaling Strategy

15

G.J. Coles and Co. and the Myer Emporium will introduce an unprecedented buying force into liquor retailing. With this buying power will eventually come big changes to businesses which rely exclusively on liquor – brewers, winemakers, wholesalers and the multitude of small liquor shops.

As a result of recent acquisitions, Myer and Coles have been thrust into a position of authority in an industry which still trades under conventions and methods which were established decades ago. Indeed, the situation is similar to that when grocery retailers were confronted with the ogre of supermarket chains. The number of small grocery operations diminished rapidly under the intense pressure from the supermarkets' focal buying strength.

At the moment, Coles and Myer emphasize that they have no immediate plans to change the liquor market. Rather, they are content to test the market's reaction to their presence through chain liquor outlets. In recognizing the growth potential of high-turnover liquor outlets, Myer and Coles made separate arrangements with a handful of the most aggressive chain liquor outlets.

The moves, aimed at larger alcohol markets, were an interesting demonstration of how two of Australia's most influential retailers often think alike and act simultaneously. On June 16, Myer's chief executive, Keith Rosenhain, announced that the company would extend its retailing activities with the acquisition of the San Remo chain of liquor outlets in Victoria. Three weeks later Coles declared that it had acquired fifty-three specialist liquor stores from Sydney's own Bacchant and hotelier Claude Fay.

The common assertion was that liquor marketing would open 'exciting new prospects' and broaden the range of goods available. The last time the two

*retailers took a risky plunge at the same time was back in the 1960s when Myer
sought control of Target and Coles wanted K-Mart. In that battle Coles won
hands-down. Myer must be anxious that in liquor retailing too Coles may have
again stolen the march.*

*Brewers and liquor wholesalers (in some cases they are one and the same)
are now finding they are compelled to deal with these heavyweight retailers in
order to maintain sales. But in doing so they merely aggravate the dramatic shift
away from traditional alcohol suppliers which have sustained them for so long.*

*At present, most of the outlets buy their beer direct from breweries and
their wine and spirits from wholesalers. The liquor industry is one of the few
remaining areas of business where the wholesalers still play an important role.
It is significant that Myer now owns a wholesaler as well as a retailer. To
compete, Coles may eventually have to follow. Some of the breweries, like
Carlton and United, own their own wholesalers and should be able to weather
the influx of the big liquor retailer. It is the small independent perhaps family-
owned and operated wholesaler which stands to lose the most if companies like
Myer and Coles become too aggressive in the liquor trade.*

*The growing tendency for drinkers to take liquor home rather than drink
it at a hotel was the main reason that Coles and Myer took the plunge into high-
turnover alcohol sales. The swing has been a long-standing concern of brewers
and hoteliers. It now has a new sense of urgency because the greater the swing
the more that hotel and brewery investments will be jeopardized. The spearhead
of Coles' push into liquor has been in New South Wales while Myer is more
aggressive in its home state. However, Victoria is the only state which effectively
legislates against beer discounting. This was implemented to protect hoteliers.*

*If it wants to use discounting as a marketing ploy, Myer will have to offer
wine at low prices instead of beer. Coles will be able to offer beer, wine and spirits
at competitive prices. Through its aggressiveness in the liquor trade, Coles now
has more than 100 liquor outlets throughout Australia and is Australia's largest
liquor retailer outside the combined force of hotel bottle shops.*[1]

One thing retailers have learned over the years, whether they sell to an elite market or a mass market, is that they are operating in an environment of accelerating change. The successful retailing formulas of yesterday may not work today, and most probably will not work tomorrow. Within the last few years major changes have occurred within the retailing industry. Myer has slipped from its premier position to third behind Coles and Woolworths, in terms of sales, but it is now re-asserting itself. David Jones, Franklins, Waltons and John Martin have changed ownership or control, as have many other retailers.

Modern retailers have to be alert to the signs of change and be prepared to shift their strategies – not too early and not too late. But even a decision to shift is not easy to implement. The large retailer is a prisoner of its own policies, which its managers have become accustomed to as the 'conventional wisdom'; it is also a prisoner of its public image, which consumers retain in their minds long after the store's reality has changed.

At the other end of the retailing spectrum is the small independent convenience or corner store, the cauldron of new enterprise. Small retailers are important for several reasons: they often create new forms of retailing which the large stores later copy, they offer greater convenience to consumers because they are everywhere, they often are more adaptable and give more personal service, and they offer a chance for people to be their own bosses and shape their own destinies.

At the same time, many persons who start small businesses are unprepared to run them. They think that all they need is a happy disposition and a warm smile; they lack technical skills and expertise. Probably the majority of new small retailers fail within five years. Both large and small enterprise are vulnerable to the winds of change.

In this chapter we focus on the institutions that make up the retailing and wholesaling sectors of the economy. We will take the viewpoint of managers of these institutions, and examine how they act and respond to marketing initiatives by consumers and manufacturers. In the two main sections, retailing and wholesaling, we will ask similar questions:

1. What is the nature and importance of retailing (wholesaling)?
2. What are the major types of retailers (wholesalers)?
3. What marketing decisions do retailers (wholesalers) make?
4. What is retailing's (wholesaling's) future?

RETAILING

Nature and Importance of Retailing

What is retailing? We all know that Woolworths is a retailer, but is this also true of an Avon lady knocking at a door, a contractor phoning a family about his services, a doctor seeing patients, a hotel offering a special weekend rate? Yes, they are all retailers. We define retailing as follows:

- *Retailing* includes all the activities involved in selling goods or services directly to final consumers for their personal (non-business) use.

Any institution that does this – whether it be a manufacturer, a wholesaler or a retail store – is doing retailing. It does not matter how the goods or services are sold (by person, mail, telephone, or vending machine) or where they are sold (in a shop, on the street, or in the consumer's home). On the other hand, a retailer or retail store is any business enterprise whose sales volume primarily comes from retailing.

Retailing is one of the major industries in Australia. Retail stores outnumber manufacturing and wholesaling establishments by more than three to one, and represent a major source of employment in the nation, with upwards of 750 000 employees. The industry, excluding motor vehicles, parts, petrol, etc., generated approximately $29 billion in sales in 1979–80.

Which are the nation's largest retailers? The five largest ones and their sales (as a percentage of all retail sales) in 1980–81 were Coles (13 per cent), Woolworths (8.5 per cent), Myer (5.5 per cent), Grace Brothers (2.9 per cent) and Safeway (2.2 per cent). In dollar terms, Coles annual sales exceed $3 billion. Other major retailers include David Jones, Franklins, Waltons, John Martin and Permewans.[2] Thus we see that the largest retailers are primarily general-merchandise department-store chains and supermarket chains.

Types of Retailers

The thousands of retailing units in this country come in all sizes and shapes. There is no one principle for classifying them, because new forms keep emerging and combining the features of different pure retailing types (e.g. a K-Mart store combines the principles of the supermarket and the discount store). While distribution functions cannot be eliminated, they can be combined in different ways to give rise to different institutional forms. All major retail innovations in the twentieth century have relied on creating new mixes of distribution functions to attain a strategic position in the marketplace.

One of the major distribution functions in retailing is 'service'. Retailing is positioned at the end of the 'bulk-breaking' process, typically catering to a very large number of individual consumers each of whom generates only a small, heterogeneous purchase mix at a time. Retailing is therefore basically labour-intensive, and the amount of service occasioned by each sale affects its overall operating cost structure. Labour costs account for 50–60 per cent of the selling costs for a full-service retailer. Hence the price savings that usually accompany self-service are likely to more than compensate consumers for serving themselves, especially for products such as groceries or everyday household goods where sales assistance is of little or no consequence.

Since there are a variety of customers with different service preferences and a variety of products with different service requirements, successful businesses may coexist with different levels of customer service. Table 15-1 distinguishes four levels of service and the retailing institutions typically employing them.

Self-service retailing in this country achieved its major growth in the 1960s. It has become institutionalized in the economy and is used by customers in all walks of life, especially for obtaining convenience goods and, to some extent, shopping goods. Self-service is the cornerstone of all discount operations. Many customers are willing to carry out their own 'locate-compare-select' process in order to save money.

At the next level is *self-selection retailing*, in which a salesperson is available for assistance if desired. Customers complete their transactions not by standing in a queue at the checkout counter but by finding salespeople and paying for the item, as in some variety stores. The operating expenses of self-selection institutions are somewhat higher than those of self-service operations because of the additional staff requirements.

In *limited-service retailing*, best exemplified by department-store chains such as Myer, the quality of sales assistance is somewhat higher because these stores carry more shopping goods and customers need more information.

Table 15-1   Classification of retailers based on the amount of customer service

Decreasing services			Increasing services
Self-service	**Self-selection**	**Limited-service**	**Full-service**
Very few services	Restricted services	Small variety of services	Wide variety of services
Price appeal	Price appeal	Shopping goods	Fashion merchandise
Staple goods	Staple goods		Specialty merchandise
Convenience goods	Convenience goods		
Warehouse retailing	Discount retailing	Door-to-door sales	Specialty stores
Grocery stores	Variety stores	Department stores	Department stores
Discount stores	Mail-order retailing	Telephone sales	
Mail-order retailing		Variety stores	
Automatic vending			

Source: Adapted from Larry D. Redinbaugh, *Retailing Management: A Planning Approach* (New York: McGraw-Hill, 1976), p. 12.

The stores also offer services such as credit and merchandise return, not always found in the previous two forms of retailing, and hence their operating costs tend to be higher.

Finally, in *full-service retailing*, exemplified by the 'classy' department stores of the 'Are You Being Served?' stereotype, customers are greeted by salespeople who are ready to personally assist in every phase of the locate-compare-select process. This type of store is valued by customers who like to be served and to develop personal relationships with store personnel. The high staffing cost, along with the fact that these stores normally carry specialty goods and slower-moving items (fashions, jewellery, cameras) and offer liberal merchandise return policies, various credit plans, free delivery, home servicing of durables, and customer facilities such as lounges and restaurants, results in high-cost retailing. Thus it is not surprising that full-service retailing has been on the decline for several decades.

Other schemes for classifying retailer types have also been proposed. Two of these schemes are shown in Figure 15-1. Gist has developed a margin-turnover classification that distinguishes retailer types according to the margins and volumes they pursue (see Figure 15-1a). A discount store, for example, works on the principle of setting low margins to draw in a large number of customers; other combinations of profitable retailing are also possible. Tigert has suggested that retailers can be classified according to assortment width and store size (see Figure 15-1b). Thus a furniture showroom warehouse is a very large store featuring a very narrow product line. Various other stores can be located in this grid.

In describing the many types of retailers, we will use the five principles of classification shown in Table 15-2: product line sold, relative price emphasis, nature of business premises, control of outlets, and type of store cluster.

Product line sold. The first basis for classifying retailing institutions is according to the product line sold, i.e. grocery stores, liquor stores, furniture stores, and so on. More broadly, we can look at the length and depth of the product assortment and distinguish

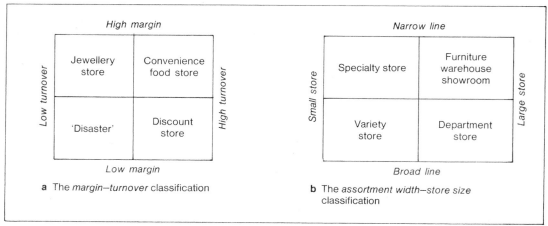

a The *margin–turnover* classification

b The *assortment width–store size* classification

Source: for 15-1a, Ronald R. Gist, *Retailing Concepts and Decisions* (New York, John Wiley, 1968), pp. 37–40; for 15-1b, adapted from Douglas J. Tigert, 'The Changing Structure of Retailing in Europe and North America' (working paper, University of Toronto, Faculty of Management Studies, 1975).

Figure 15-1 Alternative classification schemes for types of retailers

Table 15-2 Types of major retail outlets

Product line sold	Relative price emphasis	Nature of business premises	Control of outlets	Type of store cluster
Specialty store	Discount store	Mail- and telephone-	Corporate chain	Central business
Department store	Warehouse store	order retailing	Voluntary chain and	district
Supermarket	Catalogue	Automatic vending	retailer	Regional shopping
Convenience store	showroom	Buying service	cooperative	centre
Combination store,		Door-to-door	Consumer	Community
superstore, and		retailing	cooperative	shopping centre
hypermarches			Franchise	Neighbourhood
Service business			organization	shopping centre
			Conglomerchant	

some major store types. Among the most important ones are the specialty stores, department stores, supermarket, convenience store, and superstore.

Specialty store. A specialty store carries a narrow product line with a deep assortment within that line, e.g. clothing stores, sporting goods stores, furniture stores, florists and bookstores. Specialty stores can be subclassified by the degree of narrowness in their product line: a clothing store would be a single-line store; a men's clothing store would be a limited-line store; and a men's custom-made shirt store would be a superspecialty store. Some analysts contend that specialty stores will be the fastest-growing outlet in the future, to take advantage of increasing opportunities for market segmentation, market targeting, and product specialization. Two successful current examples are Sussan (women's clothing), and Just Jeans (primarily jeans).

The strong growth of specialty stores in recent years is tied to the boom of shopping centres, which typically have one or two anchor department stores and numerous specialty stores, the latter occupying 60–70 per cent of the total shopping space. Although most specialty stores are independently owned, chain specialty stores are showing the strongest growth; the most successful of these are based on specific target markets.

Department store. A department store carries several product lines – typically clothing, home furnishings and household goods – and each is operated as a separate department managed by specialist buyers or merchandisers. Examples of well-known department stores are Myer, David Jones, John Martin, and Boans.

There is some disagreement as to how the department store came about. Some writers believe that it grew out of the general store (because it carries several product lines); others believe that it grew out of the dry-goods store (because many department-store founders first ran dry-goods stores). The Bon Marche, established in Paris in 1852, is widely considered to be the first department store.[3] It introduced four innovative principles: low mark-ups and rapid turnover; the marking and displaying of merchandise prices; encouraging customers to look around without any pressure or obligation to purchase; and a liberal complaints policy. Several other stores followed, with Whiteley's in Britain (1870s) being the first to gain the reputation for carrying 'everything from a pin to an elephant', and Lewis (1870s) being the first to set up branches and employ the concept of central buying.

In Australia the earliest department stores included Foy and Gibson, and Myer at around the turn of the century.[4] They created a concept of enjoyment shopping by being housed in huge impressive buildings in fashionable central locations, with exciting displays and reputations for introducing new products. This was a far cry from going into the specialty stores of the time, which had little on display and where customers were discouraged from just browsing.

With the growth of cities, department stores developed as a major retailing institution in the central business districts (CBDs), with several stores clustering to give shoppers easy access. Specialty department stores also emerged, carrying only clothing, shoes, cosmetics, gift items, and luggage; an example is Georges in Melbourne.

Immediately after World War II, department stores experienced a relative decline in both their share of total retailing and their profitability. Many observers believe that these stores are in the declining stage of the retail lifecycle. The major factors responsible for their relative decline are: (i) increased competition among department stores, which has led to a 'trading-up' and has escalated their operating and overhead costs; (ii) increased competition from other types of retailers, particularly discount houses, specialty store chains, and warehouse retailers; and (iii) the heavy traffic, poor parking, and deterioration of central cities, along with the rapid growth of suburbs, which have made CBD shopping less appealing.

The result has been the closing of some department stores and amalgamation of others, although recently they have been waging a comeback war. Many have opened branches in suburban shopping centres, where the population growth is taking place and the parking is better. Others have added 'bargain basements' to meet the discount threat. Still others are pouring money into remodelling their stores, e.g. with a 'boutique' approach. Some are experimenting with mail-order and telephone shopping. Others, like Myer, have diversified into other store types, such as discount and specialty stores, thus becoming 'conglomerchants'. Some department stores are retrenching employees, product lines, and

customer services such as delivery, but this strategy seems destined to remove one of their major appeals compared with their competitors – namely, better service. To survive, department stores are struggling to find a way to increase their thinning profit margins.

Supermarket. A supermarket is a relatively large, low-cost, low-margin, high-volume, self-service operation 'designed to serve the consumer's total needs for food, laundry, and household maintenance products'.[5] A supermarket store can be independently owned, although most major supermarket stores are operated by supermarket chains.

The origin of the supermarket can be traced to two American sources: John Harford's introduction of the cash-and-carry Great Atlantic & Pacific Tea Company (A & P) food stores in 1912; and Clarence Saunders' Piggly-Wiggly stores which introduced, in about 1916, the principles of self-service, customer turnstiles, and checkout counters. However, supermarkets did not really become popular until the 1930s. Michael 'King' Kullen is credited with starting the first successful supermarket, a self-service, cash-and-carry grocery operation on a large scale (namely, 600 square metres of selling space as opposed to the 80 square metres in conventional stores at the time). Kullen anticipated that such a store would deliver sufficient volume to operate profitably with a gross margin of 9–10 per cent of sales, which was half that of food stores at the time. He opened his first store in August 1930 in Jamaica, New York, and it was an immediate success. In Australia, it was not until the late 1950s that grocery retailing evolved from full-service to self-service and hence to supermarkets. At this time, Coles and Woolworths diversified from variety stores into grocery retailing, largely by acquisition. Today, the four major grocery chains, Coles, Woolworths, Safeway and Franklins, operate more than 800 supermarkets and control more than 50 per cent of national grocery sales. Many supermarkets bearing names such as Foodland are independently owned and trade under a common banner.[6]

Several factors caused the rise of the supermarket in the 1950s. The mass ownership of cars made distance less important and increased weekly shopping, thus reducing the need for small neighbourhood stores. Advances in refrigeration technology meant that supermarkets and consumers could store perishables longer. Developments in packaging technology meant that food products could be marketed in storable consumer-size packages (cans and boxes) rather than distributor-size containers (barrels and crates); this stimulated pre-selling through branding and advertising, and reduced the number of salespeople needed in the store. Finally, the integration of grocery, meat, and fruit and vegetable departments made one-stop shopping feasible and attracted customers from considerable distances, thus giving stores the volume they needed for successful operation.

Over the years, supermarkets have moved in several directions to further build their sales volumes. First, they have opened larger stores – today's selling space occupying approximately 1800 square metres – with the result that most of the chains now operate larger but not necessarily more stores. Second, supermarkets have increased the number and variety of items they carry: a typical supermarket stocks about 8000 items. The most significant increase has been in the number of non-food items carried – non-prescription pharmaceuticals, beauty aids, housewares, magazines, books and toys. This 'scrambled merchandising' is continuing, and many supermarkets are moving into appliances, records, sporting goods, hardware, garden supplies and even cameras in a further effort to find high-margin lines to improve profitability. Third, supermarkets have typically upgraded their facilities through more expensive locations, larger parking facilities, carefully planned decor and architecture, longer store hours and a wide variety of customer services such as cheque-cashing and background music. Fourth, the increasing competition for customers has led supermarkets into promotional efforts in the form of heavy advertising and games of chance. Fifth, supermarkets have moved very heavily into private brands as a means of reducing their dependence on national brands and increasing their profit margins. Most of these changes have increased the supermarkets' operating costs and vulnerability to innovative competition – they are now making an operating profit of about 2 per cent on their sales.

Supermarkets have been hit hard by a number of innovative competitors (see Figure 15-2). The supermarket is typecast today as a large store selling its merchandise at medium prices: it is increasingly being challenged by other store types that meet better-defined customer needs with respect to preferred product assortments and price levels. The entire food market is becoming more refined and segmented, and is no longer likely to be dominated by one major type of food retailer. One of the major challenges to supermarkets in recent years has been the growth of fast-food outlets, with the result that Australians are now spending approximately 50 per cent of their total food budgets outside grocery stores.[7]

| | **Price** | | |
	High	Medium	Low
Narrow	Convenience stores		'Box' stores
Large		Super-markets	Discount stores
Broad		Combination stores	Superstores and hypermarches

Source: Developed from Fred C. Allvine, 'The Supermarket Challenged: New Competitive Strategies Needed', *Business Horizons*, October 1968, p. 65.

Figure 15-2 Basic store types in food retailing

Supermarkets have taken several steps to try to restore their sales volume and profitability. They have increased the number of their private brands (including generics), added more high-margined nonfood items, added delicatessen and bakery departments, and started new types of stores, particularly discount stores. While being essentially mass merchandisers, several chains are seeking to define the social-class target market better and are now designing their stores to serve specific groups.

An interesting recent development is the spread of 'supermarketing' to many other types of business, particularly in the pharmacy, home improvement, toy and sporting-goods fields. The supermarket concept, according to McCammon, involves self-service and self-selection displays; centralization of customer services, usually at the checkout counter; large-scale physical facilities; a strong price emphasis; and a broad assortment and wide variety of merchandise to facilitate multiple purchases.[8] These principles, for example, are applied by McEwan's and Nock and Kirby in the home-improvement retailing field.

Convenience store. Convenience food stores are relatively small. They are located near residential areas, are open for long hours (twenty-four hours in some cases) and seven days a week, and carry a limited line of high-turnover convenience products. Examples are local milkbars and 'delis', and expanding groups such as 7-11. Their long hours and their use by consumers mainly for fill-in purchases make them relatively high-price operations; but presumably they fill an important consumer need, and people seem willing to pay for the convenience. This form of food retailing has recently been extended to the food-petrol store, such as Food Plus run by BP and Majik Markets operated by Caltex.

Combination store, superstore and hypermarche. At the other end of the spectrum are three types of stores that are larger than the conventional supermarket. The first of these is the combination store, which is primarily a diversification of the food store into the growing pharmaceutical and prescription field. These stores are important in the United States, but it is unlikely that growth in Australia will occur due to our restrictions on the operation of pharmacies. For example, it is usually mandatory for a qualified pharmacist to be present at all times in a dispensary, and the ownership of pharmacies is usually restricted to individual pharmacists (not companies or chain operations).

The superstore tends to be larger than the conventional supermarket (3000 instead of 1800 square metres of selling space) and aims to meet the consumers' total needs for routine purchases: food products, beauty aids, personal-care products, alcoholic beverages, tobacco, housewares and hardwares, clothing such as pantyhose, magazines and books, garden products, stationery, and sewing items. In addition, the superstore may offer services such as laundry, dry-cleaning, shoe repair, and some eating facilities. The superstores' primary attraction for the investor is the 5–6 per cent higher prices over conventional supermarkets which they can charge for the wider assortment. Some leading chains such as Safeway have recently moved toward the superstore concept.

The hypermarche is even larger than the superstore, ranging between 8000 and 22 000 square metres and combining supermarket, discount and warehouse retailing principles. Its product assortment goes beyond routinely purchased goods and includes furniture, heavy and light appliances, clothing items, and many other things. The hypermarche uses a price discount appeal in contrast to the normal pricing by superstores, and also operates on warehouse principles. Many products come prepacked in wire 'baskets' direct from manufacturers, and these are stacked on five-tier metal racks to a height of four to five metres. The restocking is done by forklift trucks, which move through the wide aisles during selling hours. The basic approach is one of bulk display and minimum handling by store personnel, with discounts offered to customers who carry heavy appliances out of the store themselves. The original hypermarche was opened by Carrefour in a suburb of Paris in 1963, and it was an immediate success. The real boom occurred in the late 1960s and early 1970s, particularly in France and Germany where a few hundred of them now operate. Some hypermarches were opened in Canada, but were not very successful because supermarkets were already overdeveloped. American chains are proceeding cautiously, preferring to open superstores instead, although a few operations such as J. C. Penney's Treasury and Jewel's Grand Bazaar have adopted some of the hypermarche's operating principles. None has yet appeared in Australia (although Safeway uses the name Hypermart for its biggest stores), but Permewan Wright may be first with a Brisbane venture in conjunction with Pick 'n Pay of South Africa. The use of wire baskets or bins is gaining acceptance.

Service business. Here we want to briefly mention those business enterprises whose product line is service rather than goods. Service retailers include hotels and motels, banks, airlines, private schools and hospitals, cinemas, restaurants, repair services, and various personal services such as barber and beauty shops, dry cleaners, and funeral homes.

Service retailers in Australia are currently growing at a faster rate than retailers of goods. Each service industry has its own drama. Banks have introduced new ways to distribute their services efficiently (e.g. the use of automated tellers), and some institutions offer a telephone system for paying bills. Health maintenance organizations (HMOs) promise to revolutionize the way consumers get and pay for their health services. The amusement industry has spawned a host of 'historic reconstructions' designed to turn fantasies into realities (e.g. Old Sydney Town, Sovereign

Hill). Groups such as Transcendental Meditation and Weight Watchers have applied franchise and chain-organization principles to mass-distribute personal growth (or reduction) services. And H. & R. Block has built a franchised network of accountants and tax specialists ready to help consumers pay as little as possible to the government. We will say more about the nature of services marketing in Chapter 20.

Relative price emphasis. Another way to distinguish retail forms is on the basis of their price image and pricing policy. Most stores are middle-of-the-road pricers offering normal levels of customer service. Some stores offer shoppers higher-quality goods and/or more customer service, along with higher prices, e.g. Gucci, which justifies its high prices by saying 'You will remember the goods long after the prices are forgotten'. Still another group, discount stores, have specialized in selling goods for less than their normal prices; this is made possible by running lower-cost, lower-service operations. Discount stores will be examined here, along with two offshoots, warehouse stores and catalogue showrooms.

Discount store. A discount store sells standard merchandise at lower prices than conventional merchants by accepting lower margins and working on higher volume. The mere use of discount pricing and specials from time to time does not make a discount store; nor does the selling of cheap and inferior goods at low prices. A true discount store exhibits five elements: (i) it regularly sells at prices substantially lower than those prevailing in high-margin, low-turnover outlets; (ii) it emphasizes national brands, so that low price does not suggest inferior quality; (iii) it operates on a self-service, minimum-facilities basis; (iv) the location tends to be a low-rent area drawing customers from relatively long distances; and (v) the fixtures are spartan and functional.[9]

In recent years, intense competition among

discount houses, and between discount houses and department stores, has led many discount retailers to trade up. They have improved their decor, added new lines such as clothing, added more services such as easy returns, and opened new branches in suburban shopping centres – all leading to higher costs and thus high prices. Furthermore the department stores often cut their prices to avoid losing sales to the discounters, with the distinction between these two types of stores progressively blurring.

Today's most successful general merchandise discount chain is K-Mart, which was originally a joint venture between Coles and K-Mart (United States), but now wholly owned by Coles. The US parent company opened the first K-Mart in 1962, to replace its withering variety stores, and now has 1208 outlets. K-Mart has been opening eight to ten stores per year in Australia, and now has more than eighty throughout the country. K-Mart's success is based on sticking to discount traditions: decor is minimal; sales staff is sparse; and consumers wander about a huge one-storey building to find what they want, put their selections into shopping carts, and wheel them to checkout counters. Shoppers can choose from 15 000 specific items, including many national brands rather than the 'seconds' and 'irregulars' featured by some other discount stores.

Discount retailing has moved beyond general merchandise into specialized forms such as discount sporting-goods stores and discount stereo-equipment stores. Discount food retailing has been among the most interesting developments: chains such as Franklins, Jewel, and Permewan's Half-case have achieved success with limited assortment and/or few customer services or amenities.

Warehouse store. A warehouse store is a 'no-frills', discount reduced-service operation which seeks to move high volume at low prices. In its broad form, it includes hypermarches on the one hand and food-barn dis-count stores on the other. One of its most interesting forms is the furniture showroom warehouse; conventional furniture stores have long used warehouse sales to clear out old stock from time to time, but it took two New Yorkers to refine the idea into a new merchandising concept. The Levitz brothers got the idea in 1953, and by 1977 they had built sixty-one furniture warehouse showrooms. Shoppers enter a football-field-sized warehouse located in a low-rent suburban area. They pass through the warehouse section where they see a fantastic amount of inventory piled in neat tiers: approximately 52 000 items worth about $2 million. They enter the showroom section of the warehouse, which contains approximately 200 settings in which the furniture is attractively displayed. Customers make their selections from floor samples and place them with salespeople. By the time the customer pays for the purchase, leaves, and drives to the loading entrance, the merchandise is ready. If heavy goods are purchased, they can be delivered in a few days (compared with the many weeks of delay with conventional furniture stores) or loaded on the customer's vehicle at a savings of many dollars.

The whole operation is targeted to buyers of medium-priced brand-name furniture who are seeking discount prices (usually 10–20 per cent less than the prices charged by conventional outlets) and immediate availability. The shoppers enjoy the wide brand selection and low prices, but often complain about limited customer service. Levitz stores have attracted a number of competitors, notably the Wickes Corporation as well as units started by some of the major department-store chains hurt by the new approach. The profit picture of these furniture warehouse showrooms is mixed because there are high inventory expenses, high promotional expenditure is needed to attract sufficient traffic to their out-of-the-way locations, and often there are too many competitors.[10]

The largest Australian counterpart is the

Saba Furniture World outlet at Dandenong (Victoria) which has a one-hectare showroom on a two-hectare site. Here half the floorspace is taken by 200 room settings, and approximately $2 million is spent on television advertising each year.[11]

Catalogue showroom. A catalogue showroom applies catalogue and discounting principles to a wide selection of high-mark-up, fast-moving, brand-name goods. These include jewellery, power tools, luggage, cameras and photographic equipment. These stores emerged in the United States in the late 1960s, and have become one of American retailing's hottest new forms, even posing a threat to the traditional discounter which has moved too much into improved decor, more service, and higher mark-ups.

The catalogue showrooms issue four-colour catalogues, often 500 pages long, and supplement them with smaller seasonal editions. They are available in the showroom and are also mailed to past buyers. Each item's list price and discount price are shown; the customer can order an item over the phone and pay delivery charges or drive to the showroom, examine a sample firsthand, and buy it out of stock. In this way, catalogue showrooms differ from traditional catalogue merchandisers whose catalogues are primarily vehicles for 'in-home' shopping, where discounts do not exist and customers must wait for days or weeks before they receive the merchandise.

The customer who buys at the catalogue showroom has to put up with certain inconveniences, such as driving some distance, standing in line to see a particular item (many are locked in cases), waiting for the item to be supplied from the back room, and finding little after-service if there are problems. However, the rapid growth of this form of retailing indicates that customers are eager for their savings and willing to put up with the disadvantages. Catalogue showrooms make their money by carrying primarily national brands in nonfashion-goods categories, leasing stores in low-rent areas, doing with one-third fewer salespeople, minimizing opportunities for shoplifting by their case display, and operating largely on a cash basis. Whether this style of operation will emerge in Australia remains to be seen.

Nature of business premises. Although the overwhelming majority of goods and services are sold through stores some observers foresee that by the end of this century as much as a third of all general merchandise retailing will be done through non-store channels.[12] Others go further and predict robot retailing, where customers can order their goods using home computers and receive or pick them up without stepping into stores.[13] Here we will examine the major forms of non-store retailing: mail- and telephone-order retailing, vending machines, buying services, door-to-door selling and in-house parties.

Mail- and telephone-order retailing. Mail- and telephone-order retailing covers any selling that uses the mail or telephone to get orders and/or facilitate delivery of the goods. Mail-order itself is as old as the postal system. Although it originated in the mailed order of a customer to a manufacturer or merchant, it later took the form of merchants' attempting to stimulate custom by sending out catalogues, primarily to farmers living in rural areas where the variety of goods was limited. Today this takes several forms:

1. *Mail-order catalogue.* Here the seller mails a catalogue to a select list of customers and makes the catalogue available on its premises, either at no charge or at a nominal charge. This approach is used by few Australian firms, although there is some suggestion that it may increase as it has in the United States. Dick Smith Electronics, now part of Woolworths, claims to operate 'Australia's most famous mail order – direct buying catalogue', with over 3000 items 'from home computers through to

telephones'. Dick Smith has also pioneered direct computer-to-computer ordering by customers via the telephone lines.[14]

2. *Direct response.* Here the direct marketer runs an ad (in a newspaper, magazine, or on radio or television) describing some product, and the customer can write or telephone for it. The marketer chooses those media that maximize the number of orders for a given amount of advertising dollars. This strategy is best suited to specialty retailers dealing in a specific product market, such as records and tapes, books and small appliances.

3. *Direct mail.* Here the direct marketer sends single mail pieces – letters, leaflets, and foldouts – to prospects whose names are on mailing lists of high-potential buyers of that product category; the mailing lists are purchased from specialized brokerage houses. Direct mail (called 'junk mail' by its critics) has proved very successful in promoting books, magazine subscriptions, and insurance, and is increasingly being used to sell novelty items, clothing and even gourmet foods.[15] Australia Post is very active in promoting this activity, and has commissioned many publications (usually free to inquirers) to assist prospective users.[16]

4. *Telephone selling.* Direct marketers are increasingly using the telephone to sell everything from home-repair services or newspaper subscriptions to zoo memberships. Some telephone marketers have developed computerized systems where households are dialled automatically and computerized messages presented (which Telecom frowns on). Telephone selling has incurred the opposition of several groups, which are proposing laws to ban or limit it.

Several factors have contributed to the recent increase in mail- and telephone-order selling. The movement of women into the work force has substantially cut down the shopping time available to them. Various factors have made shopping less pleasant: the petrol situation and the spiralling costs of driving; traffic congestion and parking headaches; shoppers retreating to the suburbs and averse to visiting urban shopping areas; a lack of sales help, and the need to queue at checkout counters. In addition, many chain stores have dropped slower-moving specialty items and created an opportunity for direct marketers to promote these. The development of 'free' phone numbers, and the willingness of some firms to accept telephone orders at night or on Sundays, have also boosted this form of retailing.

Automatic vending. Automatic vending (also called automatic merchandising or robot retailing) through coin-operated machines has been a major post-World War II growth area in the United States but has had slower growth in Australia. The concept of automatic vending is not new, and one study cites a 215 BC book describing an Egyptian coin-actuated device for selling sacrificial water.[17] In the 1880s, the American Tutti-Frutti Company began installing chewing-gum machines at railway stations. But today's machines have come a long way, and have benefited from the space-age and computer technology: they have, for example, overcome the problem of requiring prices that conform to common coinage denominations, and the newest machines incorporate note-changers that can discriminate between notes of different denominations, dispense merchandise, and return the correct change. Equally significant is the considerable variety of merchandise to which auto-vend has been successfully applied. Although the bulk of sales are still generated by impulse goods with very high convenience value (cigarettes, soft-drinks, confectionery, newspapers and hot beverages), many other products (such as hosiery, cosmetics, food snacks, hot soups and food, paperbacks, record albums, film, T-shirts, insurance policies, shoeshines, and even fishing worms) are being vended successfully.

Vending machines are found everywhere – in larger retail stores, service stations and cafeterias, and on campuses. They are usually owned by a company that leases space in favourable locations and services the machines.

To customers, vending machines offer the advantages of twenty-four-hour selling, self-service, and less damaged merchandise. At the same time, automatic vending is a relatively expensive channel, and merchandise prices are often 15 to 50 per cent higher. Vendor costs tend to be high because of frequent restocking at widely scattered locations, frequent machine breakdowns, and the high pilferage rate in certain areas. For the customer, the biggest irritations are malfunctioning, machine breakdowns and out-of-stocks, and the fact that merchandise cannot be returned.

Basically, automatic vending is still most feasible only for small, fairly standardized, low-unit-value, convenience items of well-known presold brands. In non-merchandise fields, however, there have been some extensive developments. Vending machines supplying entertainment services – pinball machines, slot machines, and juke boxes – are being followed by computer games. A highly specialized area in which very rapid development is taking place is banking services. The automatic teller has revolutionized common bank transactions by allowing customers fully automated, extended-hour service for many deposits, withdrawals and transfers of funds – not only on bank premises but also in shopping malls and office buildings.

It has been prophesied that automatic vending will eventually develop into the fully automated store, i.e. where all items are purchased by coin, with one attendant or no attendants present. Several experiments in automated stores were conducted by department stores in the late 1950s and early 1960s without much success. A totally different concept in auto-mated store retailing was tested in Europe in the late 1960s. Such stores display only samples on the shelves, next to each being a slot into which the customer inserts a key (received on entering the store) which electronically registers the purchase. The order is assembled and ready for pick-up in the short time required for checkout; computer control and telecommunications are central to the system. For all practical purposes, however, the fully automated store has been a matter of research and anticipation only, and has had little impact on any major field of retailing. Only in one field has it been a resounding success – the coin-operated, automated laundry store. It appears that the future of automation in retailing may bypass the fully automated store and the really revolutionary developments come in 'in-home' shopping through interactive telecommunication systems and highly automated order-processing, billing and warehouse facilities.

Buying service. A buying service is a storeless retailer serving specific clienteles – usually the employees of large organizations such as schools, hospitals, unions and government agencies. The organization's members become members of the buying service, entitled to buy from a selective list of retailers who have agreed to give discounts. Thus a customer seeking a video recording machine would get a form from the buying service, take it to an approved retailer, and buy the appliance at a discount. The retailer would then pay a small fee to the buying service. Somewhat different are the Australian Buying Advisory Service (ABAS) and other organizations which cater to a general membership by offering advice on where to buy the cheapest products.[18]

Door-to-door retailing. This form of selling – which started centuries ago with itinerant peddlers – has many companies selling either door to door, or office to office, or at home sales parties. Pioneers include vacuum-cleaner companies like Electrolux, and household product companies like Rawleigh's; encyclopaedia companies have used door-to-door selling for years, with World Book emerging as a leader by enlisting and training schoolteachers to sell its encyclopaedias part time. Door-to-door selling improved its image considerably with Avon's entry into the industry, with its concept of the homemakers' friend and beauty consultant – the Avon lady. Tupperware helped popularize the home sales parties method of selling, whereby friends are invited to a party in someone's home where Tupperware is available for purchase.

The resurgence of door-to-door selling indicates that it meets the needs of people for convenience and personal attention. The prices of items are not low, since door-to-door selling is expensive (the salespersons receive 20–50 per cent commission), and there are the costs of soliciting and managing the sales force across widely dispersed geographic areas. The future of door-to-door retailing is uncertain. With many Australian households today consisting of single-person or two-person families (with both members working full time), the likelihood of anyone being at home during the day is rapidly diminishing: with the new telecommunication technologies expected to proliferate in the next ten years, the door-to-door salesperson may very well be replaced by a home computer.

Control of outlets. Retailing institutions are also classified according to their form of ownership. Most retail stores are independent, and account for the majority of all retail sales. There are, however, several other forms – the corporate chain, voluntary chain and retailer cooperative, consumer cooperative, franchise organization and conglomerant. Data are scarce and often outdated, but it seems that the ten largest retailers account for about 25 per cent of national sales, and that the top 100 retailers control about one-third of all sales by value.

Corporate chain. The chain store is one of the most important retail developments of the twentieth century. The idea of one merchant or company owning and operating several stores is in itself not new: the Fuggers of Augsburg had branches in scores of European cities in the fifteenth century, and the Mitsui chain was operating in Japan in the seventeenth century. The first chain stores emerged in Australia in the 1870s, with Washington H. Soul Pattinson, the New South Wales pharmacy group, being one of the pioneers. At the turn of the century department stores emerged strongly, with Foy and Gibson also establishing their own manufacturing facilities in Melbourne, and Sidney Myer opening his first store in Bendigo. In 1914 the radical George Coles opened his first 'threepence, sixpence and one shilling' store in the Melbourne suburb of Collingwood, while Woolworths was founded in Sydney in 1924. Coles' turnover reached £1 million in 1928, and by 1932 a chain of twenty-nine variety stores had been opened throughout Australia.

Gist has defined a chain store as two or more outlets that are commonly owned and controlled, sell similar lines of merchandise, have central buying and merchandising, and may use a similar architectural motif.[19] Each characteristic deserves comment. Scholars are not in agreement as to how few units make up a chain. Common ownership and control distinguishes the corporate chain from similar forms such as voluntary chains and franchise organizations, i.e. a corporate chain unit sells similar lines of merchandise, whereas a merchandising conglomerate combines several corporate chains under common ownership. Central buying and merchandising means that headquarters plays a key role in deciding the chain's product assortment, placing bulk orders for the goods to get quantity discounts, distributing the goods to the individual stores, and establishing pricing, promotion and other standardizing policies for the units. Finally, chains often develop a similar architectural motif to increase their unit's visibility and identifiability in the public eye. Corporate chain organizations have appeared in all types of retail operations: supermarkets, discount, variety, specialty and department stores.

The success of the corporate chains is based on their ability to achieve a price advantage over independents by moving toward a higher volume and lower margins. Chains achieve their efficiency in several ways. First, their sheer size allows them to buy in huge quantities to take maximum advantage of quantity discounts and lower transport costs. At various times they were accused of obtaining prices from manufacturers that bettered the normal quantity discounts, but this was challenged by the Trade Practices Act. Most authorities now question whether the chains' lower prices were in fact founded on their bulk purchasing power. Second, chains were able to develop superior operational capabilities by hiring superior managers and developing specialized management practices in the area of sales forecasting, inventory control, pricing and promotion. Third, the chains achieved a true integration of wholesaling and retailing functions, whereas the independent retailers were always dealing with many different wholesalers. Fourth, the chains were able to achieve promotional economies by buying advertising that benefited all their stores and whose cost was spread over a very large volume. Fifth, the chains permitted their units some degree of decentralized authority to meet variations in consumer preferences and competition in local markets. Probably the major threat to a chain's success consists of maintaining too much centralization and inflexibility in a rapidly changing environment.

Voluntary chain and retailer cooperative. The corporate chains were so successful that they produced various reactions, most importantly a competitive survival response in the independents, who began to form two major types of associations: the voluntary chain (a wholesaler-sponsored group of independents engaged in bulk buying and common merchandising) and a retailer cooperative (a cooperative agreement between independent retailers who set up a central buying organization). The voluntaries and cooperatives were described in Chapter 14; they gained the needed merchandising economies and programmes, and were soon able to meet the price challenge of the corporate chains. The point has been reached where the operations of corporate chains, voluntary chains and retailer cooperatives are so similar that the major difference is chiefly the question of ownership.

Consumer cooperative. A consumer cooperative (or co-op) is any retail firm that is owned by its customers. Consumer co-ops are started by the residents of a community when they feel that local retailers are charging excessive prices or providing poor-quality products. The residents contribute money to start their own store, vote on its policies and elect a group to manage it. The store may set low or normal prices, but members receive a patronage dividend based on the individual level of their purchases. A number of the most successful cooperatives are ideological, and several are found in educational communities. In Australia, consumer cooperatives have succeeded in areas such as credit unions, but they have never become an important force in general distribution. The opposite is true in some European countries, especially Scandinavia and Switzerland. A striking example is Migros in Switzerland, a consumer cooperative that accounts for 11 per cent of the entire Swiss retail volume. Migros was founded in 1925 by Gottlieb Duttweiler as a corporate chain in the grocery business, dedicated to challenging entrenched high-mark-up competitors in the grocery field. He was so successful that in 1946 he decided to turn Migros into a customer cooperative by selling one share of stock to each of his 85 000 registered customers. Today Migros is a huge federation of 440 branch stores, seventy-four specialty stores, and numerous other enterprises essentially owned by its customers.

Franchise organization. A franchise organization is a contractual association between a franchiser (manufacturer, wholesaler, or service organization) and franchisees (independent businesspeople who buy the right to own and operate one or more units in the franchise system). The main distinction between franchise organizations and other contractual systems (voluntary chains and retailer cooperatives) is that retail franchises are normally based on some unique product or service, method of doing business, trade name, goodwill or patent, that the franchiser has developed.

Two other distinctions can be drawn. The franchiser's compensation can be complex, may include an initial fee, a royalty on gross sales, rental and lease fees (on equipment and fixtures supplied by the franchiser), a share of the profits, and a regular licence fee. In a few cases franchisers have also charged management consulting fees, but usually such services are an integral part of the package deal, since one of the most important objectives of the sponsor is to ensure a minimum quality of operation and service at the franchisee level. For example, a local franchise can expect to pay from $1000 to $25 000 as an initial fee or to purchase minimum stock, royalties of from one per cent to 12 per cent of turnover, plus an advertising levy. Thus, establishment costs of the following size can be expected for some local franchises: $35 000 for Crazy Daves lighting; $45 000 for Smokes 'n' Things; $130 000 for Chicken Spot; $200 000 for Computalign; and $85 000 for the Bra Shop.[20]

The other distinction is that there are usually very specific terms on which the franchised product can be used or dispensed. These are often the subject of controversy, as when petrol-station franchisees face oil companies (their franchisers) as competitors, or when motor-vehicle franchisers try to prevent their franchisees (car dealers) from selling competing products.

Conglomerchant. Conglomerchants (also called merchandising conglomerates) are free-form corporations that combine diverse retailing lines and forms under central ownership, along with some integration of their distribution and management functions.[21] Major conglomerchants include Coles, Woolworths, Myer and John Martin.

In the 1980s, diversified retailing is growing stronger and is being adopted by more of the corporate chains. Whereas in the 1970s they concentrated on deepening their major business line, they are now looking for new types of retail businesses to launch. The major question will be whether diversified retailing produces management systems and economies that can make their separate retail lines more successful.

Type of store cluster. Another principle for retail classification is whether consumers face an isolated store or a clustered group of stores. Most stores today cluster together in shopping districts, because of zoning ordinances and also to offer aggregate convenience, namely, one-stop shopping. Just as supermarkets and department stores save consumers time and energy in finding what they need, so do clustered stores. The four main types are the central business district, the regional shopping centre, the community shopping centre, and the neighbourhood shopping centre.

Central business district (CBD). Until the late 1950s central business districts were the dominant form of retail cluster. Every large town and city had a CBD in which were located the department stores, specialty stores, banks and major cinemas; smaller business districts would also be found in neighbourhood and outlying areas. In the 1950s people began their great migration to the suburbs, giving rise to an explosive development of suburban shopping centres to serve their needs. Suburbanites shopped less in the CBD, wishing to avoid the heavy traffic, expensive parking, and deteriorating urban scene; this in turn accelerated the rate of urban blight, and forced centrally located merchants to open branches in the growing suburban shopping centres and try to revitalize the city centre by building shopping malls and car parking areas, and renovating their stores. Some CBDs have made a comeback, but others are in a state of slow and possibly irreversible decline.

Regional Shopping Centre. A shopping centre is defined as 'a group of commercial establishments planned, developed, owned and managed as a unit related in location, size and type of shop to the trade area that it services, and providing on-site parking in definite relationship to the types and sizes of stores it contains'.[22] Of these, the regional shopping centre is the most dramatic and competitive in relation to the CBD and neighbourhood shopping areas.

A regional shopping centre is like a mini-city centre, and contains from forty to more than 100 stores. To be profitable, it must serve a population of at least 100 000 customers who live within thirty minutes' driving time. In its early form, the regional shopping centre often contained two strong department stores at either end of a mall and a balanced set of specialty stores between the anchor stores. This arrangement encouraged comparison shopping: a customer wishing to buy jeans could compare the offers of Myer, Target, Just Jeans and others. Regional shopping centres have become more elaborate over the years, with all the stores being located in an enclosed mall, many malls having two storeys, and many centres having three or four large stores in one complex. Good design encourages freely moving traffic where all the stores can get exposure.

Community shopping centre. A community shopping centre contains fifteen to fifty retail stores serving between 20 000 and 100 000 residents, 90 per cent of whom live within 2.5 kilometres of the centre. One primary store is normally found, usually a branch of a department store or a variety store. The shopping centre is also likely to include a supermarket, convenience goods stores, professional offices, and sometimes a bank. The primary store will usually be located at the corner of the L in L-shaped shopping centres, and in the centre in the case of linear shopping centres. The stores nearest to the primary store normally sell shopping goods, and the other stores normally sell convenience goods.

Neighbourhood shopping centre. The most common type of store cluster is the neighbourhood shopping centre. These contain five to fifteen stores and serve a population of less than 20 000 residents. Customers live within walking distance or no more than a five-minute drive away. These are convenience-shopping centres: the supermarket is the principal tenant, and there are several service establishments such as a milkbar or delicatessen, pharmacy and hairdresser. In contrast to the larger shopping centres, this is usually an unplanned strip of stores.[23]

Retailer Marketing Decisions

Having looked at the various types of retailers, we will now examine the major types of marketing decisions made by retailers, specifically decisions in the areas of target market, product assortment and services, price, promotion and place.[24]

Target market decision. The first and most important decision facing a retailer consists of determining the target market – until this is defined in demographic and psychographic terms, the retailer cannot make precise decisions on product assortment, store decor, advertising messages and media, price levels, and so on. Some stores are able to define quite narrow groups as their target market, but too many retailers – both large and small – have not clarified their target or are trying to satisfy incompatible markets and satisfying none of them well. Even Myer, which serves so many different people, must develop a better definition of which groups it will make its major target customers so that it can achieve more precision in its product assortment, prices, locations and promotion with these groups.

A retailer should periodically carry out marketing research to make sure that it is delivering the expected satisfactions to its target market. Consider a store that seeks to attract discriminating shoppers, but has an image among such shoppers as shown by the solid line in Figure 15-3. The store is not appealing to its target market, and it has the choice of either going after a mass market or redesigning itself into a 'classier store'. Suppose it does the latter, and some time later a sample of its customers are interviewed for their perception of the store. The current image is now the one shown by the dashed line in Figure 15-3, i.e. the store has succeeded in bringing about a

congruence between its target market and the store's image.

Product assortment and services decision. The modern retailer has to make decisions on three major product variables in retailing: product assortment, services mix, and store atmosphere.

The *product assortment* chosen by the retailer must match the shopping expectations of the target market. In fact, it becomes a key element in the competitive battle among similar retailers. The retailer has to decide on product assortment width (narrow or wide) and depth (shallow or deep). Thus in the restaurant business, a restaurant can offer a narrow and shallow assortment (small snack bars), a narrow and deep assortment (delicatessen), a wide and shallow assortment (cafeteria), or a wide and deep assortment (large restaurants). Another dimension is the quality of the goods: the customer is interested in the

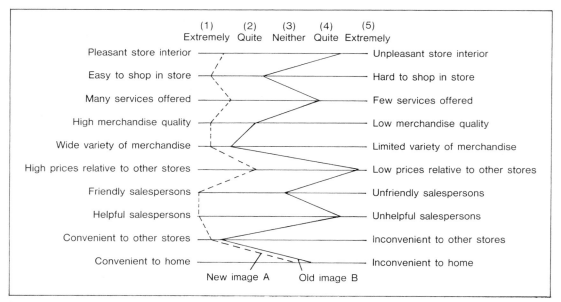

Source: Adapted from David W. Cravens, Gerald E. Hills & Robert B. Woodruff, *Marketing Decision Making: Concepts and Strategy* (Homewood, Ill.: Richard D. Irwin, 1976), p. 234.

Figure 15-3   A comparison between the old and new image of a store seeking to appeal to a class market

range of choice, but is even more interested in the quality of the product.

Retailers also must make decisions on the *mix of services* they will provide. The old neighbourhood grocery stores offered their customers home delivery, credit and conversation, services that today's modern supermarkets have often reduced or eliminated. Table 15-3 lists some of the major services that retailers can offer; the service mix is one of the key tools of nonprice competition.

The *store's atmospherics* is a third element in its product arsenal. Every store has a physical layout that makes it hard or easy to move around. Every store has a 'feel' – one is dirty, another charming, a third palatial, a fourth sombre. The store must embody a planned atmosphere that suits the target market and leans it toward purchase. A funeral parlour should be quiet, sombre and peaceful, and a discotheque should be bright, loud and vibrating; the two should not be confused. The atmosphere is designed by creative people who know how to combine visual, aural, olfactory and tactile stimuli to achieve the desired effect.[25]

Price decision. The prices established by retailers are important for the selection of target market and reflecting the quality of goods carried, the services offered, and the desired price image. The cost of merchandise is the basis of their pricing, and the ability to buy intelligently is a key ingredient in success: retailers can often make as much money through smart buying as through smart selling. Beyond this, they must price carefully in a number of other ways. Low mark-ups may be set on some items so they become traffic builders or loss leaders, in the hope that customers will buy additional items that bear a higher mark-up once they are in the store. In addition, retail management has to be adept in its use of mark-downs on slower-moving merchandise. Shoe retailers, for example, might expect to sell 50 per cent of their shoes at the normal mark-up, 25 per cent at a 40 per cent mark-up, and the remaining 25 per cent at cost. Their initial pricing anticipates these expected mark-downs.

Promotion decision. Retailers use the normal promotional tools – advertising, personal selling, sales promotion, and publicity – to reach consumers. Advertising is a major tool, and retailer advertising can be found in newspapers and magazines, and on radio and television; it is often supplemented by hand-delivered circulars and direct-mail pieces. Personal selling requires careful training of the salespeople in how to greet customers, meet their needs, and handle their doubts and complaints. Sales promotion may take the form of in-store demonstrations, prizes, and visits by celebrities.

Table 15-3 Typical retail services

Prepurchase services	Postpurchase services	Ancillary services
1. Accepting telephone orders	1. Delivery	1. Cheque cashing
2. Accepting mail orders (or purchases)	2. Regular wrapping (or bagging)	2. General information
3. Advertising	3. Gift wrapping	3. Free parking
4. Window display	4. Adjustments	4. Retaurants
5. Interior display	5. Returns	5. Repairs
6. Fitting rooms	6. Alterations	6. Interior decorating
7. Shopping hours	7. Tailoring	7. Credit
8. Fashion shows	8. Installations	8. Rest rooms
9. Trade-ins	9. Engraving	9. Baby attendant service
	10. COD delivery	

Source: Carl M. Larson, Robert E. Weigand & John S. Wright, *Basic Retailing* (Englewood Cliffs, N.J.: Prentice-Hall, 1976), p. 364.

Place decision. The retailers' choice of locations is a key competitive factor in their ability to attract customers. For example, customers primarily choose the banks that are nearest to them. Department-store chains, oil companies, and fast-food franchisers are particularly careful in making location decisions and in using advanced methods of site selection.

The Future of Retailing

Retailing is one of the most dynamic and challenging areas of the economy. Today's retailer, looking ahead to tomorrow, has to take into account the following major trends: (i) the slowdown in population growth and economic growth; (ii) the rapidly increasing cost of capital, labour and energy; (iii) changing consumer lifestyles, shopping patterns, and attitudes toward shopping; (iv) the emergence of new technologies such as computerized checkout, electronic shopping and more automatic vending; (v) the growing strength of major retailers in the total retail picture; and (vi) the rise of consumerism and environmentalism, and the increase in government regulations affecting retailing. Clearly, these trends are going to call for more than good merchandising skills: top management will need to be skilled in designing and implementing profit performance systems. The key need will be to find ways to increase retail productivity.

The search for more productivity in the later 1980s will favour the development of retailing forms that keep costs down. Many innovations have come about in the past as solutions to retailing problems of high cost and high prices; they have been explained by the wheel of retailing hypothesis.[26] According to this hypothesis, many new types of retailing institutions begin as low-status, low-margin, low-price operations which become effective competitors of more conventional outlets which have become complacent over the years. Their success gradually leads them to upgrade their facilities and offer additional services, which increases their costs and forces price increases until they finally resemble the conventional outlets that they displaced. They, in turn, become vulnerable to still newer types of low-cost, low-margin operations. This hypothesis appears to explain the original success and later troubles of department stores, supermarkets and, more recently, discount houses. On the other hand, it does not explain the growth of suburban shopping centres and automatic vending, both of which started out as high-margin and high-cost operations.

Nevertheless, one can be sure that new retailing forms will emerge to meet new needs.

Table 15-4 Lifecycles of retail institutions (United States)

Retail institutions	Early growth	Maturity	Approximate time required to reach maturity
Department stores	Mid-1860s	Mid-1960s	100 years
Variety stores	Early 1900s	Early 1960s	60 years
Supermarkets	Mid-1930s	Mid-1960s	30 years
Discount department stores	Mid-1950s	Mid-1970s	20 years
Fast-food service outlets	Early 1960s	Mid-1970s	15 years
Home improvement centres	Mid-1960s	Late 1970s	15 years
Furniture warehouse showrooms	Late 1960s	Late 1970s	10 years
Catalogue showrooms	Late 1960s	Late 1970s	10 years

Source: From Bert C. McCammon Jr, 'The Future of Catalog Showrooms: Growth and Its Challenges to Management' (working paper, Marketing Science Institute, 1973), p. 3.

Their longevity, however, is likely to be less than that of previous great forms such as the department store and the supermarket. Table 15-4 lists the lifecycle characteristics of some major retailing institutions in the United States, and indicates that the more recent ones are reaching their maturity much faster.[27] Although Australia's experience has lagged somewhat, the same trend is evident.

WHOLESALING

Nature and Importance of Wholesaling

Wholesaling includes all activities involved in selling goods or services to those who are buying for purposes of resale or business use. Thus any sales and accompanying activities undertaken by one person or firm to sell to another person or firm where the buying is not for personal use can be referred to as wholesaling. A retail bakery that occasionally sells pastry to local hotels is engaging in wholesaling, not retailing, at that point. In this chapter the term wholesalers will be confined to those persons and firms that are primarily engaged in such activity – this excludes manufacturers and farmers, for example, because they are primarily engaged in production, and it excludes retailers.

A number of major differences may be noted between wholesalers and retailers. First, wholesalers deal with customers who buy something for resale or use in production, whereas retailers are selling to customers who are buying for personal consumption. This explains why wholesalers normally locate in less-accessible and less-attractive areas where rents are lower. They also tend not to be promotion-minded, because they are dealing with hardheaded buyers who wish to make money or save money. Second, wholesale transactions are usually larger than retail transactions, and wholesalers must become much more involved with sophisticated materials-handling and information systems. Third, there are different government laws and regulations for wholesalers and retailers.

Why are wholesalers used at all in the economic system? Conceivably, manufacturers could bypass them and sell directly to retailers or consumers. The answer lies in several efficiencies that wholesalers bring about. First, small manufacturers with limited financial resources cannot afford to develop direct-selling organizations. Second, even manufacturers with sufficient capital may prefer to use it primarily to expand production rather than carry out expensive distribution. Third, manufacturers recognize that wholesalers are typically more efficient than themselves because of the wholesalers' scale of operation in distribution, their wider number of retail contacts, and their specialized skills. Fourth, manufacturers of single or limited lines find that retailers who carry many lines prefer to buy assortments rather than deal directly with every single manufacturer.

Thus retailers, manufacturers and other businesses are generally drawn to wholesalers, although in certain situations the wholesalers may be bypassed. Wholesalers are used because they are able to efficiently perform one or more valued function, such as:

1. *Selling and promoting.* Wholesalers provide a sales force enabling manufacturers to reach many small customers at a relatively low cost. The wholesaler has more contacts and is often more trusted by the buyer than is the distant manufacturer. In addition to personal and telephone selling, wholesalers also send out catalogues, promotional fliers and brochures.
2. *Buying and assortment building.* Wholesalers are able to select items, buy them, and build assortments needed by their customers, thus saving the customers considerable work.
3. *Bulk-breaking.* Wholesalers provide customers with savings through their ability to

buy in truckload lots and then sell smaller quantities adapted to the customers' varying needs.

4. *Warehousing.* Wholesalers provide a warehousing service, holding inventory until goods are ordered, thereby reducing the inventory costs and risks to both suppliers and customers.

5. *Transportation.* Wholesalers can provide quicker delivery to buyers because they are closer.

6. *Financing.* Wholesalers finance their customers by granting credit, and finance their suppliers by ordering early and paying their bills on time.

7. *Risk-bearing.* Wholesalers absorb some of the total risk in the channel by taking title and being responsible for theft, damage, spoilage and obsolescence.

8. *Market information.* Wholesalers supply useful information to their suppliers and customers regarding competitors' activities, new products, imminent price developments, and so on.

9. *Management services and counselling.* Wholesalers often help retailers improve their operations by training their salespeople, helping with layouts and displays, and setting up systems for accounting and inventory control.

Thus we see that wholesalers have value for manufacturers, retailers and other business establishments. Numerous major economic developments have contributed to wholesaling's growth over the years, including: (i) the growth of mass production in large factories located away from the principal users of the output; (ii) the growth of production in advance of orders rather than in response to specific orders; (iii) an increase in the number of levels of intermediate producers and users; and (iv) the increasing need for adapting products to the needs of intermediate and final users in terms of quantities, packages and forms.[28]

Types of Wholesalers

According to the 1968–69 business census, there were more than 30 000 wholesaling establishments in Australia, with a total annual sales volume of $22 billion. These wholesalers differ considerably in whether they take title to goods, the number and type of functions they perform, their method of operation, their size, and the range and kinds of goods they handle. This makes their classification somewhat difficult. Wholesalers can be classified into four major groups (see Table 15-5): merchant wholesalers take title to the goods; brokers and agents do not take title to the goods; manufacturers' sales branches and offices are manufacturers' wholesaling operations; miscellaneous wholesalers account for the remaining specific areas.

Table 15-5   Classification of wholesalers

Merchant wholesalers

Full-service wholesalers
  Wholesale merchants (general merchandise, general line, specialty line)
  Industrial distributors
Limited-service wholesalers
  Cash-and-carry wholesalers
  Truck wholesalers
  Drop shippers
  Rack jobbers
  Producers' cooperatives
  Mail-order wholesalers

Agents and brokers

Brokers
Agents (manufacturer's agents, selling agents, purchasing agents, commission merchants)

Manufacturers' and retailers' branches and offices

Sales branches and offices
Purchasing offices

Miscellaneous wholesalers

Agricultural assemblers
Petroleum bulk plants and terminals
Auction companies

Merchant wholesalers. Merchant wholesalers are independently owned businesses that take title to the merchandise they handle – in different trades they may be called jobbers, distributors or mill-supply houses. They are the largest single group of wholesalers, accounting for more than 50 per cent of all wholesaling (in sales volume and in number of establishments). Merchant wholesalers can be subclassified into two broad types: full-service wholesalers and limited-service wholesalers.

Full-service wholesalers. Full-service wholesalers provide such services as carrying stock, using a sales force, offering credit, making deliveries, and providing management assistance. They include both wholesale merchants and industrial distributors.

- *Wholesale merchants.* Wholesale merchants sell primarily to retailers and provide a full range of services. They vary mainly as to the width of the product line they carry. General merchandise wholesalers carry several lines to meet the needs of both general retailers and single-line retailers. General-line wholesalers carry one or two lines of merchandise in a greater depth of assortment, e.g. hardware wholesalers, pharmaceutical wholesalers, and clothing wholesalers. Specialty wholesalers carry only part of a line but this in great depth, e.g. health-food wholesalers, seafood wholesalers, and automotive item wholesalers. They offer customers the advantage of more choice and greater product knowledge.
- *Industrial distributors.* Industrial distributors are merchant wholesalers who sell to manufacturers rather than retailers. They provide several services, such as carrying stock, offering credit, and providing delivery. They may carry a broad range of merchandise (often called a mill-supply house), a general line, or a specialty line. Industrial distributors may concentrate on such lines as maintenance, repair and operating supplies (MRO items); original equipment supplies (OEM) such as ball bearings and motors; or equipment, such as hand and power tools, and fork trucks.

Limited-service wholesalers. Limited-service wholesalers offer fewer services to their suppliers and customers. They take several different forms.

- *Cash-and-carry wholesalers.* Cash-and-carry wholesalers have a limited line of fast-moving goods which they sell to small retailers for cash. Besides not providing credit, they normally do not deliver. A small seafood retailer, for example, normally drives every workday at dawn to a wholesale fish market, buys several crates of fish, pays on the spot, and drives his merchandise back to his store and unloads it.
- *Truck wholesalers.* Truck wholesalers (also called van salespeople) primarily perform a selling and delivery function. They carry a limited line of semi-perishable merchandise (such as milk, bread, snack foods), which they sell for cash as they make their rounds of supermarkets, small groceries, hospitals, restaurants, factory cafeterias, milkbars and hotels.
- *Drop shippers.* Drop shippers are usually found in bulk industries such as coal, timber and heavy equipment. They do not carry inventory or handle the product: once an order is placed with them, they find a manufacturer who ships the merchandise directly to the customer on the agreed terms and time of delivery. The drop shipper assumes title and risk during the period from acceptance of the order to its delivery to the customer. Because drop shippers do not carry inventory, their costs are lower and the savings are realized by their customers.
- *Rack jobbers.* Rack jobbers primarily serve grocery and pharmacy retailers, mostly in the area of nonfood items. They send out

delivery trucks to stores, set up the items (e.g. toys, paperbacks, hardware items, health and beauty aids), price goods, keep them fresh, set up point-of-purchase displays, and keep inventory records. Rack jobbers often sell on consignment, which means that they retain title to the goods and bill the retailers only for items sold to consumers. Thus they provide such services as delivery, shelving, inventory carrying, and financing. They do little promotion because the products they carry are branded and are often highly advertised.

- *Producers' cooperatives.* Producers' cooperatives are owned by farmer-members who assemble farm produce to sell in local markets. Any profits they make are normally distributed to members at the end of the year. They often attempt to improve product quality and promote a co-op brand name, such as Sunwhite rice, or Riverland oranges.
- *Mail-order wholesalers.* Mail-order wholesalers send catalogues to retail, industrial and institutional customers featuring jewellery, cosmetics, specialty foods and other small items. Their main customers are businesses in small outlying areas, and no sales force is maintained. The orders are filled and sent by mail, truck or other efficient means of transport.

Agents and brokers. Agents and brokers differ from merchant wholesalers in two ways: they do not take title to goods, and they tend to perform even fewer functions than limited-service merchant wholesalers. Their main function is to facilitate buying and selling, and for this they will earn a commission of anywhere from 2 to 6 per cent of the selling price. Like merchant wholesalers, they generally specialize by product line or customer types.

Brokers. Brokers perform very few functions, the chief one being to bring buyers and sellers together. They seek out buyers or sellers and assist in negotiation, being paid by the party who sought their services. They do not carry any inventory, provide any financing or assume any risk. The most familiar examples are food brokers, real-estate brokers (agents), insurance brokers, and stockbrokers.

Agents. Agents represent either buyers or sellers on a more permanent basis. There are several types.

- *Manufacturer's agents.* These representatives are more numerous than any other type of agent wholesaler. They represent two or more manufacturers of complementary lines, and enter into a formal written agreement covering pricing policy, territorial areas, order-handling procedure, delivery service and warranties, and commission rates. Presumably they are knowledgeable about each manufacturer's product line, and use their extensive knowledge of customers and customer preferences in their area to sell that product. Manufacturer's agents are used in such lines as clothing, furniture, and electrical goods. Most are small businesses, with only a few employees who are skilled salespeople. They are hired by small manufacturers who cannot afford to maintain their own field sales force, and by large manufacturers who want to open new territories or need representation in territories that cannot support a full-time salesperson.
- *Selling agents.* Selling agents are given contractual authority to sell the entire output of a manufacturer, where the latter is not interested in selling or feels unqualified. The selling agent serves as a sales department and has significant influence over prices, terms and conditions of sale. The selling agent normally has no territorial limitations. Selling agents are found in such product areas as textiles, industrial machinery and equipment, coal and coke, chemicals and metals.
- *Purchasing agents.* Purchasing agents generally have a long-term relationship with

buyers and make purchases for them, often receiving, inspecting, warehousing and shipping the merchandise to the ultimate buyers. One type consists of resident buyers in major clothing markets, who look for lines suitable for small retailers in small cities. They are knowledgeable and provide helpful market information to clients as well as obtaining the best goods and prices available.

- *Commission merchants.* Commission agents take physical possession of products and negotiate sales, usually on a short-term basis. They are used most often in agricultural marketing by farmers who cannot or do not want to sell their own output and do not belong to producers' cooperatives. A commission merchant might take a truckload of commodities to a central market, sell it for the best possible price, deduct a commission and expenses, and remit the balance to the producer.

Manufacturers' and retailers' branches and offices.

The third major type of wholesaling consists of operations conducted by sellers or buyers themselves.

Sales branches and office. Manufacturers often set up their own sales branches and offices to obtain better control of inventory, and improved selling and other promotion. Sales branches carry inventory and represent an alternative to using merchant wholesalers. They are found in such industries as timber and automotive equipment and parts. Sales offices do not carry any inventory and represent an alternative to using outside agents and brokers. They are most noticeable in drygoods and notion industries. Sales branches and offices are often much larger than the corresponding wholesalers and agents would be.

Purchasing offices. Many retailers set up purchasing offices in major market centres, either interstate or overseas, which perform a role similar to that of brokers or agents but are part of the buyer's organization.

Miscellaneous.

A few specialized wholesalers are found in certain sectors of the economy.

Agricultural assemblers. Agricultural assemblers collect farm products from farmers and build them into larger lots for shipment to food processors, bakers and government. By taking advantage of bulk transport rates and differences in area market prices, the assembler makes a profit.

Petroleum bulk plants and terminals. Petroleum bulk plants and terminals specialize in selling and delivering petroleum products to service stations, other retailers, and organizational users. Many are owned by major petroleum producers (in which case they are manufacturer's sales branches), and others are owned by independent businesspeople (in which case they are merchant wholesalers).

Auction companies. Auction houses are important in certain industries where buyers want to see and inspect goods prior to purchase, as in the tobacco and livestock markets. The buyers bid against each other and the highest bidder gets the products if the bid is over a predetermined minimum.

Wholesaler Marketing Decisions

Wholesalers must make decisions on their target-market product assortment, and service, pricing, promotion and place.

Target market. Wholesalers, like retailers, have to develop a better definition of their target market and not try to serve everyone. They can choose a target group of customers according to size criteria (e.g. only large retailers), type of customer (e.g. convenience-food stores only), need for service (e.g. customers who need credit), or other criteria. Within the target group, they can identify the more profitable customers and seek to design stronger offers and build better relationships with them. They may propose automatic re-ordering systems, set up management training and advisory systems, and even sponsor a voluntary chain. They may discourage less-profitable customers by requiring larger orders or placing extra charges on smaller orders.

Product assortment and services. The wholesalers' 'product' is the assortment that they carry: they are subject to great pressure to carry full lines and have sufficient stock for immediate delivery. This can reduce profits, however, and wholesalers are increasingly settling for 80–90 per cent coverage only; they are increasingly studying the profits of the different lines and carrying only the more profitable ones. Many wholesalers are grouping their items on an ABC basis, with A standing for the more profitable items and C for the least profitable. Inventory-carrying levels are varied for the three groups, and the wholesaler is devoting more time to selling the more profitable items.

Wholesalers also have to re-examine which services count most in building strong customer relationships and which should be dropped or charged for. The key is not simply matching the services provided by competitors but finding a distinct mix of services valued by customers.

Pricing. Wholesale pricing calls for marking up the cost of goods by a conventional percentage, say 20 per cent, that will cover the wholesaler's various expenses. Expenses may average 17 per cent of the gross margin, leaving a profit margin of approximately 3 per cent; in grocery wholesaling the average profit margin is often less than 2 per cent. Wholesalers have to experiment with new approaches to pricing: they may find it profitable to cut their margin on some lines in order to win important new customers; they may consider asking the supplier for a special discount that can be turned into an opportunity to increase the supplier's sales. Wholesalers need to develop suitable pricing systems so that customers will be satisfied and will become more loyal to them.

Promotion. Most wholesalers are not promotion-minded, either for themselves or for their suppliers. Their use of trade advertising, sales promotion, publicity and personal selling is largely haphazard. Personal selling is particularly behind the times, in that wholesalers still see it as the task of a single salesperson talking to a single customer instead of a team effort to sell, build and service major accounts. As for nonpersonal promotion, wholesalers would benefit from adopting some of the image-making techniques used by retailers. They need to develop an overall promotional strategy, and make greater use of supplier promotion materials and programmes in ways that will be to their advantage.

Place. Wholesalers typically locate in low-rent, low-rates areas, and their materials-handling systems and order-processing systems often lag behind the available technologies. Progressive wholesalers have, however, been making time and motion studies of such procedures: the ultimate development is the automated warehouse where orders are entered directly into a computer, the items are picked up by mechanical devices and conveyed on a belt to the shipping platform for assembly. Many wholesalers are also turning to electronic data-processing for such functions as accounting, billing, inventory control, and forecasting, and they are alert to other technological developments that save office costs.

The Future of Wholesaling

Changes in wholesaling have been less dramatic than changes in retailing, but they are no less important. In the nineteenth century, wholesalers held the dominant position in marketing channels. Most manufacturers were quite small, and depended on major wholesalers for the distribution of their product to the many small retailers who dotted the land. The wholesaler's power began to diminish in the twentieth century as manufacturers became larger and giant chains and franchise systems appeared in retailing. Large manufacturers sought ways to sell direct to the major retailers, and the major retailers sought ways to buy direct from the manufacturers. Although little utilized the opportunity to go direct increased the power of the manufacturers and retailers relative to that of the wholesalers and forced the latter to find ways of being more efficient. Although wholesalers declined in importance in the 1950s, and were thought to be doomed by the growth of chain operations, they have since stabilized their position.

Manufacturers usually have the option of bypassing wholesalers, or replacing an inefficient wholesaler with a more dynamic one. The major complaints that manufacturers make about wholesalers are as follows: (i) they do not aggressively promote the manufacturer's product line, acting more like order-takers; (ii) they do not carry enough inventory, and therefore fail to fill customers' orders fast enough; (iii) they do not supply the manufacturer with up-to-date market and competitive information; (iv) they do not attract high-calibre managers and bring down their own costs; and (v) they charge too much for their services.

These complaints are justified in many cases: few wholesalers have adapted or responded well to the rapidly changing world. According to Lopata:

> Technological advances, product line proliferation, changing retail structures, and social adjustments are only a few of the real problems that complicate the wholesaler's life. Each improved product passing through the wholesale level generates a new demand for investments in warehouse space, market analysis, and sales training, and for myriad adjustments in the wholesaler's information systems. Each major

retailing shift designed to satisfy customer needs obliges him to adjust his selling patterns, to review his customer service levels, to study product assortments, and to revise his strategies.[29]

Progressive wholesalers are those who are willing to change their ways to meet the challenges of chain organizations, discount houses, and rising labour costs. They are adapting their services more to the needs of target customers, and finding cost-reducing methods of transacting business.

SUMMARY

Retailing and wholesaling have spawned many kinds of institutions to meet the various needs of customers and accommodate the various characteristics of products. A glimpse of the drama and challenge of these two sectors has been presented in this chapter.

Retailing includes all the activities involved in selling goods or services directly to final consumers for their personal, nonbusiness use. Retailing is one of the major industries in Australia. Retailers can be classified in several ways: according to the product line sold (specialty stores, department stores, supermarkets, convenience stores, combination stores, superstores, hypermarches and service businesses); according to the relative emphasis placed on price (discount stores, warehouse stores, and catalogue showrooms); according to the nature of the business premises (mail- and telephone-order retailing, automatic vending, buying services, and door-to-door retailing); according to who controls the outlets (corporate chains, voluntary chains, retailers' or consumers' cooperatives, franchise organizations, and conglomerchants); and according to the type of store cluster (central business districts, regional shopping centres, community shopping centres, and neighbourhood shopping centres). The various retailers make basic decisions about their target market, product assortment and services, pricing, promotion and place. The future of retailing will be extremely challenging, and requires improved professional management and increased productivity.

Wholesaling includes all the activities involved in selling goods or services to those who are buying for the purpose of resale or for business use. Wholesalers are necessary in the economic system to help manufacturers deliver their products efficiently to retailers and industrial users across the nation. Wholesalers can perform many functions, including selling, buying and assortment building, bulk-breaking, warehousing, transporting, financing, risk-bearing, supplying market information, and providing management services and counselling.

Wholesalers fall into four groups. Merchant wholesalers take possession of the goods. They may be subclassified as full-service wholesalers (wholesale merchants, industrial distributors) and limited-service wholesalers (cash-and-carry wholesalers, truck wholesalers, drop shippers, rack jobbers, producers' cooperatives, and mail-order wholesalers). Agents and brokers do not take possession of the goods but are paid a commission for facilitating buying and selling. Manufacturers' and retailers' branches and offices are wholesaling operations conducted to bypass the wholesalers. Miscellaneous wholesalers include agricultural assemblers, petroleum bulk plants and terminals, and auction companies. Wholesaling is just holding its own in the economy. Progressive wholesalers are adapting their services more to the needs of target customers and are seeking cost-reducing methods of business.

QUESTIONS FOR DISCUSSION

1. What is the major difference between retailers and wholesalers? Explain by using an example of each.

2. Compare and contrast two types of retail clothing stores, classified according to the product line sold.

3. Briefly discuss the types of retailers that sell food products. How has retailing in this area changed in the last twenty years?

4. Describe a local warehouse store. What factors contributed to its growth?

5. Door-to-door retailing will decline in the late 1980s. Comment.

6. If friends of yours were planning to open a greeting-card shop, which type of store cluster would you recommend that they select? Why?

7. Is there a difference between the approach taken in retailer marketing decisions and that taken in manufacturer marketing decisions? Explain.

8. The major distinction between merchant wholesalers and agents or brokers is that the former offer more services to the buyer. Comment.

9. Would a small manufacturer of lawn and garden tools seek a manufacturer's agent or a selling agent to handle the merchandise? Why?

10. Why do you think the promotion area of marketing strategy has been traditionally weak for wholesalers?

NOTES

1 Robin Harris, 'Myer and Coles Ready to Tackle Hotels', *Business Review Weekly*, 1–7 August 1981, p. 31.

2 See *Inside Retailing*, 3 August 1981, p. 1; and 17 November 1980, p. 16.

3 Ernest Samhaber, *Merchants Make History* (New York, Harper & Row, 1964), pp. 345–48.

4 See, for example, *The Retail Industry* (Melbourne: IBIS Research Services, 1978); Ian Perkin, '50 Years of Retailing', *National Bank Monthly Summary*, December 1977, pp. 28–32; 'An Introduction to the Retail Industry in Australia', *Developments in Manufacturing Industry*, December 1976, pp. 7–9; 'Major Trends in Australia's Retail Industry', *Journal of Industry and Commerce*, July 1977, pp. 4–8.

5 The quoted part of the definition is from Walter J. Salmon, Robert D. Buzzell, Stanton G. Cort & Michael R. Pearce, *The Super Store – Strategic Implications for the Seventies* (Cambridge, Mass.: Marketing Science Institute, 1972), p. 83.

6 See *Foodweek's Top 20 Traders* (Sydney: Philip Luker, 1981).

7 Pam Mawbey, 'Pepsico Adds Spice to Aust's Growing Takeaway Markets', *Australian Financial Review*, 23 January 1981, p. 23.

8 See Bert McCammon, 'High Performance Marketing Strategies' (unpublished paper).

9 Based on Ronald R. Gist, *Retailing Concepts and Decisions* (New York: John Wiley, 1968), pp. 45–56.

10 See Jonathan N. Goodrich & Jo Ann Hoffman, 'Warehouse Retailing: The Trend of the Future?', *Business Horizons*, April 1979, pp. 45–50.

11 'Acres of Furniture in Giant New Showroom', *Inside Retailing*, 2 November 1981, p. 14.

12 Leo Bogart, 'The Future in Retailing', *Harvard Business Review*, November–December 1973, p. 26.

13 Belden Menkus, 'Remote Retailing a Reality of 1985?', *Chain Store Age Executive*, September 1976, p. 42.

14 'Dick Smith "First" With Electronic Shopping', *Age*, 29 September 1981, p. 29.

15 For an excellent text on direct-mail techniques, see Bob Stone, *Successful Direct Marketing Methods* (Chicago: Crain Books, 1975).

16 See, for example, Vin Jenkins, *Direct Mail Advertising in Australia* (Melbourne: Australia Post, 1979).

17 G. R. Schreiber, *A Concise History of Vending in the USA* (Chicago: Vend, 1961), p. 9.

18 See Ken McGregor, 'Buying Group Expands', *Australian Financial Review*, 2 January 1981, p. 10.

19 See Ronald R. Gist, *Marketing and Society: Text and Cases* (Hinsdale, Ill.: Dryden Press, 2nd edn. 1974), p. 334.

20 See 'Entrepreneurs Get the Best Odds Through A Franchise', *Age*, 23 November 1981, pp. 12–13 (Money Guide supplement).

21 See Rollie Tillman, 'Rise of the Conglomerchant', *Harvard Business Review*, November–December 1971, pp. 44–51.

22 This Urban Land Institute definition can be found in Roger A. Dickinson, *Retail Management: A Channels Approach* (Belmont, Calif.: Wadsworth, 1974), p. 9.

23 For an interesting and quite detailed review of retailing in a major city see *Retailing in Canberra* (Canberra: National Capital Development Commission, 1981). An earlier study of continuing value is R. J. Johnston & P. J. Rimmer, *Retailing in Melbourne* (Canberra: Research School of Pacific Studies, Australian National University, 1969).

24 Two government reports which examine aspects of retailing and wholesaling are Prices Justification Tribunal, *Processed Food Industry* (Melbourne: Commonwealth Government Printing Unit, 1979); and *Food Marketing Systems in New South Wales* (Sydney: NSW Government Food Marketing Working Party, 1979).

25 For more discussion, see Philip Kotler, 'Atmospherics as a Marketing Tool', *Journal of Retailing*, Winter 1973–74, pp. 48–64.

26 For additional articles on the future of retailing, see William R. Davidson, Albert D. Bates & Stephen J. Bass, 'The Retail Life Cycle', *Harvard Business Review*, November–December 1976, pp. 89–96; Albert D. Bates, 'The Troubled Future of Retailing', *Business*

Horizons, August 1976, pp. 22–28; and Malcolm P. McNair & Eleanor G. May, 'The Next Revolution of the Retailing Wheel', *Harvard Business Review*, September–October 1978, pp. 81–91.

27 Malcolm P. McNair, 'Significant Trends and Developments in the Postwar Period', in A. B. Smith (ed.) *Competitive Distribution in a Free, High-Level Economy and Its Implications for the University* (Pittsburgh: University of Pittsburgh press, 1958), pp. 1–25. Also see the critical discussion by Stanley C. Hollander, 'The Wheel of Retailing', *Journal of Marketing*, July 1960, pp. 37–42. For other theories of retail change, see Ronald R. Gist, *Retailing Concepts and Decisions* (New York: John Wiley, 1968), Ch. 4.

28 David A. Revzan, *Wholesaling in Marketing Organization* (New York: John Wiley, 1961), pp. 10–11.

29 Richard S. Lopata, 'Faster Pace in Wholesaling', *Harvard Business Review*, July–August 1969, p. 131.

Marketing Communications Strategy

16

What do Dame Edna Everage, golfer Jack Newton and Japan's first fast-breeder atomic reactor have in common? In case you haven't noticed, they are all being used to raise the profile of some of the lesser known brands of photocopying machines in Australia.

Following in the footsteps of the Nashua brand, which stepped into the spotlight three years ago via some television advertisements featuring actor Orson Welles, are the marketers of Mita, Toshiba and U-Bix machines. Two have decided to go the same way as Nashua by using a well-known personality to draw attention to their products. Moore Copystar Pty Ltd, the Melbourne-based importer and distributor of Japanese-produced Mita copiers, has launched a $250 000 plus advertising campaign in major metropolitan newspapers with Dame Edna Everage as its spokesperson. This follows the appointment of a new advertising agency, Clemenger Harvie in Melbourne, around six weeks ago. Mita sales director, Mr Gerald Williams, said this move was prompted by the recognition that around 20 per cent of a salesman's upfront selling time was devoted to 'telling people who we are'.

Mita copying machines have been manufactured in Japan since 1934 and marketed in Australia since 1975. Mr Williams claims Mita holds in excess of 10 per cent of the bond-paper copier market (the machines being advertised) and at least 50 per cent of the coated-paper market.

The first personality selected to lift Mita copiers out of obscurity was Professor Julius Sumner Miller who is deemed to have a lot of credibility in the technical sphere. He is depicted demonstrating the law of gravity in a current television commercial for Cadbury chocolate. In the end it was decided to drop *the proposed serious stance in favour of a more light-hearted approach via the use of comedian Barry Humphries' best known stage character, Dame Edna Everage. During his current Australian tour, Mr Humphries has also agreed to appear as himself in a television commercial for Maxwell House coffee.*

The Mita campaign consists of two different full-page press advertisements, one headed 'Dame Edna candidly discusses Mita photocopiers' and the other 'Mita. It's not your Everage photocopier'. Emphasis is placed on the smallest copier in the range, the DC-131. The campaign, which commenced on 20 September, will continue into the new year. Like that conducted throughout this year by ABE Copiers Pty Ltd for its U-Bix range using golfer Jack Newton, it has been primarily designed to assist salesmen. ABE has spent around $300 000 on its print and television campaign plus golf-related promotional activities.

The company using a picture of Japan's first fast-breeder atomic reactor to promote its photocopying machines is Toshiba which, although well-known in the electronics field generally, is a relative newcomer in the copier market. The aim of the current print campaign, according to a spokesman for Toshiba's advertising agency, Harris Robinson Courtenay in Sydney, is to give prospective customers confidence in their competence and dependability. 'If we didn't believe we could make a much better plain paper copier we would have stuck with atomic reactors', is the stance adopted throughout the campaign. Other examples of Toshiba's scientific achievements used include Japan's Bullet Train and the mechanism of the gates for Australia's Snowy River project.[1]

Modern marketing calls for more than developing a good product, pricing it attractively, and making it readily accessible to target customers. The company must also manage its impressions in the marketplace. Its products, employees and actions will communicate something, and what is communicated must not be left to chance. Every company is inevitably drawn into the role of communicator and promoter.

Companies have responded by training their sales personnel to communicate friendliness and knowledge. They hire advertising agencies to develop effective ads; sales-promotion specialists to build high-incentive sales programmes; and public-relations firms to create image-building campaigns. For most companies the question is not whether to promote, but how much to spend and in what ways.

The modern company manages a complex marketing communications system (see Figure 16-1), this communications mix – advertising, sales promotion, publicity, and personal selling – being used to reach intermediaries, consumers and various publics. Its intermediaries also develop a communications mix to reach consumers and various publics; consumers engage in word-of-mouth communication with each other and with other publics. Meanwhile each group issues communication feedback to every other group. The four major tools in the marketing communications mix are:

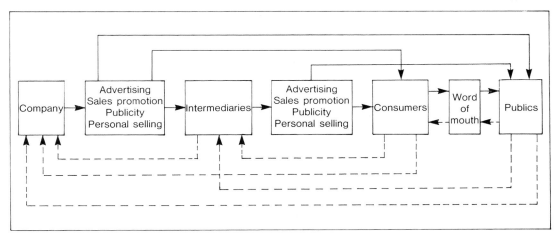

Figure 16-1   The marketing communications system

- *Advertising:* any paid form of nonpersonal presentation and promotion of ideas, goods or services by an identified sponsor.
- *Sales promotion:* short-term incentives to encourage purchase or sale of a good or service.
- *Publicity:* nonpersonal stimulation of demand for a good, service or business unit by planting commercially significant news about it in a published medium or obtaining favourable presentation on radio, television or the stage, not paid for by the sponsor.
- *Personal selling:* oral presentation in a conversation with one or more prospective purchasers for the purpose of making sales.[2]

Within each category are found specific 'promotools' such as sales presentations, point-of-purchase displays, specialty advertising, trade shows, fairs, demonstrations, catalogues, literature, press kits, posters, contests, premiums, coupons and trading stamps. At the same time we should recognize that communication goes beyond these specific tools – the product's styling and price, the package's shape and colour, the salesperson's manner and dress, and so on, all communicate something to buyers. The whole marketing mix,

not just the promotional mix, must be orchestrated for maximum communication impact.

This chapter examines two major questions:

1. What are the major steps in developing effective communications?
2. How should the promotional mix be determined?

Chapter 17 will examine the strategic use of the mass-communication tools of advertising, sales promotion, and publicity. Chapter 18 will focus on personal communications strategy through the sales force.

STEPS IN DEVELOPING EFFECTIVE COMMUNICATION

Marketers need to understand how to use communication, which involves the eight elements shown in Figure 16-2. Two of these elements represent the major parties in a communication – sender and receiver. Two others represent the major communication tools – message and media. The remaining four represent major communication functions – encoding, decoding, response and feedback. These elements can be defined as follows:

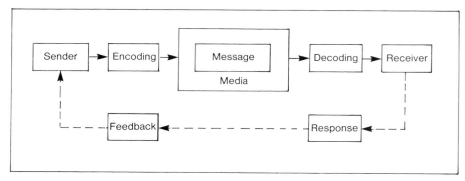

Figure 16-2 Elements in the communication process

- *Sender:* the party sending the message to another party (also called the source or communicator).
- *Encoding:* the process of putting thought into symbolic form.
- *Message:* the set of symbols that the sender transmits.
- *Media:* the paths through which the message moves from sender to receiver.
- *Decoding:* the process by which the receiver assigns meaning to the symbols transmitted by the sender.
- *Receiver:* the party receiving the message sent by another party (also called the audience or destination).
- *Response:* the set of reactions that the receiver has after being exposed to the message.
- *Feedback:* the part of the receiver's response that the receiver communicates back to the sender.

This model underscores the key factors in effective communication. Senders must know what audiences they want to reach and what responses they want. They must be skilful in encoding messages that take into account how the target audience tends to decode messages. They must transmit the message over efficient media that reach the target audience. They must develop feedback channels so that they can know the audience's response to the message.

We will examine the elements in the communication model mainly in terms of the planning flow (from target audience back to the communicator). The marketing communicator must do the following: (i) identify the target audience; (ii) clarify the response sought; (iii) choose a message; (iv) choose the media; (v) select source attributes; and (vi) collect feedback.

Identifying the Target Audience

A marketing communicator must start with a clear target audience in mind: this may comprise potential buyers of the company's products, current users, deciders, or influencers; it may consist of individuals, groups, particular publics, or the general public. The target audience will critically influence the communicator's decisions on *what* is to be said, *how* it is to be said, *when* it is to be said, *where* it is to be said, and *who* is to say it.

Clarifying the Response Sought

Once the target audience is identified, the marketing communicator must define the target response that is sought. The ultimate response is, of course, purchase behaviour, but this is the end result of a long process of consumer decision-making. The marketing communicator needs to know the state of the target audience at present, and to which state it should be moved.

Any member of the target audience may be in one of six buyer readiness states with respect to the product or organization: awareness, knowledge, liking, preference, conviction or purchase.

Awareness. The first thing to establish is how aware the target audience is of the product or organization. The audience may be completely unaware of the entity, know only its name, or know one or two things about it. If most of the target audience is unaware, the communicator's task is to build awareness, perhaps even just name recognition. This calls for simple messages repeating the name. Even then, building awareness takes time.

Knowledge. The target audience may be aware of the entity but not know much about it. In this case the communicator's goal will be to effectively transmit some key information about the entity. After waging a campaign, it can sample the target audience members to measure whether they have little, some or much knowledge of the entity, and the content of their knowledge. The particular set of beliefs that make up the audience's picture of an entity is called the image. Organizations must periodically assess their public images as a basis for developing communication objectives (see Chapter 20).

Liking. If the target audience members know the entity, the next question is how they feel about it. We may imagine a scale covering dislike very much, dislike somewhat, indifferent, like somewhat, like very much. If the audience holds an unfavourable view of the entity, the communicator has to find out why and then develop a communications campaign to build up favourable feeling. If the unfavourable view is rooted in real inadequacies of the entity, a communications campaign would not do the job; the task would be to first improve the entity and then communicate its quality. Good public re-

lations call for 'good deeds followed by good words'.

Preference. The target audience may like the entity but may not prefer it to others. In this case the communicator's job is to build the consumers' preference, by touting the quality, value, performance and other attributes of the entity. The communicator can check on the success of the campaign by subsequently surveying members of the audience to see if their preference for the entity is stronger.

Conviction. A target audience may prefer a particular entity but not develop a conviction about buying it. The communicator's job is to build conviction that buying the product is the right thing to do – this is a challenging communications task.

Purchase. A member of the target audience may have conviction but may not quite get around to making the purchase. He or she may be waiting for additional information, may plan to act later, and so on. A communicator in this situation must lead the consumer to take the final step, which is called 'closing the sale'. Possible devices include offering the entity at a low price if bought now, offering a premium, offering an opportunity to try it on a limited basis, or indicating that the entity will soon be unavailable.

The six states simplify to three stages known as the cognitive (awareness, knowledge), affective (liking, preference, conviction), and behavioural (purchase). The communicator normally assumes that buyers pass through these stages in succession on the way to purchase, and thus the task is to identify the stage common to most of the target audience and develop a communication message or campaign that will move them to the next stage. It would of course be nice if one message could move the audience through all three stages, but this rarely happens. Most communicators try to find a cost-effective communication approach to moving the target audience one stage at a time; the critical thing is to know where the audience is and what the next feasible stage is.

Some marketing scholars have challenged the idea that a consumer passes through cognition to behaviour in this order; Ray, for example, has suggested that some consumers pass from cognition to behaviour to affect[3] (as where a student hears of a particular disco, goes there without much feeling, and afterwards develops a strong liking for, or dislike of, the place). Ray has also suggested that sometimes consumers pass from behaviour to affect to cognition. Thus a student may sign up for a course that he or she knows nothing about except that friends are taking it, develop a favourable feeling, and finally begin to understand the subject. Each version of the sequence has different implications for the role and influence of communications on behaviour.

Choosing a Message

Having defined the response being sought from the target audience, the communicator can move on to developing a message or creative strategy. An ideal message is one that would manage to get attention, hold interest, arouse desire and obtain action (known as the AIDA model). In practice, few messages will take the consumer all the way from awareness through purchase, but the AIDA framework does suggest some desirable qualities.

Formulating the message will require solving three problems: what to say (content), how to say it logically (structure), and how to say it symbolically (format).

Message content. The communicator has to determine what message will produce the desired response in the target audience. This has been called the appeal, theme, idea or unique selling proposition: it amounts to formulating some kind of benefit, motivator, identification,

or reason why the audience should think or do something.

Three types of appeals may be distinguished. *Rational appeals* aim at serving the audience's self-interest – they attempt to show that the product will yield the expected functional benefits. Examples would be messages demonstrating a product's quality, economy, value or performance.

Emotional appeals are designed to stir up some negative or positive emotion that will motivate product purchase. Communicators have worked with fear, guilt and shame appeals, especially in connection with getting people to start doing things they should (e.g. brushing their teeth, having an annual health checkup) or stop doing things they shouldn't (e.g. smoking, overimbibing, drug abuse, overeating). Advertisers have found that fear appeals work up to a point, but if there is too much fear the audience will ignore the message.[4] Communicators have also used positive emotional appeals such as love, humour, pride and joy. Evidence has not established that a humorous message, for example, is necessarily more effective than a straight version.[5]

Moral appeals are directed to the audience's sense of what is right and proper. They are often used in messages exhorting people to support such social causes as a cleaner environment, equal rights for women, and aiding the disadvantaged; they occur less frequently in connection with everyday products.

Message structure. A message's effectiveness also depends on its structure. The three major issues in message structure are conclusion drawing, one- versus two-sided arguments, and order of presentation.

Conclusion drawing raises the question of whether the communicator should draw a definite conclusion or leave it to the audience to decide. Drawing a conclusion is normally more effective, except when the communicator is seen as untrustworthy, the issue is very simple or personal, and/or the audience is highly intelligent.[6] Conclusion drawing seems best suited to complex or specialized products where a single and clear use is intended.

One- or two-sided arguments raise the question of whether the communicator should only praise the product or also acknowledge some of its shortcomings. It may appear that a one-sided presentation would be more successful – this is the dominant approach in sales presentations, political contests, and child-rearing – but the answer is not clear-cut. The major conclusions are that: (i) one-sided messages tend to work best with audiences who are favourably disposed to the communicator's position, whereas two-sided arguments tend to work best with audiences who are opposed; (ii) two-sided messages tend to be more effective with better-educated audiences; and (iii) two-sided messages tend to be more effective with audiences who are likely to be exposed to counter-propaganda.[7]

Order of presentation raises the question of whether communicators should present their strongest arguments first or last. Presenting the strongest arguments first has the advantage of establishing attention and interest, which may be especially important in newspapers and other media where the audience does not attend to all of the message. However, it means an anticlimactic presentation. If a captive audience is involved, as in a sales presentation or conference, then a climactic presentation may be more effective. In a two-sided message, the issue is whether to present the positive argument first (primacy effect) or last (recency effect). If the audience is initially opposed, it appears that the communicator would be well advised to start with the other side's argument – this tends to disarm the audience, and allows the speaker to conclude with the strongest argument.

Message format. The communicator must be able to convey the message in an effective format. If the message is to be carried in print, elements such as headline, copy, illustration and colour must be developed. Advertisers are adept at using such attention-getting devices as novelty and contrast, arresting pictures and headlines, distinctive formats, message size and position, and colour, shape and movement.[8] If the message is to be carried over the radio, the communicator has to carefully choose words, voice qualities (speech rate, rhythm, pitch, articulation), and vocalizations (pauses, sighs, yawns). The 'sound' of an announcer promoting a used car has to be different from one promoting a soft, comfortable bed mattress. If the message is to be carried on television or given in person, then all of these elements plus body language (nonverbal clues, such as facial expressions, gestures, dress, posture and hairstyle) must be planned.[9] If the message is carried by the product or its packaging, the communicator has to pay attention to texture, scent, colour, size and shape.

> It is well known that colour plays an important communication role in food preferences. When homemakers sampled four cups of coffee that had been placed next to brown, blue, red and yellow containers (all the coffee was identical, although this was unknown to the homemakers), 75 per cent felt that the coffee next to the brown container tasted too strong; nearly 85 per cent judged the coffee next to the red container to be the richest; nearly everyone felt that the coffee next to the blue container was mild, and the coffee next to the yellow container was weak.

Choosing Media

The communicator can now turn to the selection of efficient media or channels of communication. Channels of communication are of two broad types, personal and nonpersonal.

Personal communication. Personal channels are of three types. Advocate channels consist of company representatives directly contacting buyers in the target market. Expert channels consist of independent persons with expertise (consultants, authorities) making statements to target buyers. Social channels consist of neighbours, friends, family members, and associates who may communicate with target buyers. This last channel is also known as word-of-mouth influence, and it is the most persuasive in many product areas.

Personal influence generally tends to be most telling for products that are expensive or risky; buyers will go beyond mass-media sources to seek the opinions of knowledgeable people. Personal influence is also telling for products that are highly social and visible.

Companies can take several steps to stimulate personal influence channels to work on their behalf: (i) identify influential individuals or companies and devote extra effort to them; (ii) create opinion leaders out of certain persons, by supplying them with the product on attractive terms or selecting them as company representatives; (iii) work through community influentials such as disc jockeys, student leaders, and presidents of women's organizations; (iv) let the advertising itself feature testimonials by influentials; and (v) develop advertising that is high in 'conversation value'.[10]

Nonpersonal communication. Nonpersonal channels carry influence without direct contact. Three types of nonpersonal channels can be distinguished. Mass and selective media consist of newspapers, magazines, radio, television, and outdoor posters or billboards. Mass media are aimed at large, often undifferentiated, audiences; selective media are aimed at specialized audiences. Atmospheres are environments designed to create or reinforce the buyer's leanings toward purchase or consumption of the product. Thus dentists, lawyers and boutiques each design their places of work to communicate confidence and other attributes that might be valued by clients.[11] Events

are occurrences designed to communicate particular messages to target audiences. Public-relations departments often arrange events such as news conferences or grand openings to achieve specific communication effects on an audience.

Although personal communication is often more effective than mass communication, mass media may be the major way to stimulate personal communication. Mass communications affect personal attitudes and behaviour through a two-step flow-of-communication process: 'Ideas often flow from radio and print to opinion leaders and from these to the less active sections of the population.'[12]

This two-step communication flow has several significant implications. First, it says that mass media's influence on mass opinion is not as direct, powerful and automatic as supposed. It is mediated by opinion leaders, persons who are members of primary groups and whose opinions tend to be sought out in one or more areas. Opinion leaders are more exposed to mass media than are the people they influence. They are the carriers of the messages to people who are less exposed to media, thus extending the influence of the mass media; or they may carry altered or no messages, thus acting as gatekeepers.

Second, the concept of opinion leaders challenges the notion that persons are influenced in their consumption styles primarily by a 'trickle-down' effect from the higher-status classes. Since people primarily interact with others in their own social class, they pick up their fashion and other ideas in this way – from people like themselves who are opinion leaders.

A third implication is that the mass communicator may disseminate messages more efficiently by using a lower advertising budget and directing it specifically at opinion leaders, letting them carry the message to others. A pharmaceutical firm, for example, may direct new product promotion to influential doctors.

Selecting Source Attributes

A communicator's effect is also influenced by how the audience perceives the communicator. Marketers have known for years that messages delivered by highly credible sources will be more persuasive: pharmaceutical companies will arrange for doctors to testify about their products' benefits because doctors have high credibility; antidrug crusaders will use former drug addicts to warn students against drugs, because ex-addicts have higher credibility than teachers; other marketers will hire well-known personalities such as newscasters or athletes to deliver their messages.

The three factors commonly thought to underlie source credibility are expertise, trustworthiness and likeability.[13] Expertise is the degree to which the communicator is perceived to possess the necessary authority for what is being claimed. Advocacy by doctors, scientists and professors ranks high in relation to their field of specialization. Trustworthiness is related to how objective and honest the source is perceived to be. Likeability is related to how attractive the source is to the audience. Qualities such as candour, humour and naturalness tend to make a source more likeable.

The most highly credible source would obviously be a person who scored high on all three dimensions.

Collecting Feedback

After the message has been disseminated, the communicator must research its effects on the target audience. This generally involves asking members whether they recognize or recall the message; how many times they recall seeing it; what points they recall; how they felt about the message; and their previous and current attitudes toward the product and company. Ultimately the communicator would like to collect behavioural measures of audience response, such as how many people bought, liked and talked to others about the product.

An example of feedback measurement is shown in Figure 16-3. Here, 80 per cent of the total market are aware of brand A, 60 per cent have tried it, and 20 per cent of those who have tried it are satisfied. This indicates that the communication programme is effective in creating awareness but the product fails to meet expectations. On the other hand, only 40 per cent of the total market are aware of brand

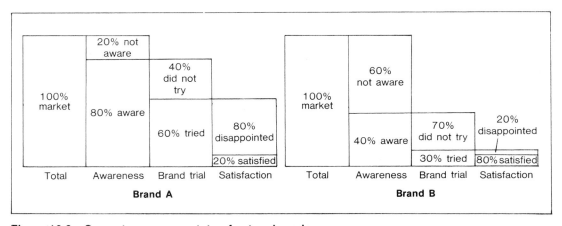

Figure 16-3   Current consumer states for two brands

B, only 30 per cent have tried it, and 80 per cent of those who have tried it are satisfied. In this case the communication programme needs to be strengthened to take advantage of the brand's satisfaction-generating power.

SETTING PROMOTIONAL BUDGET AND MIX

We have looked at the steps involved in planning a specific communication directed at a specific target audience. But how does the company decide on the total promotion budget and its division among the major promotional tools? We turn now to these questions.

Establishing the Total Promotional Budget

One of the most serious marketing questions facing company management is how much to spend on promotion. Management finds it easier to make budget decisions on plant, equipment and supplies; promotion is seen as a guessing game. Many years ago a leading marketer said: 'I know that half of my advertising is wasted. Unfortunately, I don't know which half.'

One thing is clear: industries, and companies within industries, differ considerably in how much they spend on promotion. Total promotional spending may amount to 30–50 per cent of total sales in the cosmetics industry and only 15–20 per cent in the industrial machinery industry. Within an industry, low- and high-spending companies will be found. Philip Morris, for example, was a high spender in the wine industry with Ben Ean and Liebfrauwine, the first and third top-selling Australian wines. However, Kaiser Stuhl was a low spender on Summer Wine, which largely attained its second top-selling status because of its price positioning.[14]

How do companies decide on their total promotional budget? The most common approach is to set the budget as a percentage of sales, either this year's sales or next year's projected sales. The percentage chosen is one that management feels can be afforded and is reasonable in relation to what competitors are spending. This approach, however, begs the question of whether the company is overspending or underspending – unless it has some way to determine the relation between total promotional expenditures and sales, it is flying blind. The company should seriously consider cutting its promotional percentage when it has few new products or things to say, and raise it in the opposite circumstances.

There are also companies that base their promotional budget on competitors' expenditures. They may eye some competitor and decide to spend more, less or the same. They often choose to spend the same, assuming that this will neutralize the competitor's impact, but they should really spend more or spend less depending on their objectives and the relative potency of the other elements in their marketing mix.

Other companies prefer to build their promotion budget by setting communication objectives and tasks, which then suggest the necessary communication tasks. The costs of the tasks are added, and the total promotion budget becomes the sum of the separate required costs.

The weight promotion should receive in the total marketing mix (as opposed to product improvement, lower prices, more services, and so on) depends on where the company's products are in their lifecycle, whether the products are essentially commodities or are highly differentiable, whether the products are routinely needed or have to be 'sold', and other considerations. In theory, the total promotional budget should be established where the marginal profit from the last promotional dollar just equals the marginal profit from the last dollar in the best non-promotional use. Implementing this principle, however, is another thing.

Establishing the Promotional Mix

Companies also have to decide how to split their total promotional budget among the main promotional elements. The most striking fact about the various promotional tools is their internal substitutability and their substitutability with other marketing-mix elements: it is possible to achieve a given sales level by increasing advertising expenditures, personal selling, or sales promotion; it is also possible to achieve the same sales level by product improvement, lower prices, or additional customer services. This substitutability explains why marketing departments are increasingly trying to achieve administrative coordination of all of the tools of communication and other areas of marketing.

The theory of choosing the optimal promotional mix is as follows. Suppose management is about to split the promotional budget between advertising and sales promotion. Figure 16-4a shows that there are an infinite number of promotional mixes of these two elements, i.e. every point on the *A-S* plane is a possible promotional mix. If the company has a fixed total budget, say K, it can spend all the money on advertising or on sales promotion or on any of the mixes in between shown on the constant-budget line. If, on the other hand, the company wants a particular split between advertising and sales promotion, it can settle for any mix shown on the constant-mix line up to its budget.

Associated with every possible marketing mix is a resulting sales level. Three sales levels are shown in Figure 16-4a. The marketing mix (A_1S_1) – calling for a small budget and a rough equality between advertising and sales promotion – is expected to produce sales of Q_1. The marketing mix (A_2S_2) involves the same budget, with more expenditure on advertising than sales promotion; this is expected to produce slightly higher sales, Q_2. The mix (A_3S_3) calls for a larger budget but a relatively equal splitting between advertising and sales promotion, and with a sales estimate of Q_3.

For a given marketing budget, the money should be divided among the promotional tools in a way that gives the same marginal profit on the last dollar spent on each tool. A geometrical version of the solution is shown in Figure 16-4b: a constant-budget line indicates

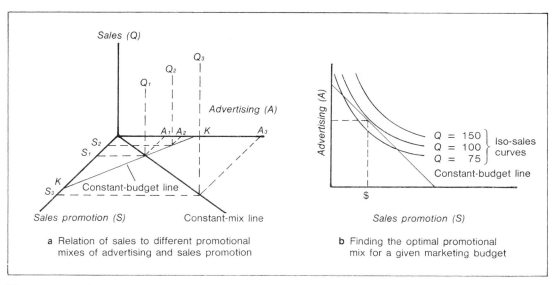

a Relation of sales to different promotional mixes of advertising and sales promotion

b Finding the optimal promotional mix for a given marketing budget

Figure 16-4 The sales function associated with two marketing-mix elements

all the alternative promotional mixes that could be achieved with this budget. The curved lines are called iso-sales curves, and show the different mixes of advertising and personal selling that would produce a given level of sales. It is a projection, into the *A-S* plane, of the set of points resulting from horizontal slicing of the sales function shown in Figure 16-4a at a given level of sales. Figure 16-4b shows iso-sales curves for three different sales levels: 75, 100 and 150 units. Given the budget line, it is not possible to attain sales of more than 100 units. The optimal promotional mix is shown at the point of tangency between the budget line and the last-touching iso-sales curve about it. Consequently the promotional mix $(A^{\star}S^{\star})$, which calls for somewhat more advertising than promotion, is the sales-maximizing (and in this case profit-maximizing) promotional mix.

Again, the challenge is one of putting the theory into practice: management must be able to estimate the amount of sales that would be produced by different combinations of promotional-mix elements. Certain factors have a major influence on which promotional elements will have the most impact. These factors are reviewed below.

Type of product. Historically there has been a considerable difference in the communication mix used by consumer and industrial marketers. The mix differences are illustrated in Figure 16-5a. Advertising is widely felt to be the most important promotional tool in consumer marketing, and personal selling the most important promotional tool in industrial marketing. Sales promotion is considered to have an equal, though smaller, importance in both markets. Publicity is considered to have an even smaller, but equal, importance in both markets.

This view leads some marketers to act as if advertising were unimportant in industrial marketing and as if personal selling were unimportant in consumer marketing. These con-

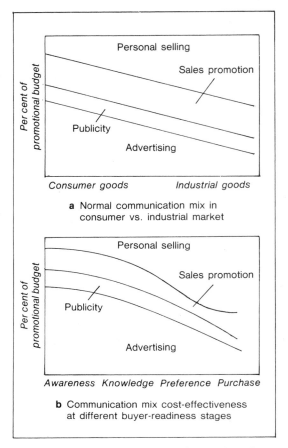

a Normal communication mix in consumer vs. industrial market

b Communication mix cost-effectiveness at different buyer-readiness stages

Figure 16-5 Communication mix as a function of type of product and buyer readiness stage

clusions are erroneous, however. While sales calls will normally have more impact than advertising in industrial-marketing situations, advertising can perform such useful functions as awareness building, comprehension building, efficiency reminding, development of prospect leads, legitimation, and product reassurance. Morrill has shown, in the case of commodity marketing, that the combination of advertising and personal selling increased the sales-per-call by 23 per cent over those achieved with no advertising. The total promotional cost as a percentage of sales was reduced by 20 per cent.[15] Levitt's research has

Exhibit 16-1 Role of Corporate Advertising in Industrial Marketing

A study conducted by Theodore Levitt sought to determine the relative roles of the company's reputation (built mainly by advertising) and its sales presentation (personal selling) in producing industrial sales. The experiment consisted of showing various groups of purchasing agents different filmed sales presentations of a new, but fictitious, technical product for use as an ingredient in making paint. The variables were the quality of the presentation and whether the salesperson represented a well-known company, a less-known but creditable company, or an unknown company. The reactions and ratings of the purchasing-agent groups were collected after the films and then again five weeks later. The findings were as follows:

1. A company's generalized reputation has a positive influence on sales prospects in improving the chances of: (i) getting a favourable first hearing; and (ii) getting an early adoption of the product. Therefore, to the extent that corporate advertising can build up the company's reputation (other factors also shape its reputation), this will help the company's sales representatives.
2. Sales representatives from well-known companies have an edge in getting the sale, provided that their sales presentation is up to the expected standard. If, however, a sales representative from a lesser-known company makes a highly effective sales presentation, this can overcome the disadvantage. To this extent, smaller companies may find it better to use their limited funds in selecting and training better sales representatives rather than in advertising.
3. Company reputations tend to have the most effect where the product is complex, the risk is high, and the purchasing agent is less professionally trained.

Source: Theodore Levitt, *Industrial Purchasing Behaviour: A Study in Communications Effects* (Boston: Division of Research, Harvard Business School, 1965).

shown that advertising can play an important role in industrial marketing (see Exhibit 16-1).

Conversely, personal selling can make a strong contribution in consumer-goods marketing. It is not simply the case that 'salespersons put products on shelves and advertising takes them off': well-trained salespeople can sign up more dealers to carry the brand, influence them to devote more shelf-space to it, and encourage them to cooperate in special promotions.

Push or pull strategy. Companies vary in their preference for a push or pull strategy. A push strategy calls for using the sales force and trade promotion to push the product through the channels: the manufacturer pushes the product into the wholesalers' hands, and the wholesalers push the product on to the retailers' shelves, and it is hoped that the retailers have sufficient incentive to push the product on to the consumers. A pull strategy calls for spending a lot of money on advertising and consumer promotion to build up consumer demand for the product. If effective, consumers will go to their retailers and ask for the product, thus pulling it through the system; the retailers, upon hearing that the company is planning to spend lots of money to build demand, are likely to agree to carry the product even though at a lower margin.

Companies differ in their predilection for push or pull. Uncle Ben's relies more heavily on push, and many of its competitors on pull. Avon concentrates on personal selling, whereas Revlon spends heavily on advertising. In selling vacuum cleaners, Electrolux spends heavily on a door-to-door sales force while Hoover relies more on advertising. This strategy choice clearly influences the funds spent on the different promotional tools.

Buyer readiness stage. Promotional tools differ in their cost-effectiveness in producing different customer responses. Figure 16-5b shows the general findings that have emerged from a number of studies.[16] Advertising, followed by sales promotion and publicity, are the most cost-effective tools in building buyer awareness, more than 'cold calls' from sales representatives. Advertising is highly cost-effective in producing knowledge, with personal selling coming in second. Buyer preference is influenced most by personal selling, followed by advertising. Finally, buyer purchase is primarily influenced by sales calls, with help from sales promotion. The buyer readiness stage is thus an important factor in formulating the promotional mix.

Product lifecycle stage. The different promotional elements perform with varying degrees of effectiveness at different stages of the product lifecycle. In the introduction stage, advertising and publicity are cost-effective in producing high awareness, and sales promotion is useful in promoting early trial. Personal selling is relatively expensive, although it must be used to get the trade to carry the product.

In the growth stage, advertising and publicity continue to be potent, but sales promotion can be reduced because incentives for trial are less needed.

In the mature stage, sales promotion tends to increase relative to advertising. Buyers know the brands and need only a reminder level of advertising unless there are some new things worth saying about the product.

In the decline stage, advertising is cut down to a reminder level, publicity is eliminated, and salespeople give the product only minimal attention. Sales promotion, however, might continue strongly.

Size of the total promotional budget. The size of the organization's promotional budget affects which promotional tools will be emphasized. Small organizations with low budgets cannot hope to spend much on television advertising or other expensive advertising media. They will rely on such things as publicity, direct mail, and personal selling. Non-profit organizations in particular will rely heavily on 'volunteers' as their promotional arm.

Responsibility for Marketing Communications Planning

Members of the marketing department hold different opinions as to how much to spend on the various promotional tools. The sales manager finds it hard to understand how the company could get more value by spending $80 000 to buy twenty exposures of a thirty-second television commercial in the five major capital cities, than by hiring three additional sales representatives for a whole year. The public relations manager feels that the company can gain by transferring some of the advertising budget to publicity.

Historically, companies left these decisions to different people; but today companies are moving toward the concept of integrated communications, which calls for: (i) developing a corporate position, such as marketing communications director, who has overall responsibility for the company's persuasive communication efforts; (ii) working out a philosophy of the roles of different promotools, and the extent to which they are to be used; (iii) keeping track of all promotional investments by product, promotool, stage of product lifecycle, and observed effect, as a basis for improving subsequent effective use of each tool; and (iv) coordinating the promotional inputs when major compaigns take place.

Coordinating promotional activities promises to achieve more consistency in the company's meaning to its buyers and publics. It places a responsibility in someone's hands – where none existed before – to unify and manage the company's image as it comes through numerous activities. It leads to the determination of a total marketing communications strategy aimed at showing how the company can help customers solve their problems.

SUMMARY

Marketing communications is one of the four major elements of the company's marketing mix. Its instruments – advertising, sales promotion, publicity and personal selling – have separate and overlapping capabilities, and their effective coordination requires careful definition of communication objectives.

In preparing specific marketing communications, the communicator has to understand the eight elements of any communication process: sender, receiver, encoding, decoding, message, media, response and feedback. The communicator's first task is to identify the target-audience members and their characteristics. Next, the communicator has to define the sought response, whether it is awareness, knowledge, liking, preference, conviction or purchase. Then a message must be constructed containing an effective content, structure and format. Then media must be selected, for both personal and nonpersonal communication. The message must be delivered by someone with good source credibility, i.e. who scores high on expertise, trustworthiness and likeability. Finally the communicator must monitor how much of the market becomes aware and tries the product, and is satisfied in the process.

The company has to decide how much to spend for total promotion. The most popular approaches are to set the promotional budget as a percentage of sales, to base it on competitors' expenditures, or to base it on an analysis and costing of the communication objectives and tasks.

The company also has to split the promotional budget among the major promotional tools. If management knew the sales associated with different promotional mixes, it could choose the optimal mix. In practice, companies are influenced by the type of product, whether they prefer a push or pull strategy, the buyer's readiness stage, the product lifecycle stage, and the size of the total promotional budget. The interactions of the different promotional activities require organizational coordination for maximum impact.

QUESTIONS FOR DISCUSSION

1. Apply the four major tools in the marketing communication mix to a professional sports team.
2. What two parties are used in any marketing communication? Discuss how they relate to McDonald's.

3. How would the six buyer-readiness states relate to your last purchase of beer or a soft-drink?

4. Which type of message content is used by the following marketers?
   • OTC international telephone service
   • Holden
   • Keep Australia Beautiful organization
   • General Electric.

5. What major types of communication channels can an organization utilize? When should each be used?

6. State whether the following individuals are credible sources for marketing communication: (a) Dennis Lillee; (b) Jana Wendt. Why?

7. How might a company set its promotional budget? Discuss the advantages of each approach.

8. The type of product being marketed has no relationship to the communication mix employed by the marketer. Comment.

9. Who should have responsibility for marketing communications planning? Why?

NOTES

1 Pam Mawbey, 'Dame Edna Finds Herself Some Unusual Bedfellows', *Australian Financial Review*, 20 October 1981, p. 27.

2 These definitions, with the exception of the one for sales promotion, are from *Marketing Definitions: A Glossary of Marketing Terms* (Chicago: American Marketing Association, 1960). The AMA definition of sales promotion covered, in addition to incentives, such marketing media as displays, exhibitions and demonstrations that can better be classified as forms of advertising, personal selling, or publicity. Some marketing scholars have also suggested adding *packaging* as a fifth element of the promotion mix, although others classify it as a product element.

3 Michael L. Ray, *Marketing Communication and the Hierarchy-of-Effects* (Cambridge, Mass.: Marketing Science Institute, November 1973).

4 Michael L. Ray & William L. Wilkie, 'Fear: The Potential of an Appeal Neglected by Marketing', *Journal of Marketing*, January 1970, pp. 55–56; and Brian Sternthal & C. Samuel Craig, 'Fear Appeals: Revisited and Revised', *Journal of Consumer Research*, December 1974, pp. 22–34.

5 See Brian Sternthal & C. Samuel Craig, 'Humour in Advertising', *Journal of Marketing*, October 1973, pp. 12–18.

6 Carl I. Hovland & Wallace Mandell, 'An Experimental Comparison of Conclusion-Drawing by the Communication and by the Audience', *Journal of Abnormal and Social Psychology*, July 1952, pp. 581–88.

7 See C. I. Hovland, A. A. Lumsdaine & F. D. Sheffield, *Experiments on Mass Communication* (Princeton, N.J.: Princeton University Press, 1948), Vol. III, Ch. 8.

8 For a discussion of these devices, see James F. Engel, Roger D. Blackwell & David T. Kollat, *Consumer Behaviour* (Hinsdale, Ill.: Dryden Press, 3rd edn, 1978), pp. 346–48.

9 See Ray Sutton, 'Watch It – Your Body is Telling Us Everything', *Australian Financial Review*, 4 December 1981, pp. 53–4. Sutton refers to Alan Pease's *Body Language*, Camel Publishing.

10 These and other points are discussed in Thomas S. Robertson, *Innovative Behaviour and Communication* (New York: Holt, Rinehart & Winston, 1971), Ch. 9.

[11] See Philip Kotler, 'Atmospherics as a Marketing Tool', *Journal of Retailing*, Winter 1973–74, pp. 48–64.

[12] P. F. Lazarsfeld, B. Berelson & H. Gaudet, *The People's Choice* (New York: Columbia University Press, 2nd edn, 1948), p. 151.

[13] See John C. Mahoney, 'Attitude Measurement and Formation' (paper presented at the American Marketing Association Test Market Design and Measurement Workshop, Chicago, 21 April 1966).

[14] See David Farmer, 'The "Big 25" in the Bubbles and Sweet Stakes', *Australian Financial Review*, 20 November 1981, p. 37*ff*.

[15] *How Advertising Works in Today's Marketplace: The Morrill Study* (New York: McGraw-Hill, 1971), p. 4.

[16] 'What IBM Found about Ways to Influence Selling', *Business Week*, 5 December 1959, pp. 69–70; and Harold C. Cash & William J. Crissy, 'Comparison of Advertising and Selling', *The Psychology of Selling* (Flushing, N.Y.: Personnel Development Associates, 1965), Vol. 12.

Advertising, Sales Promotion and Publicity Strategy

17

Palm trees bent, light showers threatened and a stiff onshore breeze at Cairns had public relations men anchoring the bottom of the slide presentation screen beside the swimming pool. Spotlit under a beach umbrella for protection against cool showers rather than hot sun, GMH's top men were presenting their new TE Gemini, its salient features flickering through the thick, humid air on to the screen. Perched on the motel roof in the breeze, two of GMH's photographic staff manned the spotlight and worked the slide projectors. It was all part of the lavish $15 000 announcement for the new small car with which GMH hopes to retain its leadership of the Australian small car market.

It had started thirty-six hours before when twenty-five journalists jetted to Cairns to learn of the latest GMH little car which was being assembled in Brisbane at the Acacia Ridge plant, 3000 km further south. To overcome jet lag, GMH had chartered next day some light, twin-engined planes for a day trip to Lizard Island on the Barrier Reef to see the marlin boats in action and snorkel among the beauties of Australia's best known coral. There was sun cream and sandshoes in case they'd been forgotten further south. (Melbourne that day had 27 degrees and perfect sunshine in contrast to the far north's threatening rain.)

The razzamatazz was to launch the new TE Gemini, which is claimed to give 10 per cent better fuel economy than the old model. Its engine innards were flicked on to the screen before the pressmen after a barbecue. The hard sell started at 6 a.m., GMH's usual reveille time. We were shown the new suspension, different spring and shock-absorber rates, new seats, improved sound insulation. On the outside, the looks of the car have been altered with a new nose and tail; the passenger cabin remains unchanged in shape.

Finally the prices – $5324 for the S, $5574 for the SL and $5943 for the new top-of-the-range SL/X – were announced. These were increased $16, $47 and $83 over those of the previous model. 'We had to keep the price of the Gemini under $6000 to avoid marketing problems', GMH's sales director, John Loveridge, said.

Gemini sales have soared to overtake the Toyota Corolla as best seller in the little car market – 19 045 in 1978, an estimated 29 700 this year and a projected figure of more than 30 000 next year. The small car market segment – and Gemini had more than 30 per cent of it – was expected to grow by 11 000 next year, GM spokesmen said.

The lights flickered, the screen was rolled up, to the PR men's relief, and the cars rolled on, in the flesh. There was a sedan and a new 'youth-oriented' panel van, the Gipsy, for fuel-conscious, get-away-from-it-all surfies.

All the fuss threatened to obscure the importance of the little car. It was billed as GMH's small, four-cylinder car for the 1980s, when fuel efficiency would count for more than engine power.

Summing up: Plenty of palm trees, barbecues, coral and pools couldn't dim the appeal of this little car, which I think will retain its market lead through its better mechanicals and claimed lower fuel thirst.[1]

To promote the Gemini, GMH does many things in addition to spending more than $1 million per year on mass-media advertising. Substantial resources are devoted to sales-promotion activities, such as feting interested parties at new-car launchings, and to securing favourable editorial coverage in the media, such as the newspaper article resulting from the Cairns launch. The three mass-promotion techniques of advertising, sales promotion, and publicity are examined in this chapter.

ADVERTISING

Advertising consists of nonpersonal forms of communication conducted through paid media under clear sponsorship. This major form of marketing communication runs up a bill of over $2 billion each year in Australia. It is a tool by no means restricted to commer-cial firms; advertising is used by museums, fund-raisers and various social organizations to bring messages about themselves and their causes to various target publics. In fact, one of the largest advertising spenders is a non-profit organization – the Australian government.[2]

Within the commercial sector, the major product groups in terms of national expenditure in all media are food, motor vehicles and accessories including fuel, household equipment and appliances, travel, toiletries and industrial materials.[3] Two of Australia's largest advertisers are Colgate-Palmolive and Reckitt & Colman, with Colgate spending more than $12 million (8 per cent of sales), and Reckitts spending $20 million (over 5 per cent of sales) each year.[4] The Philips electrical company is also a big spender, at about $14 million per year.[5] The biggest advertisers include the major retailers, with reported expenditures of $16 million by Waltons and $22 million by

Woolworths in 1981.[6] However, the retailers' advertising budgets may be only about 2 per cent of sales.

Advertising comes in many forms and has many uses. It involves magazine and newspaper space, radio and television, outdoor displays (posters, signs, skywriting), direct mail, novelties (matchboxes, blotters, calendars), cards (car, bus), catalogues, directories and circulars. It can be used for such diverse purposes as long-term buildup of the organization's image (institutional advertising), long-term buildup of a particular brand (brand advertising), information dissemination about a sale, service or event (classified advertising), announcement of a special sale (sale advertising), and advocacy of a particular cause (advocacy advertising).

Because of the many forms and uses of advertising, it is difficult to make generalizations about its distinctive qualities as a component of the promotional mix. Yet the following qualities can be noted:[7]

1. *Public presentation.* Advertising, unlike personal selling, is a highly public mode of communication. This confers a kind of legitimacy on the product and also suggests a standardized offering. Because many persons receive the same message, buyers know that their motives for purchasing the product will be publicly understood.
2. *Pervasiveness.* Advertising is a pervasive medium that permits the seller to repeat a message many times. It also allows the buyer to receive and compare the messages

---

Exhibit 17-1 Historical Milestones in Advertising

Advertising is not a new activity of modern industrialism but goes back to the very beginnings of recorded history. The diggings of archaeologists in the countries rimming the Mediterranean Sea have turned up evidence of the use of signs to announce various events and offers. The Romans painted walls to announce forthcoming gladiatorial contests, and the Phoenicians painted murals on prominent rocks along trade routes extolling the wares they sold, a precursor of modern outdoor advertising. In Pompeii, a wall has been found praising a politician and asking for the people's votes.

Another early form of advertising was the use of town criers. During the 'golden age' of Greece (the fifth century B.C.), town criers were paid to circulate through the streets of Athens announcing the sale of slaves, cattle and other goods, as well as making public announcements. An early 'singing commercial' used in ancient Athens went as follows: 'For eyes that are shining, for cheeks like the dawn/For beauty that lasts after girlhood is gone/For prices in reason, the woman who knows/Will buy her cosmetics of Aesclyptos.' The town criers were the forerunners of radio as an advertising medium and the car loudspeakers used by modern political candidates.

The third early form of advertising was the mark placed by artisans on their individual goods, such as pottery. As the reputation of a particular artisan spread, through word of mouth, buyers began to look for his distinctive mark just as trademarks and brand names are used today. They would pay a premium: Osnabruck linen was carefully controlled for quality and commanded a price 20 per cent higher than that of other Westphalian linens. As production became more centralized and markets became more distant, the mark or identifying name took on more significance.

Exhibit 17-1 (continued)

However, the turning point in the history of advertising was 1450, the year Gutenberg invented the printing press: no longer did advertisers have to produce extra copies of a sign by hand. The first known printed advertisement in the English language appeared in 1478.

Starting in 1622, an important new medium gave advertising a substantial forward push, namely, the first English newspaper, the *Weekly News*. Later Joseph Addison and Richard Steele published the *Tatler* and became devotees of advertising. Addison included this advice to copywriters: 'The great art in writing advertising is the finding out the proper method to catch the reader, without which a good thing may pass unobserved, or be lost among commissions of bankrupts.' The 14 September issue of the *Tatler* in 1710 contained competitive ads for razor strops and patent medicine which attempted to convince the readers of the products' superiority over competing products.

Advertising had its greatest growth in the United States rather than England. Benjamin Franklin is often called the father of American advertising because his *Gazette*, first published in 1729, attained the largest circulation and advertising volume of any paper in colonial America. Several factors contributed to America's becoming the cradle of advertising. First, American industry led in the mechanization of production, which created surpluses and the need to convince consumers to buy more. Second, the development of a fine network of waterways, highways and roads made feasible the transportation of goods and advertising media to the countryside. Third, the establishment in 1813 of compulsory public education led to the decline of illiteracy and the growth of newspapers and magazines. The invention of radio and, later, television created two more amazing media for the dissemination of advertising. Australian advertising followed the international pattern, deriving many aspects from British and American developments. Substantial growth occurred from about 1850.

Source: Based on information in John S. Warner, Willis L. Winter Jr & Sherilyn K. Zeigler, *Advertising* (New York: McGraw-Hill, 4th edn, 1977), pp. 10–17; and other sources including *Golden Anniversary Book 1928–78*, a special issue of *Advertising News*, 17 November 1978, which profiles the Australian experience.

of various competitors. Large-scale advertising by a seller says something positive about the seller's size, popularity and success.

3. *Amplified expressiveness.* Advertising provides opportunities for dramatizing the company and its products through the artful use of print, sound and colour. Sometimes the tool's very success at expressiveness may, however, dilute or distract from the message.

4. *Impersonality.* Advertising, in spite of being public, pervasive and expressive, cannot be as compelling as a company sales representative. The audience does not feel obliged to pay attention or respond; advertising is only able to carry on a monologue, not a dialogue with the audience.

Advertising's roots lie in early history (see Exhibit 17-1). Although it is now thought of as primarily a marketing tool used in private-enterprise economies, it can be found virtually everywhere in the world including socialist countries (see Exhibit 17-2) and developing nations.[8] Evidently, modern economies find advertising a cost-effective way to disseminate messages, whether it be to build brand preference for a drink such as Coca-Cola in over 150 countries of the world or to motivate a developing nation's people to drink milk or practise birth control.

To handle advertising, four different organizational arrangements can be used. In small companies, advertising is the responsibility of a single person in the sales department, who might handle other functions as well and oc-

Exhibit 17-2 Advertising in the Soviet Union

Who ever would have thought that more than 100 advertising agencies would be plying their trade today in the USSR? Certainly not Marx. According to traditional Marxist-Leninist doctrine, advertising is a tool of capitalist exploitation: it siphons off the surplus value belonging to underpaid workers, and puts it in the hands of overpaid white-collar workers who are nonproductively employed writing jingles.

Yet there has been an impressive growth of advertising agencies in the USSR. The initial argument was that these agencies exist to develop advertising to support Soviet goods in competitive export markets but in fact many advertisements also appear in print and broadcast media reaching Russian consumers. Another rationale was established at the 1957 Prague Conference of Advertising Workers of Socialist Countries, which made three points as to how advertising was to be used: (i) to educate people's tastes, develop their requirements, and thus actively form demand; (ii) to help the consumer by providing information about the most rational means of consumption; and (iii) to help to raise the culture of trade. Furthermore, Soviet advertising is to be ideological, truthful, concrete and functional. The Soviets claim that their advertising does not indulge in devices used in the West: ads will not use celebrities, only experts will be used to promote a product; they will not use mood advertising; they will not create brand differentiation where none exists.

Experts think that the main use of Soviet advertising is to help industry move products that come into excess, in cases where the Soviets do not want to do the logical thing, cut prices.

Exhibit 17-3 What is an Advertising Agency and How Does It Work?

Advertising agencies first appeared at the end of the nineteenth century, in the form of salespeople and brokers who worked for various media and received a commission for selling advertising space to companies. As the competition for advertising business grew, the salespeople began to attract customers by helping them compose and prepare their advertisements. This tie strengthened to such a point that today's agencies are closer to the advertisers than to the media.

An advertising agency today is an independent company that provides advertising services and sometimes general marketing services to its clients. There are several reasons why even a company that has a strong advertising department may want to use an advertising agency. Most significantly, agencies are able to employ specialists in the technical preparation and placement of advertising, who often perform the necessary tasks better than the firm's own staff. Second, an agency brings an outside perspective to bear on the company's problems, as well as a broad range of experience derived from working with a diverse set of clients and situations. Third, because of the way in which agencies are often

Exhibit 17-3 (continued)

paid for their work (see below), use of an agency may cost a firm surprisingly little. Fourth, since a firm is free to cancel its business with an agency at any time, an agency has more incentive to perform effectively and efficiently than does a permanent advertising department.

An advertising agency is typically organized around four departments: *creative*, which handles the development and production of ads; *media*, which selects media and places ads in them; *research*, which determines audience characteristics and wants; and *account service*, which handles the public relations and business activities of the agency. Each account is supervised by an account executive, and personnel in each department are assigned to work on several accounts. Some of the larger agencies are able to assign departmental personnel to only one account, and these persons become experts on the product being promoted.

New business is sometimes attracted to an agency because of its reputation or size. Generally, however, a limited number of agencies are invited to compete for a firm's account by developing and presenting a 'mini-ad-campaign' for the product. Each agency makes a private presentation, and the firm then selects one agency to handle its advertising.

Compensation to advertising agencies has primarily been in the form of commissions, although some has been in the form of fees. Typically, an agency receives a commission of 10–12.5 per cent of the cost of the media time or space it purchases for its client. Thus an advertising agency may buy $60 000 of magazine space for a client; the magazine bills the advertising agency for $54 000 ($60 000 less 10 per cent), and the agency then bills the client for the full $60 000, keeping for itself the $6000 commission. If the client bought the space directly from the magazine, it would have to pay the full $60 000 because these commissions apply only to accredited advertising agencies.

This is obviously a practice held over from the days when the agencies were working for the media, and it has created growing dissatisfaction on the part of both advertisers and agencies. Large advertisers complain that they pay more than smaller ones for the same services, simply because they place more advertising. All advertisers are uncomfortable with the fact that the incentives might drive agencies away from low-cost media and short advertising campaigns. Agencies are unhappy because they often find it necessary to perform extra services for an account without receiving additional compensation. Today there is a growing trend toward compensation on either a straight-fee basis or by a combination of commission and fee. A fee of 7.5 per cent is commonly added to the media commission of 10 per cent, yielding total compensation for the agency of 17.5 per cent of the nominal media cost.

Other trends have also buffeted the advertising agency industry in recent years. Full-service advertising agencies are encountering increasing competition from limited-service agencies (those specializing, for example, in media buying, advertising writing, or advertising production). Economic trends have increased the power of the business managers in agencies, who are demanding more profit-mindedness from the creative staff. Some advertisers have also begun to form their own inhouse agencies, thus pulling some longstanding accounts away from agencies. Finally, the Trade Practices Commission and other public policy-makers have recently expressed the opinion that agencies must share equal responsibility with the client for deceptive advertising, which would make them liable for financial penalties or the cost of corrective ads. These trends will effect some changes in the industry in future years, but advertising agencies provide a highly demanded service and can be expected to endure.

casionally work with an advertising agency. Large companies tend to set up a separate advertising department, whose head reports to the marketing manager. In some cases the advertising department will be small in that it will rely primarily on a hired advertising agency to create, test, and place advertising. The advertising department's job is to develop the total budget, approve agency ads and campaigns, and perhaps handle direct-mail advertising, dealer displays, and other forms of advertising not ordinarily performed by the agency. In other cases, especially in retail organizations, the advertising department will be large and will perform all the tasks without the help of an advertising agency. Advertising agencies, however, have several advantages and have become an important part of the Australian advertising scene (see Exhibit 17-3).[9]

In developing an advertising campaign, marketing management must make five important decisions. These are shown in Figure 17-1, and are examined in the following sections.

Objectives Setting

Before an advertising budget and programme can be developed, advertising objectives must be set. These must flow from prior decision-making on the target market, market positioning, and marketing mix. The marketing mix strategy defines the job that advertising has in the total marketing plan.

At the same time, there are many specific communication and sales objectives that can be assigned to advertising. Colley has distinguished fifty-two possible advertising objects in his *Defining Advertising Goals for Measured Advertising Results*.[10] He outlines a method called DAGMAR (after the book's title for turning advertising objectives into specific measurable goals. An advertising goal is a specific communication task, to be accomplished amongst a defined audience in a given period of time. The various possible advertising objectives may be sorted according to whether their aim is to inform, persuade or remind.

The *inform category* includes such advertising objectives as telling the market about a new product, suggesting new uses for a product, informing the market of a price change, explaining how the product works, describing various available services, correcting false impressions, reducing consumers' fears, and building a company image. This includes pioneering advertising, which seeks to build primary demand (i.e. demand for a product

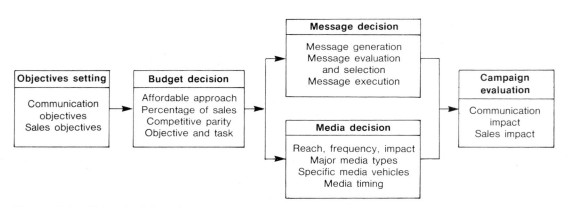

Figure 17-1 Major decisions in advertising management

category): it informs the target market about what the product is, what it does, and where it is available; it does not emphasize the brand name or compare brands. An example would be advertising sponsored by the yoghurt industry to inform consumers about the food's nutritional benefits and many uses.

The *persuade category* includes such advertising objectives as building brand preference, encouraging switching to the advertiser's brand, trying to change the customer's perception of the importance of different product attributes, persuading the customer to purchase now, and persuading the customer to receive a sales call. This category includes competitive advertising, whose purpose is to build selective demand (i.e. demand for a particular brand): it attempts to promote uses, features and benefits of a brand that may not be available from other brands. Some competitive advertising has moved into the category of comparison advertising, which seeks to establish the superiority and one or more product characteristics of a brand through specific comparison with others in the product class.[11] Comparison advertising is increasingly being used by advertisers of deodorants, toothpastes, tyres, household cleaners, and cars.

The *remind category* includes such advertising objectives as reminding consumers that the product may be needed in the near future, reminding them of where to buy it, keeping it in their minds during off-seasons, and maintaining its top-of-the-mind awareness. This category includes reinforcement advertising, which seeks to assure current users that they have made the right choice. Motor vehicle companies' ads will often depict satisfied customers enjoying some special feature of the bought make.

Budget Decision

After setting the advertising objective, the company has to establish budgets for individual-product and overall advertising.

The company wants to spend the least needed to attain the communication and sales goals, but this is difficult to determine. Four of the most common methods used to arrive at advertising budgets are described below.

Affordable method. Many companies set the advertising budget on the basis of what they think the company can afford. One advertising executive explained this method as follows: 'Why it's simple. First, I go upstairs to the controller and ask how much they can afford to give us this year. He says a million and a half. Later, the boss comes to me and asks how much we should spend, and I say "Oh, about a million and a half." Then we have an advertising appropriation.'[12] Setting budgets in this manner is tantamount to saying that the relationship between advertising expenditure and sales results is at best tenuous. If the company has sufficient funds, it should spend them on advertising as a form of insurance.

The basic weakness of the affordable approach is that it leads to a fluctuating advertising budget, which makes it difficult to plan for long-range market development.

Percentage-of-sales method. Many companies set their advertising expenditures at a specified percentage of sales (either current or anticipated) or of the sales price. A number of advantages are claimed for this method. First, advertising expenditures are likely to vary with what the company can 'afford'. This pleases the more financially-minded members of top management, who feel that expenses of all types should bear a close relationship to the movement of corporate sales over the business cycle. Second, this method encourages management to think in terms of the relationship between advertising cost, selling price, and profit per unit. Third, it encourages competitive stability to the extent that competing firms spend approximately the same percentage of their sales on advertising.

In spite of these advantages, the percentage-of-sales method has little to justify it. It uses circular reasoning in viewing sales as the cause of advertising rather than the result. It leads to an appropriation set by the availability of funds rather than by opportunities; it discourages experimentation with countercyclical advertising or aggressive spending. The dependence of the advertising budget on year-to-year fluctuations in sales militates against the planning of long-range advertising programmes. The method does not provide a logical basis for the choice of a specific percentage, except what has been done in the past, what competitors are doing, or what the costs will be. Finally, it does not encourage the constructive development of advertising appropriations on a product-by-product and territory-by-territory basis, but instead suggests that all allocations be made at the same percentage of sales.

Competitive-parity method. Some companies set their advertising budgets specifically to match competitors' outlays, i.e. to maintain competitive parity. This thinking is illustrated by the executive who asked a trade source: 'Do you have any figures which other companies in the builders' specialties field have used, which would indicate what proportion of gross sales should be given over to advertising?'[13]

Two arguments are advanced for this method. One is that competitors' expenditures represent the collective wisdom of the industry. The other is that maintaining a competitive parity helps to prevent advertising wars.

Neither of these arguments is valid. There are no a priori grounds for believing that competition is using more logical methods for determining outlays. Advertising reputations, resources, opportunities and objectives are likely to differ so much among companies that their budgets are hardly a guide for another firm to follow. Furthermore, there is no evidence that appropriations based on the pursuit of competitive parity do in fact stabilize industry advertising expenditures.

Knowing what competition is spending on advertising is undoubtedly useful information. But it is one thing to know this and another to follow it blindly.

Objective-and-task method. The objective-and-task method calls upon advertisers to develop their budget by defining their advertising objectives as specifically as possible, determining the tasks that must be performed to achieve these objectives, and estimating the costs of performing these tasks. The sum of these costs is the proposed advertising budget.

Following Ule, we will use an example to show how the objective-and-task method can be used by a new alcoholic beverage, Plonk (name fictitious), to establish the necessary advertising budget.[14] The steps are as follows:

1. *Establish the market-share goal.* The advertiser wants 8 per cent of the market: if there are 5 million alcohol drinkers, this means the company wants to attract 400 000 regular Plonk drinkers.
2. *Determine the percentage of the market that should be reached by Plonk advertising.* The advertiser hopes to reach 80 per cent (4 million drinkers) with its advertising.
3. *Determine the percentage of aware drinkers that should be persuaded to try the brand.* The advertiser would be pleased if 25 per cent of aware drinkers (1 million drinkers) tried Plonk. This is because it estimates that 40 per cent of all triers, or 400 000 persons, would become loyal users. This is the market goal.
4. *Determine the number of advertising impressions per one per cent trial rate.* The advertiser estimates that forty advertising impressions (exposures) for every one per cent of the population would bring about a 25 per cent trial rate.

5. *Determine the number of gross rating points that would have to be purchased.* A gross rating point is one exposure to one per cent of the target population. Since the company wants to achieve forty exposures to 80 per cent of the population, it will want to buy 3200 gross rating points.

6. *Determine the necessary advertising budget on the basis of the average cost of buying a gross rating point.* To expose one per cent of the target population to one impression costs an average of $200. Therefore 3200 gross rating points would cost $640 000 (= $200 ×3200) in the introductory year.

This method has the advantage of requiring management to spell out its assumptions about the relationship between dollars spent, exposure levels, trial rates and regular usage. Its major limitation is that the market-share goal is established on the basis of what management wants, rather than derived from a profit-maximizing approach to sales.

Other decision models. Advertising researchers have recently proposed more advanced models for setting advertising budgets. These models call for estimating the advertising sales-response function, i.e. the relationship between different possible levels of advertising expenditure and resulting sales (see Chapter 4). For example, Vidale and Wolfe estimated this function through a statistical analysis of past data on advertising and sales for a range of products.[15] John Little recommended the use of advertising experiments in different markets to discover the impact of varying levels of advertising expenditure on sales.[16] Ackoff and Emshoff used experimental procedures in the case of a brand of beer, and were able to show the brewer how it could substantially increase its market share without increasing its ad budget.[17] We expect to see the further use of mathematical models to arrive at sound advertising budgets.

Message Decision

Given the advertising goals and budget, management must develop a creative strategy. Advertisers and their agencies go through three steps: message generation, message evaluation and selection, and message execution.

Message generation. Message generation involves developing a number of alternative messages that will help the product achieve its desired positioning in the market.

Creative departments use different methods to generate ideas for effective advertising messages. Many proceed inductively, gathering ideas from consumers, dealers, experts and competitors. Today there is increasing interest in deductive frameworks for generating advertising messages. Maloney proposed one possible framework (see Table 17-1). He suggested that buyers may be expecting any of four types of reward from a product – rational, sensory, social or ego-satisfaction – and may visualize these from results-of-use experience, product-in-use experience, or incidental-to-use experience.[18] Crossing the four types of rewards with the three types of experience generates twelve types of advertising messages.

Message evaluation and selection. The task of selecting the best message out of a large number of possibilities calls for evaluation criteria. Twedt has suggested that contending messages be rated on three scales: desirability, exclusiveness and believability.[19] He believes that the communication potency of a message is the product of all three factors, i.e. if any of the three has a low rating, the message's potency will be greatly reduced.

The message must first say something desirable or interesting about the product. This is not enough, however, since many brands will be making the same claim. Therefore the message must also say something exclusive or distinctive that does not apply to every brand in the product category. Finally, the message must be believable or provable.

Table 17-1 Examples of twelve types of appeals

Type of potentially rewarding experience	Potential type of reward			
	Rational	*Sensory*	*Social*	*Ego-Satisfaction*
Results-of-use experience	1. Get clothes cleaner	2. Settles stomach upset completely	3. When you care enough to serve the best	4. For the skin you deserve to have
Product-in-use experience	5. The flour that needs no sifting	6. Real gusto in a great light beer	7. A deodorant to guarantee social acceptance	8. The shoe for the young executive
Incidental-to-use experience	9. The plastic pack keeps the cigarette fresh	10. The portable television that's lighter in weight, easier to lift	11. The furniture that identifies the home of modern people	12. Stereo for the man with discriminating taste

Source: Adapted from John C. Maloney, 'Marketing Decisions and Attitude Research', in George L. Baker Jr, *Effective Marketing Coordination* (Chicago: American Marketing Association, 1961).

Message execution. The impact of a message depends not only upon what is said but also upon how it is said. In fact, message execution can be decisive for those products that are essentially the same, such as detergents, cigarettes, coffee and beer. The advertiser must put the message across in a way that will win the attention and interest of the target audience.

To guide the development of message execution, the advertiser usually prepares a copy-strategy statement describing the objective, content, support and tone of the desired ad. Here is such a statement for a product called Gold Rush Biscuits.

The *objective* of the advertising is to convince biscuit-users that now, for the first time, they can buy a canned biscuit that's as good as homemade – Gold Rush Biscuits.

The *content* consists of emphasizing the following product characteristics of the Gold Rush Biscuits:

1. They look like homemade biscuits.
2. They have the same texture as homemade biscuits.
3. They taste like homemade biscuits.

Support for the 'good as homemade' promise will be twofold:

1. Gold Rush Biscuits are made from a special kind of flour (soft wheat flour) traditionally used for homemade biscuits but never before used in commercial biscuits.
2. The use of traditional Australian biscuit recipes.

The *tone* of the advertising will be news announcement, tempered by a warm, reflective mood emanating from a look back at traditional Australian baking quality.

It is the task of the creative people to find style, tone, words and format factors that make for effective message execution. Any message can be put across in many different *styles*, as the following examples show:

1. *Slice of life.* This shows one or more persons using the product in a normal setting. A family might be shown at the dinner table expressing satisfaction with a new brand of biscuit.

2. *Lifestyle.* This emphasizes how a product fits in with a lifestyle. The ad for Black

Douglas Scotch shows David Frost holding a glass of Scotch in one hand and a beautiful woman with the other, casually dropping his Rolls-Royce keys on the coffee table.

3. *Fantasy.* This creates a fantasy around the product or its use. A perfume ad features a barefoot woman in a floaty dress coming out of an old French barn, crossing a meadow, and confronting a handsome young man on a white steed, who carries her away.

4. *Mood or image.* This builds an evocative mood or image around the product, such as beauty, love or serenity. No claim is made about the product except through suggestion.

5. *Musical.* This shows one or more persons or cartoon characters singing a song or jingle involving the product. Many tea ads have used this format.

6. *Personality symbol.* This creates a character that represents or personifies the product. The character might be animated (Mr Sheen) or real (Ronald McDonald, Colonel Sanders).

7. *Technical expertise.* This shows the care that the company exercises, and the experience it has had, in selecting ingredients or manufacturing the product. Some wine and coffee ads use this approach.

8. *Scientific evidence.* This presents survey or scientific evidence that the brand is preferred to or outperforms one or more other brands. For years, Colgate toothpaste has featured scientific evidence to convince toothpaste buyers of its superior cavity-fighting properties.

9. *Testimonial evidence.* This features a highly credible or likeable source endorsing the product. It could be a celebrity like Dennis Lillee or Ron Barassi (Hertz Rent-a-Cars), or 'ordinary people' saying how much they like the product.

The communicator must also choose an effective *tone* for the ad. Some firms' advertis-ing, for example, is consistently positive in its tone: their ads say something superlatively positive about the product in the clearest possible way, and humour is avoided so as not to take attention away from the message. Other ads may typically take on a humorous and self-deprecating tone.

Words that are memorable and attention-getting must be found. This is nowhere more apparent than in the development of headlines and slogans to lead the reader into an ad. There are six basic types of headlines: news ('New Boom and More Inflation Ahead . . . and What You Can Do about It'); question ('Have You Had It Lately?'); narrative ('They Laughed When I Sat Down at the Piano, but When I Started to Play!'); command ('Don't Buy Until You Try All Three'); 1-2-3 ways ('12 Ways to Save on Your Income Tax'); and how-what-why ('Why They Can't Stop Buying').[20]

Format elements such as size, colour and illustration can make a difference in an ad's impact as well as its cost. A minor rearrangement or alteration of mechanical elements within the advertisement can improve its attention-gaining power by several points. Larger-size ads gain more attention, though not necessarily by as much as their difference in cost. The use of four-colour illustrations instead of black and white increases ad effectiveness and also ad cost.

Media Decision

The advertiser's next task is to find efficient advertising media to carry the message.

Deciding on reach, frequency and impact. Before selecting media, the advertiser must determine the desired reach, frequency and impact needed to achieve the advertising objectives:

1. Reach. This is the question of how many persons in the target audience should be exposed to the ad campaign during the specified period of time. For example, the advertiser might seek to reach 70 per cent of the target audience during the first year.

2. Frequency. This is the question of how many times the average person in the target audience should be exposed to the message within the specified time period. For example, the advertiser might seek an average exposure frequency of three. Krugman has argued that fewer than three exposures to a message may be insufficient to have an effect, and more than three exposures may be wasteful.[21]

3. Impact. This is the question of the quality of impact that the exposure should have. Messages on television typically have more impact than messages on radio because television stimulates sight as well as sound. Within a media form such as magazines, the same message in one magazine (say, *Playboy*) may deliver more credibility than in another (say, *Western Farmer and Grazier*). For example, the advertiser may seek a quality exposure of 1.5 where 1.0 is the value of an exposure in an average medium.

Now suppose the advertiser's product might appeal to a market of one million consumers. The goal is to reach 700 000 consumers (= 1 000 000 × .7). Since the average consumer will receive three exposures, 2 100 000 exposures (= 700 000 × 3) must be sought. Since high-impact exposures of 1.5 are desired, a rated number of exposures of 3 150 000 (= 2 100 000 × 1.5) must be bought. If a thousand exposures of this impact cost $10, the advertising budget will have to be $31 500 (= 3150 × $10). In general, the more reach, frequency and impact the advertiser seeks, the higher the advertising budget will have to be.

Choosing among major media types. The media planner must examine the major media types for their capacity to delivery reach, frequency and impact. Profiles of the major ad-

vertising media are shown in Table 17-2: the major media types, in order of their advertising volume, are newspapers, television, direct mail, magazines, radio and outdoor. Each medium has certain advantages and limitations, and professional planners must choose between them by considering several variables, the most important ones being:

1. *Target-audience media habits.* For example, radio and television are the most effective media for reaching teenagers.
2. *Product.* A product like women's dresses might be shown to advantage in colour magazines, and Polaroid cameras might best be demonstrated on television. Media types have different potentialities for demonstration, visualization, explanation, believability and colour.
3. *Message.* A message announcing a major sale tomorrow will require radio or newspapers. A message containing a great deal of technical data might require specialized magazines or mailings.
4. *Cost.* Television is very expensive, and newspaper advertising is inexpensive. What counts, of course, is the cost-per-thousand exposures rather than the total cost.

Advertisers must periodically re-evaluate different media to determine what they are getting for their money. For a long time, television enjoyed the supreme position in the media mix, and magazines and other media were neglected. Then media researchers began to notice television's reduced effectiveness due to increased clutter: advertisers have been beaming shorter and more numerous commercials at the television audience, resulting in poorer attention and impact. Furthermore, television advertising costs have been rising faster than those for other media. Several companies have found that a combination of print and television ads often does a better job than television commercials alone.

Table 17-2 Profiles of major media types

Medium	Volume in millions (1980)*	Example of cost (1981–82)	Advantages	Limitations
Newspapers	$657	$4760 for one page, weekday, in the *Australian*	Flexibility; timeliness; good local market coverage; broad acceptance; high believability	Short life; poor reproduction quality; small 'pass-along' audience
Television	$555	$3052 for 30 seconds on 'Sale of the Century' (GTV 9)	Combines sight, sound, and motion; appealing to the senses; high attention; high reach	High absolute cost; high clutter; fleeting exposure; less audience selectivity
Direct mail	$432	$200 for the names and addresses of 1000 businesses	Audience selectivity; flexibility; no ad competition within the same medium: personalization	Relative high cost; 'junk mail' image
Magazines	$166	$9900 for one page, four-colour, in *Women's Weekly*	High geographic and demographic selectivity; credibility and prestige; high-quality reproduction; long life; good pass-along readership	Long ad purchase lead time; some waste circulation; no guarantee of position
Radio	$145	$130 for 30 seconds on the 2SM breakfast session	Mass use; high geographic and demographic selectivity; low cost	Audio presentation only; lower attention than television; non-standardized rate structures; fleeting exposure
Outdoor	$140	$112 per month for a 6.5 m × 3 m poster in Melbourne	Flexibility; high repeat exposure; low cost; low competition	No audience selectivity; creative limitations

*The source for Column two is *Advertising Expenditure in Main Media 1980* (St Leonards, NSW: Commercial Economic Advisory Service of Australia, 1981).

On the basis of these characteristics, the media planner has to decide how to allocate the given budget to the major media types. For example, a firm launching a new biscuit mix may decide to allocate $300 000 to daytime television, $200 000 to women's magazines, and $100 000 to daily newspapers in the major markets.

Selecting specific media vehicles. The next step is to choose the specific media vehicles that would produce the desired response in the most cost-effective way. Consider the category of women's magazines, for example, which includes *Cosmopolitan, Family Circle, Home Journal, Women's Weekly, Woman's Day, New Idea, Cleo* and others. The media planner turns to several volumes put out by Australian Advertising Rate and Data Service (AARDS), which provide circulation and costs for different ad sizes, colour options, ad positions, and quantities of insertions.[22] Beyond this, the media planner evaluates the different magazines on qualitative characteristics such as credibility, prestige, geographic editioning, reproduction quality, editorial climate, lead time and psychological impact. A final judgement must be made as to which specific vehicles will deliver the best reach, frequency and impact for the money.

The cost-per-thousand criterion. Media planners calculate the cost per thousand persons reached by a particular vehicle. If a full-page, four-colour advertisement in the *Bulletin* costs $2200 and the magazine's estimated readership is 660 000 persons, then the cost of reaching each one thousand persons is $3.33. The same advertisement in *Newsweek* may cost $1600 but reach only 360 000 persons, at a cost per thousand of $4.44. The media planner would rank the various magazines with the lowest cost per thousand.

The cost-per-thousand criterion provides a crude initial measure of a media vehicle's exposure value, to which several adjustments have been applied. First, the measure should be adjusted for audience quality. For a baby-lotion advertisement, a magazine read by 1000 young mothers would have an exposure value of 1000, but if read by the same number of old men would have a zero exposure value. Second, the exposure value should be adjusted for the audience attention probability. Readers of *Vogue*, for example, pay more attention to ads than readers of *Newsweek*. Third, the exposure value should be adjusted for the editorial quality (prestige and believability) that one magazine might have over another.

Media planners are increasingly using more sophisticated measures of media effectiveness and employing mathematical models to determine the best media mix. Many advertising agencies use a computer programme to select the initial media, and then make further improvements based on subjective factors that could not have been put into the model.[23]

Deciding on media timing. The advertiser has to decide how to schedule the purchased advertising over the year (macroscheduling) and within shorter segments of time (microscheduling).

Macroscheduling. Here the challenge is to strategically schedule the advertising expenditures over the year in response to such factors as the seasonal pattern of industry sales and expected competitive plans or developments. If industry sales of a particular product peak, for example, in December and wan in March, a seller in this market has three broad options. The firm can vary its advertising expenditures to follow the seasonal pattern, vary expenditures to oppose the seasonal pattern, or hold its expenditures constant throughout the year. The vast majority of firms tend to pursue a policy of seasonal rather than constant or counterseasonal advertising. Even here, the firm faces options. It has to decide whether its advertising expenditures should lead or coincide with seasonal sales; and whether expenditures should be more intense than, proportional to, or less intense than the seasonal amplitude of sales.

Microscheduling. Here the challenge is to allocate the purchased advertising over a short period of time to obtain the maximum impact. Suppose the advertiser wants to schedule thirty spot radio announcements within the month of September and is trying to choose the particular times. One way to classify the multitude of possibilities is shown in Figure 17-2. The left side of the figure shows that advertising messages for the month can be concentrated in a short period ('burst' advertising), dispersed continuously throughout the month, or dispersed intermittently. The top side of the figure shows that advertising messages can be beamed with a level frequency, a rising frequency, a falling frequency, or an alternating frequency.

The advertiser's problem is to decide which of these twelve general patterns would be the most effective distribution plan for the messages. This decision depends upon the advertising objectives in relation to the nature of the product, target customers, distribution channels, and other marketing factors. Consider the following cases:

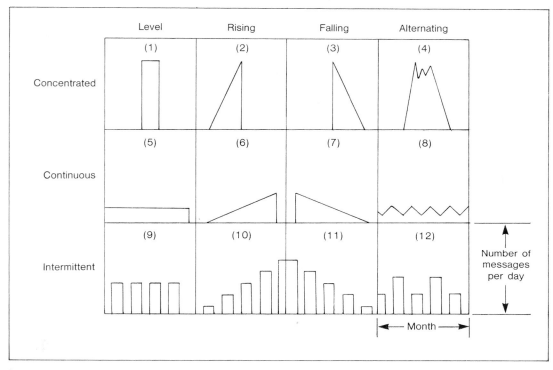

Figure 17-2   Classification of advertising timing patterns

A retailer wants to announce a preseason sale of skiing equipment. She recognizes that only certain people will be interested in the message. Furthermore she recognizes that the target buyers only need to hear the message once or twice to know whether they are interested. Her objective is to maximize the reach of the message, not the repetition. She decides to concentrate the messages on the days of the sale at a level rate, but varying the time of day to avoid the same audiences. She uses pattern 1.

A muffler manufacturer-distributor wants to keep his name before the public, but he does not want his advertising to be too continuous because only 3 to 5 per cent of the cars on the road need a new muffler at any given time. He has therefore chosen to use intermittent advertising. Furthermore, he recognizes that Friday is payday for many potential buyers, and this would influence their interest in replacing a worn-out muffler. He therefore sponsors a few messages

on a midweek day and more messages on Friday. He uses pattern 12.

The timing pattern should take into account three general factors. *Buyer turnover* expresses the rate at which new buyers appear in the market; the higher this rate, the more continuous the advertising should be to reach the new buyers. *Purchase frequency* is the number of times during the period that the buyer buys the product; the higher the purchase frequency, the more continuous the advertising should be to keep the brand on the buyer's mind. The *forgetting rate* is the rate at which the buyer forgets the brand in the absence of stimuli; the higher the forgetting rate, the more continuous the advertising should be to keep the brand in the buyer's mind.

In launching a product, advertisers must make a choice between ad continuity and ad pulsing. Continuity is achieved by scheduling exposures evenly within a given time period; pulsing (or flighting) refers to exposures scheduled unevenly over the same period. Thus fifty-two exposures could be scheduled continuously at one a week throughout the year, or flighted in several concentrated bursts. Those who favour pulsing feel that the audience will learn the message more thoroughly and that money could be saved.

Once the decisions are made on the media vehicles and their timing they should be displayed in a chart to give a bird's-eye view of the total schedule. According to the sample schedule shown in Figure 17-3, 'As the World Turns' will be used each weekday except for the summer months; 'The Mike Walsh Show' will be used three times a week throughout the year; *Family Circle* will be used at the beginning of each month except for the summer months; and the *Reader's Digest* will be used every month.

Campaign Evaluation

The planned advertising campaign should be evaluated before, during and after its launch.

Researchers have developed several techniques to measure the communication and sales effects of advertising.

Communication effect. Here research seeks to discover whether the advertising is achieving the intended communication effects. There are various ways to evaluate the communication effectiveness of, say, an individual ad before or after it has been printed or broadcast. The purpose of ad pre-testing is to make improvements in the advertising copy to the fullest extent possible prior to its release. There are three major methods of ad pre-testing:

1. Direct ratings. Here a panel of target consumers or advertising experts examines alternative ads and fills out rating questionnaires. Sometimes a single question is raised, such as 'Which of these ads do you think would influence you most to buy the product?'. A more elaborate form may also be used, which calls for ratings of the ad's attention strength, read-through strength, cognitive strength, affective strength and behavioural

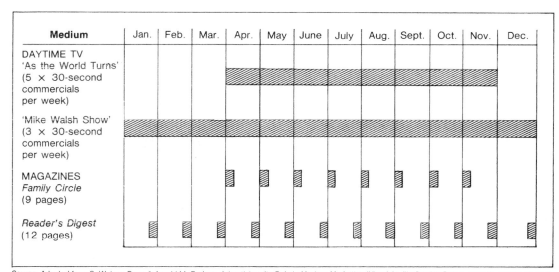

Source: Adapted from S. Watson Dunn & Arnold M. Barban, *Advertising: Its Role in Modern Marketing* (Hinsdale, Ill.: Dryden Press, 4th edn, 1978), p. 523.

Figure 17-3   A sample media schedule

strength. The underlying theory is that an effective ad must score high on all of these properties if it is ultimately to stimulate buying action; too often ads are evaluated only on their attention- or comprehension-creating abilities. At the same time, it must be appreciated that direct rating methods are less reliable than hard evidence of an ad's actual impact on target consumers. Direct rating scales help primarily to screen out poor ads rather than identify great ads.

2. Portfolio tests. Here respondents are given a dummy portfolio of ads and are told to take as much time as they want to read them. After putting them down, the respondents are asked to recall the ads they saw – unaided or aided by the interviewer – and to play back as much as they can about each. The results are taken to indicate an ad's ability to stand out and its intended message to be understood.

3. Laboratory tests. Some researchers assess the potential effect of an ad through measuring physiological reactions – heart beat, blood pressure, pupil dilation, perspiration – through such equipment as galvanometers, tachistoscopes, size-distance tunnels, and pupil dilation measuring equipment. These tests at best measure the attention-getting power of an ad rather than any impact it has on beliefs, attitudes or intentions.

There are two popular ad post-testing methods, the purpose of which is to assess the actual communication impact of the ad after it has appeared in media:

1. Recall tests. Recall tests involve finding persons who are regular users of the media vehicle and asking them to recall advertisers and products contained in the issue under study. They are asked to recall or play back everything they can remember, and may or may not be aided by the administrator. Recall scores are prepared on the basis of their responses and are used to indicate the power of

the ad to be noticed and retained. Consider the following example:

A television campaign for Katies winter fashions, produced by the Sydney advertising agency Magnus Nankervis and Curl, has created a new day-after recall record. Burke Marketing Research found the commercials drew a massive 69 per cent recall compared with a 'norm' for apparel products of 26 per cent. This is the highest recall recorded in more than 3000 tests by Burke in Australia and the U.S. during the last three years. In that time the highest recall on a commercial in Australia has been 51 per cent with 54 per cent the top rating in the U.S. 'Norm's Poem', part of the Life Be In It campaign produced by the Monahan Dayman Adams advertising agency registered the 51 per cent. The Katies commercials, which have a Hollywood-musical flavour, first went to air on April 1 in conjunction with the high rating Academy Awards program on the Nine Network. Burke managing director, Mr. Graham White, says the accompanying program or commercial environment has little bearing on how well people remember a particular commercial. He claims commercial recall hinges 90 per cent on how creatively the message is presented.[24]

2. Recognition tests. Recognition tests call for sampling, say, the readers of a given issue of a magazine, asking them to point out what they recognize as having seen and/or read. For each ad, three different readership scores may be prepared from the data: (a) *noted*, the percentage of readers who say they have previously seen the advertisement in the particular magazine; (b) *seen/associated*, the percentage of readers who say they have seen or read any part of the ad that clearly indicates the names of the product or service of the advertiser; and (c) *read most*, the percentage of readers who not only looked at the advertisement but say that they read more than half of its total written material. Some organizations also furnish *adnorms*, i.e. the average scores for each product class for the year, and separately for men and women for each magazine, to enable advertisers to evaluate their ads in relation to competitors' ads.

Sales effect. Communication-effect research undoubtedly helps advertisers improve the quality of message content and presentation, but it reveals little about how much sales may be affected, if at all. What sales conclusion can the advertiser draw in learning that a recent campaign has increased brand awareness by 20 per cent and brand preference by 10 per cent? What has the advertiser learned about the sales productivity of its advertising dollar and therefore how much to spend?

The sales effect of advertising will generally be more difficult to measure than the communication effect, because sales are influenced by many factors besides advertising (e.g. the product's features, price and availability, and competitors' actions). The fewer or more controllable these other factors, the easier it is to measure advertising's impact on sales: it is easiest to measure this in mail-order situations, and hardest to measure in brand- or corporate-image-building advertising. Efforts to measure the sales impact of advertising usually follow one of two approaches.

1. The historical approach. This involves the researcher in fitting past company sales to past company advertising expenditures on a current or lagged basis using advanced statistical techniques. For example, Montgomery and Silk examined the impact of three sales techniques – direct mail, samples and literature, and journal advertising – on the sales of a pharmaceutical firm.[25] Their statistical results indicated that the firm was overdoing direct mail and underspending on journal advertising in allocating its advertising funds.

2. Experimental design. Du Pont, for example, was one of the earliest American companies to design an experiment to measure the effects of varying levels of advertising expenditure on sales. In the case of Du Pont paint, management thought that the advertising budget was too low.[26] It classified fifty-six sales territories according to their market share (high, average or low): within one group Du Pont spent the normal amount for advertising in one-third of the group; in another third, two and one-half times the normal amount; and in the remaining third, four times the normal amount. At the end of the experimental period, Du Pont was able to estimate how many extra sales were created by higher levels of advertising expenditure. Du Pont found that higher levels of advertising expenditure led to increased sales at a diminishing rate; and that the sales response was less pronounced in the areas where Du Pont had a higher market share.

Advertising clearly involves major sums of money that can easily be misspent if companies fail to take the proper steps, i.e. defining the advertising objectives; making careful budget, message and media decisions; and evaluating the campaign results. Advertising is also an area of considerable public attention and scrutiny, which stems from its power to influence lifestyles and opinions. In recent years, advertising has been subjected to increasing regulation designed to ensure that it performs responsibly. If marketers are to be effective in their use of advertising and other elements of promotion, they must be aware of public policy developments affecting promotion (see Exhibit 17-4).

SALES PROMOTION

Sales promotion comprises a wide variety of tactical promotional tools designed to stimulate earlier and/or stronger target market response in the short term. These can be subclassified into tools for consumer promotion (e.g. samples, coupons, money-refund offers, prices-off, premiums, contests, trading stamps, demonstrations), trade promotion (e.g. buying allowances, free goods, merchandise allowances, cooperative advertising, push

Exhibit 17-4 Promotion Decisions and Public Policy

The 'misleading or deceptive conduct' and 'false representations' sections of the Trade Practices Act have spawned many prosecutions and indicate the care that must be exercised by marketers when designing and executing a programme of persuasive communications. For example, C.V. Holland Pty Ltd was fined $4000 for falsely representing the mileage in a second-hand motor vehicle displayed for sale.

Even when there is no intention of misleading, a false statement will lead to conviction. Spare Parts and Reconditioning Co. Pty Ltd was fined $500 after a 1965-model Mini car was advertised as a 1968 model. The court observed 'Parliament has provided that even an honest mistake does not excuse a false description unless it is proved that the seller took reasonable precautions and exercised due diligence to avoid false description.'

Advertisers must also be careful that their claims cannot be misinterpreted. John Martin & Co. Ltd advertised shoes as 'top quality' meaning to refer to the brand which was in fact a top brand; the shoes were in fact 'seconds', and the company was fined $2000. Power Machinery Pty Ltd was fined for stating that its electric welding machines had the approval of the State Electricity Commission (SEC) although there was no regulation stipulating that such machines needed approval by the SEC before being used. Similarly, Sharp Corporation was fined $100 000 for advertising that its microwave ovens had been tested by the Standards Association of Australia; and Prudential Assurance Co. Ltd was fined $10 000 for representing benefits that a type of superannuation did not have. 'World Series Cricket' had an injunction applied against it not to use the expression 'supertests' in advertisements, because 'sufficient people would be misled into thinking that supertests were matches developed by organizers of what they had previously known as test matches'. Suppliers have to be careful in the way advertisements are framed, and avoid all ambiguities. For instance, it is likely that a price reduction advertised as being below manufacturer's recommended price, but in fact higher than that normally charged, will be regarded as misleading. Organizations have been fined for making false or misleading statements concerning the need for goods and services. Medical Benefits Fund of Australia Ltd was fined $2500 for stating in a brochure 'If you want to be treated by your doctor in hospital — contribute to Table 10 or 12', when there was no need to contribute to these tables to receive the service mentioned.

False statements could be made by resellers about the existence of warranties provided by manufacturers while advertisers should be careful about statements concerning the effect of a warranty. A statement that a product was guaranteed against defects for two years might be considered misleading if it did not state that the guarantee applied to parts only, and that other costs (e.g. labour and transport) had to be paid by the purchaser — as is often the case. A brochure issued by Sperry Rand (Australia) Ltd stated that an electronic calculator was guaranteed for twelve months. When a customer bought one of the calculators she found a ticket attached to the calculator stating the guarantee was for ninety days. The company was fined $2000.

Some selling methods have brought about many complaints rom consumer groups in recent years, and have also been prohibited by the Trade Practices Act. Inertia selling is the practice of forwarding unsolicited goods to a customer with an indication that, if the goods are not returned by a specified date, it will mean that the consumer has agreed to buy them at the stated price. Consumers were often confused as to their rights, and felt

> **Exhibit 17-4** (continued)
>
> bound to pay or return the goods at their own cost. Suppliers are now forbidden to assert a right to payment for unsolicited goods, and must therefore be careful – when they cannot fulfil an order for a specific good – not to send similar but not identical goods instead.
>
> Referral selling, often used in the marketing of home improvements, is a scheme whereby the consumer is promised a discount on the price of services and goods supplied, calculated on the number of sales of similar services resulting from referrals made by the consumer. Very often the discount amounted to nothing or very little. Referral selling is now illegal, even if the discounts were up to the expectation of the consumer. The prohibition of 'coercion and undue harassment in connection with the supply of goods at a place of residence' is designed to get rid of certain forms of high-pressure sales tactics.
>
> Bait advertising is also prohibited under the Trade Practices Act. Here the seller offers or advertises an exceptionally good buy, and then finds some excuse for not selling the advertised item but selling something else: this includes refusing to sell the product, claiming it is already sold out, disparaging its features, demonstrating a defective one, or imposing unreasonable delivery dates or service terms.

money, dealer sales contests) and sales-force promotion (e.g. bonuses, contests, sales rallies). Although such tools are a motley collection, they have two distinctive qualities:

1. *Insistent presence.* Many sales-promotion tools have an attention-getting, sometimes urgent, quality that can break through habits of buyer inertia towards a particular product – they tell buyers of a chance that they won't have again to get something special. This appeals to a broad spectrum of buyers, particularly to the economy-minded, with the disadvantage that this type of buyer tends to be less loyal to any particular brand in the long run.
2. *Product demeaning.* Some of these tools suggest that the seller is anxious for the sale. If they are used too frequently or carelessly, they may lead buyers to wonder whether the brand is desirable or reasonably priced.

Sales-promotion tools are used by a large variety of organizations, including manufacturers, distributors, retailers, trade associations, and various non-profit institutions. As examples of the last, churches sponsor bingo games, theatre parties, testimonial dinners and raffles.

Various factors have contributed to the rapid growth of sales promotion, particularly in consumer markets.[27] Internal factors include the following: (i) promotion has become more acceptable to top management as an effective means to stimulate sales; (ii) more product managers are qualified to use sales-promotion tools; and (iii) product managers are under greater pressure to obtain quick sales response. External factors include the following: (i) the number of brands has increased; (ii) competitors have become more promotion-minded; (iii) inflation and recession have made consumers more deal-oriented; (iv) trade pressure for more manufacturers' deals has grown; and (v) there is a belief that advertising efficiency has declined due to costs, media clutter, and government control.

No single purpose can be advanced for sales-promotion tools, since they are so varied in form: a free sample stimulates consumer trial; a free management-advisory service cements a long-term relationship with a retailer. Overall, sales-promotion techniques make three contributions to exchange relationships:

* *Communication*, i.e. they gain attention and usually provide information that will, it is hoped, lead to trying the product.
* *Incentive*, i.e. they incorporate some concession, inducement or contribution designed to represent value to the receiver.
* *Invitation*, i.e. they include a distinct invitation to engage in the transaction now.

Incentive promotions are adopted by sellers to attract nonbrand users to try the brand, and/or to reward brand-loyal users for their loyalty. Since both types of buyer will buy during the promotion period, both purposes are served, although the primary purpose is usually to attract nonbrand users to the brand. The nonbrand users are of two types, those who are loyal to other brands and those who tend to be brand switchers. Incentive promotions primarily attract the brand switchers, because brand-loyal users of other brands do not always notice or act on the promotion. Since brand switchers are what they are, sales promotions are unlikely to turn them into brand-loyal users. Incentive promotions used in markets of high brand similarity produce a high sales response in the short run but little permanent gain; they are more likely to alter market shares permanently in markets of high brand dissimilarity.

Sellers usually think of sales promotion as an activity designed to break down brand loyalty, and advertising as an activity designed to build up brand loyalty. Therefore an important issue for marketing managers is how to divide the budget between promotion and advertising: companies may be found dividing their funds in a ratio of anywhere from 20:80 to 80:20 on sales promotion and advertising, respectively. This ratio has been rising over the past few years in response to consumers' heightened sensitivity to price. Management should resist letting this ratio get too high.

When a brand is on deal too much of the time, the brand image is diluted and the consumer begins to think of it as a cheap brand. No one knows when this happens, but probably there is risk in putting a well-known brand on deal more than 30 per cent of the time. In fact, dominant brands should use dealing infrequently, since most of it only gives a subsidy to current users.

Prentice has suggested that sales-promotion tools can be divided into two groups, those that are 'consumer franchise building' and those that are not.[28] The former impart a selling message in the deal, e.g. free samples, coupons which include a selling message, and premiums which are related to the product. Tools that do not build consumer franchise include price-off packs, consumer premiums not related to a product, contests and sweepstakes, consumer refund offers, and trade allowances. Sellers are urged to use franchise-building promotions whenever possible because they enlarge the consumers' understanding of the brand.

Ultimately, sales promotion seems most effective when used in conjunction with advertising.

> In one study, point-of-purchase displays related to current TV commercials were found to produce 15 per cent more sales than similar displays not related to such advertising. In another, a heavy sampling approach along with TV advertising proved more successful than either TV alone or TV with coupons in introducing a product.[29]

Major Decisions in Sales Promotion

A company that is considering sales promotion must follow a six-step process: establish the sales-promotion objectives, select the appropriate tools, develop and then pre-test the sales-promotion programme, implement and control it, and evaluate the results.

Establishing the Sales-promotion Objectives

Sales-promotion objectives are derived from basic marketing-communication objectives, which in turn are derived from more basic marketing objectives developed for the product. Within this context, the specific objectives set for sales promotions will vary with the type of target market. For consumers, objectives include encouraging more usage and purchase of larger-size units by users, building trial among non-users, and attracting trial by other brand users. For retailers, objectives include inducing retailer stocking of new items or larger volume, encouraging off-season buying, encouraging stocking of related items, offsetting competitive promotions, building brand loyalty, and gaining entry into new retail outlets. For the sales force, objectives include encouraging support of a new product or model, encouraging more prospecting, and stimulating sales in the off-season.

Selecting the Sales-promotion Tools

A wide range of sales-promotion tools are available to accomplish the various objectives. The selection decision must take into account the type of market, sales-promotion objectives, competitive conditions, and cost-effectiveness of each tool. The main tools are described below.

Samples, price packs, and premiums. These techniques make up the bulk of consumer promotions and account for more dollars than any other set of sales-promotion tools. *Samples* are offers of a free sample or trial of a product to consumers.[30] The sample might be delivered door to door, received in the mail, picked up in a store, found attached to another product, or featured in an advertising offer. Sampling is the most effective *and* expensive way to introduce a new product. For example, when S. C. Johnson introduced

Agree creme rinse and conditioner, it distributed more than a million samples via women's magazines and in-cinema giveaways. Similarly, when Chesebrough-Ponds launched Cream & Cocoa Butter skin lotion it spent more than $40 000 on sachet inserts in *New Idea*. The samples are typically offered in trial-size containers rather than regular sizes: a recent trend is for manufacturers to introduce these into stores to be sold at a low price (although these are not technically samples).

Price packs (also called cents-off deals) are offers to consumers of a certain amount of money off the regular price of a product, flagged on the label or package. The price pack may take the form of a reduced-price pack, which is single packages sold at a reduced price; a multiple pack, which is two or more packages sold at a reduced price (such as two for the price of one); or a branded pack, which is two related products banded together (such as a toothbrush and toothpaste). Price packs are very effective in stimulating short-term sales, even more so than coupons.

Premiums are items of merchandise that are offered at a relatively low cost, or free, as an incentive or bonus to purchasers of a particular product. A with-pack premium accompanies the product inside (in-pack) or outside (on-pack) the package. The package itself, if a re-usable container, may serve as a premium. A free-in-the-mail premium is an item that the company will mail to consumers who send in a request for it together with a proof of purchase, such as a boxtop. A self-liquidating premium is an item that the company will sell at well below its normal retail price to consumers who request it; it is called self-liquidating because the company usually recovers the cost of the sales promotion. A recent trend is for manufacturers to offer consumers all kinds of premiums bearing the company's name.[31]

Point-of-purchase displays and demonstrations. Called POP, this sales-promotion technique covers displays and demonstrations that take place at the point of purchase or sale (i.e. next to the merchandise). A large cardboard display figure of Bernard King or Jimmy Hannan located near Coles' meat department is an example. Unfortunately, many retailers do not like to handle the thousands of displays, signs and posters that they receive from manufacturers each year, even when the manufacturer's sales force offers to set them up. Manufacturers are responding by creating better-quality POP materials, and tying them in with television or print messages for reinforcement.

Trade promotion. Manufacturers have worked out a number of techniques for securing the cooperation of wholesalers and retailers, usually in the form of a benefit such as profit or personal gain. Manufacturers may offer a buying allowance, which is a short-term offer of cents-off on each case or carton purchased during a stated period of time. The purpose is to encourage dealers to buy an item or quantity they might otherwise ignore. It is often used to introduce a new product and compensate buyers for the trouble of adding it to their stock. The buyers can use the buying allowance for immediate profit, advertising, or price redemptions. They may receive the buying allowance as a cheque ('bill-back') or as a deduction from the face of the invoice ('off-invoice').

Manufacturers may, alternatively, offer a merchandise allowance, which is a short-term contractual agreement to compensate the dealer for featuring the manufacturer's products. An advertising allowance compensates dealers for featuring the manufacturer's product in their newspaper ads, radio programmes or handbills. A display allowance compensates them for carrying or building special displays of the product. The compensation is made upon 'proof of performance'.

Manufacturers may also offer free goods, which are extra cases of merchandise offered to intermediaries who buy a certain quantity. Another technique is to offer push money, which is cash or gifts to dealers or their sales force to 'push' the manufacturer's goods. For example, a manufacturer may offer a dealer's salespersons $10 for each appliance sold. Many retailers do not like push money, and it can also be expensive for manufacturers because they pay on all of their sales whether the salespersons pushed their products or not.

Manufacturers also make use of specialty advertising, which consists of gift items that carry the company's name and help to reinforce a relationship between the manufacturer and distributors. Advertising specialties include pens, pencils, calendars, paperweights, matchbooks, memo pads, ashtrays, rulers and many other items. These are either mailed to the intermediaries or delivered in person by sales representatives. They generally succeed in enhancing the manufacturer's image in the distributors' minds.[32]

Business conventions and trade shows. Industry trade associations organize annual (or more frequent) conventions for their members and typically sponsor a trade show at the same time. Those who sell to this particular industry are invited to participate in the trade show to display and demonstrate their products to association members. The vendors who participate in the trade show expect several benefits, including developing new sales leads, maintaining customer contact, introducing new products, meeting new customers, and selling more to present customers.[33]

Contests, sweepstakes and games. These devices present to consumers, dealers or sales forces an opportunity to win something (e.g. cash prizes, trips or goods) as a result of luck or extra effort. In the consumer area, a contest calls for consumers to submit an entry – a jingle, estimate, suggestion – to be examined by a panel of judges who will select the best entries. A sweepstake merely calls for consumers to submit their names to be included in a drawing of prize winners. A game calls for consumers to receive something every time they make a purchase – such as bingo numbers, missing letters – which may or may not help them win a prize. On the other hand, sales contests describe contests aimed at dealers or the sales force that take the form of a competition to induce them to redouble their sales efforts over a stated period, with prizes going to the top performers.

Developing the Sales-promotion Programme

A sales-promotion programme involves more than selecting one or more promotions. The marketer must make additional decisions as to size of incentive, conditions for participation, distribution vehicle for promotion, duration of promotion, timing of promotion, and overall budget.

Size of incentive. The marketer has to determine the most cost-effective size of the incentive. A minimum size will be necessary if the promotion is to be successful; beyond this, a higher incentive level will produce more sales response but at a diminishing rate. Some of the larger consumer-packaged-goods firms have a sales-promotion manager who keeps records on the effectiveness of different promotions used throughout the company, and correlates their incentive value with the sales response to gain insight into the sales-response function. As a result, the sales-promotion manager can recommend incentive levels with a degree of expertise that would not normally be possessed by individual brand managers who only carry out one or two promotions a year.

Conditions for participation. Incentives may be made available to everyone or to select groups. For example, a premium may be made available to only those who return boxtops or other evidence of previous consumption; sweepstakes may be limited to certain States and not made available to families of company personnel, or persons under a certain age. By carefully choosing conditions for participation, the seller can selectively discourage those who are unlikely to become regular users of the product. On the other hand, if the conditions are too restrictive only the most loyal or deal-prone consumers will participate.

Distribution vehicle for promotion. The marketer must decide how to promote and distribute the promotion programme to the target audience. Suppose the promotion is a coupon for use in ordering a self-liquidating premium. Such a coupon could be distributed in the package, store, mail or advertising media, each of which involves a different level of reach and cost. For example, in-pack coupons primarily reach current users, whereas mailed coupons can be directed at nonbrand-users, although at a greater cost.

Duration of promotion. If sales promotions are offered for too short a period, many prospects may not be able to take advantage, since they may not be repurchasing at the time or may be too busy with other things. If the promotion runs for too long, on the other hand, customers may begin to view this as a long-term price concession – the deal will lose some of its 'act now' force, and also raise questions about the brand's real quality. According to one researcher, the optimal frequency is about three times per quarter, and optimal duration is the length of the average purchase cycle.[34]

Timing of production. A schedule of sales promotion will usually be constructed by brand managers, and must be approved by sales and divisional management in terms of total divisional marketing strategy. The schedule is a planning instrument and requires careful coordination of production, sales and distribution. At the same time, some unplanned promotions will also be needed and require preparation on short notice.

Total sales-promotion budget. The total budget for sales promotion can be developed in two ways. It may be built from the ground up, where the marketer decides on various promotions to use during the year and estimates the cost of each. The cost of a particular promotion consists of the administrative cost (printing, mailing and promoting), the incentive cost (cost of premium or cents-off, including rate of redemption) and the expected number of units that will be sold on deal. In the case of an in-pack premium, the cost must include the procurement and packaging of the premium offset by any price increase on the package.

A more common way to arrive at a sales-promotion budget is to use a conventional percentage of the total budget for advertising and sales promotion. For example, toiletries may receive 20–40 per cent of the total budget, whereas packaged goods may get as much as 30–60 per cent. These percentages vary substantially for different brands in different markets, and are influenced by both the product lifecycle stage and competitors' expenditures on sales promotion.

Organizations with multiple brands should ensure that brand budgets are coordinated: although not all sales-promotion activities can be preplanned, coordination gives cost-saving advantages.

Strang, in his study of seventeen leading US consumer-goods manufacturers and advertising agencies, found three major planning inadequacies in sales promotion: (i) lack of consideration of cost-effectiveness; (ii) use of simplistic decision rules, such as extensions of last year's spending, percentage of expected sales, maintenance of a fixed ratio to advertising, and the 'left-over approach'; and (iii) advertising and sales-promotion budgets being prepared independently.[35]

Pre-testing the Sales-promotion Programme

Sales-promotion pre-tests should be conducted whenever possible to determine if the tools are appropriate, the size of the incentive is optimal, and the method of presentation is effective. A survey by the American Premium Advertisers Association indicated that fewer than 42 per cent of premium offerers ever tested the premiums' effectiveness.[36] Yet promotions can usually be tested quickly and inexpensively: groups of consumers can be asked to rate different possible deals according to their preference, or trial tests can be run in limited geographical areas.

Implementing and Controlling the Sales-promotion Programme

Effective control of sales promotions requires specific goals and implementation plans for individual promotions. Programme implementation must cover two critical time factors, lead time and sell-off time. Lead time is the time necessary to bring the programme to the point of announcing the deal. Sell-off time begins at the date of release and ends when approximately 90–95 per cent of the deal merchandise is in the hands of consumers (one to several months later, depending on the deal duration).

Evaluating the Sales-promotion Results

Evaluation is a crucial requirement for improving any programme. According to Strang, however, 'evaluation of promotion programs receives . . . little attention. Even where an attempt is made to evaluate a promotion, it is likely to be superficial . . . Evaluation in terms of profitability is even less common.'[37]

Manufacturers can use any of four methods to measure sales-promotion effectiveness: sales performance movement, analysis of consumer-panel data, consumer surveys, and experimental studies.

The most common evaluation technique consists of comparing sales performance before, during and after a promotion. Suppose a company has a 6 per cent market share in the pre-promotion period, which jumps to 10 per cent during the promotion, falls to 5 per cent immediately afterwards, and rises to 7 per cent some time later. In this case the promotion evidently attracted new triers as well as more purchases by existing customers; after the promotion, sales fell as consumers worked down their inventories. The long-run rise to 7 per cent indicates, however, that the company gained some new users. In other cases the brand's share may return to the pre-promotion level, indicating that the promotion only altered the time pattern of demand rather than the total demand.

Consumer-panel data could be used to examine the kinds of people who responded to the promotion and what they switched to after the promotion. A study by Dodson, Tybout and Sternthal found that deals generally enhance brand switching, the rate depending on the type of deal. Furthermore, consumers generally return to their preferred brands after the deal.[38]

If more information is needed, surveys may be conducted to learn how many consumers recall the promotion, what they thought of it, how many took advantage of it, and how it affected their subsequent brand choices.

Sales promotions may also be evaluated through carefully arranged experiments that vary such attributes as incentive value, duration, and distribution media. Some large companies test alternative strategies in selected market areas with each of their national promotions.

Thus we see that sales promotion can play an important role in the total promotion mix. Although it tends to be used on an ad-hoc and residual basis by many firms, it could be used more systematically and effectively.

PUBLICITY

Another major marketing-communications tool is publicity. Publicity has been defined as the activity of 'securing editorial space, as divorced from paid space, in all media read, viewed or heard by a company's customers or prospects, for the specific purpose of assisting in the meeting of sales goals'.[39] To the extent that an organization can create events and news around a marketable entity, it is using publicity.

Almost anything can be publicized. Publicity is used to promote various brands, products, persons, places, ideas, activities, organizations and even nations. For example, trade associations have used publicity to rebuild interest in such staple products as eggs, milk and potatoes. Publicity is commonly used to launch new products and brands, as well as to rekindle interest in mature ones. Organizations with low visibility have used publicity to attract more attention; others with poor public images have used publicity to describe positive things they have done. Nations have employed publicity to attract more tourists, foreign investment or international support. The appeal of publicity is based on its three distinctive qualities.

1. *High credibility*. News stories and features seem to most readers to be authentic, media-originated reports. They have a higher degree of credibility than if they were to come across as being sponsored by a seller.
2. *Off guard*. Publicity can reach many potential buyers who otherwise avoid salespeople and advertisements, if the message is packaged as news rather than as a sales-directed communication.
3. *Dramatization*. Publicity has, like advertising, a potential for dramatizing a company or product.

Publicity is part of a larger concept, that of public relations. Today's public relations practitioners perform the following functions:[40]

1. *Press relations.* The aim of press relations is to place newsworthy information into the news media to attract attention to a person, good or service.
2. *Product publicity.* Product publicity involves various efforts to publicize, through news media and other means, specific products and happenings related to products.
3. *Corporate communications.* This activity covers internal and external communications to draw attention to and promote understanding of the institution.
4. *Lobbying.* Lobbying refers to the effort to influence legislators and government officials in order to defeat unwanted legislation and regulation or to promote wanted legislation and regulation.
5. *Counselling.* Counselling is the provision of general advice to the company about what is happening in society and what the company might do in the way of changing its ways or improving its communications.

Since publicity is part of public relations, those skilled in publicity are usually found not in the company's marketing department but in its public-relations department. The latter is typically located at corporate headquarters rather than in the various divisions; and its staff is so busy dealing with various publics – shareholders, employees, parliamentarians and local government officials – that publicity to support product marketing objectives may be neglected. One frequent solution is to establish a publicity unit within the marketing department.

Publicity is often described as a marketing stepchild because it is relatively underutilized in relation to the real contribution it can make. Publicity has in many cases had a memorable impact on public awareness that advertising alone could not have accomplished (or accomplished at the same low cost). The company does not pay for the space or time in the media; it does pay for the staff time used to develop the stories and induce the media to use them, but this is minimal. If the company has a real story to tell, it could be picked up by all the news media and be worth millions of dollars in equivalent advertising. Furthermore, it would be more credible as news than if it were delivered as advertising.

What kinds of factors indicate that publicity would have a high potential in the total promotional mix? Here are the main ones:

1. *Newsworthiness.* Products that can support interesting stories acceptable to news editors are the best candidates for publicity.
2. *Stimulus for sales force and dealers.* Publicity can be useful in boosting the enthusiasm of the sales force and dealers if this is lacking. For example, news stories appearing about a new product before it is launched will help the sales force gain a hearing from retailers.
3. *Need for credibility.* Publicity introduces an element of credibility by communicating the message in an editorial context. Credibility is needed by new products as well as mature products that the market has questioned.
4. *Small budget.* Publicity, while it is not without cost, tends to cost less in producing exposures than does direct-mail and media advertising. The smaller the company's marketing-communications budget, the stronger the case for using imaginative publicity to neutralize the advantage of a competitor who has more money to spend on advertising.

Major Decisions in Publicity

When considering when and how to use product publicity, management should establish the publicity objectives, choose the publicity messages and vehicles, and evaluate the publicity results.

Establishing the Publicity Objectives

The first task is to set specific objectives for the publicity. As an example, suppose a group of South Australian wine producers hired a public-relations firm to create a publicity programme to support two major marketing objectives: (i) to convince Australians that wine drinking is a pleasurable part of good living; and (ii) to improve the image and market share of South Australian wines among all wines. The following publicity objectives could be established: (i) to develop magazine stories about wine and get them placed in top magazines (the *Bulletin, Reader's Digest*) and newspapers (food columns, feature sections); (ii) to develop stories directed to the medical profession on wine's many health values; and (iii) to develop special programmes for the young adult market, student market, governmental bodies and various ethnic communities.

Where possible, these objectives should be translated into specific goals for audience response variables, so that results can be evaluated at the end of the campaign.

Choosing the Publicity Messages and Vehicles

The publicist next sets about determining whether there are any interesting stories to tell about the product. As an example, suppose a college of advanced education with a low visibility adopts the objective of achieving more public recognition. The publicist will review the college's various components to see whether any natural stories exist. Do any staff members have unusual backgrounds, or are any working on unusual projects? Are any new and unusual courses being taught? Are any exceptional students with unusual backgrounds enrolled? Are any interesting events taking place on campus? Is there a story about the architecture, history or aspirations of the college? Usually a search along these lines will uncover hundreds of stories that can be fed to the press with the effect of creating much more public awareness of the college. Ideally, the stories chosen should symbolize the kind of college this college wants to be, i.e. they should support its desired market positioning.

If the number of good stories is insufficient, the publicist then dreams up newsworthy events that the college could sponsor – creating rather than finding news. Ideas might include hosting major academic conventions, featuring well-known speakers, and developing news conferences: each event is an opportunity to develop a multitude of stories directed to relevant media vehicles and audiences.

Event creation is a particularly important skill in publicizing fund-raising drives for non-profit organizations. Fund-raisers have developed a large repertoire of special events, including anniversary celebrations, art exhibits, auctions, benefit evenings, bingo games, sales (cakes, books), contests, dances, dinners, fairs, fashion shows, parties in unusual places, phonathons, rummage sales, tours and walkathons. No sooner does one type of event get created, such as a walkathon, than competitors spawn new versions such as readathons, bikeathons and jogathons.

Implementing the Publicity Plan

Implementing publicity requires a great deal of care. A great story is easy to place in the media, for example, no matter who does the placing; but most stories are less than great and may not get past busy editors. One of the chief assets of publicists is that they are often ex-journalists who know a number of media editors and know what they want, i.e. interesting, well-written stories, and easy access to sources of further information. Publicists look at media editors as a market to satisfy so that these editors will in turn be inclined to use their stories.

Publicity also requires extra care when it

Exhibit 17-5 Publicizing Publicity

The following newspaper story is a good example not only of the type of publicity achieved by a campaign, but also of the various components of a particular publicity programme:

Australian city dwellers may not believe milk comes from cardboard cartons, but a survey commissioned by the United Dairy Farmers of Victoria has found them to be ignorant of the contribution made by agriculture to the economy

The results of the survey carried out by Saulwick Weller and Associates were released yesterday at a media lunch and conference called to announce a national campaign aimed at educating city Australians and bridging the communication gap between rural and urban people.

The campaign, called Operation Farmlink, officially began this week and will continue until the end of the month.

The survey found that:

- Two-thirds of the people questioned couldn't name a farmer organization;
- 85 per cent couldn't name one farm leader (those named included Malcolm Fraser and Doug Anthony — politicians, not farm leaders);
- Two-thirds favoured support for farmers if their incomes fell below a certain level. One-third believed farmers should leave the land if they couldn't make a profit;
- Most people were confused about subsidies or simply didn't know which rural industries receive support;
- 78 per cent believed modern farming needed large amounts of capital;
- 21 per cent thought anyone can make a go of farming.

Operation Farmlink, which incorporates Dairy Week (25 March–1 April) is a voluntary and cooperative effort by individuals and organizations concerned with agriculture.

The survey found that 41 per cent of city people thought mining was the greatest contributor to national wealth.

However, mining makes up 30 per cent of Australia's export income and about 8 per cent of gross domestic product, while agriculture contributes 44 per cent of the country's export income and 11.5 per cent of its gross domestic product.

Activities during the Farmlink campaign will include:

- Serving breakfast to 2500 children in five metropolitan primary schools;
- Open house at 400 Victorian farms on 25 March, National Farm Sunday;
- Essay competitions and school excursions;
- Visits to Farmworld — an agricultural market and showpiece property near Warragul;
- Shopping centre promotions;
- Life Be In It farm picnic and family fun day including sheep-shearing demonstrations and a gumboot-tossing contest;
- Press photographer award;
- Distribution of more than 200 000 copies of a 32-page Farmlink newspaper;
- Presentation of dinner, supper, breakfast and lunch to city radio announcers.

Source: Barbara Hooks, 'Farmers Strive for Recognition', *Age*, 14 March 1979, p. 14.

involves staging special events such as testimonial dinners, news conferences and national contests. Publicists need a good head for detail, and the ability to come up with quick solutions when things go wrong.

Evaluating the Publicity Results

Because publicity is typically used with other marketing communication tools, its contribution is hard to separate and measure. In the case of a new product, however, publicity is often used before the other tools come into action and thus its contribution is easier to evaluate.

Publicity is designed with certain audience-response objectives in mind, and these form the basis of what is measured. The easiest and most common measure is the number of exposures created in the media. Most publicists supply the client with a 'clippings book' showing all the media that carried news about the product and a summary statement such as the following:

> Media coverage included 350 column centimetres of news and photographs in thirty-five publications with a combined circulation of 7.4 million; 250 minutes of air time on twenty-nine radio stations and an estimated audience of 6.5 million; and sixty-six minutes of air time on sixteen television stations with an estimated audience of 9.1 million. If this time and space had been purchased at advertising rates, it would have amounted to $104 700.[41]

The purpose of citing the equivalent advertising cost is to make a case for publicity's cost-effectiveness, since the total publicity effort must have cost less than $104 700. Furthermore, publicity usually creates more reading and believing than ads.

However, an exposure measure does not indicate how many people actually read, saw or heard the message, and what they thought afterwards. Furthermore, there is no information on the net audience reached, since publications have overlapped readership. A better measure calls for finding out what change in product awareness, comprehension and attitude occurred as a result of the publicity campaign (after allowing for the impact of other promotional tools). This requires the use of survey methodology to measure the before/after levels of these variables. Sales and profit impact is the most satisfactory measure, if obtainable.

SUMMARY

Three of the four major tools of promotion are advertising, sales promotion, and publicity. They are mass-marketing tools, as opposed to personal selling which targets one or a few buyers at most.

Advertising is the use by a seller of paid media to communicate persuasive information about its goods, services or organization; it is a potent promotional tool. Australian marketers spend over $2 billion annually on advertising, in its many forms – national, regional, local; consumer, industrial, retail; product, brand, institutional; and so on. Advertising decision-making is a five-step process consisting of objectives-setting, budget decision, message decision, media decision, and campaign evaluation. Advertisers should establish clear goals as to whether advertising is supposed to inform, persuade or remind buyers. The advertising budget can be established on the basis of what is affordable, as a percentage-of-sales, on the basis of competitors' expenditures, or on the basis of objectives and tasks. The message decision calls for generating messages, evaluating and selecting among them, and executing them effectively. The media decision calls for a number of steps: defining the reach, frequency and impact goals; choosing among major media types; selecting specific media vehicles; and scheduling the media over the year and in shorter time periods. Finally, campaign evaluation calls for continuous researching of the communication and sales effects of advertising programmes before, during and after they are run.

Sales promotion covers a wide variety of short-term incentive tools – such as coupons, premiums, contests, and buying allowances – designed to stimulate consumer markets, the trade, and the organization's own sales force. Sales-promotion expenditures have been growing at a faster rate than advertising in recent times. The effective use of sales-promotion calls for the following steps: establishing objectives; selecting tools; developing, pre-testing, implementing and controlling the sales-promotion programme; and evaluating the results.

Publicity – which is the securing of free editorial space or time – tends to be the least utilized of the major marketing communication tools, although it has great potential for building awareness and preference in the marketplace. Three main steps are involved in publicity work: establishing objectives, choosing the message and vehicles, and evaluating the results.

QUESTIONS FOR DISCUSSION

1. What kinds of organizational arrangement can be used for advertising? Give an example of each.

2. The major objective of advertising is to inform. Comment.

3. If Johnson & Johnson were introducing a new brand of shampoo, what method would the company use to set the advertising budget? Why?

4. Explain the major aspects of the message decision and relate them to a specific product.

5. Which media would the following organizations utilize for their advertising?
   a) your secondary school is trying to raise funds from past students and parents for a new addition to the library
   b) K-Mart wants to promote its Easter sale nationally
   c) White Wings is going to advertise a new type of cake mix
   d) the Red Cross blood bank wants to attract more donors
   e) a small restaurant is promoting a new luncheon menu
   f) a car dealership wants to publicize its convenient location.

6. If advertisers a, c, d and f in question 5 wanted to evaluate their campaigns, how would you suggest they do it?

7. Sales-promotion tools are only effective when used for consumer promotion. Comment.

8. Which sales-promotion tools are most widely utilized for supermarket products? Why?

9. How might Edgell evaluate the success of its national sales promotion campaign?

10. What distinguishes publicity from all other forms of promotion?

11. Discuss how you would develop a publicity campaign for the Anti-Cancer Council or Weet-Bix.

NOTES

1 Extracted from Christopher De Fraga, 'Palm Trees, Pools and PR Men – GMH Launches a New Car', *Age*, 30 October 1979, p. 36.

2 Pam Mawbey, 'Spending by Commonwealth Lifted by 32.5 pc', *Australian Financial Review*, 8 December 1980, p. 11.

3 *Advertising Expenditure in Main Media 1980* (St Leonards, NSW: Commercial Economic Advisory Service of Australia, 1981).

4 See '600 Top Ad Budgets', *Advertising News*, 18 December 1981, p. 19*ff*.

5 Pam Mawbey, 'Former Agency Chief in Element at Philips', *Australian Financial Review*, 24 February 1981, p. 50.

6 Pam Mawbey, 'Waltons' $16m Comedy Act', *Australian Financial Review*, 21 August 1981, p. 15; Valerie Lawson, 'How Fortune Lost Big W in the Advertising Account Move of the Year', *Australian Financial Review*, 14 November 1980, p. 33.

7 See Sidney J. Levy, *Promotional Behaviour* (Glenview, Ill.: Scott, Foresman, 1971), Ch. 4.

8 See R. R. Walker, 'East is Red . . . with Coca-Cola Signs and Home-Grown Pitches', *Age*, 6 June 1979, p. 22.

9 For two very useful local publications, see Kenneth Fowles & Norman Mills (eds), *Understanding Advertising – An Australian Guide* (Kensington, NSW: TAFE Educational Books, 1981); and *Advertising*, No. 27 in the Department of Industry and Commerce Managing the Small Business Series (Canberra: Australian Government Publishing Service, 1980).

10 See Russell H. Colley, *Defining Advertising Goals for Measured Advertising Results* (New York: Association of National Advertisers, 1961).

11 See William L. Wilke & Paul W. Farris, 'Comparison Advertising: Problem and Potential', *Journal of Marketing*, October 1975, pp. 7–15.

12 Quoted in Daniel Seligman, 'How Much for Advertising?', *Fortune*, December 1956, p. 123.

13 Albert Wesley Frey, *How Many Dollars for Advertising?* (New York: Ronald Press, 1955), p. 49.

14 G. Maxwell Ule, 'A Media Plan for "Sputnik" Cigarettes', *How to Plan Media Strategy* (American Association of Advertising Agencies, 1957 Regional Convention), pp. 41–52.

15 M. I. Vidale & H. B. Wolfe, 'An Operations-Research Study of Sales Response to Advertising', *Operations Research*, June 1957, pp. 370–81.

16 John D. C. Little, 'A Model of Adaptive Control of Promotional Spending', *Operations Research*, November 1966, pp. 1075–97.

17 See Russell L. Ackoff & James R. Emshoff, 'Advertising Research at Anheuser-Busch, Inc. (1963–68)', *Sloan Management Review*, Winter 1975, pp. 1–15.

18 John C. Maloney, 'Marketing Decisions and Attitude Research', in George L. Baker Jr (ed.), *Effective Marketing Coordination* (Chicago: American Marketing Association, 1961), pp. 595–618.

19 Dik Warren Twedt, 'How to Plan New Products, Improve Old Ones, and Create Better Advertising', *Journal of Marketing*, January 1969, pp. 53–57.

20 See 'Powerful Headlines Uncover Basic Wants', *Marketing Insights*, 19 May 1969, pp. 16–17.

21 See Herbert E. Krugman, 'What Makes Advertising Effective?', *Harvard Business Review*, March–April 1975, p. 98.

22 See *Australian Advertising Rate and Data Service – Consumer Press Edition* (Chippendale, NSW: Thomson Publications, published monthly). Other editions cover television, radio, newspapers, and other print media.

[23] See Dennis H. Gensch, 'Computer Models in Advertising Media Selection', *Journal of Marketing Research*, November 1968, pp. 414–24.

[24] *Australian Financial Review*, 14 July 1981, p. 21.

[25] David B. Montgomery & Alvin J. Silk, 'Estimating Dynamic Effects of Market Communications Expenditures', *Management Science*, June 1972, pp. 485–501.

[26] See 'E. J. Du Pont de Nemours & Co.: Measurement of Effects of Advertising', in Robert D. Buzzell, *Mathematical Models and Marketing Management* (Boston: Division of Research, Graduate School of Business Administration, Harvard University, 1964), pp. 157–79.

[27] Roger A. Strang, 'Sales Promotion – Fast Growth, Faulty Management', *Harvard Business Review*, July–August 1976, pp. 115–24.

[28] See Roger A. Strang, Robert M. Prentice & Alden G. Clayton, *The Relationship between Advertising and Promotion in Brand Strategy* (Cambridge, Mass.: Marketing Science Institute, 1975), Ch. 5.

[29] Strang, 'Sales Promotion', p. 124.

[30] Most of the definitions in this section have been adapted from John F. Luick & William Lee Siegler, *Sales Promotion and Modern Merchandising* (New York: McGraw-Hill, 1968).

[31] For further reading, see Carl-Magnus Seipel, 'Premiums – Forgotten by Theory', *Journal of Marketing*, April 1971, pp. 26–34.

[32] See Walter A. Gaw, *Specialty Advertising* (Chicago: Specialty Advertising Association, 1970).

[33] See Suzette Cavanaugh, 'Setting Objectives and Evaluating the Effectiveness of Trade Show Exhibits', *Journal of Marketing*, October 1976, pp. 100–105.

[34] Arthur Stern, 'Measuring the Effectiveness of Package Goods Promotion Strategies' (Paper presented to the Association of National Advertisers, Glen Cove, February 1978).

[35] Strang, 'Sales Promotion', p. 119.

[36] Russell D. Bowman, 'Merchandising and Promotion Grow Big in Marketing World', *Advertising Age*, December 1974, p. 21.

[37] Strang, 'Sales Promotion', p. 120.

[38] Joe A. Dodson, Alice M. Tybout & Brian Sternthal, 'Impact of Deals and Deal Retraction on Brand Switching', *Journal of Marketing Research*, February 1978, p. 79.

[39] George Black, *Planned Industrial Publicity* (Chicago: Putnam Publishing, 1952), p. 3.

[40] Adapted from Scott M. Cutlip & Allen H. Center, *Effective Public Relations* (Englewood Cliffs, N.J.: Prentice-Hall, 3rd edn, 1964), pp. 10–14.

[41] Adapted from Arthur H. Merims, 'Marketing's Stepchild: Product Publicity', *Harvard Business Review*, November–December 1972, pp. 111–12.

Personal Selling and Sales Management Strategy

18

Derek Crossley, 42, describes himself as a 'commercial' salesman, a man who sells one machine to a small company, a solicitor or an accountant. Tall, carefully coiffured and exquisitely shod in woven leather, Crossley shows little of his eight years in the Grenadier Guards. 'About all that is left now is a tremendous capacity for self-discipline,' he said.

'When I started selling photocopiers it was with Rank Xerox. Nobody had ever heard the name. In those days the salesmen were all ratbags. Cowboys,' said Crossley. 'Now photocopiers are like Japanese cars. They all have extras so you are selling improvements and modifications of what has gone before.'

But Crossley says he is hopelessly in love with them. When he goes home, he and wife, Pamela, 38, spend much of their time together talking about photocopiers. 'She knows more about photocopy machines than most of the people selling them,' said Crossley.

When friends visit, the topic is usually photocopiers. Many of these friends have bought machines from him. There is even a photocopier in the Crossley home — waiting for a buyer.

Derek Crossley says he must force himself to control his enthusiasm for the machines each time he explains them to a potential customer.

To sell more photocopiers than anyone else in Australia, Crossley employs a canvasser, Frances Durand, to do his leg-work for him. Each morning she takes a lift to the top of a city building, then works her way down, trying to establish a foothold for Crossley. When there is even the slightest interest, Crossley follows up, demonstrating the machines he thinks will do the job best. Then comes the proposal . . . the package deal. 'If they're not interested then I cut my losses and move on,' said Crossley. 'I lose more deals than anyone else in the business because I canvass more people. I feel like the fastest gun in the West — everyone wants to cut me down,' said Crossley.

Crossley believes he is doing no more than any other salesman should be doing. Canvass a territory with the methodical tenacity of an armoured division 'grid-iron' firing. Show that the product is the best of its kind. See the job through. Ensure the customer is satisfied. And make sure everyone around you is an enthusiast.

Last year, John Linton sold more than $30 million worth of computers. 'I would rather sell a computer than do anything else,' says Linton. 'I love my children but I began very early to realise I would rather be selling computers than taking my kids to the beach. If I have a holiday, I am desperate to get back to work.'

For John Linton, the pursuit of a computer buyer is a combination of excitement, competition, intellectual agility, guts and achieving what others say is impossible. 'Probably the key to my success is creativity. To listen to a customer for half an hour, then be able to relate my computer's ability with his interests — golf, gardening, cars — anything,' explained Linton. 'My early interest in amateur theatrical helps, and I am a voracious reader. That makes it easier to relate to a person's background and explain my computer in a way he can understand,' he said.

John Linton believes getting to the top and staying there takes more than dedication. There has to be total flexibility and the guts to make those decisions on the spot. 'Most heads of computer firms have some accountancy background, and in explaining the deal I have made on their behalf I tend not to tell them everything,' he said. 'I only answer questions because I believe there are some things about any deal they do not want to know and perhaps worry about. Like the guarantees and the kind of computer program, links and conversions which I know can be done, but which others will say are impossible,' said Linton.

Like Derek Crossley, John Linton has others to do the spadework. Being national sales manager helps Linton into the managing director's office. 'After all, they are not going to see just any salesman, and they are the only ones who can buy million dollar computers,' he said.[1]

Every organization has one or more persons who have responsibility for contacting and selling to prospects and customers. We call this group the sales force. Sales forces are found not only in most business organizations but in non-profit organizations as well. Churches form membership committees who are responsible for attracting new members. The NSW Agriculture Department Extension Service consists of agricultural specialists who try to educate and sell farmers on the latest technology. Hospitals, museums and other organizations use a staff of fund-raisers to contact prospective donors and sell them on supporting the organization.

The traditional term used to describe the persons in the sales force is salesmen. However, this term is becoming obsolete because of the increasing number of women who are taking on sales responsibilities. We will use the terms sales representatives and salespersons, although salesmen will occasionally be used where appropriate. Many other terms have come into use to describe people who work in sales, including account executive, sales consultant, field representative, manufacturer's representative, agent, service representative, and marketing representative.

There are probably more stereotypes about sales representatives than about any other group. 'Salesman' is likely to conjure up an image of Arthur Miller's pitiable Willy Loman in *Death of a Salesman* or Meredith Willson's cigar-smoking, back-slapping, joke-telling Harold Hill in *The Music Man* – a glib, boisterous character always ready with a glad hand and a racy story. Sales representatives are typically pictured as loving sociability, in spite of some recent evidence that many sales representatives actually dislike it. They are criticized for aggressively foisting goods on people, in spite of the fact that buyers often search out sales representatives.

Actually the term sales representative covers a broad range of positions in our economy, within which the differences are often greater than the similarities. McMurry devised the following classification of sales positions:

1. Positions where the salesperson's job is predominantly to deliver the product, e.g. milk, bread, heating oil.
2. Positions where the salesperson is predominantly an inside order-taker, e.g. the haberdashery salesperson standing behind the counter.
3. Positions where the salesperson is also predominantly an order-taker but works in the field, as the packing-house, soap or spice salesperson does.
4. Positions where the salesperson is not expected or permitted to take an order but is called on only to build good will or to educate the actual or potential user . . . the distiller's 'missionary person' or the medical 'detailer' representing an ethical pharmaceutical house.
5. Positions where the major emphasis is placed on technical knowledge, e.g. the engineering salesperson who is primarily a consultant to the 'client' companies.
6. Positions which demand the creative sale of tangible products like video recorders, word processors, engineering plastics and refractory bricks.
7. Positions requiring the creative sale of intangibles, such as insurance, advertising services, or education.[2]

The positions move along a spectrum ranging from the least to the most creative types of selling. The former call primarily for maintaining accounts and taking orders, while the latter require hunting down prospects and creating new sales. Most of the discussion here will deal with the more creative types of selling.

Personal selling is the most effective tool at certain stages of the buying process, particularly in building up buyers' preference, conviction and action. The reason is that personal selling, when compared with advertising, has three distinctive qualities:[3]

1. *Personal confrontation.* Personal selling involves an alive, immediate and interactive relationship between two or more persons. Each party is able to observe each other's needs and characteristics at close hand, and make immediate adjustments.

2. *Cultivation.* Personal selling permits all kinds of relationships to spring up, ranging from matter-of-fact relationship to personal friendship. In most cases the sales representative must use art to woo the buyer: the representative will at times be tempted to put on pressure or to dissemble to get an order, but will normally keep the customer's long-run interests at heart.

3. *Response.* Personal selling makes the buyer feel under some obligation for having listened to the sales talk or using up the sales representative's time. The buyer has a greater need to attend and respond, even if the response is a polite 'thank you'.

These distinctive qualities come at a cost. Personal selling is a company's most expensive contact and communication tool, costing $50–150 per sales call. In 1971, there was an estimated 420 000 sales representatives in Australia,[4] with firms spending almost $8 billion (thousand million) on personal selling.

We now turn to the major decisions facing company management in building and managing an effective sales force as part of the total marketing mix. These steps are shown in Figure 18-1 and are examined in the following sections.

ESTABLISHING SALES-FORCE OBJECTIVES

The sales force is part of the marketing mix and is capable of achieving certain marketing objectives better than other marketing tools. Companies have described their sales-force objectives in different ways. For example, IBM wants its sales representatives to be responsible for 'selling, installing and upgrading' customer computer equipment; BHP wants its sales representatives to be responsible for 'developing, selling and protecting' accounts. It appears that sales representatives are expected to perform as many as six tasks for their company:

1. *Prospecting.* Sales representatives are expected to find and cultivate new customers.

2. *Communicating.* Sales representatives are supposed to be skilful in communicating information about the company's products and services to existing and potential customers.

3. *Selling.* Sales representatives are expected to be effective in the art of 'salesmanship' – approaching, presenting, answering objections, and closing sales.

4. *Servicing.* Sales representatives must provide various services to the customers – consulting on their problems, rendering technical assistance, arranging financing, and expediting delivery.

5. *Information-gathering.* Sales representatives are expected to carry out market research and intelligence work, and supply sales reports on their customer calls.

6. *Allocating.* Sales representatives are expected to evaluate customer profitability and advise the company on allocating scarce products to their customers in times of shortage.

Companies are becoming increasingly specific, and often recommend how much time should go into each activity. Dixon describes one company that advises its sales representatives to spend 80 per cent of their time with current customers, and 20 per cent with

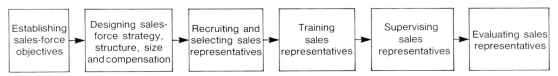

Figure 18-1   Major steps in sales-force management

Exhibit 18-1 Milestones in the History of Selling and Salesmanship

Robert Louis Stevenson observed that 'everyone lives by selling something'. Selling is one of the world's oldest professions. Paul Hermann described the discovery of a Bronze Age (circa 1000 B.C.) travelling salesman's sample case: '. . . a solid wooden box, 26 inches in length, containing in specially hollowed compartments various types of axe, sword blades, buttons, [etc.]'. Early sellers and traders were not always held in high esteem, however. The Roman word for *salesman* meant 'cheater', and Mercury, the god of cunning and barter, was regarded as the patron deity of merchants and traders.

The buying and selling of commodities flourished over the centuries and became institutionalized in market towns. In time, itinerant pedlars began to carry goods to people in their homes. This was the case in nineteenth-century Australia, the nation's first salesmen being pedlars who carried pots, pans, candles, chairs, etc. on horseback or by wagon. They travelled from town to town, often sleeping in the bush or in barns; frequently they were warmly welcomed, since they brought not only goods but news of the outside world to isolated families.

The first organized transport for sales representatives (or commercial travellers as they were then called) was provided by Cobb & Co., whose coaches travelled between the principal cities. Around the coast ships provided an alternative means of travel, even if slow by modern standards (the round trip between Sydney and Newcastle took three to four days). By 1900 these forms of transport were supplemented by the railway, which provided the basic State structure for distribution which essentially still exists today. During this era, the role of the sales representative started to expand and became more professional. A greater emphasis was placed on advising retailers and users on new products, new uses for existing products, and new management practices.

After World War II, Australia experienced a period of high economic growth which brought many changes in the selling environment. Radio had been introduced in the 1930s, as had the car; television and computers were introduced in the 1950s. Today, air travel makes a round trip to Brisbane possible in a day.

Although the basis of selling remains unaltered – i.e. creating a want, making a sale, establishing a relationship with a customer – the demands on the sales representative have multiplied. With increased competition, market segmentation and specialization, and increased analysis of the market, sales representatives must give increased emphasis to customer service and problem-solving expertise.

---

prospects; 85 per cent of their time selling the established products, and 15 per cent selling the new products.[5] If norms are not established, sales representatives will tend to spend most of their time selling established products to current accounts and neglect important market-development activities.

As companies become more market-oriented, they require their sales forces to carry out more marketing tasks. The traditional view is that salespeople produce the targeted sales volume and the company worries about profits – that their training should primarily consist of learning the art of salesmanship. The newer view is that sales-people should produce customer satisfaction and company profit; they should be skilled in analysing sales data, measuring market potential, gathering market intelligence, and developing marketing strategies and plans. The sales representatives need analytical marketing skills, and this becomes especially critical at the higher levels of sales management. Marketers believe that a marketing-oriented rather than sales-oriented sales force will be more effective in the long run.

DESIGNING SALES-FORCE STRATEGY

Once the company establishes its sales-force objectives, it is ready to face questions of sales-force strategy, structure, size and compensation.

Sales-force Strategy

Sales-force strategy is developed by the company through understanding the customers' buying process and thus determining how best to position itself against competitors. The first thing to clarify is the type of selling situation that must be handled by the sales force, of which five types may be distinguished:

1. *Sales representative to buyer.* Here a single sales representative talks to a single prospect or customer, in person or over the phone.
2. *Sales representative to buyer group.* Here a sales representative appears before a buying committee to make a sales presentation about a specific product.
3. *Sales team to buyer group.* Here a team (such as a company officer, sales representative and sales engineer) makes a sales presentation to a buying group.
4. *Conference selling.* Here the sales representative brings resource people from the company to meet one or more buyers to discuss problems and mutual opportunities.

5. *Seminar selling.* Here a company team of technical people conducts an educational seminar for a technical group in a customer company, about recent developments. The aim is to enhance customer knowledge and loyalty rather than to make a specific sale.

Thus the sales representative does not necessarily handle the whole selling job, but may serve as a 'matchmaker' bringing together company and customer personnel.[6] The sales representative may also act as the 'account manager', initiating and facilitating interactions between various people in the buying and selling organizations. Selling is increasingly becoming a matter of teamwork, requiring the support of other personnel, such as top management, which is increasingly becoming involved in the sales process, especially when national accounts or major sales are at stake;[7] technical people, who often work with the sales representatives to supply technical information needed by the customer before, during or after the purchase of the product; customer service representatives, who provide installation, maintenance and other services to the customer; and an office staff consisting of sales analysts, order expediters, and secretarial personnel.

Once the company clarifies the type of selling it must perform, it can use either a direct or a contractual sales force. A direct (or company) sales force consists of full- or part-time paid employees who work exclusively for the company. This category includes inside sales personnel, who conduct their business from their offices using the telephone and receiving visits from prospective buyers; and field sales personnel, who travel and visit customers. A contractual sales force consists of manufacturer's reps, sales agents, or brokers, who are paid a commission on the sales they obtain.

Sales-force Structure

Part of sales-force strategy is how to structure the company's sales force to have maximum impact on the market. This is relatively simple if the company sells only one product line to one end-using industry with customers found in many locations – the answer would be a territorial-structured sales force. If the company sells many different products to many types of customers, it might have to develop product- or customer-structured sales forces. These alternatives are discussed in the following paragraphs.

Territorial-structured sales force. In the simplest sales organizations, each representative is given an exclusive territory in which to represent the company's full line. This sales structure has a number of advantages. First, it results in a clear definition of the salesperson's responsibilities. As the only salesperson working the territory, he bears the credit or blame for area sales to the extent that personal selling effort makes a difference. This tends to encourage a high level of effort, especially when management is able to gauge fairly accurately the area's sales potential. Second, responsibility for a definite territory increases the sales representative's incentive to cultivate local business and personal ties. These ties tend to improve the quality of the sales representative's selling effectiveness and personal life. Third, travel expenses are likely to be relatively small, since each sale representative's travel takes place within limited bounds.

Along with this structure goes a hierarchy of sales-management positions. Several territories will be supervised by a district sales manager, the several districts will be supervised by a regional sales manager, and the several regions will be supervised by a national sales manager or sales director. Each higher-level manager takes on increasing marketing and administrative work in relation to the time available for selling; in fact, they are paid for their management skills rather than their selling skills. The new sales trainee, in looking along the career path, can hope to eventually become a sales representative, then a district manager and, depending on ability and motivation, be promoted to the higher levels of sales or general management.

The territorial form of sales organization works quite well in companies that have a relatively homogeneous set of products and customers. As their products and markets become diversified, however, they find this form less and less effective. At the heart of the problem is the fact that the sales representative, to be effective, must know the company's products and markets, but that there is a clear limit to the amount of knowledge that can be acquired about different types of products and customers.

Product-structured sales force. The importance of sales representatives' knowing their products, together with the development of product divisions and management, has led many companies to structure their sales force along product lines. Specialization of the sales force by product is particularly warranted where the products are technically complex, highly unrelated, and/or numerous.

The mere existence of different company products, however, is not a sufficient argument for specializing the sales force in this way. A major drawback may exist if the company's separate product lines are bought by many of the same customers: this means that company sales personnel travel over the same routes, and each uses up valuable time waiting in the outer office to see the customer's purchasing agents. These extra costs must be weighed against the benefits that may result from the higher level of customer service and more knowledgeable product representation.

Customer-structured sales force. Companies often specialize their sales forces along customer lines. Separate sales forces may be set up for different industries, for major versus smaller accounts, and for current versus new-business development. The most obvious advantage of customer specialization is that each sales force can become more knowledgeable about specific customer needs. At one time General Electric's sales representatives specialized in certain products (fan motors, switches, and so forth), but it later changed to specialization in markets, such as the air-conditioning and automotive markets, because customers viewed the products in these more general contexts. A customer-specialized sales force can sometimes also reduce total sales-force costs. A large pump manufacturer at one time used a single sales force of highly trained sales engineers to sell to both original equipment manufacturers (who needed to deal with technical representatives) and jobbers (who did not). Later the company split its sales force and provided the jobber market with less highly trained representatives.

The major disadvantage of customer-structured sales forces arises if the various types of customers are scattered evenly throughout the country. This means an overlapping coverage of territories, which is always more expensive.

Complex sales-force structures. When a company sells a wide variety of products to many types of customers over a broad geographical area, it often combines several principles of sales-force structure. Sales representatives may be specialized by territory-product, territory-customer, product-customer or, ultimately, territory-product-customer. A sales representative may then be responsible to one or more line managers and/or one or more staff managers.

Which type of sales-force structure an organization adopts will depend on the size of the organization and the competitive situation it faces. Consider a company which makes a range of products in each of three areas – adhesives, plastics and chemicals. Adhesives are sold to consumers via hardware shops and industrial users, primarily the car industry. Plastic mouldings are sold to consumers and industry, primarily the electronics industry.

The only chemical products are pool chemicals sold to ultimate consumers. If the sales force is organized by territory, one representative has a defined geographic region, say Brisbane, and is responsible for marketing all the products of the company to all customers. He must be able to talk knowledgeably with design engineers in the electronics industry on Monday, and with pool-chemical retailers on Tuesday. Obviously this is no easy task with the increasing complexity and sophistication of products.

If, on the other hand, the sales force is organized by product, one sales representative is responsible for a range of products (say, plastic moulding). This representative will thus visit a customer in Brisbane on Monday, and one in Adelaide on Tuesday. This is because there are insufficient electronics firms in Brisbane to keep a representative busy for more than the one day per week.

As can be seen, any way of structuring the sales force will represent a compromise between cost and necessity of providing the level of sales support demanded by customers.

Sales-force Size

Once the company clarifies its sales-force strategy and structure, it is ready to consider the question of sales-force size. Sales representatives are amongst the most productive and expensive assets in a company, and increasing their number will increase both sales and costs.

Most companies use a workload approach to establish the size of their sales force.[8] This method consists of the following steps:

1. Customers are grouped according to their annual sales volume.
2. Desirable call frequencies (number of sales calls on an account per year) are established for each class. They reflect how much call intensity the company seeks in relation to competitors.

3. The number of accounts in each size class is multiplied by the corresponding call frequency, to arrive at the total workload for the country in sales calls per year.
4. The average number of calls a sales representative can make per year is determined.
5. The number of sales representatives needed is determined by dividing the total annual calls required by the average annual calls made by a sales representative.

Suppose the company estimates that there are 1000 'A' accounts and 2000 'B' accounts in the nation; and that A accounts require thirty-six calls a year and B accounts twelve calls. This means the company needs a sales force that can make 60 000 calls a year. Assuming that the average sales representative can make 1000 calls a year, the company would need sixty full-time representatives.

Sales-force Compensation

To attract the desired number of sales representatives, the company has to develop an attractive compensation plan. Sales representatives and management tend to seek different and often conflicting objectives, which (it is hoped) are reconciled by the plan. Sales representatives would like a plan that provides income regularity, reward for above-average performance, and fair payment for experience and longevity. On the other hand, an ideal compensation plan from management's point of view would emphasize control, economy and simplicity. In the light of these conflicting objectives, it is understandable why compensation plans exhibit a tremendous variety, not only between industries but also between companies within the same industry.

Management must determine the level and components of an effective compensation plan. The level of compensation must bear some relation to the 'going market price' for the type of sales job and abilities required.

One broadly based study of sales-force compensation, covering industrial goods, consumer goods and services reported a medium salary in 1979 of $15 000.[9] By contrast, an office-equipment company was reported to have average earnings for the sales force of $30 000 with a high of $60 000 and a low of $17 000.[10] If the market price for sales manpower is well defined, the individual firm has little choice but to pay the going rate. To pay less would not bring forth the desired quantity or quality of applicants, and to pay more would be unnecessary. More often, however, the market price for sales manpower is not well defined. For one thing, company plans vary in the importance of fixed and variable salary elements, fringe benefits, and expense allowances. Furthermore, data on the average take-home pay of sales representatives working for competitive firms can be misleading because of significant variations in the average seniority and ability levels of the competitors' sales force. Published comparisons of industry-by-industry sales-force compensation levels are infrequent and generally lack sufficient detail.

The company must also determine the components of compensation – a fixed amount, a variable amount, expenses, and fringe benefits. The fixed amount, which might be a salary or a drawing account, is intended to satisfy the sales representatives' need for some stability of income. The variable amount, which might be commissions, bonuses or profit-sharing, is intended to stimulate and reward greater effort. Expense allowances enable the sales representatives to undertake selling efforts that are considered necessary or desirable. Fringe benefits, such as paid holidays, sickness or accident benefits, pensions and life insurance, are intended to provide security and job satisfaction.

Top sales management must decide which elements should be in the compensation plan and their relative importance. A popular rule seems to favour making about 70 per cent of the salesperson's total income fixed and allocating the remaining 30 per cent among the other elements. But the variations around this average are so pronounced that it can hardly serve as a sufficient guide in planning. For example, fixed compensation should have more emphasis in jobs with a high ratio of non-selling duties to selling duties and in jobs where the selling task is technically complex. Variable compensation should have more emphasis in jobs where sales are cyclical and/or depend on personal initiative.

Fixed and variable compensation taken alone give rise to three basic types of sales-force compensation plans – straight salary, straight commission, and combination salary and commission. In one study, 37 per cent of the companies paid straight salary, 3 per cent paid straight commission, and 60 per cent paid salary plus commission.[11]

RECRUITING AND SELECTING SALES REPRESENTATIVES

Having established the strategy, structure, size and compensation of the sales force, the company has then to begin recruiting, selecting, training, supervising and evaluating sales representatives. Various strategies and policies guide these decisions.

Importance of Careful Selection

At the heart of a successful sales-force operation is the selection of effective sales representatives. The performance levels of an average and a top sales representative are quite different: in the example quoted earlier, the range in sales-force earnings suggests a wide range in sales abilities.

Beyond the differences in sales productivity are the waste caused by hiring the wrong person. In one study of sales recruitment and selection, some 36 per cent of the companies reported an annual turnover rate of greater than 10 per cent.[12] Given the cost of recruiting and training a new sales representative, high labour turnover represents a significant financial drain on the organization.

What Makes a Good Sales Representative

Selecting a good sales representative would not be a problem if one knew exactly what to look for. If ideal sales representatives are outgoing, aggressive and energetic, it would not be too difficult to check for these characteristics in applicants. But a review of the most successful sales representatives in any company is likely to reveal that many are introverted, mild-mannered and far from energetic; they will also include men and women who are tall and short, articulate and inarticulate, well groomed and slovenly.

Nevertheless, the search for the magic combination of traits that spells sure-fire sales ability continues unabated. The number of lists that have been drawn up is countless; most of them recite the same qualities.

Mayer and Greenberg offered one of the shortest lists of traits exhibited by effective sales representatives.[13] Their seven years of fieldwork led them to conclude that the effective salesperson has at least two basic qualities: empathy, the ability to feel as the customer does; and ego drive, a strong personal need to make the sale. Using these two traits, they were able to make fairly good predictions of the subsequent performance of applicants for sales positions in three different industries.

It may be true that certain basic traits may make a person effective in any line of selling. From the viewpoint of a particular company, however, these basic traits are rarely enough. Each selling job is characterized by a unique set of duties and challenges: one has only to think about selling insurance, computers and cars to realize the different educational, intellectual and personality requirements that would be sought in the respective sales representatives.

How can a company determine the characteristics that its prospective sales representatives should 'ideally' possess? The particular duties of the job suggest some of the characteristics to look for in applicants. Is there a lot of paper work? Does the job call for much travel? Will the salesperson confront a high proportion of refusals? In addition, the traits of the company's most successful sales representatives suggest additional qualities to look for. Some companies compare the traits of their best sales representatives with those of their poorest sales representatives to see which characteristics differentiate the two groups.

Recruitment Procedures

After management has developed general criteria for new sales personnel, it must try to attract a sufficient number of applicants. The most frequent source of new sales representatives in Australia is newspaper advertisement, followed by internal sources and employment agencies.[14] Internal sources are particularly important for the company that seeks technically oriented representatives. Tertiary institutions are used infrequently as a source of new sales representatives, yet with the increased concern being expressed about the educational qualifications of representatives, and the lack of graduate employment opportunities in these areas, this is likely to be a more important source in the future. Students with science or engineering training are likely to be wooed more seriously by larger technically oriented companies.[15]

Applicant-rating Procedures

Recruitment procedures, if successful, will attract more applicants than the company needs, and the task becomes one of selecting the best applicants. Selection procedures range from a single informal interview to prolonged testing and interviewing, not only of the applicant but of the applicant's family.

The criteria used for the selection of sales representative include intelligence, education, experience, demonstrated selling ability and personal attributes.[16] In the study of Australian companies by Collins, attributes such as appearance, personality and a demonstrated track record in sales were noted as the most important criteria. For technically oriented representatives, education and intelligence would be more important. Historically, sales representatives have been predominantly male but with the passage of equal opportunity legislation, selling will provide more opportunities for women.

TRAINING SALES REPRESENTATIVES

In an effort to increase sales-force productivity, companies are turning to formal sales training. Several factors have convinced sales management that extended training may add more value than cost. The sales representative of today is selling to more cost-conscious and value-conscious buyers. Furthermore, he is selling a host of products which are often loosely related and sometimes technically complex; more reports are expected. The company wants to be represented by a mature and knowledgeable sales representative.

IBM is a leading exponent of the value of training. New sales representatives undertake a very extensive training programme which lasts for up to fifteen months, interspersing classroom discussion with on-the-job training. Continuing education of existing personnel is also emphasized, with every sales representative undergoing about twenty days of formal training each year.[17]

The purpose of the training is to create the following knowledge, skills and attitudes in the sales force:

1. *The sales representative should know the company and identify with it.* Most companies devote the first part of the training programme to describing the history and objectives of the company, the organizational set-up and lines of authority, the names of the chief officers, the company's financial structure and facilities, and the company's chief products and sales volume.

2. *The sales representative should know the company's products.* The sales trainee is shown how the products are produced and how they function.

3. *The sales representative should know customers' and competitors' characteristics.* The sales representative is introduced to the different types of customers and their needs, buying motives and buying habits. He learns about the company's and competitors' strategies and policies.

4. *The sales representative should learn how to make effective sales presentations.* The sales representative is trained in the basic principles of salesmanship. Part of the training time is used to develop the representative's personality and interpersonal skills. In addition, the company outlines the major sales arguments for each product, and some go so far as to provide a sales script.

5. *The sales representative should be introduced to field procedures and responsibilities.* The sales representative should know how to divide time between active accounts and potential accounts how to use the expense account, prepare reports, and route effectively.

Principles of Salesmanship

One of the major objectives of sales-training programmes is to provide instruction in the art of selling. The sales-training industry today involves expenditure of millions of dollars in courses, books, videotapes and other materials. Many thousands of copies of books on selling are purchased every year, bearing such provocative titles as *How to Outsell the Born Salesman, How to Sell Anything to Anybody, The Power of Enthusiastic Selling, How Power Selling Brought Me Success in Six Hours, Where Do You Go from No. 1?,* and *1000 Ways a Salesman Can Increase His Sales.* One of the most enduring books is Dale Carnegie's *How to Win Friends and Influence People.*

All of the sales-training approaches are designed to convert a salesperson from a passive order-taker into a more active order-getter. Order-takers operate on the following assumptions: (i) customers are aware of their own needs; (ii) they cannot be influenced or would resent any attempt at influence; and (iii) they prefer salespersons who are courteous and self-effacing.

In training salespersons to be order-getters, either a sales-oriented approach or a customer-oriented approach may be used. The first trains the salesperson to be adept in the use of high-pressure selling techniques, such as those used in selling encyclopaedias or cars: overstating the product's merits, criticizing competitive products, using a slick presentation, selling yourself, and offering some concession to get the order on the spot. The assumptions behind this form of selling are that: (i) the customers are not likely to buy except under pressure; (ii) they are influenced by a slick presentation and ingratiating manners; and (iii) they will not regret the transaction after signing the order, or if they do, it doesn't matter.

The other approach attempts to train sales personnel in customer problem-solving. Here the salesperson studies the customer's needs and wants, and proposes profitable solutions. An example would be a sales representative who examines a customer's situation and proposes a plan that would make or save the customer money – i.e. doing what is good for the customer, not what is immediately good for the salesperson. The assumptions behind this approach are that: (i) customers have latent needs that constitute opportunities for the sales representative; (ii) they appreciate good suggestions; and (iii) they will be loyal to sales representatives who have their long-term interests at heart. Certainly the problem-solver is a more compatible image for the salesperson under the marketing concept than the hard seller or order-taker.

Most sales-training programmes view the selling process as a set of steps that the salesperson has to carry out, each involving certain skills. These steps are shown in Figure 18-2 and are discussed below.[18]

Prospecting and qualifying. The first step in the sales process is to identify prospects. Although the company can offer some guidance, the sales representatives need skill in developing their own leads. This may be achieved in the following ways: asking current satisfied customers for the names of other potential buyers; cultivating other referral sources, such as suppliers, dealers, non-competing sales representatives, bankers, and trade association executives; joining organizations where there is a high probability of meeting or learning about new prospects; engaging in activities that are likely to increase the salesperson's visibility; examining various data sources (newspapers, directories) in search of names; using the telephone and mail to track down leads; and dropping in unannounced on various offices (cold canvassing).

Sales representatives also need to know how to screen the leads to avoid wasting valuable time. Prospects can be qualified by examining their financial ability, volume of business, special requirements, locations, and likelihood of continuous business. The salesperson should phone or write to prospects to see if they are worth pursuing further.

Pre-approach. The salesperson must learn as much as possible about the prospect company (what it needs, who is involved in the purchase decision) and its buyers (their personal characteristics and buying styles), consulting standard sources (such as *Kompass* and trade directories), acquaintances and others. The salesperson should determine call objectives, which might be to qualify the prospect, gather information or make an immediate sale. Another task is to decide on the best approach, which might be a personal visit (possibly with a respected intermediary), a phone call, or a letter. The best timing should be thought out because many prospects are especially busy at certain times of the year. Finally, the salesperson should give some thought to an overall strategy.

Approach. The salesperson must know how to meet and greet the buyer to get the relationship off to a good start. The important factors are appearance, opening lines, and follow-up remarks. The salesperson is encouraged to wear clothes similar to what buyers usually wear, such as open-necked shirts and no ties in Western Australia; show courtesy and attention to the buyer; and avoid distracting mannerisms, such as pacing the floor or staring at the customer. The opening line should be positive and pleasant, such as 'Mr Smith, I am Bill Jones from the ABC Company. My company and I appreciate your willingness to see me. I will do my best to make this visit profitable and worthwhile for you and your company.' This might be followed by some light talk to further the acquaintance, some key questions, or the showing of a display or sample to attract the buyer's attention and curiosity.

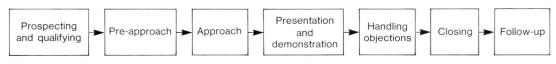

Figure 18-2 Major steps in effective selling

Presentation and demonstration. After getting acquainted and 'sizing up' the buyer, the salesperson attempts to tell the company 'story', showing how the product will make or save money for the buyer. The salesperson covers the features of the product, but concentrates on selling its benefits – the aim is to demonstrate the want-satisfying characteristics of the company and its products. The salesperson will follow the AIDA formula in presenting the product: get attention, hold interest, arouse desire and obtain action.

Companies use three different styles of sales presentation. The oldest is the *canned approach*, which is a memorized sales talk covering the main points deemed important by management. It is based on stimulus-response thinking, i.e. that the buyer is passive and can be moved to purchase by the use of the right words, pictures, terms and actions. Thus an encyclopaedia salesperson might describe the encyclopaedia as 'a once-in-a-lifetime buying opportunity' and show some four-colour pages of sports pictures hoping to trigger an irresistible desire for the encyclopaedia on the part of the buyer. Canned presentations are used primarily in door-to-door and telephone canvassing, and have generally been abandoned by other companies in favour of more flexible approaches.

The *formulated approach* is also based on stimulus-response thinking, but attempts to identify the buyer's needs and buying style before using a formulated approach. In this approach the salesperson does some presenting at the beginning and attempts to draw the buyer into the discussion in a way that will indicate the buyer's needs and attitudes. As these are picked up, the salesperson moves into a formulated presentation that is appropriate to that buyer and shows how the product will satisfy that buyer's needs. It is not canned but follows a general plan.

The *need-satisfaction approach* does not start with a prepared presentation but rather with a search for the customer's real needs. The customer is encouraged to do most of the talking so that the salesperson can ascertain his real needs and respond accordingly. The need-satisfaction approach calls for good listening and problem-solving skills. This approach is well described by an IBM sales representative:

> I get inside the business of my key accounts. I uncover their key problems. I prescribe solutions for them, using my company's system and even, at times, components from other suppliers. I prove beforehand that my systems will save money or make money for my accounts. Then I work with the account to install the system and make it prove out.[19]

Sales presentations can be improved considerably with various demonstration aids, such as booklets, flip charts, slides, movies and product samples. To the extent that the buyer can participate by seeing or handling the product, he will better remember its features and possibilities.

Handling objections. Customer will almost always pose objections during the presentation or when asked to place an order. This resistance may take a psychological or a logical form. Psychological resistance includes resistance to interference, preference for established habits, apathy, reluctance to give up something, unpleasant associations with the other person, a tendency to resist domination, predetermined ideas, dislike of making decisions, and neurotic attitude toward money.[20] Logical resistance might consist of objections to the price, delivery schedule, or certain products or company characteristics. To handle these objections, the salesperson uses such techniques as maintaining a positive approach, trying to have the buyer clarify and define the objections, questioning the buyer in such a way that he answers his own objections, denying the validity of the objections, and turning the objection into a reason for buying. The salesperson needs training in the broader skills of negotiation, of which handling objections is a part.[21]

Closing. In this step the salesperson attempts to close the sale. Some salespeople never get to this stage, or they do not do it well. They lack confidence in themselves, their company or the product, feel guilty about asking for the order, or do not recognize the right psychological moment to close the sale. Salespersons need to be trained in recognizing specific signals from the buyer, including physical actions, comments and questions indicating a possible readiness to close. Salespersons can then use one of several techniques. They can ask the prospect for the order, recapitulate the points of agreement, offer to help the secretary write up the order, ask whether the buyer wants A or B, get the buyer to make minor choices such as the colour or size, or indicate what the buyer will lose if the order is not placed now. The salesperson may offer the buyer specific inducements to close, such as a special price, an extra quantity at no charge, or a gift.

Follow-up. This last step is necessary if the salesperson wants to ensure customer satisfaction and repeat business. Immediately after closing, the salesperson should attempt to complete any necessary details on delivery time, purchase terms, and other matters. The salesperson should also consider scheduling a follow-up call when the initial order is received to make sure there is proper installation, instruction and servicing. This visit is designed to detect any problems, to assure the buyer of the salesperson's interest and service, and to reduce any cognitive dissonance that might have arisen.

SUPERVISING SALES REPRESENTATIVES

The new sales representative is given more than a territory, a compensation package, and training – he is given supervision. Supervision is the fate of everyone who works for someone else; it is the expression of the employers' natural and continuing interest in the activities of their agents. Through supervision, employers hope to direct and motivate the sales force to do a better job.

Directing Sales Representatives

Companies differ in the extent to which they try to prescribe the activities of their sales representatives. Much depends upon the nature of the selling job. Sales representatives who are paid mostly on commission and are expected to hunt down their own prospects, are generally left on their own. Those who are salaried and must cover a definite set of accounts are likely to receive substantial supervision.

A major purpose of supervision is to help the sales representatives use their time effectively and efficiently. The effective use of time means initial sound decisions about which customers and prospects to spend the time on; the efficient use of time means that the sales representatives plan their call time so as to maximize the ratio of selling to non-selling time.

Surveys indicate that, on average, sales representatives spend only 15–20 per cent of their working day in face-to-face selling. The rest of the time is spent on a variety of non-selling activities such as travelling, waiting and report-writing. If the average selling time could be raised from 15 per cent to 20 per cent, this would represent a 33 per cent increase in effective selling time.

Developing customer targets and call norms. Most companies classify their customers into account types reflecting their respective sales volume, profit potential and growth potential. They establish a certain desired number of calls per period that their

---

Exhibit 18-2 How Efficiently Do Companies Manage
Their Sales Force?

There is much evidence of inefficiency in the way companies manage their sales forces. A survey of 257 Fortune '500' companies in the United States revealed the following:

- 54 per cent have not conducted an organized study of sales representatives' use of time, even though most respondents felt that this represents an area for improvement.
- 25 per cent do not have a system for classifying accounts according to potential.
- 30 per cent do not use call schedules for their sales force.
- 51 per cent do not determine the number of calls it is economical to make on an account.
- 83 per cent do not determine an approximate duration for each call.
- 51 per cent do not use a planned sales presentation.
- 24 per cent do not set sales objectives for accounts.
- 72 per cent do not set profit objectives for accounts.
- 19 per cent do not use a call report system.
- 63 per cent do not use a prescribed routing pattern in covering territories.
- 77 per cent do not use a computer to assist in time and territorial management.

---

sales force should make to each account type. Thus A accounts may receive nine calls a year; B, six calls; and C, three calls. The exact levels depend upon competitive call norms and expected account profitability.

The real issue is how much sales volume could be expected from a particular account as a function of the annual number of calls made to that account. Lodish describes an approach, based on an interactive computer model, to help sales representatives allocate their time to customers.[22] Individual representatives are asked to estimate the response from specific customers to different levels of call frequency. The estimates are then used by the model to develop the best pattern of call allocation, taking travel time into consideration.

Developing prospect targets and call norms. Companies generally specify how much time their sales force should spend prospecting for new accounts (e.g. representatives may be directed to spend 25 per cent of their time prospecting, and to stop calling on a prospect after three unsuccessful calls).

There are various reasons why many companies try to set up a minimum requirement for the canvassing of new accounts. If left alone, many sales representatives will spend most of their time in the offices of current customers. Current customers are better-known quantities – the sales representatives can depend upon them for some business, whereas a prospect may never deliver any business or deliver it only after many months of effort. Unless sales representatives receive a bonus for opening new accounts, they may avoid this activity; some companies rely on a salaried missionary sales force to open new accounts.

Using sales time efficiently. Sales representatives should know how to schedule sales calls and use their time efficiently. One tool is the preparation of an annual call schedule, showing which customers and prospects to call on in which months, and which activities to carry out (e.g. participating in trade shows, attending sales meetings, and undertaking marketing research).

The other tool is time-and-duty analysis, to determine how to use sales-call time more efficiently. The sales representative's time is spent in the following ways:

- *Travel.* The time spent in travel, between rising in the morning and arriving at a lodging in the evening, may in some jobs amount to as much as 50 per cent of total time. Travel time can be cut down by substituting faster for slower means of transport – recognizing, however, that this will increase costs. More companies are encouraging air travel (commercial or private) for their sales force in order to increase their ratio of selling to total time.
- *Food and breaks.* Some portion of the sales force's workday is spent in eating and in taking breaks. If this involves dining with a customer, it will be classified as selling time.
- *Waiting.* Waiting consists of time spent in the outer office of the buyer. This is dead time unless the sales representative uses it to plan or to fill out reports.
- *Selling.* Selling is the time spent with the buyer in person or on the phone. It breaks down into 'social talk' (the time spent discussing other things) and 'selling talk' (the time spent discussing the company and its products).
- *Administration.* This is a miscellaneous category consisting of the time spent in report writing and billing, attending sales meetings, and talking to others in the company about production, delivery, billing, sales performance, and so on.

Companies are constantly seeking ways to help their sales representatives use their time more efficiently. This takes the form of training them in the effective use of the telephone ('phone power'), simplifying the record-keeping forms and requirements, using the computer to develop call and routing plans, and supplying marketing research reports on the customer.

Motivating Sales Representatives

A small percentage of representatives in any sales force can be expected to do their best without any special prompting from management. To them, selling is the most fascinating job in the world; they are ambitious and self-starters. But the majority of sales representatives on nearly every sales force require personal encouragement and special incentives to work at their best level. This is especially true of creative field-selling, for the following reasons:

1. *The nature of the job.* Selling is a job offering frequent frustration. Sales representatives usually work alone, their hours are irregular, and they are often away from home. They confront aggressive, competing sales representatives, they have an inferior status relative to the buyer, they often do not have the authority to do what is necessary to win an account, and they lose large orders that they have worked hard to obtain.
2. *Human nature.* Most people operate below capacity in the absence of some special incentive. They will not 'kill themselves' without some prospect of financial gain or social recognition.
3. *Personal problems.* The sales representative, like everyone else, is occasionally preoccupied with personal problems, such as sickness in the family, marital discord, or debt.

Management can affect the morale and performance of the sales force through its organizational climate, sales quotas, and positive incentives.

Organizational climate.

Organizational climate describes the feeling that the sales representatives get from their company regarding their opportunities, value, and rewards for good performance. Some companies treat their sales representatives as if they were of minor importance; others treat them as the prime movers, and offer unlimited opportunity for income and promotion. The company's attitude toward its sales representatives acts as a self-fulfilling prophecy: if they are held in low opinion, there is much turnover and poor performance; if they are held in high opinion, there is little turnover and high performance.

The quality of personal treatment from the sales representative's immediate superior is an important aspect of the organizational climate. An effective sales manager keeps in touch with the members of the sales force through regular correspondence and phone calls, personal visits in the field, and evaluation sessions in the office. At different times the sales manager is the sales representative's boss, companion, coach and confessor.

Sales quotas.

Many companies set sales quotas for their representatives. These specify quotas for total sales as well as quotas for individual products. Their compensation is often, though not always, related to their degree of quota fulfilment.

Sales quotas are determined each year in the process of developing the annual marketing plan. The company first decides on a sales forecast that is reasonably achievable. This becomes the basis of planning production, workforce size, and financial requirements. Then management establishes sales quotas for all of its regions and territories, which typically add up to more than the sales forecast in order to stretch the sales managers and salespeople to their best effort. If they fail to make their quotas, the company may nevertheless make its sales forecast.

Each field sales manager takes the assigned quota and divides it up among the sales representatives. There are three schools of thought on quota setting. The high-quota school sets quotas that are above what most sales representatives will achieve but still possible for all. Its adherents are of the opinion that high quotas spur extra effort. The modest-quota school sets quotas that a majority of the sales force can achieve. Its adherents feel that the sales force will accept the quotas as fair, attain them, and gain confidence in doing so. Finally, the variable-quota school thinks that individual differences among sales representatives warrant high quotas for some and modest quotas for others.

Positive incentives.

Companies use a number of positive motivators to stimulate sales-force effort. Periodic sales meetings provide a social occasion, a break from routine, a chance to meet and talk with 'company brass', and a chance to air feelings and identify with a larger group. Companies also sponsor sales contests when they want to spur the sales force to make a special selling effort. Other motivators include honours and awards, profit-sharing plans, and special holidays overseas.

EVALUATING SALES REPRESENTATIVES

We have been describing the feedforward aspects of sales supervision – the efforts of management to communicate what the sales representatives should be doing, and to motivate them to do it. But good feedforward requires good feedback. And good feedback means getting regular information from and about sales representatives to evaluate their performance.

Sources of Information

Management obtains information about its sales representatives through a number of channels. Probably the most important source of information is the sales representative's periodic reports; other sources include personal observation, customers' letters and complaints, and conversations with other sales representatives.

A distinction can be drawn between sales reports that represent plans for future activities and those that represent write-ups of completed activities. The best example of the former is the salesperson's *work plan*, which most representatives are required to submit for a specified future period, usually a week or a month in advance. The plan describes the calls they will make and the routing they will use, encouraging the sales force to plan and schedule their activities, informing management of their whereabouts, and providing a basis for comparing their plans with their accomplishments. Sales representatives can be evaluated on their ability to 'plan their work and work their plan'. Occasionally, management contacts individual sales representatives after receiving their plans to suggest improvements.

Companies moving towards annual marketing planning in depth are beginning to require their sales representatives to draft an annual *territory marketing plan*, in which they outline their programme for developing new accounts and increasing business from existing accounts. The formats vary considerably, some asking for general ideas on territory development and others for detailed volume and profit estimates. This type of report casts sales representatives into the role of market managers and profit centres; the plans are studied by sales managers and become the bases for rendering constructive suggestions to sales representatives, and developing branch sales objectives and estimates for higher-level management.

Several reports are used by sales representatives to write up their completed activities and accomplishments. Perhaps the best known is the *call report* in which the salesperson records pertinent aspects of his or her dealings with a customer, including competitive products used, best time for calling, degree and type of resistance, and future account promise. Call reports help to keep sales management informed of the salesperson's activities, indicate the status of the customers' accounts, and provide information that might be useful in subsequent calls.

Sales representatives also report *expenses* incurred in the performance of selling duties, for which they are partly or wholly reimbursed. The objective from management's standpoint is, first, to exercise control over the type and amount of expenses and, second, to have the requisite data for income-tax purposes. It is also hoped that the sales representatives will exercise more care in incurring expenses when they must report them in some detail. Some companies also require from their sales representatives a report on new business secured or potential new business, a report on lost business, and a report on local business and economic conditions.

These reports supply the raw data from which management can extract key indicators of sales performance. The key indicators are: (i) average number of sales calls per salesperson per day; (ii) average sales-call time per contact; (iii) average revenue per sales call; (iv) average cost per sales call; (v) entertainment cost per sales call; (vi) percentage of orders per hundred sales calls; (vii) number of new customers per period; (viii) number of lost customers per period; and (ix) sales-force cost as a percentage of total sales. An analysis of these statistics will raise useful questions: Are sales representatives making too few calls per day? Are they spending too much time per call? Are they spending too much on entertainment? Are they closing enough orders per hundred calls? Are they producing enough new customers, and holding on to the old customers?

Formal Evaluation of Performance

The sales force's reports, along with other reports from the field and the manager's personal observations, supply the raw materials for formally evaluating members of the sales force. Formal evaluation procedures lead to at least three benefits. First, they lead management to develop specific and uniform standards for judging sales performance. Second, they lead management to draw together all its information and impressions about individual sales representatives, and make more systematic, point-by-point evaluations. Third, they tend to have a constructive effect on the performance of sales representatives – who know that they will have to sit down one morning with the sales manager and explain certain facets of their routing or sales-call decisions, or their failure to secure or maintain certain accounts.

Salesperson-to-salesperson comparisons.

One type of evaluation frequently made is to compare and rank the performance of the various sales representatives. Such comparisons, however, can be misleading. Relative sales performances are meaningful only if there are no variations from territory to territory in the market potential, workload, degree of competition, company promotional effort, and so forth. Furthermore, sales are not the best denominator of achievement. Management should be more interested in how much each sales representative contributed to net profits, which cannot be known until the sales representatives' sales mix and sales expenses are examined. A possible ranking criterion would be the sales representative's ratio of actual to potential contribution to company net profits: a ratio of 1.00 would mean that the sales representative delivered the potential sales in his or her territory. The lower a sales representative's ratio, the more supervision and counselling he needs.

Current-to-past-sales comparisons. Another common type of evaluation is to compare a sales representative's current performance with past performance. This should provide a more direct indication of progress.

The sales manager can learn many things about John Smith from the information in Table 18-1. One of the first things to note is that Smith's total sales increased every year (line 3). This does not necessarily mean that Smith is doing a better job: the product breakdown shows that he has been able to push the sales of product B further than those of product A (lines 1 and 2), and according to his quotas for the two products (lines 4 and 5) this increased sales of B may have been at the expense of product A. According to gross profits (lines 6 and 7), the company earns about twice as much on A as B, as a ratio to sales. The picture begins to emerge that Smith may be pushing the higher-volume, lower-margin product at the expense of the more profitable product. In fact, although he increased total sales by $1100 between 1978 and 1979 (line 3), the gross profits on his total sales actually decreased by $580 (line 8).

Sales expense (line 9) shows a steady increase, although total expense as a percentage of total sales seems to be under control (line 10). The upward trend in Smith's total dollar expense does not seem to be explained by any increase in the number of calls (line 11), although it may be related in part to his success in acquiring new customers (line 14). However, there is a possibility that in prospecting for new customers he is neglecting present ones, as indicated by an upward trend in the annual number of lost customers (line 15).

The last two lines show the level and trend in Smith's sales per customer, and the gross profits on his sales per customer. These figures become more meaningful when they are compared with overall company averages. For example, if John Smith's average gross profit per customer is lower than the

Table 18-1 Form for evaluating sales representative's performance

Territory: Southern   *Sales Representative:* John Smith

	1976	1977	1978	1979
1. Net sales product A	$251 300	$253 200	$270 000	$263 100
2. Net sales product B	$423 200	$439 200	$553 900	$561 900
3. Net sales total	$674 500	$692 400	$823 900	$825 000
4. Per cent of quota product A	95.6	92.0	88.0	84.7
5. Per cent of quota product B	120.4	122.3	134.9	130.8
6. Gross profits product A	$ 50 260	$ 50 640	$ 54 000	$ 52 620
7. Gross profits product B	$ 42 320	$ 43 920	$ 55 390	$ 56 190
8. Gross profits total	$ 92 580	$ 94 560	$109 390	$108 810
9. Sales expense	$ 10 200	$ 11 100	$ 11 600	$ 13 200
10. Sales expense to total sales (%)	1.5	1.6	1.4	1.6
11. Number of calls	1 675	1 700	1 680	1 660
12. Cost per call	$ 6.09	$ 6.53	$ 6.90	$ 7.95
13. Average number of customers	320	324	328	334
14. Number of new customers	13	14	15	20
15. Number of lost customers	8	10	11	14
16. Average sales per customer	$ 2 108	$ 2 137	$ 2 512	$ 2 470
17. Average gross profit per customer	$ 289	$ 292	$ 334	$ 326

company's average he may be concentrating on the wrong customers or not spending enough time with each customer. Looking back at his annual number of calls (line 11), it may be that Smith is making fewer annual calls than the average salesperson. If distances in his territory are not much different, this may mean he is not putting in a full workday, is poor at planning his routing or minimizing his waiting, or spends too much time with certain accounts.

Qualitative evaluation of sales representatives. The evaluation usually extends to the salesperson's knowledge of the company, products, customers, competitors, territory and responsibilities. Personality characteristics – such as general manner, appearance, speech and temperament – may also be rated, and the sales manager may consider any problems in motivation or compliance. Since an almost endless number of qualitative factors might be included, each company must decide

what would be most useful to know. It also should communicate these criteria to the sales representatives so that they are aware of how their performance is judged and can make an effort to improve it.

SUMMARY

Most companies utilize sales representatives, and many companies assign them the pivotal role in the creation of sales. The high cost of this resource calls for an effective process of sales management consisting of six steps: establishing sales-force objectives; designing sales-force strategy, structure, size and compensation; recruiting and selecting; training; supervising; and evaluating.

As an element of the marketing mix, the sales force is capable of achieving certain marketing objectives effectively. The company has to decide on the proper mix of activities for the sales force, drawn from the following: prospecting, communicating, selling and servicing, information-gathering, and allocating. Under the marketing concept, the sales force is expected to acquire skills in marketing analysis and planning as well as traditional selling skills.

Given the sales-force objectives, sales-force strategy answers the question of what type of selling would be most effective (solo selling, team selling, etc.), what type of structure would work best (territorial, product- or customer-structured), how large the sales force should be, and how it should be compensated (pay level, and pay components such as salary, commission, bonus, expenses and fringe benefits).

Sales representatives must be recruited and selected on the basis of scientific procedures, to hold down the high costs of hiring the wrong persons. Sales-training programmes are becoming more elaborate, and are designed to familiarize the salesperson with the company's history, products and policies, the characteristics of the market and competitors, and the art of selling. The art of selling involves training salespeople in a seven-step process: prospecting and qualifying, pre-approach, approach, presentation and demonstration, handling objections, closing, and follow-up. The salesperson needs supervision and continuous encouragement because he must make many decisions and is subject to many frustrations. Periodically, the salesperson's performance must be formally evaluated to help him do a better job.

QUESTIONS FOR DISCUSSION

1. How does personal selling differ from advertising?

2. Relate the six tasks of selling to a car sales representative.

3. In what alternative ways can a sales force be structured? Relate each to a specific company that sells industrial products.

4. A combination of straight salary and commission is probably the best way to compensate a sales force. Comment.

5. What two personal qualities do you think are most important in a successful sales representative? Why?

6. You have just been hired by the World Book Encyclopaedia Company as a salesperson for the summer. Discuss how you would progress through the steps involved in effective selling.

7. What are the major tasks required of those who supervise sales representatives?

8. How would the World Book sales manager (see question 6) go about evaluating your selling job at the end of the summer?

NOTES

1 Diane Willman, 'The life of a salesman', *Australian Financial Review*, 20 February 1981, pp. 31–2.

2 Robert N. McMurry, 'The Mystique of Super-Salesmanship', *Harvard Business Review*, March–April 1961, p. 114.

3 See Sidney J. Levy, *Promotional Behaviour* (Glenview, Ill.: Scott, Foresman, 1971), pp. 65–69.

4 Australian Bureau of Statistics, *Census 1971* (Canberra: AGPS).

5 See William R. Dixon, 'Redetermining the Size of the Sales Force: A Case Study', in Martin R. Warshaw (ed.), *Changing Perspectives in Marketing Management* (Ann Arbor: University of Michigan, Michigan Business Reports, 1962), No.37, p. 58.

6 P. T. FitzRoy & G. Mandry, 'The new role for the salesmen – Manager', *Industrial Marketing Management*, 4, 1975, pp. 37–43.

7 William H. Kaven, *Managing the Major Sale* (New York: American Management Association, 1971); and Benson P. Shapiro & Ronald S. Posner, 'Making the Major Sale', *Harvard Business Review*, March–April 1976, pp. 68–78.

8 Walter J. Talley, 'How to Design Sales Territories', *Journal of Marketing*, January 1961, pp. 7–13.

9 *Survey of Salesforce Compensation Practices* (Caulfield: Marketing Department, Caulfield Institute of Technology, Melbourne, 1980).

10 'Year Round motivation scheme for sales and service staff', *Rydge's*, June 1978, p. 99.

11 *Survey of Salesforce Compensation Practices*, p. 15.

12 M. J. S. Collins, *Sales Force Recruitment and Selection* (Caulfield: Department of Marketing, Caulfield Institute of Technology, Melbourne, 1977).

13 David Mayer & Herbert M. Greenberg, 'What Makes a Good Salesman?', *Harvard Business Review*, July–August 1964, pp. 119–25.

14 Collins, p. 8.

15 R. J. Luscombe, 'The Failing Sale of Selling', *Rydge's*, June 1979, pp. 105–10.

16 Collins, p. 10.

17 'How the elite salesmen are trained', *Rydge's*, April 1978, pp. 75–78.

18 Some of the following discussion is based on W. J. E. Crissy, William H. Cunningham & Isabella C. M. Cunningham, *Selling: The Personal Force in Marketing* (New York: John Wiley, 1977), pp. 119–29.

19 Mark Hanan, 'Join the Systems Sell and You Can't Be Beat', *Sales and Marketing Management*, 21 August 1972, p. 44. Also see Mark Hanan, James Cribbin & Herman Heiser, *Consultative Selling* (New York: American Management Association, 1970).

20 Crissy, Cunningham & Cunningham, pp. 289–94.

21 Chester L. Karrass, *The Negotiating Game* (Cleveland: World Publishing, 1970).

22 L. M. Lodish, 'Callplan: An Interactive Salesman's Call Planning System', *Management Science* 18, No. 4, December 1971, pp. 25–40.

Part 5

Marketing's Role in Society

International Marketing

19

When Crown Corning found itself with increased manufacturing capacity as a result of productivity gains and little hope of lifting sales in a slack domestic market, there was only one way to go — export. Today, as a result of superior technology, aggressive pricing and a very professional marketing approach, Crown Corning is doing its version of coals to Newcastle by exporting drinking glasses to Scandinavia and Germany, not to mention the USA and South-East Asia. Export sales in the current year are expected to reach $2.5 million, about 8 per cent of the company's total consumer business. General manager Don Allan believes exports can grow to as much as 15 per cent of the total.

He admits to having been 'somewhat a cynical Australian' when the previous general manager, an American, told him on joining the company that Crown Corning's technology was world class, if not world superior. 'I could not quite conceive how we would have built up a body of technical knowledge in this country that had reached such a standard. I remember telling him that when I see someone saying they want to buy a lot of our glass because it's better, and when someone pays me real money for our technology, then I'll believe it's valuable. Now it has come home to roost on two counts. The Germans tell us we are giving them a better quality glass than they expected — better than their other suppliers — and are now paying us a premium. The technology enquiry came to us because the world's major manufacturer of the equipment most of the industry uses told them we were the people who know how to operate their equipment best. So I am convinced.'

The company has not got all its eggs in the export business, although Don Allan confesses to a particular fascination for the export side. On the domestic *scene the company is riding the gourmet boom and consumer demand for better and brighter products by promoting Corningware.*

But it's the export market which offers the real growth opportunities, Allan believes. 'As far as Australian industry is concerned, unless you re-invent the wheel or do something really outstanding, the growth opportunities in this country are modest at best. We've made a commitment that we are in the export business come hell or high water and we are not going to walk away from it.'

Allan offers this advice to would-be exporters:

1. *The first essential is need — you have to be convinced it is an important need in your business.*
2. *You have to get your employees committed to the belief that they have products which are acceptable in world markets — and that requires almost a missionary approach.*
3. *Choose good people to staff your export department.*
4. *Don't appoint a distributor until you're convinced you've got the best one available, and don't commit yourself long-term until he has proved himself. Give him your maximum support.*
5. *You must make an absolute commitment to export. You cannot use export to fill the slack in domestic orders, and then turn off the tap when you're squeezed by domestic demand.*
6. *Don't sit on your hands and wait for Government subsidies and help. You must be able to export viably, and make profit out of it. If you get Government subsidies as well, that's fruit for the sideboard but don't depend on it.*[1]

Mixed feelings about expanding abroad have been a factor keeping many Australian companies from taking an aggressive world posture. Domestic marketing is generally simpler and safer: managers do not have to learn another language, deal with a different currency, face political and legal uncertainties, or adapt the product to a different set of needs and expectations.

There are two main factors that might draw Australian companies into international marketing. First, they might be pushed into it by a weakening of marketing opportunities at home. Growth in the Australian market has slowed considerably in the last few years, with the annual rate of increase of GDP dropping to 3–4 per cent. But Australia is located on the edge of one of the most rapidly growing regions of the world – the western Pacific basin – and international operations are thus the only way to satisfy corporate growth objectives. Pressure may also be exerted by the federal government, who encourages firms to export in order to earn foreign exchange and reduce the trade deficit. For other firms, cost-effective operations involve building a plant with a capacity far greater than the total Australian market: the woodchipping operations of Associated Pulp and Paper Manufacturers are geared to world markets, as are the smelting operations of Alcoa and Comalco.

Secondly, Australian companies might be pulled into international operations by growing opportunities for their products in other countries. Nicholas International may see opportunities for its products in Germany or Switzerland, or any other of the 100 countries in which the company operates.

AUSTRALIAN EXPORTS

Exports from Australia account for about 16 per cent of GDP, i.e. of all goods and services produced in Australia. This compares with 6 per cent in the United States and 36 per cent in Belgium. As can be seen from Table 19-1, Australia generally exports more than is imported and thus has a positive balance of trade. But if we include the so-called invisibles – travel, insurance, shipping, repatriation of earnings, etc. – the net result is a current account deficit. This deficit is met by private capital inflow and government borrowing.

Australian exports are predominantly derived from the agricultural and mining sectors of the economy, as can be seen from Table 19-2 where exports are grouped by major commodity class. Table 19-3 shows the exports for seven agricultural and mining products which, as can be seen, account for a high proportion of total Australian exports.

Table 19-4 indicates the destination of exports, by country or by trade group. The most important trading partner for Australia is Japan, which in 1978–79 accounted for approximately 35 per cent of Australian exports. Japan is a major market for such products as beef, sugar, woodchips, iron and other ores, and coal. The European Economic Community (EEC) – comprising Belgium, Denmark, France, Germany, Italy, Netherlands and the United States – is another major customer. The Association of South-East Asian

Table 19-1   Australian balance of payments ($ million)

	Exports	Imports	Balance of trade	Net invisibles	Balance on current account
1976–77	11 447	10 345	1 102	3 088	− 1 986
1977–78	12 026	11 165	861	3 370	− 2 510
1978–79	14 075	13 493	582	3 856	− 3 274
1979–80	18 581	15 829	2 751	4 320	− 1 569
1980–81	18 933	19 141	− 208	4 683	− 4 891

Source: Australian Bureau of Statistics, *Balance of Payments June 1981*, Cat. No. 8364.0.

Table 19-2   Australian exports by commodity class ($ million)

Class	Description	1974–75	1975–76	1976–77	1977–78	1978–79
0	Food and live animals	2 964	3 090	3 472	3 671	4 124
1	Beverages, tobacco	19	21	21	27	30
2	Crude materials	2 146	2 578	3 461	3 955	4 598
3	Mineral fuels	895	1 231	1 498	1 730	1 848
4	Animal, vegetable oils	56	68	75	109	134
5	Chemicals	479	619	782	220	308
6	Manufactured goods	1 150	1 002	1 342	1 335	1 798
7	Machinery, transport	565	496	483	547	673
8	Miscellaneous manufacturers	125	120	140	181	228
9	Others					
	Total exports	8 726	9 640	11 652	12 270	14 243

Source: Australian Bureau of Statistics, *Australian Exports, Country by Commodity, 1980*, Cat. No. 5411.0.

Table 19-3 Australian exports, selected commodities ($ million)

	1978	1979	1980
Beef	970	1 537	1 256
Wheat	763	1 514	1 965
Wool	1 112	1 325	1 296
Raw sugar	474	446	966
Iron ore	908	1 008	1 160
Other ores	1 297	1 563	2 066
Coal	1 480	1 607	1 681

Source: Australian Bureau of Statistics, *Australian Exports, Country by Commodity, 1980,* Cat. No. 5411.0.

Table 19-4 Australian exports by country ($ million)

Japan	2 456	3 192	3 959	3 896	4 108
ASEAN	727	660	772	856	1 090
EEC	1 336	1 431	1 916	1 719	2 012
UK	475	406	540	482	571
USA	831	968	1 009	1 289	1 789
Total	8 726	9 640	11 652	12 270	14 243

Source: Australian Bureau of Statistics, *Australian Exports, Country by Commodity, 1980.* Cat. No. 5411.0.

Nations (ASEAN) – made up of Indonesia, Malaysia, Philippines, Singapore and Thailand – is also emerging as a major trading partner for Australia. The United Kingdom, historically a major customer for Australia, now accounts for only about 4 per cent of total exports.

The 1960s saw the beginning of a trend for US and European companies to expand the geographic extent of their activities. Many companies have gone into world marketing on such a large scale that they are called *multinationals*, e.g. Exxon, BP, Shell, GM, Ford, IBM, Xerox, Honda and Sony operate in many countries of the world.

Several Australian enterprises have followed the same strategy. Nicholas International (with brands such as Aspro, Staminade) operates in more than 100 countries: in 1980, 36 per cent of sales were in the United Kingdom, 19 per cent in the rest of Europe, 4 per cent in the United States and only 23 per cent in the Pacific (which includes Australia). Mr Rupert Murdoch has expanded his press interests into the United Kingdom and the United States; Thomas National Transport (TNT) has expanded rapidly into the United States and Canada; and Mayne Nickless has moved into the United States and the United Kingdom with its security and computer services.

In the same period, an increasing number of overseas companies have entered the Australian market. In addition to the multinationals mentioned earlier, such companies include Alcoa, Utah, Coca-Cola, Kraft, ICI, Philips and Cadbury-Schweppes. The presence of multinationals is the subject of intense political debate in Australia, with concern being expressed about Australia's ability to control its own destiny in such circumstances. At the same time, the multinationals are responsible for significant social benefits in terms of technology transfer, management skills and access to capital. A significant proportion of funds needed for the development of our mineral resources, for example, has been generated overseas.

Management in the local subsidiaries, particularly marketing management, may find their activities tightly controlled and circumscribed. To the extent that the overseas parent is pursuing an integrated worldwide strategy, it may retain control of marketing decisions such as product design, new product development and pricing; managers in Australia are thus responsible for implementing a strategy which has been developed on a worldwide basis.

One may ask whether international marketing really involves any principles that have not been examined in discussions earlier in this book. Obviously similar principles will apply in the setting of marketing objectives, choosing target markets, developing marketing positionings and marketing mixes, and carrying out marketing control. But the differences between nations may be so great that the international marketer must master special environmental factors and institutions and be prepared to drop some of the most basic assumptions about how people respond to marketing stimuli.

We now turn to the basic decisions that a company faces in considering international marketing (see Figure 19-1).

APPRAISING THE INTERNATIONAL MARKETING ENVIRONMENT

Before deciding to sell abroad, a company will have to acquire a thorough understanding of the international marketing environment. This has undergone significant changes since 1945, creating new opportunities as well as new problems. The most significant changes

are: (i) the internationalization of the world economy, reflected in the rapid growth of world trade and investment; (ii) the gradual erosion of the dominant position of the United States, and attendant problems of an unfavourable balance of trade and a falling value of the dollar in world markets; (iii) the rising economic power of Japan in world markets; (iv) the establishment of an international financial system offering improved currency convertibility; (v) the shift in world income, since 1973, to the oil-producing countries; (vi) the increasing trade barriers put up to protect domestic markets against foreign competition; and (vii) the gradual opening up of major new markets, namely China, the USSR, the Arab countries and the western Pacific nations.[1]

The International Trade System

The Australian company looking abroad must start with an appreciation of the international framework for world trade and finance. In attempting to sell to another country, the firm will face various trade restrictions. The most common trade restriction is the *tariff*, which is a tax levied by the foreign government against certain imported products and normally based on the goods' weight, volume or value. The tariff may be designed to raise revenue (revenue tariff) or to protect domestic firms (protective tariff). The exporter may also face a *quota*, which sets limits on the amount of goods that the importing country will accept in certain product categories. The purpose of a quota is to conserve on foreign exchange and

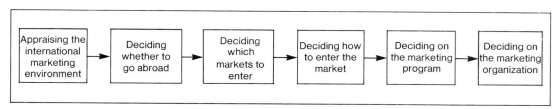

Figure 19-1   Major steps in international marketing

protect local industry and employment. An *embargo* is the ultimate form of quota, in that imports in prescribed categories are totally banned. Trade is also discouraged by *exchange control*, which regulates the amount of available foreign exchange and its exchange rate against other currencies. The Australian company may also confront a set of *non-tariff barriers*, such as foreign discrimination against Australian company bids, and product standards that discriminate against foreign products (e.g. overly high health or safety standards).

At the same time, certain forces in the international economy seek to liberalize and foster trade between nations, or at least between some nations. The General Agreement on Tariffs and Trade (GATT) is an international accord that has reduced the overall level of tariffs throughout the world on six different occasions. In addition, certain countries have formed economic communities, the most important of which is the EEC (more popularly known as the Common Market). The EEC's members are the major western European nations, and they are striving to reduce tariffs within the community, reduce prices, and expand employment and investment. The EEC has taken the form of a customs union, which is a free trade area (no tariffs facing the members) that imposes a uniform tariff for trade with non-member nations. The next move would be towards a true common market or economic union in which all members would operate under the same trade policies, as is the case within the United States. Since the formation of the EEC, other economic communities have been formed, notably the Latin American Free Trade Association (LAFTA) and the Association of South-East Asian Nations (ASEAN).

Each nation within the international community has unique features that must be understood. A nation's readiness for different products and services, and its general attractiveness as a market to foreign firms, depend on its economic, politico-legal, cultural and business environment.

Economic Environment

In considering possible export markets, the international marketer must study each country's economy. Two economic characteristics in particular reflect a country's attractiveness as an export market.

The first is the country's industrial structure, which shapes its goods and service requirements, income levels, employment levels, and so on. Four types of industrial structure may be distinguished:

1. Subsistence economies. In a subsistence economy, the vast majority of people are engaged in simple agriculture. They consume most of their output and barter the rest for basic goods and services. For obvious reasons, they offer few opportunities for exporters.

2. Raw-material exporting economies. These economies are rich in one or more natural resources but poor in other respects. Much of their revenue comes from exporting these resources. Examples are Chile (tin and copper), Congo (rubber), and Saudi Arabia (oil). These countries are good markets for extractive equipment, tools and supplies, materials-handling equipment, and trucks. Depending on the number of foreign residents and wealthy local rulers and landholders, they are also a market for western-style commodities and luxury goods.

3. Industrializing economies. In an industrializing economy, manufacturing is beginning to play a role of some importance, probably accounting for somewhere between 10 and 20 per cent of the country's gross national product. Examples include Egypt, the Philippines, India, Brazil, Singapore, Taiwan and Hong Kong. As manufacturing increases, the country relies more on imports of textile raw materials, steel and heavy machinery, and less on imports of finished textiles, paper products and cars. Industrialization tends to create a new rich class and a small but growing middle class, both demanding new types of goods, some of which can be satisfied only by imports.

4. Industrial economies. Industrial economies have built up their industrial base to the extent that they become exporters of manufactured goods and investment funds. They trade manufactured goods between themselves, and also export them to other types of economies in exchange for raw materials and semi-finished goods. The large and varied manufacturing activities of these nations, and their sizeable middle class, make them rich markets for all sorts of goods.

The second economic characteristic is the country's income distribution, which is related to industrial structure but is also affected by the political system. The international marketer can distinguish countries with five different types of income distribution pattern: (i) very low family incomes; (ii) mostly low family incomes; (iii) very low and very high family incomes; (iv) low, medium and high family incomes; and (v) mostly medium family incomes. Consider the market for Lamborghinis, a car which costs more than $60 000. The market would be very small in countries with income patterns described in (i) or (ii); the largest single market for Lamborghinis is in fact Portugal (iii), the poorest country in Europe but one with a number of wealthy status-conscious families.

Politico-legal Environment

Nations differ greatly in the favourableness of their politico-legal environment for imports and foreign investment. At least four such factors should be considered by the marketer who is trying to determine whether to do business in a particular country.

Attitudes toward international buying. Some nations are very receptive – indeed encouraging – to foreign firms; others are very hostile. As an example of the former, Singapore offers generous incentives in the form of tax holidays and duty-free imports of raw materials and capital goods; the most favourable incentives are granted to pioneer firms and firms producing for export. On the other hand, India has a complex set of registration procedures, limited equity for overseas companies, strict control over the remittance of profits, stipulations that a high percentage of the management team be nationals, and so on. IBM and Coca-Cola made a decision to leave India because of all the 'hassles'.

Political stability. One must consider not only the host country's present political climate but also its future stability. Governments change hands, sometimes quite violently; and even without a change in government, a regime may decide to respond to new popular feelings. The foreign company's currency holdings may be blocked, import quotas or new duties may be imposed or, at worst, its property be expropriated. Where political instability is high, international marketers may still find it profitable to do business with the host country, but the situation will affect their mode of entry. They will favour export marketing to direct foreign investment, keep their foreign stocks low, and convert their currency rapidly. As a result, the people in the host country pay higher prices, have fewer jobs, and get less-satisfactory products.[2]

Monetary regulations. Sellers want to realize profits in a currency of value to them. In the best situation, the importer can pay either in the seller's currency or in hard world currencies. Short of this, sellers might accept a blocked currency if they can buy other needed goods in that country or goods that they can sell elsewhere for a needed currency. In the worst case they must take their money out of the host country in the form of relatively unmarketable products that they can sell elsewhere only at a loss. Besides currency restrictions, a fluctuation exchange rate also leads to unusual risks for the exporter.

Government bureaucracy. A fourth factor is the extent to which the host government runs an efficient system for assisting foreign companies: efficient customs-handling procedures, market information, and other factors conducive to doing business. Perhaps the most common shock to Australian business executives is the extent to which various impediments to trade exist, all of which disappear if a suitable payment (bribe) is made to some official(s).

Cultural Environment

Perhaps the most difficult aspect of international markets is the consumer buying preferences and patterns, which are full of surprises:

- The average Frenchman uses almost twice as many cosmetics and beauty aids as does his wife.
- The Germans and the French eat more packaged, branded spaghetti than the Italians.
- Italian children like to eat a bar of chocolate between two slices of bread as a snack.
- Women in Tanzania will not give their children eggs for fear of making them bald or impotent.

Industrial buying styles vary tremendously:

- South Americans are accustomed to talking business in close physical proximity with other persons – in fact, almost nose to nose. The Australian business executive retreats, but the South American pursues. And both end up being offended.
- Australian executives frequently complain of the difficulty of negotiating with the Japanese, although the reasons are embedded in Japanese culture. The *ringi*

system – circulating a proposal to all interested parties for their approval – frequently makes decision-making a time-consuming process. Management in Japan is both top-down and bottom-up, so the chief executive rarely makes quick decisions.
- In France, wholesalers do not care to promote a product – they simply ask their retailers what they want today, and deliver it. If an Australian company builds its strategy around the French wholesaler, it is almost always bound to fail.

Each country (and even regional groups within each country) has cultural traditions, preferences and taboos that must be carefully studied by the marketer.[3]

DECIDING WHETHER TO GO ABROAD

Companies initially become involved in international marketing in one of two ways. In some cases someone – a domestic exporter, foreign importer, foreign government – solicits the company to sell abroad. In other cases the company starts to consider the idea of its own volition: it might face overcapacity, or simply see better marketing opportunities in other countries than at home.

Before going abroad, the company should try to define its international marketing objectives and policies. First, it should decide what proportion of foreign to total sales it will ultimately seek. Most companies will start small when they venture abroad: some will plan to stay small, seeing foreign operations as a small part of their business; others will have more grandiose plans, seeing foreign business as ultimately equal to or even more important than their domestic business.

Second, the company must choose between marketing in a few countries and marketing in many countries. A company with a fixed budget for international expansion has the choice of entering only a few foreign markets and developing them well (market concentration) or entering several markets, each on a smaller scale (market proliferation). In the United States, the Bulova Watch Company made the latter choice and expanded into more than 100 countries in the late 1960s and early 1970s: it spread itself too thin, however, made profits in only two countries and lost about $40 million.

Third, the company must decide on the types of country it wants to market in. The types that are attractive will depend on the product, geographical factors, income and population, political climate, and numerous other factors. The seller may have a predilection for certain country groups or parts of the world.

DECIDING WHICH MARKETS TO ENTER

After developing a list of possible export markets, the company will have to find some procedure for screening and ranking them. Normally the candidate countries should be ranked on several criteria, such as market size, market growth, cost of doing business, competitive advantage, and risk level. The core of the ranking procedure is to try to determine the probable rate of return on investment in each market. Five steps are involved:[4]

1. Estimate of current market potential. The first step is to estimate current market potential in each candidate market. This calls for using existing published data supplemented by primary data collected through company surveys and studies of various kinds. The Department of Trade and Resources and several large banks are increasing the amount of information available about foreign markets.

2. Forecast of future market potential. The firm also needs a forecast of market potential. This is complicated because the market analyst is usually insufficiently versed in the eco-

nomic, political, cultural and business currents of another country. Many foreign countries do not show the stability of government, currency or law that permits reliable forecasting.

3. Forecast of sales potential. Estimating the company's sales potential requires forecasting its probable market share. The normal difficulties of forecasting market shares are compounded in a foreign environment. The foreign company will find itself competing with other foreign companies as well as with home-country firms. It has to estimate how the buyers will feel about the relative merits of its product, selling methods and company. Even if the buyers are impartial, their government may put up barriers in the form of quotas, tariffs, taxes, specifications or even outright boycotts.

4. Forecast of costs and profits. Costs will depend on the company's contemplated entry strategy. If it resorts to exporting or licensing, its costs will be spelled out in the contracts; if it decides to locate manufacturing facilities abroad, its estimation will require an understanding of local labour conditions, taxes, trade practices, and stipulations regarding the hiring of nationals as key employees. After estimating future costs, the company subtracts them from estimated company sales to find company profits for each year of the planning horizon.

5. Estimate of rate of return on investment. The forecast income stream must be related to the investment stream to derive an implicit rate of return. The estimated rate of return should be high enough to cover both the company's normal target return on its investment, and the risk and uncertainty of marketing in that country. The risk premium must incorporate not only the chance that the basic estimates of sales and costs may be wrong but also the chance that unanticipated monetary changes (devaluation, blocked currency) and political changes (future discrimination against foreign business firms, or even expropriation) may occur.

DECIDING HOW TO ENTER THE MARKET

Once a company decides that a particular foreign market represents an attractive opportunity, its task is to determine the best mode of entering that market. Here it has three major strategies: exporting (home production and selling abroad), joint venturing (joining with foreign companies in some way), and direct investment abroad.[5] Each succeeding strategy tends to involve more commitment, risk and possible profits. The three strategies are shown in Figure 19-2, with the various relevant options.

Export

The simplest way for a company to enter a foreign market is through export, on either of two levels. Occasional exporting is a passive level of involvement where the company may export surpluses from time to time and sell goods to resident buyers representing foreign companies. Active exporting takes place when

the company makes a commitment to expand exports to a particular market. In either case the company continues to produce all of its goods at home, and may or may not modify them for the export market. Exporting involves the least change in the company's product lines, organization, investments or mission.

A company can export its product by either hiring independent international marketing middlemen (indirect export), or assuming direct responsibility for selling to the foreign buyers or importers (direct export).

Indirect export. Indirect exporting involves the use of home-based export agents of various forms. It has several advantages for the firm that is just beginning its export activities. Less investment is required, as the firm does not have to develop an overseas sales force or set of contacts. It also generally involves less risk as the export agent brings some know-how and services to the relationship and the seller is thus likely to make fewer mistakes. One particular form of agent is the cooperative organi-

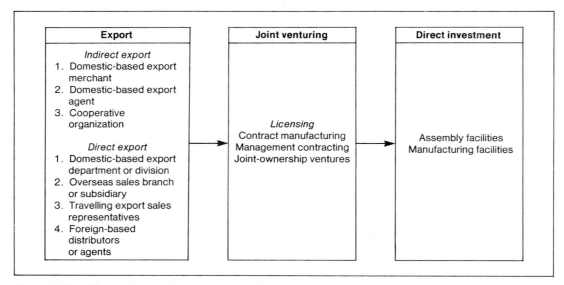

Figure 19-2 Alternative market entry strategies

zation, which carries on exporting activities on behalf of several producers and is partly under their administrative control. This form is often used by producers of primary products for foreign sale: the Australian Wheat Board, for example is responsible for all the overseas marketing of Australian wheat.

Direct export. Most companies elect to undertake their own export activity, to permit greater control. The investment and risk are somewhat greater, but so is the potential return. There are several ways in which the company can carry on direct exporting activity:

1. *Domestic-based export department or division.* This consists of an export sales manager with some clerical assistants. They carry on the actual selling, and draw on regular company departments for marketing assistance in such areas as advertising, credit and logistics. This may evolve into a self-contained export department or sales subsidiary carrying out all the activities involved in export, and possibly be operated as a profit centre.
2. *Overseas sales branch or subsidiary.* This may be established in addition to, or instead of, a domestic export department. An overseas sales branch allows the manufacturer to achieve greater presence and programme control in the foreign market. It handles sales distribution, may handle warehousing and promotion, and often serves as a display centre and customer-service centre.
3. *Travelling export sales representatives.* The company may decide to have one or more home-based sales representatives travel abroad at certain times to take orders or find business.
4. *Foreign-based distributors or agents.* Foreign-based distributors would buy and own the goods; foreign-based agents would sell the goods on behalf of the company. They may be given exclusive rights to represent the manufacturer in that country, or only general rights.

Australian companies frequently adopt a combination of the above, as the following example demonstrates. Ausonics Pty Ltd is a Sydney-based firm specializing in the manufacture of ultrasonic tissue scanners, with some 80 per cent of sales being exported.[6] The company has two overseas subsidiaries, located in Switzerland and the United States, which are responsible for maintaining an inventory of spare parts, providing operator training and engineering support. Agents and distributors are used in other countries such as Japan, Israel and New Zealand. Ausonics provides a high level of dealer support (literature, video-cassettes, etc.), and a company engineer accompanies the first piece of equipment going to a distributor's territory for installation.

Joint Venturing

A second broad method of entering a foreign market is to join with nationals in the foreign country to set up production and marketing facilities. Joint venturing differs from exporting in that some production facilities are set up abroad, and it differs from direct investment in that an association is formed with someone in that country. Three types of joint venture may be distinguished.

Licensing. Licensing is a comparatively simple way for a manufacturer to become involved in international marketing. The licensor enters an agreement with a licensee in the foreign market, offering the right to use a manufacturing process, trademark, patent, trade secret, or other item of value for a fee or royalty. The licensor gains entry into the market at little risk; the licensee gains production expertise, or a well-known product or name, without having to start from scratch. Coca-Cola has carried out its international marketing activities by licensing bottlers around the world – or, more specifically, *franchising* bottlers, because it supplies the syrup needed to produce the product.

Licensing has potential disadvantages in that the firm has less control over the licensee than if it had set up its own production facilities. Furthermore, if the licensee is very successful, the firm has forgone these profits and, if and when the contract ends, may find it has set up a competitor. To avoid these dangers the licensor must establish some advantage, a key to which is remaining innovative so that the licensee is dependent.

Management contracting. Here the domestic firm agrees to supply the management know-how to a foreign company that is willing to supply the capital, i.e. the domestic firm is really exporting management services rather than products. This arrangement is used by the Hilton hotel system in undertaking to manage hotels throughout the world.

Management contracting is a low-risk method of getting into a foreign market, and it starts yielding income right from the beginning. The arrangement is especially attractive if the contracting firm is given an option to purchase some share in the managed company within a stated period. On the other hand, the arrangement is not sensible if the company could put its scarce management talent to better uses, or if there are greater profits to be made by undertaking the whole venture. Management contracting prevents the company from setting up its own operations for a period of time.

Joint-ownership ventures. An increasingly popular arrangement consists of foreign investors' joining with local investors to create a local business of which they share ownership and control. The investor may buy an interest in an existing operation, or the two parties may form a new business venture.

From the point of view of the foreign inves-tor, a joint venture may be necessary or desirable for economic or political reasons. Economically, the firm may find it lacks the financial, physical or managerial resources to undertake the venture alone. The foreign government may, on the other hand, require joint ownership with local companies as a condition for entry.

Joint ownership can have certain drawbacks for the partners if there is disagreement over investment, marketing or other policies. One partner may wish to invest earnings for growth while the other works to pay these out in dividends. The firms with a minority interest are effectively locked in, with little control over the future of the venture. Furthermore, joint venturing can hamper the plans of a multinational company seeking to carry out specific manufacturing and marketing policies on a worldwide basis. The agreement may also make it difficult for the foreign firm to enter other markets where its partner already operates.

Direct Investment

The ultimate form of involvement in a foreign market is investment in foreign-based assembly or manufacturing facilities. Companies just new to the market would be well advised to avoid this scale of participation at the outset. However, as experience is gained through export channels, and if the foreign market appears large enough, foreign production facilities offer distinct advantages. The company may secure these advantages partially through licensing or joint-ownership ventures, but if it wants full control (and profits), it may give serious consideration to direct investment.

The advantages of direct investment are several. First, the firm may secure real cost economies in the form of cheaper labour or raw materials, government investment incentives, freight savings, and so on. Second, the firm will gain a better image in the host country because it demonstrates its concern with that country's future. Third, the firm develops a deeper relationship with government, customers, local suppliers and distributors, enabling it to better adapt its products to the local market. Fourth, the firm retains full control over the investment and can therefore develop manufacturing and marketing policies that serve its long-term international objectives.

The main disadvantage is that the firm has exposed a large investment to certain risks, such as blocked or devalued currencies, worsening markets, or expropriation. In some cases, however, the firm has no choice but to accept these risks if it wants to operate effectively in the host country.

DECIDING ON THE MARKETING PROGRAMME

Companies that operate in one or more foreign markets must decide how much, if at all, to adapt their marketing mix to local conditions. Here we will examine their product, promotion, price and distribution options.

Product

Keegan distinguished five possible strategies involving the adaptation of product and pro-

motion to a foreign market (see Figure 19-3).[7] Here we will focus on the three product options.

The first strategy, *straight extension*, means introducing the product to the foreign market without any change. Top management says to its marketing people: 'Take the product as it is and find customers for it.' The first step, however, should be to determine whether the foreign consumers use that product. Deodorant usage among men ranges from 80 per cent in the United States, to 55 per cent in Sweden, 28 per cent in Italy, and 8 per cent in the Philippines. Many Spaniards do not use common products as butter and cheese.

Straight extension has been used successfully by Coca-Cola to introduce its soft-drinks everywhere in the world, but it has failed for some other producers. Straight extension is a tempting strategy because it involves no addition R & D expense, manufacturing retooling, or promotional modification; but it can be costly in the long run.

The second strategy, product *adaptation*, involves altering the product to meet local conditions or preferences. Thus Heinz varies its baby-food products: in Australia it sells a baby food made from strained lambs' brains; and in the Netherlands, one made from strained brown beans. Ausonic's tissue scanners are designed specifically for the needs of export markets, especially with regard to the

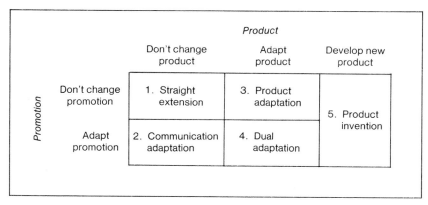

Figure 19-3   Five international product and promotion strategies

voltage and frequency of the electrical power supply.

The third strategy, product *invention*, calls for creating something new. Backward invention is the reintroducing of earlier product forms that happen to be well adapted to the needs of that country. The National Cash Register Company reintroduced its crank-operated cash register, that could sell at half the cost of a modern cash register, and sold substantial numbers in less-developed countries. This illustrates the existence of international product lifecycles, i.e. different countries are at different stages of readiness to accept a particular product.[8] Forward invention is the creation of a completely new product to meet a need in another country. For example, there is an enormous need in less-developed countries for low-cost high-protein foods: companies such as Pillsbury, Nestlé and Monsanto are researching the food needs of these countries, formulating new foods, and developing mass-communication programmes to gain product trial and acceptance. Product invention would appear to be the costliest of all strategies, but the payoffs to the successful firm also appear to be the greatest.

Promotion

Companies face two options with respect to their promotion strategy abroad. They can either use the same promotion strategy used in the home market or change it for each local market.

Consider message, for example. Many multinational companies favour using a highly standardized advertising theme and approach in order to create worldwide impact.[9] A classic case is Pepsi's use of the 'Pepsi generation' theme for several years in its worldwide advertising, which gave the company international recognition. The theme may be carried out literally everywhere, or be adapted in minor ways for local conditions. The latter is more common because of variations in cultural

norms and taboos. For example, colours in an advertisement might have to be modified to avoid taboo colours in other countries: purple is associated with death in most of Latin America; white is a mourning colour in Japan; and green is associated with jungle sickness in Malaysia.

Other companies will let their international division and subsidiaries develop an ad from scratch, feeling that the optimum appeal should be found for each market. For example, a bicycle company may use a pleasure appeal to sell its bicycles in the United States and a safety appeal in Scandinavia.

In the case of media, much more international adaptation is normally required. The company will find that media availabilities differ considerably from country to country. For example, commercial television time in Germany is only available for about an hour each evening, and marketers must buy time months in advance; in Sweden, commercial television time is non-existent. Commercial radio does not exist in France and Scandinavia; magazines are a major medium in Italy, and a minor one in Austria; newspapers are national in the United Kingdom, and local in Spain and the United States.

Price

Manufacturers often price their products lower for the foreign market than for the domestic market, for a number of reasons. The foreign market may be one of low incomes, and a low price is necessary if the goods are to sell. A manufacturer may use a low price to build market share against domestic and other foreign competitors, or may simply want to 'dump' excess goods that have no market at home. Australian manufacturers frequently claim that foreign competitors from Europe, Scandinavia or Japan are dumping their product on the Australian market, generally when world markets suffer a reversal.

Manufacturers do not have much control over the retail prices charged by the foreign intermediaries who carry their products. Many foreign intermediaries prefer high mark-ups, even though this means selling fewer units; they also like to buy on credit, which increases the manufacturer's cost and risk.

Distribution Channels

The international company must take a whole-channel view of the problem of getting its product to the final users or consumers, i.e. it must see the channel of distribution as an integrated whole, from the manufacturer on one end to the final user or buyer on the other.[10] Figure 19-4 shows the three major links between the seller and ultimate buyer. The first link, seller's headquarters organization, supervises the channels and is part of the channel itself. The second link, channels between nations, does the job of getting the products to the overseas markets. The third link, channels within nations, is extremely pertinent – too many manufacturers fail to observe what happens to their product once it arrives in the foreign market. If the channels there are weak or inefficient, the target customers fail to achieve satisfaction and the company fails to achieve its international objectives.

With respect to consumer goods, within-nation channels of distribution vary considerably from country to country, in terms of both the number and type of intermediaries serving each foreign market. The Japanese distribution system is one of the most complex in the world, with a high level of involvement by wholesalers: to introduce a consumer product to Japan may involve selling to a trading company, who sells to a primary wholesaler, who in turn sells to a secondary wholesaler, who finally sells to retailers. All of these distribution levels may result in a doubling or tripling of the price to the Japanese consumer over the price to the importer.[11]

Another important difference is the size and character of retail units abroad. Whereas large-scale retail chains dominate the scene in Australia, most foreign retailing is in the hands of many small independent retailers. In Thailand, hundreds of thousands of retailers operate tiny shops or sell in open markets; their mark-ups are high, but the real price is often brought down through haggling. Large-scale retail chains such as supermarkets could conceivably bring down prices, but they are difficult to introduce to developing countries because of many economic and cultural resistances.[12] People's incomes are low, and they consequently prefer to shop daily for small amounts rather than weekly for large amounts. They do not have the storage and refrigeration space to keep food for several days. Packaging is not well developed because it would add too much to the cost. Consumers like to see and handle the food and often distrust packaged items. These and other factors have kept large-scale retailing from spreading rapidly in developing countries.

With respect to industrial goods, within-nation channels in advanced countries re-

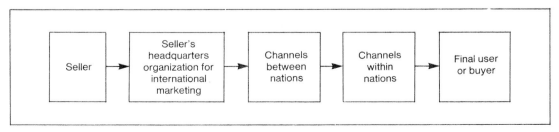

Figure 19-4   Whole-channel concept for international marketing

semble those found in Australia. In the less-developed countries, importers are strong and the fate of foreign companies is generally in their hands. If companies seek their own distributors, they must carefully sort out the good ones from the poor ones. Often the company has to offer exclusive distribution to a local distributor, and its success in this market is thus tied up with how well it has chosen its distributor.

Companies must thus decide how standardized their marketing programmes should be. In favour of standardization is the lower cost of developing uniform products and marketing programmes; against it is the greater adaptation of the company's products and marketing programmes to local needs. Each company must decide. Beecham tries to make its advertising programme uniform; Nestlé, on the other hand, varies its advertising programme in different countries. A recent survey of twenty-seven leading multinationals in consumer-packaged-goods industries reached the following conclusion: 'To the successful multinational, it is not really important whether marketing programmes are internationally standardized or differentiated; the important thing is that the *process* through which these programmes are developed is standardized. At the heart of this process is the annual marketing planning system they use.'[13]

DECIDING ON THE MARKETING ORGANIZATION

Companies manage their international marketing activities in different ways. The different organizational arrangements often parallel their degree of involvement in international marketing.

Export Department

A firm usually starts international marketing in response to a few orders that come in fortuitously. At first it simply ships out the goods. If international sales expand, the company usually organizes an export department consisting of a sales manager and a few clerical assistants; and as sales increase further this staff is expanded to include various marketing services so that it can go after business more aggressively and not depend on the domestic staff. If the firm moves beyond exports into a programme of joint ventures or direct investment, the export department will no longer serve these purposes.

International Division

Many companies eventually become involved in a number of different international markets and ventures. A company may export to one country, license to another, have a joint-ownership venture in a third, and own a subsidiary in a fourth, and it may eventually create an international division or subsidiary with responsibility for all of its international activity. The international division is headed by an international division manager, who sets goals and budgets and is given total responsibility for the company's growth in that area.

International divisions are organized in a variety of ways. Usually the corporate staff consists of functional specialists in marketing, manufacturing, research, finance, planning and personnel, and will plan for and provide services to various operating units. The operating units may be organized according to one or more of three principles. First, they may be geographical organizations, e.g. reporting to the international division manager may be managers for different areas such as North America, Japan, Europe, Africa and Asia. The area managers are responsible for a sales force, sales branches, distributors and licensees in their respective areas. The operating units may also be product-group organizations, with a director responsible for worldwide sales of each product group and able to draw on specialists for expertise on different areas.

Finally, the operating units may be international subsidiaries, each headed by a managing director and with various subsidiary chief executives reporting to the manager of the international division.

A major disadvantage of the international-division concept is that the corporation's top management may think of it as just another division and never fully appreciate and plan for global marketing. Top management may not give the division the attention it deserves, and in difficult times may cut its budget.

Multinational Organization

As discussed earlier, several firms have passed beyond the international division organization and become truly multinational organizations. They stop thinking of themselves as national marketers who venture abroad, and start thinking of themselves as global marketers. This means the top corporate management and staff are involved in the worldwide planning of manufacturing facilities, marketing policies, financial flows and logistical systems. The various operating units around the world report directly to the chief executive, not to the head of an international division; the company trains its executives in worldwide operations, not just domestic *or* international. Management talent is recruited from many countries, components and supplies are purchased where they can be obtained for least cost, and investments are made where the anticipated returns are greatest.

Major companies will undoubtedly have to go multinational in the 1980s if they are to grow. As foreign companies continue to invade the home market with some success, home companies will have to move aggressively into those international markets best suited to their distinctive products and competencies. They will have to evolve from ethnocentric companies, i.e. treating their foreign operations as secondary to their domestic operations, to geocentric companies which view the entire world as a single market.[14]

SUMMARY

Companies are drawn into international marketing for a variety of reasons. Sometimes they are pushed in by inadequate or poor opportunities in the home market, and sometimes they are pulled in by superior opportunities abroad. International competition is becoming fiercer, and – given the risks – companies need a systematic way to make their international marketing decisions.

The first step is to appraise the international marketing environment, particularly the international trade system. In considering a particular foreign market, its economic, politico-legal and cultural characteristics must be assessed. Second, the decision to go abroad must be considered in terms of what proportion of foreign to total sales the company will seek, whether it will do business in a few or many countries, and what types of country it would want to market in. The third step is to decide which particular markets to enter, which calls for making a hard evaluation of the probable rate of return on investment against the level of risk. Fourth, the company has to decide how to enter each attractive market – through export, joint venturing, or direct investment. Many companies start as exporters, move to joint venturing, and finally undertake direct investment as their overseas business expands. Companies must next decide on the extent to which their products, promotion, price and distribution should be adapted to individual foreign markets. Finally, the company must develop an effective organization for pursuing international marketing. Most firms start with an export department and graduate to an international division. A few pass this stage and develop a multinational organization, which means that worldwide marketing is planned and managed by the top officers of the company.

QUESTIONS FOR DISCUSSION

1. In appraising the international marketing environment, the foreign country's economy is the most important consideration for the firm. Comment.

2. Discuss the relevant aspects of the politico-legal environment that might affect Myer's reported decision to open retail outlets in Asia.

3. What steps are involved in deciding which markets to enter? Relate these to a consumer-product example.

4. Briefly discuss the three major strategies that a firm might use to enter a foreign market.

5. How does licensing differ from the other joint-venture possibilities?

6. The price of products sold in foreign markets is usually lower than in the domestic market. Why?

7. Which type of international marketing organization would you suggest for the following companies?
   - a small manufacturer of toys, which is going to market its products in Europe
   - Comalco, which is contemplating selling ingot aluminium in Indonesia.

NOTES

1 Michael Batten, 'Crown Corning takes on the competition in their own markets', *Rydge's In Marketing*, October 1979, pp. 34–6.

2 For a system of rating the political stability of different nations, see F. T. Haner, 'Rating Investment Risks Abroad', *Business Horizons*, April 1979, pp. 18–23.

3 For further examples, see David A. Ricks, Marilyn Y. C. Fu & Jeffery S. Arpan, *International Business Blunders* (Columbus, Ohio: Grid, 1974).

4 See David S. R. Leighton, 'Deciding when to Enter International Markets', in Victor P. Buell (ed.), *Handbook of Modern Marketing* (New York: McGraw-Hill, 1970), Sec. 20, pp. 23–28.

5 This discussion of entry strategies is based on Gordon E. Miracle & Gerald S. Albaum, *International Marketing Management* (Homewood, Ill.: Richard D. Irwin, 1970), Chs 14–16.

6 'Ultrasonic Medical Equipment Maker "exports to survive" ', *Overseas Trading*, 11 April 1980, pp. 213–14.

7 Warren J. Keegan, 'Multinational Product Planning: Strategic Alternatives', *Journal of Marketing*, January 1969, pp. 58–62.

8 Louis T. Wells Jr, 'A Product Life Cycle for International Trade?', *Journal of Marketing*, July 1968, pp. 1–6.

9 Ralph Z. Sorenson & Ulrich E. Wiechmann, 'How Multinationals View Marketing Standardization', *Harvard Business Review*, May–June 1975, pp. 38–54.

10 See Miracle & Albaum, pp. 317–19.

11 See William D. Hartley, 'How Not to Do It: Cumbersome Japanese Distribution System Stumps US Concerns', *Wall Street Journal*, 2 March 1972, pp. 1, 8.

12 However, see Arieh Goldman, 'Outreach of Consumers and the Modernization of Urban Food Retailing in Developing Countries', *Journal of Marketing*, October 1974, pp. 8–16.

13 Sorenson & Wiechmann, p. 54.

14 See Yoram Wind, Susan P. Douglas & Howard V. Perlmutter, 'Guidelines for Developing International Marketing Strategies', *Journal of Marketing*, April 1973, pp. 14–23.

20

Marketing of Services, Organizations, Persons, Places and Ideas

In 1980 the Health Commission of New South Wales established a new staffing position: Director of the Division of Health Promotion. Later that year Ms J.M. Hefferan was appointed to the position. This appointment raised a number of eyebrows within other State departments of health and in the community at large. Why should a health department engage in promotion and marketing?

Until recent times the emphasis on community health care was directed towards the eradication of disease and the countering of existing health problems within the community. This appointment can be seen as leading an initiative into preventative medicine.

The skills of social marketing are being used to encourage people to lead more healthy lives and hence call less on medical services. It could be argued that these expenditures on social marketing will cost the community far less than if action was only taken after illness occurred.

The Director of the Division of Health Promotion leads a team of health educationalists, journalists and artists, and is responsible for the development of a wide range of health-promotion resource materials. In addition she provides consultative assistance to the regional directors of health in New South Wales, regarding their health-promotion programmes and the in-service training offered to health educators.

Marketing initially developed as a discipline in connection with selling physical products such as toothpaste, cars, steel and equipment. In talking about marketing, there is a tendency to emphasize physical goods because they are more tangible and familiar. This focus causes people to overlook the many other types of entities that are subject to marketing analysis, planning and control. The purpose of this chapter is to examine the increasing applications of marketing concepts to entities other than physical goods – namely, services, organizations, persons, places and ideas.

SERVICES MARKETING

Comparisons on the importance of service industries in different countries are shown in Tables 20-1 and 20-2. The data show that the service sector is of considerable importance in most countries, particularly in those with higher income levels.

During the decade to 1972 the proportion of total employment represented by services increased in countries at all levels of per capita income. Also, the relative importance of this sector appears to be increasing, as shown by the substantial increases in the employment share of services in Australia and other countries during the period.

Table 20-2 provides a comparative picture of the service sector contribution to Domestic Product.

Australia with 64 per cent of Domestic Product originating from the service sector in 1973 is similar to the average of the higher income countries.

Service industries are quite varied. The entire government sector – courts, employment services, hospitals, loan agencies, military services, police and fire departments, post office, regulatory agencies, and schools – is in the service business. The private non-profit sector, with its art galleries and museums, chari-

ties, churches, schools, foundations and hospitals, is in the service business. A good part of the business sector – airlines, banks, computer services, hotels, insurance companies, law firms, management consulting firms, medical practices, cinemas, plumbers and real-estate firms – is based on the provision of services. Furthermore, new types of service firms keep popping up all the time:

For a fee, there are now companies that will balance your budget, baby-sit your philodendron, wake you up in the morning, drive you to work, or find you a new home, job, car, wife, clairvoyant, cat feeder, or gypsy violinist. Or perhaps you want to rent a garden tractor? A few cattle? Some original paintings? Or maybe some hippies to decorate your next cocktail party? If it is business services you need, other

Table 20-1 Service sector size: share of employment by annual per capita income, 25 countries, 1960–62 and 1970–72

Per capita annual GDP in US$ (1973)	Number of countries	Average service sector share of employment (per cent)	
		1960–62	*1970–72*
5482	Australia	60	67
5000 or more	6(a)	56 (47–64)	64 (62–71)
3000–4999	8(b)	50 (43–67)	58 (53–67)
1000–2999	3(c)	36 (30–43)	45 (41–43)
Under 1000	8(d)	24 (13–47)	30 (15–56)

Source: Bureau of Industry Economics, *Features of the Australian Service Sector*, Research Report 1, 1980, p. 8.

Notes:
(a) USA, Sweden, West Germany, Canada, Australia, Denmark.
(b) Norway, France, Belgium, Japan, Finland, Austria, UK, Israel.
(c) Italy, Portugal, Greece.
(d) Mexico, Chile, Turkey, South Korea, Philippines, Thailand, India, Indonesia.
Figures in parentheses show the range.
The countries included in Tables 20-1 and 20-2 differ because of differences in the availability of data.

companies will plan your conventions and sales meetings, design your products, handle your data processing, or supply temporary secretaries or even executives.[1]

Nature and Characteristics of a Service

We define a service as follows:

- A *service* is an activity or benefit that one party can offer to another that is essentially intangible and does not result in the ownership of anything. Its production may or may not be tied to a physical product.

Thus renting a hotel room, depositing money in a bank, travelling by plane, visiting a psychiatrist, having a haircut, having a car repaired, watching a professional sport, seeing a movie, having clothes dry-cleaned, getting ad-

vice from a lawyer, all involve buying a service. Services have a number of characteristics that must be considered when designing service-marketing programmes.

Intangibility. Sales are intangible, i.e. they cannot be seen, tasted, felt, heard or smelled before they are bought. A patient walking into a psychiatrist's office cannot know the content or value of the service in advance: under the circumstances, purchase requires having faith in the service provider.

Service providers can do certain things to improve the client's confidence. First, they can try to increase the service's tangibility by a number of devices. A plastic surgeon may, for example, make a drawing or clay model showing the changes the operation will make in the patient's appearance. Second, service providers can place more emphasis on the benefits of the service rather than just describing its features. Thus a university admissions officer may talk to prospective students about the marvellous jobs its graduates have found, instead of merely describing life on the campus. Third, service providers can put brand names on their service to increase confidence, such as the Diners Club credit card, the Commonwealth Bank bankcard and Transcendental Meditation. Fourth, service providers can use a highly regarded celebrity to personalize and create confidence in the service, as banks and other firms offering financial services do in their advertising from time to time.

Table 20-2   Service sector size: share of domestic product by annual per capita income, 25 countries, 1963 and 1973

Per capita annual GDP in US$ (1973)	Number of countries	Average service sector share of domestic product (per cent)[a]	
		1963	*1973*
5482	Australia	63	64
5000 or more	6[b]	61 (50–66)	62 (49–66)
3000–4999	6[c]	62 (54–70)	62 (53–67)
1000–2999	4[d]	63 (45–84)	62 (46–77)
Under 1000	9[e]	49 (36–68)	52 (41–72)

Source: Bureau of Industry Economics, *Features of the Australian Service Sector*, Research Report 1, 1980, p. 9.

Notes:

(a) In constant prices.

(b) USA, Sweden, West Germany, Canada, Australia, Denmark.

(c) Norway, France, Belgium, Finland, Austria, UK.

(d) Italy, Singapore, Greece, Portugal.

(e) Mexico, Chile, Turkey, Tunisia, South Korea, Philippines, Thailand, India, Indonesia.

Figures in parentheses show the range.

Inseparability. A service is inseparable from the source that renders it, whether the latter be a person or a machine. In other words, production and consumption occur simultaneously in a service, whereas a physical product exists whether or not its source is present. Consider going to a Rolling Stones concert. The entertainment value is inseparable from the performer – it is not the same service if an announcer tells the audience that Mick Jagger is indisposed and therefore his record will be played instead, or that Barry Humphries will appear. What this means is that the number of people who can buy this particular service – watching Mick Jagger perform live – is limited to the amount of time that Mick Jagger wants to give concerts, until such time as means are found to clone him. Thus strong consumer preferences can considerably limit the scale of operation of the service firm.

Several strategies exist for getting around this limitation. The service provider can learn to work with larger groups. Management educators, for example, work both on a one-to-one basis and with small groups. The more sought-after and distinguished scholars, however, attract large groups to venues such as hotel ballrooms where they can then be exposed to the 'master'. The service provider can learn to work faster – the psychotherapist can spend thirty minutes with each patient instead of fifty minutes, and thus see more patients. The service organization can also train more competent service providers and build up client confidence in them, as H. & R. Block has done with its national network of trained tax consultants.

Variability. The same service can be highly variable, depending not only on *who* is providing it but *when* it is being provided. A heart-transplant performed by Dr Christiaan Barnard is likely to be of higher quality than the same operation performed by a recently graduated MD, and Dr Barnard's service quality can vary depending on his energy and mental set at the time of the operation. Purchasers of services are aware of their high variability, and engage in normal risk-reducing behaviour by talking to others and trying to select the best provider.

Service firms can take two steps to ensure high and consistent quality in their business.

The first consists of developing a good personnel selection and training programme. Airlines, banks and hotels spend substantial sums of money to train their personnel to provide uniform and courteous service – one is supposed to find, for example, the same friendly and helpful personnel in every Qantas aircraft. This is not without creating some 'role strain', since the personnel are under cross-pressure to be friendly and work fast at the same time. The second step consists of developing adequate customer-satisfaction monitoring systems. The main tools for this are suggestion and complaint systems, customer surveys, and comparison shopping.[2]

Perishability. Services cannot be stored. Although a car can be kept in inventory until it is sold, the revenue from an unoccupied seat on the Southern Aurora on a particular Sydney–Melbourne trip is lost for ever. The reason many doctors charge patients for missed appointments is that the service value only existed at that point when the patient did not show up. The perishability of services is not a problem when demand is steady, because it is easy to staff the services in advance; but when demand fluctuates considerably, service firms have difficult problems. For example, bus companies have to use much more equipment because of peak demand during rush hours than they would if transport needs were constant throughout the day.

Service organizations have several means available to try to produce a better match between demand and service capacity. Sasser has described several strategies for managing demand and supply.[3] On the demand side:

1. *Differential pricing* can be used to shift demand of some segments from peak to off-peak periods. Examples include low-priced, stand-by air fares and special reduced day rates at fitness centres.
2. *Non-peak demand can be developed*, as, for

example, when special summer events are staged at Thredbo village to attract summer visitors to a predominantly winter resort.

3. *Complementary services* can be developed during peak time to provide alternatives to waiting customers, such as cocktail lounges to sit in while waiting for a table in a restaurant, and automatic tellers in banks.

4. *Reservation systems* are a way to pre-sell service and know how much is needed, and are used extensively by airlines, hotels and doctors.

On the supply side:

1. *Part-time employees* can be used to serve peak demand, as when universities and colleges add part-time teachers when enrolment goes up, and restaurants call in part-time waitresses when needed.

2. *Peak-time efficiency routines* can be introduced, such as employees' performing only essential tasks during peak periods.

3. *Increased consumer participation* in the tasks can be used, as when consumers fill out their own medical records or bag their own green groceries.

4. *Shared services* can be developed, as when several hospitals agree to limit and share medical-equipment purchases.

5. *Facilities with built-in expansion possibilities* can be developed, as when an amusement park buys surrounding land in case it is needed for later expansion.

Classification of Services

Services can be classified in several ways. First, to what extent is the service *people-based* or *equipment-based*? A psychiatrist needs a minimum of equipment, perhaps a couch, whereas a pilot needs an expensive piece of equipment called an aeroplane. In people-based services, we can distinguish between those involving professionals (accounting, management consulting), skilled labour (plumbing, car repairs) and unskilled labour (janitorial service, lawn care). In equipment-based services, we can distinguish between those involving automated equipment (automatic car-washes, vending machines), equipment operated by relatively unskilled labour (taxis, cinemas), and equipment operated by skilled labour (aeroplanes, computers).[4] Even within a specific service industry, different service providers vary in the amount of equipment they use – contrast the Bushwackers band with their simple instruments and the Rolling Stones with their tonnes of audio equipment. Sometimes the accompanying equipment adds value to the service (stereo amplification), and sometimes it exists to reduce the amount of labour needed (automatic car-washes).

Second, to what degree is the *client's presence* necessary to the service? Brain surgery involves the client's presence, but a car repair does not. To the extent that the client must be present, the service provider has to be considerate of his needs. Thus hairdressers will invest in their shop's decor, play background music, and engage in conversation if the client desires it.

Third, what about the *client's purchase motive*? Does the service meet a personal need (personal services) or a business need (business services)? For example, fitness centres charge different prices for their programmes according to whether they are serving private individuals or providing a prepaid service to the employees of a particular company. Service providers can develop different service offers and marketing programmes for personal service versus business service target markets.

Fourth, what about the *service provider's motives* (profit or non-profit) and *form* (private or public)? These two characteristics, when crossed, produce four quite different types of service organizations (see Figure 3-1). Clearly the marketing programmes of, say, a private hospital will differ from those of a charity-funded hospital or a public hospital.

The Extent and Importance of Marketing in the Service Sector

Service firms typically lag behind manufacturing firms in their development and use of marketing. George and Barksdale surveyed 400 service and manufacturing firms and concluded that:

> . . . in comparison to manufacturing firms, service firms appear to be: (i) generally less likely to have marketing mix activities carried out in the marketing department; (ii) less likely to perform analysis in the offering area; (iii) more likely to handle their advertising internally rather than go to outside agencies; (iv) less likely to have an overall sales plan; (v) less likely to develop sales training programmes; (vi) less likely to use marketing research firms and marketing consultants; and (vii) less likely to spend as much on marketing when expressed as a percentage of gross sales.[5]

Why have service firms neglected marketing? Several reasons can be given. Many service businesses are small (shoe repairs, barbershops) and do not use management techniques such as marketing, which they think would be expensive or irrelevant. There are also service businesses (law and accounting firms) that are averse to the idea of marketing, believing that it is unprofessional to apply marketing planning to their services and even prohibiting or restricting it in their code of ethics.[6] Other service businesses (private schools and hospitals) had so much demand for years that they had no need for marketing until recently.

Today, as competition intensifies, as costs rise, as productivity stagnates, and as service quality deteriorates, an increasing number of service firms are taking an interest in marketing. They can profit by studying the few service industries that have already moved into marketing. Airlines were one of the first service industries to formally study their customers and competition, and take positive steps to make the travellers' trips easier and more pleasant. They first had to build people's confidence in air travel, and then try to outperform each other in preflight, inflight and postflight services to win customer loyalty. Banks and building societies represent a service industry that moved from hostility to active use of marketing in a relatively short period of time. At first they saw marketing mainly as promotion and friendliness, but they are now setting up marketing organizations, information, planning and control systems.[7] One of their strategies was to lure marketers from top marketing companies to bring in marketing sophistication as soon as possible, although this was not without some tension between financial and marketing departments.[8] Many banks and building societies have redesigned their 'atmospheres' for comfort and/or style, extended their service hours, increased the number of service products, and so on. In other service industries – such as tax consultancy, stockbrokerage, insurance and accommodation – the marketing concept has come in unevenly, with some firms taking major marketing steps (H. & R. Block, Eagle Star Insurance) but most others lagging behind.

As competition becomes keener, more marketing sophistication will be needed in service marketing. One of the main agents of change will be product marketers who decide to move into service industries because they see that this is where the economy is moving. Myer moved into services marketing with partial ownership of a travel company and full ownership of a large marketing-research firm. Xerox Corporation operates a major business in sales-management training (Xerox Learning), and Elders IXL has moved into television and radio.

One of the main needs in services marketing is to find ways to increase productivity. Since the service business is highly labour-intensive, costs have been accelerating, as exemplified by the soaring costs of hospital services. Many people incorrectly assume that little can be done to increase productivity in service businesses, but there are five possible approaches. The first is to have service providers work harder or more skilfully for the same pay; working harder is not a likely solution, but more skilful work can be achieved through better selection and training procedures. The second is to increase the quantity of service by surrendering some quality. The third is to add capital-intensive equipment to increase delivery capabilities. Levitt has recommended that management adopt a 'manufacturing attitude' toward the production of services, as represented by the assembly-line principles that McDonald's applied to fast-food retailing, culminating in the 'technological hamburger'.[9] Commercial dishwashing, jumbo jets, cinema complexes, and automatic tellers in banks all represent technological solutions to expanded service. The fourth is to reduce or remove the need for a service by inventing a product solution, as where television substituted for outside entertainment, the wash-and-wear shirt reduced the need for the commercial laundry, and penicillin reduced the need for tuberculosis sanitariums. The fifth approach is to design a more effective service that eliminates or reduces the need for a less effective service: the 'Life. Be In It.' campaign may reduce the need for more expensive curative medical services later on; word processors replace more expensive assistance in, for example, the legal profession.

Marketing-mix Decisions for Service Firms

Almost everything we have already said in this book about marketing-mix decisions applies to service firms as well as product firms. To illustrate this we will examine the dry-cleaning industry, and consider its product, price, place and promotion opportunities.

Product. Product planning is a challenging area for a service organization. A dry-cleaner offers to clean work clothes, recreation and business wear, blankets and drapes. The cleaner needs certain 'star' services to attract heavy users (e.g. ski-wear) and it needs some 'cash cows' (industrial garment contracts) to pay for some of its 'question marks' (home delivery) and 'dogs' (shoe-repair service). The manager has to be hard-headed about whether to keep an expensive but optional service, e.g. opening on Thursday and Friday nights until 9 p.m. Another aspect of product planning calls for customer feedback (complaint systems) so that the manager can be sure of rendering a quality product.

Price. Service industries must be more imaginative in their *pricing*. Many set their prices as a straightforward mark-up over cost (car mechanics), and others charge what the traffic will bear (restaurants). Yet there are many other ways of pricing that might meet the financial needs of the service provider and/or the clients. Dry-cleaners, for example, could vary their charges depending upon how quickly clothes are to be returned. Alternatively, discounts could be given for cash in advance of service as a means of achieving better cash flow and control. Quantity discounts could also be offered, as could special rates on those days of the week that attract less than full capacity. Arrangements could be made with large community groups so that they were offered special deals for their custom. There are many creative pricing approaches available to a service industry.

Place. Service providers have several options with respect to service *delivery systems*, although this is not always fully appreciated. Many people think that because services are intangible, inseparable and perishable, the concepts of intermediaries and physical distribution are not relevant. Consider, however, the services offered by a dry-cleaner. The major delivery system for dry-cleaning services is the shop front occupied by the salesperson. The owner hires the salesperson to deliver the service to customers face to face, but there are several different options available. An expansion-minded dry-cleaner could offer agencies in other shopping centres with retailers who would be willing to take the service on as a supplementary activity. A dry-cleaning company could establish its own retail shops in other centres and bring the garments for cleaning back to the shop with the processing equipment. These non-processing shops are known as dry stores. The next step would be to establish full processing plants in those dry stores where the market demand warranted it. Finally it may consider offering a home pick-up and delivery service for the segment of the market that is willing to pay for this convenience.

Promotion. Finally, service organizations have many opportunities as regards *promotion* of their business. Promotion can be used to build interest in the service, to differentiate the firm's offer from competitors' offers, and to build the organization's overall image. Service organizations can make extensive use of publicity, personal selling, advertising and even sales promotion.

Our dry-cleaner, for example, may rely on public relations to obtain local publicity. He may photograph customers who are celebrities and display the photographs in the shop or have them printed in the local press. Personal selling will be used extensively if industrial contracts are sought. For counter staff, there may be a need for training on how to deal with the customer and how to suggest other services.

Advertising might take the form of window displays, coupon discounts distributed in letterboxes, and advertising in local or business papers. For the industrial market, special brochures might be produced and direct mail actively engaged in.

Sales promotion might take the form of distributing paperweights advertising the firm's name to industrial buyers, or promotional coat-hangers given to retail customers.

One firm in Melbourne, City Wide Work Garment Service, offers prospective industrial buyers free consulting advice on garment control and maintenance systems as a promotional technique.

ORGANIZATION MARKETING

We will use the term organization marketing to describe those activities undertaken to create, maintain or alter attitudes and/or behaviour of target audiences toward particular organizations. Thus we do not mean the normal marketing activities undertaken to sell the organization's products and services, but rather those undertaken to sell the organization itself. Organization marketing has traditionally been the responsibility of the public-relations department. This is evident from the following widely used definition of public relations:

- *Public relations* is the management function which evaluates public attitudes, identifies the policies and procedures of an individual or an organization with the public interest, and plans and executes a programme of action to earn public understanding and acceptance.[10]

It has been argued that public relations is essentially marketing management shifted from a product to an organization.[11] Many of the same skills are needed: knowledge of audience needs, desires and psychology; skill at communication; an ability to design and execute programmes aimed at influence. The recognition of the similarities, or at least complementarities, between marketing and public relations has led several companies to combine both functions under single control.

The general methodology of organization marketing consists of three steps: (i) assessing the current image of the organization;

(ii) determining a desirable image for it; and (iii) developing a marketing plan for bringing about the desired image.

Image Assessment

No fruitful work can be achieved with an organization's image until research is conducted to determine how the organization is seen by its various key publics. The organization might be quite pleased with its measured image, and simply want to do the work necessary to maintain it; on the other hand, the organization might discover that it has some serious image problems, in which case its interest lies in correcting and improving its reputation.

Image assessment calls for developing a survey instrument to measure the organization's image amongst its major publics. One part of the survey will establish the visibility-favourability position, and the other will measure the content of the organization's image. One such survey was undertaken in 1979 in an endeavour to better understand attitudes to building societies.[12] It discovered that the banks retained their traditionally superior image, and were seen as offering the greatest security and variety of services.

Building societies suffered from a suspicion that large-scale withdrawal of funds was not as easy as it appeared. Although they were seen as offering attractive interest rates, there was a prevailing concern as to their security. Credit unions, which operate on a smaller scale using word of mouth or private promotion were little understood by the public: approximately one-quarter of the sample in the study associated the terms with 'buying on credit – a Bankcard kind of thing'.

Figure 20-1a illustrates the results of measuring the visibility-favourability images of five American management-consulting firms. The two firms in quadrant I are in the best position – firm 1, in particular, is highly visible and enjoys the highest repute. Firm 3 in quadrant II also has high repute, but is less well known: its marketing need is to increase its visibility so that more people will know how good it is. Firm 4 in quadrant III is less well regarded than the preceding firms, but fortunately not many people know about it. This firm should maintain a low profile and introduce improvements in its management-consulting practice designed to attract more approval. If effective, firm 4 will move to quadrant II, from which it can then seek more publicity. Finally, firm 5 in quadrant IV is

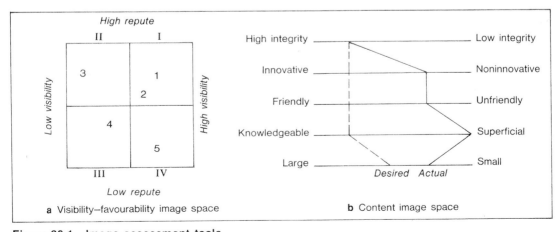

a Visibility–favourability image space

b Content image space

Figure 20-1 Image assessment tools

worst off in that it is seen as a poor service provider *and* everyone knows about this. The firm's best course of action is to try to reduce its visibility (which would move it to quadrant III) and then plan to move successively to quadrants II and I. Of course, this would take several years – if the firm ever accomplished it at all. Thus it should be clear that a firm's initial position in the visibility-favourability space defines the basic type of strategy it should pursue.

The second part of the image study is designed to reveal the content of the organization's image, and one of the major tools used here is the semantic differential.[13] The semantic differential involves identifying a set of appropriate object attributes and stating each in bipolar terms: respondents are asked to place a mark on each scale, according to their impression of the degree to which the object possesses that attribute. The researcher then averages the responses on each scale and represents this by a point: the points of the various scales are connected vertically, forming an image profile of the object.

Suppose firm 4 in Figure 20-1a finds its image profile to be that shown by the solid line in Figure 20-1b. Firm 4 is regarded as being high in integrity but not particularly innovative, friendly, knowledgeable or large. The firm will either be surprised to learn this or recognize its validity; in either case, the firm knows that these weaknesses handicap its growth and profitability.

The firm should recognize that its 'average' image, as shown in Figure 20-1, is probably not its image with every key public and even within one. An organization's image should be separately examined for each key public, and little marketing effort need be applied where this is acceptable. The image consistency should also be examined within each key public: the firm may want its image to be highly specific or may prefer it to be somewhat varied.

Image Choice

The next step calls for the organization to identify the image that it would like to have. It must be realistic and not aim for the 'impossible'. Let us assume that management-consulting firm 4 decides that a feasible and desirable image is that shown by the dashed line in Figure 20-1b. The firm is pleased with its integrity standing, but would like to be seen as more innovative, friendly and knowledgeable, as well as larger. It might place different weights on each image component so that it can concentrate on improving the more important ones. It might even seek to cultivate somewhat different images among different publics, as long as they are broadly consistent.

Image Planning and Control

At this point firm 4 has to develop a marketing plan that will eventually shift its actual image toward the desired one. If it wants to put most of the planning weight on increasing its reputation as a knowledgeable firm, and really lacks knowledgeable consultants, then the key step is to hire better consultants. If the firm has highly knowledgeable consultants but they are not very visible, then its task is to give them more exposure, e.g. they should be encouraged to join business and trade associations, give speeches, write articles, develop public seminars on 'hot' new topics, and sponsor awards that draw favourable attention to the firm and suggest their interest in advancing knowledge in the industry.[14]

From time to time the firm must re-survey its publics to see whether its activities have succeeded in improving its image. The job cannot be accomplished overnight because of the limitation of funds and the 'stickiness' of public images; but if the firm is making no progress, it should be concerned that either its substance or its image communications are deficient.

We have illustrated the methodology of organization marketing using the example of a management-consulting firm. Following are additional examples of organizations' taking concrete steps to improve their image among key publics:

- *Police force.* Police departments are often criticized by community groups. They have responded in a number of ways. Programmes are launched in which police officers visit schools, appear on television, and try in other ways to improve their image. Special exhibitions are mounted from time to time, explaining their operations. Various police-force administrators are beginning to talk about the use of market research (What does the public want from us?) and better distribution (where to locate police services in relation to crime rates).

- *Churches.* Churches have a long-standing interest in the problem of developing and maintaining believers. Missionary and evangelical work represents this tradition in its pure form; at certain points in history, enthusiasm for religious conversion reached unusual proportions, as in the Inquisition. Today the methods of attracting and maintaining members are more subtle. A book entitled *Successful Church Publicity* discusses the various problems of church marketing under such topics as 'publicizing the right message', 'slanting publicity toward prospects', 'word-of-mouth publicity', 'direct-mail campaigns', 'outdoor signs', 'chimes and sound systems'.[15] The Billy Graham organization is probably the most sophisticated evangelical organization in its use of modern campaign concepts involving words, music and celebrities, all orchestrated to inspire an outburst of religious feeling.

PERSON MARKETING

In addition to products, services and organizations, persons are also marketed. Person marketing consists of activities undertaken to create, maintain or alter attitudes and/or behaviour toward particular persons. The three most common types of person marketing are celebrity marketing, political-candidate marketing, and personal marketing.

Celebrity Marketing

Celebrity marketing has a long history going back to the Caesars; in recent times it has been most conspicuously associated with the build-up of movie stars and entertainers. Hollywood actors and actresses would hire press agents to promote their stardom. For a retainer, the press agent would manage to get frequent mentions and pictures of the star in the mass media and also schedule the star's appearance in highly visible locations and conventions. At one point in his career, Bing Crosby owed 60 per cent of every dollar he made to other people, including a personal manager, business manager, road manager, lawyer, and record company. One of the great promoters was the late Brian Epstein, who adroitly managed the Beatles' rise to stardom and, in the process, received a larger share of the money than any of them. The Australian Robert Stigwood is currently one of the most successful international operators in this sphere. Today celebrities are promoted not by single press agents but by entire organizations.

Celebrity marketers cannot work miracles – much of course depends on the talent and personality of the star. If the star is a born promoter, there is no limit. Elton John is said to have made the most money in the history of the music business: besides selling more than 42 million albums, his concerts are always packed. Elton wears one of several hundred pairs of glasses, pounds the piano with his feet, bats tennis-balls in the crowd, and hires actors to wander around the stage dressed as Frankenstein or Queen Elizabeth. Whether these are his ideas or those of his manager, he is able to carry them off.

Celebrity marketers all recognize that celebrity lifecycles are quite varied and often limited (see Figure 20-2). The head of marketing for Polygram, an international record conglomerate, likens a performer's career to a crate of strawberries that must be packaged, brought to the market, and sold before they spoil and become worthless. Mike Gormley, US publicity director for Mercury Records, describes a typical meeting: 'We get together every six weeks. We'll go down our sales figures. If we decide a group is getting "no action" – meaning no airplay or sales – we'll drop them. If promotion doesn't get results, you don't just throw away more money.'[16] Some 'has-been' celebrities, such as Eddie

Fisher, will try to make a comeback, but they find that it is a long road back to the top.[17]

Political-candidate Marketing

In Australia the marketing of political candidates is still emerging, but in the United States it has become a major industry and an area of specialization. Every few years the public is treated to an endless number of campaigns attempting to put various candidates for local, State and national offices in the best light. During the 1972 American presidential election year, the various candidates for all offices managed to spend over $US400 million in less than two months – on media advertising, direct mail and telephone, and other campaign methods.

Political campaigns have increasingly been compared to marketing campaigns: the candidate goes into the voter market and uses

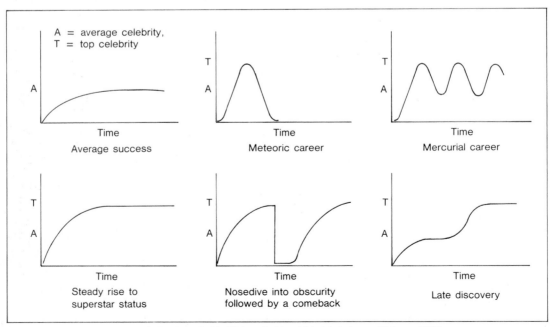

A = average celebrity,
T = top celebrity

Average success

Meteoric career

Mercurial career

Steady rise to superstar status

Nosedive into obscurity followed by a comeback

Late discovery

Source: Charles Seton, 'The Marketing of a Free Lance Fashion Photographer' (unpublished student paper, 20 January 1978).

Figure 20-2 Celebrity career lifecycles

modern marketing techniques, particularly marketing research and commercial advertising, to maximize voter 'purchase'. The marketing analogy is more than coincidental. The very essence of a candidate's interface with the voters is a marketing one, not only in recent times but far back into the past. Candidates seeking to win elections cannot avoid marketing themselves. The only question is how to do it effectively. Certainly the major political parties in Australia have, in recent years, been undertaking and studying marketing research to help them with their campaigns.

Interest in the marketing aspects of elections has been stimulated to a large extent by the spectacular growth in political advertising. There has also been a substantial growth of scientific opinion-polling (i.e. marketing research), and computer analysis of voting patterns (i.e. sales analysis). The subtleties of the marketing approach go beyond the rising expenditure levels and the use of certain information and planning approaches. They are delineated in a series of popular books, such as White's *The Making of the President 1960* and McGinness's *The Selling of the President 1968*.[18] In a quieter way, several scholarly works have also noted the marketing character of political elections.[19]

It would be a gross mistake to think that election campaigns have taken on a marketing character only in recent years. Prior to the new methodology, candidates sought office through the handshake, baby-kissing, teas and speech-making. They still use these methods – the new methodology is not the introduction of marketing methods into politics but rather an increased sophistication and acceleration of their use. According to Glick:

> The personal handshake, the local fund-raising dinner, the neighbourhood tea, the rally, the precinct captain and the car pool to the polls are still very much with us ... the new campaign has provided a carefully coordinated strategic framework within which the traditional activities are carried out in keeping with a Master

Plan. It centers on a shift from the candidate-controlled, loosely knit, often haphazard 'play-it-by-ear' approach to that of a precise, centralized 'team' strategy for winning or keeping office. Its hallmarks include the formal strategic blueprint, the coordinated use of specialized propaganda skills, and a more subtle approach to opinion measurement and manipulation. And, though there is a world of difference between selling a candidate and merchandising soap or razor blades, some of the attributes of commercial advertising have been grafted into the political process.[20]

Political candidates seeking election start with marketing research to identify and understand the major marketing segments and the major issues of concern to each. They and their advisers then develop a candidate concept, consisting of a political philosophy, choice of issues and positions, a personal style, and a description of the candidate's background and qualifications. The next step calls for developing a communication and distribution strategy involving the use of mass and selective media, scheduled personal appearances, and the assistance of volunteers and party workers. Through these marketing tools the candidate is prepared to wage a good fight for votes, with the ultimate outcome determined by the voters.[21]

Personal Marketing

Personal marketing encompasses the efforts of individuals to create certain impressions about themselves in the minds of others. Erving Goffman considers impression management a ubiquitous human trait,[22] and Erich Fromm observes that 'in order to have success it is not sufficient to have the skill and equipment for performing a given task but that one must be able to "put across" one's personality in competition with many others'.[23] Gilbert and Sullivan gave this advice: 'If you wish in the world to advance/ Your merits you're bound to enhance/ You must stir it and stump it, and blow your trumpet/ Or, trust me, you haven't a chance.'

Personal marketing takes on higher-than-normal importance during job interviewing, public appearances, and romantic courtship. Many books have been written advising job-seekers (whether they be tertiary students, professors and lecturers, or seasoned executives) how to write better curricula vitae and conduct better interviews. Gootnick, for example, provides the following advice:

1. *Pre-interview.* Arrive a little earlier to get into the right frame of mind; if you will be late, phone the interviewer; look businesslike.

2. *Interview opening.* Use the interviewer's name and apply a firm handshake; flow with the small talk and be relaxed.

3. *Interview development.* Start developing why you are interested in the job, and your qualifications.

4. *Interview closing.* Summarize your key credentials, express enthusiasm, express appreciation, and ask what the next step will be.

5. *Post-interview.* Record the key points about the company on paper and evaluate your own success on appearance, oral communications skill, and social skill. Send a 'thank you' letter in about five days expressing appreciation and reiterating your key qualifications.[24]

Clearly, the whole framework resembles that of a sales presentation.

In the United States in 1974, company recruiters were surveyed as to the importance of different candidate attributes and ranked them as follows: (i) personality and leadership potential; (ii) motivation and clear-cut goals; (iii) maturity and previous business (or military) experience; (iv) communication skills; (v) analytical ability; (vi) reputation of the school; and (vii) grades.[25] Among the things that most hurt in an interview are poor appearance; inability to express oneself; poor listening skills; lack of common courtesy; lack of preparation for interview; lack of confidence, interest and enthusiasm; conceit and overconfidence; being evasive, deceitful and dishonest; high-pressure selling; and being long-winded or abrupt.[26]

The key point is that the job-seeker must see the recruiting company as a buyer and try to understand the buyer's motives and buying criteria. Then it is up to the job-seeker to determine whether he has the necessary qualifications and wants to use personal marketing to get the job. The objective is not to falsify one's true self, which would eventually catch up with the person on the job, but to project oneself in as favourable a light as possible given what business firms look for in applicants. A person who cannot succeed in this is probably mismatched to a corporate business career in the first place.

Interestingly enough, at the same time that job-seekers are marketing themselves, so is the recruiting company. A recruiter who is interested in a specific candidate will try to impress the candidate and position the company favourably against other companies. The recruiter and the job-seeker will try equally hard to understand each other's choice criteria.[27] Thus while the job-seeker is doing personal marketing, the company is doing organizational marketing.

> To help job-seekers and ambitious executives, a cottage industry of 'image doctors' has sprung up to give business pros advice about everything from what to wear to what to say and how to say it. For a sizeable fee, these consultants will lower the pitch of your voice, remove your accent, correct your 'body language', modify your unacceptable behaviour, eliminate your negative self-perceptions, select your wardrobe, restyle your hair, and teach you how to speak off the cuff or read a speech without putting your audience to sleep.[28]

The various personal-image consultants, who take on both corporate and individual clients, consist of speech and public appearance trainers, dress consultants, and personal public-relations consultants.[29]

PLACE MARKETING

Place marketing involves activities undertaken to create, maintain or alter attitudes and/or behaviour toward particular places. Five types of place marketing can be distinguished.

Domicile Marketing

Domicile marketing involves the effort to develop and/or promote the sale or rental of single-family dwellings, flats and other types of housing units. Domicile marketing has traditionally relied on classified ads and real-estate agents. Advanced marketing practices have recently emerged in connection with home-unit selling and the development of total communities.[30] Large builders attempt to research housing needs, and develop products attuned to the price ranges and preferences of specific market segments. Some high-rise apartments have been built for the young set, others for the geriatric set – filled with the features, symbols and services appropriate to each. Entire housing communities have been designed with specific lifecycle and/or lifestyle groups in mind. Increasingly TV advertising, direct mail and larger newspaper and journal advertisements are replacing traditional means of promotion.

Business-site Marketing

Business-site marketing involves the effort to develop, sell or rent business sites or properties such as plants, stores, offices and warehouses. Larger developers have become quite sophisticated in researching business needs and responding with total real-estate solutions, such as industrial parks, shopping centres, and new office buildings. Most States operate departments concerned with promoting industrial development, which try to sell the advantages of local circumstances to companies and may offer to fly prospects to the site when necessary. The Victorian Department of State

Development, Decentralization and Tourism, for example, has flown prospective investors to Portland – an area that the government wishes to develop because of its deep sea port facilities.

Land-investment Marketing

Land-investment marketing involves efforts to develop and sell land for investment purposes. The buyers – companies, doctors, small investors, speculators – plan to sell the land when it rises sufficiently in value. Land-investment marketing has been instrumental in developing large parts of the Gold Coast. Over the years, land developers have worked out elaborate marketing programmes involving mass-media advertising and publicity, direct mail, personal sales calls, free dinner meetings, and even free flights to the site.

Holiday Marketing

Holiday marketing involves the effort to attract holidaymakers to various spas, resorts, cities, States and even whole nations. The effort is carried on by travel agents, airlines, motor clubs, oil companies, hotels, motels, and various government units.

Holiday marketers have classified tourists into major types and scrutinized their behaviour in order to develop more targeted communication appeals.[31] Today almost every city and State in the nation is in the business of advertising and publicizing its tourist attractions. Bikini-clad meter maids are a promotional device used by the Gold Coast to publicize the area to southern Australians during the winter months. In the case of Tasmania the establishment of a casino assisted in attracting more tourists and convention traffic to the State; this has been a factor in the proposals to legalize casinos in New South Wales and Queensland.

Overseas, some places are using marketing

techniques just as strenuously to demarket themselves. In the United States, Florida's Palm Beach is letting its beach erode to discourage tourists; Oregon has put out some negative statements about its weather; Yosemite National Park is considering prohibiting snowmobiles, conventions and private cars; and several European countries, such as Finland and France, could consider discouraging tourists from holidaying in certain areas where they feel the ravages of mass tourism exceed the revenues. Some conservationists believe that such a strategy should be implemented on the more popular parts of the Great Barrier Reef to ensure that the attraction is not damaged.

Nation Marketing

Nations engage in continuous public-relation activities to win a favourable image among the citizens of other countries. The day-to-day job is carried on by the information officers attached to embassies. One officer said his job was to 'project the true image of his country'[32]; others describe this work as propaganda, which is defined as 'the deliberate attempt by some individual or group to form, control or alter the attitudes of other groups by the use of the instruments of communication, with the intention that in any given situation the reaction of those so influenced will be that desired by the propagandist'.[33] Arthur E. Meyerhoff, the managing director of an advertising agency in the United States, observed:

> We have not effectively applied our sales techniques to selling ourselves and our ideas to other countries . . . the job has never been given to the people who know how to do it. These are people who have popularized cornflakes and automobiles, and they are skilled in the art of persuasion, which is the basis for successful propaganda.[34]

IDEA MARKETING

One further application of marketing theory is to the marketing of ideas. Meyerhoff's comment in the preceding paragraph suggests marketing the idea of American democracy more effectively to other nations: in one sense, all marketing is the marketing of ideas, whether it be the idea of brushing one's teeth, the idea that Colgate is the most effective decay preventer, or anything else. Here, however, 'idea marketing' will be used to cover efforts to market ideas as such; and we will further confine our discussion to the marketing of social ideas.

Social ideas are embodied in public health campaigns to reduce smoking, alcoholism, drug abuse, and overeating; environmental campaigns to promote wilderness protection, clean air, and resource conservation; and a myriad of other campaigns such as family planning, women's rights, and racial equality. This idea has been called social marketing, and it is defined as follows:[35]

- *Social marketing* is the design, implementation and control of programmes seeking to increase the acceptability of a social idea, cause or practice in a target group(s). It utilizes market segmentation, consumer research, concept development, communications, facilitation, incentives, and exchange theory to maximize target-group response.

Social marketing, in contrast to ordinary business marketing, has the characteristics of a change technology rather than a response technology. In trying to get smokers to stop smoking, social marketing seems to be based on the selling concept rather than the marketing concept. But consumer orientation is not ignored: to try and formulate an effective marketing plan to encourage people to give up smoking, the social marketer tries to understand why smokers smoke, what pleasures they get, and what difficulties they have in trying to stop.

Social marketing may have various objectives: (i) to produce understanding (knowing the nutritional value of different foods); (ii) to trigger a particular one-time action (participating in a mass immunization campaign); (iii) to attempt to change behaviour (car seat-belt campaigns); (iv) to change a basic belief (convincing people to prefer socialism).

Social marketing calls for much more than public advertising. Many public campaigns fail because of the tendency to assign advertising the primary, if not the exclusive, role in accomplishing social objectives. This ignores the marketing truism that a given marketing objective requires coordination of the promotional mix with the goods-and-service mix and the distribution mix. Wiebe, in a study of four social campaigns in the United States, showed how their differential success was related to how closely they resembled the conditions of selling a normal product or service.[36] The great success of an evening radio marathon to sell government bonds was due, in Wiebe's opinion, to the presence of force (patriotism), direction (buy bonds), mechanism (banks, post offices, telephone orders), adequacy and compatibility (many centres to purchase the bonds), and distance (ease of purchase). These easily translate into factors such as product, price, place and promotion. The other three social campaigns – recruiting civil defence volunteers, stimulating people to take steps to help juvenile delinquents, and arousing citizens against crime – met with much less success because of the lack or mishandling of product, price, place or promotion variables.

Any organization with a cause can approach its task by developing a marketing plan. Thus social marketing may be said to take place if the Melbourne-based Hospital Benefits Association sponsors a campaign against alcohol and drug dependency, or if Comalco sponsors a campaign calling upon people to dispose of their empty soft-drink containers in a responsible manner. Furthermore, the concepts and techniques making up social marketing are available to all sides of an issue. We cannot call it 'social marketing' if we agree with the cause, and 'propaganda' if we disagree with it: groups in favour of, *and* opposed to abortion can both use social marketing.

The social marketer, in designing a strategy for social change, goes through a normal planning process. The first step is to define the social-change objective, e.g. 'to reduce the number of teenage smokers from 60 per cent to 40 per cent of the teenage population within five years'. The next step is to analyze the beliefs, attitudes, values and behaviour of the target group – here teenagers – and identify key segments of this market who would respond to different approaches. An analysis is also made of the major competitive forces that support teenage smoking. This is followed by concept research, in which the social marketer generates and tests alternative concepts that might be effective in dissuading teenagers from smoking (see Exhibit 20-1). The next step is channel analysis, in which the social marketer identifies and assesses the most effective communication and distribution approaches to the target market. This is followed by formal development of both a marketing plan and an organization to carry it out. Finally, provision is made to regularly monitor results and take corrective action when called for.

Social marketing is still too new for its effectiveness to be evaluated in comparison with other social-change strategies. Social change is hard to produce with any strategy, let alone one that relies on voluntary response. The ideas of social marketing have been mainly applied in the areas of family planning,[37] environmental protection,[38] energy conservation, improved nutrition, road safety, and public transport, with some encouraging successes. More applications will have to take

Exhibit 20-1 Can Social Marketing Reduce Cigarette Smoking?

The weight of scientific evidence demonstrates a link between cigarette smoking and such medical ailments as lung cancer, heart disease, and emphysema. Most cigarette smokers are aware of the bad effects of cigarette smoking. The problem is one of formulating and distributing solutions that will give them the means or will to reduce their cigarette dependence. The four P's suggest several possible types of solutions:

1. *Product*
   a) Require manufacturers to add a tart or bitter ingredient to the tobacco.
   b) Find a way to further reduce the tar and nicotine in cigarettes (e.g. develop better filters).
   c) Find a new type of tobacco that tastes good but does not have harmful ingredients (e.g. lettuce leaf).
   d) Find or promote other products that will help people relieve their tensions (e.g. chewing-gum).

2. *Promotion*
   a) Increase fear of early death among smokers.
   b) Create guilt or shame among cigarette users.
   c) Strengthen some other goal of smokers that supersedes their satisfaction from smoking.
   d) Urge smokers to cut down the number of cigarettes they smoke or to smoke only the first half of the cigarette.

3. *Place*
   a) Make cigarettes less accessible.
   b) Make cigarettes unavailable.
   c) Make it easier for cigarette smokers to find places offering help, like anti-smoking clinics.
   d) Make it harder to find public places that allow cigarette smoking.

4. *Price*
   a) Raise substantially the price of a packet of cigarettes.
   b) Raise the cost of life and health insurance to smokers.
   c) Offer a monetary or other reward to smokers for each period they forego smoking.

Anti-smoking campaigns appear to be worthwhile. However, social marketers should be aware of some unanticipated secondary consequences. People who stop smoking have a tendency to eat more and gain weight. Overweight is estimated to shorten people's lives by approximately fourteen years, whereas smoking is estimated to shorten people's lives by seven years. Liquor, interestingly enough, is estimated to shorten consumers' lives by four years. This may suggest that the social marketer should either leave the smoker alone or encourage the smoker to stop smoking and start drinking.

place before we can actually determine social marketing's potential as a tool for social change.

SUMMARY

Marketing was first developed in connection with products, but has been broadened in recent years to cover other 'marketable' entities, i.e. services, organizations, persons, places and ideas.

Australian society is in an era when the majority of people are employed in service industries (as is also the case in the United States). Services can be defined as activities or benefits that one party can offer to another that do not result in the ownership of anything; services are intangible, inseparable, variable and perishable. Services can be classified according to whether they are people-based or equipment-based, whether the client's presence is necessary, whether the client is a consumer or business, and whether the service provider is a profit or non-profit firm in the private or public sector. Service industries have lagged behind manufacturing firms in adopting and using marketing concepts, but rising costs and increased competition have forced them to search for new ways to increase their productivity. Marketing can make a contribution by applying more systematic planning to service concepts and their pricing, distribution and promotion.

Organizations can also be marketed. Organization marketing describes those activities undertaken to create, maintain or alter attitudes and/or behaviour of target audiences toward particular organizations. It calls for three steps: (i) assessing the organization's current image; (ii) determining a desirable image; and (iii) developing a marketing plan for bringing about the desired image.

Person marketing consists of activities undertaken to create, maintain or alter attitudes and/or behaviour toward particular persons. The three most common types are celebrity marketing, political-candidate marketing, and personal marketing.

Place marketing involves activities undertaken to create, maintain or alter attitudes and/or behaviour toward particular places. The five most common types are domicile marketing, business-site marketing, land-investment marketing, holiday marketing, and nation marketing.

Idea marketing involves efforts to market ideas. In the case of social ideas it is called social marketing and consists of the design, implementation and control of programmes seeking to increase the acceptability of a social idea, cause or practice in a target group. Social marketing goes further than public advertising in that it coordinates advertising with the other elements of the marketing mix. The social marketer proceeds by defining the social objective, analysing consumer attitudes and competitive forces, developing and testing alternative concepts, developing appropriate channels for the idea's communication and distribution and, finally, monitoring the results. Social marketing has been applied in the areas of family planning, environmental protection, anti-smoking campaigns, and other public issues.

QUESTIONS FOR DISCUSSION

1. Relate the four distinctive characteristics of services to a service that you have purchased recently.

2. Producers of services have historically been more marketing-oriented than producers of products. Comment.

3. Explain how the distribution channel is important to the following service marketers:
   - Arthur Andersen (a large accounting firm)
   - Armaguard (the Mayne Nickless security service)
   - Joe's Repair Shop
   - a local drama group.

4. What is the primary purpose of an individual responsible for organization marketing? Explain.

5. How would you apply 'personal marketing' to your attempt to secure a job?

6. The only places that can effectively be marketed are those that people enjoy visiting. Comment.

7. What distinguishes social marketing from social advertising? Explain.

NOTES

[1] 'Services Grow While the Quality Shrinks', *Business Week*, 30 October 1971, p. 50.

[2] For a good discussion of quality-control systems at the Marriott Hotel chain in the United States, see G. M. Hostage, 'Quality of Control in a Service Business', *Harvard Business Review*, July–August 1975, pp. 98–106.

[3] See W. Earl Sasser, 'Match Supply and Demand in Service Industries', *Harvard Business Review*, November–December 1976, pp. 133–40.

[4] See Dan R. E. Thomas, 'Strategy Is Different in Service Businesses', *Harvard Business Review*, July–August 1978, p. 161.

[5] William R. George & Hiram C. Barksdale, 'Marketing Activities in the Service Industries', *Journal of Marketing*, October 1974, p. 65.

[6] James Hearne & Christine Beckingsale, 'How the Professional can use Marketing', *Rydge's in Marketing*, 7 January 1981, p. 12.

[7] See Daniel T. Carroll, 'Ten Commandments for Bank Marketing', *Bankers Magazine*, Autumn 1970, pp. 74–80. In Australia, this change has been hastened by the deregulation of the finance industry (following the 1981 Campbell Report), and the amalgamation of banks.

[8] See G. Lynn Shostack, 'Banks Sell Services – Not Things', *Bankers Magazine*, Winter 1977, pp. 40–50. The experience has been similar in Australia, although nothing has yet been published on this trend.

[9] Theodore Levitt, 'Product-Line Approach to Service', *Harvard Business Review*, September–October 1972, pp. 41–52; also see his 'The Industrialization of Service', *Harvard Business Review*, September–October 1976, pp. 63–74.

[10] *Public Relations News*, 27 October 1947.

[11] For this argument, see Philip Kotler & William Mindak, 'Marketing and Public Relations', *Journal of Marketing*, October 1978, pp. 13–20.

[12] A private report, entitled 'Attitudes to Building Societies', commissioned by the Victorian Building Societies' Association.

[13] The semantic-differential technique was originally presented in C. E. Osgood, C. J. Suci, & P. H. Tannenbaum, *The Measurement of Meaning* (Urbana, Ill.: University of Illinois Press, 1957). For a discussion of various image-measurement techniques, see Philip Kotler, *Marketing for Nonprofit Organizations* (Englewood Cliffs, N.J.: Prentice-Hall, 1975), pp. 131–37.

[14] For additional ways to market the services of a professional services firm, see Philip Kotler & Richard A. Connor Jr, 'Marketing Professional Services', *Journal of Marketing*, January 1977, pp. 71–76.

[15] Carl F. H. Henry, *Successful Church Publicity: A Guidebook for Christian Publicists* (Grand Rapids, Mich.: Zondervan Publishing House, 1943).

[16] 'In the Groove at Mercury Records', *Chicago Daily News*, Panorama magazine, 16 October 1976.

[17] John E. Cooney, 'Eddie Fisher Discovers That Regaining Fame is a Daunting Goal', *Wall Street Journal*, 20 February 1978, p. 1.

[18] Theodore White, *The Making of the President 1960* (New York: Atheneum, 1961); and Joe McGinness, *The Selling of the President 1968* (New York: Trident Press, 1969).

[19] See E. Glick, *The New Methodology* (Washington, D.C.: American Institute for Political Communication, 1967); and Dan Nimmo, *The Political Persuaders: The Techniques of Modern Election Campaigns* (Englewood Cliffs, N.J.: Prentice-Hall, 1970).

[20] Glick, p. 1.

[21] For an elaboration, see Kotler, *Marketing for Nonprofit Organizations*, Ch. 19, 'Political Candidate Marketing', pp. 365–88.

[22] Erving Goffman, *The Presentation of Self in Everyday Life* (New York: Doubleday Anchor Books, 1959), p. xi.

[23] Erich Fromm, *Man for Himself* (New York: Holt, Rinehart & Winston, 1947), pp. 67–116.

[24] David Gootnick, *Getting a Better Job* (New York: McGraw-Hill, 1978).

[25] 'Grading the Recruit', *MBA Magazine*, March 1974, p. 43.

[26] Gootnick, op. cit.

[27] Orlando Behling, George Labovitz & Marion Gainer, 'College Recruiting: A Theoretical Base', *Personnel Journal*, January 1968, pp. 13–19.

[28] Jacqueline A. Thompson, 'The Image Doctors: A Guide to the Personal Packaging Consultants', *MBA Magazine*, September 1977, p. 1.

[29] For a list of firms, see Thompson, pp. 24, 25, 28, 29.

[30] For a description of the marketing of 'The Woodlands', a new town in Texas, see Betsy D. Gelb & Ben M. Enis, 'Marketing a City of the Future', in *Marketing Is Everybody's Business* (Santa Monica, Calif.: Goodyear, 1977).

[31] See William D. Perreault, Donna K. Darden & William R. Darden, 'A Psychographic Classification of Vacation Life Styles', *Journal of Leisure Research*, 9, No. 3 (1977), pp. 208–24.

[32] Yair Aharoni, 'How to Market a Country', *Columbia Journal of World Business*, Spring 1966, pp. 41–49.

[33] Terrence H. Qualter, *Propaganda and Psychological Warfare* (New York: Random House, 1962), p. 27.

[34] Arthur E. Meyerhoff, *The Strategy of Persuasion: The Use of Advertising Skills in Fighting the Cold War* (New York: Berkley Publishing, 1968), pp. 14–15.

[35] See Philip Kotler & Gerald Zaltman, 'Social Marketing: An Approach to Planned Social Change', *Journal of Marketing*, July 1971, pp. 3–12.

[36] G. D. Wiebe, 'Merchandising Commodities and Citizenship on Television', *Public Opinion Quarterly*, Winter 1951–52, pp. 679–91.

[37] See Eduardo Roberto, *Strategic Decision-Making in a Social Program: The Case of Family-Planning Diffusion* (Lexington, Mass.: Lexington Books, 1975).

[38] See Karl E. Henion II, *Ecological Marketing* (Columbus, Ohio: Grid, 1975).

Marketing and Society

21

When the Clemenger network of advertising agencies conducted a national research study into the 'everyday problems of the average Australian',[1] it found that the following problems were the 'top 40' in terms of people being either quite concerned or very concerned about them.

The top problems	Quite concerned (%)	Very concerned (%)
1. High prices of food	18	73
2. High cost of repairs in relation to initial cost of the article	20	70
3. Too many strikes	14	70
4. High personal income tax	16	66
5. Re-pricing of old stock in supermarkets to today's prices	16	65
6. Light penalties for law-breakers	21	64
7. High unemployment, especially among young people	21	64
8. The best television programmes showing at the same time on different channels	22	63
9. Too many television commercials	21	63
10. Prices no longer an indication of quality	23	62

11. Union members lack say in union decisions	17	62
12. Packaging that adds too much to the cost of products	24	61
13. Showing the best television programmes only during rating weeks	21	61
14. Pollution in our cities	25	60
15. Excessive wage demands	18	60
16. Rising prices and declining quality of cars	20	59
17. Government making it too easy for people not to work	18	59
18. The absence of secret ballots in union matters	15	59
19. Higher postal charges with reduced postal services	22	58
20. Too many faulty new cars	21	57
21. Having to watch the same television commercial more than twice in one hour	20	57
22. Advertising on television that 'yells' at you	18	57
23. Poor television programmes over the Christmas/New Year period	18	57
24. High cost of financing land/housing	15	57
25. Poor standards of driving and road courtesy	27	56
26. Too few good television programmes	27	56
27. Lack of interest and attention by retail staff	26	56
28. Poor quality taken too much for granted	30	55
29. Union leaders caring only about their particular members, not workers generally	21	55
30. Sales staff that don't know enough about what they are selling	25	54
31. Workers becoming lazy	25	54
32. Clothing that is poorly made	25	54
33. Waiting for service in shops	23	54
34. The high cost of petrol	19	54
35. Service work not carried out properly	25	53
36. Poor television on Friday and Saturday nights compared to the rest of the week	23	53
37. People not taking pride in their work	30	52
38. Not enough permanent accommodation for the old and infirm	25	52

39. *Children leaving school without the basic skills*	24	52
40. *Prices in Australia that are kept high by tariff barriers*	23	52

Although reactions to this list will vary, the principal response will probably be to wonder at the apparent priorities of our fellow Australians, particularly the preoccupation with television. However, a closer scrutiny of the list reveals the substantial dissatisfaction with many areas of marketing activity.

Responsible marketers seek to interpret buyer wants and respond with appropriate products, priced to yield good value to the buyers and profit to the producer. The marketing concept is a philosophy of service and mutual gain – its practice leads the economy by an invisible hand to satisfy the diverse and changing needs of millions of consumers.

Not all marketing conforms to this theory. Some individuals and companies engage in questionable marketing practices; and certain private marketing transactions, seemingly innocent in themselves, have profound implications for the larger society. Consider the sale of cigarettes. In theory, companies should be free to sell cigarettes and smokers should be free to buy them. However, this transaction is tinged with public interest. First, the smoker may be shortening his own life. Second, this places a burden on the smoker's family, and on society at large. Third, other people in the presence of the smoker may have to inhale the smoke and may experience discomfort and harm. This is not to say that cigarettes should be banned; rather it shows that private transactions may involve profound questions of public policy.

The businessperson can easily brush aside public policy questions by pointing to the great wealth created in Australia by its mass-production and mass-consumption philosophy. Surely a few excesses, abuses and wastes are a small price to pay for the cornucopia of material goods enjoyed in this country.

But this attitude is dangerous. If the public feels there are things wrong with marketing, it is folly to ignore these feelings. For reasons of both self-interest and conscience, marketers should critically examine their role in society.

This chapter will consider the macro-consequences of micromarketing behaviour. It will address the following questions:

1. What are the most frequent social criticisms levelled against private marketing activity?
2. What steps have private citizens taken to try to curb or correct alleged marketing ills?
3. What steps have legislators and government agencies taken to try to curb or correct alleged marketing ills?
4. What steps have enlightened companies taken to carry out socially responsible marketing?
5. What principles might guide future public policy toward marketing?

SOCIAL CRITICISMS OF MARKETING

Aspects of marketing which are subject to social criticism can be classified according to whether they are alleged to hurt individual consumers, society as a whole, or other business firms. We will examine the major criticisms in the following paragraphs.

Marketing's Impact on Individual Consumer Welfare

Critics have accused the Australian marketing system of harming consumers through high prices, deceptive practices, high-pressure selling, shoddy or unsafe products, planned obsolescence, and poor service to disadvantaged consumers.

High prices. Many critics charge that the Australian marketing system causes prices to be higher than they would be under more 'sensible' arrangements. They point to three different factors.

High costs of distribution. A longstanding accusation is that product prices are inflated by greedy intermediaries who apply mark-ups substantially beyond the value of their services. This criticism is an ancient one: Plato held that shopkeepers practised acquisitive rather than productive arts and brought nothing new into existence; Aristotle condemned shopkeepers as making their profit at the expense of the buyer. These views persisted into the Middle Ages, with the Church placing various restrictions on intermediaries.

One of the most thorough contemporary studies of distribution costs appeared in 1939 in the book *Does Distribution Cost Too Much?*[2]. The work was undertaken after it was observed that selling and distribution costs rose from 19.8 per cent of product costs in 1850 to 50.4 per cent of product costs in 1920. The authors concluded that distribution did cost too much and pointed their finger at '. . .

duplication of sales efforts, multiplicity of sales outlets, excessive services, multitudes of brands, and unnecessary advertising . . . misinformed buying on the part of consumers . . . and, among distributors themselves, lack of a proper knowledge of costs, too great zeal for volume, poor management and planning, and unwise price policies'.[3]

How do retailers answer these charges? First, they argue, intermediaries undertake a lot of work that would otherwise have to be performed by the manufacturers or the consumers. Second, the rising mark-up covers the provision of improved services that consumers want: more convenience, larger stores and assortment, longer trading hours, return privileges, and so on. Third, the costs of operating stores, such as personnel and utilities, keep rising and forcing retailers to raise their prices. Fourth, competition in much of retailing is so intense that margins are actually quite low: for example, supermarket chains are barely left with one per cent profit on their sales after taxes.

High advertising and promotion costs. Modern marketing is also accused of pushing up prices because of the heavy use of advertising and sales promotion. First, 'commodity' products – petrol, aspirin, coffee, sugar, flour, cigarettes – are branded and heavily promoted by manufacturers to create psychological differentiation. For example, a dozen tablets of a well-known brand of aspirin sell for the same price as 100 tablets of lesser-known brands. Critics feel that if commodity products were sold in bulk, their prices would be considerably lower. Second, with slightly differentiated products – cosmetics, detergents, toiletries – the costs of packaging and promotion can amount to 40 per cent or more of the manufacturer's price to the retailer. Much of the packaging and promotion adds psychological rather than functional value to the product. Furthermore, many retailers undertake their own promotional efforts – advertising, games of chance, and so on –

thereby adding several more cents to retail prices.

Businesspeople answer these charges with the following observations. First, consumers are not interested only in the functional aspects of products. They buy concepts, such as products that make them feel affluent, beautiful or special, and the manufacturer's task is to develop concepts for which consumers are willing to pay. Consumers usually have the option of buying purely functional versions of the product at a lower price. Second, branding exists to give confidence to buyers – a brand name signifies a certain quality, and consumers are willing to pay for well-known brands even if they cost a little more. Third, heavy advertising is necessary simply to inform potential buyers of the existence and merits of a brand. If consumers want to know what is available on the market, they must expect manufacturers to spend large sums of money on advertising. Fourth, advertising and other promotion is necessary for the individual enterprise because competitors are doing it. The individual enterprise would risk its survival if it did not match competitive expenditures at some level to gain and hold 'share of mind'. At the same time, companies are very cost-conscious about promotion and try to spend their money wisely. Fifth, heavy sales promotion is necessary from time to time because goods are produced ahead of demand in a mass-production economy; special incentives have to be offered to buyers to clear excess inventories.

Excessive mark-ups. Critics charge that certain business sectors are particularly guilty of marking up goods excessively. They point to

Exhibit 21-1 No Free Lunch?

As the man who did more to elevate the humble roll of film to the exalted status of the Hills hoist and Victa lawn-mower, Mr Neil Cottee has developed some rather astonishing thoughts on his achievement. Mr Cottee, who pioneered the free-replacement-film sales gimmick at Pacific Film more than a decade ago, an idea the marketers have clung to ever since, now sees it as the major evil in the industry.

Last week Mr Cottee broke five months of silence since his retirement from Pacific Film in August to issue some stern words on the direction of the photo-finishing industry in Australia. And in particular he attacked his promotional baby, a free replacement film, as a confidence trick. 'The Australian public is still being subjected to rip-offs that are quite astounding . . . there is no such thing as a free lunch and there is no such thing as a free film,' Mr Cottee said last week. The costs of the so-called free film are being passed onto the consumer, 'prints are 40 cents – they should not be more than 25 cents or 30 cents'.

Speaking from his Bowral, New South Wales, property – his home since he abandoned city living – he was at first reluctant to criticize the industry. But when pressed he said he disagreed with the management methods of all the major companies in the Australian industry – including the company he founded, Pacific Film. When he introduced the free-replacement film notion fourteen years ago it was 'a good promotional idea' but 'not even a first-year marketing student would expect it to last 14 years. I was agitating to kill free film a few years ago.'

Source: Denny Groth, 'Cottee Looks Beyond Pacific', *Australian Financial Review*, 8 January 1980, pp. 1, 4.

the pharmaceutical industry, where a pill costing five cents to manufacture may cost the consumer forty cents; they point to the pricing tactics of funeral homes, which prey on the emotions of bereaved relatives;[4] they point to the high prices of television and car repairs. The alleged exploitation is dramatized from time to time in books with such provocative titles as *The Ugly Face of Australian Business, The Poor Pay More, The Hucksters, The Permissible Lie, The Innocent Consumer vs. the Exploiters, The Thumb on the Scale or the Supermarket Shell Game,* and *100 000 000 Guinea Pigs.*

Businesspeople respond to these criticisms with the following observations. First, there are unfortunately some unscrupulous business-owners who take advantage of consumers: they should be reported to consumer-affairs bureaus and other agencies set up to protect consumers. Second, most business-owners deal fairly with consumers because they want continuing business. Third, consumers often overlook the justification for high prices: for example, pharmaceutical mark-ups cover not only the cost of purchasing, promoting and distributing existing medicines, but also the huge costs spent in the search for new and improved medicines.

Deceptive practices. Businesspeople are often accused of engaging in deceptive practices, i.e. leading consumers to believe they will get more value than they actually do. Certain industries account for a disproportionate share of these complaints. Amongst the worst offenders are certain insurance companies (alleging that policies are 'guaranteed renewable' or underwritten by the government), publishing companies (approaching subscribers under false pretences), mail-order land-sales organizations (misrepresenting land or improvement costs), home-improvement contractors (using bait-and-switch tactics), automotive repair shops (advertising ultra-low repair prices and then 'discovering' a necessary major repair),

home-freezer plans (falsely representing the savings), correspondence schools (overstating employment opportunities after course completion), vending-machine companies (falsely guaranteeing top locations), studios offering dance instruction (signing up elderly people for lessons beyond their life expectancy), and companies selling medical devices (exaggerating therapeutic claims).

Three types of deceptive practices may be distinguished. *Deceptive pricing* includes such practices as advertising 'factory' or 'wholesale' prices falsely, or advertising a large price reduction from list where the list was artificially high. *Deceptive promotion* includes overstating the product's attributes, misrepresenting the guarantees, falsely photographing the product's accomplishments, luring the customer to the store for a bargain that is out of stock or downgraded by the salesperson, and running rigged contests. *Deceptive packaging* includes exaggerating the apparent contents of a package through a subtle design, not filling the package to the top, advertising cents-off on the package when it is the normal price, and describing the size in misleading terms.

Deceptive practices in these areas have given rise to legislative and administrative remedies. In 1974 the Trade Practices Act gave the Trade Practices Commission clear powers to regulate unfair or deceptive acts or practices, and the commission has since published several guidelines. The toughest problem remains in the area of trying to distinguish between puffery and deception in advertising.

Defenders of advertising freedom offer three arguments. First, most businesspeople avoid deceptive practices because such practices would harm their businesses in the long run – if consumers did not get what they were promised, they would patronize more reliable entrepreneurs. Second, most consumers recognize exaggerated advertising and exercise a healthy scepticism when they buy. Third, advertising puffery is intrinsic to communicating a product concept, is practised by all institutions in society, and actually makes life more interesting. According to Theodore Levitt:

> There is hardly a company that would not go down in ruin if it refused to provide fluff, because nobody will buy pure functionality . . . Worse, it denies . . . man's honest needs and values. If religion must be architectured, packaged, lyricized, and musicized to attract and hold its audience, and if sex must be perfumed, powdered, sprayed, and shaped in order to command attention, it is ridiculous to deny the legitimacy of more modest, and similar, embellishments to the world of commerce . . . Many of the so-called distortions of advertising, product design, and packaging may be viewed as a paradigm of the many responses that man makes to the conditions of survival in the environment. Without distortion, embellishment, and elaboration, life would be drab, dull, anguished, and at its existential worst . . . I shall argue that embellishment and distortion are among advertising's legitimate and socially desirable purposes; and that illegitimacy in advertising consists of falsification with larcenous intent.[5]

But this attitude serves to accentuate the consumerist demand for accurate and complete information so that 'rational' choices, even if on 'irrational' grounds, can be freely made in fuller possession of the facts.[6] To proffer 'larcenous intent' as the limit on falsification is merely to further obscure the search for honesty and openness in marketing.

High-pressure selling. Another criticism is that salespeople in certain industries apply high-pressure selling techniques (hard sell) that induce people to buy goods they had no thought of buying. It is often said that such goods as encyclopaedias, insurance, real estate, and jewellery are sold, not bought. The salespeople in these industries are trained in delivering smooth canned talks to entice purchase. They work hard at selling, because of sales contests promising big prizes to those who turn in the best performance.

Businesspeople recognize that buyers can often be talked into buying things they did not initially want or need. This is the reason for proposed legislation requiring door-to-door salespeople to announce their purpose at the door – i.e. to sell a product. Buyers are also allowed a 'three-day cooling-off period' in which they can cancel their contract after rethinking it; they can take their complaints to consumer-affairs bureaus when they feel that undue selling pressure was applied.

According to the Victorian Director of Consumer Affairs, in the motor-vehicle industry

> . . . by far the largest contributing factor to complaints is the absence of any sales morality in some dealerships. This in turn gives rise to a cut-throat competition amongst some dealers.
>
> In many instances it is a matter of 'swim or sink'. In some car yards management adopts a procedure known as a 'head count' whereby the number of consumers who visit those yards is counted and this number is then compared with the number of sales made for the day. If the percentage does not compare favourably, then the sales staff are held to task for allowing too many people to leave the yard without having been sold a car. Statements have been made to inspectors that management adopt the policy that consumers are never 'just looking', and that they never come back once they are allowed to leave the yard without committing themselves. Such a policy exerts a pressure on the sales staff to proceed in a ruthless manner towards prospective purchasers and to disregard ethical business sales practices.
>
> The argument presented to the Ministry on a number of occasions is that some consumers are plain 'wood-ducks' (a term adopted by the trade for consumers with a low sales resistance and a high gullibility), and that if they do not sell a vehicle to these types of people whenever they walk into a car yard, then in the following day or two some other dealer will. They further claim that if they consider such ethical issues as sales morality, then their competitors may not do so, and again they would lose sales.[7]

Shoddy or unsafe products. Another criticism is that products often lack the quality they should have. One type of complaint is that products are not made well, or used to be made better: 'If [the consumer] somehow escapes rattles, pings, loose buttons or missing knobs, there probably will be dents, mismatched sizes, static, fluttering, leaking or creaking.'[8] Cars are the subject of a disproportionate number of complaints; other products that are singled out include colour-television sets, various appliances, and clothing. While it cannot be proved that quality has deteriorated over the years – perhaps consumers have become more sophisticated or selective – many persons think that many products fall short on quality.

A second type of complaint concerns whether certain products deliver any benefit, e.g. consumers were shocked to hear that dry breakfast cereal may have little nutritional value. Robert B. Choate, a Washington nutritional specialist, told a US Senate subcommittee:

> In short, [the cereals] fatten but do little to prevent malnutrition . . . The average cereal . . . fails as a complete meal even with milk added . . . It is apparent . . . that we humans are viewed not as beings to be nourished, but as suckers to be sold . . . these comments gain importance when one understands the extent to which children demand foods hucksltered to them on television.[9]

Choate added that consumers could often get more nutrition by eating the cereal package than the contents.

A third type of complaint centres around the safety characteristics of products. For years consumer groups have been reporting various hazards found in tested products – electrical dangers in appliances, carbon-monoxide poisoning from room heaters, finger risks in lawn-mowers, and faulty steering in cars.

Altogether, product quality has been a problem in certain industries for a number of reasons, including occasional manufacturer indifference, increased product complexity, poorly trained labour, and insufficient quality control.

On the other hand, several forces also lead manufacturers to have an interest in producing good quality. First, as they add more products to their line, large manufacturers become increasingly concerned with their reputations. A customer who has had a bad or disappointing experience with one of their products may avoid buying any others in the future. The concern with customer satisfaction is reinforced by the increased intensity and sophistication of competitors and the spread of the marketing concept. Second, large retailers are increasingly trying to develop their own name for quality, and they express this both in the national brands they select to sell and in their own private brands. Third, consumer groups are standing in the wings to point out poor-quality products and penalize companies for unsafe ones. No company wants bad publicity. In addition to consumer groups, various laws and government agencies are empowered to protect consumers against substandard or unsafe products.

Planned obsolescence. Critics have charged that producers in certain industries cause their products to become obsolete before they actually need replacement. Three types of obsolescence can be distinguished.

Planned style obsolescence means a deliberate policy by manufacturers to change users' ideas of acceptable appearance, and make them dissatisfied with their present goods. At different times, manufacturers of clothing, cars, furniture and even homes have been accused of this: the annual style change of passenger cars is considered a prime offender.

Planned functional obsolescence means a deliberate policy by manufacturers to 'withhold fully developed attractive features whose present absence and subsequent introduction may be used to encourage an earlier replacement of

Exhibit 21-2   Do You Recall?

Keith Bradshaw was watching the list of names grow. Their blue felt-pen capitals were filling his last display board; red-headed pins representing each name were sprouting in all areas on his wall map of Melbourne. Somewhere in Port Phillip Bay someone had written 'Ballarat, Swan Hill, Warrnambool, Bendigo, Ocean Grove, Moe' and the names of other towns that red pins could not reach.

'Lofty' Bradshaw is the Victorian Health Commission's chief health surveyor and it was his job to puzzle over those names. What had given all these people abdominal pain, diarrhoea and a high temperature? What made them vomit and dehydrate? Bacteria called salmonella newport, said the lab. Right. But how were all these widely dispersed people linked? The old, old question: Was it something they ate? Answer, almost certainly. But what?

As Keith Bradshaw watched the list of names spill to a sheet tacked on the back of another display board, he began to see the high proportion of 'migrant' or 'Mediterranean' names. In one of the columns beside each name was a list of foods that victims could remember eating. One product seemed to warrant a closer look. Salami.

Last Monday, about lunchtime, the manager of Tibaldi Smallgoods (Australia) Pty Ltd, Mr John Caprioglio, received a visit from health inspectors. They looked through the plant in Lens Street, Coburg, and asked about food preparation. They left with samples of salami from some of the twenty types the company produces. That afternoon one of Tibaldi's employees hurried to tell Mr Caprioglio about a radio report which had said the Health Commission was warning people not to eat Tibaldi salami. 'I just about collapsed,' he said.

Production and deliveries stopped and media inquiries started. Meetings were held and the company brought in International Public Relations Pty Ltd (IPR), to advise it. Results of tests on food samples from the factory and faecal specimens from the staff were not expected for a week. As the company's co-founder, Mr Frank Tibaldi, said on Tuesday, to be embroiled in a salmonella scare was 'disastrous'.

Australia's largest salami manufacturer would soon be losing $20 000 to $30 000 a day. The effect on the reputation of the business that was started with a hand mincer in Carlton in 1934 could not be calculated. Health inspections showed no defect in the factory practices, checks were started to trace the abattoirs that supplied Tibaldi with pork and beef and the company waited for results of tests on food samples and specimens from staff.

The reaction of the Tibaldi company when it was named by the Health Commission on Monday was hardly typical. Companies usually retreat into their shell leaving only their 'no comment' showing. Whether they are subsequently shown to be a source of an outbreak or not is irrelevant.

Tibaldi did the reverse. On Tuesday at least one reporter and one photographer were given a guided tour of the factory by Mr Frank Tibaldi. They were accompanied by an IPR representative. Mr Tibaldi explained the mincing and boning rooms and pointed out that the place was very clean, was it not? He led the way into huge drying rooms with thousands of salami sausages hung on racks. He cast an arm proudly at a room full of prosciutto, a cured ham, and called it 'the Rolls-Royce of smallgoods'.

Mr Caprioglio said that had the company decided to shut the shutters after being named, it would have been interpreted as an admission of guilt when Tibaldi had nothing to hide. Close to midnight on Tuesday, after a meeting with health staff that afternoon, the

Exhibit 21-2 (continued)

company issued a statement jointly with the acting assistant director of public health, Dr John Harrison. It said in part: 'There was no imputation of fault on the part of Tibaldi Smallgoods (Australia) Pty Ltd, for the recent outbreak of salmonella.' The company was co-operating and had re-cleaned its premises as a precaution, the statement said.

On Wednesday Mr Caprioglio said he was feeling the strain. The company's Adelaide plant had received crank calls. He also received calls from retailers pledging their support.

By Thursday evening it was confirmed that three previously unopened Tibaldi salami sausages – one from a wholesaler and two from shops – contained salmonella newport. The difficult search for abattoirs that had supplied the company with raw meat was incomplete. Yesterday, Mr Caprioglio said that the company would recall the salami that had been withdrawn from sale since Tuesday.

This outbreak has shown the need for speed and accuracy in pinpointing suspect sources. It has also highlighted at least one obstruction to this. Health Commission spokesmen have repeated this week that the lack of date stamps on Tibaldi products had made it extremely difficult to sort out which batches are suspect.

Source: Paul Chadwick, 'Health Alert', *Age*, 15 August 1981, p. 23.

the product . . .'[10]. Suppose the manufacturers of motor vehicles had a whole set of improvements – with respect to safety, pollution reduction, fuel economy, handling – that they could introduce today but withheld deliberately.

Planned material obsolescence means that manufacturers deliberately choose materials and components that are subject to higher breakage, wear, rot or corrosion. For example, many drapery manufacturers have switched to using a higher percentage of rayon in their drapes. They argue that rayon reduces the price of the drapes and has a better holding power; critics suggest that substituting rayon will cause the drapes to fall apart after two cleanings instead of four.

Businesspeople answer these charges as follows: First, consumers like style changes, they get tired of their old goods – they like to have a new look in clothing or a car. No one has to buy the new look: obviously if enough people did not like it, it would not take over. Second, companies withhold new functional features when they are not adequately tested, when they add more cost to the product than consumers are willing to pay, and for other good reasons. They do this at the risk of having a competitor introduce the new feature and steal the market. Third, companies often substitute new materials in the effort to lower their own costs and consumer prices. They do not deliberately design their products to break down earlier, because they would risk losing their customers in doing so. Fourth, much of so-called planned obsolescence is really the working out of dynamic competitive and technological forces in a free society, leading to ever-improving goods and services.

Marketing's Impact on Society-as-a-whole

The marketing system has also been accused of contributing to some social 'bads' in Australian society – specifically, excessive materialism, false wants, insufficient social goods, cultural pollution, and excessive political power.

Exhibit 21-3 Thou Shalt Cast Out Consuming Devils

Once, there were 10 commandments. Recently, Christians have been inspired to write another 10. Ten commandments to fight the consumerism of the 80s are pinned to walls in parishes around Melbourne and taped to fridges in Christian homes. Called '10 points for a simpler lifestyle', they include: living on the poverty line for a month; staying out of shops; giving part of your pay packet away; and making television commercials a family joke. They were first published in *See*, a Melbourne Anglican newspaper.

The 10 suggestions have come from a group of Anglican clergymen appointed by the Archbishop of Melbourne, the Most Reverend Robert Dann, at the request of the diocesan synod. Even the eight members of the committee on Christian lifestyle that came up with the suggestions acknowledged the impossibility of fulfilling all 10. A committee member, Bishop Gerald Muston, said he had been trying to resist the urge to go into shops. The points are presented as a game.

Number One urges Christians to live on the poverty line for a month. The committee writes: 'Of course it's not really possible to do this when we have all the trappings of affluence around us. But decide as a family for one month to housekeep as if you were on the poverty line as many Australians are. For instance, if you are a family of four, try limiting your food spending to $40 a week.'

Number Two suggests a different way of using money. 'In the first month, take $10 a week from your pay and put it aside. In the second month, take $20 a week and put it aside. At the end of two months you will have $120. Find someone who needs it, and give it to them.'

Number Three: Decide for a month that your entertainment will be free.

Number Four: As a family competition for one month, deduct marks every time you go to a shop. Refuse to make a local shopping centre your entertainment on Friday nights. When you do shop, buy at smaller shops or in bulk. Buy selectively. Eliminate highly processed and fast foods.

Number Five: Try a little hospitality. Set out to ask home some people you would not normally invite.

Number Six: Make TV commercials a family joke. Decide as a family which is the most outrageous commercial for the week. Teach children to be critical of the enormous advertising pressures on them.

Number Seven: Leave your car in the garage. Walk whenever you can. Use public transport and put pressure on the government to make it better.

Number Eight: You don't need all those clothes. Don't be fooled into adding to them. Learn to live with a smaller, more basic wardrobe. Buy or make good-quality garments and use them until they wear out.

Number Nine: See how much you can recycle. Divide rubbish into disposable and compost, and put the compost on the garden to enrich the soil. See how little garbage you can put out each week.

Number Ten: Try a little moderation. The Bible commends it. Don't be put off by extremists at either end.

Source: Louise Carbines, 'Thou Shalt Cast Out Consuming Devils', *Age*, 3 September 1981, p. 1.

Excessive materialism. The business system has been accused of creating a lopsided interest in material possessions. People tend to judge others by what they own rather than by what they are; people are not considered successful unless they own a substantial home, two cars, and the latest clothes and appliances.

Most people enter the materialistic race with great vigour. Only a few, however, win the big prizes; many others drop out along the way; some vigorously repudiate the system. The emphasis on material accumulation leaves many people unhappy or frustrated. According to the New Left:

> We oppose the depersonalization that reduces human beings to the status of things . . . Loneliness, estrangement, isolation describe the vast distance between man and man today. These dominant tendencies cannot be overcome by better personnel management, nor by improved gadgets, but only when a love of man overcomes the idolatrous worship of things by man.[11]

Some of this may be changing – dominant value systems tend to breed countercultural groups and values. An increasing number of Australians are losing their drive for possessions, particularly (and ironically) the more affluent. They are relaxing more, playing more, and learning to get along with less. 'Small is beautiful' and 'less is more' describe the developing ideology; greater emphasis is being placed on cultivating close relationships and simple pleasures than on being 'hooked on things'.

False wants. This dominant interest in 'things' is not seen as a natural state of mind but rather one created by advertising. Business hires agencies to stimulate people's desires for goods; they use the mass media to create materialist models of the good life. Conspicuous consumption on the part of some, creates invidious desires in others. People work harder to earn the necessary money. Their purchases increase the output and productive capacity of the industrial state which, in turn, makes greater use of advertising to stimulate desire for industrial output. Thus people are seen as a manipulated link in the cycle between production and consumption. Wants come to depend on output. This is what Galbraith calls the 'dependence effect':

> The control or management of demand is, in fact, a vast and rapidly growing industry in itself. It embraces a huge network of communications, a great array of merchandising and selling organizations, nearly the entire advertising industry, numerous ancillary research, training and other related services and much more. In everyday parlance this great machine, and the demanding and varied talents that it employs, are said to be engaged in selling goods. In less ambiguous language it means that it is engaged in the management of those who buy goods.[12]

And Marcuse:

> 'False' [needs] are those which are superimposed upon the individual by particular social interests. Most of the prevailing needs to relax, to have fun, to behave and consume in accordance with the advertisements, to love and hate what others love and hate, belong to this category of false needs.[13]

These quotations probably exaggerate the power of business to synthesize and stimulate wants. It may be possible to brainwash some people in a prisoner-of-war camp, or in a totalitarian society where all the means of persuasion are under state control and no counterpropaganda is permitted. Under normal social conditions, however, the individual is exposed to conflicting lifestyles and value systems through personal experience and the mass media. Some of the mass advertisers' intended effect is diminished by gatekeepers who screen out or change the messages before they reach large sections of society. In addition, persons have elaborate perceptual defences against the mass media – selective attention, perception, distortion and retention. The mass media are most effective when they appeal to existing needs rather than attempt to create new ones – which is hard to call manipulation. Furthermore, people tend to be information-seekers with respect to the more consequential purchases, which makes them less reliant on single advocate sources. Even inconsequential purchases, which may be triggered off by advertising messages, lead to repeat purchase only if the product performance meets the expectations. Finally, the high failure rate of new products removes credence from the claim that companies – even the biggest and most sophisticated ones – are able to manage demand.

On a deeper level, our wants and values are influenced not only by marketers but also by family, peer groups, religion, ethnic background, and education. If Australians are highly materialistic, this arose out of basic socialization processes that go much deeper than the influence of business and mass media.

Insufficient social goods. Business has been accused of overstimulating demand for private goods at the expense of public goods. In fact, as private goods increase they require a proportional complement of public services that is not usually forthcoming:

> An increase in the consumption of automobiles requires a facilitating supply of streets, highways, traffic control, and parking space. The protective services of the police and the highway patrols must also be available, as must those of the hospitals. Although the need for balance here is extraordinarily clear, our use of privately produced vehicles has, on occasion, got far out of line with the supply of the related public services. The result has been hideous road congestion, an annual massacre of impressive proportions, and chronic colitis in the cities.[14]

Thus private consumption leads to a 'social imbalance' and 'social costs' that neither the producers nor the consumers appear willing to pay for. Some way must be found to restore a social balance between private goods and public goods. Manufacturing firms could, for example, be required to bear the full social cost of their operations, that is, they would build such costs into their price. Where buyers did not find the private goods worth the price, those firms would go out of existence and the resources would move to other uses that could support the sum of the private and social costs.

Cultural pollution. Critics charge the marketing system with creating cultural pollution. Our senses are constantly being assaulted by advertising noise: serious programmes are interrupted by commercials; serious printed matter is lost between pages of ads; magnificent landscapes are marred by posters and signs. These interruptions intrude sex, power or status continuously into people's consciousness.

Yet it appears that the flood of advertising strikes people in different ways. In a study of consumer attitudes toward advertising, Bauer and Greyser found that advertising was a low-salience topic, something like the daily weather.[15] Although people occasionally complain about it, they are not too serious in their complaints. Only 15 per cent of the 1856 persons interviewed thought advertising needed change, and these tended to be people who see a need for change in many institutions. The average respondent tended to 'pay some attention' to about seventy-six ads in an average day, and did not find more than 16 per cent of them annoying or offensive. Some people thought that the best part of television programming was the ads!

Businesspeople usually answer the charges of commercial noise with these arguments. First, they hope that their ads largely reach only the target audience. But because of mass-communication channels, some ads are found to reach people who have no interest in the product and are therefore left bored or irritated. People who buy magazines addressed to their own interests – such as *Cleo* or *Playboy*

– rarely complain about the ads because they advertise products of interest. Second, ads are responsible for making commercial radio as well as television a free medium, and for keeping down the costs of magazines and newspapers. Most people are happy to accept the commercials as a small price to pay.

Excessive political power. Another criticism against business is that it wields too much political power;[16] there are parliamentarians who stand ready and able to protect particular industries' interests against the public interest. Business is also accused of having too much power over the mass media, neutralizing its freedom to report independently and objectively. As stated some years ago by one critic: 'How can *Life, Post,* and *Readers Digest* afford to tell the truth about the scandalously low nutritional value of most packaged foods . . . when these magazines are being subsidized by such advertisers as General Foods, Kellogg's, Nabisco, and General Mills? The answer is *they cannot and do not.*'[17]

The various industries in Australia do attempt to promote and protect their interests. They have a right to representation in parliament and the mass media, although it is possible for their influence to become too extensive and controlling. Fortunately, many powerful business interests thought to be untouchable have been tamed in the public interest – for example, advertising of cigarettes via electronic media was banned in the 1970s (although sports sponsorship largely avoided the ban). Business control over the media is also changing as more sponsors share the costs for major shows and as the media themselves become more courageous in featuring editorial material designed to interest different segments of the market. This does not mean that the charge of excessive power in the hands of business is invalid, but that countervailing forces operate to check and offset these powerful interests.

Marketing's Impact on Other Businesses

Critics have also charged that many companies, in their zeal for profits, ride roughshod over other companies. Large firms are accused of taking over or ruining small firms, thus leading to less competition. Three types of problems are identified: anti-competitive mergers, artificial barriers to entry, and predatory competition.

Anti-competitive acquisition. A recurrent accusation against the business system is that many firms expand by acquiring other firms rather than by internally developing new and needed products. Within a certain time period, the nine leading ethical drug companies in the United States developed eight new businesses internally and acquired sixteen others.[18]

Acquisition is a complicated subject. Acquisitions can be beneficial to the society under the following circumstances: (i) when the acquiring company gains economies of scale leading to lower costs and lower prices; (ii) when a well-managed company takes over a poorly managed company and improves its efficiency; and (iii) when an industry that was fairly non-competitive becomes competitive after acquisition takes place. Other acquisitions can be harmful, particularly when a vigorous young competitor is absorbed and fewer firms come to dominate the major share of the business.

Barriers to entry. Critics have charged that modern marketing practices often create substantial barriers to entry in certain industries. These may be in the form of patents, substantial promotion requirements, tie-ups of suppliers or dealers, and so on.

The regulators of competition recognize that some barriers to entry are associated with real economies of large-scale enterprise; others could be challenged by both existing law and new legislation. For example, some critics have suggested putting a progressive tax on advertising expenditures to reduce the impact of selling costs, a particularly prevalent barrier to entry.

Predatory competition. In certain instances firms go after other firms with the intention of hurting or destroying them, setting their prices below costs, threatening to cut off business with suppliers, or disparaging the competitor's products.

There are various laws to prevent predatory competition. The difficulty at times is to establish that the intent or action was really predatory.

CITIZEN ACTIONS TO REGULATE MARKETING

Since business has historically been seen as the real or alleged cause of many economic and social ills, it is not surprising that grassroots movements have arisen from time to time to discipline business and call for legislative remedy. The two major anti-business movements have been consumerism and environmentalism.

Consumerism

Put simply, consumerism is an organized movement of concerned citizens and government to enhance the rights and power of buyers in relation to sellers. Traditional sellers' rights include:

1. The right to introduce a product in any size and style, provided it is not hazardous to personal health or safety; or, if it is, to introduce it with the proper warnings and controls.
2. The right to price the product at any level, provided there is no discrimination among similar classes of buyers.
3. The right to spend any amount of money to promote the product, provided it is not defined as unfair competition.

4. The right to formulate any product message, provided it is not misleading or dishonest in content or execution.
5. The right to introduce any buying incentive schemes they wish.

Traditional buyers' rights include:

1. The right not to buy a product that is offered for sale.
2. The right to expect the product to be safe.
3. The right to expect the product to be what is claimed.

Comparing these rights, many believe that the balance of power lies on the sellers' side. It is true that the buyer can refuse to buy any product, but it is generally felt that buyers are really without sufficient information, education and protection to make wise decisions in the face of highly sophisticated sellers. Consumer advocates therefore call for the following additional consumer rights:

4. The right to be adequately informed about the more important aspects of the product.
5. The right to be protected against questionable products and marketing practices.
6. The right to influence products and marketing practices in directions that will enhance the quality of life.

Each of these proposed rights leads to a whole series of specific proposals by consumerists. The right to be informed includes such things as the right to know the true interest rate on a loan (truth in lending), the true cost per standard unit of competing brands (unit pricing), the basic ingredients in a product (ingredient labelling), the nutritional quality of foods (nutritional labelling), the freshness of products (open dating), and the true benefits of a product (truth in advertising).

The proposals related to additional consumer protection include the strengthening of consumers' positions in cases of business fraud, the requiring of more safety to be designed into products, and the issuing of greater powers to existing government agencies.

The proposals relating to quality-of-life considerations include regulating the ingredients that go into certain products (detergents, petrol) and packaging (soft-drink containers), reducing the level of advertising and promotional 'noise', and creating consumer representation on company boards to introduce consumer welfare considerations in business decision-making.

Exhibit 21-4 Consumerism and Australia

A leading consumer activist outlined the evolution of consumerism as follows:

The need for consumer protection in any country is closely related to the rate of change in the marketplace. Change is accompanied by a natural resistance to change; by the difficulties involved in making new kinds of value judgments and often by a lack of understanding of financial, marketing and technological innovations — in fact, by any inability to adapt. A recent example is the abolition of resale price maintenance by the Trade Practices Act in 1974. This is still the target of considerable criticism by the people that it benefits, for they cannot understand that the same product can have many prices, depending on the overheads and efficiency of any particular retailer.

Consumer protection necessarily followed the industrial revolution, when the marketplace changed from being the source of locally produced goods of known materials produced by known growers and tradesmen to being a source of new products made of unknown materials by unknown and distant manufacturers. The then accepted doctrine of *caveat emptor* — 'let the buyer beware' — had to change simply because the buyer was, in many cases, unable to judge whether the goods were of merchantable quality or even fit for the purpose for which they were acquired. The change was slow and after 100 years of industrial activity the English Sale of Goods Act, 1893, became law.

Catalysts for development

The increase in manufacturing activity and the irresponsible behaviour of the advertising industry were the catalysts for the development of consumer organizations as we know them today. In 1927 in the United States, Stuart Chase and Frederick Schlink published a best-selling book called *Your Money's Worth*, which showed how difficult it was to get your money's worth in a marketplace flooded with that joint product of advertising and manufacturing — the 'national brand' — and rife with fraud and misrepresentation. They proposed some possible remedies, one of these being a clearing house for consumer market information. In 1929 an organization called 'Consumers Research' was founded, with Schlink as its director.

In 1935 the staff of Consumers Research tried to introduce unionism into the organization, but Schlink opposed it. Some of the employees then broke away and formed 'Consumers' Union', a democratically organized consumer research and testing body. In order to grow, Consumers' Union had to resort to direct mail advertising because newspapers and

Exhibit 21-4 (continued)

magazines of the 1930s (and even up to the 1950s) refused to accept its advertising. One reason for this was that its 'Not Acceptable' rating of various products was viewed by the publishers as an attack on other advertisers.

Consumers' Union grew from 3000 subscribers in 1930 to 2 200 000 in 1975. Similar organizations were formed in other countries, in some cases with government assistance. In Australia, the Australian Consumers' Association was founded in 1959 and now has nearly 200 000 subscribers (to its magazine *Choice*). Consumer organizations in the United States of America, Australia, Belgium, and United Kingdom and the Netherlands formed an international body, the International Organization of Consumers Unions as a clearing house for consumer test information. It has now developed into an international forum for consumer affairs problems and represents consumers' interests to many international agencies and organizations. It has a membership of 103 private consumer associations and government-financed consumer councils and similar bodies in forty-five countries.

In 1964 the Victorian Parliament passed the Consumer Protection Act and established the first government consumer protection agency in Australia. In July 1969 the New South Wales Parliament established the first government agency specifically empowered to receive and deal with complaints. The other States and Territories followed suit, the last, the Australian Capital Territory Consumer Affairs Ordinance, being gazetted in May 1973.

In October 1973 the federal government established the Interim Commission of Consumer Standards as the first step in carrying out of its election policy. In its final report that commission recommended, inter alia, that it should be succeeded by a statutory commission, and that an appropriate Act be passed giving the commission wide powers for consumer protection. Federal responsibility for consumer affairs was transferred to the Minister of Science in April 1975 and the Bill for an Australian Consumer Protection Authority lapsed with the change in government in November 1975. In December 1975 a new department of business and consumer affairs was established. Since then the government has established the Commonwealth/State Consumer Products Advisory Committee to recommend regulations under the Trade Practices Act relating to consumer products, and the National Consumer Affairs Advisory Council to advise the Minister for Business and Consumer Affairs on relevant matters of commonwealth responsibility.

All of these bodies have been established to fulfil the demonstrated need for consumer protection — protection from producers of goods and suppliers of services, who, in the main, control their own particular segment of the economy and use this control to further their own interests. In too many cases their own interests conflict with the public good, and we, the borrowers, the hirers, the owners, the parents, the patients, the shoppers and the tenants all suffer.

What of tomorrow?

There are many challenges facing consumer organizations in Australia; probably the most important is to have recognized consumer representation on every authority and body making decisions that affect consumers. Too many of these bodies, when they control their own destinies, satisfy their public consciences by having token consumer representation. Some examples are the Advertising Standards Council, where the chairman personally appointed the five 'public' members, and the Press Council which nominated its own consumer representatives. Where the power to appoint resides with a minister it happens only too often that the persons appointed are those that he or his department will feel comfortable with.

Exhibit 21-4 (continued)

A vital objective is for consumers to be able to have the opportunity to influence government legislative and administrative policy in relevant areas. The coalition government has gone part way towards this by letting Bills lie before Parliament or circulating 'exposure drafts' of Bills for comment. The Australian Labor Party has gone further by evolving a clear policy whereby all departments will issue 'Consumer Impact Statements' when making proposals that have significant effects on consumers so that informed responses can be generated.

The next most important objective is for consumers to be able to submit properly researched, representative views to all inquiries and commissions conducting hearings that will result in recommendations affecting consumers. One must realize that every industry submission to such inquiries is paid for by the public in the price that it pays for the goods and services of that industry. The only source of funding for the consumers' views is from revenue, because consumer organizations do not sell a product whose price can be loaded to pay for representation.

There must be sufficient government assistance to ensure that government does hear the views of consumers as well as the views of those who tend to behave as if they own the marketplace. A recent example of this attitude is the statement by Bruce McDonald, Chairman of the Advertising Federation of Australia, when commenting on the intervention of the Australian Federation of Consumer Organizations in the Prices Justification Tribunal inquiry into the Colgate-Palmolive application for an increase in prices based on increased advertising costs. Mr McDonald said: 'I remind all bureaucratic peacocks that it's our garden in which they're strutting, and they are only there by our invitation.'

Education necessary

Another important objective is to ensure that consumer education is fostered throughout the formal education system and encouraged outside it. People have to be taught to use the techniques of value analysis in purchasing goods and services, to understand money management, to know their legal rights and responsibilities, to understand how the economy works and the probable effects of bounties, quotas, subsidies and tariffs on employment and on their own purchasing power. In a recent survey of the public, consumer activists and businessmen in America, there was overwhelming support for all high-school students to be required to study consumer affairs. This was the only question of nearly ninety in a survey where there was complete agreement. The coalition government has promised to establish a task force on consumer education sponsored by the Department of Business and Consumer Affairs and the Commonwealth Curriculum Development Centre. It will be asked to make specific recommendations on the action that should be taken, particularly at the commonwealth level, to remedy the existing deficiencies in the primary, secondary and tertiary education areas.

One important aspect of consumer education was identified in the Trade Practices Commission Report: 'It would be unrealistic to expect a consumer education programme to be able to change spending habits quickly. But over the longer term progress may be achieved through consumer education in getting for the lower income consumer more value for his limited income. It may at least assist him towards maximizing the benefits of consumer credit consistent with other demands upon his limited income.'

Source: Michael J. Vernon, 'Looking Forward and Back', *AFCO Quarterly*, December 1977, pp. 2–4.

Environmentalism

Whereas consumerists focus on whether the marketing system is efficiently serving consumer needs and wants, environmentalists focus on the impact of modern marketing on the environment and the costs that are borne in serving these consumer needs and wants. In 1962 Rachel Carson's *Silent Spring* presented a documented criticism of pesticidal pollution of the environment.[19] It was no longer a matter of wasted resources but one of human survival. In 1970 the Ehrlichs coined the term 'eco-catastrophe' to symbolize the harmful impact of certain business practices on the environment.[20] And in 1972 the Meadowses and others published *The Limits to Growth*, which warned people, through the evidence of systems simulation, that the quality of life would eventually decline in the face of unchecked population growth, spreading pollution, and continued exploitation of natural resources.[21]

These concerns underpin the movement known as environmentalism: an organized movement of concerned citizens and government to protect and enhance people's living environment. Environmentalists are concerned with mining, forest depletion, factory smoke, billboards and litter; with the loss of recreational opportunity; and with the increase in health problems due to bad air, water, and chemically sprayed food.

Environmentalists are not always against marketing and consumption; sometimes they simply want them to operate on more ecological principles. They think that the goal of the marketing system should not be the maximization of consumption or consumer choice or consumer satisfaction as such, but rather the maximization of life quality. And life quality means not only the quantity and quality of consumer goods and services, but also the quality of the environment.

Environmentalists want environmental costs formally introduced into the decision making of producers and consumers. They favour the use of tax mechanisms and regulations to impose the true social costs of anti-environmental business and consumption activity. Requiring business to invest in anti-pollution devices, taxing non-returnable bottles, banning high-phosphate detergents, and other measures are viewed as necessary to lead businesses and consumers to move in directions that are environmentally sound.

Environmentalists are in many ways more critical of marketing than are consumerists. They complain that there is too much wasteful packaging, whereas consumerists feel the latter has certain conveniences. Environmentalists feel that mass advertising leads people to buy more than they need, whereas consumerists worry more about deception in advertising. Environmentalists dislike the proliferation of shopping centres, whereas consumerists welcome new stores and more competition.

Thus environmentalism is a more radical challenge to current marketing philosophy than consumerism. It does not accept the sacredness of consumer sovereignty and satisfaction; it rejects the marketing concept of 'finding needs and filling them' because this ignores societal and ecological considerations. Environmentalists are ready to question consumer needs and wants, and intervene to prevent environmental abuse. Consumption is not, in their minds, the be-all and end-all of human existence.

Environmentalism has hit certain industries hard. Steel factories and public utilities have been forced to invest in pollution-control equipment and costlier fuels. The motor-vehicle industry has had to introduce expensive emission-control devices in cars. The soap industry has had to research and develop low-phosphate detergents. The packaging industry has been required to develop ways to reduce litter and increase biodegradability in its products. The petroleum industry has had to formulate new low-lead and no-lead petrols. Naturally, these industries are inclined to resent environmental regulations, especially when formulated and imposed too rapidly to allow the companies to make the proper adjustments; they have had to absorb large costs and pass them on to buyers.

As for marketers, their life has become more complicated. They have to investigate more carefully the ecological properties of the product and its packaging; they have to raise prices to cover environmental costs, knowing this will make the product harder to sell. Yet there is no turning back to the 1950s and 1960s when few managers worried about the effect of product and marketing decisions on the quality of the environment. It was partly that indifference that led to the growth of environmentalism in the first place.[22]

PUBLIC ACTIONS TO REGULATE MARKETING

Citizen agitation against specific marketing practices will usually stimulate public policy debate and lead to legislative and judicial proposals. Some legislators will see these issues as important and will draft bills. The bills will be subjected to prolonged debate, many will be defeated in the process, others will be substantially modified and sometimes made 'toothless', and a few will emerge in really workable form.

We alluded to many of the laws bearing on marketing in Chapter 7. The task is to translate these and other laws into understandings

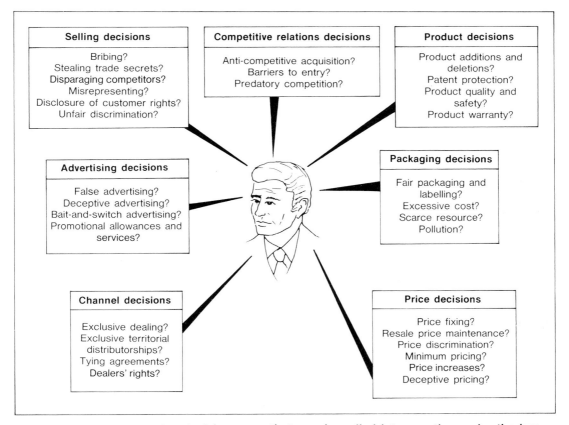

Figure 21-1   **Major marketing decision areas that may be called into question under the law**

that marketing executives have as they make decisions in the areas of competitive relations, products, price, promotion, and channels of distribution. Figure 21-1 summarizes the major issues in each area facing members of management as they do their marketing planning. The specific dos and don'ts have already been reviewed in each of the appropriate chapters.

BUSINESS ACTIONS TOWARDS SOCIALLY RESPONSIBLE MARKETING

Initially, many companies actively opposed consumerism and environmentalism. They thought that many of the criticisms of the marketing system were either unjustified or unimportant. They resented the power of strong consumer leaders to point an accusing finger at their products and cause their sales to plummet; they also resented proposals that appeared to increase business costs more than they helped the consumer. They felt that most consumers would not pay attention to unit pricing or ingredient labelling, and that the doctrines of advertising substantiation, corrective advertising and counteradvertising would stifle advertising creativity. They felt that the consumer was better off than ever, that large companies were very careful in developing safe products and promoting them honestly, and that new laws would only lead to new constraints and higher seller costs that would be passed on to the consumer in higher prices. Thus many companies opposed the consumer movement and lobbied vigorously against new legislation.

At the present time, most companies have come around to accepting the new consumer rights in principle. They might oppose certain pieces of legislation on the ground that such measures are not the best way to solve a particular consumer problem, but they recognize the consumers' right to information and protection. Here we want to examine responsible and creative business responses to the changing marketing environment and marketing opportunities. We first examine a concept of enlightened marketing and then the issue of marketing ethics.

A Concept of Enlightened Marketing

A concept of enlightened marketing grows out of the concept of enlightened capitalism. Two centuries ago Adam Smith, in his *Wealth of Nations*, attempted to show that freedom of enterprise and private property would result in a dynamic and progressive economy. His basic postulate was that people will naturally pursue their self-interest and, if given the freedom to do this, they and the society will benefit. Through free enterprise, entrepreneurs will put their resources into the areas of highest profit opportunity. Profits are usually high where needs must be met; as resources move in, costs would be brought down through healthy competition. The system would be characterized by efficiency and flexibility; it would be guided, by the 'invisible hand' of the price system, to produce needed goods without resort to government bureaucracy and direction.

This system is of course subject to abuse when companies do not follow the rules of proper business behaviour – those that try to destroy competitors, raise barriers to entry, and gain the protection and favours of legislators are not competing fairly. Hence a concept of enlightened capitalism is needed in which businesspeople would recognize that their long-run interests would be best served by self-reliant and honest activity within the rules of the system. Enlightened marketing holds that the company's marketing should support the best long-run performance of the marketing system. Enlightened marketing, as such, embodies five principles.

Consumer-oriented marketing. The company should view and organize its marketing

Exhibit 21-5 Future Government Regulators May Put Harder Questions to Marketers

The trend toward increased regulation of company marketing activity may lead to the spectre of new government commissions being formed. Here is a scenario of the critical questions that new government commissions might put to businesspeople in the future.

A company developing a new product may have to get the approval of a *Federal Products Commission*. Commission members are likely to put the following questions to the company:

- Is the new product sufficiently different from existing products?
- Are the product differences, if any, of sufficient benefit to the buyers and society?
- Is the product relatively safe and healthful for the user?
- Is the new product designed for minimum ecological harm?
- Is the production process minimally polluting?

A *Federal Advertising Commission* will want to approve all major ads. Commission members will raise the following questions:

- Does the ad tell the truth about the product?
- Does the ad use humanistic or base appeals?
- Is the level of company or industry advertising expenditures excessive from a social point of view?

A *Federal Distribution Commission* would have the responsibility for protecting the retail environment in which products and services are sold. Commission members are likely to ask the following questions:

- Is the new outlet necessary?
- Are the outlet's location and design suitable?
- Are the outlet's merchandising policies in the best interest of the consumers?

A *Federal Fair Price Commission* will try to make sure that the prices charged for goods and services are 'fair' to the buyer. Commission members will ask the following questions:

- Is the price clearly stated in a standard unit before the purchase is made?
- Does the price yield an undue profit to the seller over a long period?
- Does the price reflect all the social costs created by the product?

No one really wants to see these commissions established because they mean bureaucratic interference with the working of the free market. The irony is, however, that the questions are good ones that marketers should, ideally, ask themselves. Indeed, to the extent that marketers manage to produce good products, advertising and distribution, and avoid excessive pricing, there will be less of a basis for a popular movement to create these commissions.

activities from the consumers' point of view. It should strive to effectively and efficiently sense, serve and satisfy a defined set of needs of a defined group of customers.

Innovative marketing. The company should continuously search for real product and marketing improvements. The company that overlooks new and improved ways to do things will eventually find itself challenged by a company that has done so.

Value marketing. The company should put most of its resources into value-building marketing investments. A number of things marketers do – one-shot sales promotions, minor packaging changes, advertising puffery – may in the short run raise sales, but add less value to the consumer than real efforts to improve the product's features, convenience, availability, information, and so on. Consider the following example:

> Kundenkreditbank is a large and profitable chain of consumer banks in Germany. Its chairman, Stefan Kaminsky, made the decision to target the bank to serve primarily working-class customers. He developed a careful mission statement for the bank. Instead of saying that the bank would engage in loans, deposits, cheque accounts, and safekeeping, or that it would meet consumers' financial needs, he adopted a consumer-enhancement mission: the bank would help consumers increase their total assets so they could achieve a higher standard of living. This mission meant that Kaminsky's bank had to be ready to offer a high level of customer service and advice. This led to the notion that his own employees should be well trained and well acquainted with their customers; they should know their customers as well as lawyers or doctors know their clients or patients. It would not be amiss for a customer to phone the banker at home in the evening because of a pressing problem. Kaminsky decided that his branches should never have more than six employees. If a branch's size grows beyond the service ability of six employees, a new branch is opened nearby. When he hires the branch manager, Kaminsky says: 'I want you to understand that you will be in this branch for thirty years. These employees are your family. You will be rewarded for good performance through salary increases and bonus participation in the income earned by your branch. The government shares in the income, the shareholders share in the income, and the employees share in the income. Even the customers will share.' So the branch manager does not look forward to being rewarded by moving to headquarters. The result is that the branch manager digs deep roots in the community. The branch bank operates like a club. In one section of the bank is a table with consumer reports and cassettes to help consumers buy goods and brands more carefully. The bank's personnel do everything they can to help the customers increase their assets.

Sense-of-mission marketing. The company should define its mission in broad social terms rather than narrow product terms. When a company defines a social mission, company personnel feel better about the nature and importance of their work and have a clearer sense of direction. Consider the following statement of mission by the International Minerals and Chemical Corporation:

> We're not merely in the business of selling our brand of fertilizer. We have a sense of purpose, a sense of where we are going. The first function of corporate planning is to decide what kind of business the company is in. Our business is agricultural productivity. *We are interested in anything that affects plant growth, now and in the future.*[23]

Societal marketing. An enlightened company will make its marketing decision by considering not only the consumers' wants and the company's requirements, but also the long-run interests of consumers and society. The company is aware that neglecting the last two considerations is a disservice to consumers and society.

Alert companies have recognized societal problems as the basis for opportunities. As stated by Drucker, consumerism is:

... the shame of the total marketing concept. It is essentially a mark of the failure of the concept ...

Consumerism means that the consumer looks upon the manufacturer as somebody who is interested, but who really doesn't know what the consumer's realities are ... *Consumerism actually should be, must be, and I hope will be, the opportunity of marketing. This is what we in marketing have been waiting for.*[24] [Emphasis added]

The aim of a societally oriented marketer is to design not only pleasing products but also salutary products. The distinction is made clear in Figure 21-2. Current products can be classified according to their degree of immediate consumer satisfaction and long-run consumer benefit. Desirable products are those that combine high immediate satisfaction and high long-run benefit, such as tasty, nutritious breakfast foods. Pleasing products are those that give high immediate satisfaction but may hurt consumer interests in the long run, such as cigarettes. Salutary products are those that have low appeal but are also highly beneficial to the consumer in the long run, such as low-phosphate detergents. Deficient products are those that have neither immediate appeal nor salutary qualities, such as a bad-tasting patent medicine.

The company might as well forget about deficient products because too much work would be required to give them pleasing and salutary qualities. On the other hand, the company should invest its greatest effort in developing desirable products – e.g. new foods, textiles, appliances, and building materials – which combine intrinsic appeal and long-run benefit. The other two categories, pleasing and salutary products, also present a considerable challenge and opportunity to the company.

The challenge posed by pleasing products is that they sell extremely well but are not in the consumer's ultimate interests. The opportunity is therefore to formulate some alteration of the product that adds salutary qualities without diminishing any or too many of the pleasing qualities. For example: (i) a company developed and promoted a phosphate-free laundry detergent that became a big-selling brand; (ii) Pepsi-Cola developed a one-way plastic soft-drink bottle that is biodegradable; and (iii) Mobil Oil developed and promoted no-lead and low-lead petrols in response to the oil shortage. The challenge posed by salutary products is to add some pleasing qualities so that they will become more desirable in the consumers' minds.

Marketing Ethics

Even with the best of intentions, marketers will face many moral dilemmas; it will not often be clear what is the best thing to do. Since not all executives will have the finest moral sensitivity, it is important that the company develop explicit corporate marketing policies. Policies are 'broad, fixed guidelines that everyone in the organization must adhere to, and that are not subject to exception'.[25] They cover distributor relations, advertising standards, customer service, pricing, product development, and general ethical standards.

Even the finest set of guidelines cannot anticipate or resolve all the ethically difficult situations confronting the marketer. Consider Howard Bowen's classic questions about the marketer's responsibilities:

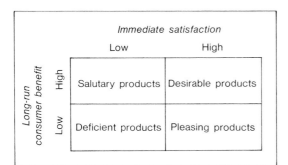

Figure 21-2   Classification of new-product opportunities

Should he conduct selling in ways that intrude on the privacy of people, for example, by door-to-door selling . . . ? Should he use methods involving ballyhoo, chances, prizes, hawking and other tactics which are at least of doubtful good taste? Should he employ 'high pressure' tactics in persuading people to buy? Should he try to hasten the obsolescence of goods by bringing out an endless succession of new models and new styles? Should he appeal to and attempt to strengthen the motives of materialism, invidious consumption, and 'keeping up with the Joneses'?[26]

Table 21-1 lists fourteen ethically difficult situations that marketers could well face during their careers. If they decide in favour of the immediate sales-producing actions in all

Table 21-1   Some morally difficult situations in marketing

1. You work for a cigarette company, and up to now have not been convinced that cigarettes cause cancer. A recent report has come across your desk that clearly establishes the connection between cigarette smoking and cancer. What would you do?

2. Your R & D department has modernized one of your products. It is not really 'new and improved', but you know that putting this statement on the package and in the advertising will increase sales. What would you do?

3. You have been asked to add a stripped-down model to the low end of your line that could be advertised to attract customers. The product won't be very good, but the sales representatives could be depended upon to persuade buyers to buy the higher-priced units. You are asked to give the green light for developing this stripped-down version. What would you do?

4. You are interviewing a former product manager in a competitor's company You are thinking of hiring him. He would be more than happy to tell you all the competitor's plans for the coming year. What would you do?

5. One of your dealers in an important territory has had family troubles recently and is not producing the sales he used to. He was one of the company's top producers in the past. It is not clear how long it will take before his family trouble is resolved. In the meantime, many sales are being lost. There is a legal way to terminate the dealer's franchise and replace him. What would you do?

6. You have a chance to win a big account that will mean a lot to you and your company. The purchasing agent hinted that he would be influenced by a 'gift'. Your assistant recommends sending a colour-television set to his home. What would you do?

7. You have heard that a competitor has a new product feature that will make a big difference in sales. He will have a hospitality suite at the annual trade show and unveil this feature at a party thrown for his dealers. You can easily send a snooper to this meeting to learn what the new feature is. What would you do?

8. You are eager to win a big contract, and during sales negotiations you learn that the buyer is looking for a better job. You have no intention of hiring him, but if you hinted that you might, he would probably give you the order. What would you do?

9. You have to make a choice between three ad campaigns outlined by your agency for your new product. The first (A) is a soft-sell, honest information campaign. The second (B) uses sex-loaded emotional appeals and exaggerates the product's benefits. The third (C) involves a noisy, irritating commercial that is sure to gain audience attention. Preliminary tests show that the commercials are effective in the following order: C, B and A. What would you do?

10. You are a marketing manager working for a beer company, and you have learned that a particularly lucrative State is planning to raise the minimum legal drinking age from 18 to 21. You have been asked to join other breweries in lobbying against this bill, and to make contributions. What would you do?

11. You want to interview a sample of customers about their reactions to a competitive product. It has been suggested that you invent an innocuous name like the Marketing Research Institute and interview people. What would you do?

12. You produce an antidandruff shampoo that is effective with one application. Your assistant says that the product would turn over faster if the instructions on the label recommended two applications. What would you do?

13. You are interviewing a capable female applicant for a job as sales representative. She is better qualified than the men just interviewed. At the same time, you suspect that some of your current salesmen will react negatively if she is hired, and you also know that some important customers may be ruffled. What would you do?

14. You are a sales manager in an encyclopaedia company. A common way for encyclopaedia representatives to get into homes is to pretend they are taking a survey. After they finish the survey, they switch to their sales pitch. This technique seems to be very effective and is used by most of your competitors. What would you do?

Exhibit 21-6   A Code of Conduct for Australian Managers?

Foreshadowing moves by other States, the Victorian division of the Australian Institute of Management has introduced a code of conduct and guide to good management practice. The moves follow a national council meeting last year which recommended that the States investigate and discuss the value of a code.

Queensland, Western Australia and South Australia have moved on codes of conduct and other States may do so. Queensland has a code similar to Victoria's, being printed for distribution to members, Western Australia is drawing one up and South Australia has a draft code which it hopes to distribute to members early next year. New South Wales has no immediate plans for a code and Canberra has a membership requirement that members abide by ethical practice.

The executive director of AIM (Victoria), Mr Ron Gilchrist, said he thought younger managers particularly would welcome some guidance on management practice. The code says members should at all times discharge allotted and accepted responsibilities as a manager with integrity and observe the standards in the guide to good management practice. It also says members should not misuse authority or office for personal gain, they should comply with the laws of Australia and operate within the spirit of those laws and, in their personal conduct, should not injure the standing and reputation of the AIM.

The guide to good management practice elaborates on the manager's responsibilities as a person, to his organization and to the community. These include respecting the confidentiality of information, accepting work only that managers believe they are competent to do, the development of communication, delegation of authority wherever possible, and acceptance of the responsibility of subordinates. Managers should also make every endeavour to conserve the environment.

A major feature of the code and guide is that they are not enforceable. The president of AIM (Victoria), Mr J. H. Curtis, said that although the code was binding it was not intended to use it as an instrument of discipline against members. 'The code's major value lies in its declaration of good intentions by way of a statement of accepted standards of behaviour', Mr Curtis said.

Mr Gilchrist said he had anticipated criticism of the code as 'window dressing'. 'Some malicious people would say that this is just window dressing and doesn't mean anything', he said. But, although he had expected this criticism it had not eventuated. Members and companies had reacted well and Melbourne University was planning to use the code in a management course.

Although the code was intended to be a guide for managers, AIM also hoped it would improve managers' standing in the community. 'We must accept that to society, the standard of business ethics is not seen to be very high', Mr Gilchrist said. 'I do not believe that society sees that business conducts itself in a highly ethical manner. I think society is kind of suspicious that there is cheating and unethical behaviour and bribery and all sort of things going on.' Mr Gilchrist said he felt this reputation was undeserved.

The code was based on similar codes from management organizations overseas, including those in Thailand and Britain.

Source: Kerry O'Shea, 'Victoria Sets National Example with AIM Code of Conduct', *Australian Financial Review*, 4 November 1980, p. 16.

fourteen cases, their marketing behaviour might well be described as immoral or amoral. On the other hand, if they refuse to go along with *any* of the actions, they might be ineffective as marketing managers and unhappy because of the constant moral tension. Obviously managers need a set of principles that will help them determine the moral gravity of each situation and how far they can go in good conscience.

All ethical philosophies deal with one or more of three characteristics of the act: they judge either the act itself (moral idealism), the actor's motives (intuitionism), or the act's consequences (utilitarianism).

Moral idealism is the most rigid in that it postulates certain acts to be bad under all (or most) circumstances. Moral idealism gives marketing managers the most definite answers to most of the questions raised in Table 21-1. They would refuse to hear private information or spy on competitors, deceive customers, and so on. As one executive put it, 'I would refuse to do anything that I would be ashamed to admit to on national television.' By refusing to let the ends justify the means, these executives would derive a greater feeling of correct conduct.

Intuitionism is less rigid, leaving it up to individual managers to sense the moral gravity of the situation. If managers feel that their motives are good and that they are not out to hurt anyone, they are taking an intuitive approach to these morally difficult situations.

Utilitarianism is the most deliberative of the three systems, seeking to establish the moral locus not in the act or the motives but in the consequences. If the consequences of the act (both good and bad) to the individual and society represent a net increase in society's happiness, or at least not a net decrease, the act is right.

Ultimately each marketer must choose and work out a philosophy of proper behaviour. Every moral system is predicated on some conception of the good life and the relation of one's welfare to that of others. Once the marketer works out a clear philosophy and set of principles, these will help cut through the many knotty questions posed by marketing and other human activities.

Marketing executives of the late 1980s will find their jobs full of challenges. They will face abundant marketing opportunities opened up by technological advances in solar energy, home computers and robots, cable television, modern medicine, and new forms of transport, recreation and communication. At the same time, forces in the socio-economic environment will increase the constraints under which marketing can be carried out. Those companies that are able to pioneer new values and practise societally responsible marketing will have a world to conquer.

PRINCIPLES FOR FUTURE PUBLIC POLICY TOWARD MARKETING

Finally, we want to consider a set of principles that might guide the formulation of public policy related to marketing. Too often, various laws are passed to correct specific abuses without considering them in the context of a larger set of objectives that the society wants to achieve through its marketing system. Here we will propose seven basic principles on which the marketing system and public policy might be modelled.

The Principles of Consumer and Producer Freedom

To the maximum extent possible, marketing decisions should be made by consumers and producers in relative freedom.

There are three possible levels of *producer freedom* in a society. The first is where producers have no freedom to decide what to produce, in that the state prescribes or approves all products. The second level is where producers are free to produce whatever they think

Exhibit 21-7 Constructive Responses to Consumerism

In 1974 Professors Greyser and Diamond surveyed major American companies to learn what steps they took to respond to consumerism. They found that 51 per cent upgraded product quality and performance standards; 26 per cent established industry product standards; 24 per cent increased research commitments to better identify consumer wants and needs; 23 per cent modified products for greater safety, ease of use, and repair; 22 per cent made postsale follow-up calls on consumers; 20 per cent supported industry self-regulation efforts; 19 per cent made advertisements more informative; 16 per cent developed owner's manuals on product use, care and safety; 15 per cent created new organizational positions to deal with consumer affairs; and 14 per cent provided more informative product labelling.

In developing constructive consumer programmes, a major issue is how to bring consumer influence into the company decision-making process. In addition to the usual steps of surveys and suggestion and complaint systems, further positive steps can be taken. A major supermarket chain appointed a consumer advisory board consisting of twenty-five women shoppers, who hold monthly meetings with the chain's high-level managers. A large number of leading manufacturers have created a consumer-affairs unit that handles customer inquiries and complaints, disseminates information to customers, deals with consumer interest groups, and acts as a consumer ombudsman. The consumer-affairs unit also carries out a consumer-affairs audit to determine how well the company is serving customers. It reports its findings to management for constructive response.

Source: Stephen A. Greyser & Steven L. Diamond, 'Business Is Adapting to Consumerism', *Harvard Business Review,* September–October 1974, p. 57; E. Patrick McGuire, *The Consumer Affairs Department: Organization and Functions* (New York: Conference Board, 1973); and *Consumerism: The Corporate Response* (Melbourne: John Clemenger, 1975).

the market wants, with the exception of certain product categories for which they must gain approval (e.g. addictive drugs, dangerous medicines, pornography, explosives, and so on). The third level is where producers are free to produce anything the market will pay for.

Similarly, there are three possible levels of *consumer freedom*. The first is where consumers have no freedom to decide what to consume: they must live in prescribed homes, eat prescribed food, wear prescribed clothing, and participate in prescribed rituals and recreations. The second level is where consumers are free to consume whatever is available, with the exception of certain product categories that are banned or require special permission (as described above). The third level is where consumers are free to buy and consume anything that the producers are willing to offer.

There is a tendency to find producer and consumer freedom at approximately the same level in different societies. Examples of level-one societies are monasteries, kibbutzim, tribal groups, highly religious communities, and communist societies. Here production and consumption patterns are precisely determined. Citizen satisfaction is likely to be high because individuals have a limited concept of material and cultural alternatives, and the tensions of human choice are not present. The possibility of self-actualization is particularly unavailable.

Level-two societies describe most modern industrial states that permit most things to be produced and consumed. These societies have active entrepreneurial classes seeking to learn what consumers want and responding with a large variety of goods and services. When active producer competition is present, consumers generally enjoy a high degree of choice and satisfaction with the available products and services. Their greatest dissatisfaction is felt in product categories that are restricted or unavailable, and in social goods that are scarce relative to private goods.

Level-three societies, i.e. that impose hardly any restrictions on either production or consumption, are rare, although certain societies have more freedom than others. Consider a normally restricted product category such as pornography: here Spain is at level one, Australia at level two, and Denmark is at level three. It is rare to find any nation at level three in all product categories.

This principle assumes that a high level of marketing freedom is important if a marketing system is to deliver a high level of life quality. People are able to achieve satisfaction in their own terms rather than those defined by someone else; it leads to a closer matching of products to desires, and therefore the chance of greater fulfilment. High freedom for producers and consumers is the cornerstone of a dynamic marketing system. But further propositions are necessary to implement this freedom and to prevent the social dysfunctions of absolute freedom.

The Principle of Curbing Potential Harm

The political system intervenes in producer or consumer freedom only if serious harm would occur in the absence of intervention. As far as possible, transactions freely entered into by producers and consumers are their private business, not the concern of third parties, except in the case of transactions that harm, or threaten to harm, one or both of the parties or a third party. This principle is widely recognized as grounds for government intervening in transactions. The major issue is whether there is real and sufficient actual or potential harm to justify the intervention. For this, it is necessary to distinguish five different levels of harm that might result from a private transaction.

The *no-harm situation* describes the case where neither the production nor the consumption of the product or service harms producers, consumers, third parties, or society in the short or long run. This will serve as a benchmark case: the more immediate the harm, the lower the level number.

Level-one harm is where the production of the good is a source of short- or long-run harm to those who produce it. Workers are hurt when they are subjected to noxious or dangerous processes or to excessively long hours. Child-labour and factory-safety laws have been passed to reduce the likelihood of harm to those engaged in production.

Level-two harm is where the consumption or use of the goods can cause immediate harm to the consumer, whether through ignorance or intention. This type of harm justifies the banning or regulation of unsafe drugs, materials, toys, and so on. The amount of regulation varies with the potential severity, incidence and imminence of the harm.

Level-three harm is where the consumers are gratified by the product but harmed in the long run: it has been used, for example, to justify restriction or prohibition of pornographic materials or cigarettes. Thus it is argued that the consumer of pornographic material will suffer degradation of character or the smoker of cigarettes will lose his health. There is an implication that this may in turn cause others to suffer – family or other citizens – but the primary emphasis is on protecting the specific consumer from being harmed through ignorance or indifference. There is a serious question, however, of how far the state should be allowed to intervene in such cases: the possibilities range from simple advertisement of the danger (e.g. requiring cigarette manufacturers to include the following statement on their cigarette packages: 'Warning: Smoking is a Health Hazard', to restricting consumption (e.g. to certain groups, or in the amount available for consumption per period), to outright prohibition. The mood of the times is toward increased government responsibility for informing the public of the potential harm of the product.

Level-four harm is where neither the producers nor the consumers are harmed in the short or long run, but adjacent third parties are harmed during or after production or consumption. This may include persons living or travelling near the place of production or consumption who may inhale the bad air, be exposed to physical danger (through high voltage or dangerous equipment), or be exposed to sights or sounds that may cause physical or mental pain. For example, there are growing proposals to limit smoking to certain areas of a public facility, or pornography to certain areas of a city.

Level-five harm is where neither the producers nor the consumers are harmed, but society suffers in the long run: the major example is environmental pollution caused by unregulated production or consumption. Pollution grows arithmetically or geometrically with industrial development, and tends not to be regulated until a nation satisfies the basic needs of its people; it is viewed as a small price to pay for rapid economic development when per-capita incomes are low. Many developing nations either have no laws regulating pollution or carefully avoid enforcing the laws so as not to discourage investment. In industrially advanced nations, the abundance of material goods and the growing scarcity of clean air, water and nature are prompting

regulation and enforcement to reduce this source of societal harm.

In examining the five levels of potential harm, levels one and two are almost universally recognized as justified areas of regulation by the state because they involve imminent and serious potential harm to producers or consumers. Level three is coming under increasing regulation, as reform organizations exert pressure on the state to regulate or at least inform users of the potential long-run harm from the use of certain products. Levels four and five are just beginning to be regulated in the more advanced countries. The society that is trying to maximize life quality will probably become more active in regulating levels three, four and five where the long-run negative effects are substantial.

The Principle of Meeting Basic Needs

The marketing system should serve the needs of disadvantaged consumers as well as affluent consumers. In a free-enterprise system, producers produce goods for markets that are willing and able to buy. If certain groups lack purchasing power they may go without essential goods, causing harm to their physical or psychological well-being.

The social imbalance of goods and services appears in both poor and rich nations. Some groups in the population are able to obtain a great quantity of goods, while other groups struggle to obtain the basic requisites of food, clothing and shelter; social services such as medical care and education are also ill distributed.

The two common solutions to the problem of unbalanced social output are illustrated in the USSR and Scandinavia. The Russian solution calls for a complete determination by the state of the mix of goods and services, through the mechanism of central planning. The state attempts to supply goods in the order of their need priority, making sure that everyone has a basic level of food, clothing, shelter, medical care, and education; surplus resources are invested in the development of less-necessary goods and services.

The Scandinavian solution calls for preserving the principle of producer and consumer freedom, but using economic and political interventions to bring social output closer into line with need priorities. Through high and progressive income taxes, the surplus incomes of the rich are transferred to the poor through welfare payments and improved social services. The system eliminates extremes of income: most people are in the middle, enjoying basic amenities; 'higher goods and services' are looked forward to by all inhabitants rather than the few.

Many of the free nations of the world are moving toward the Scandinavian solution, although it is recognized that this creates in its wake greater government bureaucracy, some loss of freedom, and some loss of individual incentive.

The Principle of Economic Efficiency

The marketing system strives to supply goods and services efficiently and at low prices. Every society is characterized by scarce resources in relation to the population's needs and wants. The extent to which these needs and wants can be satisfied depends upon the efficiency with which the existing resources are used. Inefficiency or waste exists if the society could produce the same output with fewer resources, or more output with the same resources – the cost is measured by the satisfaction that consumers would have enjoyed from the goods that have not been produced.

Free economies and centrally planned economies use different principles to achieve efficiency. Free economies rely on active producer competition and informed buyers to make a market efficient. Competitors are assumed to be profit maximizers who develop products, prices and marketing programmes attuned to buyer needs and values, and watch costs carefully. Buyers are assumed to be utility maximizers who are aware of competitive products, prices and qualities, and choose carefully. The presence of active competition and well-informed buyers is assumed to keep quality high and prices low.

The centrally planned economy thinks of efficiency in terms of accurate forecasting of consumer and industry demand, and the arrangement of methods and capacities to mass-produce the required goods and services at low cost. A premium is placed on production efficiency through group incentives and bonuses; there is less attention paid to consumer efficiency in terms of information, waiting time, and assortment choice.

The Principle of Innovation

The marketing system encourages authentic innovation. An effective marketing system makes provision for continual investment in both process and product innovation. The former seeks to bring down the cost of production and distribution; product innovation seeks to formulate new products to meet evolving consumer needs and desires.

Product innovation raises the issue of distinguishing between authentic and trivial innovation. Marketers tend to be concerned with the market's acceptance of new features and styles, not with whether the innovation represents a genuine contribution to human welfare. Much of what is called innovation is simply imitation of other brands with a slight difference to provide a talking-point. The consumer may confront ten brands in a product class, but have far less real choice than implied by the number of brands. This disproportion between the number of brands and the number of really different products is known as the problem of brand proliferation. An effective marketing system is one that encourages real product innovation and differentiation to meet the preferences of different market segments. However, it relies mainly on exhortation and consumer education rather than interfering with the principle of maximum producer and consumer freedom.

The Principle of Consumer Education and Information

The marketing system invests heavily in consumer education and information, as a means to increase long-run consumer satisfaction and welfare. The principle of economic efficiency requires that the society actively invest in consumer education and information. This is particularly important in technologically advanced nations, where goods and brands are confusing because of their abundance and conflicting claims, and therefore the consumer must have some way of evaluating product differences and making intelligent choices. This may appear to be self-evident but many modern nations provide woefully inadequate consumer education and information. In fact, four levels of 'consumer investment' can be found.

Level-one consumer investment is where there is little or no manufacturer information, government information, or private consumer organization information, and little or no consumer education. This level characterizes most economies at the start of their industrial development, and the situation is one of 'buyer beware'.

Level-two consumer investment is where there is some manufacturer-supplied information in the form of branding and labelling, but little or no government or private information. Most of the manufacturer-supplied information is promotionally rather than educationally oriented. Consumer education is underdeveloped, taking the form of a few home-economics courses poorly taught and held in low esteem by the education establishment.

Level-three consumer investment is where there is more manufacturer information, some government publications directed to help consumers recognize values in major product categories, and some private consumer organizations' ratings of products available to subscribers. Consumer education in the public schools is taught with more competence but still is a minor part of the curriculum. This is generally the level of consumer investment found currently in Australia.

Level-four consumer investment is where full manufacturer information is required by law (such as nutritional labelling and freshness dating in the case of foods), and more accurate manufacturer advertising exists because of vigorous enforcement of truth-in-advertising legislation. Private consumer organizations and the government are also active in disseminating product information and evaluations, and lean hard on manufacturers to provide better information and better products. Finally, the schools have consumer-education programmes that run for several years and train future citizens in the purchase of foods, drugs, cars, appliances, fabrics, insurance, banking service, and so on. This level of consumer investment is currently found in Sweden.

The Principle of Consumer Protection

The marketing system must supplement consumer education and information with consumer protection in certain product areas and market practices. Consumer education and information cannot do the whole job of protecting consumers. Modern products are often so complex technologically that even trained consumers cannot buy them with confidence: consumers will not be able to discern whether a colour-television set has too high a level of radiation, whether a new car is designed with adequate safety, and whether a new drug product is without dangerous side-effects. Therefore it is necessary for a government agency to review and render a verdict on the safety levels of products in many classes, notably foods, pharmaceuticals, toys, appliances, fabrics, motor vehicles, and housing. Failure to pursue this actively would lead to an increase in the number of deaths and disabilities. Even well-intentioned producers often do not recognize product faults until they are pointed out.

Consumer protection also stretches to cover production and marketing activities that are environmentally destructive. Here the consumers may readily buy products and fail to understand the consequences of their consumption, not only on the quality of the land and water but on the kind of air they breathe. Consumer protection also covers the prevention of deceptive practices and certain high-pressure selling techniques in situations where the consumer acting alone would be defenceless.

The assumption behind these seven principles is that the goal of the marketing system is not to maximize producers' profits or total consumption or consumer choice, but rather to maximize life quality. That is, how well can the citizens of a society satisfy their basic material needs, experience a high availability of varied and good-quality products, enjoy their physical environment, and find satisfaction in their cultural environment? Since the marketing system has a major impact on the quality of life, it must be managed on principles consistent with improving the quality of life.

SUMMARY

A marketing system should function to sense, serve and satisfy consumer needs, and enhance the quality of their lives. In endeavouring to meet consumer needs, businesspeople may take certain actions that are not to everyone's liking or benefit. The marketing system has frequently been criticized, and marketing executives should be fully aware of this.

Marketing's impact on consumer welfare has been criticized for high prices, deceptive practices, high-pressure selling, shoddy or unsafe products, and planned obsolescence. Marketing's impact on society has been criticized for excessive materialism, false wants, insufficient social goods, cultural pollution, and excessive political power. Marketing's impact on business competition has been criticized for anti-competitive acquisition, high barriers to entry, and predatory competition.

These felt abuses of the marketing system have given rise to various citizen-action movements, the most important being consumerism and environmentalism. Consumerism is an organized social movement seeking to strengthen the rights and power of consumers vis-à-vis sellers. Resourceful marketers will recognize it as an opportunity to serve consumers better through providing more consumer information, education and protection. Environmentalism is an organized social movement seeking to minimize the harm done by marketing practices to the environment and quality of life. It calls for intervening in consumer wants when their satisfaction would create too high a cost to the environment.

Citizen action has led to the passage of many new laws designed to protect consumers in the area of product safety, truth in packaging, truth in lending, and truth in advertising.

While many businesses initially opposed these social movements and laws, most of them now realize that there is a need for positive consumer information, education and protection. Some companies have gone further and have pursued a policy of enlightened marketing based on the principles of consumer orientation, innovation, value creation, social mission, and societal orientation. They have also formulated company policies and guidelines, and have described ways in which their executives can deal with moral dilemmas.

Future public policy must be guided by a set of principles that will improve the marketing system's contribution to the quality of life.

The set of principles calls for relative consumer and producer freedom, intervention only where there is potential harm, arrangements to adequately meet basic consumer needs, the practice of economic efficiency, emphasis on authentic innovation, and the provision of consumer education, information and protection.

QUESTIONS FOR DISCUSSION

1. Which two criticisms of marketing's impact on individual consumer welfare are the most legitimate? Briefly defend your position.

2. Critics of marketing's impact on society are really condemning our business system rather than just the area of marketing. Comment.

3. If the Trade Practices Commission were proposing to restrict mergers between large (over $2 billion in sales) companies, which criticisms of marketing's impact on other business would this help to alleviate? Why?

4. How does consumerism differ from environmentalism? Which poses the greater threat to marketing? Explain.

5. Discuss the five principles of enlightened marketing.

6. Ethical issues facing marketing will decrease in the late 1980s. Comment.

7. If you were the marketing manager at a chemical company, how would you deal with the principle of curbing potential harm with regard to water pollution?

8. How might the scarcity of natural resources, including energy, affect the principles of economic efficiency and innovation in the future?

9. What relationship exists between the principles of consumer education and information, and consumer protection? Which will be the dominant one in the next ten years? Why?

NOTES

1 *The Silent Majority* (Melbourne: John Clemenger, 1977).

2 Paul W. Stewart & J. Frederick Dewhurst (with Louis Field), *Does Distribution Cost Too Much?* (New York: Twentieth Century Fund, 1939).

3 Ibid., p. 348.

4 See Jessica Mitford, *The American Way of Death* (New York: Simon & Schuster, 1963); and Timothy Hall, *The Ugly Face of Australian Business* (Sydney: Harper & Row, 1980).

5 Theodore Levitt, 'The Morality(?) of Advertising', *Harvard Business Review*, July–August 1970, pp. 84–92.

6 For an interesting comparative study, see Grahame R. Dowling, 'Information Content in US and Australian Television Advertising', *Journal of Marketing*, Autumn 1980, pp. 34–37.

7 *Report of the Director of Consumer Affairs 1978* (Melbourne: Government Printer, 1979), p. 49.

8 'Rattles, Pings, Dents, Leaks, Creaks – And Costs', *Newsweek*, 25 November 1968, p. 92.

9 'The Breakfast of Fatties?', *Chicago Today*, 24 July 1970.

10 Gerald B. Tallman, 'Planned Obsolescence as a Marketing and Economic Policy', in L. H. Stockman (ed.) *Advancing Marketing Efficiency*

(Chicago: American Marketing Association, 1958), pp. 27–39.

[11] Mitchell Cohen & Dennis Hale (eds), *The New Student Left* (Boston: Beacon Press, rev. edn, 1969), pp. 12–13.

[12] John Kenneth Galbraith, *The New Industrial State* (Boston: Houghton Mifflin, 1967), p. 200.

[13] Herbert Marcuse, *One-Dimensional Man* (Boston: Beacon Press, 1964), pp. 4–5.

[14] John Kenneth Galbraith, *The Affluent Society* (Boston: Houghton Mifflin, 1958), p. 255.

[15] Raymond A. Bauer & Stephen A. Greyser, *Advertising in America: The Consumer View* (Boston: Graduate School of Business Administration, Harvard University, 1968).

[16] See, for example, *The Corporate Dilemma* (Melbourne: John Clemenger, 1980), Part I.

[17] From an advertisement for *Fact* magazine, which does not carry advertisements.

[18] Mack Hanan, 'Corporate Growth through Venture Management', *Harvard Business Review*, January–February 1969, p. 44.

[19] Rachel Carson, *Silent Spring* (Boston: Houghton Mifflin, 1962).

[20] Paul R. & Ann H. Ehrlich, *Population, Resources, Environment: Issues in Human Ecology* (San Francisco: W. H. Freeman, 1970).

[21] Donnella H. Meadows, Dennis L. Meadows, Jorgen Randers & William W. Behrens III, *The Limits to Growth* (New York: Universe Books, 1972).

[22] See Norman Kangun, 'Environmental Problems and Marketing: Saint or Sinner?', in Jagdish N. Sheth & Peter L. Wright (eds), *Marketing Analysis for Societal Problems* (Urbana: University of Illinois, 1974).

[23] Gordon O. Pehrson, quoted in 'Flavoured Algae from the Sea', *Chicago Sun-Times*, 3 February 1965, p. 54.

[24] Peter Drucker, 'The Shame of Marketing', *Marketing/Communications*, August 1969, pp. 60, 64. (Italics supplied).

[25] Earl L. Bailey, *Formulating the Company's Marketing Policies: A Survey* (New York: Conference Board, Experiences in Marketing Management, No. 19, 1968), p. 3.

[26] Howard R. Bowen, *Social Responsibilities of the Businessman* (New York: Harper & Row, 1953), p. 215.

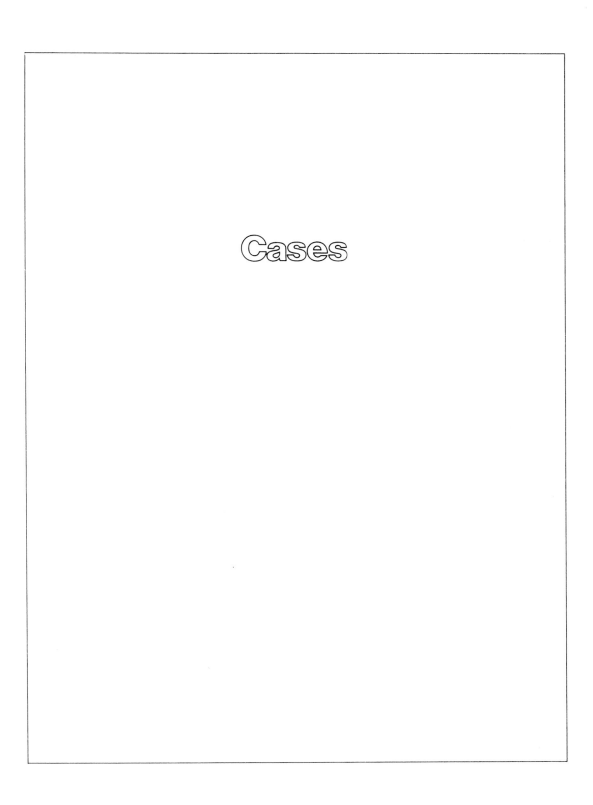

Cases

CASE 1 Harcourt Special Accommodation House

In 1976, Pam Proctor and a friend decided to seek a business venture to utilize a small amount of idle funds and provide a source of interest. A rest home was considered suitable, as one of the prospective partners had experience in this field. Harcourt was selected from a number of other rest homes on the market, after investigations over a four-month period. The pre-tax return on capital indicated by the existing lessees for taxation purposes was 50 per cent. Bed occupancy had been stable at 96 per cent over the previous twelve months. A feasibility study undertaken by accountants Arthur Young & Co. suggested that the business was sound and of attractive potential, and the partners secured bank finance for the remaining portion of the leasehold price.

Harcourt was located at 300 High Street, Windsor, an older residential and commercial suburb about 5 kilometres from central Melbourne. Registered under the State Health Act, 1958 and governed by the Special Accommodation House Regulations, 1974, it had bed space for twenty-two elderly ladies. Bedrooms ranged from single to sharing for four persons. The premises had originally been a family home of the Victorian era, converted to comply with regulations by previous lessees. Although in need of maintenance, the facilities and location appeared most suitable. Windsor had many services catering for the needs of the elderly. Prahran Market and shopping centre was within two kilometres. Housing Commission flats and homes for the elderly were also in close proximity. Further details of the Prahran local government area are given in Appendix II.

The business was purchased and the partnership took over on April Fool's Day 1976, with three and a half years remaining of a four-year lease. The length of this lease at the time of negotiation was considered quite reasonable in the light of economic conditions.

The partnership was dissolved after six months, as the working partner remarried and decided to move interstate. However, Pam Proctor continued to operate the business, employing a manageress. She felt that Harcourt provided a necessary service for elderly persons whose relatives were no longer able or willing to tend them. Whilst some elderly persons may require hospitalization or full nursing care, many are ambulant and continent but at risk or insufficiently capable of caring for themselves. Such persons did not require the facilities of a nursing home, but merely rest-home care as provided by Harcourt. Another need catered for was after-care, for elderly persons recovering after hospitalization.

Pam described the role of Harcourt in the following manner: 'Harcourt aims to provide a homely atmosphere where residents share a sense of belongingness, permanency and security. Uprooting the elderly from familiar surroundings is one of the greatest health hazards they face. The potential for companionship is plentiful, limited only by the personal disabilities of residents such as hardness of hearing, limited mobility, and so on. All physical needs are amply catered for. Meals are excellent, rooms are heated, cleanliness is regarded as essential. There is colour television. Safety requirements are foremost. To avoid potential accidents, residents are assisted with bathing and other hazardous activities as required. Medications and health needs are handled with meticulous care. As much care is taken as possible to provide mental comfort, although this is not possible in all circumstances, particularly when residents regard themselves as having been "abandoned" by their families.'

Harcourt had had an impressive history of occupancy. Pam felt that the need for rest-home care would increase in the future, as advances in preventive and rehabilitative medicine have increased the proportion of elderly people in the community. Australian government statistics indicated that the proportion of the Australian population aged 65 years and over rose from 4.5 per cent in 1921, to 8.75 per cent in 1977. By 1991, it was expected to increase to about 10 per cent. A home for elderly females was considered to be additionally secure, as wives often outlived their husbands by a considerable number of years. For instance, Pam discovered that in 1975 there were 191 410 more females than males in the 65-and-over age group in Australia.[1]

However, difficulties associated with occupancy levels became evident during the last half of 1977, when one bed was often vacant and occasionally two beds were vacant. Since late 1977 the problem has been of increasing concern, and currently some sixteen beds were occupied on average. However, to date, the business had been able to support its bank-loan repayments.

Pam felt that an apparent change in industry conditions was primarily responsible. She noticed that during 1979, a relatively large percentage (16 per cent) of Melbourne special accommodation houses were advertised for sale in the *Age*, and advertisements of bed vacancies in private hospitals also began to appear. Bed numbers in private hospitals appeared to be rising, and Pam felt that medical-benefit provisions enabled recoupment of such costs, and thus represented a cheaper alternative for an elderly person and her relatives.

Rest-home care was not subsidized by the government, and special accommodation houses tended to base their charges on the age pension. Residence at Harcourt absorbed most, if not all, of the single pension, depending upon whether single or shared facilities were occupied. Families may have found it cheaper to send an elderly relative to a nursing home for intermittent 'hospital holidays' to obtain relief from the continual responsibility of caring. During the hospital stay, the entire pension could have been saved to help defray any excess required for subsequent hospitalization.

Another influence on the occupancy levels of rest homes was federal government provision of capital assistance for self-contained accommodation. Domiciliary care facilities had also been improved at the local-council level, Windsor/Prahran being no exception. Nearby Caulfield Council had established live-in care centres such as Heathlands Community Centre. Facilities comprised individual accommodation with *en suite* facilities for forty-eight elderly persons in a modern and attractively landscaped environment. Although the ingoing fee was reputed to be $5500, Pam heard that this was waived for needy cases. The weekly rate was a mere $37, as Heathlands received a Council subsidy. Thus charges were significantly lower than at rest homes such as Harcourt, and lengthy waiting lists had been reported at similar facilities in Chelsea, Knox and Springvale.

The possibility of inappropriate classification by doctors, and consequent acceptance of patients by nursing homes, was suggested by a social-worker friend as another possible cause of falling rest-home occupancy levels. She reported that 'light' nursing patients were eagerly accepted by nursing homes, as this reduced the staff workload. Although not presently in need of extensive nursing or hospitalization, these patients were encouraged to apply in advance due to waiting lists and to enter at a stage when rest-home care would have amply catered to their

[1] Statistics derived from *Report of the Committee on Care of the Aged and the Infirm* (Canberra: Australian Government Publishing Service, 1977).

current needs. The Australian Department of Health had responsibility for reclassifying nursing-home patients, but budgetary restrictions permitted department doctors only to visit these homes about once every six to nine months. Hence there were delays in reclassification which could have caused some flow of patients from nursing homes to special accommodation houses such as Harcourt.

Pam used to receive inquiries from social workers at the various public hospitals and local doctors regarding vacancies at Harcourt, but the rate of inquiries had been falling. Whilst the business had initially been able to charge in excess of the pension, the highly competitive nature of the industry now made this impossible. Internal differentiation in fee levels according to beds per room was one recent action taken by Harcourt management to improve its competitiveness. However, no new avenues had been explored as regarded contacting potential residents.

Pam had acknowledged problems pertaining to the lessee-owner relationship: there had been problems renegotiating the lease, and she was currently uncertain whether the owner would extend beyond the eighteen months remaining. Although the premises needed painting inside and outside, it appeared impractical to upgrade the premises given the lack of current profits and uncertainty of tenure. She felt that Harcourt may have currently been regarded as of average standard compared with the widely varying range of competing rest homes.

Pam was unhappy with current profitability, which merely enabled her to pay monthly mortgage obligations and running costs. However, she felt that sale of the business should not be considered in the short term unless the lease were renegotiated. She had heard that sale was easier if the freehold or a substantial lease term was offered to enable potential buyers to recoup capital and profits before facing the uncertainty of lease renewal.

To convert Harcourt to a nursing home would necessitate extensive modifications to comply with requirements of the Hospitals and Charities Commission. Upgrading of facilities would be expensive, available space for patients would be reduced from the current twenty-two beds, and a specific proportion of trained staff would be required. Problems could also have occurred in obtaining the permission of the owner and council approval.

This did not appear to be a viable option if the business continued to be operated at the current premises. However, Pam recognized that a strategy must be devised to improve profitability and avert a potential cash-flow problem.

APPENDIX I PRIVATE HOSPITALS AND NURSING HOMES

Most private hospitals are privately owned and administered along profitable business lines, although some may best be described as non-profit organizations with their ownership resting mainly in religious denominations.

Private hospitals accommodate short-term and acutely ill patients, and private nursing homes accommodate patients requiring constant nursing care for an indefinite period. Patients may be the frail aged, bed-ridden, near bed-ridden, or totally dependent children.

Private hospitals and nursing homes must always be staffed according to regulations under the Victorian Health Act, e.g. the ratio of qualified nursing and domestic staff to patients must not be allowed to fall below a determined level.

In June 1979, nursing-home and rehabilitation beds available in State, voluntary and private hospitals totalled approximately 12 400, while hostels accommodated approximately 7500 persons. Since the provision of beds alone could not adequately serve disabled or elderly persons, community health centres, improved domiciliary services, and more day hospitals are being established. Day hospital attendances approximated 345 000 during 1978–79.

Elderly persons in the Melbourne metropolitan area receive dental care at the clinic in the Royal Dental Hospital of Melbourne. Treatment is also provided at clinics established in eighteen major country centres and in geriatric centres.

Meals-on-wheels services at 30 June 1979 were provided by eighty-two hospitals in cooperation with a number of organizations, supplying 120 meals-on-wheels areas.

Welfare Services

The aim of the home-help service, senior citizens' clubs, and municipal welfare officers engaged in welfare for the aged is to assist them in pursuing independent lives in their own surroundings for as long as possible. Duties of a home help are to maintain the household's routine, assist with household chores, do the shopping and prepare meals. Assessment of charges is made according to the person's ability to pay. Health Commission advisers are available to discuss problems and they make regular visits to municipalities for this purpose.

Elderly citizens' clubs provide facilities for fostering social companionship for the elderly, and supply the environment for them to make new friends and take a renewed interest in life. Municipal councils are paid a subsidy through the Health Commission to establish and maintain these clubs, which provide activities such as carpet bowls, billiards, crafts and entertainment. Services such as hot meals and chiropody help maintain health and comfort, meals-on-wheels being confined to housebound elderly persons. Routine visits are made by assistant advisers to municipal councils to discuss existing clubs, the implementation of new services, or the formation of new clubs. Regular discussions are conducted with club members in an attempt to broaden club activities and instil a sense of responsibility in members.

A welfare officer, subsidized by the Health Commission, is employed by a municipal council to ensure the development, coordination and continuing provision of welfare services appropriate to the needs of the elderly, to supervise existing services, foster cooperation, promote purposeful activity within elderly citizens' clubs, and help the elderly realize that aid is available.

Nursing-home Benefits Arrangements

The current nursing-home benefits arrangements are the result of major changes introduced by the Commonwealth Government on 1 October 1977.

At 8 November 1979, the basic nursing-home benefit in Victoria was payable up to a maximum of $22.70 per day. In addition, an extensive care benefit of $6 per day was payable.

Prior approval for the admission of patients to participating nursing homes must be obtained from the Commonwealth Department of Health. Approval for admission also acts as approval for the payment of basic benefits; it is also required for the payment of extensive care benefits.

The Commonwealth government pays the appropriate benefits on behalf of uninsured patients accommodated in participating nursing homes. Private health-insurance organizations pay the appropriate benefit on behalf of insured patients accommodated in participating nursing homes.

Patients pay a prescribed minimum contribution towards accommodation costs. This contribution is now set at 87.5 per cent of the single pension, plus supplementary assistance. At 8 November 1979, the rate of contribution was $7.85 per day for participating nursing-home patients. These rates may be waived or reduced in cases of financial hardship.

The rates of benefit now payable, when combined with the prescribed minimum patient contribution, are designed to cover fully the approved fees charged for 70 per cent of the beds in non-government nursing homes.

Nursing-home inspections are conducted to ensure that patients are receiving the appropriate level of nursing care and to ensure that the patient classifications are correct. The National Health Act includes provisions under which the construction of new nursing homes or extensions to existing approved premises require departmental approval.

The Commonwealth government has maintained its control over nursing-home fees by continuing to make it a condition of approval under the National Health Act that participating nursing homes cannot charge fees in excess of those determined by the Commonwealth Department of Health.

Nursing home benefits paid (Victoria) ($000)

	1974–75	1975–76	1976–77	1977–78	1978–79
Commonwealth government	36 631	43 019	51 831	55 922	50 505
Private health funds	2 882	3 963	3 244	17 676*	31 142*
Total benefits paid	39 513	46 982	55 075	73 598	81 647

* The increase in benefits paid by the private health insurance funds is due to the change in the nursing-home arrangement from 1 October 1977

Source: Adapted from the *Victorian Year Book No. 94* (Victoria: Australian Bureau of Statistics), pp. 623–40.

APPENDIX II   CITY OF PRAHRAN: COMPARATIVE STATISTICAL SUMMARY

	City of Prahran	Melbourne Statistical Division
Population (1976)	50 900	2 672 000
Annual rate of growth in population (%)	– 2.34	+ 1.22
Age structure, percentage of total population:		
Under 15 years	15.2	26.6
15–29 years	31.0	26.0
30–44 years	18.6	18.8
45–59 years	15.4	16.0
60 and over	19.9	12.6
Family type, percentage of total number of families:		
Head only	50.7	20.3
Head and spouse only	19.5	21.6
Head, spouse and children	12.8	28.6
Household ownership, percentage of total occupied private dwellings:		
Ownership	37.6	69.6
Private tenancy	46.4	20.1
Public tenancy	6.0	2.9

Source: Melbourne and Metropolitan Board of Works, *Comparative Local Statistics, Melbourne Statistical Division,* August 1981.

Question

Review the alternatives open to Harcourt Special Accommodation House and prepare a comprehensive marketing plan for Pam Proctor.

CASE 2 The Bee Bee Biscuit Company Ltd

The Bee Bee Biscuit Company Ltd (for 'better baked' biscuits) is today one of the leading biscuit manufacturing groups in Australia. From its origins in 1851 as a manufacturer of ship's biscuits, expansion has occurred into all Australian States, Papua-New Guinea and Singapore. Its diversified operations include a jam company, a flour-milling division, an engineering firm, a crumpet company, cardboard containers, dog food and a transport division.

Numerous generations of the families responsible for the firm's growth have built between them an impeccable reputation for quality. However, the prices of the quality ingredients used in its products have been rising recently. Profitability has been patchy due to a difficult business environment. The industry is highly competitive and both manufacturers and retailers have been involved in heavy promotional activity. Product proliferation strategies have been undertaken by all major biscuit manufacturers.

Objectives

The Bee Bee Biscuit Company has certain values and objectives, which have been built up since its foundation. Of prime importance is that efficiency is never to be substituted for quality: the company has built up a reputation for home-made, high-quality products, and this must be maintained.

The present goal may be summarized as profitable sales growth. Market share has recently been eroded, and plant is currently underutilized. However, the company ethos does not permit sales growth or increased efficiency at the expense of product quality.

In this atmosphere, and in fear of a further decline of its market share, Bee Bee Biscuits decided to launch a new biscuit in the hope of securing its position in the market.

New-Product Development Procedure

The Bee Bee Biscuit Company utilizes a standard new-product development procedure, encompassing the following stages:

Stage 1. Examination and analysis of the Grocery Research Index to determine possible unexploited market niches.

Stage 2. Interfirm biscuit comparisons.

Stage 3. Definition of the product concept — in this case, the need for a nutritious, high-energy biscuit.

Stage 4. Prototype development. The new-product development department, bakers, the testing laboratory and the sales department liaise to design the product: a round, glucose-creamed mould-cut biscuit. The advertising manager compiled a list of alternative names, and employees and management selected the name 'Sports'. This was believed to depict a nutritious food that provides high energy to the consumer who leads an active life. Packaging in a small eight-pack, with individual pouches, was expected to generate greater sales through repeat purchasing. Management selected a blue-and-white pack design, which clearly stated the company name and ingredients. The sugar content was emphasized, so that people would realize that 'Sports' generated a high energy level. The biscuit itself was not featured, as it was thought that this would detract from the eye appeal.

Stage 5. Trial. Having received approval from the new-product committee to proceed with the new biscuit, consumer taste tests were conducted at a Melbourne suburban shopping complex. A sample of 200 respondents, primarily female, tendered generally favourable comments, suggesting improvements that could be made to enhance the biscuit. The suggestions were considered by the committee, which concluded that many of the comments were not relevant to the marketing of 'Sports'.

Stage 6. Commercialization. First, the price was determined. Provisional costings were made: the company knew that people were usually prepared to pay from 90 cents to $1.20 depending upon the quality of the biscuit. 'Sports' were definitely in the more expensive range and of comparatively high quality. As the biscuits were a branded product, in an attractive package and supported by advertising, it was thought that consumers could be willing to pay $1.10 for a packet of eight biscuits. This price was expected to generate a net margin of 30 per cent, somewhat higher than margins for the majority of lines (averaged net margin 22 per cent).

An advertising budget of $180 000 was set, and a campaign based on the 'nutritious, home-made, high-energy' theme developed by the advertising manager. Advertising objectives were stated as follows:

- the establishment of 'Sports' as an entirely new biscuit;
- emphasis on home-made goodness and nutritious/high-energy value;
- strong identification of the Bee Bee Biscuit Company name.

Media selection included magazines, radio and television. Magazines were included because full-page colour spreads were believed to enhance product appeal through visual means. Copy strategy involved presentation by women who lead an active life. Radio and television were to have a supplementary, more minor role.

The advertising campaign opened with a full-page colour spread in the *Australian Women's Weekly* on 1 November 1980. Free advertising materials, which were modified versions of the press advertisements, were made available in all stores.

Market-demand Measurement

Estimates were made of volume requirements based on daily reports of sales ex-warehouse. At the end of the first thirteen weeks, the biscuit became part of the company range. An estimated and an actual sales report had been constructed for the period, and these figures were compared.

Estimated sales figures were usually based on past performance of a similar biscuit in the product range. As there was no biscuit to fill this requirement, management had to use a biscuit that was quite different in form, quality and appeal. Sales estimates were based on the following assumptions:

- *Opening order.*
  Total number of retail food outlets in Victoria presently ordering from Bee Bee Biscuits = 5000.

One-half of Victorian outlets (2500) would buy an average of two cases as opening order = 5000 cases
Each case cost $13.20
Sales revenue = 5000 × $13.20 = $66 500.
- *Projected annual sales.*
It was assumed that one-half of the Victorian stores would continue to buy two cases per week.
- *Annual sales revenue.*
2500 × 52 = 130 000 × $26.40 = $3 432 000.

Bee Bee Biscuits thought this to be a conservative estimate of sales, but it was considered to be sufficient for 'Sports' to yield a valuable contribution to the company's profits. When distribution was eventually extended to other States, considerably higher sales were expected in the long term.

Distribution

Sales representatives were briefed concerning product details. This was necessary as they had not been involved in the development of 'Sports'. Distribution was to be through the normal retail channels and was timed for late spring so that retailers would have time to stock up for the Christmas holiday trade. The presentation to retailers was made by a series of trade nights, the aim being to impart a strong product image.

Epilogue

As early as ten weeks after the commencement of advertising, the company noticed that sales were not reaching expectations. After six months, the prospect of failure was becoming more and more apparent.

Tom Smith, senior executive in the marketing department was given the task of preparing recommendations to overcome the failure of the biscuit. He must explain why 'Sports' failed and what marketing-mix changes might have prevented this. He must determine whether to keep 'Sports' on the market or delete it from the product range. His brief indicated certain broad options which could be examined:

1. To retain 'Sports', but reduce the price and cut the promotional budget substantially.
2. To withdraw 'Sports' from the market immediately, so as to cut losses as quickly as possible.
3. To retail 'Sports' in the product range and relaunch it.

Question

Prepare a critique of the Bee Bee Biscuit Company's new-product development procedure and its marketing strategy for 'Sports'. Examine the options facing Tom Smith and devise your own recommendations for the future marketing of 'Sports'.

CASE 3 Taurina Takes a Tumble

Summer 1980 will long be remembered as the summer of the natural wonder — mineral water. Whether it be taken straight, mixed with fruit juice, wine or whisky, consumers using the product belong to a rapidly expanding group in Australia.

In Europe it is anything but new. Its been around since Hannibal crossed the Alps in 218 B.C. Now the French consume an annual average of 50 litres per head of the population, whilst the European average exceeds 30 litres.

A European meal-table is rarely seen without the adornment of a bottle of mineral water — whether as a refreshing drink or as a substitute for poor local water. It is even considered chic to bathe or wash with mineral water. Perhaps nowhere is it as popular as in Italy, where some 2500 different brands are on the market.

Mineral water has recently flooded the US and UK markets at a staggering rate. In the United States, consumption has flourished from 0.5 litre per capita in 1973 to 1.9 litres in 1981, mainly due to the concentrated efforts of Apolinaris from France.

Following on the heels of this worldwide excitement, an Australian company prepared to make an adventurous assault on the local market under the Taurina brand. The product was derived from Helidon in Queensland, which had been given the highest accolades from sample tests carried out in Italy. Initial market research was undertaken at a cost of $14 000. Results indicated that a number of people in the prospective target market had a negative attitude towards mineral water. To start with there was low awareness of mineral water in its generic form. Then, many Australians who did know the product had lingering prejudice that mineral water was an antiquated European habit.

The research highlighted that 51 per cent of existing consumption was undertaken by migrants, although they represented only 30 per cent of the population.

In 1980, a history-making New South Wales test-market launch was achieved with Taurina Spa becoming the first-ever heavily advertised mineral water. The promotion, including a complete package revamp, was built around television/radio personality John Laws and the slogan of 'Mother Nature's soft-drink'. The concept was innovative, bold and expensive with a media launch cost of $400 000. Taurina Spa's strategy was designed to 'skim the cream' off the $4 million soft-drink market. In the words of the marketing manager at the time, 'What we are trying to do is to take the product out of the freak category and give it general use both as a straight drink and as a sophisticated mixer.'

The New South Wales launch exceeded all expectations. Sales in dollar terms for that market tripled within a few months, of which Taurina Spa took a massive 46 per cent of the total market. This marked the beginning of a rolling launch around Australia on a State-by-State basis.

In Victoria an arrangement was entered into with H.J. Heinz Australia Ltd, primarily to distribute the product. A two-pronged strategy was developed through two of its subsidiaries, with Epicure to sell direct to large wholesalers and the Stanley wine company to sell direct to individual grocery outlets, liquor shops, hotels, winebars and restaurants. The logic of the link with a wine marketer was based on the blending of wine and soda water known as 'spritzer' — an extremely popular drink overseas, and expected to take on in Australia.

By late 1980, the flood gates were opened as new brands such as Boon Spa, Deep Spring, Bisleri, Vichy and Apolinaris gushed on to the market. All jostled and elbowed to develop a unique position in the marketplace.

Cadbury Schweppes was an early entrant, with their 1250 ml bottle of manufactured mineral water made to a prescribed recipe unlike the natural waters of all other brands. They heavily emphasized the Schweppes label and stressed their balanced formula.

Hepburn Spa was another that had an entrenched market position. Established for over 100 years it held 70 per cent of the market for most of the last decade. For the last five years distribution had been through supermarkets. Like Schweppes and most other brands it was positioned as a natural and refreshing alternative to soft-drink.

The stage was set for the champagne of mineral waters to make an entrance — Perrier. Packaged in a small 385 ml green bottle compared with most others in the 750 ml family size, its position was uniquely aimed at the highest-priced market segment. Its retail price was around $1 per bottle compared with an average 40 cents for a 750 ml alternative.

Taurina Spa had achieved its objectives by expanding the total mineral-water market and capturing a large share of it. However disaster struck on 19 February 1981. The New South Wales Health Commission, after analyzing Taurina Spa, found that it contained substances that could be injurious to health: within a week the company had withdrawn the product from sale.

(*Note*: The Taurina Spa product currently on the market is sourced from three locations in New South Wales and Victoria. Australia Consolidated Press owns 75 per cent of the company; the remaining 25 per cent is held by Taurina Spa Pty Ltd.)

Questions

1. (a) What are the reasons for the changes in demand for mineral water in the United States and the United Kingdom?
   (b) Do these factors apply in Australia?
2. What market segment is Taurina Spa attempting to capture? How does this differ from Perrier's target market?
3. As marketing manager of Taurina, what steps would you have recommended after the product was banned from sale?
4. Develop an action blueprint for products in a similar situation.

CASE 4 Cool Profits in the Room Air-conditioning Market

In recent years, major retailers and discount stores have searched for new product opportunities in growth markets. To some extent they have found one in dishwashers even though the husband-and-wife washing and drying combination still prevails in most households. More recently, retailers have been pinning their hopes on room air-conditioners (RACs) as a major growth opportunity.

Since 1972, RACs (wall and window mounted, mobile, fascia, split consoles and ducted; see Appendix I) have enjoyed a combined annual growth of 15 per cent and in 1980–81 Australian retail sales registered $155 million or 160 000 units (see Appendix II). This is about half the size of the refrigerator market. Of this, $20 million worth was purchased by government instrumentalities, major project builders, mining-town developers and air-conditioning contractors. The remainder was distributed by retailers and RAC specialists mainly to consumer markets.

The market penetration level for RACs is still below 10 per cent of all Australian households. This compares with a market penetration level of 55 per cent in the United States, where they are often purchased like a television set at the local department store. The US company Carrier, in fact use the slogan 'Carry home a Carrier today'.

RACs were first purchased by Australian consumers in small quantities in the early 1950s. Sales expanded from that time until the late 1960s, but large-scale growth was hampered by the initial cost of the units and high operational costs. By the early 1970s, significant breakthroughs had occurred in manufacturing technology which resulted in a more reliable product which was also energy-efficient.

Many makes of RAC, particularly those purchased in Melbourne, had a reverse-cycle capability allowing them to be used for both heating and cooling purposes. Significant sales had been achieved with these units since the oil crisis of the late 1970s, when many consumers substituted them for their uneconomical oil heaters. As an example, using November 1981 prices, an oil heater was 60 per cent more expensive to run than a standard window-type RAC. Gas, which was by far the cheapest form of heat at 33 per cent lower than the operating cost of a RAC, attracted the majority of consumer demand as the market moved away from oil heaters.

Industry experts believe that RACs are now out of the luxury class. Retail prices for a standard wall unit are comparable to other discretionary purchases such as replacement refrigerators, colour-television sets, stereo units and package holidays. Most of these have a relatively high market penetration rate, and so industry observers forecast that RACs are poised at the beginning of the growth stage of their product lifecycle. Manufacturers believe that some categories of RAC have become impulse purchases, with sales peaks closely related to hot or humid weather. This particularly applies to small window and mobile units.

Email Air, which has 45 per cent of the national RAC market, expects the following growth patterns in retail sales to emerge over the next five years.

Category	Sales 1980–81 ($ million)	Annual average growth rate (%)	Estimated sales 1985–86 ($ million)*
1. Evaporative coolers (mobile type only)	11	2	12
2. Small window type (below 13 000 BTUs)	38	16.5	81
3. Large window type (above 13 000 BTUs)	39	9	60
4. Wall-hung fascia (above 13 000 BTUs)	23	20	57
5. Split consoles (including wall & ceiling types)	12	25	37
6. Ducted (including cost of duct work)	32	30	119
Total	155	19	366

* Expressed in 1980–81 dollar terms

Victorian Market

The summer of 1980–81 was a bumper season for RACs, with many leading manufacturers and retailers experiencing stockouts by November and December. Industry observers believed that this was caused by the unseasonally hot and humid weather. Melbourne consumers, who normally prefer reverse-cycle models, were prepared to purchase cooling-only units because of stock shortages, even though the price difference was only about $30.

In terms of unit sales, the Victorian market represented approximately 26 per cent of the national total, whilst Melbourne accounted for 70–75 per cent of the Victorian market.

Distribution

Over recent years, significant changes have occurred in the market regarding the distribution strategies of the major local manufacturers.

In 1977 Carrier, which held 25 per cent of the national RAC market had 400 retail accounts but reduced that to thirty-two dealers accounting for 85 per cent of their sales. Its stronger rival Email Air, with a 45 per cent market share, followed a similar strategy and now operates through five dealers (see Appendix IV for national market shares).

The flood of imports which now represents a major share of the market (Appendices V and VI) has led to the development of private brands for the major retailers. These are typically imported from Israel or South-East Asia and are usually the lowest-priced units on the market. The general tariff rate applicable to imported RACs is 25 per cent for developed nations and only 15 per cent for those classified as developing. In a study conducted by the Industries Assistance Commission in 1975, it was noted that some local manufacturers claimed that several South-East Asian countries were dumping small window-type RACs on the Australian market.

Because of the ease of entry into the lower-priced end of the market, both in manufacturing and importing, competition has been ruthless and profit margins small.

Pricing

The lower end of the market is considered to be highly sensitive and dominated by imported models. The table below outlines the average price ranges for the major product categories for 1981.

Evaporative coolers	$ 220– 350
Small window type	$ 250– 400
Large window type	$ 400– 600
Wall-hung fascia	$1200–1500
Split consoles	$2200–3000
Ducted	$2500–5000

Recently, noise legislation became an important factor in determining the types of units produced and subsequently purchased. Each State and Territory now has legislation which can be called upon to prevent a person using any noisy device which disturbs neighbours unnecessarily. Considerable development work has been undertaken by manufacturers to reduce the noise level of units. It is unlikely that this noise impediment can be fully overcome for wall and window RACs.

APPENDIX I PRODUCT DESCRIPTION

1. *Evaporative coolers*
   These provide cool air only, and reduce the air temperature by a forced air-circulation method.

2. *Window units*
   These box-type RACs are inserted into the wall or window of a room that requires temperature and humidity control. They have a relatively low purchase, installation and operating cost. Units with a reverse-cycle capability may be used for heating as an alternative to fuels such as gas, oil and kerosene.
   The major drawback of this unit is its lack of flexibility to heat and/or cool more than one room. A further problem is its noise both inside and outside the room.

3. *Wall-hung fascia*
   Fascia units are an improved version of the window/wall unit. Because of design and manufacturing modifications there is very little noise during operation inside or outside the room. These are much more attractive than the wall/window model.

4. *Split units*
   Split units separate the air-outlet panel from the motor, the cool or hot air being transmitted through pipes, which means that an outlet can be placed anywhere in the house and not necessarily against a wall. They may be pre-set for the desired temperature and operation time, and computer readouts are available on temperature and humidity conditions within the room. The location of the motor outside the house ensures silent internal operation.

5. *Ducted*
   This is an expansion of the split-unit system, with a number of air outlets being provided. To a large extent each installation is tailor-made to the specific requirements of the owners: the number of outlets and size of room influences the nature of air-conditioner plant required.

APPENDIX II TOTAL INDUSTRY STATISTICS, 1980 (AUSTRALIA)

	Total	Cooling	Reverse cycle
Small			
½ hp	23 000	23 000	—
¾ hp			
Other			
1 hp	30 000	18 000	13 000
1½ hp	31 000	9 000	23 000
1¾ hp	33 000	8 000	22 000
2 hp	43 000	12 000	32 000
Total other	137 000	47 000	90 000
Total Australian	160 000	70 000	90 000

Note: 10 000 BTU equals one horsepower (hp)

APPENDIX III VICTORIAN RAC UNIT SALES

Year (January/January)	Unit sales
1976–77	14 900
1977–78	24 060
1978–79	21 688
1979–80	27 000

APPENDIX IV NATIONAL MARKET SHARES, 1980 (%)

Email Air	45	(imports a major proportion)
Carrier	25	
Dunn Air	15	
Other (including imports)	15	
	100	

APPENDIX V LOCAL RAC PRODUCTION

1975–76	32 059
1976–77	41 006
1977–78	41 649
1978–79	45 454
1979–80	61 430

Source: Australian Bureau of Statistics, *Production Bulletin: Electricity, Gas and Electrical Appliances*, Cat. No. 8357.0.

APPENDIX V RAC IMPORTS

Electric portable refrigerative (not exceeding 12.7)*
Australian Commodity Classification No. 719.12.05

Year to date	Units	Value FOB ($000)
Nov. 1980–81	50 327	11 126
1979–80		
1978–79		
1977–78	48 931	10 147
1976–77	46 544	7 552
1975–76	19 756	3 526
1974–75	85 072	12 361
1973–74	36 578	5 117
1972–73	5 258	803
1971–72	6 559	881
1970–71	3 402	431
1969–70	2 669†	436†
1968–69	3 458†	322†

* Kilojoules/hour (1 Btu = 1.06 kj). (One British Thermal Unit (Btu) is the heat required to raise one pound of water one degree fahrenheit. One joule is the amount of force required to accelerate one kilogram mass one metre per second.)

† Figures for 1969–70, 1968–69 include categories 719.12.03 and 719.12.06 (Australian Bureau of Statistics classification).

Source: Australian Bureau of Statistics, *Overseas Trade, Australia, Part I, Exports and Imports*, Cat. No. 5409.0, various issues.

Question

A Melbourne-based businessman has an option to take the Victorian agency for a Japanese RAC manufacturer. The Japanese company has a reputation outside Australia for producing high-quality units, and if desired can compete in each of the RAC product categories.

You have been asked by the prospective agent to provide marketing advice. In particular you are required to detail the market segments that exist for RACs, and the appropriate product-mix strategy for the Japanese units. These details should form part of a marketing plan which will be submitted to the prospective agent.

CASE 5 Le Monde Tailoring

In the mid-1950s, Mr Fryde left his native Hungary and migrated to Australia. His training was as a tailor, a flourishing trade in Hungary, so he began work in Sydney as a full-time employee of already established tailors before later tailoring for his circle of friends.

In 1959 he set up shop in Oxford Street, Darlinghurst, and later moved his business to Elizabeth Bay. The business was proving to be quite profitable and a loyal clientele was being established. In 1965, rental premises were secured in Double Bay, an area renowned for its specialty shops catering to affluent residents and tourists. Double Bay appeared to offer more passing traffic than Elizabeth Bay, being a popular shopping centre for the sophisticated and wealthy Sydney shopper.

The move was successful and widened the number of Mr Fryde's regular clients. Their positive word-of-mouth recommendations regarding the quality and service of Le Monde Tailoring had now become the major source of new clients.

The shop in Double Bay comprised a workshop at the rear, containing machinery and trimmings (accessories required to make garments) and the front section contained a range of menswear, materials and the fitting room.

The range and stock of menswear was not extensive, being valued at approximately $2500 and consisting of shirts, ties, socks, singlets, underwear, cufflinks, handkerchiefs, pyjamas, shaving coats, jumpers, braces, cravats and cummerbunds. These items were from local sources, and prices were comparable with local specialty shops but dearer than department stores.

Although Mr Fryde tailored only for men, he provided an alteration service for both men and women. Because fashions changed and clients tended to be fashion-conscious, clothing tended to be altered to keep up with the fashion, especially the cut of trousers and lapels. Alteration business was also generated by the nearby dry-cleaning establishment, which subcontracted work to Mr Fryde.

The clientele of Le Monde Tailoring totalled approximately 400, including those who brought their clothes for alterations. The great majority were professional people: doctors, lawyers, engineers, company directors. Some data had been collected which reflected the high socio-economic status of a sample of twenty-five clients (see Appendix I). As might be expected, these were the people who could afford hand-tailored suits and required a touch of individuality in their dress. They expected a higher standard than off-the-rack garments: quality tended to encompass fabric, style, fitting and finishing. A wide range of quality European fabrics were available. Clients, having selected a fabric, had a number of fittings. Unlike ready-made suits, tailored suits were largely hand-sewn, although fusing (a gluing technique) had been partially substituted.

A significant difference between a tailor-made suit and a ready-made suit was the number of hours it took to make. A hand-tailored suit took about forty hours, but substitution of labour by capital in the clothing industry had enabled mass-produced suits to be made in about four hours.

Reflecting the skill and time inputs of tailoring, prices of tailored suits were relatively dear in comparison with off-the-rack pricing. According to Mr Fryde, price depended very much upon the type and quality of fabric chosen. For example a Vicuna/cashmere mixture could cost $900 per metre. Average prices were:

Two-piece suit	$500
Three-piece suit	$550
Trousers	$100–200
Sports coat	$350–400
Full-length coat	$500–600

However, one could pay just as much for a ready-made outfit. Valentino, Dior, Yves Saint Laurent and Pucci were examples of high priced clothes primarily reflecting brand names rather than garment quality. Other world-famous brands such as Chesterberry, Davenza and Aquascutum may also have been priced well above made-to-measure outfits.

Over the years, the number of employees of Le Monde Tailoring had varied. The peak was six full-time and three part-time employees. The present shortage of skilled tailors had severely affected Mr Fryde's business, and he had no full-time employees and only two part-time employees.

Interestingly, not one of his employees had been Australian-born. This was typical of the tailoring and clothing industry in general, where migrants of European background dominated the work force. Mr Fryde felt that Australians had not entered the tailoring trade because of a lack of encouragement and the absence of an effective apprenticeship scheme.

The demand for Le Monde tailored garments had increased, especially since relocation in Double Bay, but with the number of employees falling and a general lack of skilled workers available, Mr Fryde was unable to cater to the demand for his services. The option of training employees was not attractive, because of the high costs involved and the lack of restrictions to entry in the tailoring industry: There was no requirement for certain years of apprenticeship training nor issuance of a certificate as in the hairdressing industry. Mr Fryde explained that if he did train someone, after six months or so the trainee could leave and probably find a job on full pay.

Although faced with the probability of losing some of his clients to other tailors, due to the waiting period that manpower shortages had created, there was little scope for improving efficiency by substituting capital input for labour input. This would have entailed abandoning traditional tailoring, according to Mr Fryde.

There seemed little doubt that tailoring in the traditional sense was a dying trade, and consequently fewer and fewer small tailoring businesses existed. The shortage of skilled workers was not the only problem in the industry. In general, the demand for tailor-made clothes had declined: more people were buying off-the-rack, due to generally cheaper prices and convenience of purchase. Individual requirements could be satisfied by comparison shopping, and fitting rooms and personalized attention by sales staff enabled evaluation of style, suitability and harmony with one's self-concept. To some degree the perceived risk may have been less with ready-to-wear than with tailored outfits, and the time taken to complete the purchase may have been less. The current range of sizes, and the provision of an alteration service by most department and specialty stores, enabled most persons to be fitted accurately.

Although the demand for tailored clothing had probably declined mainly for more price-elastic shopping goods, the availability of more upmarket off-the-rack items in specialty shops and department stores may have been affecting demand for tailoring services. Another factor commonly believed to have contributed to a declining market potential locally was the availability of tailoring services in tourist destinations such as Hong Kong and Singapore, increasingly popular on family and business itineraries.

However, Mr Fryde's problem was of over-full rather than declining demand. His high quality reputation and personalized service had generated a loyal and substantial clientele, resident in the immediate vicinity of his Double Bay premises or in Woollahra, Point Piper, Bellevue Hill, Darling Point, Rose Bay and Vaucluse.

Mr Fryde wished to continue providing the same level of expertise and service in the satisfaction of clothing needs of his clientele. However, as each suit may take him forty hours to complete, his output was currently constrained by the lack of full-time employees. He believed the scarcity of skilled workers precluded any manpower expansion. He could think of no other method of increasing the supply of tailoring services which would not jeopardize his objective of offering traditional quality tailoring.

During the recent festive season, his brother-in-law Maurice Spink and family visited the Fryde's Centennial Park home. The conversation finally broached business matters, and Mr Fryde mentioned his concern. Maurice Spink was familiar with the growth of Le Monde Tailoring and promised to consider feasible alternatives for aligning supply and demand. Although Maurice Spink's experience lay in jewellery rather than tailoring, Mr Fryde was most hopeful that when they next met Maurice's more detached stance would have generated a variety of novel approaches to the solution of his perceived business problem.

APPENDIX I   CLIENT PROFILE

	Percentage of total clientele
Income	
$20–30 000	36
$31–40 000	16
$41–50 000	24
$51–60 000	8
$60 000 +	16

Age

30–39	28
40–49	16
50–59	20
60 +	36

Nationality

Australian	80
American	12
Other	8

Car driven

Australian manufacture	20
European manufacture	64
Other	16

Permanent dwelling location

Double Bay and Bellevue Hill	22
Woollahra, Paddington	20
Rose Bay	19
Point Piper	14
Vaucluse	12
Darling Point	7
Other	6

Employment

Company executive	32
Company owner	20
General practitioner/specialist	16
Lawyer/barrister/solicitor	8
Investor	16
Other	8

Question

You have been asked to prepare a marketing strategy for Mr Fryde. Determine what additional information you might need in order to do this. Assuming you can obtain most of this information, what seems the best strategy to recommend to Mr Fryde?

CASE 6   The Lychee Tree Restaurant

In 1963, Peter Chin and his wife Mabel opened a restaurant specializing in Malaysian and Asian cuisine at Waitara, an upper North Shore suburb of Sydney.

The premises had a seating capacity of 100, somewhat larger than many Asian restaurants, and the proprietors felt confident that profitable operations were possible in this location. The surrounding suburbs were affluent, with middle- to upper-class residents, and there were no comparable restaurants in the area. Any other Asian-style restaurants tended to specialize in Cantonese food, but there were no such restaurants on the Pacific Highway at Waitara (see Appendix I).

The Chins' intention was to offer both take-away and eat-in facilities, and a BYO licence was obtained so that customers could enjoy their own selection of wines with the meal. The Chins expected that patronage would be derived from both local residents and passing traffic, as the Pacific Highway is a major northern outlet for traffic to and from Newcastle and the Hunter Valley. Traffic from Parramatta connected with the Pacific Highway at Pearce's Corner, near the restaurant site, and the spread of population to outlying northern suburbs (such as Hornsby, Castle Hill, Baulkham Hills, Westleigh, Asquith and Mt Colah) had increased traffic flows on the highway. Young families resident in such suburbs could be expected to have an interest in and appreciation of quality Malaysian cuisine.

Prior to the opening day, advertisements were lodged in the *North Shore Times* and the *Hornsby Advocate* announcing the new restaurant and introducing the proprietors. Regular advertisements were also lodged in the restaurant guide in the *Sydney Morning Herald*. An article by food correspondent, Bill Smith, appeared in the *North Shore Times* one month after the restaurant opened.

Fortunately for Peter and Mabel, the Lychee Tree has been well patronized by local residents over the years, and promotional activities have been scaled down as profits have been up to their expectations. Promotion has recently been confined to infrequent sponsorship of community sporting groups, and no media advertising has been undertaken over the past few years.

Although business activity has been low during weekdays and Sundays, Peter feels that this lull is suffered by all businesses in the suburbs; sales on Fridays and Saturdays have constituted 70 per cent of total sales. Lunch is offered five days per week, and dinner six days a week (the restaurant closes on Mondays). Appendix II gives further details of the sales pattern; Appendix III summarizes sales data for the year ended 30 June 1980.

December has tended to be the busiest month, but above-average sales have generally been recorded in November, August and May. The slackest month has tended to be February, and March and April have been fairly quiet. Peter was not sure if such fluctuations were experienced by other restaurants, but felt that families tended to eat out more often during holiday periods. The cold weather in June and July had not appeared to depress business, contrary to the popular belief that people will venture out less during the winter months.

Peter attributed the success of the restaurant to the extensive menu, moderate prices, friendly service, and attractive and casual surroundings; he felt that the lack of formality appealed to family groups. Mabel provided much assistance with menu planning, and adjusted the range of dishes to provide more variety for regular patrons. However, the Chins believed that certain, infrequently ordered dishes should remain on the menu to provide a balanced offering of authentic Malaysian cuisine. The number of dishes offered is set out in Appendix IV.

Prices have tended to be slightly lower than two nearby Cantonese restaurants, although they vary for individual dishes. The Chins attempted to set prices to generate an overall target profit. According to Peter, although the price of an individual item should theoretically be set to reflect the demand for it, difficulties could arise in predicting the effect of any price variation upon demand. Patrons were buying not only the food but service and entertainment — a 'total experience'. Nearby restaurants may be somewhat different in such respects, so strict price comparisons may be of limited usefulness. The two closest Cantonese restaurants did offer a set-price menu, and one also provided private rooms for special group bookings.

Recently, Peter heard of an application being approved by Hornsby council for a restaurant to be operated at Waitara on the Pacific Highway, only eight doors from the Lychee Tree. This new Chinese restaurant was to have a seating capacity of 200.

Peter and Mabel felt very concerned that their custom might be eroded, perhaps only temporarily as people tried the new restaurant. The uneven pattern of business presently experienced by the Lychee Tree could compound the effect of any downturn due to competition. The new restaurant was apparently to be opened in December, normally their busiest month.

Mabel's nephew David, a marketing student and part-time employee at the Lychee Tree, felt that customer research might help uncover patronage motives, new opportunities for customer satisfaction, menu selection, price perceptions, restaurant image and present customer characteristics. Such information, he said, would help Peter and Mabel to devise a marketing strategy to counter the competitive threat.

It was thus decided that a simple questionnaire should be administered to patrons on weeknights, as it would have been more difficult during the busy period and may have been disruptive to patrons. David agreed to personally interview patrons during the first week of October, and summarize the survey results. The questionnaire, administered to 100 patrons, is included as Appendix V; the results are summarized in Appendix VI.

APPENDIX I ASIAN RESTAURANTS IN NEARBY SUBURBS

Golden Lantern Restaurant, Turramurra
Hing Foi Chen Restaurant, Pymble
Banquet Chinese Restaurant, Turramurra
Bright Pearl Chinese Restaurant, Asquith
Lotus Inn, Wahroonga
House of Chan, Hornsby
Loong Cheong Restaurant, Hornsby
Very Good Chinese Restaurant, Pymble

Source: Yellow Pages, 1981.

APPENDIX II SALES PATTERNS OF THE LYCHEE TREE

	Estimated daily sales ($)	Slack* period ($)	Peak† period ($)	Estimated annual sales ($)	Sales mix (%)
Lunch					
Take-away	18	5.40	12.60	4 500	1.5
Table service	50	15.00	35.00	12 500	4.3
Dinner					
Take-away	225	67.50	157.50	67 500	23.7
Table service	666	199.80	466.20	199 800	70.2
Total	959	287.70	671.30	284 300	100.0

* Below average sales generally occurred on Tuesdays, Wednesdays, Thursdays and Sundays

† Approximately 70 per cent of total sales occurred on Fridays and Saturdays

APPENDIX III LYCHEE TREE SALES DATA, YEAR ENDED 30 JUNE 1980

	$	%
Sales	284 300	100
Cost of goods sold	113 720	40
Gross profit	170 580	60
Wages, other costs	124 000	43.6
Net profit	46 580	16.4

APPENDIX IV LYCHEE TREE MENU

The Lychee Tree Restaurant provided an extensive menu, with twenty-five specialties. Ordinary dishes included:

Courses	No. of dishes offered
Entree	13
Soup	9
Main Dishes: Rice and omelettes	9
Steak	7
Chicken	12
Seafood	6
Prawns	7
Satay and curries	11
Pork	6
Sweets	5
Drinks	9

This Menu was written in English and easily read. Dishes were not numbered.

APPENDIX V QUESTIONNAIRE FOR LYCHEE TREE PATRONS

1. Sex: Male_____ Female_____ (observation)
   Age: Young_____ Middle_____ Old_____ (observation)
   Marital status: Married_____ Single_____ (observation)
   _____ for classificatory purposes _____

2. How did you find out about the Lychee Tree Restaurant?

   Pass by_____ Personal contacts_____ Media_____

3. How long does it take to travel to the restaurant?

4. Why did you decide to come today? [Probe]

5. Reasons for patronizing?

   Food_____ Price_____ Location_____
   Service_____ Atmosphere_____

6. Do you frequent the restaurant?

7. Have you been to another similar restaurant lately? If yes, which restaurant?

8. What is the occupation of the head of the family?

9. Have you any criticism of the restaurant?

10. How would you classify the prices here, in comparison with similar restaurants?

   Above_____ Below_____ Equivalent_____

APPENDIX VI   SURVEY RESULTS

Awareness of the restaurant

Virtually all of the respondents heard about the Lychee Tree through friends and acquaintances. Only one in twenty had become aware of the restaurant by walking or driving past. A further 5 per cent of respondents recalled seeing advertisements.

Recommendation	90%
Advertising	5%
Pass by	5%

Patronage motives

The two most frequently mentioned reasons for dining at the Lychee Tree Restaurant were 'good' or 'excellent' food and 'reasonable price'. Most respondents mentioned more than one reason.

Food	90%
Price	85%
Service	45%
Atmosphere	44%
Location	5%

Analysis of awareness and patronage motives yielded the following response data:

	Location	Food	Service	Price	Atmosphere	Total response
Advertising	1	4	—	—	—	5
Pass by	1	2	2	2	1	8
Recommendation	5	46	11	40	16	118
Total response	7	52	13	42	17	131

Frequency of patronage

These data yielded three broad groupings of respondents, deemed 'heavy users', 'light users' and 'triers'. Heavy and light users are regular patrons, but the light users patronize the restaurant no more than six times per year. Triers are new patrons. Some 85 per cent of respondents were regular customers, one in two being classified as heavy users. Only one in seven respondents had not previously dined at the Lychee Tree.

Price perception

Responses were classified according to frequency of patronage. Overall, 51 per cent of respondents said that prices were equivalent to competitors' prices, 35 per cent believed prices to be lower, and 13 per cent felt that prices were higher than at similar restaurants.

Customers	Above	Below	Equal	Total
Heavy users (50%)	2	8	10	20
Light users (35%)	2	2	6	10
Triers (15%)	1	3	3	7
Total	5	13	19	37
Percentage	13	35	51	100

Menu selections

Respondents' menu selections were also recorded. Generally, each patron had an entree or soup and one main course. The popular dishes were Canton Special (23.7 per cent) and poultry dishes (16.6 per cent). Rice, although popular, was considered a side dish. Beverage sales indicated that approximately half of the respondents brought their own wine.

Menu Selections

First course		Second course		Third course	
Entree	80%	Canton Special	27.3%	Sweets	26.2%
Soup	20%	Steak	6.3%	Beverages	44.2%
		Poultry	16.6%		
		Seafood	8.5%		
		Pork	7.2%		
		Malaysian cuisine	7.8%		
		Rice	20.5%		

Questions

1. What problems confront the proprietors of the Lychee Tree Restaurant?
2. Has appropriate action been taken to overcome these problems?
3. Describe the successive steps in the marketing research process. Comment on these five aspects of the Lychee Tree survey research.
4. Devise a marketing strategy for the Lychee Tree Restaurant.

CASE 7 Quality Oil

In 1971 in the State of Victoria, the annual motor-spirit market amounted to 600 million gallons. The market was divided amongst three main categories of supplier.

The first group accounting for nearly 60 per cent of industry sales comprised the companies Shell, BP and Mobil. These companies had an extensive network of their own retail outlets, which they generally leased to individual operators. They had vast resources available based on their international structure, and each operated oil refineries in Australia. Of the three, Mobil, although not the largest, was considered the aggressive marketer at both the wholesale and retail level.

The second category of supplier was a group of smaller companies. Their sales were of roughly equal size to each other. Two of these firms – Quality Oil and Ampol – were solely Australian-based companies while the others – Caltex and Esso – were part of international groups. Their total share of market was in the vicinity of 30 per cent. These companies also operated refineries in Australia.

The balance of the market was made up of Amoco – another international company but recently established in Australia – IOC and XL Petroleum. The latter two companies were new on the Australian scene. They had Australian management and were exploiting an opportunity to import and market petroleum refined in Japan at a cheaper price than that offered by the established suppliers.

The majority of service stations were owned by the major companies. Leases were offered a standard retail margin of 8.1 cents per gallon and, depending upon the gallonage sold through the outlet, larger margins could be negotiated. Independent service-station owners generally contracted themselves to an oil company for a specific period and undertook to only sell that brand.

During the early part of 1971, some independent owners had contracted themselves to IOC and XL and were benefiting from higher margins than were offered by the traditional sources. As acknowledged discounters, the IOC and XL retail outlets demonstrated to other retailers that there was money to be made by offering discount prices. Their gallonage sales rose dramatically to the detriment of other retail outlets.

The result had been that other independent owners selling other brands of petrol had followed suit and discounted prices to their subsequent benefit from increased sales. Lessees not offering discounts had a difficult job to maintain their sales. The growth in imports of motor spirit had repercussions on motor-spirit sales achieved by the companies with Australian refineries and they reacted by offering discounts to lessees and independents.

By July 1971, discounting was rife in the Melbourne metropolitan area. Mobil had unilaterally taken their price to 8 cents per gallon off the normal retail price and had in effect established a new retail price. All other companies followed suit. Independent retailers with higher margins and lower costs went down even further in their discounting and were offering a discount of 10–12 cents a gallon. Two were offering a discount of 14 cents a gallon. The basis of discounting was that, for a consumer discount of 8 cents, the oil company contributed five-eighths of the discount and the retailer was expected to contribute three-eighths.

Discounting at these levels was placing a major strain on Quality Oil with their brand of motor spirit 'Silver Fur'. Unlike some of the international companies they did not have the resources to offset the drastic drop in gross profit being experienced in local trading. They were having difficulty withstanding this price competition.

Quality, along with other well-established wholesalers, had in the past oper-ated on a gross margin of 10 cents a gallon. The present level of discounting meant that they were giving away 5 cents of this.

By mid-July 1971, Mr Joseph, the General Manager of Quality, felt that action had to be taken. Mobil's unilateral reductions were hurting Quality badly. He believed that 'Silver Fur' buyers were loyal to the company and that by returning prices to their previous level the company's fortunes could be improved. He recognized that some customers might be lost but assessed that sales could fall significantly without affecting present profit levels.

Mr Joseph felt that loyalty to 'Silver Fur' was tied to the quality of the service his company had always offered consumers through retail outlets. Other com-panies and lessees, in reducing margins, had been forced to reduce the services offered the consumer. He felt that 'Silver Fur' appealed to the family man who lived in the suburbs.

He therefore decided that the company should cease discounting. As an added inducement to regular customers he decided to run a competition. Mr Joseph felt that he knew the Australian character. Australians liked to gamble and also liked to help their fellow man. He therefore decided on a competition that contained these elements. A fortnightly contest open to all Quality Oil petrol buyers was devised. $10 000 was to be given away fortnightly, and both the prize-winner and his favourite charity would benefit.

In the middle of July Mr Joseph announced his scheme publicly. It received wide media coverage and he was interviewed on news programmes and current-affairs programmes. This extensive free publicity was supplemented by extra advertising expenditure on television and in the press announcing the Quality Oil policy.

Questions

1. Do you agree with Mr Joseph's insights into consumer buyer behaviour?
2. As a retailer of 'Silver Fur' brand what would be your reaction to this move by Quality?
3. What other marketing strategies could be considered in this market situation?
4. Does the economic theory relating to the behaviour of oligopolies have any relevance to this case?

CASE 8 Canterbury Canvas Centre Pty Ltd

Canterbury Canvas Centre was a privately owned manufacturer, retailer and re-pairer of canvas and vinyl goods. Annexes, camper-trailer tent sections, and occasional custom-order tents constituted its major manufacturing lines. Other goods included utility tonneau covers, utility and trailer canopies, tarpaulins, signwriters' banners, and tent alterations. Most of these were retailed at premises in Canterbury Road, Forest Hills, an eastern suburb of Melbourne. Some work was also performed for industrial direct end users.

Recently, the retail assortment had been widened with the addition of the Primus range of outdoor goods, including tents, stoves, lamps, portable refrigerators, coolers, drink dispensers, sleeping bags, portable toilets, air beds, luggage and sundry camping accessories.

Margins were higher on self-manufactured goods than on goods purchased for resale. With the latter goods, such as Primus products, stockholding tended to cause a drain on working capital. The financial position of Canterbury Canvas Centre was strained by the seasonal nature of the retail canvas trade and the limited credit available from major local suppliers of canvas. Typically, some 50 per cent of sales were achieved between October and December, 25 per cent between January and April, and the balance over the remainder of the year. Tarpaulin sales, however, were higher in winter than summer, but currently not substantial enough to offset production peaks. With its present assortment, Canterbury Canvas Centre faced underutilization of capacity over the majority of the year, which adversely impacted upon its financial position.

In 1979, the manufacturing operations were relocated in a factory in Bayswater, releasing more space for display purposes in the Forest Hills premises. Productive capacity could now potentially expand threefold. Incremental costs would be restricted to certain variable costs, due to current underutilization of fixed capital equipment. An additional three or four machinists would each receive $300 per week wages and consume some $600–$800 worth of material during a forty-hour week. Power costs would increase, but no extra machinery or benchspace would be required. If more than four extra machinists were employed, an extra employee for cutting would also be required.

However, the owners of Canterbury Canvas Centre were uncertain where the best opportunities for expansion lay. The increase in total sales in the last two years had barely kept pace with inflation. Sales of caravan annexes had been declining in recent years, reflecting the slump in new-caravan sales. Camper-trailer tent sections and repair work had shown sales growth, and there might be potential for increased penetration of the tarpaulin market. As promotional efforts had been limited in the past, the owners also felt that a well-designed and executed promotional strategy may be able to boost sales, even in the caravan annexe market.

Media used in the past included billboards and newspapers. Several local newspapers and a metropolitan morning daily had been used with minimal success. The owners had sometimes been pleased with the response to advertisements in the Caravan and Trailer section of Saturday's *Age*. However, lacking any employee with marketing expertise, no coordinated marketing or promotional strategy had been devised. The effectiveness of existing advertising thus could not be measured, as no objectives or goals had been expressed. No sales-promotion activity had ever been undertaken.

The stated objectives of the owners were the profitability, survival and growth of the firm, but profitability had not been satisfactory. The financial position had however improved since the mid-1970s, when the liquidation of a client company caused substantial bad debts. At the same time an employee had set up in opposition, taking certain clients and employees with him. The credit policy of Canterbury Canvas Centre evolved in this period, reflecting the owners' concern with survival during such stressful times.

Settlement terms were as follows. All retail sales or repairs were cash-on-delivery. Wholesale customers were generally offered seven-day credit terms. A few larger firms were granted thirty days for settlement, while occasional customers were expected to settle on delivery. Government authorities and schools were granted credit on signed order.

Planning was also difficult due to the paucity of market data. No government statistics were available, and firms in the industry were many and diverse in nature. There was no trade organization or magazine. Typically, trends were recognized only after the event, and planning was reactive. The owners tended to rely upon intuition, as information sources internal to the firm were limited in breadth, detail and timeliness. For instance, no information was available regarding segment characteristics, other than sales by product line.

The following information was provided relating to the major market segments.

Caravan annexes. Because of the lack of statistical information, caravan registration figures were used as a surrogate to ascertain trends in the caravan annexe market. It should be noted firstly that annexes were complements, and not all caravan owners decided to purchase an annexe. Also, caravan registration figures included used vans sold and re-registered, and excluded on-site vans. Automatic re-registrations of caravans were not included. Finally, annexes could be purchased as replacements of existing annexes. Monthly caravan registrations for Victoria are given in Appendix I.

Details of other Melbourne-based caravan-annexe manufacturers are given in Appendix II. Canterbury Canvas Centre faced competition from both canvas and aluminium annexes. The latter tended to threaten the sales of larger canvas annexes, but were substantially dearer for smaller sizes: for example, a 7-metre canvas annexe would typically retail for $600–$800, whereas an aluminium annexe might cost $1500–$2000. Canterbury Canvas Centre appeared to be quite competitive with other canvas-annexe manufacturers according to a recent price comparison (see Appendix III).

Broadly, the new annexe market was declining but the replacement market was rising. The owners expected the market to be stable but cheaper annexes to gain in popularity. Currently, Canterbury Canvas Centre annexes were made of the same material as other competing canvas annexes (Bradmill and Brella). Although Canterbury Canvas Centre had initially developed the 'pop-top' annexe, other manufacturers now offered almost identical units. Thus, its early market lead had been eroded in the absence of effective promotional and competitive strategies.

Tarpaulins. Canterbury Canvas Centre had manufactured tarpaulins for transport operators, but there might be the potential to supply the home-renovation market or begin renting out tarpaulins. Little was known of the market, although it was believed to be growing. One attractive characteristic was that purchasers normally paid cash rather than requiring credit.

Details of competition were not available. However, none of Canterbury Canvas Centre's close competitors was in this market.

Camper-trailer tent sections. Presently, the firm supplied these both wholesale and retail. Replacement demand was a sizeable proportion of retail sales. (Appendix IV lists certain competitors; it should be noted that some firms subcontracted to Canterbury Canvas Centre.) No data were available for this product line, but growth prospects were believed to exceed that of tarpaulins for transport vehicles, as the latter demand was likely to be affected by regulations for food-transport vehicles requiring solid bodies.

Other product lines. Two areas not presently covered by Canterbury Canvas Centre were government tender work, and the manufacture and repair of canvas household blinds. The former might be attractive, being non-seasonal, but the latter might be too competitive. Another possible growth area, according to the owners, was swimming-pool covers.

APPENDIX I   CARAVANS REGISTERED IN VICTORIA

	1970–71*	1971–72	1972–73	1973–74	1974–75	1975–76	1976–77	1977–78	1978–79
Aug.		529	680	932	802	986	1153	871	660
Sept.		552	584	849	963	1400	1235	928	714
Oct.		566	1220	1305	1092	1444	1465	1026	706
Nov.		688	1054	1332	1049	885	1236	888	718
Dec.		1270	1141	930	932	1596	1376	733	669
Jan.	863	618	1026	1342	1233	1482	1331	1123	616
Feb.	310	293	519	740	1242	1090	1326	891	996
March	408	633	637	869	719	1437	1136	791	488
April	543	568	715	786	798	1435	502	844	528
May	417	523	956	1110	1332	1461	1161	980	614
June	351	457	645	810	1092	1281	1318	854	478
July	425	531	706	817	1263	981	1068	631	698

* No figures are available prior to January 1971

Source: Australian Bureau of Statistics, *Motor Vehicle Census*, Cat. No. 9302.2, various issues.

APPENDIX II   MELBOURNE-BASED CARAVAN ANNEXE MANUFACTURERS

Annexe manufacturers which competed directly or indirectly with Canterbury Canvas Centre were as follows:

- *Tebbs Canvas Products Pty Ltd.* Located in Futura Road, Dandenong, this firm specialized in the wholesale market, and represented indirect competition.
- *Peter Bedggood Industries Pty Ltd.* Located nearby in Ringwood, this firm competed directly with Tebbs in supplying annexes to industrial consumers. Recently, however, it had commenced advertising at retail level and had been taking in general canvas work.
- *Campbell Heep Industries Pty Ltd.* This Burwood firm was potentially a direct competitor of Canterbury Canvas Centre, but currently appeared to be concentrating on the household and industrial blinds and awnings market.
- *Casavilla Holiday Equipment.* As a manufacturer of permanent aluminium annexes, this Montrose firm catered to a somewhat different target market. Its price range was considerably higher. Recently, however, Casavilla had been advertising a new 'pop-top' annexe, and it was possible that it may decide to enter the annexe market on a wider scale.
- *Alum Annexe Pty Ltd.* A direct competitor of Casavilla, this West Heidelberg firm manufactured aluminium annexes for permanent living.

APPENDIX III   COMPARATIVE RETAIL PRICES OF CARAVAN ANNEXES

Prices for annexes of various sizes are given. It should be noted that, although the canvas quality is identical between manufacturers, optional extras may vary the final price. For instance, Canterbury Canvas Centre provided two windows at the quoted prices, but customers purchasing from Tebbs were charged an additional $40 for a second window. Peter Bedggood did not offer the option of a second window.

Annexe size	Manufacturer		
	Canterbury Canvas	Tebbs	Peter Bedggood
	($)	($)	($)
3-metre	425	425	435
4-metre	443	437	448
5-metre	520	498	510
6-metre	567	539	552
7-metre	650	n/a	637

APPENDIX IV   MANUFACTURERS OF CAMPER-TRAILER TENT SECTIONS

Local competitors of Canterbury Canvas Centre included:

- *Jayco Caravans (Recreation Industries) Pty Ltd.* This Noble Park firm manufactured its own camper-trailers and tent sections. Its replacement canvas sections tended to be cheaper, probably due to its volume of production. It tended to supply sections only for its own vehicles, not for other brands of camper-trailers.
- *Siddons Leisure Products Pty Ltd.* This Bendigo firm tended to supply sections only for its own vehicles. The firm did subcontract some repair work to Canterbury Canvas Centre.
- *ACT Cruiser, Consort, Comet.* The manufacturer of these units had ceased production, but existing units generated a replacement market of considerable size.
- *Trail Blazer.* These units were also nearing the age when tent-section replacement would be necessary, and the manufacturer had ceased business.
- *Golf.* These units were relatively new, and there was little immediate likelihood of replacement sales of tent sections.
- *Bushwalker.* Although the local distributor was no longer importing these units, current stocks were high. There appeared to be no prospects for replacement sales of tent sections.
- *Adventure Camper Centre Pty Ltd.* This Clayton firm specialized in the repair of camper-trailers, and subcontracted tent repair work to Canterbury Canvas Centre.

Question

Prepare a comprehensive marketing strategy for Canterbury Canvas Centre Pty Ltd.

CASE 9 Civil Engineering Ltd: Building Products Division

The building-products division of Civil Engineering Ltd was part of a large, well-established Australian public company engaged in the manufacture of steel products and accessories.

This division of CivEng had its head office in Clayton, an outer south-eastern suburb of Melbourne, but also operated in other States. In Sydney, the division was represented by a sales manager, construction supervisor, engineer and a draftsman. In Brisbane, one sales manager was responsible for all Queensland work. In Adelaide and Perth, representatives provided leads which were followed up by the Melbourne office. All fabrication work was carried out at the Clayton plant, which was located on a 3-hectare lot.

The main activity of the building-products division (BPD) was the fabrication and construction of single-storey, pitched-roof, portal-frame steel buildings, ranging from 12.2 metres to 76.2 metres in clear span. The most obvious physical feature of most of these buildings was their 'three plate weld' construction, proven to be very economical in so far as substantially less material was used during fabrication. The building also featured 'Z' section purlin and girt systems which were cold-rolled on the premises using high-strength lightweight steel.

The basis of building design was, in accordance with the latest methods, using computers for structural analysis and construction was based upon standardized building components. However, building size was completely flexible which allowed the development of structures to suit most requirements.

In order to sell its buildings as a complete package deal, roof and wall sheeting was produced to architecturally designed steel panels, which were available in two profiles and could be either galvanized or in a Colourbond range.

The services offered by BPD included the design, supply, fabrication, delivery to site, and the erection of steelwork and fixing of sheetwork on site. However, clients may avail themselves of only some of these services depending upon their particular requirements.

In selling its buildings, BPD always endeavoured to include the sale of its sheeting. However, this was not always possible. For instance, in New South Wales, CivEng sheeting was not very competitive so the structural steel was sold and the sheeting obtained from other suppliers. To counter this loss in sheeting sales, loose sheeting was often sold to private individuals for garages, sheds and other domestic purposes, and replacement sheeting for old or damaged portions was sold to industrial and commercial clients.

Although few firms offered complete package deals with respect to engineering, drawing, fabrication and erection, BPD faced intense competition from small steel fabricators, consultant engineers and architects. These competitors provided only part of the product and subcontracted the rest to other firms. The main users of CivEng services are summarized in Appendix I, and they were canvassed by BPD's sales representatives on a regular basis.

The main supplier of structural steel to CivEng was BHP, which provided approximately 70 per cent of total supplies, while local steel merchants and overseas purchases provided the remainder. Coils used in the production of sheeting were supplied by John Lysaght Ltd, a subsidiary of BHP, and the supply of purlin strip was shared equally between BHP and Lysaght. The various accessories necessary for the completion of projects were obtained from a number of local and overseas suppliers and manufacturers.

Disruptions to the continuity of supply affected BPD, threatening completion of projects and increasing their cost as supplies had to be obtained at higher prices from local merchants. As a result, BPD's costs began to escalate and its profit margin declined. Similar problems with sheeting supplies had also occurred.

The Victorian sales team comprised two representatives, who were responsible for acquiring all contracts in Victoria, South Australia, Western Australia and Tasmania. Their activities included regular personal calls to established clients and mailing brochures to prospects. Contracts were otherwise obtained through word-of-mouth recommendation, repeat custom, and the checking of industrial land sales in newspapers and technical journals. Until February 1981, when a new board of directors was elected, little promotional and advertising expenditure had been undertaken, except for the production of brochures and the occasional advertisement in the *Age*. In New South Wales and Queensland, which had only one sales representative each, similar forms of advertising and sales promotion were undertaken but expenditures were even lower. This was quite surprising, as New South Wales accounted for about 60 per cent of all national contracts.

The new board of directors had indicated dissatisfaction with BPD's performance, and wished to implement a marketing strategy to improve both market share and profitability. A report was commissioned from Andro Consulting Services on market prospects and conditions in the fabrication and construction industry. Also, a decision was reached to lease premises owned by Metalmaster, a medium-sized fabricator, with an option to buy at the end of the twelve-month period. The major attraction was Metalmaster's 'beamline', which would enable BPD to fabricate a greater variety of buildings, including multistorey structures, and lower labour costs for projects requiring repetitive work.

One of the major problems associated with leasing and possibly acquiring Metalmaster was that its present owner, who was nearing retiring age, had not undertaken any recent promotion and work flow had dropped considerably. CivEng was not sure how it could generate sufficient work to keep the Metalmaster facilities fully utilized. The higher overheads associated with the use of the beamline had been responsible for the recent failure of a Brisbane firm — potential cost savings would only be realized by CivEng if the value of work in progress could be substantially increased.

The new board of directors had also shown concern that nearly 60 per cent of contracts were being won in New South Wales, where BPD's sheeting was not very competitive, and margins were lower due to reliance upon supplies from other sheeting manufacturers. Also of concern were reports that Queensland was expected to have higher growth rates over the next few years, as BPD currently had only one sales representative in that State.

The board thus recommended, in addition to a strategy review, a national assessment of the sales force and a report on the optimal distribution of representatives and location of offices in all States.

APPENDIX I   MAIN USERS OF CIVENG SERVICES

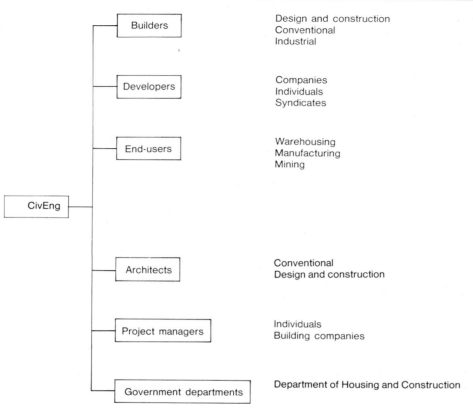

Builders	Design and construction Conventional Industrial
Developers	Companies Individuals Syndicates
End-users	Warehousing Manufacturing Mining
Architects	Conventional Design and construction
Project managers	Individuals Building companies
Government departments	Department of Housing and Construction

APPENDIX II   SUMMARY OF REPORT FOR THE BUILDING-PRODUCTS DIVISION OF CIVENG

The building and construction industry is a cyclical industry. Affected by recession in the mid-1970s, prospects for the next few years are for an improvement due to stronger economic growth, favourably impacted by resource development.

The overall outlook for 1980–81 is for strong expansion in activity led by private sector growth. Statement Number 2, of the Treasurer (Mr Howard) also forecasts that business fixed investment will grow as much as 20 per cent. Strong growth is expected in plant and equipment expenditures, as well as other building and construction activity.

However, prospects for the Victorian economy are not so bright. Experiencing slower population growth than many other States, and more heavily dependent upon manufacturing industry, the main plus-factor is the growth of decentralized industry. Other influences on the level of building and construction activity include present market stock, the growth rates and profitability of businesses, and their needs to relocate due to shifts in location, demand, or government incentives. The decentralization of population to areas such as Albury-Wodonga creates a need for shopping centres, power, roads and other amenities.

Production of structural steel has declined over the last decade, although this has not been uniform on a State basis (see Appendix III). In Victoria and New South Wales, it has reflected the downturn in commencements of major commercial buildings in Melbourne and Sydney. Over the next few years New South Wales is likely to experience significant increases, along with Queensland and Western Australia: the Victorian market, despite developments at Portland and the Latrobe Valley, will grow relatively slowly.

The market is also being redefined by competition from alternative materials and substitution of new technologies.

Technological developments

Computer-aided design and manufacturing now offers systems for the structural-steel industry — for punching or drilling sections, or even producing a complete steel frame for a building or other structure, by simply keying in a code number to a computer.[1] These systems can produce up to 1000 tonnes of structural steel a month with just one or two people. These are known as 'beamlines', and were developed by Peddinghaus and Fabriline.

Other developments on the local front include a simplified method of connection developed by the Australian Institute of Steel Construction, documented in a manual entitled *AISC Standardized Structural Connections*. The use of such systems will create savings in design time for engineers, and enable simplified detailing, efficient fabrication using standardized components, and speedier erection of structures. Cost savings estimated for a single-storey portal-frame structure constructed in Sydney were reported to be close to 50 per cent.[2].

Competition from concrete

Steel has been experiencing competition primarily from concrete, and any substitution between the two materials will depend upon relative structural characteristics, preference trends and building design. Considerable restructuring of the steel-fabrication industry has resulted from competition from reinforced and prestressed concrete in the post-war period. The use of structural steel for high-rise and commercial buildings has also tended to decline due to the impact of fire regulations.

Locational flexibility of the industry

Fabricators tend to situate near areas of high population density, from which they draw their work force; relocation to areas of higher market growth could be uneconomic for potential 'one-only' contracts. However, transport costs will affect the ability of distant firms to tender competitively. Thus location, coupled with transport costs, tends to limit the geographic size of the market (see Appendix IV for comparative domestic and international freight rates).

Some firms, tendering for work beyond their geographic market, have successfully subcontracted less complex work. This tends to improve flexibility, but depends upon the existence of excess capacity amongst local fabricating shops. Capacity utilization of fabricating firms is expected to rise over the next few years. Thus there could be difficulties subcontracting, especially in Sydney which is already under-served.

---

[1] *Manufacturer's Monthly*, 15 March 1979, pp. 41–2.
[2] Ian Macphee (Minister for Productivity), 'Productivity in Australia's Metal Manufacturing Industries', Australian Institute of Metals Lecture, Melbourne, 16 May 1978.

Competition

Steel fabrication and erection is highly competitive, and margins tend to be low: it is not uncommon for firms to make a return-on-sales of 2 or 3 per cent. Opportunities for differentiation tend to lie more with ancillary services than the physical product. Many larger firms now offer a complete design, fabrication and erection package.

Most work is gained by competitive tender. Because many smaller fabricators have underutilized capacity and clients may be large firms, pressure tends to be exerted on prices. As costs of key inputs have tended to rise faster, the industry is subject to a cost-price squeeze.

Profits tend to be volume-sensitive, although a key factor is consistency of work flow rather than greater absolute turnover. The introduction of standardized components and computerized estimation, quotation and design potentially enables realization of scale and experience effects. Scale economies are particularly relevant to the ten or twelve large firms which have installed automatic beamlines.

Price tends to be the most important marketing-mix variable. A typical tender situation usually sees a few high tenders, several close tenders and some cheaper prices. The job does not necessarily go to the cheapest quote, as the reputation of the firm and its financial viability are also important considerations. It is important to customers that work will proceed on schedule and be completed: small firms which undercut may go to the wall before finishing a job.

Conclusion

Taking the served market concept for the industry in which CivEng participates, the present attractiveness of this industry was low to medium because of factors such as low margins, cyclicality, low capacity utilization, sensitivity of demand to price and strong bargaining power, both upstream and downstream. Business position was medium, reflecting share

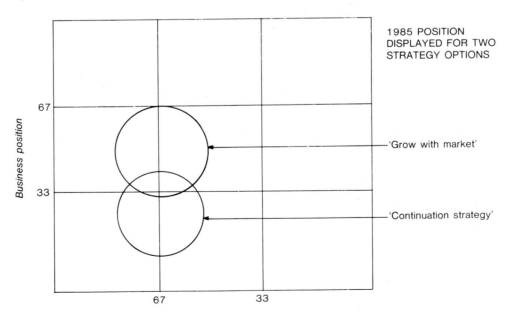

Market attractiveness

in served market, good functional capabilities, present technological position, capacity utilization and cost position.

On the assumption of no change in strategy, business position would fall over the next few years, due to factors such as location and capacity limitations. However, industry attractiveness is expected to increase greatly as the size and growth rate of the market increase, enabling greater capacity utilization and cost savings through scale and experience effects. Details of the construction of the portfolio display are included in Appendix V.

In the light of this evaluation of future trends in the fabrication and construction industry, it is therefore recommended that current strategies be re-examined.

APPENDIX III   PRODUCTION OF FABRICATED CONSTRUCTION STEEL (AUSTRALIA)

	1966–67	*1976–77*		*1977–78*	
	(%)	(tonnes)	(%)	(tonnes)	(%)
New South Wales	44.6	181 324	38.6	152 059	35.2
Victoria	23.3	84 934	18.1	92 265	21.4
Queensland	9.7	86 616	18.4	70 944	16.4
South Australia	10.0	42 881	9.1	39 690	9.1
Western Australia	10.3	62 889	13.4	65 524	15.3
Tasmania	2.1	9 782	2.1	11 341	2.6
ACT	—	1 388	0.3	*	*
	100.0	469 814	100.0	431 823	100.0

* Included in NSW figures

Source: Australian Bureau of Statistics, *Production Bulletin No. 8, Miscellaneous Products*, Cat. No. 8364.0, various issues.

APPENDIX IV   COMPARATIVE FREIGHT RATES ($)

Within Australia*

From plants located at	*To sites located at*		
	Gladstone (Qld)	Ranger (NT)	Port Hedland (WA)
Melbourne	85.00	170.00	220.00
Sydney	60.00	160.00	210.00

Overseas locations to Australian sites

From plants located at	*To sites located at*	
	Gladstone† (Qld)	Port Hedland‡ (WA)
United Kingdom	165.00	215.00
Japan	83.00	135.00
India	95.00	145.00

* Rates per tonne are based on average steelwork not exceeding dimensions of 13 m × 2.5 m × 2.5 m. If these dimensions are exceeded, rates may increase by 100 per cent.
† Rates include shipping to Brisbane and transport by road to site ($20)
‡ Rates include shipping to Fremantle and transport by road to site ($70)
Note: If specific requirements are known, it could be possible to ship direct to the port concerned. Also, charter shipping would reduce the rates above.

Source: Submission by Johns Perry Limited to the IAC Enquiry into Structured Steel, Sydney, 1980, p. 109.

APPENDIX V   BPD: PROJECTED BUSINESS PORTFOLIO

Current position

Industry attractiveness factors

	Score	×	Weight	=	
Large market	1.0		10		10
Growth rate 6% p.a. at constant prices	.5		10		5
Price sensitivity of demand	.0		10		—
Cyclicality	.0		10		—
Bargaining power upstream and downstream	.5		10		5
Low concentration	1.0		5		5
Substitution by new technology, other materials	.5		10		5
Low margins	.0		10		—
Low capacity utilization	.5		10		5
Scale and experience effects limited	.5		5		2.5
Government building regulations slowing down final demand	.5		5		2.5
35-hour week, unions	.0		5		—
			100		40

Business position factors

	Score	×	Weight	=	
Share in served market	.5		10		5
Low influence on market	.0		10		—
Bargaining power downstream	.5		5		2.5
Competitive position	.5		5		2.5
Functional capabilities	1.0		10		10
Vulnerability to new technology	.5		10		5
Level of integration	.5		10		5
Scale, experience	.5		10		5
Capacity utilization	1.0		10		10
Skills, technology	.5		5		2.5
Good relationships with unions	1.0		5		5
Little influence on government — IAC, building regulations	.0		10		—
			100		52.5

Portfolio display five years hence

Industry attractiveness factors

	Score	×	Weight	=	
Large market	1.0		10		10
Growth rate	1.0		10		10
Price sensitivity of demand	.0		10		—
Cyclicality (not important)	1.0		5		5
Bargaining power upstream and					
downstream	.5		10		5
Concentration low	.5		10		5
Substitution by new technology,					
materials	.5		10		5
Low margins but cost savings	.5		10		5
Scale, experience	1.0		10		10
Capacity utilization	1.0		10		10
Government influence	.5		5		2.5
			100		67.5

Business position factors

	Score	×	Weight	=	
Market share	.5		10		5
Low influence on market	.0		10		—
Location	.0		10		—
Bargaining power downstream	.5		5		2.5
Competitive position	.5		5		2.5
Functional capabilities	1.0		5		5
Vulnerability to new technology	.5		10		5
Level of integration	.5		5		2.5
Scale, experience	.5		10		5
Capacity utilization	.0		10		—
Skills, technology	.5		5		2.5
Good relationships with unions	.5		5		2.5
Influence on government	.0		10		—
			100		32.5

Question

Prepare a marketing plan for Building Products Division of CivEng.

CASE 10 International Pharmaceuticals (Aust) Pty Ltd

This case was prepared by Dr Rollyn Graham, Senior Lecturer in Physical Distribution Management, Chisholm Institute of Technology.

It's 7 a.m. on Monday morning and Frank Halloran is alone in the office. This is his first day as materials manager for the Australian operations of the large multinational firm, International Pharmaceuticals.

Halloran's accounting background, analytical mind and willingness to make staff cuts has earned him a reputation as a trouble-shooter and Young Turk. He was appointed largely because of his knowledge of the new computer-based inventory control and materials requirements systems, his reputation for getting things done, and his rapport with other members of top management.

Now, Halloran reads his notes from the Friday meeting with Harold Deakin, the Australian managing director. 'Resolve the agency question and reduce inventories.'

Background

International Pharmaceuticals (Australia) Pty Ltd (IPA) established its reputation through the manufacture and sale of prescription drugs (called ethical products). Two of these drugs became extremely popular and are currently amongst the most frequently prescribed drugs in the world.

Unfortunately, the international patents on these two compounds will expire within the next two years. The research and development department is investigating new compounds, but as a hedge IPA decided to enter the non-prescription, over-the-counter (OTC) market.

Cough-and-cold preparations, vitamins, sun-care products and women's hair preparations were selected as product lines. Unseasonably mild winters in both Sydney and Melbourne were blamed for the relatively low sales of the new cough-and-cold preparations, but management hopes that a hot summer will stimulate sales of the new sun-care line.

IPA also manufactures and markets a line of bulk chemicals, primarily fertilizers, and a range of specialized diagnostic equipment and reagents. These lines are profitable, but represent less than 25 per cent of total sales.

Appendix I presents a partial organization chart for IPA. The pharmaceuticals division is primarily a marketing operation concerned with specific product lines. Manufacturing support is provided by the technical division. The materials department is responsible for the administration of the sales offices and warehouses in each of the capital cities (except Hobart, where there is an agency), purchasing in support of the manufacturing programme, overall inventory control and production planning based on sales forecasts.

Until three years ago, IPA distributed its pharmaceutical products through one large company which also distributed products of IPA's competitors. Because of the seemingly high cost of this arrangement, IPA decided to distribute directly to customers (chemists and hospitals) from IPA warehouses in capital cities and from selected agents in country centres.

Agents in country centres take orders from customers and arrange delivery. Although stocks are held at the agent's facility, IPA retains full title to the goods and is responsible for billing all customers. Most agents also act as agents or wholesalers for competing products.

Agency Question

Independent agencies distribute IPA pharmaceutical products in Darwin, Hobart, Canberra, Newcastle, Wagga, Townsville and Wollongong (see Appendix II).

Several agencies have written to IPA headquarters complaining about receiving customer queries concerning new IPA products which have not yet been released. These agencies stated that in future they would refer these customers to IPA in Sydney because they were not being paid to provide an inquiry service.

The previous materials manager has proposed that the agency agreements be terminated. According to his suggestion, Darwin and Townsville customers would be supplied directly from Brisbane; Newcastle, Wagga and Wollongong customers would be supplied from Sydney; and Hobart customers would be supplied directly from Melbourne. The issue is not yet resolved, and has become known as 'the agency question'. Headquarters warehousing manager Leonard Harman is opposed to the suggestion, and has prepared the data shown in Appendix III.

Halloran has scheduled discussions with the people directly involved in the distribution process: Joshua Herbert, Sydney warehouse superintendent; Kevin Gumley, manager of inventory control and production planning; Terry Smith, marketing manager for OTC pharmaceuticals; and Richard Harris, marketing manager for ethical pharmaceutical products; Jerry Freeth, financial controller.

Interview with Joshua Herbert, Sydney Warehouse Superintendent

Mr Herbert conducted a tour of the raw-materials and packaging warehouse. Halloran's first impression upon entering the warehouse was that it was incredibly stocked — with more than 90 per cent of the available rack space being utilized. The warehouse itself was spotlessly clean.

Surrounding the 'Goods Inwards' bay of the raw-materials warehouse was the quality-control area. Incoming goods were stored in this area until they were cleared by quality control. Herbert stated that quality control could take anywhere from one day to two months to perform the necessary tests. Halloran made a cursory inspection of the stored items, and found one which had been awaiting clearance for over eight months. When asked why the material had been there for so long, Herbert replied, 'Well, it's probably taken quality control that long to do the checks.' Halloran asked if there was a follow-up on items which had been in quality control for a substantial period of time. Herbert replied, 'Sometimes, when production is stirring to get the goods out. Otherwise, no. On this particular item there has been no stirring from production.'

Herbert was not aware of the quality-control clearing procedures, or the accounts against which goods in this area were held. He commented that whatever account it was, it would be distorted by the fact that it included the value of returned merchandise.

Herbert said that goods held in the quality-control area could not be touched until quality control approved them for use. Once approved, a special sticker was placed upon the merchandise; staff were told not to move any goods without this sticker. There was no formal location system in the quality-control area.

Once approved, the goods went into the main warehouse. Again, Halloran's first reaction upon entering this warehouse was to note the very high volumetric utilization: there were, at most, five empty racks in the entire warehouse.

A board system was used for the location control, and bin cards were also established for individual items. Individual items were identified by assay numbers issued by quality control, and separate numbers were always assigned to individual batches. Typically, the items were identified by both their individual pallet number and their batch number. The pallet number indicated when goods had arrived, and staff could cross-reference by batch number in case there were quality problems. Goods were stored in random locations and the FIFO (first in–first out) system was policed by the board system. Except for an area containing a range of minor items, only one item was stocked in each bay location. A large percentage of the storage space in the warehouse was dedicated to packaging materials, especially cardboard outers and sundry bottles.

The dispatch dock and the receiving dock were one and the same. Herbert indicated that they had encountered no particular problems with this arrangement, except that it was difficult to dispatch goods when a semi-trailer arrived with many pallets to be unloaded.

A direct pallet exchange was used with suppliers, i.e. when suppliers arrived they were immediately reimbursed the number of pallets involved in the unloading.

Herbert and Halloran then travelled over to the finished-goods warehouse. There were two warehouses – the Sydney operations and the central warehouse – to ensure so-called 'fair share' distribution. The 'fair share' system was introduced to ensure that all States received equitable delivery of finished goods from the factory. Herbert was unhappy with this system because it often required double handling, to move the goods first into the central warehouse and then through the door back into the Sydney warehouse. He thought that this was unnecessary. Because the most distant States were given shipping priority, Sydney often waited up to three weeks for deliveries – and since Sydney is the major sales area, Herbert felt that this was not very efficient.

Distribution from the Sydney warehouse was effected by contract carriers with two 2-tonne trucks and one 3-tonne truck. In addition, IPA had two one-tonne trucks of its own to service the local area. The contract carriers serviced the rest of the Sydney Metropolitan area, and were paid a per-carton rate:

No. of cartons	Rate
1–30	$1.00
31–45	0.75
46 +	0.50

The standard of service was generally good. If customers rang by 4 p.m., delivery was made on the next working day. Typically, the trucks were loaded in the late afternoon and went out the next morning. Customers received the goods in the morning unless there were a great many deliveries for that particular day.

Herbert said that IPA shipped approximately 8000 cartons per month from the Sydney warehouse. The average drop was approximately one and a half cartons; eighty drops per day was a very heavy run. Herbert indicated that total transport costs for the three contract carriers were of the order of $1200 per week.

For deliveries within New South Wales, IPA uses Jetaway: they can achieve overnight delivery to 90 per cent of customers provided the merchandise reaches

Jetaway by 3.45 p.m. the preceding afternoon. For interstate transfers of material, Jetaway, Ansett and TNT are used. Narcotics are always sent by air if possible.

A problem can occur in the finished-goods warehouse if customers specify a common batch. If IPA has insufficient stock on a partial pallet to satisfy that order, they must break into another pallet. When this happens repeatedly, IPA ends up with a number of partial pallets of the same product, but with different batch numbers.

Once goods have been picked up and packed for delivery, the warehouse or customer is telexed as to what is coming. This advice is cross-referenced with the customer's pro-forma number and the carrier's consignment note. If items are not on the telex, then the consignee knows that there has been a stock-out or some other problem. IPA warehouses provide a form indicating when they received the goods and the condition of the goods. They also fill in when they were supposedly shipped, using the telex as the date. These forms are then sent back to the warehouse manager, who uses them to maintain a monitoring system for carrier performance.

Most of the carriers guarantee delivery. For local deliveries from the Sydney warehouse, Herbert receives the drivers' route sheets bearing signatures from the customers indicating receipt of the goods.

At the finished-goods warehouse, complete stocktakes are performed twice a year as well as monthly cyclical stocktakes of selected items.

Interview with Kevin Gumley, Manager of Inventory Control and Production Planning

Mr Kevin Gumley sat in his office, surrounded by bound volumes of computer output, as he explained the inventory control and production planning systems to Halloran.

Gumley said that the system used for the inventory control of raw materials was a net materials-requirement planning package supplied by IBM and modified to a major extent by IPA. Gumley said that there was no major problem with the system itself, but the manner in which it was used did cause major problems. IPA's international headquarters in Antwerp required a sixteen-month forecast of the production plan so that global import and export movements could be planned. Unfortunately, the marketing forecast this far out was very inaccurate, especially with regard to over-the-counter products.

For all purchases other than overseas imports, updates of the next twelve-months' production plan were input every three months to match the plant capacity, the production plan and the marketing forecast. Actual production followed a two-week firm programme and a further tentative two-week programme. This system could, however, cause problems in that purchasing of the raw materials was based upon the longer-range forecast, while material usage followed the short-term programme. Gumley said that there was no auditing of the actual production programme against the production plans which initiated purchases.

Gumley claimed that inventory control was very different because the market forecasts were invariably optimistic. This resulted in over-buying of raw materials, particularly packaging materials such as printed cartons and bottles. According to Gumley, sales forecasts for new products were typically in error by factors of two, three and even ten; occasionally the forecast would err on the low side, but this was very rare. Out of a total inventory of approximately $8 million of finished goods, Gumley estimated that $1.8 million was useless.

Gumley explained that IPA had approximately $17 million of stock on hand, including raw materials, work in progress and finished goods. The total annual sales were $35 million which, with a 40 per cent mark-up, corresponded to a cost of goods sold of about $25 million.

Gumley commented that the marketing people were complaining of serious shortages of fast-moving items, especially in the OTC product range. Ethical products did not seem to present such a problem because the demand for them was much more amenable to statistical forecasts.

Gumley indicated that inter-warehouse movement accounted for approximately 8—12 per cent of the total stock movement, about half of this being planned (e.g. narcotics always came out of the Sydney warehouse).

Gumley felt that many of the current problems would be solved by the new computer system. He described how it would work: if the stock on hand of an item was less than the re-order point, the central warehouse would ship three-quarters of a month's usage plus the back-orders. When queried by Halloran, Gumley replied that there was no seasonality in the reimbursement calculations to determine the re-order points. Halloran was certain the computer programme had the option of using season factors, but he said nothing.

Gumley continued his description of the new system. In cases of shortages, clerks would consult the marketing department and then attempt to 'fair share' the items that were in stock. The new system, once introduced, would give automatic service-level calculations: target service levels would be set by the marketing department, and the computer system would translate these into safety stocks. Based on the deviation between forecast and actual sales, the input target service level, and an input limit on the lead time (usually set at the first quartile) the computer would automatically calculate the re-order point.

According to Gumley, the finished goods represented 65—70 per cent of the value of goods stored in IPA warehouses. All inventories were considered to be national and no records were kept of the location of stockholdings. Gumley noted that there could be serious shortages in one market area even though the national stocks were excessive: there was no system for anticipating shortages in local markets so as to be able to initiate inter-depot movement before a stock-out occurred.

When Halloran asked about the stock-turn rates, Gumley replied that he did not use them — in fact, he didn't have any information which broke down the stock on hand into various product lines. There was no regular report detailing the value of inventory associated with the various product divisions. Gumley went on to say that product divisions paid attention to the stocks of finished goods, but received no feedback concerning the stock held in the raw-materials warehouse which was dedicated to their lines, especially packaging materials.

Halloran left Gumley's office with the impression that production control, inventory control and purchasing all appeared to view marketing as an enemy. There was certainly a tendency to shift the blame for excess stocks in that direction. There did not seem to be a cooperative approach towards solving the problems for IPA as a whole.

Interview with Terry Smith, Marketing Manager for OTC Pharmaceuticals, and Richard Harris, Marketing Manager for Ethical Pharmaceutical Products

Halloran's initial discussion here concerned advantages and disadvantages of wholesalers, direct supply and agencies. Smith stated that wholesalers in the various markets provided two deliveries daily to customers in their area. However, when asked whether wholesalers or direct supply provided the better profit contribution, Smith and Harris believed that there was higher contribution from direct distribution and agencies. Halloran silently wondered whether, when all costs were considered, there was perhaps higher profit contribution from the wholesalers.

Halloran then asked what was the effect on sales of using either agencies or wholesalers. Smith and Harris did not agree. Smith felt that agencies provided services which Halloran knew they were not providing (e.g. answering queries from customers on the viability and availability of new product lines). Smith observed that OTC products tended to be quite heavy and thus the provision of short delivery times via air transport could be very expensive. Harris said air transport might be viable for ethical products. When asked whether or not delivery time was important for the various product lines, he stated that delivery time was important for ethical products. Smith felt that a delivery time of less than five working days for OTC products was necessary.

Smith and Harris confirmed Halloran's suspicions that customer delivery standards did not exist – such a service was not considered to be a competitive factor. Smith and Harris believed that it would be impossible to monitor customer service with the present system. It was suggested that one way to improve service would be for IPA to telephone customers, on a rotary system, to ask what orders they needed rather than to rely on the customers making contact. It was pointed out that the staff requirements for this would be fairly substantial.

Smith and Harris then turned the discussion to the questions of back-order policy and procedures. Customers were not notified when an item was back-ordered for them, which led them to double-order: having failed to receive the product from IPA they then ordered it from a local wholesaler, and when IPA finally supplied the back-order customers typically sent this order back. Smith and Harris felt very strongly that customers should be notified about back-orders, and Halloran agreed that there could be a significant problem because nobody was in charge of both local warehousing and local sales operations.

Discussion then turned to the so-called forward-order system, i.e. where representatives placed orders for delivery at a future time. Halloran observed that representatives often held the forward order until near delivery times, and pointed out that the system would only work if representatives forwarded the orders as they were received.

Smith and Harris stated that sales forecasting was done on a national basis only, with no breakdown into local territories.

Harris indicated that changes to the national health service listings were also a problem. Often, the listing would simply specify changes to pack size and IPA was expected to comply immediately – they had no flexibility, and were unable to plan. When IPA planned to introduce a new pack size, Smith and Harris said they tried to sell out stocks of the old size in the finished-goods warehouse. They admitted that they did not consider the packaging stocks in the raw-materials warehouse, but claimed that they were never told what those stocks were. Both Smith and Harris felt that distribution costs and the costs of carrying inventory should be viewed simply as a cost of doing business, i.e. be allocated as an overhead.

At the end of the discussion, Halloran's general impression was that Smith and Harris were very sales-oriented. They did not seem to fully appreciate the necessity of controlling the working capital tied up in inventories. His suspicions about a lack of communication between marketing staff and the inventory control and production planning unit was reinforced. The marketing people had been mainly concerned about the few times that production facilities had been unable to keep up with demand for a product that had 'taken off'; they did not seem concerned about the fact that, in many cases, the product had not taken off and demand had in fact been much lower than anticipated.

Interview with Jerry Freeth, Financial Controller

Mr Freeth was particularly concerned with the value of inventory tied up in new OTC products which had not taken off in accordance with sales expectations. Freeth felt that a more detailed marketing plan was needed, whereby the forecast would be phased month by month and the plan would allow for holding down sales if the product in fact took off. To allow for high sales, production should run up inventories of substitutable products, for which demand was steady, before the product was launched. If demand for the new product did take off, they could then curtail production of the substituted product and change over to the new one. If it didn't take off, overtime on the production facility could be eliminated and the stocks of the substitutable item could be allowed to run down.

Freeth emphasized that the substitutable item would have a reasonably smooth sales pattern, which would ensure that IPA would not be left with large amounts of inventory. Over-stocks of the substitutable product were recoverable, but this was not necessarily the case with new products.

Freeth again emphasized the problems associated with the basic unpredictability of seasonal items. In the case of sun-care products, a rainy summer would substantially decrease the amount sold; similarly, a pleasant winter would drive down the sales of cough-and-cold prescriptions. Since these items tended to bear expiry dates, there was an enormous risk associated with carrying inventories. Freeth believed that the change-over cost, on the production line, from one item to the next was quite high, but this had not been quantified. There were no established procedures for minimizing the costs of holding inventory plus the cost of the inventory change-overs, to cope with seasonal-product unpredictability.

Freeth had recently introduced a system whereby damages, spoilages and obsolete stocks were charged to the product-line divisions. For example, if there were $1 million of obsolete stock disposed of, Freeth would report how much was due to skin-care products, other OTC lines, or ethical lines. Freeth reacted favourably to Halloran's idea of allocating the cost of carrying inventory to the various product divisions. He felt that such a procedure would certainly encourage the product divisions to be somewhat less over-optimistic in their sales forecasts for new products.

Freeth was concerned about what he considered to be a somewhat cavalier attitude towards the introduction of new products by the product divisions. He quoted an example concerning the cough-and-cold product range. The marketing people had decided to market the product in a nice clear bottle to display its nice blue colour. The product was not tested in the new container, however, and a yellow residue appeared along the top of the bottle which looked less than pleasing to the eye. The product therefore had to be recalled and re-packaged, but unfortunately the product division had decided on an English-manufactured bottle which was slightly off-size and for which there was no market in Australia. Freeth had recently authorized the disposal of $130 000 worth of these bottles — he was quite upset that such a marketing decision could have been taken without first having tested the product.

Freeth noted that he had come from a company that was perhaps overly market-research orientated; nonetheless, he was concerned that there was no market research within IPA. In his opinion, this lack was very evident in the manner in which new products were introduced into the market; Freeth claimed that five out of every six new products introduced by IPA failed.

From a financial planning and political point of view, Freeth stated that it would not be possible to write off $2 million dollars worth of obsolete stock in one year. However, he felt that a planned write-off of $250 000–$500 000 a year for two or three years would be possible.

The discussion then turned to the possibility of changes to the overall operating procedures of IPA. First, Freeth indicated that the cost of closing agencies would only be the cost of lost sales, as the contracts allowed for cancellation on three months' notice by either party.

Halloran then explored the possibility of introducing major new data-processing systems. Freeth said that top management felt that the current systems needed cleaning up, so that in the near term funds would be allocated for this purpose rather than for implementing new systems.

Finally, Freeth noted that the cost of direct distribution is a sales deduction and does not appear on operating reports as a distinct item. He agreed with Halloran that this procedure was not desirable.

Halloran returned to his office at 6.30 p.m. He realized that Harold Deakin's directive, 'Resolve the agency question and reduce inventories' was a very tall order indeed. He placed three sheets of paper on his desk. He labelled them 'Symptoms', 'Causes' and 'Possible solutions'. Then he began to write.

Questions

1. What, if any, are the problems associated with the distribution/marketing interface? Suggest possible solutions.
2. What role does the sales forecast play in enhancing or degrading distribution performance?
3. What initiatives should be taken, and by whom, in formulating a customer-service policy?
4. What fundamental issues are involved in, and what additional information is required for, the resolution of the 'agency question'?

APPENDIX I   ORGANIZATION CHART

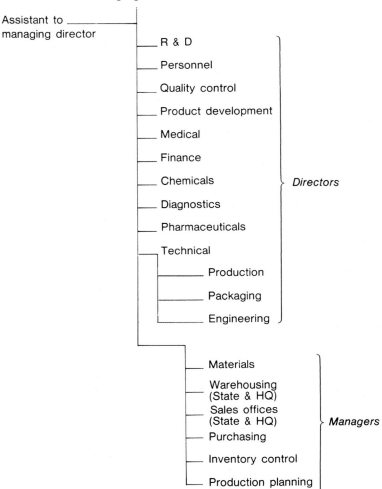

Managing director

Assistant to managing director

- R & D
- Personnel
- Quality control
- Product development
- Medical
- Finance
- Chemicals
- Diagnostics
- Pharmaceuticals
- Technical
  - Production
  - Packaging
  - Engineering

} *Directors*

- Materials
- Warehousing (State & HQ)
- Sales offices (State & HQ)
- Purchasing
- Inventory control
- Production planning

} *Managers*

APPENDIX II   AGENCY DATA

	Darwin	Hobart	Canberra	Newcastle	Wagga	Townsville	Wollongong
Sales per week ($ value)	700	8 800	5 500	18 000	4 600	5 100	6 500
No. of orders per week	6	68	65	117	52	42	65
Average inventory ($ value)	6 000	80 000	56 000	72 000	39 000	35 000	48 000
Commissions paid per week	46	512	339	934	300	350	187
Transport of weekly stock replenishment ($ cost)	30	30	30	30	20	45	11
Damaged and outdated stock per week ($)	—	1.30	—	9.03	—	—	—

APPENDIX III   AGENCY DATA PREPARED BY WAREHOUSING MANAGER

Average parcel weight per order	5 kg
Current orders per week:	
Sydney	651
Melbourne	524
Brisbane	280
Adelaide	207
Perth	132
Estimated delivery cost per parcel ($)	
Brisbane to Darwin	6.80
Brisbane to Townsville	10.05
Sydney to Canberra	3.20
Sydney to Newcastle	3.05
Sydney to Wollongong	3.05
Sydney to Wagga	3.25
Melbourne to Hobart	5.14
Packaging material cost per parcel ($)	0.20
Inventory carrying cost (% per annum)	24

CASE 11   Bonzer Beverages Pty Ltd

Bonzer Beverages was situated in Cotham Road, Kew, an eastern suburb of Melbourne. It commenced business in 1940, and grew profitably until the mid-1960s, but the retirement of the owner resulted in falling market share and eventual losses.

In 1978, the freehold property was purchased by a management consultant who decided to continue the business and replace certain outdated, inefficient machinery. Under new management, monthly sales increased substantially from $40 000 in 1978 to $75 000 in 1980. Net after-tax profit was in the vicinity of $30 000 in the latter years (see Appendix I for details on a unit basis).

Bonzer Beverages had very low overheads, employing twelve part-time sales representatives whose other duties involved areas of production. There was a production manager, a marketing manager, and two sales managers (one of whom dealt with wholesale sales and canvassing, whilst the other had responsibility for home deliveries). Bonzer Beverages spent only a small amount on advertising, as it was believed sales representatives were more effective.

Bonzer Beverages encompassed both wholesale and retail cordial sales. Home delivery had originally comprised its main business, but in recent years wholesaling to hospitals, restaurants, cafes, catering services, milkbars, schools, football clubs and cinemas had grown to account for 95 per cent of its sales revenue. Bonzer Beverages did not supply supermarkets, in contrast to major competitors such as Cadbury-Schweppes Australia Ltd and Cottee's General Foods Ltd. It had a fleet of eight trucks, and depots in thirteen Melbourne locations in addition to its Kew premises (see Appendix II).

The soft-drink market is highly competitive, reputedly suffering from vast over-capacity.[1] In recent years, some firms had fallen casualty to this competition although smaller firms still survived in a market dominated by large, sometimes multinational firms. (Production and industry data are presented in Appendices III, IV and V). Bonzer Beverages presently supplied an extremely narrow product range compared with major Victorian competitors.

In recent years, many soft-drink companies had diversified into cordial production, for instance Noddy's Soft Drinks and Slade's Soft Drinks; large companies such as Life Savers Pty Ltd had diversified into soft-drinks and fruit juices. Certain segments of the refreshment market had experienced rapid growth. Increasing numbers of health-conscious Australians had enthusiastically adopted the many local and imported brands of mineral water, regarded as status beverages with a clean, zesty, healthy image.[2]

Competition from fruit juices and flavoured milk had also caused the soft-drink market to be in the doldrums. The juices and flavoured milk currently bore no sales tax, compared with the 15 per cent impost on soft-drinks. Advances in packaging (such as the Tetra Brik), large promotional budgets, competitive pricing and widespread availability in supermarket and convenience outlets had further fostered consumer acceptance of juices and flavoured milks, especially amongst younger age-groups. The social acceptability, healthiness and convenience of these beverages, generally stressed in advertising copy, had enabled rapid adoption and growth of this segment.

Amongst refreshment producers, competition for shelf-space in supermarket outlets was keen. Buyers tended to be unable to accommodate the many competing brands, and smaller companies with low market shares faced almost insuperable problems gaining store acceptance. The growth of generics had been another factor impacting adversely upon branded beverages acceptance by supermarket buyers.

Bonzer Beverages tended to be somewhat lower in price than other brands available in Victoria, especially for customers purchasing in bulk (see Appendix VI).

---

[1] *Rydge's In Marketing*, November 1980, p. 43.
[2] *Beverages Journal*, June 1980, p. 9.

Management aimed to project an image of value for money and to offer high product quality at a reasonable price.

The objectives of management currently stressed increased market share, which they believed would positively impact upon profitability, due to the underutilization of capacity at current sales volume (85 per cent utilization). One means of increasing sales volume was believed to be exporting, and recently a trial shipment had been dispatched to Papua-New Guinea. A marketing consultant had been engaged to evaluate the market potential of Papua-New Guinea and Fiji, and management was hopeful that market development would enable greater growth of Bonzer than would continued dependence on the Victorian market.

Bonzer Beverages management had considered the possibility of trying to gain supermarket distribution, especially as they faced cost pressures with their existing distribution system. However, the odds appeared almost insuperable for a small firm.

Another possibility which they had been considering was entry of the fruit-juice market. Although management could allocate funds to this venture, it was felt that much more market research should be undertaken prior to reaching any firm decision. The fruit-juice market appeared to be an attractive, higher-growth market, but Bonzer Beverages feared that it was already dominated by large firms, and highly competitive. However, the move may have had defensive benefits in enabling Bonzer to compete better in its core market of cordial manufacture.

The costs of market entry were expected to be high. Refrigeration equipment for storage at the plant cost $10 000; sizeable advertising and promotional expenditures could be necessary, especially if new channels such as supermarkets were to be utilized. Bonzer was uncertain how many of its existing customers would require fruit juices and select it as a supplier.

Due to underutilized capacity at present, no additional expenses other than direct materials were expected to be incurred for the first 10 000 units per week; direct labour would also not affect incremental costs up to this volume. However, above 10 000 units per week direct labour was estimated to cost 2.5 cents per unit.

Certain costings had been performed for fruit-juice production, although no decision had been made as to packaging style or sizing and thus additional plant requirements were unclear. It was expected that retail prices would have to be competitive with other brands available in Victoria (see Appendix VII).

Bonzer's managing director and owner, Mr McKenzie, felt that fruit-juice production might be unattractive if the margin per unit was lower than for cordial production. However, he realized that costings were premature when product and process decisions had yet to be clarified. He was also awaiting the feasibility study for cordials export to Papua-New Guinea and Fiji. Although capital availability appeared to permit both options to be explored and developed simultaneously, the expertise of the existing management team, whose main task had been sales rather than fully fledged consumer and international marketing, may have posed a constraint on Bonzer's successful strategy implementation. However, Mr McKenzie could see no reason to employ a qualified and experienced marketing man until it was clear what direction the firm's future strategy should take.

APPENDIX I   COST AND PROFIT ANALYSIS (CORDIALS)

		Cost (cents)
Average selling price		92
Less		
Unit material	72	
Direct labour	3	
Manufacturing, finance, overheads	3	
	——	78
Gross margin per unit		14
Less		
General overheads (sales department, accounting department, dispatch manager, administration expenses)	4	
Advertising and distribution	4	8
	——	——
Net profit per unit		6

APPENDIX II   BONZER BEVERAGES: MARKET COVERAGE

Suburban depots

Footscray	Ringwood
Sunshine	Glen Waverley
Williamstown	Clayton
Preston	Moorabbin
Doncaster	St Kilda
Templestowe	South Melbourne
Blackburn	

Market coverage (local government areas)

Box Hill	Melbourne
Brighton	Moorabbin
Brunswick	Northcote
Camberwell	Nunawading
Caulfield	Oakleigh
Coburg	Port Melbourne
Collingwood	Prahran
Doncaster and Templestowe	Preston
Essendon	Richmond
Fitzroy	Ringwood
Footscray	St Kilda
Hawthorn	Sandringham
Heidelberg	South Melbourne
Kew	Sunshine
Malvern	Waverley
	Williamstown

APPENDIX III   BEVERAGE MANUFACTURING ESTABLISHMENTS

ASIC code	Description	No. of establishments at 30 June 1980	Turnover ($000)	Value added ($000)
2185	Soft-drinks, cordials and syrups	190	548 361	190 519
2186	Beer	23	687 950	317 997
2187	Malt	23	117 717	30 887
2188	Wine and Brandy	171	345 534	141 684
2189	Alcoholic beverages nec	7	13 931	8 059
218	*Total beverages and malt*	414	1 713 493	689 144

Source: Australian Bureau of Statistics, *Manufacturing Establishments, Details of Operations by Industry Class, Australia, 1979–80*. ABS Catalogue No. 8203.0.

APPENDIX IV   SOFT-DRINKS, CORDIALS AND SYRUPS: PRODUCTION, IMPORTS AND EXPORTS (1977–78)

		Sales and transfers out of goods produced in Australia	Imports	Exports of Australian produce
ASIC code	Description	Value ($000)	Value for duty ($000)	Value F.O.B. ($000)
	Industry of origin: Class 2185 Soft-drinks, cordials and syrups			
2185.05	Aerated, carbonated and non-carbonated soft-drinks; cordials and syrups; manufactured ice; flavoured or coloured sugars, syrups and molasses (except sweetened fruit juices)	442 887	950	5 000
	Aerated and carbonated waters:			
2185.05.05	Canned	144 565	n/a	4 868
2185.05.10	Bottled and bulk	178 991	n/a	67
2185.05.15	Other	119 331	n/a	64
2185.10	Preparations for making non-alcoholic beverages (except flavouring essences)	3 131	1 281	n/a

Source: Australian Bureau of Statistics, *Comparable Commodity Statistics of Production, Imports and Exports, Australia, 1977–78*; ABS Catalogue No. 1310.0.

APPENDIX V PRODUCTION OF SELECTED NON-ALCOHOLIC BEVERAGES

Commodity code	Item	Unit of quantity	1977–78 (census year) Production Quantity	Sales and transfers out Quantity	Value ($000)	1978–79 (census year) Production Quantity	Sales and transfers out Quantity	Value ($000)
	Liquid whole milk, cream and skim milk:							
	Graded, tested or chilled:—							
	Liquid whole milk	'000 l	1 058 964	607 458	69 108	1 152 748	579 459	74 691
	Separated, standardised i.e. pasteurised, sterilised, homogenised, etc.:—							
	Liquid whole milk:—							
	Pasteurised whole milk (incl. homogenised but excl. flavoured and standardised milk):—							
051.86	Bulk	'000 l	1 609 025	226 903	45 837	1 598 826	219 832	50 672
051.91	Packed	'000 l		1 360 613	376 072		1 375 773	429 015
051.92	Flavoured whole milk	'000 l	42 926	41 951	18 449	67 346	68 040	31 146
051.74	Standardised milk	tonne	1 817 917	61 227	9 346	1 775 920	96 325	11 382
	Fruit juice, natural:—							
	Single strength (total production incl. that used for concentrating and for making other products such as fruit drinks, soft drinks, etc.):—							
074.61	Apple	'000 l	30 572	11 091	2 988	28 451	11 694	2 860
074.65	Citrus	'000 l	118 539	41 087	17 213	102 787	33 714	15 512
074.67	Grape	'000 l						
074.68	Mixed fruits	'000 l	37 875	40 350	14 330	55 001	37 889	15 075
074.69	Pineapple	'000 l						
074.63	Blackcurrant	'000 l	10 596					
074.79	Other	'000 l						
	Total fruit juices, single strength	'000 l	197 582	92 528	34 531	186 239	83 297	33 447
	Concentrated:—							
074.82	Grape must	'000 l	760	217	162	3 039	589	711
	Citrus:—							

Commodity code	Item	Unit of quantity	1977–78 (census year)			1978–79 (census year)		
			Production Quantity	Sales and transfers out Quantity	Value ($000)	Production Quantity	Sales and transfers out Quantity	Value ($000)
074.85	In terms of single strength Apple:—	'000 l	77 154	61 378	24 174	70 642	53 406	18 018
074.78	In terms of single strength Other:—	'000 l	18 564	13 232	1 813	14 326	13 508	3 287
074.87	In terms of single strength	'000 l	14 019	9 196	1 463	15 340	5 390	1 193
	Aerated and carbonated waters (incl. soda water, non-excisable brewed beers and non-excisable mixed beverages)*							
171.03	Canned	'000 l	364 648	366 466	144 565	354 277	368 535	157 365
171.04	Bulk	'000 l	2 539	2 604	1 029	2 295	2 606	1 347
	Bottled:—							
171.07	In returnable bottles	'000 l	419 051	422 057	116 265	368 513	372 305	113 355
171.08	In non-returnable bottles	'000 l	212 426	192 839	61 696	260 672	255 344	88 077
	Cordial and syrups:—							
171.06	Fruit juice†	'000 l	78 180	79 273	39 184	77 052	82 878	41 964
171.10	Other (imitation and flavoured)	'000 l	37 288	35 529	22 106	32 140	30 184	19 970
171.14	Cordial extract, concentrated (excl. essences)	'000 l	985	1 107	1 600	675	676	1 056
	Non-carbonated drinks:—							
075.01	Containing at least 25% by volume of pure fruit juice	'000 l	125 007	124 509	51 238	100 996	100 143	44 595
075.11	Containing less than 25% by volume of pure fruit juice	'000 l	9 174	9 193	3 635	25 861	25 909	11 447
171.22	Powder flavours for soft drinks (excl. saline powder and powder flavour for milk drinks)	'000 kg	730	718	1 531	2 397	2 180	3 901
	Cider and perry:—							
172.13	Non-alcoholic	'000 l	4 696	4 303	2 503	5 341	5 002	3 026

* Excludes beverages which are only slightly carbonated and which are commonly packed in non-pressure type containers and alcoholic mixed drinks (mixtures of spirits and aerated waters)

† Containing at least 25% by volume of pure fruit juices

Source: Australian Bureau of Statistics, Manufacturing Commodities, *Principal Articles Produced, Australia 1977–78 and 1978–79*, ABS Catalogue No. 8303.0.

APPENDIX VI   COMPARATIVE RETAIL PRICES OF CORDIAL

2 litres
Farmland	All flavours	$1.25
Cottees	Varied flavours	$1.30–$1.40
Jeneric	All flavours	$1.30
Kia-ora	All flavours	$1.44
Bonzer*	All flavours	$1.30

750 ml
Cottees	Varied flavours	$0.62–$0.70
Kia-ora	All flavours	$0.75
Bonzer†	All flavours	$0.65

* If purchased in bulk, Bonzer Beverages price is reduced to 97 cents per 2-litre container
† Bonzer Beverages also supply 4-litre bottles, offered by very few other manufacturers

APPENDIX VII   RETAIL FRUIT-JUICE PRICES

Bonzer Beverages: estimated price

Orange juice (premium quality)
2 litres	$1.20
4 litres	$2.15
10 litres	$4.00 (plus $3.00 container deposit)

Orange juice (caterers' pack)
4 litres	$1.55
10 litres	$3.65 (plus $3.00 container deposit)

Orange drink
2 litres	83 cents
4 litres	$1.45
10 litres	$3.00 (plus $3.00 container deposit)

Orange and mango drink
2 litres	87 cents

Apple juice, grapefruit juice, lemon drink
2 litres	$1.20

Typical retail prices of competing brands

Spring Valley	Apple juice (2 litres)	$1.65
Glen Park	Apple juice (2 litres)	$1.45
Big O	Orange juice (2 litres)	$1.45
Valencio	Orange juice (2 litres)	$1.45
	Grapefruit juice (2 litres)	$1.45
Prima	Apple Orange/Mango } (250 ml) Tropical Grapefruit	$0.28
Berri	Orange } (850 ml) Grapefruit	$0.75

Question

Prepare a marketing strategy for Bonzer Beverages, including a consideration of at least the following issues:

1. Describe the impact of the options of export marketing, fruit-juice market entry, and supermarket outlet entry on business definition and market coverage.
2. Do you think Bonzer Beverages should remain a market specialist?
3. Should Bonzer Beverages investigate interstate cordial markets, rather than consider the somewhat bolder step of export marketing?
4. Should Bonzer Beverages enter the fruit-juice market?

CASE 12 Taken to the Cleaners

For many years Spotless Ltd was the major force in the retail dry-cleaning industry in Victoria. In the late 1970s, the company decided on a major strategic change and proceeded to dispose of its one-hour dry-cleaning plants. Coinciding with this move, it purchased a majority holding in Ensign Holdings Ltd. Ensign was the largest dry-cleaning company catering for the garment cleaning needs of industry and commerce.

The retail dry-cleaning plants being disposed of by Spotless were shopfront factories located in strip shopping centres. Garments were taken over the counter as well as through agencies dispersed around each plant's local geographic area. Ancillary services offered at the retail outlets included garment and shoe repairs, dyeing, laundry, suede and drape cleaning. These were in addition to standard and deluxe dry-cleaning. Plant staff numbers ranged from two to ten or twelve depending on store traffic and the business generated through agencies. Agencies carried the full range of services offered by the processing plant, although same-day cleaning was typically offered instead of one-hour service.

The Spotless sale of retail outlets attracted the interest of Norm Beatty along with many other businessmen. Norm had no experience in this field. After completing his undergraduate business-studies course he had worked for five years as an account executive with a major advertising agency in Melbourne. Norm believed that dry-cleaning, along with many other personalized services, were growth opportunities for the 1980s, and that dry-cleaning could provide the vehicle for his entrepreneurial launch.

On the advice of his accountant he purchased two plants in the blue-collar western suburbs of Melbourne. Although within six kilometres of each other, both shopfronts were located in strip shopping centres that were declining in popularity and offered very little passing trade. Two large regional shopping centres in the vicinity attracted the majority of shoppers.

After twelve months of savouring the joys of running his own business, Norm's attitude can be best summarized in the following comments:

'The biggest problem I'm facing is the seasonality of the business. During winter we make reasonable profits but summer months drag us down with low sales and huge holiday payments. We have no ability to pass on cost increases over the counter. Last year my expense items increased by 26 per cent, whilst prices moved up by 8 per cent. Most of the costs are fixed, such as rent, plant leases and even wages. Our agencies expect anything from 33.3 per cent to 50 per cent discount and I have to do all their work. Another year like the last one, and I'll be back at the advertising agency earning a real wage.'

Most small businessmen can find something to grizzle about, but Norm's predicament seemed to give an accurate account of a genuine industry problem.

To increase over-the-counter sales (see Appendices I and II), Norm called extensively on his advertising skills using consumer bulk-purchase coupons, point-of-sale specials and competitions. As a desperate measure he even engaged in a price war with local competitors.

In an attempt to improve his year-round cash flow and utilize plant capacity, which was running at about 75 per cent at both stores during the peak season, Norm was giving serious thought to following Spotless's move into the industrial market. This would be done by contracting with local companies to provide an adjunct to the domestic cleaning business.

Although the machinery at each plant was reasonably old, he felt that overalls and other light protective garments could be processed with domestic garments. No facilities existed at either of the plants to handle laundry work — white garments in particular, which usually accounted for a small percentage of all industrial contracts. Hence he felt that he was limited in the type of work that could be handled. Furthermore, industry sources confirmed that 80 per cent of companies requiring laundry or dry-cleaning services preferred to operate under a garment rental scheme. This service allowed the cleaning company a contracted quantity of garments to be repaired and cleaned over a fifty-two week period. The main drawback to a small operator was the capital cost in purchasing garments.

Prices charged under a garment rental scheme averaged $1.60 per garment. Because no additional capital cost was required by a cleaner offering a clean-and-repair service on the customer's garments, strong competition existed from some small domestic dry-cleaners as well as the established larger companies. Prices were often forced down to as low as 90 cents per garment for the clean-and-repair service. As the customer owned the garments, he was not compelled to have a predetermined quantity cleaned. This meant that during the annual company shut-down, quantities for cleaning would slump dramatically.

Norm knew of a friend who imported protective workwear from China and was willing to sell overalls and dustcoats at $11 each. Significant cost savings were available in the industrial business: variable costs were about 25 cents per unit for industrial work, compared with 55 cents for a domestic garment. Although domestic garments average $2.20 retail price, they required a number of costly processes such as spotting, hand-finishing, pressing and quality packaging.

In consultation with experienced dry-cleaners, Norm was advised that it was difficult to combine domestic and industrial dry-cleaning on a long-term basis. The discolouration of the cleaning solvent, and wear and tear on the machinery, often had a detrimental effect on the standard of the domestic work. Plant A, however, was considered to be more suited to handle soiled industrial work than was Plant B, because of the type of solvent used and plant layout.

APPENDIX I ANNUAL SALES BREAKDOWN,
1981

	Plant A	Plant B
Shop sales	30 000	45 000
Agents	75 000	55 000

APPENDIX II AGENCY SALES BREAKDOWN, 1982

Agent No.	Plant A ($)	Agent No.	Plant B ($)
1	8 000	5	1 000
2	2 000	6	2 500
3	1 500	7	14 000
4	3 500	8	22 000
		9	4 000
		10	1 000
		11	4 500
	15 000		55 000

Questions

1. What factors will influence the long-term demand for domestic dry-cleaning?
2. Was a price war a sensible strategy?
3. What opportunities exist to expand the domestic cleaning business?
4. What is the buying behaviour of industrial companies purchasing cleaning services?
5. If you were Norm, what would you do?

CASE 13 Sales Call (Part 1): Feltons of Everton

*This case was prepared by Mr M. J. S. Collins of the David Syme Business School
at the Chisholm Institute of Technology.*

Feltons is a long-established electrical appliance business in Everton Park. It recently changed hands and the new proprietor, Geoff Odell, has had long experience in retailing radio and television. However he has not made any changes to the shop yet. This outlet is about 225 square metres, with display windows on either side of the front door which opens out on to a narrow street in the main shopping area. There is no competition in the immediate surrounds.

George Thomas, the local representative, parks his car, walks straight across the street to Feltons and notes as he enters the store that the display windows look a little tatty but that the right-hand one at least shows a few Philips hairdryers among the shavers. He walks past the television sets and hi-fi models to the counter, carrying a briefcase containing pamphlets and an order book. He walks up to the assistant by the cash register and says:

REP: Hello, I'm from Philips and wondered if Mr Odell was free?

ASST: I'll go and get him.

As he waits, George puts up a Philips display card on the shaver cabinet and rearranges some of the shavers. The manager comes down steps into the main shop area and shakes hands.

REP: How are things, Geoff?

MGR: Crook! The market is flat. No one is buying. There is no sign of a Christmas pick-up yet . . . Would you like to come up into the office?

George nods and follows Geoff upstairs into a small back office with a window looking down into the shop. Geoff Odell sits down behind his desk, on which stands a calculator, a heap of pamphlets strewn around, a pad and a telephone.

MGR: Yes, things are certainly bad. The election has dampened everything down . . . people are waiting to see what will happen. Maybe they will go on a spree after it when they know who gets in.

REP: But isn't that just another excuse? Last month it was the power dispute and . . .

MGR: I think you have a point there. There's always something going on. But I read in a recent buying survey that whereas a year ago people were buying televisions first, with washing machines and refrigerators next and then stereo, they have dropped stereo further down replacing it with dishwashers, freezers, and now even microwave ovens.

At this point, potential customers entered the shop below and the manager went down to give a hand. George sat and waited until he returned five minutes later.

MGR: Sorry about that, but let's get down to business. What have you got to tell me?

REP: I've brought in some brochures and sales material for you Geoff, which I think you will like.

He hands over various colour blurbs on Philips television and audio models, together with a small cut-out depicting the Philips seal peering into the television.

MGR: [as he pushes these materials to one side] Thanks, but as you know, George, I'm not buying any Philips TVs yet. When I took over this store a few months back I had to buy the stock which included a lot of dead stuff. You probably saw I had three GEs down there which have been here for over a year, so I am offering them at very low prices to get them off my books before I start buying again. Also as a member of Retravision I buy Rank Arena first up.

REP: But we are also one of approved Retravision suppliers, you know.

MGR: I know, but that is the only outlet for Rank Arena whereas you have many others. It is only right that I give support to Rank Arena first.

REP: I understand that, but did I tell you last time I called that we are offering a special discount if you undertake to order a certain number of TVs? Let me show you our range.

He hands across the latest Philips catalogue featuring both brown and white goods. Geoff starts flicking through the pages and picks out the new 550 cm colour TV.

MGR: How much would I pay for that?

REP: Er, I think that would be around $695.

MGR: Of course that's what's wrong with this game. How can I compete when Quilpie takes so little profit that he just cuts the guts out of the market. The whole pricing set-up is wrong. He possibly gets no more than $2 out of a $700 set, and to achieve the high turnover he needs he has ruined the market for all of us. It's all right for you manufacturers, you just put up your prices, but it's us as retailers who suffer − it's our margins that are squeezed, not yours. You still get your 10 per cent and I hear you are giving special deals to social clubs now, is that right?

REP: Just like you, we have to get turnover too, and groups that can buy significant quantities of appliances can get discounts.

MGR: What about Willy Herman? Does he get a special deal from you people?

[Geoff's nearest competitor is a Herman store which was recently completely re-built and modernized.]

REP: No. They get just the same as any other member of NARTA. But have a look through this catalogue, there may be something you want to buy.

MGR: Are your prices about to go up? The National rep was in here yesterday and told me that they'll be putting up their prices by 8 per cent early in the near year.

REP: I don't know, but if you order now you will get them at current prices less our special discount.

The manager starts thumbing through the catalogue and stops when he sees the new videotape recorder model.

MGR: What is the price on this? I have a local doctor who was recently inquiring if I could get one for him. They can get tapes these days to keep them up to date on medical developments.

REP: The price is around $900.

MGR: Does that include tax? How do I go about getting him a tax exemption? Do I have to apply?

REP: Yes. When you confirm the model you want, you give us the details and complete the tax exemption form. The price would be about 25 per cent off but I don't know exactly.

MGR: 'Hmmm . . . these look interesting. [He points to the first white goods page.] I intend to go into these to get my turnover. How much are the dishwashers?

REP: As you know, I don't deal in those so I can't tell you what they'd be . . . but what can I put down for you in the audio field?

MGR: As I said before, I'm placing no orders as I am overstocked. I won't buy more than half the value of my monthly sales and I have already done that for this month.

REP: Well you certainly need a Philips on your floor.

MGR: Oh yes, I will get one in as soon as I can. I do have customers who ask for them. Oh well, I guess that's it! Thanks for the pamphlets and this. [He points to the catalogue.] I'll see next time you drop by. Cheers!

Representative leaves the premises. He is pleased with the call. Although he has not got an order, he feels he's prepared the ground well and established a good working relationship. The rep gets into the car, remembers he must call in on Eldorado Electrics in the next suburb, before lunch as promised, and so drives straight off for his next call.

Questions

1. What were the call objectives for the sales representative?
2. To what extent were they achieved?
3. How do you rate the performance of the sales representative?
4. List five objections raised by the store owner and describe how you would have handled them.
5. What follow-up procedure would you recommend to the sales representative?

Sales Call (Part 2): Herveys of Nundah

Tom Fielding is a proprietor of the small electrical-goods bulk store, Herveys, in Nundah. The shop is a deep narrow-fronted one at the end of the main shopping area. On the pavement outside he has several large cartons, two air-conditioners and a refrigerator. Inside, stock is piled high on the shelves and refrigerators line one wall. The floor is crammed with both white and brown goods, some still in cartons. There is little display material but there is large lettering across the front window announcing discounts. The floor is uncarpeted.

The representative, George Thomas, enters the shop to find the proprietor engaged with a sales representative from Email, and therefore stays down in the front area out of earshot. Whilst waiting George takes a look at the stock on the floor, noting that there is only one Philip's appliance – a dishwasher. He checks it over and sees there is a deep scratch on the left-hand panel. He then assesses the competitor stock on the floor and makes a mental note of a space along one of the walls, the number of sold stickers on appliances, and the large amount of stock.

With the departure of the competitor representative, and after a friendly word with one of the sales assistants, George makes his way up the narrow passage between refrigerators, washing machines, freezers, etc. to the back counter.

REP: How are you, Tom? I popped in to give you the new price lists which become effective on the first of next month. [Hands over two green sheets listing the new prices by model.] As you can see they have had to change quite a bit, but you can still order stock at the old price over the next ten days.

TOM: Thanks, George, I expected it of course. But what does that make the single-door compacts now?

REP: [pointing to the relevant line] Let me see . . . ah, yes! That's gone up to $335 whereas on your old list that was . . . $295 — so it's gone up by $40. But they have not all gone up. The 325-litre one has stayed the same and the two freezer models have actually fallen. See, here . . .

TOM: Uh-huh, anyway I'll put these in my book and . . .

REP: [interrupting] Why not put them in the nice blue folder I gave you with the pamphlets and other price lists — it keeps them all together and helps quick reference.

At this point one of the two sales assistants asks for some advice with a customer and Tom disappears for five minutes. George asks the other assistant what the pamphlet situation was and if he can replenish the brochure drawer. Given the affirmative, he distributes various single-leaf promotional sheets and then waits for Tom to return.

TOM: Sorry about that but she had a query over a hairdryer . . . anyway thanks for coming in.

REP: Well, Tom, I know you have a lot of stock on the floor but I saw that you have sold the 360 you bought when I was last in three weeks ago. You have space for a replacement there — now I know you won't want to put in an order now, but you should assess what you need before the new prices come in. It looks as though quite a lot of stock will go out this week judging by all the sold stickers.

TOM: That's right. Things are still slow, but I'm hoping they will pick up now with the warmer weather. I will get my manager, Clarrie, to look into the position later this week and he will phone if he needs anything.

REP: Fine, but what about putting in a bar fridge? We have a very good one now — let me show you a picture of it [He thumbs through his folder of plastic-covered pamphlets on Philip's models, until he finds the two-door Frig-O-Bar Model RL105S.] There, isn't that good . . .

TOM: It's too expensive. You wouldn't sell one of those around here!

REP: But it's good value. When you think that our cheaper model without all those extra features is $199 and this, with the lovely teak finish, is only $239. I think it would go all right.

TOM: Not in this area.

REP: Well, we have a lot of exciting products. I would like to get you and Clarrie into our showroom when things quieten down a bit. We have a really good display and I could then give you a lunch — it's about time I did that!

TOM: It would be a nice idea, George, but we could never both get away. There is always too much to do, but I'll get Clarrie to come down to you one of these days . . . anyway thanks for calling in.

REP: A pleasure, Tom, it's always good to come into your store. I will ring you on Friday to see what you want to order. Good selling!

George shakes hands and, as he leaves the shop, deliberately goes over to one of the assistants to remark how good it was to see him back at work, as he remembered the assistant had been off work for several months with hepatitis. George left the shop pleased with the call, and confident he would get an order on Friday. Therefore he wrote Tom's name and telephone number in his diary, before returning to the car and setting off for his next call . . .

Questions

1. What were the call objectives?
2. How far were these successfully achieved?
3. Would the order be given on Friday?
4. How well was the interview conducted?

CASE 14 Life. Be In It – How Norm Was Born

In 1975 the Victorian Department of Youth, Sport and Recreation was considering the implementation of a fitness programme. Like many similar projects around the world, it was designed to stir the population from lethargy.

The initial concept was a quick, hard-hitting get-fit campaign. The department decided that before implementing such a programme it should draw on professional marketing skills to both test the concept and assist with developing an appropriate plan and strategy. Research consultants were engaged, with an initial brief to carry out an attitudinal survey titled 'Attitudes of Victorians to Fitness and Recreation'.

Consumer research was conducted using a series of group discussions. Insights from these helped to shape a number of hypotheses which were to be subsequently tested in a statistically based sample-household survey.

Results from the group discussions clearly indicated that although the department was initially interested in 'selling' fitness, this was not what the public was likely to buy. Some early feedback showed that:

- The conscious pursuit of fitness appeared to be a non-issue for many people.

- The concept of being active had greater appeal than working hard to get fit.
- Activities such as jogging and exercising were seen as the personal domain of the fitness fanatic.

Hence, marketing research helped to understand the market. It was obvious that Victorians equated fitness with the sweaty tracksuited stereotype – one that they were not likely to embrace.

Armed with this information the department decided to suspend further action on a fitness campaign until the results of the household survey were obtained.

The household survey was based on psychographic research. Respondents replied to 103 attitudinal statements based on transcripts from the group discussions, with answers rated on scales ranging from 'strongly agree' to 'strongly disagree'.

The purpose was to assist the department in identifying the segments that made up the fitness/recreation market. Four main groups were then identified:

	Percentage of the population
Drifters	59
Tuned out	19
Tuned in: self-improvers (11%) Tuned in: self-convinced (6%)	17
Supertuned (young lions)	5
	100

Descriptions of the characteristics of the people within each group were developed.

- *Drifters (59 per cent)*. Fitness is a non-issue to this group. They would prefer to listen to a record or go out to dinner than work hard to keep fit. They do, however, understand the benefits of being active.
- *Tuned out (19 per cent)*. Many of these people learned that they were failures at sport at school. They still remember the P.T. (Physical Torture) programmes of those days and their incompetence and embarrassment in participating in them.
- *Tuned in (Self-improvers, 11 per cent)*. Members of this group are relatively active and strongly support getting fit. They tend to be active in order to 'look good' and 'get on'.
- *Tuned in (Self-convinced, 6 per cent)*. Members of this group are representative of the typical fitness fanatic: they are vitally fit, know how to stay fit, and are usually willing to tell you how to go about achieving the same level of fitness.
- *Supertuned – young lion (5 per cent)*. Those in this group are unconsciously very active and consequently extremely fit. They are typically in the younger age-groups.

An examination of these groups highlighted that nearly 80 per cent of the population was not interested in fitness. It was clear that the department's new task was to broaden the community's concept of activity. A strategy had to be developed that would show that activity could be increased without pain. The inactive had to be made to think about activity, whilst the active had to be encouraged to remain so.

Following further refinement of the objectives and strategies, an advertising agency was selected to communicate the message. Monahan Dayman Adams was the successful advertising agency; a director, Phillip Adams, described his creative rationale as follows:

> The Australian has a strong anti-authoritarian streak and prefers to offer irreverent advice from the outer than to participate in physical activity. This suggests that a sense of humour is an important ingredient in any attempt to communicate with your fellow citizens. It also facilitates genuine communication. A good-humoured approach to the problem breaks down hostilities, prejudice and intellectualized resistance. A government programme postulated on good humour is hard to brand authoritarian . . .
>
> . . . Any attempt to get Victorians doing push-ups en masse is foredoomed to failure whereas a reasonable percentage of them may well be persuaded to push themselves away from the dinner table, or to cut their intake of carbohydrates . . .
>
> . . . The programme will offer people useful but amusing suggestions as to how they can escape from their self-imposed restrictions. We will offer them life instead of mere existence. Show them that life can be a little more enjoyable and suggest that they in fact Be-In-It.

Questions

1. Why, in the first instance, were group discussions used by the Department of Youth, Sport and Recreation?
2. Was it appropriate or necessary to follow this research with a household survey?
3. Discuss how you would select:
   (a) individuals to participate in the group discussions;
   (b) persons to be interviewed in a random sample of households?

Glossary

Absolute product failure   A product failure that loses money and whose sales do not cover the variable costs.

Accelerator principle   A small change in consumer demand leads to a large increase in industrial demand.

Administered vertical marketing system   Achieves coordination of successive stages of production and distribution not through common ownership but through the size and power of one of the parties within the system.

Advertising   The use of paid media by a seller to communicate persuasive information about its goods, services, or organization.

Advertising goal   A specific communication task to be accomplished among a defined audience in a given period of time.

Agents   Business firms — such as manufacturer's representatives and brokers — that are hired by producers and find buyers and negotiate sales but do not take title to the merchandise.

Attitude   A person's enduring favourable or unfavourable cognitive evaluations, emotional feelings, and action tendencies toward some object or idea.

Backward integration   A company's seeking ownership or increased control of its supply systems.

Belief   A descriptive thought that a person holds about something.

*****Brand**   A name, term, sign, symbol, or design, or a combination of them which is intended to identify the goods or services of one seller or group of sellers and to differentiate them from those of competitors.

*****Brand mark**   That part of a brand which can be recognized but is not utterable, such as a symbol, design, or distinctive colouring or lettering.

*****Brand name**   That part of a brand which can be vocalized — the utterable.

Buyer   Anyone who might conceivably buy a given product.

†**Buying centre**   All those individuals and groups who participate in the purchasing decision-making process, who share some common goals and the risks arising from the decisions.

Closed-ended question   A question in which the possible answers are supplied.

---

*The definitions preceded by an asterisk are from *Marketing Definitions: A Glossary of Marketing Terms* (Chicago: American Marketing Association, 1960).

†The definitions preceded by a dagger are from Frederick E. Webster, Jr., and Yoram Wind, *Organizational Buying Behavior* (Englewood Cliffs, N.J.: Prentice-Hall, 1972).

Cognitive dissonance theory Almost every purchase is likely to lead to some postpurchase discomfort, and the issues are how much discomfort and what will the consumer do about it.

Company demand The company's sales resulting from its share of market demand.

Company marketing opportunity An attractive arena of relevant marketing action in which a particular company is likely to enjoy superior competitive advantages.

Company marketing system The set of major participants, markets, and forces that make up the company's marketing environment.

Company sales forecast The expected level of company sales based on a chosen marketing plan and assumed marketing environment.

Company sales potential The limit approached by company demand as company marketing expenditure increases in relation to competitors.

Concentration strategy A marketing strategy in which the firm concentrates its resources only in the strongest markets and channels while phasing out its efforts elsewhere.

Concentric diversification A company's seeking to add new products that have technological and/or marketing synergies with the existing product line; these products will normally appeal to new classes of customers.

Conglomerate diversification A company's seeking to add new products that have no relationship to the company's current technology, products, or markets; these products will normally appeal to new classes of customers.

Consumerism An organized social movement seeking to strengthen the rights and power of consumers vis-à-vis sellers.

Consumer markets The set of individuals and households that buy products intended for personal consumption.

Containerization The putting of goods in boxes or trailers that can easily be transferred between two or more modes of transportation.

Continuation strategy A marketing strategy in which the firm continues to use the same market segments, channels, pricing, and promotion.

Contractual vertical marketing system A system in which independent firms at different levels of production and distribution integrate their programmes on a contractual basis to obtain more economies and/or sales impact that they could achieve alone.

*Convenience goods Consumer goods that the customer usually purchases frequently, immediately, and with the minimum of effort in comparison and buying.

Copyright The exclusive legal right to reproduce, publish, and sell the matter and form of a literary, musical, or artistic work.

Corporate vertical marketing system The combining of successive stages of production and distribution under a single ownership.

Cues Minor stimuli that determine when, where, and how the person responds.

Discretionary income The amount of money a person has left after paying for his or her basic food, clothing, shelter, insurance, and other necessitites.

Disposable personal income The amount of money a person has left after paying taxes.

Distribution channel The set of all the firms and individuals that take title, or assist in transferring title, to the particular good or service as it moves from the producer to the consumer. Thus a distribution channel primarily includes the merchants (because they take title) and the agents (because they assist in transferring title). The distribution channel does not include suppliers, facilitators, and marketing firms.

Distribution structure All available arrangements in a particular industry to get products from the producers to the consumers.

Diversification growth opportunities Those opportunities lying outside the current marketing channel system.

Drive   A strong internal stimulus impelling action. A drive becomes a motive when it is directed toward a particular drive-reducing stimulus object.

Drop-error   Occurs when the company dismisses an otherwise good idea because of a lack of vision of its potentialities.

Durable goods   Tangible goods that normally survive many uses.

Embargo   The ultimate form of quota in that imports in prescribed categories are totally banned.

Environmentalism   An organized social movement seeking to minimize the harm done by marketing practices to the environment and quality of life.

Environmental threat   A challenge posed by an unfavourable trend or specific disturbance in the environment which would lead, in the absence of purposeful marketing action, to the stagnation or demise of a company, product, or brand.

Evoked set   The set of alternatives that the buyer might or did consider at that stage of the decision process.

Exchange   The act of obtaining a desired object from someone by offering something in return.

Expectations-performance theory   A consumer's satisfaction is a function of the consumer's product expectations and perception of product performance.

Facilitators   Business firms — such as transport companies, warehouses, banks, and insurance companies — that assist in the logistic and financial tasks of distribution but do not take title to goods or negotiate purchases or sales.

Fads   Particular fashions that come quickly into the public eye, are adopted with great zeal, peak early, and decline very fast.

Fashion   A currently accepted or popular style in a given field. Fashions tend to pass through four stages: distinctiveness, emulation, mass fashion, and decline.

Forecasting   The art of anticipating what buyers are likely to do under a given set of conditions.

Forward integration   A company's seeking ownership or increased control of some of its dealers or distributors.

Functional marketing organization   A form of marketing organization in which the various marketing functions are headed by separate managers who report to the marketing manager.

Go-error   Occurs when the company lets a poor idea proceed to development and commercialization.

Government market   Governmental units of all types — federal, State, and local — which purchase or rent goods for carrying out the main functions of government.

Harvesting strategy   A marketing strategy in which the firm sharply reduces its expenses to increase its current profits, knowing that this will accelerate the rate of sales decline and ultimate demise of the product.

Horizontal diversification   A company's seeking to add new products that could appeal to its current customers though technically unrelated to its current product line.

Horizontal integration   The term refers to a company's seeking ownership or increased control of some of its competitors.

Human need   A state of felt deprivation in a person.

Image   The set of beliefs that a person or a group holds about an object.

Image persistence   People's continuing to see what they expect to see, rather than what is.

International markets   The set of buyers found in other countries. This set includes foreign consumers, producers, resellers, and governments.

Learning   Changes in an individual's behaviour arising from experience.

Line stretching The act of lengthening the company's product line beyond its current range.

Macroenvironment The totality of major institutions and forces that are external and potentially relevant to the firm.

Market The set of all actual and potential buyers of a product.

Market demand The term refers to the total volume that would be bought by a defined customer group in a defined geographic area in a defined time period in a defined marketing environment under a defined marketing programme.

Market development A company's seeking increased sales by taking its current products into new markets.

Market forecast The market forecast shows the expected level of market demand for the expected level of industry marketing effort and the given environment.

Marketing Human activity directed at satisfying needs and wants through exchange processes.

Marketing audit A comprehensive, systematic, independent, and periodic examination of a company's — or a business unit's — marketing environment, objectives, strategies, and activities with a view to determining problem areas and opportunities and recommending a plan of action to improve the company's marketing performance.

Marketing channel A method of organizing the work that has to be done to move products from producers to consumers.

Marketing concept A management orientation that holds that the key to achieving organizational goals consists of the organization's determining the needs and wants of target markets and adapting itself to delivering the desired satisfactions more effectively and efficiently than its competitors.

Marketing firms Business firms — such as advertising agencies, marketing research firms, and marketing consulting firms — that assist in targeting and promoting the sellers' products to the right markets.

Marketing information system A continuing and interacting structure of people, equipment, and procedures designed to gather, sort, analyze, evaluate, and distribute pertinent, timely, and accurate information for use by marketing decision makers to improve their marketing planning, execution, and control.

Marketing intelligence system The set of sources and procedures by which marketing executives obtain their everyday information about developments in the external marketing environment.

Marketing management The analysis, planning, implementation, and control of programmes designed to create, build, and maintain mutually beneficial exchanges and relationships with target markets for the purpose of achieving organizational objectives. Effective marketing management involves a disciplined analysis of the needs, wants, perceptions, and preferences of consumer and intermediary markets as the basis for effective product design, pricing, communication, and distribution.

Marketing mix The particular blend of controllable marketing variables that the firm uses to achieve its objectives in the target market.

Marketing process The managerial process of identifying, analyzing, choosing, and exploiting marketing opportunities to fulfill the company's mission and objectives.

Marketing research The systematic design, collection, analysis, and reporting of data and findings relevant to a specific marketing situation facing the company.

Marketing strategy The fundamental marketing logic by which the business unit intends to achieve its marketing objectives. Marketing strategy consists of a coordinated set of decisions on (i) target markets, (ii) marketing mix, and (iii) marketing expenditure level.

Marketing system   A set of interacting participants, markets, and flows that are involved in an organized arena of exchange.

Market management organization   A form of marketing organization in which major markets are the responsibility of marketing managers who work with the various functional specialists to develop and achieve their plans for the markets.

Market penetration   A company's seeking increased sales for its current products in its current markets through more aggressive marketing effort.

Market potential   The limit approached by market demand as industry marketing expenditure goes to infinity, for a given set of competitive prices and a given environment.

Market segmentation   The act of dividing a market into distinct and meaningful groups of buyers who might merit separate products and/or marketing mixes.

Mass marketing   A style of marketing in which the seller mass-produces and mass-distributes one product and attempts to attract everyone to its purchase.

Merchants   Business firms — such as wholesalers and retailers — that buy, take title to, and resell merchandise.

Micro-sales analysis   An attempt to determine the specific products, territories, and so forth, that failed to produce their expected share of sales.

Model bank   A collection of models that will help marketers develop better marketing decisions.

Motive   A stimulated need which is sufficiently pressing to direct the person toward the goal of satisfying the need. After the need is satisfied, the person's tension is discharged and he or she returns to a state of equilibrium.

* **Nondurable goods**   Tangible goods that normally are consumed in one or a few uses.

Open-ended question   A question that the respondent is free to answer in his or her own words.

Organization   A social unit characterized by explicit goals, definite rules and regulations, a formal status structure, and clear lines of communication and authority.

†**Organizational buying**   The decision-making process by which formal organizations establish the need for purchased products and services, and identify, evaluate, and choose among alternative brands and suppliers.

Organization marketing   Those activities undertaken to create, maintain, or alter attitudes and/or behaviour of target audiences toward particular organizations.

Partial product failure   A product failure that loses money but its sales cover all the variable costs and some of the fixed costs.

‡**Perception**   The process by which an individual selects, organizes, and interprets information inputs to create a meaningful picture of the world.

Physical distribution   The tasks involved in planning and implementing the physical flows of materials and final goods from point of origin to points of use or consumption to meet the needs of customers at a profit.

Political system   The term refers to the forms and institutions by which a nation is governed. It consists of an interacting set of laws, government agencies, and pressure groups that influence and constrain the conduct of various organizations and individuals in the society.

Price leader   A product that is priced below its normal markup or even below cost. It is used to attract customers to the store in the hope that they will buy other things at normal markups.

Price-taking market   A market where each seller must charge the going price.

---

‡This definition is from Bernard Berelson & Gary A. Steiner, *Human Behavior: An Inventory of Scientific Findings* (New York: Harcourt Brace Jovanovich, 1964), p. 88.

Pricing strategy The task of defining the rough initial price range and planned price movement through time that the company will use to achieve its marketing objectives in the target market.

Primary data Data that are originally collected for the specific purpose at hand.

Producer markets The set of organizations that buy products for the purpose of using them in the production process to make profits or achieve other objectives.

Product Anything that can be offered to a market for attention, acquisition, use, or consumption that might satisfy a need. It includes physical objects, services, persons, places, organizations, and ideas.

Product assortment *See* Product mix.

Product concept (i) A management orientation that assumes that consumers will favour those products that offer the most quality for the price, and therefore the organization should devote its energy to improving product quality. (ii) A particular subjective consumer meaning that a company tries to build into a product idea.

Product development The term refers to the company's seeking increased sales by developing new or improved products for its current markets.

Product-differentiated marketing A style of marketing in which the seller produces two or more products designed to look different from each other and competitors' products.

Product idea A possible product, described in objective and functional terms, that the company can see itself offering to the market.

Product image The particular subjective picture that consumers actually acquire of the product.

Production concept A management orientation that assumes that consumers will favour those products that are available and affordable, and therefore the major task of management is to pursue improved production and distribution efficiency.

****Product item** A distinct unit within a product line that is distinguishable by size, price, appearance, or some other attribute. The item is sometimes called a stockkeeping unit, a product variant, or subvariant.

****Product line** A group of products within a product mix that are closely related, either because they function in a similar manner, are sold to the same customer groups, are marketed through the same types of outlets, or fall within the given price ranges.

Product management organization A form of marketing in which products are the responsibility of product managers who work with the various functional specialists in the company to develop and achieve their plans for the product.

****Product mix** The set of all product lines and items that a particular seller offers for sale to buyers.

Public Any group that has an actual or potential interest in or impact on an organization's ability to achieve its objectives.

Publicity The securing of the free editorial space or time.

Pull strategy A strategy that calls for spending a lot of money on advertising and consumer promotion aimed at the final consumer to build up demand for the product.

Push strategy A strategy that calls for using the sales force and trade promotion to push the product through the channels.

Quota Sets limits on the amount of goods that can be imported in certain product categories.

Relative product failure A product failure that yields a profit that is less than the company's normal rate of return.

Reseller market All the individuals and organizations who acquire goods for the purpose of reselling or renting them to others at a profit.

Resellers *See* Merchants.

Retailer Any business enterprise whose sales volume primarily comes from retailing.

Retailing All the activities involved in selling goods or services directly to final consumers for their personal, nonbusiness use.

Role A set of activities that the individual is supposed to perform according to the definition and expectations of the individual and the persons around him or her.

Sales analysis The effort to measure and evaluate the actual sales being achieved in relation to the sales goals set for different managers.

Sales budget A conservative estimate of the expected volume of sales. It is used primarily for making current purchasing, production, and cash-flow decisions.

Sales quota A sales goal set for a product line, company division, or sales representative. It is primarily a management tool for defining and stimulating sales effort.

Sales-response function The likely sales volume during a specified time period associated with different possible levels of a marketing-mix element holding constant the other marketing-mix elements.

Sales variance analysis An attempt to determine the relative contribution of different factors to a gap in sales performance.

Secondary data Data that already exist somewhere, having been collected for another purpose.

Selective distortion Name given to the tendency of people to twist information into personal meanings.

Selling concept A management orientation that assumes that consumers will either not buy or not buy enough of the organization's products unless the organization makes a substantial effort to stimulate their interest in its products.

Service Any activity or benefit that one party can offer to another, is essentially intangible, and does not result in the ownership of anything. Its production may or may not be tied to a physical product.

****Shopping goods** Goods that the customer, in the process of selection and purchase, characteristically compares on such bases as suitability, quality, price, and style.

Social classes Relatively homogeneous and enduring divisions in a society which are hierarchically ordered and whose members share similar values, interests, and behaviour.

Social marketing The design, implementation, and control of programmes seeking to increase the acceptability of a social idea, cause, or practice in a target group. It utilizes market segmentation, consumer research, concept development, communications, facilitation, incentives, and exchange theory to maximize target group response.

Societal marketing concept A management orientation that holds that the key task of the organization is to determine the needs, wants, and interests of target markets and to adapt the organization to delivering the desired satisfactions more effectively and efficiently than its competitors in a way that preserves or enhances the consumer's and the society's well-being.

****Specialty goods** Goods with unique characteristics and/or brand identification for which a significant group of buyers are habitually willing to make a purchasing effort.

Statistical bank A collection of advanced statistical procedures for learning more about the relationships within a set of data and their statistical reliability.

Statistical demand analysis A set of statistical procedures designed to discover the most important real factors affecting sales and their relative influence.

Strategic business unit (SBU) Any business making up the company.

Strategic planning The managerial process of developing and maintaining a stategic fit between the organization and its changing market opportunities. It relies on developing a clear company mission, objectives and goals, growth strategies, and product portfolio plans.

Style   A basic and distinctive mode of expression appearing in a field of human endeavour.

Suppliers   Business firms and individuals who supply resources needed by the producer to produce the particular good or service.

Systems selling   The act of offering a buyer a complete system solution rather than some isolated products.

Target market   A well-defined set of customers whose needs the company plans to satisfy.

Target marketing   The act of selecting one or more of the market segments and developing a positioning and mix strategy for each.

Tariff   A tax levied by the foreign government against designated imported products.

Time-series analysis   A company forecast prepared on the basis of a statistical-mathematical analysis of past data.

Total market potential   The maximum amount of sales (in units or dollars) that might be available to all the firms in an industry during a given period under a given level of industry marketing expenditures and given environmental conditions.

***Trademark**   A brand or part of a brand that is given legal protection because it is capable of exclusive appropriation. A trademark protects the seller's exclusive rights to use the brand name and/or brand mark.

Transaction   A trade of values between two parties.

***Unsought goods**   Goods that the customer either does not know about or knows about but does not have an interest in purchasing.

Value analysis   An approach to cost reduction through the careful study of which components can be redesigned or standardized or made by cheaper methods of production.

Wholesaling   All the activities involved in selling goods or services to those who are buying for the purpose of resale or for business use.

Index